# The Theology of MISSIONS in the Puritan Tradition

A Study of Representative Puritans:
Richard Sibbes, Richard Baxter, John Eliot,
Cotton Mather & Jonathan Edwards

Sidney H. Rooy

AUDUBON PRESS
2601 Audubon Drive / P.O. Box 8055
Laurel, MS 39441-8000  USA

Orders: 800-405-3788
Inquiries: 601-649-8572
Voice: 601-649-8570 / Fax: 601-649-8571
E-mail: buybooks@audubonpress.com
Web Page: www.audubonpress.com

© 2006 Audubon Press edition

All rights reserved.

Printed in the United States

Cover design by Crisp Graphics

ISBN # 0-9742365-4-3

Original Publication:
Willam B. Eerdman's Publishing Co.
Grand Rapids, Michigan
1965

*In Memory of David*

*To my Wife*

*Custodimus etiam cum non custodimus*
**Richard Sibbes**

ACKNOWLEDGEMENTS

The completion of this dissertation marks the closing of one period of my life and the opening of another. I pause now with profound gratitude to those who have brought enrichment and blessing in the past.

The first steps on my theological journey were taken at Calvin College and Seminary. To all my professors there, I owe a debt of gratitude. I was deeply influenced by Dr. Henry Stob, who taught me for six years in the college and seminary. His breadth of vision and depth of piety have inspired me in my further study and mission work.

My next obligation is due to several professors at Union Theological Seminary and Columbia University of New York. Particularly Dr. Robert Handy provided stimulation and encouragement. Fellow pastors and church members at Midland Park and Paramus, New Jersey, taught me the importance of teamwork in the mission of the church to the unconverted and the joy of open-hearted confession of the Lord to my fellow-men.

The beginning of my studies at the Free University of Amsterdam was made possible through the Centennial Missions Scholarship provided by the members of the Christian Reformed Church. The pleasant arrangements for my wife with the Dordrecht branch of the International School and for myself as pastor of the Pilgrim Fellowship of the Reformed Church of Dordrecht made the completion of my study possible. The spiritual fellowship of the church brought us much strength, especially at the time of the loss of our son. In addition, the interdenominational character of the church work provided real points of contact with the ideas on missions and church unity set forth in this study.

Our Dutch and American friends have stood by us and have assisted in many ways. We thank them gratefully. I appreciate the time and counsel given to me by the Revs. A. Ferwerda of Amsterdam and A. Oliemans of Dordrecht. Particularly the K. van Henten family has shared so much with us these last three years that we count them as our own family. Also, the teachers of our children in Amsterdam and Dordrecht, both in the Dutch and the International schools, have been most obliging. Fellow students and American friends who have assisted with the typescript, translations, and proof reading include John Barrett, Jack Bax, John Koole, Harvey Smit, and Clarence Vos. Mrs. E. Poling gave a great deal of secretarial assistance at an earlier stage of my thesis. Mrs. Jack Bax rendered invaluable assistance in many ways, but especially in the checking of nearly all citations from the authors considered in this study.

To the staffs of the libraries of the Free University and the Municipal University of Amsterdam, the Royal Library of The Hague, and the University of Leiden, I am deeply grateful. Their courteous assistance has made my work more pleasant. The library of the University of Engineering at Delft loaned microfilm reading equipment for many months. For the use of much resource material I am indebted to the British Museum, the Dr. Williams's Library, and the Evangelical Library, all located in London. The library of the Society for the Propagation of Christian Knowledge permitted me the use of the manuscript letter of Henry Newman to John Wesley, and the Bodlian Library provided a microfilm of the *Communion of Churches* by John Eliot. I appreciated especially the readiness of the staff of the Dr. Williams's Library in answering many questions and for their long patience in the loan of the microfilms of the Baxter Ms. Treatises and Letters.

The staffs of the Missions Seminary and the Evangelism Center in Baarn graciously permitted me two years' attendance at lectures and training sessions. Through these institutions came contacts with Dutch missionaries, also at Oegstgeest and Zeist, which were contributions to my stay. Dr. H. Bergema, Rev. J. A. C. Rullmann, and Rev. H. H. Grosheide, were particularly helpful.

The two most significant and treasured contributions to my study and thesis are those of my professors at the Free University and those of my family. The lectures of Dr. G. C. Berkouwer in history of doctrine and dogmatics have enriched my understanding of the biblical teachings of redemption as they have become formulated and have been often reformulated in the life of the church. Dr. H. R. Wijngaarden has guided me to a better knowledge of human character and the problems to be faced in genuine inter-personal contact and in the communication of the gospel. The breadth of experience and vital zeal for missions of the late Dr. J. H. Bavinck belong to those incalculable constituents that strengthen one's own sense of calling. Dr. D. Nauta offered much appreciated advice.

To Dr. Johannes van den Berg, my promotor, I owe more than words can express. He has become the second professor in my life from whom the greatest formative influence has come. His willing guidance throughout this study and his constructive criticism have provided the encouragement that I needed to continue. As sympathetic pastor and friend, his presence and words of consolation have strengthened our faith in that One whose presence never fails.

Finally, I thank my family for their loving concern. My father and mother have taught and shown me the only road that brings true peace, the road of joyful service to our risen Lord. My brother John in his long illness has given me an example of hope and courage that will always be a guiding star in my life. Our children, Dianne, Paul, and Gayle, have come to view the thesis as a family project and have shouldered many household duties as their part in its completion. My wife, Mae, has contributed more than any other. She has been mother and pastor's wife; she has taught and typed; she is my faithful critic and loving inspiration. In humble gratitude I dedicate this book to her. For her and for the others the Lord has given to bless my life, I offer grateful praise.

# CONTENTS

| | | |
|---|---|---:|
| Introduction | | 11 |
| CHAPTER I. | Richard Sibbes: The Theological Foundation of the Mission | 15 |
| | Biographical Introduction | 15 |
| | A. The Conversion of Man | 18 |
| |    1. Divine Sovereignty and Human Responsibility | 18 |
| |       a. The Human Situation | 18 |
| |       b. God's Redeeming Act | 21 |
| |    2. The Right Use of Nature | 26 |
| | B. The Role of the Church | 31 |
| |    1. The Character of the Church | 31 |
| |    2. The Means of Grace | 36 |
| |    3. The Church Member as Witness | 40 |
| | C. The Redemption of the World | 44 |
| |    1. The Nature of the World | 44 |
| |    2. God's Way with the World | 48 |
| |    3. The Latter Age and the End of History | 56 |
| | Conclusion | 60 |
| CHAPTER II. | Richard Baxter: The Development of the Mission Idea | 66 |
| | Biographical Introduction | 66 |
| | A. The Conversion of Man | 71 |
| |    1. Divine Sovereignty and Human Responsibility | 71 |
| |       a. The Human Situation | 71 |
| |       b. God's Redeeming Act | 76 |
| |    2. The Right Use of Nature | 83 |
| | B. The Role of the Church | 92 |
| |    1. The Nature of the Church | 92 |
| |    2. The Means of Grace | 94 |
| |    3. The Methods of Approach | 102 |
| |       a. Witnessing by the Church Member | 102 |
| |       b. Promoting the Public Good | 108 |
| |       c. Seeking Church Unity | 111 |
| |       d. Teaching Essential Doctrine | 114 |
| | C. The Redemption of the World | 119 |
| |    1. The Need in England and Abroad | 119 |
| |    2. The Great Hindrances | 124 |
| |       a. Within the Christian Church | 125 |
| |       b. Outside the Christian Church | 129 |
| |    3. Motives for Involvement | 138 |
| |    4. Eternity and the Holy War | 140 |
| | Conclusion | 148 |
| CHAPTER III. | John Eliot: The Establishment of the Mission | 156 |
| | Biographical Introduction | 156 |
| | A. The Conversion of Man | 160 |
| | B. The Role of the Church | 170 |
| |    1. The Nature of the Church | 170 |
| |    2. The Establishment of the Indian Church | 176 |
| |       a. Small Beginnings and First Meetings | 176 |
| |          Tract One: New England's First Fruits ... (1643) | 176 |
| |          Tract Two: The Day-Breaking ... (1647) | 179 |
| |       b. Stabilization and Growth | 186 |
| |          Tract Three: The Clear Sunshine ... (1648) | 186 |
| |          Tract Four: The Glorious Progress ... (1649) | 195 |

|  |  | c. The Indian Town and Civil Government | 201 |
|---|---|---|---|
|  |  | Tract Five: The Light Appearing ... (1651) | 201 |
|  |  | Tract Six: Strength Out of Weakness ... (1652) | 205 |
|  |  | d. Preparation for Church Estate | 209 |
|  |  | Tract Seven: Tears of Repentance ... (1653) | 209 |
|  |  | Tract Eight: A Late & Further Manifestation ... (1655) | 212 |
|  |  | Tract Nine: A Further Accompt ... (1659) | 215 |
|  |  | e. Church Establishment | 217 |
|  |  | Tract Ten: A Further Account ... (1660) | 217 |
|  |  | Tract Eleven: A Brief Narrative ... (1670) | 218 |
|  | 3. Hindrances and Helps | | 220 |
|  | C. The Redemption of the World | | 224 |
|  | 1. The Divine Mission in History | | 224 |
|  | 2. The Indians and the Ten Lost Tribes of Israel | | 230 |
|  | Conclusion | | 235 |
| Chapter IV. | Cotton Mather and Jonathan Edwards: The Progress of the Mission | | 242 |
|  | A. Cotton Mather and the *Magnalia Christi Americana* | | 242 |
|  | Biographical Introduction | | 242 |
|  | 1. The Planting of the Church in America | | 252 |
|  |  | a. The Background | 252 |
|  |  | b. The Divine Mission | 258 |
|  |  | c. The American Theocracy | 261 |
|  |  | d. The Great Apostasy | 266 |
|  | 2. The Evangelization of the Indians | | 268 |
|  | 3. The Coming of the Kingdom | | 275 |
|  | Conclusion | | 279 |
|  |  | a. Mission Principles | 280 |
|  |  | b. Mission Methods | 281 |
|  |  | c. Mission Motives | 282 |
|  |  | d. A Pattern for the World | 284 |
|  | B. Jonathan Edwards and the *History of Redemption* | | 285 |
|  | Biographical Introduction | | 285 |
|  | 1. The Message of the *History of Redemption* | | 294 |
|  |  | a. God's Great Purpose for the World | 294 |
|  |  | b. God's Purpose Progressively Realized in Three Stages | 295 |
|  | 2. The Nations and Their Religions | | 299 |
|  | 3. Mission Principles in the History of Redemption | | 301 |
|  |  | a. God as Founder and Lord of the Mission | 301 |
|  |  | b. Man as Responsible Object of the Mission | 302 |
|  |  | c. Biblical Revelation as the Norm of the Mission | 304 |
|  |  | d. The Spirit in the Church as the Agent of the Mission | 306 |
|  |  | e. Establishment of the Kingdom of God as Goal of the Mission | 308 |
| Conclusion | | | 310 |
|  | A. The Conversion of Man | | 310 |
|  | B. The Role of the Church | | 317 |
|  | C. The Redemption of the World | | 323 |
| Abbreviations | | | 329 |
| Bibliography | | | 337 |
| Index of Persons | | | 342 |

# INTRODUCTION

The modern missionary movement is rooted in the various branches of Reformation theology. It is based upon a genuine concern for the conversion of souls, the expansion of the church, and the establishment of the kingdom of God. Though the object of our study only incidentally touches the influence of Roman Catholic missions of the sixteenth and seventeenth centuries, we can state that their work provided a stimulant and, in many cases, a worthy example to Protestant contemporaries. The roots of modern missions actually reach back into the early church, both as organic outgrowth and as pattern for emulation. Our concern is with one of the various roots of modern missions that is found in the seventeenth century.

The purpose of this study is to examine the theology of five Puritans in order to assess the relation of their theology to the practice of missions. Is there a relationship, or is what concern they had inconsistent with their basic theology? Is Puritanism, and *pari passu*, Calvinism, basically a theology of the elect for the elect, or is it a theology of redemption for the world? What is the nature of the church: a fellowship of the redeemed, or an agent for salvation to the unredeemed? What is God's purpose for the world; that is, what is in purview when we speak of redemption? Is it the conversion of souls, or the establishment of the elect church, or the achievement of a millennial kingdom of righteousness and peace?

These and many other questions that pressed for consideration in the seventeenth and early eighteenth centuries concern us still. The possibility of salvation for heathen who have never heard the gospel, the use of the native or the missionary's language, the financial and governmental indigence of the church, the proper use of literature and native evangelists, the problem of imposing a foreign liturgy upon a native church, and the cultural gap between evangelist and evangelized are relevant problems that face the church each generation anew.

In this study I have not simply assumed that the Puritans represent the Calvinistic tradition. Since some scholars have seen Puritanism as a diminution of Calvinism, we must be careful to understand their theology. However, that the Puritans regarded themselves as Calvinists can hardly be questioned. But do their teachings agree with those of original Calvinism? Those who are acquainted with Calvin's teaching will be able to judge for themselves in those mission-related theological subjects discussed below.

By Puritanism we understand the trend in English Protestantism that called for a restoral of Scriptural simplicity in liturgy, vestments, and church government, and that emphasized the presence and work of the Holy Spirit in the faith and life of the believer and in the church. The first was due negatively to a strong reaction against Roman Catholicism and positively to the emphasis on the Bible and the further development of the Reformation which they believed the continued working of the Spirit required. Thomas Cartwright (1535–1603) and William Perkins (1558–1602) were the key men in the first half century of the movement. Cartwright favored Genevan theology and ecclesiastical practices. Of Cartwright, Mullinger says: "But although wanting in the judgment and self-command essential in the leader of opinion and party, he gave system and method to the Puritanism of his day, and must be regarded as its most influential teacher during his lifetime." [1]

The theology of William Perkins became a sort of classic theology for the Puritans. His *Armilla Aurea*, first published in 1590 and 1592, went through fifteen editions in twenty years, including translations in Dutch, Irish, Spanish and Welsh. He set a keynote (to which we shall have occasion to refer again), when he inscribed the preface of this work, ". . . in the year of the last sufferings of the Saints."[2] The practical use of doctrine, stressed by Petrus Ramus (1515–1572), Perkins defined as "the science of living blessedly forever."[3] "Faith," he wrote, "commeth onely by the preaching of the word, and increaseth dayly by it: as also by the administration of the Sacraments, and praier." [4] To the book he appended "the order which M. Theodore Beza used in comforting afflicted consciences." Of special significance for the developing struggle between Puritanism and what would be called Arminianism [5] was his definition of the four views with regard to predestination: Pelagians believed in free will; Lutherans held that God gave grace to the elect and foresaw that reprobates would reject the gospel; semi-Pelagians and papists believed mercy was given to men on the basis of foreseen obedience, while Calvinists believed that salvation was based only on the *eternal* mercy of Christ. His fear of pro-Pelagian views was that "...whilst they goe about to ordaine universall grace, they doe not free themselves, but are rather more entangled. For most true is that saying of *Peter Martyr*: *whilst these men made grace so common to al, they turne grace into nature.*" [6] Perkins also accented Calvin's distinction between the universal external call (many are called) and the effectual call of the gospel (few are chosen).[7] Through men like John Preston (1587–1628), Richard Sibbes (1577–1635), and William Ames (1576–1633), these views were transmitted to seventeenth-century Puritanism.[8]

Here it is well to note that, especially in the seventeenth and eighteenth centuries, there was a rationalistic development in Calvinism. This development is variously referred to as hyper-Calvinism, rigid Calvinism, or high Calvinism. I can illustrate this no better than Susannah Wesley does to her son, John, in 1725, when she wrote: "The Doctrine of Predestination, as main-

---

[1] *DNB*, III 1139.
[2] *DNB*, XV 892–895, James B. Mullinger.
[3] Perkins, *Works*, I 10.
[4] *Ibid.*, 2.
[5] Arminius died in 1609; his views were condemned by the Synod of Dordrecht in 1618–1619.
[6] Perkins, *Works*, II 728.
[7] *Ibid.*, I 117.
[8] Morison, *The Intellectual Life of Colonial New England*, 160.

tained by rigid Calvinists, is shocking, and ought utterly to be abhorred; because it charges the most holy God with being the Author of Sin."[1] The phrase "as maintained by rigid Calvinists" is significant, since in her time there were some who taught so as to make them liable to such an accusation. Calvin, however, and none of the Puritans included in this study would have considered God as the author of sin, though all held to the doctrine of predestination. The "moderate" Calvinists held to human responsibility, as we shall see, as the other pole of the divine sovereignty emphasis. I have tried to make this clear in the first section of each chapter by considering man in the condition of sin, the sovereignty of grace, and human accountability.

The second section of each chapter deals with the two interdependent means by which the work of redemption is accomplished: the way in which the church and the individual Christian are to approach the unbeliever, and the way the unbeliever is to follow in order to find salvation. Particularly in the chapter dealing with Richard Baxter, there is a lengthy development of the method he believed essential to the progress of the gospel. In the chapter on John Eliot the burden of this second section comprises a full description of his establishment of the Indian church.

The third and last section of each chapter develops the Puritan outlook toward the world and indicates the place they assigned to the conversion of men in the scope of history. Here we consider the greater obstacles to the progress of mission, the motives for evangelization, and the goal of the work and of history.

Each chapter begins with a biographical introduction in order to indicate the circumstances in which the theology and work came to expression. Each chapter closes with a brief recapitulation of the primary principles, methods, motives, and the goal of missions.

The approach to the five Puritans in this study varies. The chapter on Sibbes is more theological, that on Baxter a blending of the theological with the practical, and that on Eliot basically practical. The nature of their tasks and situations are determinative to the sort of contribution they make to missions. The same holds true for Mather and Edwards, only we have not dealt with these comprehensively, as was the case with the first three, since during their period new mission ideas begin to come into the foreground. We have chosen one primary writing of each and indicated how the main lines of mission thought and practice in Puritanism are carried through.

The structure of the thesis as a whole can be seen as both chronological and logical. The ministerial work of Richard Sibbes covers the first third of seventeenth-century Puritanism. My thesis proposes that the fundamental principles of mission which are found in Sibbes reach through the whole Puritan period. Richard Baxter, whose life nearly spans the seventeenth century, shows the development of the practical implications of these principles in a way unequalled, to the best of my knowledge, by any other English Puritan. The call

---

[1] Cited by G. Nuttall in *Man's Faith and Freedom*, G. O. McCulloh, ed., 57.

of Sibbes and of Baxter for a meaningful witness for the faith by Christians bore fruit in New England. My concern is not to show that these two men are exclusively the source of the mission in New England, but rather that they, as representative of Puritanism in Old England, clearly demonstrate an emphasis on the need and the human accountability for conversion. This evangelistic emphasis can be demonstrated by the concern for the conversion of the Indians and for the conversion of unbelievers in the frontier churches. John Eliot, whose life nearly coincides with that of Baxter, made the conversion of the Indians his life-time task. Cotton Mather's life, likewise, shows consistent concern for missions to the Indian, especially during the first three decades of the eighteenth century. But his efforts, and those of the seventeenth-century Puritan ministry in New England, for the conversion of unbelievers, are most clearly shown in his "Ecclesiastical History of New-England to 1698" (*Magnalia Christi Americana*, 1702). Finally, we have chosen Jonathan Edwards (ministry 1722–1758), whose vital role in the Great Awakening and personal involvement in the Indian work are known. His *History of Redemption* is examined to determine the basic lines of his mission theology. My study concludes with a comparison of the men included in this study and of the main emphases found in their writings. These are related to some problems of modern missions.

The materials used are described under primary sources in the bibliography. The basic source for Sibbes has been his collected works, and for Baxter, his practical works and the unpublished letters and treatises found in the Dr. Williams's Library. The "missionary tracts," eleven publications (1643–1671) concerning Eliot's work and reprints of his letters, and the other writings of Eliot, have formed the basis for the third chapter. The numbering of the tracts are mine since the term "missionary tracts" is popular usage and not an official series. Contractions in common usage at the time have been resolved, e.g. $y^m$ = them, $w^{ch}$ = which, $\bar{m}$ = mm, and the old form of the s has been modernized. Since the pages in most prefaces, dedications, and epistles to the reader, and the like, in the missionary tracts, are not numbered, I have adopted my own pagination to indicate the places cited. Finally, when prefaces, etc., are completely italicized in the original, only words printed in bold face have been italicized here to indicate those words the author intended to emphasize.

CHAPTER I

# RICHARD SIBBES

THE THEOLOGICAL FOUNDATION OF THE MISSION

*Biographical Introduction*

Richard Sibbes[1] was born at Tostock, Suffolk County, in 1577, the year the Lutherans penned their Formula of Concord. Only five years had passed since Knox had died and thirteen since the death of Calvin. Matteo Ricci – the Jesuit missionary to China, John Robinson – pastor of the Pilgrims at Leiden, Justus Heurnius – Dutch missionary to the East Indies, and Bartholomé de las Casas – the Spanish conquistador, were Sibbes' contemporaries. His birthplace in Suffolk exposed him early to Puritan thought-forms. From Suffolk stemmed fugitives to Holland, Pilgrim emigrants, and nearly a hundred ministers – to be silenced in 1662. There, though his father complained of the cost, Sibbes had his early education. He was a studious lad, reading books while he walked the miles to and from school.[2] When grammar school was finished, his father, weary of expenses, bought an axe and other tools and set young Richard to work at a trade "to the great discontent of the youth, whose Genius wholy caried him another way."[3]

The local minister and an attorney sent the eighteen-year-old lad, without the consent of his father, to St. John's College at Cambridge with the necessary recommendations. Here he was partially supported by friends and partially by his father. Not long after his entrance in 1595, he was elected scholar of the college; he received his A.B. in 1599, was admitted a fellow two years later, and received his M.A. in 1602. About this time, under the preaching of Paul Baynes, Sibbes was converted[4] and began preaching.[5] By 1608 Zachary Catlin, a contemporary, calls him a preacher of note.[6] This judgment is confirmed by his election as a college preacher in 1609.[7] He received his B.D. degree in 1610, whereupon he was appointed lecturer at Holy Trinity, Cambridge. Because of his Puritan views he was deprived of both his lectureship and his professorship in 1615. Two years later, likely through the influence of high-

---

[1] "Sibbes" is spelled variously, also by himself and by his contemporaries: Sibbs, Sibs, Sybbes, Sybesius. Since "Sibbes" is used by the editor of his works, I have chosen that spelling.
[2] Alexander Grosart, "Memoir of Richard Sibbes," *The Complete Works of Richard Sibbes, D.D.*, I xxxii.
[3] Zachary Catlin, "Dr. Sibbs, his Life," *Ibid.*, cxxxv.
[4] Grosart, *op. cit.*, xxxv.
[5] Richard Sibbes, *The Complete Works of Richard Sibbes, D.D.*, I 126, "To the Christian Reader," SC, refers to sermons he has preached in London about this time.
[6] Catlin, *loc. cit.*
[7] *DNB*, 182.

positioned friends, he was chosen preacher at Gray's Inn, London. Here resided some of the most illustrious lawyers, students, and statesmen of the day.¹ While continuing to minister to fellow-residents and townsmen, he became master of St. Catherine's Hall, Cambridge, in 1626, received his D.D. in 1627, and was appointed to the curacy of Holy Trinity, Cambridge, in 1633. At Gray's Inn he remained until his death in 1635. He had never married.

Testimonies by contemporaries to Sibbes' gentle and warm spirit abound. Izaak Walton wrote in his personal copy of Sibbes' "The Returning Backslider":

> Of this blest man let this just praise be given,
> Heaven was in him before he was in heaven.²

According to Dr. Thomas Manton,³ Sibbes' manner of expression is a gift of unfolding and applying the gospel with "a native elegancy, as is not easily to be imitated."⁴ To these qualities Sibbes' sermons give evidence. His silence about himself, about his own accomplishments, even about his own conversion, breathes humility. In his sermon "A Description of Christ" he counsels men to be of Christ's disposition and to labor for humility of spirit. For us to "blazon" our own works abroad, he writes, is not the spirit of Christ.⁵ Sibbes published few of his own works. When he did, it was usually only after others had threatened to publish his sermons from defective notes. Yet in a preface to one of John Preston's works he wishes that "able men would be persuaded to publish their own works in their lifetime."⁶

Sibbes' preaching was direct application of Bible truth and had wide influence. Through it John Cotton was converted;⁷ he, in turn, was the agent of John Preston's conversion. In later years Preston and Sibbes both preached at Cambridge. Famous men, then students, must have heard his sermons: John Milton, Jeremy Taylor, George Herbert, Matthew Wren, William Gouge, Thomas Fuller, Charles Chauncey, Joseph Mede. At Gray's Inn, where he continued to preach Sundays, the names in his auditory were equally great: Bacon, Boyle, Cromwell, Drake, Nevill, Sidney, Standish, Winthrop. The greatest of these, also a resident of Gray's Inn, was Francis Bacon, whose last Essays were published during this period (1625).⁸

Besides being well-known in England, Sibbes' writings were among the most read and quoted by the Puritan fathers of New England. Elwood judges his writings, and those of John Owen, to be "the purest examples of the original Puritan spirit."⁹ Perry Miller writes:

---

[1] Grosart, *op. cit.*, xl, xli.
[2] *DNB*, 183.
[3] Thomas Manton, Puritan divine (1620–1677).
[4] Quoted by Grosart, *op cit.*, xvii.
[5] Sibbes, *op. cit.*, 30 (DC).
[6] *Ibid.*, xcviii.
[7] Cotton Mather, *Magnalia Christi Americana*, I 255; Larzer Ziff maintains that John Cotton taught more in Sibbes' tradition than in that of Perkins. Ziff, *Career of John Cotton*, 11.
[8] Grosart, *op. cit.*, xl, xli; Edmund S. Morgan, *The Puritan Dilemma*, 15.
[9] Douglas J. Elwood, *The Philosophical Theology of Jonathan Edwards*, 107.

> ...William Perkins, William Ames, Richard Sibbes and John Preston became "the most quoted, most respected, and most influential of contemporary authors in the writings and sermons of early Massachusetts."[1]

For the most part, Sibbes did not encounter great difficulty with church and royal authority for his Puritan views, except in 1615, as noted above. Twice, however, he was summoned before the Star Chamber, which served with royal authority to enforce obedience to ecclesiastical decrees and to punish offenders. The first arraignment was occasioned by a circular letter, signed by Sibbes and three others in 1627, appealing for funds to assist distressed ministers and private persons who were left homeless and poor by "the furie of the mercilesse papists in the Upper Palatinate."[2] Cries for assistance by the Protestant victims in the Thirty Years War had gone unheeded by King James. Public collections had failed. Sibbes and his friends inaugurated a private collection. For this they were severely reprimanded.

In 1633 the second summons came. This time Sibbes was found guilty of serving as one of twelve trustees (feoffees) for funds to support Puritan ministers, teachers, and students at selected places. The feoffees, in operation from 1626, were viewed by Archbishop Laud as *"the main instruments for the Puritan faction to undo the Church."*[3] Because he judged such a practice subversive to the discipline of the church, it was summarily suppressed. However, the occasion for the feoffees was the increasing official hostility to Puritan preachers, – the same hostility that motivated the great migration to New England after 1628. Sibbes' motive in establishing the fund may be sensed in these words:

> If it were possible, it were to be wished that there were set up some lights in all the dark corners of this kingdom, that might shine to those people that sit in darkness, and in the shadow of death.[4]

It is well to note here that Sibbes lived and died a minister of the Church of England. In spite of the painful trials of his friends and the bleedings of his own sympathetic conscience, his view of the times in which he lived was not altogether pessimistic: ceremonial matters were not essentials; surely the day of toleration would soon arrive. His deep personal piety gave the certainty that in life and death the course of events rested in the hands of a faithful Saviour. Sibbes' will and testament, dictated the day before his death, commences:

> ...I commend and bequeath my soule into the hands of my gratious Saviour, whoe hath redeemed it w$^{th}$ his most pretious blood, and appeares now in heaven to receave it, with humble thankes that he hath vouchsafed I should be borne and live in the best tymes of the gospell, and have my interest in the comforte of it....[5]

---

[1] Perry Miller, *Errand Into the Wilderness*, 59, quoting H. W. Clark, *Thirty-Two Divines*, 143.
[2] Grosart, *op cit.*, lviii.
[3] Laud's *Works*, III 216, 217, quoted by Grosart, *op. cit.*, lxxiv.
[4] Sibbes, *op. cit.*, I 331, SS.
[5] Quoted by Grosart, *op. cit.*, cxxviii.

A. THE CONVERSION OF MAN

*1. Divine Sovereignty and Human Responsibility*

Two aspects of conversion which recur in Sibbes' sermons are the situation of man as he stands under judgment and the redemptive activity of God. Divine sovereignty and human responsibility, he wrote, form essential parts of the converting drama in history. God is eternally active; man must be active. Conversion cannot be explained apart from either activity. "What God worketh in thee, thou must work thyself." [1] There is priority both in time and significance in God's act. God afflicts man for his sin; man cries to God; God sends deliverance; man gives thanks.[2] Both the heavenward and the earthward sides of redemption have their place.

> When God by grace enlarges the will, he intends to give the deed.... When our wills, therefore, carry us to that which God wills above all, we may well expect he will grant us what we will.[3]
> It is not sufficient that God is reconciled in Christ, because God will alway have a reflex act from man.[4]

Even "the spiritual contract between Christ and his church" makes clear that redemption requires that *"both parties must consent."*[5] God's sovereign will is neither altered nor compromised by man's act of faith. Nor is man's responsible act of faith non-essential to redemption. Both the divine and human aspects are necessary.

a. The Human Situation

The consent required of man fits his created capacity. Man is not made to be worked by spading like earth.[6] Man is made to reason, to determine, to work.[7] For this he was created. Sin complicates, if not incapacitates, these functions. No longer are they used to the glory of God and for the good of man.[8] There is no supernatural goodness in us; rather, there is enmity,[9] and men "bury that divine spark, their souls, which is capable of the divine nature."[10] The corruption of nature through Adam is multiplied by continual sinning.[11] This

---

[1] To avoid needless repetition, all citations will be from *The Complete Works of Richard Sibbes*, unless otherwise indicated. VII 510, PP.
[2] VI 136, RD.
[3] I 246, SC.
[4] VI 342, AA.
[5] II 201, S.
[6] VII 510, PP.
[7] I 23, DC; 392, UM; VI 367, FL; 412, ML.
[8] VI 318–356, AA.
[9] I 82, BR.
[10] I 150, SC.
[11] I 173–174, 231, SC; IV 441, C2C4.

opposes and excludes divine light.[1] Fallen man is dead in sin. In a sermon on Ephesians 2:1, Sibbes points out that man is dead in sin in three senses. 1. By the "sin of Adam" we were all damned. A corruption of nature results. We cannot act, think, will, or choose spiritually. 2. By a "death of sentence" upon us, not only for Adam's sin, but for actual sins of our own, we add to the condemning judgment already upon us. 3. By being "dead in law" or guilt, we are bound over into eternal death. Though "fire and brimstone" preaching is infrequent in Sibbes' sermons, his view of the implications of human sin is plain.[2]

Yet none are to "pretend impossibility" of salvation because of the crippling power of sin.[3] The cause of every man's misery is his own sin; all power of the world or hell cannot keep him there if he repent.[4] There can be no word of comfort for those who will to be evil.[5] It is our life here that determines eternity.[6] Even "the devil cannot force men to wickedness. It is their own sinful hearts which betray them into his hands."[7] Here humanity is one. "Do not every one of us bring sticks to the common fire?"[8] Sin has completely defaced the image of God in us. Man would be absolute,[9] when by reason of his natural dependence and unnatural sin he should be broken in spirit.

There is, thus, necessity for a change, either on God's part or ours. "Now who must change? God that is unchangeable, or we that are corrupt and changeable?"[10] The answer is obvious. Man is like a cracked bell. It must be recast; it is good for nothing else. So we must be set in tune again "before the soul can make any sweet harmony in the ears of God."[11] No one comes to heaven without the change of a new birth. But how is one born again? How does one change from death to life? There are two answers. The first is that a dead person cannot make himself alive; only God can do it. Without the gift of the Spirit of Christ, no one can be a Christian. God creates a new heart which can believe and trust the gospel.[12] "Nothing in heaven or earth will work out corruption, and change our dispositions, but the Spirit of Christ."[13]

> The Holy Ghost, therefore, puts us in frame by a spirit of faith, infusing a spirit of knowledge into the understanding, a spirit of obedience into the will.[14]

The second answer of Sibbes to the question how to be born again is that man is responsible for his rebirth. You ask, "What then should we do to be saved? Why, receive him: that is, believe in him now."[15] This is a direct act of faith. A close but clear distinction exists between the "direct act" of faith and the

---

[1] II 465, MF.
[2] VII 400–401, DM; cf. also I 40; II 492, 503; V 39; VI 354.
[3] I 391, UM.
[4] II 257, RB.
[5] Ibid., 308.
[6] III 126, C2C1.
[7] V 269, PF.
[8] VI 189, CCC.
[9] VI 220, GI.
[10] IV 257, EG; cf. I 411, SH-P.
[11] IV 256, EG.
[12] I 238, SC.
[13] I 177, SC.
[14] IV 449, C2C4.
[15] VII 378, WS.

"reflect act." In the direct I cast myself upon Christ; in the reflect I know that I am saved by the fruits of the Spirit.[1] The second depends upon the changeable quality of my feelings and grows or diminishes at times with my state in grace.[2] Yet the two firm grounds of faith always remain: God promises that whoever casts himself upon mercy shall be saved, and I have so cast myself.[3]

The reflect act or the fruits of faith brings the assurance of salvation to man. A close examination of one's basic desires and attitudes verifies this; trust, spiritual gifts, sympathy for good, antipathy to evil, partaking in the communion of saints, prayer, acceptance of earthly condition, desire for further grace, ability to beget other Christians, looking for the coming of Christ, – these are some of the many indications.[4] One may thus distinguish counterfeit from true faith by the religious affections.[5] They can show what we are in religion now.[6] For assurance of salvation it is not enough to know; one must also feel a desire to be saved with all one's heart in the affections.[7]

Thankfulness will be the overwhelming and compelling motive in the Christian life.[8] Not the quantity but the sincerity of fruit counts.[9] Men ought to be weighed rather than counted. Compounded as he is of both good and evil,[10] the Christian yet takes real joy in life in the knowledge that his is the way of final victory.[11] He belongs to Christ, and Christ will never forsake his own.[12]

But what of those who do not believe the gospel? We speak here only of those who have been under the hearing of the Word. Of heathen we shall speak shortly. Man from the time of Adam lives by nature in a state of separation from God.[13] This is to be under condemnation, under judgment. Therefore "if thou wilt still live in thy sins, thou shalt be damned." Rejection is based, then, on disbelief of the gospel rather than on breaking of the Ten Commandments.[14] "Men are not damned because they cannot do better, but because they will do no better; if there were no will, there would be no hell." [15]

> None are damned in the church but those that will....Such must know that the Lamb can be angry, and they that will not come under his sceptre of mercy, shall be crushed in pieces by his sceptre of power.[16]

They voluntarily purpose to live in sin;[17] in glorious times of the gospel, they have sinned against the means;[18] their own hardness has kept them from faith.[19] The evil of punishment fulfills the good of justice.[20]

The gate in religion is narrow.

---

[1] VII 213, DMHC; 378, WS; V 390, SA.
[2] VII 418, FT; V 393, SA.
[3] VII 429, FT.
[4] II 64, BO; IV 266, 279, EG; VI 9–15, FC; 352, AA; V 114–115, EP3; VI 459, 470, HC; VII 130 ,TR; 273, SAnt.
[5] II 219, BG.
[6] IV 182, GH.
[7] IV 381, C2C4; VI 98, SF.
[8] I 255, SC; 396, DS; III 331, C2C1.
[9] II 362, RB.
[10] VI 36, TH.
[11] VII 443, FT.
[12] I 98, BR; 396, DS; II 49, BO; VI 403, 407, ML.
[13] III 155–156, C2C1.
[14] *Ibid.*, 399.
[15] I 175, SC.
[16] I 73, BR.
[17] VII 524, BD; 490–491, DGC.
[18] VI 495, KDE.
[19] IV 313, C2C4.
[20] VI 86–87, SR.

...we must strip ourselves of ourselves before we can enter; if we bring any ruling lust to religion, it will prove a bitter root of some gross sin, or of apostasy and final desperation.[1]

The Lord himself threatens hell to make us lowly.[2] God uses our imaginations to our profit. As he represents heaven under terms of a banquet and a kingdom and our union with Christ as a marriage, so he presents hell under terms of wrath and fire and darkness. Because childhood is the age of fancy, we use such representations to instil the shunning of evil and the loving of good to their minds. So the Lord does also to us.[3]

Three degrees of estrangement from God exist: spiritual, physical, and eternal death.[4] If one does not get into life here, he will never attain it hereafter.[5] The offer is made; we are commanded to obey; God promises; we are invited – but if we reject all this there is eternal death.[6] A reprobate is a man who is "totally, wholly, and finally hardened, and it is joined with security and insensibleness; it is joined with obstinacy, and with contempt of the means." [7] The Word says that God hardens such a one, but the cause is from our own selves. God's part is four-fold. 1. He withholds and withdraws his melting and softening powers. 2. He takes away from us his graces, which are not natural in us. 3. He hardens by giving us to the devil, to be vexed by his troubles. 4. He hardens by propounding good objects which, meeting with a wicked heart, make it harder.[8] When a good object comes to a bad heart, its goodness is thwarted. It hardens. "So we see God cannot be impeached with the hardening of our hearts, because all the cause is from ourselves." [9]

Believer and reprobate are identifiable in the concreteness of life. What they do with the means of grace, the gospel, defines which they are. History only in small and tentative ways introduces to consciousness the depth and riches of the mystery of Eternal Will. But what is revealed coincides with that Will without denying either God's eternal counsel or man's responsible decision.

b. God's Redeeming Act

God is supreme. Redemption is of his initiation. Grace is of his dispensation Salvation is of his ordination. He established the Covenant of Grace in Christ.

> Christ was chosen before all worlds to be the head of the elect. He was predestinate and ordained by God. As we are ordained to salvation, so Christ is ordained to be the head of all that shall be saved. He was chosen eternally, and chosen in time. He was singled out to the work by God; and all others that are chosen are chosen in him. There had been no choosing of men but in him; for God saw us so defiled, lying in our filth, that he could not look upon us but in his Son. He chose him, and us in him.[10]

---

[1] I 169, SC.
[2] VII 374, WS.
[3] I 185, SC.
[4] V 234, SJ.
[5] IV 426, C2C4.
[6] III 399–400, C2C1.
[7] VI 38, TH.
[8] *Idem.*
[9] *Idem.*
[10] I 9, DC; cf. also IV 118, YA; V 12, CW.

God's choosing is founded in mercy which is at the heart of his nature.¹ Such mercy overcomes the resistance in man ² and makes him wise unto salvation.³ The Spirit of God infuses

> ...a divine nature into us, which we call the Spirit, being the seed of all grace....As in original sin there is the seed of all corruption, so in the Spirit the seed of regeneration is the seed of all grace....⁴

The Holy Spirit, thus, is crucial to conversion, since conversion is the fruit of grace. Commenting on the salutation in II Corinthians, Sibbes says:

> *Grace*, in this place, *is the free favour and love of God from his own bowels*; not for any desert, or worth, or strength of love of ours. ...We say we are justified by grace, and so do they (i.e., the "papists"). What do they mean by being justified by grace? That is, by inherent grace. We say, No; we are justified by grace; that is, by the free favour of God in Jesus Christ. ...Eternal life is χάρισμα. The word comes of χάρις, of gift. ...So from the first grace, to eternal life, which is the complement of all, all is grace.⁵

God's work of grace is wrought out through his covenant. Christ is its foundation. The fulfilling of it on our part is also of grace. He gives us faith.

> Think of faith as the first grace of the Spirit, that acteth and stirs up all other graces. It is the first, because it is the grace of union that knits us to Christ. It is the grace required in the covenant of grace.⁶

This is but another way of saying, as we noted above, that God chose Christ and us in him. Paul writes in Galatians 2:20 of "the Son of God who hath loved me, and gave himself for me." This means that "God loves some with a peculiar and a special love." A consequent question is: "Whether Christ loved all, and gave himself for all...?" ⁷ The answer is clear. He loved all mankind in one way, his own in a special way.

> Those that the Father gives in election, Christ redeems, and by redemption saves; for redemption, in regard of efficacy, is no larger than God's election.... His [Christ's] love is only to those whom God gave him, for he looks upon all he died for as they were in his Father's love. There are a company in the world whom God hates: 'Esau have I hated,' Rom. ix. 13.... Saint Paul's meaning, therefore, is not that he loved me with that love wherewith he loved all mankind. The apostle means a more special love...than he bears to all mankind.⁸

One needs always to bear in mind that Sibbes is preaching to Christians, at least to nominal ones. Frequent interjections punctuate his sermons to answer

---

¹ I 62, BR; II 325, RB; V 482, FO.
² IV 385–387, C2C4.
³ III 278, C2C1.
⁴ IV 441, C2C4.
⁵ III 16–17, C2C1.
⁶ IV 440, C2C4.
⁷ V 388–389, SA.
⁸ *Idem.*

false conclusions drawn from such a doctrine as election.[1] Belief in this truth is the fruit of faith, the highest rung of the ladder, where we cannot begin.[2] We should, therefore, leave disputing about such matters and fall to obeying the gospel.[3] God's secrets are never the rule of our obedience.[4] To make them so is to attempt to pull God's office out of his hands,[5] an impossible and vain thing for clay to do to its potter.[6] Sibbes appeals to Calvin, "a very holy man" who "out of his holiness avoided curious questions as much as he might."[7] "Dark disputes of election and predestination," Sibbes emphasizes,

> at the first especially, let them go.... Begin not with those... but see first what God hath wrought in thy heart, what affection to heavenly things; and thence from thy affections to go backward to election, and forward to glorification, there is no danger in it.[8]

God is "the Father and the God of all the elect, and only the elect, and of every one of the elect, as we say, *in solidum*."[9]

> All the passages of salvation are done by way of covenant, by way of commerce and intercourse between God and man, but God begins first. In election, indeed, we choose him; but he chooseth us first.[10]

This is a confession born only of genuine humility.[11] Its blessing comes in the assurance that God's care is full and effectual. "He cares for all as one, and for every one as if he had but one.[12]

> Our choosing... is an evidence God hath chosen us; and once chosen, ever chosen. Our actions are but reflex. He chose us, loved us, knows us, and therefore we choose, love, and know him; and these being the gifts of God to us, are without repentance on his part.

Nothing can, therefore, take this part from us.[13]

Acceptance of election, which is the confession of humility and the foundation for growth of Christian assurance, is the end fruit, not the first fruit, of faith. Men proceed wrongly from God the Father and election to Christ the Son and redemption to the Holy Spirit and sanctification. Rather, the reverse order is the only way for man to come to God.[14] God is not thereby excluded. On the contrary, he sovereignly works in this way. He must alter the will,[15] establish the means,[16] reveal unbelief to the soul,[17] and persuade powerfully and effectively.[18]

---

[1] The same holds for other revealed matters, *e.g.*, of angels and heavenly orders. VI 319, AA.
[2] VII 54, DR.
[3] VI 353, AA.
[4] V 390, SA.
[5] VI 257, RP.
[6] VI 202, CCC.
[7] V 352, CE; cf. also VII 545, ChE.
[8] IV 182, GH.
[9] VI 477, HC.
[10] *Ibid.*, 423.
[11] VI 202, CCC.
[12] VII 216, DM.
[13] VII 295, 288, MC.
[14] I 94, BR.
[15] VII 281, SG.
[16] I 83, BR.
[17] II 464, MF.
[18] IV 378, C2C4; V 242, SJ; VII 434, FT.

> This calling of his is the beginning of his golden chain of salvation. He calls us from a cursed estate to a happy communion; from death and bondage under the devil, to be kings and princes. And this is done by outward means, and inward work of the Spirit. This calling is a powerful calling, enabling them to come that are called.[1]

The inward work of the Spirit is God's affair. It is man's, however, in this respect: that God chooses to work through means, chiefly through the church and its ministers. The two-sided character of the God-to-man and man-to-God relationship is present here as always. For salvation to be achieved, there must be concurrence between heaven and earth, God and the ministers, the Spirit and the ordinances, Christ and the church.

Heaven came to earth in Christ. His life and death became the foundation of a saved earth. There was a merciful disposition in Christ joined with perfect holiness.[2] Through his blood the church began, grew, and will be brought to completion.[3] His righteousness is imputed to us.[4] Because he has conquered the world, death, hell, and sin, he is the king of the soul.[5] "Christ hath all first, and we have all from him."[6] "See thy nature abased in Christ, see thy nature glorified in Christ, see thy nature filled with all grace in Christ."[7] As he was the Son, the beloved, the one acquitted for sin, justified, and ascended, so shall we be,[8] if we will have whole Christ[9] as a king to govern us.[10]

This does not mean that Christ is to be viewed as an appeaser to the Trinity.

> ...God the Father allures and invites you when Christ doth it, because he is anointed to invite you. Think that the Father is as peaceable as Christ was, because Christ was so by his Father's appointment, by his anointing. See all the three Persons, the Father, Son, and Holy Ghost in Christ.[11]

All of salvation, from election, calling, justification, and sanctification to glorification, is in him.[12] He apprehends us with an effectual calling.[13] "Out of Christ there is no grace."[14] God approaches us in five steps, depending upon the depth of need:

> 1. Now when I see that God keeps *open house*, come who will, without denying entertainment unto any, and when God's Spirit hath wrought the will in me, and I come and take God at his word, and believe in Christ...this is faith....

---

[1] V 112, EP3.
[2] I 62, BR.
[3] I 132, SC; VII 478, DGC.
[4] I 19, DC.
[5] II 140, BO.
[6] III 27, C2C1; IV 26, CP.
[7] III 27, C2C1; V 433, FS.
[8] III 27, C2C1.
[9] Sibbes uses the phrase *whole Christ* frequently and in three senses: the acceptance of all the doctrine concerning his person and work, the complete commitment of oneself in obedient service, and the inseparable union of Christ as Head with believers in the church.
[10] III 400, C2C1.
[11] III 417, C2C1.
[12] IV, 331, C2C4; VI 351, AA.
[13] V 103–104, EP3; 242, SJ.
[14] V 191, AC.

2. Now if a man do stagger, for all that the King keeps open house, so as he will not or doth not come, then in the second place comes *invitation*. Because we are slow to believe, therefore God invites us....

3. Thirdly, Sometimes Christ meets with a slow and dull heart, lazy and careless, in a manner, what become of it;.... 'God sends an embassage to *entreat us*';... We know it might be counted a kind of indignity for the king of Spain, so great a monarch, to sue unto the Hollanders for peace, who are so far inferior unto him. This dishonour God puts up at our hands and says [sues?] unto us first, when rather it becomes us on our knees to beg for it.

4. Fourthly, If none of all this will do, then comes a further degree, *a command from the Highest*, You shall do it.... What, may one object, *must* I needs believe? Yes, thou art as strictly bound to believe, as not to murder, not to be an idolater, not to steal.

5. Fifthly, If all this will not do, then comes *threatenings*. Then God swears, that such as refuse shall never enter into his rest.[1]

God in Christ becomes a suitor to us; whereas earth should be seeking heaven, heaven seeks earth.[2] God does not use physical force to make converts.[3] In the winning, gaining disposition of Christ [4] is the sweet manner of the gospel demonstrated.[5] Satan sets out God as a terrible judge,[6] while God rejoices in conversions as monuments of his mercy.[7] He uses friendly intercourse and persuasion;[8] he entreats and commands men to come in.[9]

> God persuades the soul *sweetly of the truth*, by showing a man the goodness of it, and the suitableness to our condition, and the reasons of it, how they agree to our nature. He doth not force the soul, but doth it with reasons and arguments sweetly.[10]

Sin has completely defaced the image of God in man. He no longer lives in right relation to God, nor can he. Reconciliation is possible only by grace. "Nothing in heaven or earth will work out corruption, and change our dispositions, but the Spirit of Christ, clothing divine truths with a divine power to this purpose." [11] Through his Son, God redeems man, and through his Spirit, God awakens sin-deadened hearts. Man, on the other hand, must choose for God; he must respond to grace. Apparently, some of Sibbes' auditors objected that the above two answers were inconsistent. This he repeatedly disavows. There can be no contradiction in God; there is only lack in our powers of comprehension.

---

[1] VII 378–380, WS.
[2] VI 112, SuS.
[3] VI 313, VV.
[4] IV 262, EG; I 29, DC; 79, BR.
[5] V 506, FO.
[6] VI 379, FL.
[7] I 284, SC.
[8] I 39, BR.
[9] VI 484, HC; VII 484, DGC.
[10] VII 435, FT.
[11] I 177, SC.

## 2. The Right Use of Nature

There is a natural knowledge of God. Every creature, every benefit, every chastisement, has a voice to say–"seek God."

> Everything hath a voice. We know God's nature somewhat in the creature, that he is a powerful, a wise, a just God. We see it by the works of creation and providence; but if we should know his nature, and not his will towards us–his commanding will, what he will have us do; and his promising will, what he will do for us–except we have a ground for this from God, the knowledge of his nature is but a confused knowledge; it serves but to make us inexcusable, as in Rom. i. 19, *seq.*, it is proved at large.[1]

What God is in himself, his power and wisdom, we can discover from nature; one not in Christ still has God as Father in creation and providence.[2] What God is in relation to us, must be revealed.[3]

The knowledge the heathen as natural man possesses is of a negative kind. He knows that to trust in the creature is vanity. The Stoics knew that, but they were ignorant of where to place their confidence.[4] The heathen knows the vanity of the world. Plutarch and Seneca, and the rest, had fine speeches on the passing nature of things, but they lacked communion with God.[5] The heathen by the use of discretion and knowledge saw there was nothing in the world to give true happiness. Yet they had not the grace of trust.[6] The heathen out of the strength of moral discourse and outward experience can tell you that all earthly things are perishing. But for the affirmative part, paganism is blind.[7]

Natural man, so defined, is not restricted to the pagans. The Church of England and Christian lands are well stocked with such folk: idolaters see the vanity of false gods well enough; in Italy thousands of the "wittier and learneder" sort see the folly of their religion; and in England learned men discourse on the evils of popery, but in their own lives are no better for it. "A negative Christian is no Christian.... There must be a positive as well as a negative religion; a cleaving to God as well as a forsaking of idols." [8]

Conflicts constantly arise in the natural soul. Contrary passions, such as pride resulting in assertion and covetousness demanding restraint, fight not only against God and reason but against each other. Contrary affections strive for supremacy, anger calling for revenge and fear of the law frustrating the soul. The natural conscience reasons degrading passion to subjection in order to maintain self-respect. Gospel truth impels unconverted hearts to resist sins in order to quiet disturbed consciences.[9] These conflicts in carnal men are found not only in the dregs of society but among the refined sort, who desire eminence in the world. So men

---

[1] VI 112, SuS.
[2] VI 454, HC.
[3] VI 253, 255, RP.
[4] II 291, RB.
[5] III 57, C2Cl.
[6] VI 252, RP.
[7] VI 363, FL.
[8] II 291, RB.
[9] I 152, SC.

> ...bury that divine spark, their souls, capable of the divine nature, and fitter to be a sanctuary and temple for God to dwell in, than by closing with baser things to become base itself.[1]

Through the conscience every man in the world has a rule.

> In the soul there is a treasury of rules by nature. The word doth add more rules, the law and the gospel. And that part of the soul that preserves rules is called intellectual, because it preserves rules. All men by nature have these graven in the soul. And therefore the heathen were exact in the rules of justice, in the principles which they had by nature, grafted and planted in them.
>
> Now because the copy of the image of God, the law of God written in nature, was much blurred since the fall, God gave a new copy of his law, which was more exact. Therefore the Jews, which had the word of God, should have had more conscience than the heathen, because they had a better general rule. And now we having the gospel too, which is a more evangelical rule, we should be more exact in our lives than they.[2]

There are thus three degrees or ranks of men in the world under which all men may be comprehended: 1. the estate of nature, 2. the estate of man under the spirit of bondage under the law, and 3. the estate of grace under the gospel.[3]

Men in the estate of nature have the negative kind of knowledge of which we have spoken. To these, as to all, God has given a spark of reason which makes the use of concepts and understanding of things possible. The intellect "is the engine whereby we do all things as men and are capable of the grace of God."[4] There is

> ...a divine instinct, power, and faculty in men, that nothing here can suffice; which shews, that there is a place to satiate the will and the understanding, and fill the affections; that there is a condition which shall make a man fully happy.[5]

There are "*some beams of excellency in every creature*. There is somewhat of God in every creature." [6]

Man is made for a better life, but he will not go into "a better estate, to the heat, to the sunbeams to warm him. He will not seek for the favour of God, to be cherished with the assurance of his love." [7] The worst judgment at the last day will be not ignorance, but the refusal to know.[8] Gentiles are obstinate persons.[9] Because they erred grossly in the first table of the law, God gave them over to err in the second.[10] The heathen want a god, so they make one of fire and another of water. They take instruments for the real thing; means for the end.[11]

---

[1] I 150, SC.
[2] III 210, C2Cl.
[3] V 359, LF.
[4] VI 152–153, RD.
[5] V 360, LF.
[6] II 147–148, BO.
[7] VI 221, GI.
[8] III 213, C2Cl.
[9] III 514, C2Cl.
[10] VII 368, SP.
[11] III 49, C2Cl.

In spite of this folly, God has a general love for all mankind.[1] He answers the outward cry of the heathen outwardly; but without the knowledge of God in Christ, they are in great misery.[2] "How pitiful is it to live in places where means of salvation are not, that have no light shining in their hearts at all?"[3] "Can the love of God be in them? No."[4] Apart from Christ there is no grace.[5] The seeds of the law are in our nature, but there are none of the Spirit, for these are supernatural.[6]

Many nominal Christians are actually still in the state of nature. They have never so much as entered the second degree or rank of men, those under the law. Not that they did not know the law; contrariwise, they had been under the preaching of the gospel besides. Yet they cherish the principles of nature in common with the heathen;[7] they reject the gracious offer of mercy. God sees better conduct in a pagan than in such a one.[8] "Most of our ordinary people are worse than pagans."[9] The heathen is better than a hypocrite.[10] "Negative infidelity [of heathen and infidels] is, as it were, no sin in comparison."[11] It is negative in that no means for salvation was present. Not that the heathen shall escape judgment. As the heathen

> ...sin without the gospel, so shall they be damned without the gospel. The rule of their damnation shall be the law of nature written in their hearts; for this is an undoubted truth, *no man ever lived answerable to his rule*; and therefore God hath just ground of damnation to any man, even from this, that he hath not lived answerable to...his own conscience. So that we need not fly to reprobation, etc.[12]

Before a man can come from nature to grace, he must come under the law. Therefore out of love for the souls of men God set forth the law.

> God gave the law, not to damn men but in love to men, that thereby they might see the impurity of their natures, and lives, and the curse due to it, and so follow him forthright to Christ, from Sinai to Sion, appealing from the throne of justice to the throne of grace and mercy, the Lord Christ.[13]

In commenting on Romans 2 and 3 Sibbes points out how the Jews

> ...bragged of many excellent privileges they had above the Gentiles; as to have the law, circumcision; to be teachers of others; to have God amongst them; and [they] therefore despised the Gentiles.[14]

The apostle grants the higher degree of their knowledge but shows that in condemning the Gentiles they condemned themselves. "All the learning in the world will not set the image of God upon the soul, will not bring the soul out of darkness into the kingdom of Christ...."[15]

The three ranks in which all men are included form as well the three degrees

---

[1] V 389, SA.
[2] IV 406, C2C4.
[3] IV 354, C2C4.
[4] VI 394, ML.
[5] V 191, AC.
[6] I 391, UM.
[7] III 213, C2C1.
[8] VI 495, KDE.
[9] V 495, FO.
[10] V 183, AC.
[11] I 389, UM.
[12] *Idem.*
[13] IV 339, 340, C2C4.
[14] VII 368, WS.
[15] IV 388, C2C4.

of the man on his way to heaven.[1] His pilgrimage not only moves from nature to law to gospel, but one builds upon the other. "Grace presupposeth nature."[2] "The Gospel doth not take away or dissolve the laws of nature and reason."[3] Rather, "God works grace upon nature."

> ...though a man be spiritually dead, yet notwithstanding he hath feet to carry him to the house of God; he hath ears to hear the word of God; he hath abilities of nature upon which grace is founded.[4]

Any man living in the church without any inward change can come by common grace to the means. We must use the nature God has given us to

> ...offer ourselves to the gracious and blessed means wherein the Spirit of God may work. Therefore I beseech you, as you would be raised up out of this death, hear the noise of God's trumpet. Come within the compass of the means.... the word 'is the word of life,' because, together with the word, God conveys spiritual life.[5]

So much nature can do that is right and good. "Grace is seated in the powers of nature.... carnal sins disable nature, and so sets us in a greater distance from grace."[6] In the church redeemed natures and corrupt natures are to be found. Yet God "rains the showers of his ordinances upon all, but the benefit thereof is only to his ground, not to the reprobates."[7] He evidences a more special love for the redeemed than for mankind in general.[8]

Does reason have a use in the gospel? "Sanctified reason hath, to draw sanctified conclusions from sanctified principles."[9] Reason can show that gospel mysteries are not contrary to, though certainly above, reason, even as the light of the sun is above the light of a candle.

> The same thing may be both the object of faith and of reason. The immortality of the soul, it is a matter of faith, and it is well proved by the heathen by the light of reason. And it is a delightful thing to the soul in things that reason can conceive of to have a double light, for the more light the more comfort; to have both the light of nature, and the light of grace and of God's Spirit.[10]

The resurrection is likewise manifested by both Scripture and reason.[11]

Reason, however, has its limits. In truths altogether above itself it must yield. It cannot conceive Christ in the womb of a virgin, the joining of two natures in one, the trinity of persons in one divine nature, and the like. Here it is most reasonable for reason to yield to faith.[12] As reason corrects sense, so faith corrects reason.[13]

---

[1] IV 233, EG.
[2] III 199, C2Cl.
[3] VI 89, SR.
[4] VII 404, DM.
[5] *Idem.*
[6] V 419, FS.
[7] V 389, SA.
[8] *Idem.*
[9] V 467 FO.
[10] *Idem.*
[11] VII 317, GR.
[12] V 467, FO.
[13] V 372, LF; VII 423–425, FT.

Some one proposes: Gentiles are saved by the rule of nature, Jews by the law, and Christians by the gospel,—so all are saved. This is wrong, since salvation is only through Christ (Acts 4:12).[1] If you take away Christ, what is left? Only hell![2] It is a great fundamental error that says man can be saved in any religion, for salvation comes by knowledge which is to be found only in the church.[3]

How is the heathen in the state of nature to be brought to the gospel? Admittedly, serious obstacles arise here. In pagans there is such a distance between corrupt nature and divine grace

> ...that we must have a great deal of preparation; and though there be nothing in preparation to bring the soul to have grace, yet it brings the soul to a nearer distance than those that are wild persons.[4]

Reason which is refined and raised by education, example, and custom, breaks in some degree the force of natural corruption. It brings the soul into another nature, as it were, and yet not into a true state of grace. Yet if there come no change, after a time corruption may prevail over education.[5] It is thus possible to bring men into a civil state, which is good, but insufficient for salvation.[6] Some truths may civilize; other helps may be profitable. Still, these are all inferior works of the Spirit which may make the soul of men civil, with whom it is pleasant to converse, but this is like embalming a dead body, so long as it is not accompanied by the almighty work of the Spirit.[7]

In his "Lydia's Conversion" sermon, Sibbes comments in some detail on the works of preparation for conversion. God ordinarily prepares those he intends to turn to himself. This is usual procedure, both for works of nature, as ploughing before sowing, and for works of grace. The distance between man's nature and corruption, and grace make a rising by degrees necessary. There is no meritorious cause in our preparations. But how much preparation is necessary? Until a man's soul is so far cast down that he sets a higher price on Christ than on all the world. When the light of the Spirit brings him so far, he is prepared for conversion. This has implications for preaching to the heathen:

> Now, God in preparation for the most part civiliseth people, and ther Christianiseth them, as I may say; for the Spirit of God will not be effectual in a rude, wild, and barbarous soul; in men that are not men. Therefore they must be brought to civility; and not only to civility, but there must be a work of the law, to cast them down; and then they are brought to Christianity thereupon.
>
> Therefore they take a good course that labour to break them from their natural rudeness and fierceness.... There is no forcing of grace on a soul so far indisposed, that is, not brought to civility. Rude and barbarous souls therefore, God's manner is to bring them in the compass of civility,

---

[1] III 392–393, C2C1.
[2] III 418, C2C1.
[3] IV 318, C2C4.
[4] VII 196, DMHC.
[5] I 152–153, SC.
[6] IV 340, C2C4.
[7] IV 388, C2C4.

and then seeing what their estate is in the corruption of nature, to deject them, and then to bring them to Christianity....

For however there is no force of a meritorious cause in preparations to grace, to raise up the soul to grace.... Yet notwithstanding it brings a man to a less distance than other wild creatures that come not within the compass of the means. Therefore usually to those that use the talents of their understanding and will, that they have, well, God after discovers himself more and more.

Therefore let all be encouraged to grow more and more to courses of civility and religion, and wait the good time till God shine on them in mercy....[1]

We have noted that salvation is only of grace. Natural man knows God as the wise Creator but not as Redeemer in Christ. In negative knowledge concerning human transitoriness he abounds. Conflicts follow, a divine instinct points him to a better estate. He wills not to go. How pitiful as he kneels in darkness to his self-made gods. But far more pitiful still is the man under gospel light, yet rejecting mercy. Each shall be judged strictly according to the rule under which he lived. The law drives men to Christ or else it only condemns, as it did the unbelieving Jews. Reason may confirm some divine truths; others it yields to faith. Proper education of reason prepares nature for works of grace.

We have seen that in the relationship between divine sovereignty and human responsibility, missions is a divine prerogative, yet a prerogative requiring human response. Man is not capable of achieving redemption through natural knowledge of God. Reason, though unmeritorious, can be used as an instrument to prepare man for conversion. The question remains: whose responsibility is it to present God's sovereign command that all men repent and believe the gospel? For Sibbes, the accountability rests with the church through the preaching of the gospel and the witness of the individual member.

### B. THE ROLE OF THE CHURCH

#### 1. *The Character of the Church*

Sometimes by "church" the Word of God intends all under the regular hearing of the gospel; believers and unbelievers are included. Sometimes it is used more narrowly in referring to the bride of Christ, a peculiar people; only believers are included here.[2] Concretely we have to do with the mixed church. Ministers address both sorts of people mentioned above. The church lives in a dependent relation to the Word.[3] To all the Word of God is taught. So long as the Word is taught, we must remain in the visible church.[4] No man can do without being a member of some particular church,[5] yet no less than full sincerity of profession will do for admission to the name of Christian and the sacraments.[6] The church is a "seminary" (nursery) of young plants to get us to heaven.[7]

---

[1] VI 522, 523, LC.
[2] III 12, C2C1.
[3] III 374–375, C2C1.
[4] II 242, BG.
[5] III 12, C2C1.
[6] III 12–14, C2C1.
[7] II 235, BG; III 347, C2C1.

Every church is a particular church, so is the Church of England.[1] But all are part of the one universal catholic church.[2]

> What is the meaning of it? I believe that in all times to the end of the world there will be a company of people spread over the world, gathered out of the rest of mankind, whom Christ hath knit to himself by faith, and themselves in a holy spirit of love, of which company I believe myself to be one.[3]

The calling of the church is determined by her nature. As Christ has "two natures, God and man, in one person; mortal and immortal; greatness and baseness; infiniteness and finiteness", so the church has its scorned and base side, but it has a hidden mystical root.[4] In consonance with its inner spiritual life, it has the intrinsic duty through the ministers to preach the gospel, administer the sacraments, and ordain ministers.[5]

The magistrate, emperor, or king is responsible for the outward aspects of religious life: correcting those who do not their duties in church or commonwealth, calling church councils and public fasts, and such general religious matters.[6] Ministers and magistrates are the team God uses to bring good to men[7] and to oppose such errors as the papacy and national sins.[8] Magistrates are nursing fathers to the church;[9] ministers are watchmen to the church and physicians to the magistrates.[10] Atheistic statesmen are a contradiction in terms; religious statesmen are the best, the only good ones.[11] It was never better for the church of Christ than when such were rulers.[12] Christians should never worry first about magistrates, but about themselves. [13] When things do not go well, even when the Lord's officers come to arrest us, we must take the right course: "go to God by prayer, and entreat him who hath the hearts of kings in his hand, to incline and stir up the hearts of princes for to reform abuses." [14] The church may never succumb to the temptation to take such matters into its own hands. Yet this some of the Puritans were presuming to do.

How Sibbes regarded those who did so is pointedly stated in a letter from

---

[1] II 226, BG.     [2] V 332, CE.

[3] VI 232, RP; Observe the similarity of this definition to that of the Heidelberg Catechism of 1563, Question 54: What do you believe concerning the *holy catholic Church*?
  A. That the Son of God, out of the whole human race, from the beginning to the end of the world, gathers, defends, and preserves for Himself, by His Spirit and Word, in the unity of the true faith, a Church chosen to everlasting life; and that I am, and forever shall remain, a living member thereof.
The Heidelberg Catechism certainly was available to Sibbes and Baxter, since it was published in German and Latin at Heidelberg in 1563 and numerous times thereafter. It was published in English at London in 1572 and 1578, and at Oxford in 1588. D. Nauta lists ten additional English editions since that time. ("Die Verbreitung des Katechismus, Übersetzung in andere Sprachen, moderne Bearbeitungen," *Handbuch Zum Heidelberger Katechismus*, 38–62).

[4] V 464, FO.     [10] VI 89, SR.
[5] VI 88, SR.     [11] III 299, C2C1.
[6] VI 88–90, SR.     [12] *Idem.*
[7] I 343, CB.     [13] VI 272, SM.
[8] V 126, EP3.     [14] VI 89, SR.
[9] II 121, BO.

him written in response to one from an unnamed Puritan.[1] This man was in great trial and despondency through grave personal circumstances and for want of the communion of saints through which he could be comforted. Sibbes points out how God uses afflictions for what is good, though now we see it not, and counsels humble repentance as the way of restoration. But the monstrous sin that occasioned his friend's despondency was that of separation from God's church. God is methodical in his corrections and often does "so suite the crosse to the sinne, that you may reade the sin in the crosse."[2] The main affliction is lack of fellowship with God's people; the sin, wilful separation.

> Consider well therefore the haynousnesse of this sin, which that you may the better conceive, First, consider it is against Gods expresse Precept, charging us not to forsake the assemblies of the Saints, Heb. x. 20,25. Again, it is against our own greatest good, and spirituall solace, for by discommunicating & excommunicating our selves from that blessed society, we deprive our selves of the benefit of their holy conference, their godly instructions, their divine consolations, brotherly admonitions, and charitable reprehensions; and what an inestimable losse is this? Neither can we partake such profit by their prayers as otherwise we might: for as the soule in the naturall body conveyes life and strength to every member, as they are compacted and joyned together, and not as dissevered; so Christ conveyes spirituall life and vigour to Christians, not as they are disjoyned from, but as they are united to the mysticall body, the Church.[3]

But, Sibbes continues to his friend, you claim England is no true church, and therefore you separate. But the Church of England is easily proved to be a true church.

> First, because it hath all the essentialls, necessary to the constitution of a true Church; as sound preaching of the Gospell, right dispensation of the Sacraments, Prayer religiously performed, and evill persons justly punisht (though not in that measure as some criminals and malefactors deserve:) and therefore a true Church.
> 2. Because it hath begot many spirituall children to the Lord, which for soundnesse of judgement, and holinesse of life, are not inferiour to any in other Reformed Churches. Yea, many of the Separation, if ever they were converted, it was here with us....[4]

Though our church be corrupted by ceremonies and pestered by profane persons, such evils do not justify a rent in the church. "That were a remedy worse than the disease."[5] Besides, do not all true churches have their evils? See the seven Asian churches of Revelation 2 and 3. You may find churches across the

---

[1] A Grosart, the eitdor of Sibbes' *Works* judges the letter to have been written to Thomas Goodwin, "the patriarch of Independency." (I cxvi)

[2] I cxv.
[3] *Idem.*
[4] *Idem.*
[5] *Idem.*

sea without ceremonies; their blemishes are corruption in preachers, profanation of the Lord's Day, or something else. A mixture of wicked persons will be in the visible church to the end of the world. We cannot escape such by leaving the Church. Sibbes concludes by warning of the dire consequences of separation from the Church and urging his friend to return.

> As for wicked and prophane Persons amongst us, though we are to labour by all good meanes to purge them out, yet are we not to separate because of this residence with us: for, there will bee a miscellany and mixture in the visible Church, as long as the world endures, as our Saviour shewes by many parables: Matth. xiii. If therefore we should be so overjust as to abandon all Churches for the intermixture of wicked Persons, we must saile to the Antipodes, or rather goe out of the world, as the Apostle speaks: it is agreed by all that *Noahs* Arke was a type and embleme of the Church. Now as it had been no lesse then selfe-murder for *Noah, Sem,* or *Iaphet,* to have leapt out of the Arke, because of that ungracious *Cains* [Ham's?] company; so it is no better then soule-murder for a man to cast himself out of the Church, either for reall or imaginall corruptions. To conclude, as the Angell injoyned *Hagar* to returne, and submit to her Mistris *Sarah,* so let me admonish you to returne your selfe from these extravagant courses, and submissively to render your self to the sacred communion of this truly Evangelicall Church of *England*.
>
> I beseech you therefore, as you respect Gods glory and your owne eternall salvation, as *There is but one body and one spirit, one Lord, one Baptisme, one God and Father of all, who is above all, and through all, and in us all; so endeavour to keep the unity of the spirit in the bond of peace,* Eph. iv., as the Apostle sweetly invites you. So shall the peace of God ever establish you, and the God of peace ever preserve you, which is the prayer of
>
> *Your remembrancer at the Throne of Grace*
> R. Sibs.[1]

The unity of the church is a precious thing, a preserver,[2] a necessary act,[3] because the unity of the faith[4] and love require it.[5] "Cursed, devilish spirits oppose Christ in his members."[6] Schism and rebellion should break our hearts.[7] Fraction and disunion halt grace.[8] Discord is our enemies' melody.[9] There is too much un-churching and un-brothering in passion.[10] Mourn your sins, labour to repress strife, stop divisions.[11] Does faith make a unity only to be broken? "Oh, beloved, no!"[12] "It concerns all that are non-atheists to establish one religion."[13]

---

[1] I cxvi.
[2] I 379, CV.
[3] I 382, CV.
[4] III 375, C2C1.
[5] VI 408, ML.
[6] *Idem*.
[7] V 127, EP3.
[8] IV 255, EG.
[9] I 76, BR.
[10] I 56, BR.
[11] I 382, 379, CV.
[12] IV 447, C2C4.
[13] III 280, C2C1.

> In John xvii.21, saith our Saviour Christ there, 'I pray that they may be one as we are one'. It was the sum of that heavenly prayer, the unity of the church to the end of the world.... The Trinity should be the pattern of our unity. Because, I say, all good is in union, and all that comes from us that is accepted of God, it must be in peace and union.[1]

Although use of vestments and required liturgy had been imposed and the doctrine of predestination was not to be publicly discussed,[2] Sibbes continued preaching. So long as the Word of God could be taught, England had a true Church.[3] In this, England was gloriously blessed over the other countries in darkness.[4] For some sixty years God had continued his ministerial knocking. The time of reformation had come there through a child (Edward VI) and a woman (Elizabeth).[5] One could only pity the good men who suffered under Mary.[6] Now we are under a greater prince than any other.[7] What is the glory of England? That there are ministers to preach and administer the Word.[8] Yet it is a pitiful thing to find Christians under such a glorious light of the gospel who are so weak in prayer and frequent in sin.[9]

There are usually three degrees of persons in the church: the rotten and profane ones, those that have only a form of godliness, and imperfect Christians.[10] The church of God is his own house, but it bears a contradictory character:[11] there is a mixture of good and bad in it.[12] It is a common hospital;[13] it is weak, defective, and deformed.[14] Though some sinners may be shut out of the church,[15] ill fish always will remain in the net.[16] It will be necessary to go out of the world to avoid the mixture of evil persons.[17] Even without unbelievers in it, the church would still be a black church; the prodigal son, though erring, is still a son.[18]

It is true, there are many in the church who are only name Christians,[19] who are professors of the gospel but are not Christ's:[20] unbelievers,[21] and non-Christians,[22] who belong to the devil,[23] enemies to Christ.[24] As many marry to cloak adultery, so many join the church.[25] Others are half open to the gospel but not effectually converted.[26] They are seeming Christians lost in formality[27]

---

[1] III 194, C2C1.
[2] I lxxxiii.
[3] II 242, BG.
[4] IV 337, C2C4.
[5] VI 520, LC.
[6] VI 494, KDE.
[7] VII 533, BD; Grosart adds: "Sibbes seems from this and other tributes, to have held a high opinion of James I (VI of Scotland)." (Ibid., 534).
[8] VII 260, RPe.
[9] VI 95, SF.
[10] VII 405, DM.
[11] V 141, EP3.
[12] I 374, CV.
[13] I 57, BR.
[14] VI 135, RD; VII 539, ChE.
[15] II 160, BO, 242-243, BG.
[16] II 165-167, BO.
[17] I cxvi.
[18] I 58, BR.
[19] I 401, SH-P.
[20] II 187, BO.
[21] IV 406, C2C4.
[22] V 161, RBo.
[23] V 135, EP3.
[24] V 212, HL.
[25] II 205, S.
[26] II 68, BO.
[27] VI 427, HC.

who flee at the first sign of persecution.[1] But it is equally true that the members of Christ are sick. Each age has its own particular sins. Before it was superstition. Now it is profaneness, atheism, hardness of heart, looseness, presumption, formalism, Sabbath breaking, lying, swearing, rebelliousness, popery.[2]

We have seen how salvation begins with the conversion of man. God's primary activity does not relieve the urgency of man's personal response of faith. Salvation is usually worked by the Spirit through appealing preaching of the gospel. Some believe. They are saved by grace. Some reject. Their stubbornness secures judgment. Every believer as a member of Christ is a member of his church. That church is both good and bad. Yet to divide it is to divide Christ. Rather, the unbelievers in it should be addressed, prayers made for leaders in church and state, children instructed.

## 2. *The Means of Grace*

But how, then, is conversion effected? Sibbes answers: "The Spirit of God works it in the soul together with the word: the Spirit and the word go together."[3] The Word has through the Spirit effectual and converting power.[4] "The Spirit of God in the ordinances, in the means of salvation, stirs up the heart to answer God's call as it were."[5] The Spirit is pleased to be there with blessing when obedient hearts use the appointed means.[6] Perhaps no theme recurs more frequently in Sibbes' sermons than this: God uses means,[7] he saves through means,[8] he gives grace through means. Men are damned who despise the means.[9] Where there is a careful use of means, there will be faith;[10] where faith is, there will be a careful use of means.[11] Do you want grace? Go to the Creator and frequent the means of grace.[12] Do you want to obey the gospel? God will make the means effectual, soon or late, as surely as the angel once stirred Bethesda waters.[13]

What are the means God pleases to use for salvation? They are many: the preaching, the Word, the sacraments, obedience, prayer, meditation, good pastors and people, religious duties, even book prayers and salutations by authorized (non-papal) ministers. We know God's meaning no way except through the Word.[14] The written Word is undoubtedly true;[15] it is to teach us how God must be served, "an exact and perfect rule."[16] There are three degrees of revelation: the Scriptures are the first degree, the soul's enlightenment by the Spirit is the second, while the third will be discovered only in heaven.[17] The Old and New Testaments reveal the same religion, though clothed differently.

---

[1] I 406, SH–P.
[2] VI 496, KDE; IV 373, C2C4; V 132, EP3, 418, FS; VI 71, AM, 427, HC.
[3] VII 434, FT.
[4] IV 367–368, 377, 386, C2C4.
[5] IV 219, EG.
[6] I 23, DC; V 82–83, EP3; VI 409, ML.
[7] VI 353, AA.
[8] I 421, SH–P.
[9] VI 495, KDE.
[10] VI 380, FL.
[11] VII 476, RMJ.
[12] I 410, SH–P.
[13] I 391 UM.
[14] I 412, SH–P.
[15] III 359, C2C1.
[16] VI 499, KDE.
[17] IV 158, GH;.

The Spirit uses the Word: the Word is the vehicle of the Spirit, the Spirit is the soul of the Word. The Spirit inspires the Word, and it is guarded by the same Spirit.[1] But how do I know the Word to be the Word of God? Variously: the majesty in it, the mystery of forgiveness in it, the witness of the Spirit, the efficacy of the gospel, by experience ("There is no other principle to prove the word, but experience from the working of it"),[2] and demonstration by reason as to the probability of its truth.[3]

God's usual manner of winning souls is through the preaching, writing, and teaching of the Word by authorized ministers.[4] The vessels Christ uses are the Word and the sacraments.[5] Through these ordinances he has a special presence in the church.[6] Thus he comes to woo and to win us in the ministry.[7] The minister's calling is two-fold: preach Christ to amend the wrong in Christians, and preach to win souls for Christ.[8]

> The preaching of God's holy word...is the ministry of the Spirit. In the hearing of it the Spirit is given. If we would have the Spirit, let us attend upon the ministry of the Spirit.[9]

It is the special office of the ministry to "lay open Christ" [10] and his riches.[11] Christ, and only Christ, is the object of preaching.[12] As the Word of God is the Word of reconciliation, so the minister is the messenger of reconciliation.[13] He is God's primary means to bring men to Christ.[14] God has shined on him that he may shine on others.[15] To him belongs the honor of saving souls.[16] The minister's "calling is to bring men's souls to heaven, to be saviours of the people, to be God's own name, to be fathers."[17]

All this is true in spite of the meanness, the frailty, and the earthen character of the vessels.[18] You cannot depend upon a minister as a person for your salvation.[19] Those whose hearts are unheated do no kindling.[20] Yet those who despise the ministers despise Christ,[21] for they are his ambassadors.[22] It is the elevated task of the Word that makes attendance upon preaching so urgent: a curse upon those who practice private devotions at the expense of public worship.[23] We lost salvation by ear, we must come to it again by hearing.[24] We have two teachers who must concur for salvation, an inward and an outward one: God

---

[1] "Verbum est vehiculum Spiritus, inspirat verbum, et ab eodem Spiritus anima verbi. Spiritus Spiritu custoditur." (VII 558, ACN).
[2] II 495, MF.
[3] Idem.
[4] IV 309, C2C4; VI 526, LC.
[5] II 33, BO.
[6] VI 125, SuS.
[7] II 68, BO.
[8] V 128, EP3; II 142, BO.
[9] VII 545, ChE.
[10] II 168, 185, BO.
[11] VII 257, RPe.
[12] III 369, C2C1; V 509, FO.
[13] III 508, C2C1.
[14] III 319–320, C2C1.
[15] IV 336, YA.
[16] III 319, C2C1.
[17] IV 358, C2C4; II 204, S.
[18] IV 354ff, C2C4; VI 423, HC.
[19] IV 387, C2C4.
[20] III 320, C2C1.
[21] III 372, C2C1.
[22] II 493, MF.
[23] VI 423, HC.
[24] VI 422, HC.

and ministers.[1] Since "grace comes by declaring,"[2] ministers are to woo[3] plainly with the Word and with native simplicity.[4] Sibbes counsels ministers to be both gentle or sharp as the need might require,[5] but to exercise themselves with care. It will not do to kill an insect on the forehead with a hammer.[6] The heart is changed by reasons fetched from Christ.[7]

Since all grace comes by understanding in the soul,[8] man usually comes to God motivated by a sense of dependence or by an attraction to his goodness.[9] Motives of fear of judgment, of death, or damnation are usually short-lived and ineffective.[10] It is true that some need damnation sermons. Men are like children who get themselves dirty, then cry when washed. If gentleness and mildness will not do, do not spare fiery words.[11] Christ came with sweetness, but John the Baptist was austere; "The reason of God's making use of men of severe dispositions is, because of the different natures of men, whereof some can better relish one nature than another." [12]

Sibbes' own mild and persuasive approach is abundantly shown in his sermons. He uses scriptural texts of invitation such as "whosoever will" and "come unto me" innumerable times. But as often he addresses sinners directly:

> God is so willing to come.[13]
> I beseech you, love Christ.[14]
> Unless you repent, you shall perish.[15]
> How is it with you? [16]
> Labour now to be acquainted with God.[17]
> Think what damnation is, I beseech you.[18]
> Labour, labour, get into Christ.[19]
> Open your hearts.[20]
> Let no one be disconsolate, Christ and the promises are open to all.[21]
> All people that will come may, none excluded.[22]
> God offers himself if you will come in.[23]

This confronting men with the gospel invitation, on the one hand, and the insistance on divine priority in the redemptive act, also for the individual, on the other hand, must be seen, not as contradictory, but as the human and divine sides of the matter. These are not contrary to, but beyond, the powers of human reason, as we shall note later.

---

[1] IV 393, C2C4.
[2] I 28, DC, 161, 168, SC; II 68, BO.
[3] III 317, C2C1.
[4] III 233, C2C1.
[5] I 53, BR.
[6] I 55, BR.
[7] IV 378, C2C4.
[8] VI 525, LC.
[9] IV 195–196, GH.
[10] III 130, C2C1; VII 296, MC.
[11] III 490–492, C2C1.
[12] VII 281, SG.
[13] III 155, C2C1. This series of references are indirect quotations.
[14] I 393, UM.
[15] II 496, MF.
[16] III 126, C2C1.
[17] III 325, C2C1.
[18] IV 102, JR.
[19] VI 408, ML.
[20] VI 424, HC.
[21] III 400, C2C1.
[22] II 446, MF.
[23] IV 484, HC.

The sacraments bring grace to us. Christ's body is offered spiritually in communion [1] and nourishment is given to believing participants.[2] Frequent observance is needed by hungry souls.[3] Baptism, like communion, without faith is a seal to a blank.[4] The outward sign of baptism may be, but ought not to be administered to believer and unbeliever alike. True baptism, the inward united with the outward, saves us.[5]

One might, at this point, ask the altogether relevant question, what about the children born in the church and raised under the preaching of the gospel? To such, God is gracious from their childhood.[6] As part of their parents,[7] they should be baptized as included in God's promise.[8] The consequent duty devolving upon the parents is the careful instruction in the Christian faith, attempting thus to keep their children in the covenant.[9] Children ought to love God from their childhood. Their baptism, however, does not assure their salvation if they refuse to love God as they grow older. The Anabaptists are to be condemned for refusing baptism to children whom God surely accepts as his own.[10]

The young are rather to be carefully trained that they, too, may teach others. The truth is propagated by teaching. Sibbes emphasizes to students the importance of II Timothy 2:2: "What you have heard from me entrust to faithful men who will be able to teach others also." A love for the truth must be instilled in the hearts of all God's children if they are to teach others. For untaught persons, just like flutes, give no sound at all unless they are blown upon by others; and it must be seen to, that those who give shape to the studies of others do not imbue those with a dislike of the best, both of people and things. For badly dyed characters, like black wool, take no other color.... Let us therefore cherish the studies of the adolescents, so that no bee-glue may cut off the way to what the bees should take. Let it be to nobody's loss or damage that he has been brought into closer contact with piety, for what else is this than to kill, as a Herod, the Christ child in the hearts of the young? [11]

The knowledge of theology and of the arts go hand in hand. Thus students must be well instructed if they are to be teachers. Through doctrine, languages are restored to holiness. He must break the nut who will eat the kernel. And theological spears strike harder, go in deeper, when soundly brandished by muscles of logic and rhetoric.[12]

---

[1] IV 182, GH.
[2] III 325, C2Cl.
[3] II 183, BO.
[4] VI 484, HC.
[5] VII 479, DGC.
[6] I 43, BR.
[7] VII 23, UB.
[8] V 78, EP3.
[9] V 27, CW.
[10] VI 22, FC.
[11] "Indocti enim tibiarum similes nihil sonant nisi ab aliis inflati; et videndum ne qui formant aliorum studia imbuant eos odio optimorum et hominum et rerum. Male tincta enim ingenia ut nigrae lanarum nullum alium colorem imbibunt.... Foveamus ergo adolescentum studia, ne quod apes capere oportet fuci intercipiant. Nemini fraudi aut damno sit pietati fuisse addictorem; quid enim aliud hoc est quam Christum infantem in juvenum cordibus, Herodis instar, occidere?" VII 554, 555, ACN.
[12] "Et sane logicis rhetoricisque lacertis vibrata theologica tela fortius feriunt...." VII 555, ACN.

*3. The Church Member as Witness*

How do you persuade an unconverted sinner of God's love to him? The first step is to awaken him to a sense of not yet being in Christ,[1] and to the greatness of God's forgiving mercy in Christ. In discussing II Cor. 1:3, Sibbes reflects upon the phrase "Father of mercies" in its use for the unconverted. In it the sinner is to see God's first attitude as one of mercy rather than of justice. He comes freely, but only upon our admission of fault.

> ...if thou come in, never consider what thy sins have been; if thou come in, God will embrace thee in his mercy. Thy sins are all as a spark of fire that falls into the ocean, that is drowned presently. So are thy sins in the ocean of God's mercy.
> There is not more light in the sun, there is not more water in the sea, than there is mercy in the 'Father of mercy', whose bowels are opened to thee if thou be weary of thy sinful courses, and come in, and embrace mercy....
> The mercy-seat was a type of Christ, covering the law, covering the curse. Though thou be guilty of the curse a thousand times, God in Christ is merciful.[2]

If the unconverted object: "Aye, but I have abused mercy a long time; I have lived in sin, and committed great sins,"[3] the reply is at hand:

> Take sin in the aggravations, in the greatness of it, Manasseh's sin, Peter's denying of his Master, the thief on the cross, and Paul's persecution! Take sin as great as you will, he is the 'Father of mercies'. If we consider that God is infinite in mercy, and that the Scripture reveals him as the 'Father of mercies', there is no question but there is abundance, a world of comfort to any distressed soul that is ready to cast itself on God's mercy.[4]

Let such truths as these, Sibbes counsels, "allure those that are not yet in state of grace, to come under Christ's sweet and victorious government."[5] No condition is so terrible as to live in the church, yet not knowing Christ.[6] A man had better be nothing in religion than lukewarm.[7] Paul is sharper to those who are alleged Christians than to the heathen.[8] Even those who have gone far in religion may fall away and become apostates.[9] "I beseech you,... Examine what spirit is in you." [10] Present Christ's gracious invitation to all men.

> *Christ offereth himself to all in the gospel.* ... Christ offers himself to you. These are the times, this is the hour of grace. Now the water is stirring for you to enter; do but entertain Christ, and desire that he may be yours to rule you and guide you, and all will be well for the time to come.[11]

---

[1] VI 390, ML.
[2] III 35, C2Cl.
[3] III 36, C2Cl.
[4] III 37, C2Cl.
[5] I 99, BR.
[6] II 143–144, RB.
[7] VI 305, VV.
[8] V 67, EP3; cf. I 275, SC.
[9] VII 406, DM.
[10] VI 406, ML.
[11] II 187, BO.

That the individual Christian should be at the heart of the gospel's spread is no wonder. "God's goodness is a communicative, spreading goodness." [1] His goodness and grace enter into the believer. Because good is by nature diffusive, we must be of a communicative, spreading disposition.[2] Our goodness must flow out to others.[3] Or, to use the figure of grace: "wheresoever grace is, it is of a spreading nature,...communicative."[4] The best Christians are consequently, those who are communicative and diffusive, who labor to gain all men.[5] Those not heated with grace cannot kindle others.[6] What comes from a Christian? Grace and comfort to others. Let us therefore labor to have large affections, to have a spreading goodness. Communicate it far abroad to many, as far and remote, like Paul, as we can.[7]

> And then we may think that we have all things, the benefit and comfort of any true gift, when we have spirits of love to communicate it to others. These be therefore two main graces of communion, humility, and love. And when we can sweetly, humbly, and by the spirit of love communicate it to others, then we be masters of what we have, else it is not given for our good. God will blast it if we do not communicate it. God will take away that he hath from the idle servant, that will not employ his talent. I would to God more conscience were made of this, that not only ministers, but every one, would be first the cistern, and then the conduit, first get something in, and then put it out, when it is seasonable, and when we have a calling to do it.[8]

The figure of sunshine also conveys the idea of diffusion. "The sun shineth on the greater part of the world at once. The more communicable the better: the more near God and Christ."[9] God shines first, and we shine consequently on others.[10] The end of light is not to shine in our own hearts to no purpose, but to shine to others.[11] In an exposition on the text "among whom you shine as lights in the world," Sibbes says:

> These words contain another reason why the children of God ought to be unreprovable. For, saith the apostle, 'you are lights'. All God's children are lights, but so as there is an order of them. God is the ground of all light; he is the Father of lights. Christ he is the Sun of righteousness. These are the grand lights. The word of God is also a light and a lantern to light us in the dark ways of this world. From hence light is derived to the saints, who receive it from Christ by the word and Spirit. You being therefore thus enlightened, you are to converse amongst men as lights, saith the apostle.[12]

---

[1] VI 113, SuS.
[2] III 98, C2Cl.
[3] II 10, BO.
[4] II 355, RB.
[5] III 321, C2Cl.
[6] III 320, C2Cl.
[7] VI 114, SuS.
[8] IV 338–339, C2C4.
[9] IV 338, C2C4.
[10] I 260, SC.
[11] III 314, 365, C2Cl; VII 199, DMHC.
[12] V 28, CW.

> Light is a quality of surest motion. It spreads suddenly. Thus do the children of God. They communicate to others. They shine, spreading forth the grace, first of all to those that are next them, as children and friends, then to such as are further off. Those that have not this nature, that do not desire to do good to others, they are not children of the light; for it is the nature of all good to communicate.[1]

Believers must therefore stand as examples for others and shine the way to heaven;[2] they bestow grace wherever they come by example and words.[3] Talents increase with exercise. The Christian who exercises his love as a good example will make others in love with religion. Doing well to those who are evil wins indifferent ones to Christ.[4] "Of all apologies life is the best." [5] To be moody is to do a disservice to others, since it renders us ineffective in ministering.[6] Rather, if the example of the church is of such force as to convert Jews as the Scriptures promise, how much more will it be of power to make Christians.[7]

> We owe this to all, even to them that are without, to do them so much good as to give them a good example, and we wrong them when we do not, and hinder their coming on by an evil or a dead example.... For the more spreading our good is either in word, life, or conversation, the more our consciences shall be settled in the consideration of a good life well spent, our reward shall be answerable to our communication and diffusion of good.[8]

Every Christian has a divine appointment to spread the gospel. Not only the ministers, but all are to be the happy instruments to win others.[9] This greatest joy belongs to all Christians.[10] "...every Christian is a prophet.... God maketh common Christians saviours of others." [11] God wills that the message shall come from man to man.[12] "You my disciples are to encounter with the world."[13]

Witnessing is not simply an honor for the Christian,[14] nor a luxury he can afford to be without. Not to witness is to deny our possession of goodness and grace. Speaking out of a warm heart is one of the ways I may know that I am a Christian.[15] Spreading the faith, shining as lights, setting a good example in life and word,—God uses these as means for conversion. There is no room for physical persecution or compulsion.[16] Rather, prayer for laborers in the harvest[17] and personal diligence attain divine ends.

Because God has a gracious good will toward all men, we must love mankind.

---

[1] V 29, 30, CW.
[2] III 258, C2C1.
[3] III, 337 C2C1.
[4] I 404, SH–P.
[5] III 204, C2C1.
[6] VII 342, FSe.
[7] II 133, BO.
[8] II 132, BO
[9] II 165–167, BO; IV 9, CP, 342, C2C4.
[10] III 322, C2C1.
[11] IV 338, C2C4.
[12] IV 372, C2C4.
[13] VII 357, SP.
[14] III 257, C2C1.
[15] IV 29–30, CP.
[16] VI 313, C2C4.
[17] VI 527, LC.

And learn this for imitation, to love mankind. God loved mankind; and surely there is none that is born of God, but he loves the nature of man, wheresoever he finds it. He will not stand altogether, whether it be good or bad, &c. But because we are now in the way, and our state is not determined, and because God loves the nature of man, therefore every man that hath the Spirit of God loves mankind. He will labour to gain Turks, or Indians, &c., if he can, because he loves the very nature of man.[1]

A Christian enters into the life of men. It is therefore more of a sign of grace to weep for another's sin, than for our own.[2] If we love the church, we should mourn for any sins that may prejudice others' salvation. If Christ's bowels yearned with compassion for men, "shall we see so many poor souls in darkness, and our bowels not yearn?"[3]

The Christian has a spirit to seek the good of others.[4] Thus it is natural that after being gained to Christ he labors to gain others.[5] He strives to draw those who are not yet called,[6] those not yet in Christ,[7] unto him. Probably in Sibbes' day, as in ours, not everyone shared concern for sharing Christ. "O that this gaining and winning disposition," he cries, "were more in many!"[8] And again, "Can we have a greater encouragement than, under God, to be gainer of a soul, which is as much in God's esteem as if we should gain a world?"[9]

> Mercy shewed to the souls of men is the greatest mercy, and wisdom in winning of souls is the greatest wisdom in the world, because the soul is especially the man, upon the goodness of which the happiness of the whole man depends.... A Christian should have feeding lips and a healing tongue.[10]

If only everyone in his place would labor to enlarge the kingdom of God that children and servants and unbelievers may come in! If we put not out our helping hand to that for which we pray, it is a contradiction. Those that hinder the conversion of others' souls and draw them to wicked courses are on the way to hell themselves.[11] Those that labor to convert souls have greater honor in heaven.[12] The consideration of the coming day of the Lord Jesus ought to "make us digest labour, and pains, in dealing with the souls of others, in doing good, and being fruitful in our places. ...And considering that there is such a day, let us make much of the day of the Lord that is now left us."[13] Such an eschatological impulse in a communicative, spreading disposition achieves results. To discourse with others of blessed experiences under God's gracious providence is fruitful service for Christians. "God gains by that means. His glory is spread. Our grace is increased. The good of others is multiplied."[14]

---

[1] VI 349–350, AA.
[2] II 487, MF.
[3] VII 193, DMHC.
[4] VII 210, DMHC.
[5] I 54, BR.
[6] I 317, SS.
[7] II 142, BO.
[8] I 51, BR.
[9] I 192, SC.
[10] *Idem.*
[11] VII 542, ChE.
[12] III 320, C2C1.
[13] III 326, C2C1.
[14] III 98, C2C1.

Sibbes places heavy responsibility upon all Christians to spread the gospel where they are, at home or abroad. He does not yet conceive of the mission as demanding the sending of missionaries to foreign places. Rather, the individual Christian becomes God's converting instrument. His redeemed nature is outreaching. His light cannot but shine. His example converts. He is under divine orders to be converting. So without applying physical compulsion to others,[1] he witnesses,[2] he prays,[3] he does good.[4] A gracious good will to all men, love for Christ and desire to follow his example, motivates the Christian to love and to sympathize with his fellow man. A concern for common humanity, touched by the eternal dimension of God's presence and made urgent by the certainty of the Lord's coming, brings healing to sin-wounded lives. A gracious, winning disciple reveals the gracious, winning Lord.

We have considered the human predicament, born as it is in, but not from, the will of God. The redemption he appointed in Christ is mediated through the ministry of the Word and the personal witness. That gospel is addressed to the ungodly world, wherever it is to be found.

### C. THE REDEMPTION OF THE WORLD

#### 1. *The Nature of the World*

By the ungodly world, Sibbes intends those not part of the mystical Church of Christ which is the world of the elect. In a sermon on the words: "...that we should not be condemned with the world" (I Cor. xi:30–32), he defines:

> For as in the great world there is the little world–man–so in the great world of mankind, there is a little world–the world of God's people; but here it is the world of the ungodly.[5]

These are called "the world" because they are the most part of the world and because the best thing in them is the world. "They have their name from that they love. Love is an affection of union. What we love, that we are knit unto."[6] Carnal men are in love with the world, are united in their affections to it. If you

> ...anatomise a carnal man that is not in the state of grace, rip him up in his soul, what shall you find in him but the world?...You shall find little of the word of God there, and scarce any thing that is good, because the best thing in him is the world; therefore he is the world.[7]

The world of ungodly ones shall be condemned: because they set their hearts upon condemned things, because they serve a damned prince–Satan, because

---

[1] VI 313, VV.
[2] III 257, C2Cl.
[3] VI 527, LC.
[4] VI 210, GI.
[5] IV 98, JR; cf. V 516–517, FO.
[6] IV 98, JR.
[7] *Idem.*

they condemn God, because even in the church there are a company of men that will to be damned, and because the world is shut out of Christ's prayer. Someone objects: why do you so preach to us?

> We are baptized. We hear now and then a sermon! Are we the world? The world are Pagans, and Turks, and Jews, and such; perhaps papists. Such as they are the world.[1]

But Sibbes answers:

> Oh no, beloved, 'Babylon is in Jerusalem', as the father [2] saith, the world is in the city of God, the world is among you. Nay, and that part of the world that shall be deepest damned is here amongst us. For our damnation shall be deeper than the Turks' or Jews'.[3]

The first duty of the church is to see the world in its own bosom. There are many who do only the outward duty, the shell of holy duty. Such may be baptized, receive communion, hear the Word of God, but it is only outward performance. To find the life and soul of holy duty is crucial:

> ...to hear as he should; and to be moulded into the performance of it; to obey that we hear, and to come to receive the sacrament with reverence and due preparation; and to increase the assurance of salvation, and our comfort and joy.[4]

This latter is the hard part of the duty, undone by the world.

The world of the ungodly is condemned. But our thoughts are not to stray far afield when we think of damnation. They should go no further than our own congregations and the places we live. To us God speaks, to the world disguised within our churches, to the walkers on the broad and easy way. Such want, yes, resolve to be damned.

> ...in spite of God, in spite of his truth, in spite of conscience, and to despite the Spirit that awakeneth them and tells them that there is another way that they should walk in... yet they will rush on in their courses, as the horse rusheth into the battle. Say God what he will, the world will be damned.[5]

It is true the ungodly world has no part in the prayer of Christ, "in him that died to redeem us." Yet "the world will not receive the Spirit, because they maintain their own lusts."[6] The condemned nature of the world should motivate us to get our friends and our children out of the world, to repulse conformity to the unregenerate and damned world, and to examine our own affections to see if we are of Jerusalem or Babylon.[7]

The Roman Church is also part of the ungodly world. Paul warns the

---

[1] IV 99, JR.
[2] Likely in reference to Augustine in *De Civitate Dei*.
[3] *Loc. cit.*
[4] IV 100, JR.
[5] *Idem.*
[6] IV 101, JR.
[7] IV 101–103, JR.

Philippian church (Chap. 3.2) especially to beware of the dogs within the church, those who "join works of the law and Christ together, in matter of salvation."[1] Though those of whom the apostle speaks are gone, yet

> ...the same spirit is now-a-days in many... Jesuited papists... having gotten power in their hand, they persecute with fire and sword, and the most exquisite torments that they can devise.[2]

Because of papal wiles and errors, we should take heed and not deal with papists more than is necessary.[3] They use outward form and pomp to please men's imaginations.[4] They presume to forgive intended, but as yet uncommitted, sin.[5] Human tradition and authority replace that of the Word of God.[6] Mary-worship, statues and crucifixes, cloak idolatry.[7] "Hail Mary, full of grace" perverts the Greek text, which requires "freely beloved."[8] These are serious errors.

But what makes the Roman church apostate is that it gives the soul "false props" in the matter of justification.

> They would have us to trust to our own works in matter of salvation, to trust to our own satisfaction to be freed from purgatory, etc. They would have us trust to creatures, to something besides God; to trust in the mediation of saints, to be our intercessors, etc.[9]

They think that God loves us for some good which he foresees in us, or for some good we do in time by which his favor is deserved. But both are false. The cause of love can be found only in free grace.[10] Not seeing this, the Church of Rome misses the height of grace and the depth of original sin.[11] Rome has other priests and other intercessors than Christ; it joins faith and works together in justification. This is another gospel.

> ...as if Christ were not an all-sufficient Saviour...! What is the gospel but salvation and redemption by Christ alone? Gal. ii.16....Beloved, they that join works with Christ in matter of justification, err in the foundation. The very life and soul of religion consists in this....So when a man sets up a righteousness of his own, neglecting the righteousness of Christ, it is impossible he should ever be saved, living and dying in that error, Philip. iii.10.[12]

The tragic compromise of the gospel of free grace and the persecution of those who further the true gospel earn for the Roman Church the unequivocal title of "the kingdom of Antichrist."[13]

---

[1] V 66, EP3.
[2] *Idem.*
[3] *Idem.*
[4] I 179, SC; III 420, C2C1; IV 357, C2C4.
[5] I 323, SS.
[6] II 57, BO; III 364, 9, C2C1; IV 384–385, C2C4.
[7] II 287, RB.
[8] IV 244, EG.
[9] III 133, C2C1.
[10] II 318, RB; cf. III 99 C2C1.,
[11] II 302, RB.
[12] I 388, UM.
[13] VII 468, RMJ; cf. also I 471, SH–P.

In a sermon on Rev. 17:7 (For God hath put into their hearts to fulfill his will, and to agree to give up their kingdoms to the beast, until the word of God shall be fulfilled), Sibbes vividly portrays Rome's church as the beast, thrice mentioned in Revelation. It is not Rome under the heathen emperors, but under the See of Rome, the See of Antichrist which is in view. As in Apostolic times, at the return from preaching the gospel, Satan is seen falling from heaven like lightning, so now, by the preaching of the Word of God, Antichrist will be consumed.[1]

Why is it so hard to convert a papist? Though they be so mild of their own nature, yet as idolaters they are cruel. It is because their religion is "a brat, a child of their own begetting," suiting their own natural will and appetite. It is no easy matter to free the soul of such idolatry and of this "cursed disposition."[2]

One may not conclude from the foregoing that a papist cannot be saved. Many of them are. These believe the positive, fundamental truths which both of us hold together and thus reverse the grounds of their religion, holding instead to ours, which is agreeable to the Word. In life they add Roman negative doctrines to Apostolic positive ones: Apocrypha and traditions to the Scriptures, saints and angels as mediators to Christ, justification by works to that by faith, five sacraments to the two, the novelties of transubstantiation and papal supremacy to primitive Christian belief. But they die by the positive truths, seeing the vanity of their works and embracing only Christ.[3]

Papal practice should put us on our guard. There is a natural kind of popery in every man, in our own hearts. In fundamental doctrine there is too much sanctification, too little justification.[4] Men, like popes, easily excuse themselves.[5] It is we who keep Antichrist alive by atheistical impulses in our hearts, of which there is a great deal.[6] Our independence claims time for ourselves, when in reality it belongs to God.[7] In this way the apostasy of the church finds another golden head. This is a damnable thing, to forsake the golden headship of Christ over the church. Let the apostate church alone with her Antichrist.[8] Still, we keep Antichrist alive by want of zeal, squabbles, coldness, indifference in religion.[9] Thus the ungodly world enters the bosom of the church.

The ungodly in the church is our immediate and responsible concern. Damnation is an awful reality for such as reject God's love and gracious mercy. These are "dogs." All men are "dogs" by nature. That is a hard word. We should not dare to use it except the Holy Ghost does so in the gospel. But we should not be more modest than He: "...*wicked men are dogs*."[10]

Wicked men are either outside the church or inside. Outside the church all are dogs. "Mat. xv.26, 'It is not meet to take the children's bread and to cast it to dogs'."

---

[1] VII 517ff., BD.
[2] II 386, RB.
[3] III 375–379, C2Cl.
[4] I 138, SC.
[5] I 308, SS.
[6] III 324, C2Cl.
[7] III 344, C2Cl.
[8] II 150, BO.
[9] I 261, SC.
[10] V 65, EP3.

> Of this number are all Turks and Jews, who were *filii*, children, but are *canes*, dogs. We were *canes*, but now through God's mercy are come to be *filii*.[1]

Turks and Jews, the dogs outside, were once children, once were God's people, but both by the personal choice of rejection have excluded themselves for the most part from the church. They were "...aliens from the commonwealth of Israel" (Eph. 2:12).

Before the coming of Christ, the Gentiles were in misery except for some few proselytes. What were their gods but devils? They were under the kingdom of Satan. They were little better than beasts before the gospel was preached to them. To them the preaching of the gospel was a mystery; it was so even for Peter. Why did God let the Gentiles go in their own ways so many thousand years before Christ came? Were they not creatures of God even as the Jews? It is a mystery to us. Yet they sinned against the light they knew. They imprisoned the light of nature they had (Rom. 1:21). They were unfaithful in what they had. See what malicious and reprobate judgments they made. See how they despised God's people and persecuted them. Do not presume to call God to the judgment bar. They were "dogs" just as we were in the time of Julius Caesar. God delivered us from that, yet how little we give God praise. We grow weary of religion as the Jews did of manna.[2]

## 2. God's Way with the World

The world, understood in its broad sense, is the ungodly world of hypocrites and formalists in the church, papists and Jews, Turks and pagans. The church must recognize the world for what it is, but its redemptive efforts begin with the Babylon nearest by: one's own church, one's own heart. Here one begins because here God begins, in the single soul. These redemptive efforts are little at first and mixed with corruption.[3] Like the seed in Christ's parable they grow [4] both in measure and purity.[5] As in nature, growth in grace must be expected.[6] We must always be adding grace to grace [7] and one degree to another. It is characteristic of Sibbes to make the care of souls man's greatest responsibility, since the soul is man's richest possession. "The account for our own souls, and the souls of others, is the greatest account, and therefore the care of souls should be the greatest care." [8] It may be objected that sometimes Christians seem to be static or even to regress. Growth is suspended.

> God sees it needful they should grow in the root, and therefore abaseth them in the sense of some infirmity, and then they spring out amain again. As after a hard winter comes a glorious spring, upon a check grace breaks out more gloriously.[9]

---

[1] V 66, EP3; cf. 510, FO.
[2] V 510–511, FO.
[3] I 49, BR.
[4] I 90, BR; III 470, C2C1.
[5] I 62, BR.
[6] III 246, C2C1; IV 288, EG; V 108, EP3.
[7] I 124, SC.
[8] I 150, SC.
[9] IV 288–289, EG.

Then grace begets grace. It is a strange thing how great matters arise from little things. "Good things beget good things." [1] The woman of Samaria had only a small beginning in grace, but how many of her neighbors she brought to believe in Christ. So did Andrew for his brother Simon, Philip for Nathaniel, and Paul in Caesar's court.[2]

The nature of faith is the same in the church as in every particular Christian.

> In those things that we call homogeneal, there is the same nature in each quantity as in the whole, as there is the same nature in one drop of water as in the whole ocean, all is water.... So Christ bears the same respect to the church as to every particular, and to every particular as to the church.[3]

This is because all are united in Christ. One and the same Spirit is in both the whole church and every individual Christian. So the constant progress of Christ's glorious power in us until victory is attained, likewise is true of the whole body of Christians–the church. When we pray "Thy Kingdom come," we have reference first of all to Christ's kingship over and in us. The soul is his proper throne. "The kingdom of Christ in his ordinances serves but to bring Christ into his own place, our hearts." [4] Christ will achieve at length his purpose in us. "And so for the church in general, by Christ it will have its victory." [5] Again, like the individual, the church may seem to regress and suffer defeat. Here too, suffering is the conquering way as it was for Christ. His "work, both in the church and in the hearts of Christians, often goeth backward, that it may go the better forward." [6] If the church is not now what it should be, just as the individual also is not, the means of growth must be used, and we must wait patiently; perhaps the brighter time is still a way off.[7] When outward things are ill, God intends the good of the soul.[8] Christ is humbling the church for its advance.[9]

Nothing is so small as grace at first, and

> ...nothing more great or glorious in this world in the progress of time; nothing so admired of God, and pleasing unto man.... It is true both of the church and of particular graces.[10]

The apostle's *unum necessarium* is to "grow more and more to the fulness of the knowledge of Christ."[11] The church, like the individual, grows as a vine. First there are "two or three gathered" in Christ's name, then there are great congregations and families, then the church becomes a mother church to one under her shadow, and finally the new church carries its growth forward in the same manner.[12] Every Christian, every church is a vine for fruitfulness. As the vine is never the worse for pruning, so the Christian and the church for affliction.

---

[1] II 165, BO.
[2] II 165–167, BO.
[3] II 184, BO; cf. also 7, BO.
[4] I 78, BR.
[5] I 85, BR.
[6] I 85–86, BR.
[7] VII 422, FT.
[8] III 142, C2C1.
[9] V 351, CE.
[10] II 358–359, RB.
[11] V 105, EP3.
[12] II 359, RB.

> Therefore as it was the state of the Head to have no outward form or beauty, though inwardly he was all glorious.... So it is with the church of God and particular Christians; who, though in outward government they have not that policy and outward glory other governments have, yet there is an inward secret work or God's government... wherein he brings glory from shame, life by death.[1]

In every age of the church are changes reflecting its spiritual state. In most ages five are discernable: a strong desire for communion with Christ, some declining in affection, recovery and regaining of love, more severe declining of affection, return to firmer grasp on Christ than ever before, prompted by his constant affection.[2]

Again Sibbes observes, "...*there is the same regard of the whole church, and of every particular member, in regard of the chiefest privileges and graces that accompany salvation.*"[3]

God's movement of grace in the individual Christian and in the particular church likewise carries through in the world church of all ages. The mother promise to fallen mankind (Gen. 3:15) was but the first step of redemption.[4] From the beginning the church desired that Christ would come in our nature, and that "he would manifest by little and little, clearer and clearer, his coming in the flesh."[5]

> ...and accordingly he did by degrees reveal himself, as first in paradise...; then to Abraham...After that to one tribe...the tribe of Judah...; then to one family of that tribe, the house of David...; then a virgin shall conceive...; and after that...John the Baptist....So you see how Christ did reveal himself more and more by degrees unto his church.[6]
> ...*the church in general grew to knowledge by degrees*, till Christ...came.... And as the whole body mystical, so every member; we grow to knowledge by degrees.[7]

There are several great steps in the accomplishment of God's promises: 1. when the Jews came out of captivity, 2. when Christ came in the flesh, 3. when the Gentiles were called, 4. when the Jews shall be called, and 5. when the new heaven and new earth arrive.[8] It is these great cycles within God's purpose for history that give meaning to an otherwise meaningless world. In the world

> ...is a circle of human things. The times are but even as they were. Things come again upon the stage. The same things are acted. The persons indeed are changed, but the same things are acted in the world to the end of the world. The times were naught before, they are naught, and they will be so. Villany is acted upon the stage of the world continually. The former actors are gone, but others are instructed with the same devices, with the same plots. The corruption of nature shews itself in all. Only now we have the

---

[1] II 360, RB.
[2] II 6, BO.
[3] *Idem.*
[4] VI 116, SuS.
[5] II 202–203, S.
[6] II 203, S.
[7] VI 385, ML.
[8] VI 546, BL; cf. 236, RP.

advantage for the acting of wickedness in the end of the world; because, besides the old wickedness in former times, we have the new wickedness of these times. All the streams running into one, make the channel greater.¹

But the *"one sovereign Head over the whole world"* ² is at work. We should not lose ourselves in problems about the manner of creation.³ God, *Elohim*, made it. That is enough. And he continues to keep the world by what might be called "continuous creation."⁴ It cannot fail. Nothing in the world is to him or his servants absolutely evil. Everything, little or great, takes on meaning in his wise ordering and guiding of it.⁵

God continues the world for love of two things: "his truth, and his church, begotten by his truth." ⁶ "All truths are eternal truths." ⁷ They do not die as men do.

> David is dead, and Moses is dead; but this truth is not dead, 'Seek ye my face'. Paul is gone and Peter is gone. We are the Davids and the Moseses, and the Peters, and the Pauls now. Those truths that were good to them are good to us.... There is an eternal truth, that runs through all ages of the church, that hath an everlasting comfort.⁸

The Scriptures were written for all times, and its truths, setting aside the personal circumstances applied to particular men, are universal and concern everyone.

But what are these universal truths, the same fundamental truths for all ages? It is but a large explication of what has always been taught in the church. "Divine truth is always the same," ⁹ though more clearly revealed in the New Testament than in the Old. In defining the differences between Romanism and Protestantism, Sibbes draws the distinction between negative and positive truths. The latter are to be discovered in the Scriptures and the apostolic church. The negative were the later man-made additions to the gospel, some unheard of for a thousand years after Christ, some established not many years before at Trent. They included: purgatory, invocation of saints, sacraments of diverse kinds, adding tradition to Scripture, and merit to faith, transubstantiation, papal absolutism, canonization of saints.¹⁰

The positive truths are: the Scriptures as the Word of God, not the Apocrypha and the traditions; Christ as the only Mediator both for redemption and for intercession, not saints and angels; two sacraments, baptism and the Lord's supper, not five more; Christ as the Son of God and reconciler of God and man.¹¹ The personal application of the truths in the Lord's Prayer petitions and every article of the Creed brings remission of sins and life everlasting:

---

¹ III 255, C2C1.
² V 270, PF.
³ IV 315, C2C4.
⁴ I 205, SC; IV 316, C2C4.
⁵ V 270, PF.
⁶ I 305, SS.
⁷ VI 116, SuS.
⁸ *Idem.*
⁹ IV 116, SuS.
¹⁰ *Idem*; III 376, 377, C2C1.
¹¹ V 477, FO; III 375ff., C2C1.

"I believe God the Father to be *my* God, Jesus Christ *my* Saviour, the Holy Ghost *my* sanctifier."[1] There are three main parts of salvation: knowledge of our misery, knowledge of our deliverance, and a life answerable.[2]

We must labor to be established in these main points, these evangelical truths. To argue the fine, the difficult, or unrevealed points of doctrine is a barren exercise.[3] Instead we should keep little points of faith on which we differ to ourselves for the sake of the peace and good of the church, especially in view of the weaknesses of human nature.[4] Let us assent in lesser matters, maintaining the greater, as Bucer did, who refused no one who had "something of Christ."[5] We should be "zealous" in fundamental truths. "*There is one faith from the beginning of the world.* As there is one Christ, one salvation, so there is one uniform faith for the saving of our souls."[6] It is by knowledge we come to God, not by a general knowledge of divinity, but by the knowledge of him, the calling of God and Christ.[7] Compendiums are insufficient. "If we know that we must love God above all, and our neighbours as ourselves, and that Christ died for all, we know enough, more than we can practise."[8] It is through the personal knowledge of God that his truth bears fruit in the church. This is his means of advancing the church in the world.

The growth of the truth in the world has not been constant. Yet for the sake of the elect and the church, the world is continued.[9] God spares the vineyard for good vines.[10] A Christian is no sooner one with Christ, than all the powers of evil are arrayed against him. There are two grand sides in the world, two kingdoms, two seeds, two contrary dispositions.[11] The battles of men and empires are but a little part of the world drama. Two things in the world keep this world from being a hell upon earth: God's church and his cause.[12] The state of a Christian and of the church in this world is glorious because it is impregnable.[13] "If God be for us, who can be against us?"

Much in history seems to belie such optimism. Trials and afflictions are real. But to the church each bears good.[14] It is precisely through afflictions the church has been spread to the uttermost part of the world.[15] Even as Christ was first humiliated, then glorified, so it is with us. We must be "content to

---

[1] VI 477, HC.

[2] Note the similarity here to the Heidelberg Catechism, Q.2:
   Q. How many things are necessary for you to know, that you in this comfort may live and die happily?
   A. Three; the first, how great my sins and misery are; the second, how I am delivered from all my sins and misery; the third, how I am to be thankful to God for such deliverance.

[3] I 54, BR; VII 545, ChE.

[4] I 76, BR.

[5] I 57, BR; I lxxxvi [Sibbes' introduction to Paul Bayne's "Commentary on 1st Chapter of Ephesians, handling the controversy of Predestination" (1618)].

[6] VII 414, DB.
[7] VII 492–493, GG.
[8] II 190, BO.
[9] IV 466, C2C4.
[10] II 361, RD.
[11] VII 389, SPC.
[12] VII 396, SPC.
[13] VII 391, SPC.
[14] III 142, C2C1; VII 526, BD.
[15] IV 403, C2C4.

suffer first, and then be glorious."[1] "It is true in the head, it is true in the body, and it is true of every particular member of the body."[2] In all the seeming confusion of things, harmony is overcoming the discord. God is fitting and preparing. Delivery is coming. "The church and her opposites are like the scales of a balance; when one goes up, the other goes down." When God's truth conquers, the enemy will be destroyed.[3]

In the individual Christian, the Spirit ebbs and flows.[4] The same progress and regression pattern applies to the whole church.[5] "The whole days of the church are a time of persecution." It "began with blood, continues with blood, and shall end with blood."[6] But the time of suffering is when the glorious manifestation of the gospel comes. So came ten persecutions following the first general promulgation of the gospel after Christ.[7] Likewise God's judgments come upon his people, first small ones, and, if these are unsuccessful, greater. Perhaps some worthy leaders will first be taken away, pillars of the church. This is an evil sign, as are atheism, idolatry, and especially divisions and dissensions.[8]

But God does do great things. The darkness of Egypt and of Babylon were opportunities for his glorious grace.[9] "Christ and his church, when they are at the lowest, are nearest a rising."[10] After a time a spirit will enter into the church, and it shall live.

> Babylon must fall; the church must rise. Christ will enlarge his church to the end of the world.... He that raised up Jesus will raise up the church out of all its troubles.[11]

When God breaks down, it is to build up his church; when he purges, it is to cure and heal.[12]

Satan labors to cast men into a dead sleep. He deludes them with false dreams of what is good, that they are good, that tomorrow will continue as today, that no danger is near, "though God's wrath hangeth over their head."[13] So he did, beginning about Constantine's time, when the church grew secure and suffered ecclesiastical abuses to come in. So popery grew by degrees till it overspread the church.[14] God did not forsake his own.

> God hath always a church in the worst times, in the obscurest age of the church, eight or nine hundred years after Christ... when Egyptian darkness had overspread the world, and there was little learning and goodness in the world, God had always sealed ones, marked ones, that he preserved from the danger of dark times....[15]

---

[1] V 530–531, FO.
[2] III 117, C2C1.
[3] I 305, SS.
[4] IV 206, EG.
[5] II 6, BO.
[6] I 378, CV.
[7] *Idem.*
[8] I 379, CV.
[9] IV 317–318, C2C4; III 117, C2C1.
[10] I 99, BR; cf. III 158, C2C1.
[11] IV 464, C2C4.
[12] VI 321, RP.
[13] II 42, BO.
[14] *Idem.*
[15] III 461, C2C1; cf. VI 234–235, RP.

There came a second spring of the gospel. In the first great expansion by the preaching of the apostles, much good spread through the world in forty years! "How did the gospel then break out like lightning, by means of that blessed apostle Paul, who himself carried it through a great part of the world!" [1]

> And now, in the second spring of the gospel, when Luther began to preach, in the period of a few years, how many countries were converted and turned to the gospel! England, Scotland, Swethland, Denmark, the Palatinate, a great part of France, Bohemia, and of the Netherlands. How many lillies grew up here on a sudden! Sudden growths are suspected, and well they may be. But when God will bless, in a short space a great deal of work shall be done.[2]

The churches to which John and Paul wrote are gone. The gospel is now come into the western parts.[3]

The great monarchies of the world have fallen: Assyria, Persia, Greece, Rome. Noble cities have died like men, and had their periods. Only the Christian has a kingdom which cannot be shaken.[4] The history of the church of all ages shows how God's people are encircled with cruel enemies and dangers on every side. The heathen judge them a forlorn people. Yet God shows himself at such times and makes it evident that the church stands not by its own strength.[5] Then the church remembers that a "few Moseses in the mount would do more good than many soldiers in the valley."[6]

> If a company would join in an army of prayers, it were worth all the armies in the world; it would set the great God on work. He that can raise light out of darkness, what cannot he do to his poor church, if they had a spirit of prayer to set him on work! [7]

"It is God's manner, before any great work for his church, to stir up the spirits of his beloved ones to give him no rest." [8]

God uses the prayers of his people to usher in the next great thrust of the gospel. When they are humbled and prepared, the time will be ripe. We must wait quietly; his time is best.[9] We should not despair, not even of the conversion of those that are savages in distant parts of the world.

> Christ's almighty power goeth with his own ordinance to make it effectual. Since the coming of Christ, the world lies before Christ, as beloved of him, some in all nations. The gospel is like the sea: what it loseth in one place it gaineth in another. So the truth of God, if it lose in one part—if it be not respected—it gets in another, till it have gone over the whole world.[10]

---

[1] II 337, RB.
[2] *Idem*.
[3] III 11, C2Cl.
[4] II 341, RB.
[5] I 316–317, SS.
[6] I 261, SC.
[7] IV 319, C2C4; cf. IV 365, C2C4; VI 198–199, CCC.
[8] I lxxxix (Sibbes' "Recommendation," an Essay on Prayer, prefixed to Henry Scudder's "Key of Heaven, the Lord's Prayer Opened.").
[9] III 164, C2Cl.
[10] V 517, FO.

The gospel storm is gathering. Where God is truly worshipped, "God is terrible out of his holy place."[1] There is no doubt that the humiliation of God's people brought Antichrist to his knees in Germany and elsewhere. Through the "excellency of power in the word, in faith, in prayer, in fasting, in the sentence of the church," God works powerfully by the church upon others.[2]

Great men in the world think they will do great matters, but know not that what they do is to render service to the church.

> The administration of the world, it is not for the rebels that are in it, it is for those that are God's children; and he tosseth and tumbleth empires and monarchies.... All is for the elect.[3]

The creation of the world, sufferance of the wicked, continuance of heaven and earth, ordinance of civil government, providential care, reprobation, the ordinances of the ministry and sacraments,–all are reductive to the good of the little flock.[4]

What distinguishes the wicked from the "little flock" is grace, and only that.

> Do not many sit in darkness, and in the shadow of death? Is it not a grace therefore that we partake of the means of salvation? What is in us by nature better than in Turks and Pagans? or than many other people under Satan, and under popish teachers, and so rot away in their ignorance? Nothing. We differ only by the grace of God.[5]

Because he cares for the work of grace, God often corrects his people more sharply than the world. For general sins there are general corrections, but for special sins, particular visitations are frequent. "Let none think to be exempt and venture themselves from grace they have."[6] God will save his own not only from hell but from the miseries occasioned by sin on earth.[7] He has, like a physician, a special care for his own, administering according to need and saving in extremity. Rams horns, pitchers with lamps, the jawbone of an ass, and crude fishermen were means of destroying enemies and their cities from Midian to Rome. God has done great things.[8] He still does.

> All the afflictions of this world are to draw or to drive us to God, whether we will or no. As the messengers in the gospel, to force guests to the banquet with violence, Luke xiv.23; so afflictions they are to force us to God.[9]

He is working his victory for us and in us.[10] We cannot comprehend his reasons. As in election and reprobation, so there is a depth in the mystery of his providence. But "whatsoever befalls us, we may with comfort say, 'The will of the Lord be done'."[11]

---

[1] IV 389, C2C4.
[2] *Idem.*
[3] III 95–96, C2C1.
[4] *Idem*; II 423, RB.
[5] III 331, C2C1.
[6] IV 81, JR.
[7] VII 490, DGC.
[8] IV 390–391, C2C4; VI 234, RP.
[9] III 153, C2C1.
[10] V 264, PF.
[11] VII 216, DMHC.

## 3. The Latter Age and the End of History

Sibbes' sermons are frequently punctuated with expressions of concern for the persecuted church abroad. To understand his troubled mind, we need first to catch the spirit of advance that spurted new life into Protestant veins whenever the sixteenth-century Reformation came to mind. After a thousand years of decline under Satan's increasing rule,[1] darkness reigned. It was no wonder the gospel was grasped so greedily when Luther began to preach.[2] Consider what makes these times so good:

> ...the manifestation of Christ's glorious gospel, that hath shined for a hundred years and more in our church; the discovery of the means of salvation so clearly; the abundance of the Spirit with the means, making men to apprehend the means; enlightening their understandings to make use of them, and working their hearts to obedience. Look in what age these are; they are happy times.... Oh, those that lived two hundred years ago, though they were good men, if they had lived to see that that we see, and to hear that that we hear, living in the glorious lustre and sunshine of the gospel, how would it have rejoiced them.... Blessed be God... that we should be born in this generation; in the blessed time of the gospel; in this second spring of the gospel. We should bless God for it.[3]

Numerous were the descriptive phrases for the new period of history ushered in by the Reformation: the latter-spring of the gospel,[4] latter age of the church,[5] clear or glorious sunshine of the gospel,[6] glorious light of the gospel,[7] glorious times of the gospel,[8] and the latter age of the world.[9] Events had seemed to confirm such visionary optimism: Antichrist (papal power) had been brought to his knees in Germany;[10] in 1588 God had sent four winds to help achieve victory over the Spanish enemy;[11] king, church, and state had been co-ordinated through the reformation of religion;[12] commonwealths beyond the sea had prospered by proclaiming the gospel;[13] enlargement of the church had resulted;[14] progress of the gospel in England had come under Edward and Elizabeth;[15] and spirituality and comfort in the world had increased.[16]

The plight of the church in the Palatinate, in France, in Spain, in Italy was indeed sobering. Again and again Sibbes cries: Consider the state of the poor church abroad, torn by enemies without and rending itself by divisions within.[17] The church is now lying bleeding.[18] What has become of the Reformation

---

[1] IV 313, C2C4.
[2] VI 311, VV.
[3] VI 494–495, KDE.
[4] I 100, BR.
[5] I 125, SC.
[6] I 388, UM; III 393, C2C1; V 512, FO; VI 226, GI.
[7] IV 313, C2C4; VI 95, SF.
[8] VI 557, BL.
[9] VII 206, DMHC.
[10] IV 389, C2C4.
[11] I 317–318, SS.
[12] I 312, SS.
[13] III 219, C2C1.
[14] IV 255, EG.
[15] VII 469, RMJ.
[16] IV 215, EG.
[17] I 76, BR; IV 428, C2C4; VI 549, BL; VII 60, DR.
[18] V 235, SJ.

gospel?[1] A great part of God's house is on fire:[2] dreaded Charles IX, St. Bartholomew's massacre,[3] the Gunpowder Plot,[4] the great plague of 1625,[5] wars of Europe[6] all the church of God is in a state of combustion, Europe is in tumult, the church is in a narrow corner.[7]

Once, the awful possibility is mentioned: What if God leaves the church, as he did the Jews, as he may do for France and England? "...he will alway have a catholic church in the world; but he is not tied to England or France, or any country...."[8] This is but more reason to pray for the state of the church at home and abroad. "But where is the man, when he hears of news beyond the seas, that sends up sighs to God? prayer, that he would take pity upon his church?"[9] We must add reformation to our lamentations, otherwise the whole church and the commonwealth is in danger. The Christian must also weep for the sins and miseries of others.[10] "Who is so pitiful of his brethren round about as he ought?"[11] The mystical body of Christ is under persecution, souls in it are being slaughtered,[12] and we are all one society, one family, all brethren.[13] We cannot but sympathize with those beyond the seas.[14] Realistically Sibbes recognizes the darkness of the hour:

> It is true our times are not so good as they should be, and in many regards they are miserable times; and we must not murmur at this dispensation of God, if God hath so appointed that our lot shall be to live in hard and ill times. I say in some respects these are bad times; for the world, the older it grows, the worse it is. As it is in a sink, the farther it goes the more soil it gathers; so all the soil of former times are met in the sink of later times, and in that respect this generation is an ill generation.[15]

In that respect, in some respects–but not in the chief respect. We should not be discouraged about the afflicted state of the church abroad.[16] The misery is indeed great in Bohemia where there is no liberty of the gospel,[17] but in most Protestant lands, the church has leapt forward. The golden age is now.[18] The apostolic times were the virgin best times, the first springs of the gospel,[19] as

---

[1] I 135, SC.
[2] I 380, CV.
[3] I 302, SS; II 226, C2C1.
[4] I 310, SS. The gunpowder plot was an attempt of prominent Catholics to incite a Catholic rebellion by blowing up James I and parliament on November 5, 1605. The plot was revealed and its leaders, including the famed Guy Fawkes, were executed by the enraged Protestants. Evidence that the plotters were influenced by Jesuit thought intensified feeling against the latter. Thereafter a day of commemoration was held annually. G. M. Trevelyan, *England under the Stuarts*, 87–93.
[5] VI 153, RD.
[6] V 532, FO.
[7] III 187, C2C1; VI 148, RD.
[8] II 247, BG.
[9] VI 67, AM.
[10] VI 66, AM.
[11] VI 196–197, CCC.
[12] IV 428, C2C4.
[13] VI 150, RD.
[14] IV 104, JR.
[15] VI 494, KDE.
[16] V 151–152, EP3; 492, FO.
[17] III 198, C2C1.
[18] V 512, FO.
[19] II 189, BO.

such they remain our example.[1] But now once again after centuries of papal darkness, the sunshine of the gospel has returned. These are happy times indeed.

When we inquire as to God's purpose in his world, there is only one answer: his glory. In the government of the world, in the ministry and the church, is shown something of his glory. Weak means or none at all do not hinder his providence in attaining his great ends.

> God aimeth at his own glory, and it is no pride in him, because there is none above him, whose glory he should seek. And therefore it is natural for God to do all for his own glory, as it is natural for him to be holy, because he is the first cause, and the last end, of all things... Rom. xi.36. It is God's prerogative. The grace is ours. He giveth grace to us, but the glory is his own....[2]

The end of creation and redemption alike is to give God the praise. The gift of reason is intended to take in, from the beholding of the creatures, God's greatness and goodness and to give him the glory. There are second causes which bring joy and good to man. God himself subdues the disorders in our human nature for the good of society and the furtherance of his church. The just man, following his Lord's example, works to bring good to men. One way to help us to see God is to see and seek him in second causes. Such are fittest to glorify God who see second causes but move from them to the first of all.[3]

The Christian is, after all, a man of another world.[4] While here, he is a member of two worlds.[5] "A man is never safe till he be in heaven."[6] The grace that he has today is an earnest of the fullness of heaven.[7] The gospel now preached is especially a treasure for the time to come, some grapes of heaven on earth.[8] The glorious estate in heaven will be of the same kind as the life of grace here upon earth; there will only be difference in the degree of happiness.[9] Christ came once in humiliation; he will come again in glory.[10] Then the bodily resurrection will take place,[11] the second and perfect degree of justification will be given,[12] the church will be glorious within and without.[13]

More glorious times will soon come when truth is no longer heresy, nor heresy called catholic doctrine.[14] The time of that day is uncertain; God's time is best.[15] But Christ will not be long from his church.[16] The church will be "in glory ere long."[17] The place of glory is heaven, because that is where Christ is.

> Oh, if the outside, skirts, and suburbs of the palace (the stars and planets, chiefly those two great lights, the sun and moon) of this great King be so

---

[1] VII 299, CWa.
[2] IV 390, C2C4.
[3] VI 151, RD; I 177, SC; II 421, RB.
[4] I 132, SC.
[5] IV 50, SMA.
[6] III 332, C2C1.
[7] II 510, MF.
[8] IV 344, C2C4.
[9] VI 137, RD.
[10] V 140, EP3; VI 544, BL.
[11] V 146, EP3.
[12] V 492, FO.
[13] V 491, FO.
[14] I 92, BR.
[15] II 504, MF.
[16] II 171, BO.
[17] V 533, FO.

glorious, that with our eyes we cannot look upon the splendour of the same, what brightness of glory is in the chamber of presence, innermost court, and *sanctum sanctorum* itself?[1]

About the nature of heaven little can be said. And certainly nothing more ought to be said than is written. In such matters we should "tie no man to believe further than the Spirit of God shall direct him."[2] We know that when Christ comes, believers will be comforted, for their desire to be with him will be fulfilled. Unbelievers will be filled with woe, since hell will be their reward,[3] the hell of separation from God which on earth they insisted upon. We may be certain that, if we do not seek his face here, we shall not see it hereafter.[4]

The time is short in three senses. 1. The time of the world is short before the day of judgment. "Christ is at hand to judge the quick and the dead.... It was short then, it is shorter now.... We are fallen into the latter end of the world."[5] God can accomplish much quickly; he is not bound to length of time. Blessed times are approaching. Antichrist will be overthrown.[6] The fullness of the Gentiles is coming. And when they are come in, then comes the conversion of the Jews.[7]

2. The time is short for me, for you, as a particular person. When we die, our eternal destiny is set.[8] "Christ is come to us, and we every day go to him, for every day takes away part of our life." Our life should be a fitting of ourselves for him. "...what is good at the hour of death is good now."[9]

3. The season of time, the prime time, is short. The opportunity of time is shorter than life. The whole year is neither seedtime nor harvest. The tide is not always in, nor does the sun always shine. So it is in the spiritual state of things.[10] God has continued the world for believers' sakes. The church cannot die with us. The remnant of Isaiah's time shall endure to the end.[11] As God gave up the eastern empire, the glorious churches of Saint John's time, to the Turk, and those western kings to Romish Antichrist for undervaluing the gospel, so he will give us up if we do not make much of the gospel. God dealt graciously at first with "those two, the Turk and pope, [who] are twins; they had their beginning at once, about seven hundred years after Christ,"—he gave them his truth to save their souls.[12] But they chose their will above his, traditions of men for his wisdom, dross instead of gold. It was just to leave them in their lies. We should profit from their example.[13]

> So presently after the preaching of the gospel, comes the fan and the axe, or though not very presently, yet after a certain time, when our need requires it; for God will wait a while to see how we entertain his glorious gospel, and whether we walk worthy of it no not.[14]

---

[1] VII 499, GG.
[2] VII 333, GR.
[3] VI 79, SR.
[4] VI 131, SS; III 313, C2C1.
[5] IV 43, SMA.
[6] II 498, MF.
[7] V 517, FO; II 337, RD; 446, 498, 505, MF.
[8] IV 43, SMA.
[9] VII 305, CWa.
[10] IV 43–44, SMA.
[11] VI 233, RP.
[12] VII 529, BD.
[13] *Idem.*
[14] I 378, CV.

*Conclusion*

A significant variety of interpretation surrounds the theology of Richard Sibbes. About three decades ago, W. K. Jordan held that Sibbes was thoroughly Calvinistic in his doctrinal views;[1] and A. Grosart over a hundred years ago wrote: "...Sibbes avouched his Calvinism, and spoke with no bated breath of Arminianism."[2] M. Schmidt qualifies these judgments by saying that "...es wäre falsch, ihn deshalb zum Vertreter der kalvinistischen Prädestinationslehre zu machen";[3] Larzer Ziff believes him to be "ambiguously inconsistent" on predestination in that he believes in absolute election and conditional reprobation;[4] and Ola Winslow judges him to be a compromise of Calvin's teaching on the absolute sovereignty of God by his emphasis on good works.[5] August Lang calls him one of the "pietistischen Puritaner,"[6] as have others;[7] Elwood refers to him as a representative of the resurgence of mysticism in the seventeenth century;[8] and William Haller sees him as representative of, among other things, a growing insistence on the immanence of God in nature and in human life.[9] I. Morgan calls attention to Sibbes' valuation of worldly things both as good in themselves and as given to sweeten our passage to heaven;[10] and the Georges indicate his balanced Christian view on a variety of subjects: natural truth as God's gift,[11] the lawfulness of recreation,[12] the Christian character of particular callings,[13] the spiritual equality (if not superiority) of women in responsiveness to religion,[14] the priesthood of believers,[15] the *via media* on ceremonials,[16] and the catholic unity of the church.[17] We are concerned to discuss these views insofar as they are related to the missionary elements in Sibbes' theology. This we shall do by summarizing his principles, motives, methods, and goal of missions.

We call attention to three principles. First, God is the sovereign Lord of missions. This is true both for the redemption of humanity and the salvation of the individual. God's election of Christ and us in Christ is clearly seen in his predestinating act and the providential fulfillment of his over-arching purpose. For Sibbes, predestination, providence, and election are all of one piece. Together they constitute the Biblical way of ascribing redemption completely to God. God so reveals himself. We can say no more. It is true that predestination

---

[1] W. K. Jordan, *The Development of Religious Toleration in England*, 359.
[2] Grosart, *op. cit.*, I xiii.
[3] Martin Schmidt, *Der junge Wesley als Heidenmissionar und Missionstheologe*, 10.
[4] Larzer Ziff, *The Career of John Cotton*, 219.
[5] Ola E. Winslow, *Jonathan Edwards*, 147.
[6] August Lang, *Puritanismus und Pietismus*, 140-163.
[7] S. van der Linde in *Die Religion in Geschichte und Gegenwart*, Dritte Auflage, VI 14.
[8] Douglas J. Elwood, *The Philosophical Theology of Jonathan Edwards*, 144.
[9] William Haller, *The Rise of Puritanism*, 209.
[10] Irvonwy Morgan, *The Non-Conformity of Richard Baxter*, 13.
[11] Charles and Katherine George, *The Protestant Mind of the English Reformation*, 234, 347.
[12] *Ibid.*, 141.
[13] *Ibid.*, 117.
[14] *Ibid.*, 282-283.
[15] *Ibid.*, 321.
[16] *Ibid.*, 357.
[17] *Ibid.*, 374, 383, 384, 416, 417.

includes both believers and unbelievers, elect and reprobate, "*canés et filii.*"[1] If this were not so, part of the world would be excluded from the Lordship of God. No inadequacy of man to understand the relation of divine sovereignty to human responsibility justifies the exclusion of some part of finiteness from God's controlling will.

> ...redemption, in regard of efficacy, is no larger than God's election.
> ...There are a company in the world whom God hates: 'Esau have I hated, Rom. ix.13....'[2]

This point establishes the identity of Sibbes' view in main lines with the predestination teaching of Calvin. Schmidt rightly sees that the idea of God is the controlling motif for Sibbes. The heathen who came into the church were not the intellectually and morally superior Socrates and Plato, but the degenerate Corinthians. Why? "God pardons whom He will and condemns whom He will."[3] But this does not, as Schmidt affirms, differ from the Calvinistic view of predestination![4] The insistence on divine priority both in time (decrees) and in working (born of the Spirit) holds high the concept of divine transcendence over against classic mysticism.[5] There are, of course, elements of mysticism in Sibbes, elements which are found in the nature of the Christian faith and the believer's union with Christ through the indwelling of the Spirit. Elwood defines a mystic as "one who claims to know God through a form of spiritual inwardness."[6] Certainly, true mystic elements must be present in every aspect of Christian theology. But we may not forget that these elements must not be excluded from one's faith, but must be seen in the perspective of the controlling sovereignty of a transcendent God. This Elwood recognizes, but he wrongly classifies Sibbes with Francis Rous (*The Mysticall Marriage*–1635) and with John Everard (translator of *Theologica Germanica*), who tend to blur the line between the transcendence and immanence of God.[7] Sibbes does not blur the line between the Creator-Redeemer God and the creature-sinner. His sermons, the later as much as the earlier ones, state that distinction clearly; moreover, they remain explications on the Word of God in the Bible, and they set forth the objective redemption offered by Jesus Christ.[8]

---

[1] Sibbes, *Works*, V 66, EP3.
[2] *Ibid.*, 388–389.
[3] Schmidt, *loc. cit.*
[4] Joannis Calvini, *Institutio Christianae Religionis*, Book III, Chap. xxiiii has as its title: "Electionem sanciri Dei vocatione: reprobos autem sibi accersere iustum, cui destinati sunt, interitum."
[5] By classic mysticism I mean the doctrine that man can have direct communication with God and receive knowledge of spiritual truths through intuition or union with the divine.
[6] Elwood, *op cit.*, 143.
[7] Elwood, *op cit.*, 144; see W. Haller, *op. cit.*, 206–216, who does not classify Sibbes, as does Elwood, with Everard, see especially 216.
[8] It is difficult to know to what Haller refers when he states that there is a "growing insistence" on God's immanence (*op. cit.*, 209) in Sibbes. We can establish the periods of his sermons only by noting those published by himself, the first of which appeared in 1629, and the two last sermons which he preached before his death in 1635. Since his sermons

The second principle of significance for missions is: God uses means to accomplish redemption. These means include especially the church and its ordinances: the preaching of the gospel and the use of the sacraments. The minister's calling is to win men to God: "Preaching is the chariot that carries Christ up and down the world."[1] God could have converted the elect by a direct act of his Spirit; he chooses rather to use the weakest of means.[2] There is, thus, no doubt that salvation comes, not from the means, but from God Himself. How are we to receive God's Spirit and be converted? "For answer there unto; we should ever be under sanctified means."[3]

Third, man must respond to the gospel. Sibbes' strong emphasis on the sovereignty of God in predestination seems contradictory to his constant call for man's responsible choice for Christ and the godly life. He recognizes the contradiction in these two emphases. But preaching exegetically, as he does, leaves him no alternative. The Bible teaches both – a sovereign God and a responsible man. Moreover, as a Christian, his own experience was the same. He was saved completely by grace, not by works, yet he was required to make his calling and election sure. As Perry Miller has put it: "...by the absolute decree of God man was assigned to the place of freedom...."[4] And again, quoting Sibbes this time, "'Though God's grace do all, yet we must give our consent'".[5] Our consent is not to be divorced from God's power.

> ...Though it is we that answer, yet the power by which we answer is no less than that whereby God created the world and raised Christ from the dead. The answer is ours, but the power and strength is God's, whereby we answer, who performs both his part and ours too in the covenant.[6]

When man does not respond to the gospel, is the cause to be attributed to man or to God? Characteristically, Sibbes answers this question in two ways. When he describes predestination, he notes that there are differences among Reformed divines in neighboring countries on this matter: whether God's decree precedes or follows the fall. Yet, he continues, all agree: that there was an eternal separation of men in God's purpose, that this sovereign act of separation on God's part is independent of anything in the creature, and that damnation is an act

---

are not dated, we have no way of knowing when they were preached. A careful comparison of those published in 1629 with the two preached in 1635 does not indicate the sort of difference suggested by Haller. Compare, for example, the doctrinal explanation of the text "Ye believe in God, believe also in me" (*Works*, VII 346 ff.) preached in 1635, with that on the text "For this is my blood of the new testament, which is shed for many, for the remission of sins" published in 1629 .(*Ibid.*, VII 263 ff.) The persons of the Trinity, the objective nature of the atonement, divine forgiveness, and the consequent indwelling of the Spirit and union with Christ are as plain in the one as in the other. Likewise, the prefaces to books of friends, written by Sibbes, dating from 1618, indicate no change of this sort.

[1] *Works*, V 508, FO.
[2] *Ibid.*, 518, FO.
[3] *Ibid.*, VII 170, SRi.
[4] Miller, *The New England Mind*, I 233.
[5] *Ibid.*, 389; *Works*, V 515, FO.
[6] *Works*, I civ.

of divine justice based upon sin. On the one hand, foreseen sin cannot be the cause of separation, since all have sinned; and, on the other hand, the execution of the decree is founded upon sin. Here again are the two irreconcilables: divine separation and human sin.[1] Even in reprobation, Sibbes refuses to let these two poles go. But in preaching to the unbeliever, he makes it clear: man is condemned for his own sin. Here again he reflects Calvin, who entitled the chapter in his *Institutio* following those on eternal election: Election Confirmed by the Divine Call. The Destined Destruction of the Reprobate Procured by Themselves.[2] The words may sound contradictory: "The destined destruction ...procured by themselves." Sibbes was consistent in insisting both upon this doctrine and upon the fact of the mystery involved, a mystery beyond the right or necessity of a creature to question.[3] Nor does Sibbes compromise Calvin's view of sovereignty by attributing one iota of merit to good works.[4] Man must consent; all is of grace.

There are subsidiary principles for Sibbes, but these three theological principles form the foundation for the sense of mission in the Puritan tradition: the sovereign God is Lord of the mission, the divinely appointed means accomplish the mission, the response of man is the object of the mission. Compromise of the first opens the floodgates to Mysticism. Indifference to the second brings formalism or sectarianism. Blindness to the third gives birth to rationalistic orthodoxy. The crucial question was: Could Puritanism hold these elements in tension without compromising what they were sure was gospel truth? We shall have occasion to test later Puritans at this touchstone.

For Sibbes there are two primary aspects of the method for missions. The first results from the right use of the means and the second from the nature of the Christian faith. We have extensively presented Sibbes' explication of both in this chapter. They run as lines through all of his writings. The first is the verbal preaching of the gospel by the ministers and also by men in their ordinary callings: especially "merchants, and those that give themselves to navigation, they may with good success carry the gospel to all people."[5]

> Indeed, 'preaching' is the ordinance of God, sanctified for the begetting of faith, for the opening of the understanding, for the drawing of the will and affections to Christ.[6]

The one who preaches must lay open the person and work of Christ, show the sinner his true estate through the law, and then sweetly persuade him to come to Christ.[7] The power of the gospel is itself a ground to work for the conversion of savages, no matter how barbarous they be. Think what we in England were sixteen hundred years ago![8]

---

[1] *Ibid.*, lxxxv–lxxxvi. Sibbes' introduction to Paul Bayne's *Commentary on 1st Chapter of Ephesians, handling the controversy of Predestination* (1618).
[2] Calvin, *Institutio Christianae Religionis*, II 24.
[3] Vs. L. Ziff, *loc. cit.*
[4] Vs. Ola Winslow, *loc. cit.*
[5] *Works*, V 512, FO.
[7] *Ibid.*, 514.
[8] *Ibid.*, 505–506.
[9] *Ibid.*, 513.

> Let no man therefore despair; nor, as I said before, let us not despair of the conversion of those that are savages in other parts. How bad soever they be, they are of the world, and if the gospel be preached to them, Christ will be 'believed on in the world'. Christ's almighty power goeth with his own ordinance to make it effectual....[1]

The second primary method springs from the communicative and diffusive nature of faith. Faith, like light, shines; like a vine, bears fruit; like fire, warms; like God, loves. The Turks conquered to their religion by violent means, by blood.[2] We must do it by love. Schmidt puts it:

> Es könnte sein, dass Sibbs die missionarische Tätigkeit als normale Funktion des kirchlichen Lebens versteht und sie darum mit einer naiven Selbstverständlichkeit jedem Gemeindeglied zuweist.[3]

Sibbs does just that,[4] because the nature of faith requires it. Goodness spreads, talents increase, light shines, prophets speak,—so believers cannot but witness.

In a Latin sermon on 2 Tim. 1:14, preached to students at Trinity College on October 9, 1627, Sibbes sets six prescriptions for the right preservation of the deposit of the gospel committed to the church. The last two of these are *communicandum* and *propagandum*. We have already commented on the latter.[5] *Communicandum* points to the utter impossibility of defending the silence of a Christian. We are to explain the riches of Christ.

Besides, this deposit is also to be communicated; for it is a talent which is only preserved when it is expended for the use of others. For we preserve when we do not preserve. We are not produced into this world in order to be mute people, to indulge in idle speculations; to be only keepers and not stewards, to be shells and not channels: cursed is he who keeps his fruit hidden; and happy are we whose works God deigns to use in his vineyard, that we be not confused and broken rubbish and unusable instruments, but people whose industry God will have valued. Perhaps the jackdaws would be silent when the swans would sing. And everybody must have his measure distributed to him.[6]

The primary motive is for Sibbes, as for Puritanism in general,[7] the glory of God. His view of the majesty, sovereignty, and condescending love of God

---

[1] *Ibid.*, 517.
[2] *Ibid.*, 518.
[3] Schmidt, *op. cit.*, 12.
[4] *Supra*, 40ff.
[5] *Supra*, 37.
[6] "Insuper et hoc depositum communicandum est; talentum enim est quod tum custoditur cum aliorum usui impenditur. Custodimus etiam cum non custodimus. Non producimur in hanc scenam ut simus κῶφα πρόσωπα, ut speculationibus indulgeamus; ut condi simus tantum, non promi, ut conchae, non canales: maledictus qui abscondit frumentum; et faelices nos quorum opera uti dignatur Deus in vinea sua, quod non simus rejicula turba, fracta, et inutilia instrumenta, sed quorum industrium in alto loco posuerit Deus.... Tacerent forsitan graculi si canerent cygni. Cuique suum σιτομέτριον distribuendum est." (*Works* VII 554, ACN).
[7] Johannes Van den Berg, *Constrained By Jesus' Love*, 29.

in Christ leaves no other possibility. However, other motives find expression. The love of mankind as mankind and the fact of the human predicament are for the Christian, as they were for his Saviour, compelling motives to do what he can. The heathen as part of the ungodly and unbelieving world are objects of compassion. The work of missions, carried out in obedience to divine authority, has a place only in the perspective of the obedience every creature owes to his Creator and Redeemer. Sibbes views preaching to the Gentiles as a natural consequent of redemption and seldom refers to an explicit Scriptural directive to preach to them. Schmidt views the matter differently when, in comparing Sibbes' motive with that of Wesley, he says:

> Damit aber, dass die Mission für Wesley existentielle Aufgabe bedeutet, die aus der eigenen Lebensnot mit Inbrunst ergriffen wird, ist ein Fortschritt über Sibbs hinaus erreicht, für den sie unbedingtes, aber allgemeines, auch dem Willen Gottes beruhendes Gebot bleibt. Aus Autorität ist Autonomie geworden.[1]

Rather, the inner necessity of witnessing, resulting from the nature of faith, is for Sibbes a greater motive than obedience to external command, though both are certainly rooted in his biblical exegesis.

The final goal of history serves to fix our course as a star in the night. We cannot set the time or the manner of the final end of the age. We have entered the last stage of the redemptive drama. The sun moves westward, the course of the gospel as well.[2] Before Christ returns, the gospel must reach the ends of the earth. The glorious sunshine of the gospel attains divine ends: men are converted, the church grows, eternity approaches. Death is the entrance to glory, yet not death but the judgment tells the final victory. Then the purpose of history will be fulfilled for each of us, and for the whole creation as well. Men will be filled with grace and heaven with glory.

---

[1] Schmidt, *op. cit.*, 26, 27.
[2] *Works*, I 100-101, BR; V 517, FO.

CHAPTER II

# RICHARD BAXTER

THE DEVELOPMENT OF THE MISSION IDEA

*Biographical Introduction* [1]

Richard Baxter was born on November 12, 1615, at Rowton in Shropshire. Due to the gambling debts of his father, he lived ten years with his grandparents. Some time after his father's conversion through Scripture reading, the boy returned to his parental home at Eaton Constantine. The ignorance, drunkenness, and immorality of the clergy who read the Sunday lesson and taught during the week left deep scars on his sensitive spirit. The crude and meaningless manner of his confirmation at the age of fourteen by the bishop only made matters worse. However, partially because of his father's example and particularly through the reading of Bunny's *Resolution* and Sibbes' *The Bruised Reed*, Baxter was converted.

Baxter wanted university training but had to be satisfied with preparatory school at Wroxeter and private tutoring at Ludlow Castle. Actually, there was little tutoring, but he made good use of the excellent library there. He spent an unsatisfying month as apprentice page at court when he was nineteen. Here he lived at the home of the Master of Revels, Sir Henry Herbert, a brother of the poet George Herbert. Gladly he returned home from the low moral standards of the court. At home he studied and helped his father for four years. During this time his mother died.

Meanwhile, a thirst to be used in the conversion of others developed within him. In December, 1638, he was ordained deacon and began a fifty-three year ministry that spanned the reigns of Charles I, Oliver Cromwell and his son Richard, Charles II, James II, and reached into that of William III. He spent one year as usher in a school at Dudley while preaching in vacant pulpits on Sundays. Thereafter he served for two years as pastor at Bridgenorth, also in Shropshire, before accepting the position of lecturer at Kidderminster. Here in a township of three or four thousand, he exercised the chief work of his pastoral ministry first for fifteen months, and then for thirteen years after a four year interruption due to the civil war. He preached to soldiers and citizens at Coventry during the war and later served as chaplain, preaching to the living and praying with the dying, until a breakdown in health ended his service.

---

[1] Books from which the biographical material is based for the most part are: *The Practical Works of Richard Baxter*, with its introductory Essay; and *Reliquiae Baxterianae*, ed. by M. Sylvester; Alexander B. Grosart, *Representative Non-Conformists*, 107–193; Marcus L. Loane, *Makers of Religious Freedom in the Seventeenth Century*, 157–226; Hugh Martin, *Puritanism and Richard Baxter*; Frederick J. Powicke, *A Life of the Reverend Richard Baxter*, 2 vols; John Tulloch, *English Puritanism and Its Leaders*, 279–390.

While at death's door at the home of friends, he wrote most of *The Saints Everlasting Rest* during a few months in 1647 and won immediate fame. From the time of his return to Kidderminster that year until his silencing (as he calls it) in 1660, in addition to his regular work he wrote and published fifty-seven books,[1] including *The Reformed Pastor, A Treatise of Conversion,* and *A Call to the Unconverted.* From 1660 until his death in 1691 he gave himself wholly to study and writing, apart from such private and ecclesiastical activities as were allowed. The law permitted little opportunity for preaching during this period except for the last four years of his life, directly after the Declaration of Indulgence by James II. His one and a half year commitment to prison in 1684–1685 was based upon the charge that his *Paraphrase of the New Testament* was an attack on the established church and the state. The ludicrous behavior of Judge Jeffreys and the unfairness of the trial is one of the bad examples of legal conduct in a not too stable century.

For the brighter times in his youth, Baxter could thank good parents and his joy in reading. Pilfering apples with other lads from the neighbor's orchard was part of boyhood fun, as well as joining on occasion the merry-makers about the maypole near his father's house. For the most, however, he received greater pleasure from following his father's example of piety. Apart from the interruption of the war, the periods of pastoral activity were particularly rewarding to Baxter. The change for many in his parish from indifferent worship or none at all to serious-minded commitment to God brought real joy to his heart. Conversions were many, particularly among the youth. A regular visitation program of families in the parish bore much fruit. His wife, Margaret Chalton, gave him warm companionship and softened the hard edges of his life from the time of his silencing in 1662 until her death in 1681. His *A Breviate of Margaret Baxter,* written shortly after her death, breathes something of the depth of his love to her. He hardly expected to live ten years longer, but during this last difficult period there were many friends to cheer him, particularly Matthew Sylvester, whose pulpit he shared at the end and to whose care was entrusted the editing and publishing of his autobiography, *Reliquiae Baxterianae.* Throughout his life the love of reading stimulated his racing mind. Though he says he did not study after supper, his recreation was preparation of sermons and reading, likely late into the night. The two hours a day he spent walking for health's sake brought him some relief from nearly constant pain.

There were many dark shadows in his life. His weak body seemed unable to cope with the opportunity for which his mind and character qualified him. At the end he could only believe that God continued his life longer than nature was willing.[2] Already at the age of twenty-one he lay at death's door for two years. This was prophetic of the many other times in his life that he did not expect to live longer. During one of his more critical periods of illness he wrote *Dying Thoughts of Mr. Baxter* (1683). No doubt the aggravating weakness, the excruciating pain, the coughing and spitting of blood, and the constant irrita-

---

[1] According to the bibliographical list of Baxter's Works prepared by Alexander B. Grosart.
[2] Ms. Treatises IV, Item No. 117: "Elegy on the Death of Mr. Baxter."

tion of a large kidney stone in later life, contributed as much to the urgency of his preaching as "a dying man to dying men" [1] as did his Puritan theology.

Baxter's choice for a sort of Nonconformity was certainly not the least of his difficulties. Though his father had been ridiculed as a Puritan, Baxter Sr. was as much a conformist as the ancestors of both his parents had been. About 1640 Richard himself, after studying Nonconformity, chose a modified episcopacy, what he called "primitive episcopacy."[2] Bishops were all right so long as they did not act unilaterally in the life and discipline of the local church. Kneeling for the sacraments, laying on of hands by fellow pastors, and voluntary fasting were good. The use of a few days dedicated to saints of the church, the use of the Book of Common Prayer and form prayers, and the use of words such as sacrifice, priest, and altar, were indifferent matters and should not be scrupled. Baxter preferred not to use the sign of the cross and the surplice himself. But what he consistently rejected was the acknowledgement that the government of the church by diocesan bishops was divinely ordained and therefore not to be altered, as was required by the "Et cetera" oath in 1640, and the enforced subscription in matters indifferent or unlawful, as required by the Act of Uniformity in 1662.[3] That year he declined the bishopric of Hereford.

Nuttall gives two reasons why Baxter did not conform: his tender conscience for the liberty of others and his passionate concern for church unity.[4] The second will be considered later in this chapter. As to the first, Baxter could not believe, for example, that communion should be refused to those who judged it wrong to kneel, nor could he believe that ministers should be silenced for scruples against the use of the prayer book and wearing of the surplice. Episcopacy was wrong in requiring more than Scripture; Puritans were wrong in refusing what was indifferent. For Baxter Scripture itself was the only final authority.

> I doe not know of any divine Law but what is expressely or by consequence containd in the Scripture.... and no other... ought to be receiv'd or impos'd as necessary to salvation.[5]

Baxter experienced both personal and theological changes during the first half of his ministry. Before considering his view of man, the church, and the world as they relate to missions, these should be noted. In the *Reliquiae* Baxter discusses forty changes of emphasis in his person and views.[6] Many of these point to inward character changes: moderation of temper, a slower but more deliberate understanding, less desire for controversy and more emphasis upon fundamentals, increasing concern for sins of omission (e.g., lack of longing for God is worse than sins of immorality), less emphasis on grief for sin and more on love of God and joyful praise, less emphasis on regeneration and marks of sincerity

---

[1] III 1030, DT (1683).
[2] RB, II 371 (1665).
[3] Loane, *op. cit.*, 164.
[4] Geoffrey R. Nuttall and Owen Chadwick, *From Uniformity to Unity 1662-1962*, 184-185.
[5] Ms. Treatises V, Item No. 141, ff. 15-16.
[6] RB, I 124-136 (1664).

and more on God and heaven since "it is the Object that altereth and elevateth the Mind,"¹ increasing awareness of our own ignorance and the hiddenness of much truth, less trust in human opinions and more discerning use of books of men.

Other changes are more directly related to churches, to other Christians, and to the Scripture. With regard to the last, for example, early personal doubts were never about the truth of Scripture and Christianity, rather, they concerned the genuineness of faith in Christ. Later the converse was more true. His view of church communion became broader both in relation to other Protestants and Roman Catholics. External modes and forms of worship no longer limited or determined the extent of his communion. Church divisions affected him more. Apart from the sad condition of the heathen, nothing troubled him as much. However, the passage of time dimmed his hopes of unity and prosperity for the church on earth. He increasingly discounted the use of force in matters of religion. By the end of his life, prayers and efforts for the cause of the Christian faith outside England had become the most urgent of his concerns.

Baxter had several direct contacts with the mission work for the Indians in New England. From 1656 to at least 1682, Baxter corresponded with John Eliot and showed great interest in his work. Likely this personal concern for missions in New England helped to make him eager to assist in the securing of the new charter of the Corporation for the Propagation of the Gospel in New England in 1660-1662.² Though he assisted in the selection of new members to the Corporation, his own and other controversial names had to be omitted. He successfully appealed to the Lord Chancellor, with whom he was acquainted, for the return of the property belonging to the Corporation at the time of the Restoration. He appealed to the Corporation several times on behalf of Eliot and other mission projects. Especially through his friend Robert Boyle, President of the Corporation, Baxter brought influence to bear. Moreover, his own *Call to the Unconverted* was translated by Eliot and printed at the cost of the organization.³

Baxter's contact and influence in missions was much broader than New England. He encouraged Robert Boyle to contribute so that Grotius' *De Veritate Religionis Christianae* could be translated into Arabic. When it had been translated, he wrote the Dutch East India Company in 1660, suggesting that the book be spread by agents of the Company "to the end Christianity may be establisheda mong those infidels...."⁴ Of particular significance is the inspira-

---

[1] *Ibid.*, I 129 (1664).
[2] The Corporation for the Propagation of the Gospel in New England (later called the New England Company) was established by charter from Oliver Cromwell in 1649. Puritans both within and outside the established Church were active in its efforts to assist the New England mission to the Indians. For a full account of the Corporation, see William Kellaway, *The New England Company*. We consider the Corporation more fully in the next chapter.
[3] William Kellaway, *The New England Company 1649-1776*, 42, 44, 46, 88, 102, 131, 135, 143, 146.
[4] Court Minutes Book of the East India Company, Nov. 14, 1660, quoted by J. van den Berg, *Constrained by Jesus' Love*, from F. Penny, *The Church in Madras*, London, 1904, 36.

tion given by his writings to later missionaries. The father of John and Charles Wesley heard Baxter preach and said that his sermons seemed to glow with "a strange fire and pathos."[1] Young John Wesley asked Philip Doddridge for advice on reading. Doddridge pointed to Baxter as the "highest in his esteem" and his "particular favorite."[2] Wesley later thanked God for the discovery of Baxter's *Aphorisms of Justification*, of which he published an extract in 1745.[3] Both John and Charles Wesley, as well as Spurgeon, were influenced by Baxter's *Reformed Pastor*.[4] Bishop Wilson of Calcutta, in his preface to an edition of the *Reformed Pastor*, said that it was one of the best of Baxter's "invaluable practical works."[5] He appeals to the ministers of all Protestant churches of Europe and Africa to preach the blessed gospel so that "salvation of souls is the one thing we aim at, the object of desire, the ruling passion of our souls,"–only then can we "expect a general revival of religion."[6]

Isaac Watts, the Puritan hymnist *par excellence*, professed to be following Baxter's principle in preparing 'David's Psalms to be sung by Christian lips.'[7] Likely many gained a new awareness of the breadth of Christ's kingdom by Watts' hymn:

> Jesus shall reign where'er the sun
> Does his successive journeys run;
> His kingdom stretch from shore to shore,
> Till moons shall wax and wane no more.

Through Doddridge, whose dependence upon Baxter was significant,[8] William Wilberforce was converted. Wilberforce was a member of the influential Clapham sect which included in its number missionaries from India and Sierre Leone.[9] He calls Baxter's *Practical Works* a "treasury of Christian wisdom."[10] Baxter's *Call to the Unconverted* helped to bring George Whitefield to the knowledge of free grace and of the necessity of being justified by faith only.[11] Upon visiting Kidderminster, Whitefield reports: "I was greatly refreshed... to find what a sweet savour of good Mr. Baxter's doctrine, works, and discipline, remained to this day."[12] That Baxter's missionary influence extended far beyond the bounds of his life is clear; that influence touches at many points the great missionary movements of the eighteenth and nineteenth centuries. In order to understand why that influence was so great, we shall consider Baxter's views concerning the conversion of man, the role of the church in the work of redemption, and the redemption of the world.

---

[1] Loane, *op. cit.*, 183.
[2] *The Practical Works of Richard Baxter*, I Essay, xxxiv.
[3] Powicke, *op. cit.*, II 245.
[4] Martin, *op. cit.*, 210.
[5] *Practical Works*, I xxvi.
[6] *Ibid.*, xxvi-xxviii.
[7] Martin, *op. cit.*, 141–142.
[8] As Geoffrey Nuttall has clearly shown in his *Richard Baxter and Philip Doddridge*.
[9] Ernest Marshall Howes, *Saints in Politics*, 10–27.
[10] *Practical Works*, I xxvii.
[11] In August Lang, *Puritanismus und Pietismus*, 301, 302, quoting from Tyerman, *A Short Account of God's Dealings with ... Whitefield*, 1740.
[12] *Practical Works*, I xxvii.

## A. THE CONVERSION OF MAN

For Baxter nothing is more urgent than conversion. Man's meaningful involvement in history requires it. How some can be so blind to conversion as God's way for man and so irrational as to reject it, Baxter can hardly conceive. The stated object of many of his writings, and the repeated application in others, is to press for the believing response of the unconverted. God's way for man and man's to God are the key to the meaning of life and history.

### 1. Divine Sovereignty and Human Responsibility

#### a. The Human Situation

Humanity is estranged from God by sin. What is sin? Sin can have no being except that which is caused by the will of man. Whether it be called a privation or relation or *modus entis* is but a trifling philosophical question and must be treated as such.[1] The heart of sin is violating God's holy law, denying his authority, making ends of ourselves, rejecting proffered mercy, holding in contempt appointed means, debasing reason, misusing spiritual faculties, and destroying the harmony and order of the world.[2] The "grand impediment" to salvation lies in the incapability, the indisposition, and the frowardness of the human heart.[3] The radical depravity of man's moral nature [4] makes pleasing God, apart from Christ, impossible.

In the *Treatise of Self-Denial*, a sermon on Luke 9:23,24, the root of sin is presented as the corruption of man's created, holy disposition of soul by the choice of an inferior good, namely the pleasing and advancement of self. By this act reason bowed to sensuality, man became his own ultimate end. With the same sinful inclination we are all born. Instead of using all creation to God's pleasure, man uses all he possesses as fuel for self-advancement. The ordinate is grasped inordinately and subordinated to inferior ends.[5] This was the original sin.

Now "sinful, guilty, and miserable natures are propagated to all mankind."[6] Those who deny original sin and its deep-rooted effects "go against plain Scripture, reason, and the experience of mankind."[7] God does not impute to men what they are not already. We were seminally, not personally, in Adam; so is our guilt. Due difference between the principal agent and his offspring must be maintained.[8] It is certainly not incredible that unholy parents beget unholy children. Yet "no man in the world doth perish for Adam's sin alone, without his own."[9]

---

[1] Richard Baxter, *The Practical Works*, III 788, DL: KG (1663). To avoid needless repetition, all citations listed will be from *The Practical Works* unless indicated.

[2] I 86–88, CD : CEth (1673). Here Baxter shows in forty points "wherein the intrinsical malignity of sin consisteth." (page 86).

[3] II 160, RCR : Chr (1666).

[4] III 212, SER (1649); 512–513, CW (1657).

[5] III 372–373 ff., TS-D (1659); II 511, CU (1657).

[6] IV 264, PM (1672).

[7] *Ibid.*, 265.

[8] *Idem.*

[9] II 143, RCR : Chr (1666); 62–64, 73, RCR : NR (1666).

Because of his fall into sin man has lost "most" of the knowledge of God, holiness and happiness. This must be seen not only as a defect but as opposition to our proper end until grace overcomes us.[1] So the malady of the understanding is ignorance consisting of both privation and indisposition to the truth. Yet man's greatest disease lies in the will. Inordinate inclinations propagated by like acts and irrational refusal of spiritual good conspire to trap men in a web of depravity.[2]

What man has retained is "the natural power and freedom consisting in the self-determining faculty and principle."[3] What he has gained is moral inability and corruption. The knowledge of the "nature and pravity of man should teach us to...resolve all guilt and blame into the free and vitiated will of man."[4] His understanding is a dark, imperfect director, and his will is an imperfect receiver of the understanding's directions.[5] The collusion of these two makes unsanctified hearts incapable of sound faith. Small wonder that Jew and heathen reject the gospel![6]

God has determined to rule the world with the two great engines of free will and external objects.[7] By sin, free will is not taken away; man is still a man.[8] God works in a way agreeable to man's nature and present state.[9] Salvation is freely offered; nothing but our refusal can undo us.[10] God damns "none but those that will not be saved in his way: that is, that will not accept of Christ and salvation freely given them. (I speak of those that hear the gospel; for others their case is more unknown to us.)"[11] How unconceivable "that many men, and most men, should be damned, when they might be saved if they would, and will not."[12]

> We assure them, that God will never say, Depart from me, ye workers of iniquity, if they do not first by iniquity depart from God; and that God will not damn them, except they damn themselves, by the obstinate final refusing and resisting of his mercy.[13]

Not God's decree but man's sin is the cause of condemnation.[14]

For conversion and believing there is necessary a two-fold power: natural and moral. Everyone possesses the natural power. It is the faculty of understanding and of willing to which there is no physical impediment so long as the use of reason is unimpaired and the word is heard. Ability to believe and to repent belong to this power, so that all men can believe and love God if they will. The moral power is a disposition or habit in the soul to execute belief and repentance and a freedom from contrary habits; this only those who have received effectual grace possess. "Morally to be unable to believe, is no more

---

[1] II 296, UI : ChW (1655).
[2] I 84–86, CD : CEth (1673).
[3] II 808, MS-I (1661).
[4] *Idem.*
[5] II 927, RMeth (1653).
[6] II 316, UI : US (1655).
[7] II 260–261, UI : SpW (1655).
[8] I 271–272, CD : CEth (1673).
[9] III 794, DL : KG (1663).
[10] IV 486, VR (1660).
[11] II 891, RMeth (1653).
[12] IV 821, MS-I (1661).
[13] IV 1046, RM (1676).
[14] IV 868, SJ (1654); II 496, TCon (1657); 978, GGV (1671).

than to be unwilling to believe."[1] Hence, you see that only natural impotency excuses faults. He that wants to believe but cannot is excusable. None who hear the gospel can so plead. Moral impotency aggravates guilt; the more will involved, the more sin. All government and justice in the world, all rewards and punishments, all moral virtue and vice, are grounded upon this principle which rests in the will. Here all culpability lies. Hence, if a man offends willingly, he is guilty, for nature has taught all the world to bring the fault to the will.[2]

It is not difficult to recognize unconverted men. They can judge themselves. They have not felt the evil of sin, nor come to Christ for pardon, set their hearts on heaven, used the God-appointed means, or done the duties of holiness to God and mercy to man.[3] They refuse God's grace and greatest mercies, as a sick stomach refuses food and medicine.[4] There are only two kinds of men in the world: slaves of sin and servants of Christ. To be the former is to be in a miserable state; it is to be under the dominion of Satan. While men are unconverted, nothing they can do will please God.[5] They live in continual danger of damnation. They are not certain to be out of hell an hour.

> As sure as the word of God is true, every soul that goeth unconverted out of the body, is shut out of all hope of mercy for ever, and entereth into a remediless misery.[6]

As long, then, as a man remains unconverted, he has no ground for one hour's true peace and comfort. He has no sin pardoned. One sin unpardoned is enough to condemn a man forever, as one stab at the heart will kill him.[7]

God has made it clear that every one must be converted or condemned. Reasons are abundant: God says so in his word, God's judgment is righteous and men are sinners, God's holy nature does not permit the unholy soul in his presence, God has offered salvation in this life for the taking and it has been refused. Salvation without conversion is a flat contradiction, an impossibility.[8] On this all Christians—papists, Baptists, and every sect—are agreed: you must turn to God or die.[9]

Conversion basically means the same in Scripture as repentance, regeneration, sanctification, and vocation. "Vocation" refers to God's calling of men to faith, sometimes accepted, sometimes rejected. When accepted in its deepest meaning, it is called special effectual calling. Here it is the same as conversion, though more limited to the first effect on the soul. With this meaning "repentance" also agrees, though it stresses more the *terminus a quo*. Repentance points primarily back to the God from whom man has fallen, while vocation relates more to our coming to Christ as mediator. "Regeneration" and "sanctification" are both somewhat more comprehensive than conversion, repentance, or vocation. Regeneration refers to our whole new reborn state and sanctification to our whole state of devotedness to God.[10]

---

[1] II 497, TCon (1657).
[2] II 35 ff., RCR : NR (1666).
[3] II 445, TCon (1657).
[4] II 43, RCR : NR (1666).
[5] *Ibid.*, 451.
[6] *Ibid.*, 453.
[7] *Ibid.*, 450.
[8] *Ibid.*, 439, 440.
[9] II 509-515, CU (1657).
[10] II 402-403, TCon (1657).

Viewed thus, conversion is not a small matter or a simple work. It is "to break the heart for sin, and make him fly for refuge unto Christ, and thankfully embrace him as the life of his soul."[1] This is to change the bent of man's soul and life.

There are three parts to conversion. The first is the change of the mind. Natural man wastes his reason on wilfulness. Men refuse the converting grace and the infallible truth of all the Word of God. Their prayers are cold, their conference carnal, their lives careless and sinful. But the Spirit illuminates their understanding to make them turn from careless indifference to sober reflection on the truth. Ignorance is put away. Sin becomes unpleasant, the world becomes undesirable, and salvation becomes urgent. The Spirit opens the eyes to the mysteries of grace, causing the mind to know the ugliness of sin and the loveliness of God.[2]

The second part of conversion is the change of the heart or will, for which the change of mind is preparatory. The will receives a new inclination. It chooses right ends, receives Christ as he is offered in the Gospel, resolves to commit everything to the Lord and changes affections from transitory to spiritual objects. This change is not the outward civilizing of life or the restraint of a wicked work or two. The crucial question is "which way are you travelling?"[3] Sometimes this choice comes by the hearing of a sermon, but ordinarily "men stick long under conviction and half purposes, before they are thus converted."[4] By this change the old man of corrupt disposition and life becomes a new man renewed in knowledge and quality of soul, reflecting his Creator's image. Converting grace teaches how little we deserve God's mercy, how to esteem others better than ourselves, and how to become servants of all.[5]

The last part of conversion is the change that takes place in men's lives. The same God who rules and cleanses the heart must rule the life and cleanse the hands. The initial step in the spiritual life is the acceptance of the baptismal covenant, or, what is equally important, the owning of this covenant at maturity. Dedication to this covenant does not come from a sudden fear, or flash of conviction under a moving sermon, or despondency during sickness and trial; it does come resolvedly and habitually from a rooted conviction and constancy of the heart. The heart rejects sin, Satan, and the flesh as deadly enemies, and accepts a world of work, witness, and compassion for those in need.[6]

But these changes of the mind, heart, and life are what the natural man does not desire. "No rational will desireth or chooseth evil," except as a means to the good.[7] Therefore, he must prefer to think of himself as already converted,

---

[1] II 513, CU (1657); note the similarity to the whole structure of the Heidelberg Catechism here, as outlined in Question and Answer 2:
   Q. How many things are necessary for you to know, that you in this comfort may live and die happily?
   A. Three; the first, how great my sins and misery are; the second, how I am delivered from all my sins and misery; the third, how I am to be thankful to God for such deliverance.

[2] II 404–406, TCon (1657).
[3] *Ibid.*, 410.
[4] *Ibid.*, 417.
[5] *Ibid.*, 424–427.
[6] *Ibid.*, 428–433.
[7] II 7, RCR : NR (1666).

since it is unthinkable that he wants to be damned. He mistakes the true nature of conversion. He will not seek to be converted without a knowledge of his misery and how it may be resolved.[1]

That there is no salvation without conversion is abundantly and clearly indicated by the express words of Scripture. Moreover, it is the specific office of Jesus Christ to bring the ungodly back to God.

> And shall we think that Christ came on a needless errand? Believe it, sirs, as his suffering was necessary for our ransom, so was his doctrine and Spirit as necessary for our conversion, and we can no more be saved without the one than without the other. Think with yourselves whether it be a likely thing, that God should send his Son on earth by a miracle, surpassing all miracles, and this on purpose to call home straying sinful souls, if they might be saved without conversion? If it had been possible for men to be happy without holiness, and to escape misery without escaping sin, what need Christ have come to sanctify them?[2]

It was not the Lord's mind to bring men to glory without a change, nor to impute righteousness to the unconverted, nor to pretend to God that a man was just when he was not. Of this you may be sure: Christ would never have done so much to convert men, if they could have been saved without it. You may be filled with terror in the consideration of Christ, but you may be certain he will give you no hope of salvation apart from conversion.[3]

Yet the ungodly will not believe. What nonsensical reasons they put forth: if only the converted and sanctified go to heaven, it will be empty; if I go to hell, I will have much company; all men are sinners, even the converted; those who profess religion are no better than others. I am no whoremonger or drunkard, why talk to me about conversion? I do not mean harm to any one, then why should God condemn me? You make men mad by pressing them to impossible things. God is not so much concerned about what men do. The world is better off without so much ado about religion. There are so many sects, one cannot know which to choose, therefore, it is better not to be changed. Godly men are as poor, and have as much trouble as others. I am resolved to hope well, trust in God, and do as well as I can without going to very much trouble. Such empty excuses as these are shameful.

Why are men so unreasonable in matters of religion? His enemies are many: habitual inclination of nature against God, ignorance of and blindness to spiritual truths, confident wilfulness in self-salvation, slavery to lust and passion, evil company, and a deluding devil. These keep thousands unconverted, when God and Christ have done so much. The reasonableness of God's commands stands in judgment over the unreasonableness of men's disobedience.[4]

Man's wilful sin has cut him from fellowship with God and destroyed the harmony of the world. The universal human disease is ignorance of the truth and obstinate resistance to mercy. The only cure is a full conversion demanding

---

[1] II 445–448, TCon (1657).
[2] *Ibid.*, 435.
[3] *Idem.*
[4] II 524–530, CU (1657).

sorrow for sin, faith in Christ, and a thankful life of service. Mind, heart, and life must be changed. This, man under sin refuses to do. He stands under judgment.

b. God's Redeeming Act

God, not willing that man should remain in misery, sent His Son to take our nature, to become our Mediator, to die for our sins on the cross, and thus to redeem us from the curse upon sin and the power of the devil. No longer does the law, exacting perfect obedience, condemn, but a new law of grace brings pardon to repentant and believing souls. The Holy Spirit illuminates and converts the souls of the elect and enables them to proclaim the word of reconciliation. Nothing but a full-orbed Trinitarian redemption satisfies. The chain of salvation [1] binds divine acts and human means together in repairing the image of God upon the soul.

> The Father sendeth the Son; the Son redeemeth us, and maketh the promise of grace; the Holy Ghost inditeth and sealeth this gospel; the apostles are the secretaries of the Spirit, to write it; the preachers of the gospel to proclaim it, and persuade men to obey it; and the Holy Ghost doth make their preaching effectual, by opening the hearts of men to entertain it.[2]

The primary message of the gospel is one of good news and hope. No sinner dares go home and say: Despair is the preacher's message. God was not required to provide a Saviour. But he has done so. No door of mercy is shut against men; they shut it themselves. Has any minister ever said that if you turn, God will have no mercy? No, we proclaim the opposite. Life and not death, salvation and not damnation, pardon and not judgment, is the first, great, and primary doctrine that is to be proclaimed. There is indeed a message of wrath and death. But this is not the principal message. We tell you that you are under wrath, that you will be under remediless death should you refuse mercy.

> There is mercy in God, there is sufficiency in the satisfaction of Christ, the promise is free, full, and universal: you may have life if you will but turn.[3]

Only when mercy is rejected, the consequence of wrath and death must be shown. Believe the gospel, and there is no need to frighten or trouble you with the word "damnation." A hundred texts commission us to make the offer of life, to call you to believe, to extend the promise conditionally to all. The mercy of the Lord is ready to receive you. Conversion is not the mending of one's way and repairing the old house of one's life, but the changing of masters. God will be a father only to his children.

Both God and man are agents in the work of conversion. The Holy Spirit is the principal cause by which he changes men's minds and hearts from the

---

[1] Although Baxter does not use the phrase "chain of salvation," the order of redemptive acts set forth in this passage follows that of Perkins and Sibbes, *supra*.

[2] *Ibid.*, 512; cf. p. 502, the introductory sentence.

[3] *Ibid.*, 516.

creature to God in Christ. The instrumental cause is the doctrine of Christ, either read, heard, or known in some other way. Man is both the subject of the Spirit's operation and the agent of the holy duties of believing, repenting, and turning to Christ which the Holy Spirit causes him to do.[1] The *Call to the Unconverted* ends with the prayer that God will awaken men before their own sins destroy them: "...bring them to themselves, and to thy Son, before their sins have brought them to perdition." [2]

Some object to the doctrine that redemption is effective only for the elect and that the Holy Spirit must open men's hearts before they can believe. They reason thus:

> ...if God hath chosen us we shall be saved, and if he hath not, we shall not, whatsoever we do: no diligence will save a man that is not elected, and "it is not in him that willeth, nor in him that runneth, but in God that showeth mercy." Those that God will save, shall be saved, whatsoever they be; and those that he will damn, shall be damned; and no man can have grace except God give it him; for we can do nothing of ourselves....[3]

But in the Scripture to which the objector refers, the apostle does not intend to say that man's will has nothing to do with salvation. Rather, he is talking about the giving of the gospel to those in darkness and the denying of it to those who have forfeited it by their neglect. The cause of man's damnation is not God's will to condemn, but man's own sin. Grace is denied to no one who has not first deserved that denial. The reason for man's salvation is not only given in Scripture as caused by God's will, but from the faith and obedience of men. Both rewarding justice and paternal love and mercy are involved in its bestowal. The reason for God's gift of the first special grace to repent and believe is purely mercy. No man can give a convincing reason why this grace is given to Peter and not to Judas, yet we know that the denial to Judas is deserved and the grace to Peter is undeserved.

Some object further: the Scripture says, "whom he will, he hardeneth." To this Baxter answers that God hardens no man undeservedly; only when his softening grace is resisted and abused. Hardening is letting the sinner go his own way, removing the rejected Spirit, carrying providence on its just course. Thus he knows corrupt natures will be hardened, but he does not inject hardness into any heart.[4]

The conversion of man is the heart of the age-old question: how are divine sovereignty and human responsibility to be reconciled. As related to his creatures God is the "efficient cause" (OF HIM), the "dirigent cause" (THROUGH HIM), and the "final cause" (TO HIM, are all things: to whom be glory forever, Amen)–Romans x.36.[5] He is to be known in his goodness [6] and majesty [7], by his graciousness [8] and "benefices."[9] As Creator, God is our Owner and Lord; as

---

[1] II 403, TCon (1657).
[2] II 539, CU (1657).
[3] II 496, TCon (1657).
[4] *Ibid.*, 497–498.
[5] I 73, CD : CEth (1673). Reference should be Romans xi.
[6] *Ibid.*, 287.
[7] II 390, UI : AR (1655).
[8] II 891, RMeth (1653).
[9] III 800, DL : KG (1663).

Redeemer, our Ruler and King; as Regenerator and Sanctifier, our Benefactor and Father.[1]

The sovereignty [2] consequent from the Creator-creature and Redeemer—to-be-redeemed relationship, reaches purposively into history with a remedying covenant of grace for all mankind. According to this covenant, men are bound to believe, if the remedy is to be effective. "All the nations are under divine obligations...."[3] But somewhere between that divine reaching and the human obliging lies a mystery, hidden (because incomprehensible) from human eyes but open to God. There are other mysteries in the Christian faith: the Trinity, the incarnation, miracles, the resurrection, immortal life, and the like.[4] Yet here divine initiative indicates divine willingness; divine sacrifice secures the gracious covenant; and the divine gift of repentance accepts the divine invitation.[5]

Scripture teaches that election is God's eternal, antecedent act.[6] However, God's eternal acts or decrees are one in God and not subject to time as for us. This places the whole matter beyond the possibility of our understanding. We can receive it only in humanized language as we are warranted to do in Christ.

> The decree is AEternal and had no beginning...for the [decrees] there is little likelyhood they should be future, before God willed their futurity: whether they were possible before he willed their possibility; or whether he knew & willed them as possible, before he know & willed them as future, let them dispute that dare: If all these acts be one in God then there is no prius or posterius. And if there be no time in AEternity, nor it be Divisible, then p[r]e & post have there no signification, or rather contradict AEternity. And though there is no such thing in mente divina as p[r]eteritum vel futurum; & preordinatio is but ordinatio, & predestinatio but destinatio; & all this but simplex Volle....If any will speake of God after the manner of men, & confesse a necessity of so doing, & thinke it convenient to lay by mostly those metaphysicall notions, into which we have shaped the Divine p[er]fections, by Reason; & consequently not to raise or cherish fierce & dividing disputes about them, as being things quite beyond our understanding; & say that we have no one word that ends was made to exp[r]esse Gods Nature in strict p[ro]priety, & though we must speake of him in borrowed phrase....I will seek to conceive of God as he is in God-man (Christ) come downe a little nearer my conceiving.[7]

Scripture never mentions God's pardoning or glorifying any man without his fulfillment of certain spiritual conditions.[8] As God's act and not man's, election is not required of man.[9] Those who make God the physical efficient predeter-

---

[1] I 73, CD : CEth (1673).
[2] "God's absolute dominion and sovereignty over us is the very foundation of all religion." IV 792, TChr (1654).
[3] II 222–223, MR (1671).
[4] II 135, RCR : Chr (1666).
[5] I 931, RL (1661).
[6] For an involved discussion of election as it relates to the necessity of Christ's death see II 237–240, UI (1655); cf. also III 10, 11, SER (1649).
[7] Treatises, VI, Item No. 197 (=6/15), ff. 52–93.
[8] I 652, CD : CEccl (1673).
[9] *Idem*; II 237, UI (1655).

miner of every creaturely act make him as much the author of sin as of grace. They undervalue mercy as fully as do the Pelagians who make Peter no more indebted to grace than Judas.[1]

We cannot reason our way logically or temporally from God's decrees to human sin. God's decrees cause neither man's sin nor his damnation. Reprobation as an immanent act puts nothing into a person, nor does it necessitate sin and misery.[2] It did not for Adam, nor does it for us. God may decree the effect, which sinners accomplish (as in the death of Christ), and he may overrule men in their sin for good, but he cannot will or decree or cause sin itself. Nor does he decree to permit sin. To permit is merely not to hinder, which is no act; to will or to decree is a positive act.[3]

The problem of election and free will is shrouded with mystery. This is no wonder, for a Person in the Godhead is not like the persons of men which are so many substances divided from one another, nor does God talk and act like a man.[4] God's way of doing is not the same as ours; we cannot limit him to our logical categories. We do better to "keep off with reverence from concealed mysteries."[5] All our knowledge of God is but enigmatical, and as in a glass. All words we use of God are borrowed from his image on creatures. They do not signify formally the same thing in God as in us. "If you think otherwise, you will make an idol in your conception, instead of God...."[6] We must, therefore, abhor presumptuous curiosities in pretending to know the secret things of God.[7] It is sinful folly to desire to know things unrevealed and impossible to be known.[8] Above all, "we must not upon such uncertainties deny certainties, nor from some unreasonable scruples about the manner of God's working grace, deny the blessed nature of God...."[9]

In his *Call to the Unconverted*, Baxter makes plain that God in his blessedness desires the salvation of the wicked. But in order to understand this doctrine, it is necessary to make a distinction clear. The first act of the will is a simple apprehension of the understanding, that is what one naturally wills before a choosing act whereby the will compares and determines the practical act. So a ruler makes laws to be obeyed and only secondarily determines rewards or punishments as necessary consequents.[10]

Man knows God in the glass of the Word and creation. We ascribe to him understanding and will after the nature of man. So, according to the Scriptures, we distinguish between the acts of God's will and the objects of his will, though in God both are one. We dare to do this because Christ has assumed our human nature. The simple love or will of God is directed to all that is naturally or morally good, since he himself is good. In this will God desires the conversion

---

[1] I 145–146, CD : CEth (1673); cf. III 808, DL : KG (1663).
[2] II 978, GGV (1671).
[3] *Ibid.*, 979.
[4] IV 59, 36, MC (1701).
[5] I 270, CD : CEth (1673).
[6] III 627f., LF (1669).
[7] *Idem.*
[8] IV 558, TKL (1689); cf. also I 271 ff., CD : CEth (1673); II 152, RCR : Chr (1666); 385, UI : AR (1655); 689–690, SB (1662); III 3,50, SER (1649); 682, LF (1669).
[9] II 891, RMeth (1653).
[10] II 517, CU (1657); 44, RCR : NR (1666).

and salvation of all. This he, as lawgiver and ruler, sets forth in a practical will for salvation through the free grace of Christ and life which he entrusts to his messengers. They are to offer and persuade men to accept that grace. Yet, as lawgiver he resolves that those who do not turn will die. When the day of grace is past, he will as judge execute that decree. The judge does not delight in the death of a murderer, yet he must for the sake of justice fulfill the law.

> But so far God is against your damnation, as that he will teach you and warn you, and set before you life and death, and offer you your choice, and command his ministers to entreat you not to damn yourselves, but accept his mercy, and so to leave you without excuse....[1]

God as judge delights in justice, but not in the misery which the unrepentant bring upon themselves. The proofs for this are plain: the gracious nature of God; the many commands to turn and live, and the tenor of the gospel; the commission given to ministers to offer mercy and to teach the way of life, to entreat and to do all possible for the conversion of men; the course of providence whereby life is upheld and thereby a time of grace is given and rich blessings dispensed; the incarnation, suffering, and atonement.[2]

To say that Christ died only for the elect and, therefore, God's good will to the wicked is voided, cannot stand.

> For it was thy sin, and the sin of all the world, that lay upon our Redeemer; and his sacrifice and satisfaction is sufficient for all, and the fruits of it are offered to one as well as another; but it is true that it was never the intent of his mind, to pardon and save any that would not by faith and repentance be converted.[3]

Remember how Christ wept over impenitent Jerusalem, how he prayed for his persecutors from the cross. Do you think then that he delights in the death even of those who live and die in wicked unbelief? Not at all, for in Ezekiel 33:11 the Lord has confirmed by an oath that he has no pleasure in the death of the wicked, but rather that he turn and live.

The oath of God settles the issue. God desires the conversion of all. Only our ignorance cannot reconcile this truth with predestination and actual damnation of the wicked. What is confirmed by God's oath cannot be distorted or denied; rather, doubtful points must be reduced to that which is divinely-sworn truth. Who is it that does take pleasure in the sin of unbelievers? Neither God nor the godly do, but the devil, the wicked, and the flesh. "So earnest is God for the conversion of sinners, that he doubleth his commands and exhortations with vehemency; 'Turn ye, turn ye, why will ye die?'" [4] Here is the most joyful message ever preached to man. Judgment is not yet here. Mercy is offered. Turn, and it shall be yours.

First, see what preparations mercy has made for your salvation. God is ready for your salvation. Instead of a flaming sword, a curse, and offended justice,

---

[1] II 518, CU (1657).
[2] Ibid., 518–519; cf. 72, RCR : NR (1666)
[3] II 519, CU (1657).
[4] Ibid., 521.

God stands with open mercy and an offered pardon. The ministers of God, all that fear God, and even heaven itself, – all are ready for salvation, and will you, O sinner, refuse it?

Second, consider how encouraging and numerous, how earnest and dreadful, how loud and joyful, are the calls to turn and live. God himself is the principal inviter. His many instruments cry that you may hear his call and turn: the holy Scriptures, the ministers of Christ, the Spirit, the conscience, the godly by persuasions and example, the whole world and all creatures, the patient forbearance of God, all the mercies he gives, reason and the frame of human nature, and all the promises made to God in the baptismal covenant and in the sacraments.

Third, consider in what relationship you stand before God. He is your maker; you are a servant under judgment. You stand at the brink of hell.

> Sirs, you are not shut up in the darkness of heathenism, nor in the desperation of the damned. Life is before you, and you may have it on reasonable terms if you will; yea, on free-cost if you will accept it. The way of God lieth plain before you, the church is open to you, and you may have Christ, pardon, and holiness, if you will. What say you? Will you or will you not?[1]

"The Lord condescends to reason the case with unconverted sinners, and to ask them why they will die."[2] One thing is certain: no one desires misery. "...no man can be willing of any evil, as evil, but only as it hath some appearance of some good."[3] Yet God here teaches that the wicked die and are damned because they will to be so. This is so because they choose the way of love for the world that leads to hell; they reject the God-appointed means for salvation; and they do not desire the heaven of perfect love and holiness. They have no heart for such a heaven.

What is astounding is that the great God stoops to reason with man. "Why wilt thou die?" (Ezek. 33:11) Man is endowed with reason and must be dealt with accordingly. He must be persuaded and overcome by reason. God does not require what is unreasonable; all the right reason in the world is on his side. No good reason will dare to reason against the God of truth and reason. No good reason is imaginable to damn one's own soul, to cross one's ultimate end, to venture into sin, to deny one's creator.[4]

Divine election and human responsibility are somehow bridged by the Holy Spirit. He is "Christ's great Witness and Agent in the world."[5] Not by outward force or compulsion, but by his drawing power, he renews and purifies the souls of the elect.[6] Without the Spirit's regenerative work there is no salvation.[7] Till he comes, man is dead, blind, indifferent.[8] When he comes, man is illuminated, converted, quickened.[9]

---

[1] Ibid., 524.
[2] Idem.
[3] Idem.
[4] Ibid., 524–530.
[5] II 83, RCR : Chr (1666).
[6] I 65, 69 ff., CD:CEth (1673).
[7] III 62–63, SER (1649).
[8] Ibid., 71.
[9] IV 94, CF (1682).

In *The Mother's Catechism* the question is asked: "What is that Holy Ghost that Christ promised to send down?" And the answer is:

> He is the Spirit of God the Father and the Son, sent to... fit men to further their own and other men's salvations, and propagate the grace and kingdom of Christ in the world.[1]

Here not only the Spirit's saving, but also its qualifying power is the key to ongoing conversion in history. In conversion, man's reason, conscience, and will are moved only by the Spirit of God.[2] On occasion the Spirit works in extraordinary ways and in special providences; for the most, however, he follows the course of ordinary means.[3] The objective fact of his working is seen in the person of Christ, miracles, prophecy, and the redeemed life.[4] For the ordinary man the redeemed life itself confirms the Spirit's activity through regeneration,[5] in the removal of sin,[6] and the profession of Christ's name.[7] Those who oppose God, the evident light and law of nature, the Holy Scripture, holiness and purity of life, and good order, have no claim to the Spirit of God. Contrariwise, those whose soul is renewed to God's image, those who seek wisdom, holiness, love, and those whose lives are changed by the Spirit's power, know his presence.[8]

God's sovereign, active will and man's free, responsible will are mysteriously joined by the empowering Spirit. What remains "utterly uncertain" to us is how God works on man's will "inwardly" by his Spirit.[9] This problem is pinpointed by two passages in Baxter. The first analogically demonstrates that both the Spirit's activity and man's are essential to conversion.

> There is an admirable, unsearchable concurrence of the Spirit, and his appointed means, and the will of man, in the procreation of the new creature, and in all the exercises of grace, as there is of male and female in natural generation; and of the earth, the sun, the rain, the industry of the gardener, and the seminal virtue of life and specification, in the production of plants with their flowers and fruits. And as wise as it would be to say, it is not the male but the female, or not the female but the male that generateth; or to say, it is not the earth but the sun, or not the sun but the rain, or not the rain but the seminal virtue, that causeth plants with flowers and fruits: so wise is it to say, it is not the Spirit but the word and means, or it is not the word and means but the Spirit, or it is not the reason, and will, and industry of man, but the Spirit: or, if we have not wisdom enough to assign to each cause its proper interest in the effect, that therefore we should separate what God hath conjoined, or deny the truth of the causation, because we comprehend not the manner and influence – this is but to choose to be befooled by pride, rather than confess that God is wiser than we.[10]

---

[1] IV 63, MC (1701).
[2] II 297, UI : ChW (1655).
[3] II 266, UI : SpW (1655).
[4] II 98–110, RCR : Chr (1666).
[5] *Idem.*
[6] III 71, SER (1649).
[7] II 126, RCR : Chr (1666).
[8] II 298–300, UI : ChW (1655).
[9] II 891–892, RMeth (1653).
[10] I 70, CD : Ceth (1673).

The second passage comprises the entirety of a letter to one of his many critics, briefly presenting the heart of the problem.

> The dispute about free-will is one of the hardest in the world, and hath tired doctors these 1200 years; and therefore cannot be made easy to you, much less in a few words: but thus much is easy and sure:
> 1st. That all good is of God, and all our willingness to good is of his grace.
> 2ndly. The deliverance of the will from its ill disposition, and disposing it to good, is of absolute necessity to salvation; and this holy freedom no man hath further than he hath grace.
> 3rdly. The will hath a self-determining power, which is its natural freedom in all its actions.
> 4thly. Common grace enableth men to do more good and less hurt than they do; and it is for not using this power that they suffer.
> 5thly. If these short words satisfy you not, be satisfied with shorter; that all sin, and consequently punishment is of ourselves; and all grace and deliverance is from God. Obey his Spirit, and you shall shortly understand his counsel.[1]

We have seen that man is made in the image of God. Through Adam's sin and our own that image is not only defective but turned against God. Through Christ's redemption some grace is given to every man. How God's electing grace relates to the will of man, we cannot understand. The nature of the Creator precludes such understanding by the creature. What we do know is what counts: all evil is ours; all grace is God's. He tells us to believe and to obey. We must.

## 2. The Right Use of Nature

One doctrine that Baxter develops is the relation between common and special grace. Is there a qualitative difference? To what extent does natural man receive grace? Does Christ's death profit him in any way? Is it not possible through common grace to be saved? These questions have far-reaching significance for the present and future state of the heathen.

Man in his natural, perhaps one should say unnatural, fallen state retained natural good but lost moral good.[2] There is no natural being which is not good.[3] Man remains man apart from grace,[4] retaining his natural powers of the understanding and the will. However, now man's understanding suffers through ignorance and an indisposition to know the truth, and man's will is impotent apart from grace to choose the good.[5] A corrupt inclination fastens man to his present state and sets him against recovering grace. The natural

---

[1] IV 1045, "Mr. Baxter's Letter to Mr. Bromley, 1680, Containing His Judgment about Free-Will, in as few words as possible, for the satisfaction of some persons, who misunderstood some of his books."

[2] I 272, CD : CEth (1673).
[3] I 566, CD : CEccl (1673); 272, CD : CEth (1673); III 372, TS–D (1659).
[4] I 272, CD : CEth (1673).
[5] II 621, DP (1658); I 84–85, CD : CEth (1673); II 623, DP (1658).

state has become the corrupted state. "For every man that is in this state of corrupted nature, is a wicked man, and in a state of death."[1]

A natural principle of self-love certainly keeps men from wanting to be damned.[2] Nearly all men desire salvation. Not one in a thousand expects not to be saved.[3] Though non-Christian philosophers discover parcels of truth, naturally or supernaturally received,[4] no man's works please God without Christ.[5] Philosophers may understand something of heaven[6] and see a creator's hand in the world and providence,[7] yet enmity remains in every unrenewed heart until God removes it.[8]

All rational souls, though especially Christians as to holiness, are God's image.[9] This image consists in three parts: the natural substantial, the qualitative moral, and the relative honorary. The natural substantial part consists in a reason capable of knowing God, a will capable of adhering to him, and an executive power capable of serving him. This no man loses, or he would cease to be man. The moral qualitative part (holiness) consists in the wisdom of the mind (knowledge of God), the rectitude of the will (love of God), and obedience of the executive power (service of God). This part is what the Spirit restores. The relative honorary part concerns God's great relations to us as absolute owner, supreme judge, and bountiful benefactor (Father) and end, and the way we reflect these relations to subordinate creation. This part of God's image in man is only partially lost.[10]

Reason is the light of nature which sees the foundational truths of religion.[11] To "deny reason is to deny humanity."[12] Bedlam[13] is the alternative to reasonable man.[14] He who despises reason must turn into a brute.[15] Yet reason is but the eye to the law and not the law itself. Barbarous Indians and learned Romans had reason, but how far reason alone led them astray![16]

Still one can begin at no other point when dealing with those who are without the spirit. So Christ and the apostles dealt with men as rational men. Faith itself is the rational act of a rational creature. "To tell them that the Spirit testifieth it, is no means to convince them that have not the Spirit."[17] This is not to say that the book of nature is sufficient to convince men. The Spirit is absolutely essential.[18] Yet God asks no one to believe without reason; believing

---

[1] II 511, CU (1657).
[2] II 895, RMeth (1653); 834–835, MS–I (1661).
[3] III 181, SER (1649).
[4] II 1027, CSCC (1669).
[5] III 683, LF (1669).
[6] III 332, SER (1649); 984, DT (1683).
[7] III 322, SER (1649).
[8] III 797, DL : KG (1663).
[9] IV 149, CF (1682); II 35, RCR : NR (1666).
[10] RB, II 297 (1665), from a letter to John Eliot of New England, dated Nov. 30, 1663; cf. also I 156, CD : CEth (1673); II 32, RCR : NR (1666).
[11] I 247, 256, CD : CEth (1673); II 1024, CSCC (1669).
[12] I 303, CD : CEth (1673).
[13] "Bedlam" was a colloquialism for the Hospital of St. Mary of Bethlehem, a London insane asylum. It was possible to purchase a ticket to see the patients exhibited, as in a zoo.
[14] IV 736, TC (1659).
[15] II 594, DP (1658); III 88, SER (1649).
[16] III 73–74, SER (1649).
[17] *Ibid.*, 88; 84–88.
[18] *Ibid.*, 62–63.

is not an irrational or non-rational act.[1] "...the world is as God's statute book...." it belongs to the "law of nature," which "natural aptitude maketh us fit to read and practise...." [2]

Basic to the operation of the grace required for right use of reason is the redemption of Jesus Christ. His death has a two-fold dimension to all mankind and to the elect. His righteousness secured pardon conditionally for all men but is actually imputed only to true believers.[3] Christ's death is a sacrifice for all the sin of man, original and actual,

> ...not, for any man's final, predominant impenitence, infidelity, atheism, or unholiness; but for all sorts of sin, on condition of faith and repentance, actually pardoning them to penitent believers.[4]

It is thus necessary to distinguish between universal (common, general) grace and special grace. Redemption by Christ was universal, though the remedy was not. Christ's death was for all men in that he procured grace, though not equal grace, for all. We should distinguish between Christ's procurement of salvation and man's taking Christ as the object of his faith. Christ's act was sufficient for all men and conditionally applied to all men without exception.[5] All mankind is brought by Christ under a continuing covenant of grace which is repealed only by man's abuse of the grace of the covenant.

> For as a covenant of entire nature, or innocency, was made with all mankind in innocent Adam, so a covenant of grace was made with all mankind in lapsed Adam, (Gen. iii.15) in the promised seed, and renewed again with all mankind in Noah. No man can prove either a limitation of this covenant to some, (till the rest, by violating it, became the serpent's seed, at least) nor yet that ever God did abrogate it, as it was made to all the world.[6]

No man on earth is excluded from this covenant. The only reason that all are not justified and saved is that they will not accept the mercy freely offered to them.[7] Through this covenant salvation is offered to all, with personal consent the only condition to title. None are to be shut out except they who shut out themselves.[8] It is not that God cannot save, only that men will not accept his way.[9]

---

[1] II 897, RMeth (1653).
[2] II 31, RCR : NR (1666).
[3] III 676, LF (1669); II 892, RMeth (1653); III 683, LF (1669).
[4] IV 1042, RT (1667); Baxter held that it was an error to believe that Christ's death was caused only by the sins of the elect. III 672, LF (1669).
[5] Baxter adds in II 965, RMeth (1653): "I put it in terms beyond dispute, because I would not build up believer's comforts on points which godly divines do contradict (as little as may be). Yet I am past all doubt myself, that Christ did actually make satisfaction to God's justice for ALL, and that no man perisheth for want of an expiatory sacrifice, but for want of faith to believe and apply it, or for want of repentance and yielding to recovering grace."
[6] II 222, MR (1671); cf. also *Ibid.*, 221-234.
[7] II 892, RMeth (1653).
[8] IV 486, VR (1660).
[9] IV 826, TD (1659).

> God commandeth us all to believe (wicked and godly), that our sins are made pardonable by the sufficient satisfaction of Christ for them; and that God is very merciful and ready to forgive; and that he hath conditionally forgiven us all in the new covenant, making a deed of gift of Christ, and pardon, and life in him to all, on condition they believe in him, and accept what is given.[1]

A great degree of pardon is given to the world before conversion, which yet justifies and saves only believers.[2] Christ shows mercy before the sinner knows about it.[3] The common effects of Christ's redemption are manifold: the execution of the law of works is hindered; forfeited mercies are given; human nature is brought nigh to God in the incarnation; the world, the devil, death, and the grave are conquered in preparation to our conquest; a universal deed of life to all the world is made with a conditional pardon preparatory to faith; ministers, churches, and providential mercies are helps; some inward motions and assistance of the Holy Ghost is at work.[4] Of these, the

> ...great and notable common benefit, is the conditional covenant of grace; or the conditional pardon of sin, and gift of eternal life to all without exception, John iii. 16; Mark xvi.15, 16; Rom. x.9; Matt. vi.14, 15; xxii.7-9.[5]

How blasphemous to deny God's common love to fallen man and his universal pardoning covenant! How clearly is God's antecedent love shown in Christ to lost mankind in his giving a free pardon of all sin, offering life eternal, entreating men to accept, and excluding none but final refusers![6] The foundation, thus, of all our faith is the gracious nature of God, the sufficiency of Christ's sacrifice and merit, and the universal offer of life to all on condition of acceptance.[7]

Since God's universal grace is due to love of man as man,[8] revealed in the redemption of Christ, it will not do to undervalue general grace.[9] There is admirable concord between natural truths and the gospel of Christ. Love of Christ is but the means to right love of our Creator.[10] The image of the Creator is upon his world.[11] Nature and providence are God's books to teach, but they are insufficient.[12] Grace is medicinal to nature. Where natural light ends, supernatural begins. "To renounce the Christian religion is to renounce reason." [13] Reason, free-will, and self-love are not destroyed but repaired, freed, and improved by faith. Insofar as natural truths are taken up in men's religion, some good is present. Yet only the Christian religion has true reason for it; truth and goodness are God's instruments to begin conversion.[14] God's will is partly

---

[1] II 917, RMeth (1653).
[2] III 676, LF (1669).
[3] II 145, RCR : Chr (1666).
[4] II 617–617, DP (1658); cf. 71, RCR : NR (1666).
[5] III 633, LF (1669).
[6] III 68, SER (1649).
[7] III 729, LF (1669); Baxter hesitated to publish his *Universality of Redemption* to avoid giving offence, although he appealed to numerous divines who believed as he did. RB, I 123 (1664), II 206 (1665).
[8] I 164, CD : CEth (1673).
[9] *Ibid.*, 145.
[10] II 92, RCR : Chr (1666).
[11] II 304, UI : ChW (1655).
[12] II 537, CU (1657).
[13] II 271, UI : SpW (1655).
[14] *Ibid.*, 262.

revealed in nature, but wholly in Scripture.[1] Both the full and glorious truths proclaimed in Christianity and the effectual working of the Spirit are advantages over the small part of truth and the contrary affections of Mohammedans, pagans, and heathen.

That is to say, general grace is but a beginning point. Natural knowledge can be an advantage. Education and civilization can be utilized as preparatory grace.[2] Not that being civilized can be equated with being Christian![3] Due to common grace all men are in a gray condition: neither devils nor saints. Natural advantages are in themselves insufficient.[4] However, there are more preparatory helps in Christian than in non-Christian lands, such as teaching, reason, and sobriety.[5] Education moderates natural temper and customs.[6] Before learning of heaven, one must learn what it is to be a man.[7] Universal grace precedes special grace.[8] The former proceeds by degree into the latter, though there is an indiscernable point at which a moral, qualitative difference enters. So great is the likeness between the highest degree of general grace and the lowest degree of special grace that men often cannot discern between them.[9] The law of grace has a pre-supposed part: the law of nature[10] which gives introductory light and prepares for the supernatural part of the law of grace.[11] Christ came to help knowledge, for faith itself is a mode of knowing.[12]

> ...It being God's way to bring men from the *lower roome* of *Naturall wisdom*, to the *higher roome* of *Speciall Grace*, by many *Staires* or *degrees*, I think it most p[ro]bable if all that p[er]ish do breake off & turne backe before they came to [so] *high a degree* as to receive *Grace Sufficient* to the *very Justifying act of ffaith*....[13]

Not every unprepared mind is capable of the truth. A capacity and due preparation of the recipient is required. As novices learn not science in a moment, so time, discernment, and help are necessary to the understanding of the evidences of faith.[14] "The understanding, though not first in the sin, must be first in the cure."[15] Knowledge is the introductory act to love.[16] Therefore all helps of natural light are to be used.[17] The gospel is not against but fulfills natural law.[18] Sight and reason, a will and love, are part of very nature. Their exercise gives an appetite for the art of godliness and approaches toward it.[19]

---

[1] II 665, SB (1662).
[2] I 35–36, CD : CEth (1673).
[3] II 832, MS–I (1661).
[4] II 623, DP (1658); IV 1044, SA (1689).
[5] II 225, MR (1671).
[6] III 381, TS–D (1659).
[7] II 160, RCR : Chr (1666).
[8] III 729, LF (1669).
[9] II 907, 910, 965, RMeth (1653); III 176, 198, 205, SER (1649).
[10] IV 268, PM (1672).
[11] II 160, RCR : Chr (1666).
[12] *Ibid.*, 151.
[13] Ms. Treatises, V, No. 177 (= 5/47), ff. 220–265, Prop. 49.
[14] III 601, LF (1669).
[15] I 84–85, CD : CEth (1673).
[16] IV 612, TKL (1698).
[17] III 600–601, LF (1669). In RB, I 108 (1664), Baxter says: "... he that is ignorant of *Politicks* and of the *Law of Nature*, *will* be ignorant and erroneous in Divinity and the sacred Scriptures."
[18] III 605, LF (1669).
[19] III 1036, DT (1683).

Preparatory humility,[1] doubtings of self-sufficiency and fears of judgment,[2] thoughtful consideration of ends,[3] crying for mercy and relief,[4] a general and confused knowledge,[5] – all may be preparatory steps to a saving change.

> Preparatory grace usually goeth before special grace; and those that resist it, are further from the kingdom of God, than they that have it. And to him that hath (by improvement) shall be given; and in every nation, he that feareth God, and worketh righteousness, is accepted of him. Believing that God is, and that he is the rewarder of them that diligently seek him, is better than nothing, and than mere sin.[6]

God uses three glasses or seals by which he has revealed himself to man: the law of creation (nature), the law of Moses, and the law of the gospel.[7] Men know God by degrees. The lowest degree is the world of creatures alone. The second is the law and promises to the Jews and their forefathers, together with the law of nature. The third and highest degree of outward means includes the whole frame of Christian institutions with the two preceding degrees. Each of these three has a *sufficiency* of its own kind and use; nature points men to God, to the need for supernatural institutions, and to a life consistent thereto; law (Jewish) points men to a Saviour as a sacrifice for sin, to reconciliation with God, to holiness and service of God; gospel points to right belief in Father, Son, and Holy Spirit, and to love and to live unto him. The nature of the Spirit's working through these means is suited to the nature of the means, to God's ends in their appointment, and to their effect. Certainly the world is full of books about the doctrine of *sufficient* and *effectual* grace. By *sufficient* here is meant necessary, signifying the degree without which the act cannot be performed. That men have a degree of help for positive acts left undone and against sinful acts committed (e.g., lying, going to an alehouse instead of to church), no one would deny. Men who abuse the help they have by not learning even the alphabet of nature forfeit that help which would have brought them to nature's higher forms.

> But so much as I have mentioned of the help of the Spirit is given to those who do not grossly forfeit it by abuse, among the pagans of the world: and so much multitudes have attained.[8]

Before concluding the discussion on the nature of man and the differing situations in which he finds himself, we must ask: what is the possibility of salvation for those under the law of nature? This question, as with that concerning common grace, can be answered only in relation to the redemptive work of Christ, and the way in which it affects men in general.

Christ as the eternal λόγος, or wisdom of God, is throughout history the object of faith. The Jews were under the first edition of grace. They were God's peculiar, sacred people. But in Old Testament times God had other servants

---

[1] II 599, DP (1658).
[2] *Ibid.*, 647.
[3] *Ibid.*, 594.
[4] *Ibid.*, 647.
[5] *Ibid.*, 648.
[6] IV 1044, SA (1689).
[7] III 766–767, DL : KG (1663).
[8] III 692, LF (1669).

than they, though perhaps with less knowledge and faith. Christ has not diminished his mercies since his incarnation but increased them. Those who are where the gospel is not preached, and who therefore do not refuse it, are in no worse state than before the incarnation. None perish now for the mere sin of Adam, nor simply due to lack of innocency required by the first law, but each man is now condemned for refusing or abusing "some mercy purchased by Christ, which had an apt tendency to their repentance and recovery."[1]

The heathen are not under the original covenant of works, as Adam was, for this would leave them hopeless as devils.[2]

> Heathens and infidels are not left unredeemed under the remediless curse, and covenant of innocency, which we broke in Adam; but are all brought by the redemption wrought by Christ under a law or terms of grace.[3]

The law of nature, not the law of Moses, bound all men. So the covenant of grace was made with all men in Adam (Gen. 3:15) and Noah. The Jews were God's specially chosen people. They were advanced in dearness to him. But they were not the only people who professed to worship the true God. This no Scripture denies, and charity would hope for the best. The Scripture intends to give a history only of God's special people, the Jews, but alludes to others who likely also believed: Shem and his kingdom, Melchizedek as king and priest, Job and his friends, Ishmael's and Esau's posterity, Abraham's offspring by Keturah, passages in Jonah about Nineveh, Japheth and his seed. We know little of other kingdoms in the world. We must take heed of concluding, as the proud Jews were apt to do, that, because they were a privileged nation, the redeemer under the law of grace to Adam had no other churches in the world.[4]

But what of those who know not the incarnate Christ? That those who reject him as offered cannot be saved is clear. However, "all those shall be saved (if such there be) who never had sufficient means to know Christ incarnate, and yet do faithfully perform the common conditions of the covenant of grace as it was made with Adam and Noah...."[5] This does not mean men are saved without Christ;[6] his grace is absolutely necessary. However, the knowledge of Christ *incarnate* is a different question. Men were saved by him four thousand years before his incarnation. There is no salvation today "but by Christ the Saviour of the world; though there be more mercy from Christ, than there is faith in Christ."[7]

> No man could ever be saved without believing in God as a merciful, pardoning, saving God, though many have been saved who knew not the person of Christ, determinately. For he that cometh to God must believe that God is, and that he is the rewarder of them that diligently seek him; who is no respector of persons, but in every nation, he that feareth God and worketh righteousness is accepted of him.[8]

---

[1] II 222–225, MR (1671); I 719, 720, CD : CEccl (1673).
[2] II 145, RCR : Chr (1666); 223, MR (1671).
[3] II 979, GGV (1671).
[4] I 719–720, CD : CEccl (1673).
[5] *Ibid.*, 720; II 73, RCR : NR (1666).
[6] II 225, MR (1671).
[7] I 721, CD : CEccl (1673).
[8] *Idem*; II 74, RCR : NR (1666).

Baxter concludes the first part of his *Reasons of the Christian Religion* by indicating that all men shall be judged by the law which they received from God to live by. Not for truths never revealed will men be condemned. Nor for those, men had no means to know. Such physical impossibilities are not matters for condemnation. For if by the means available any are brought to godliness, to love of God "*in sensu composito,*"[1] to a holy and obedient life, "God will not condemn such persons, though they want a supernatural revelation of his will."[2]

The rejection of those with only natural revelation but who do not love God is not because they rejected sufficient helps of mercy for such love. Rather, it is because God would have drawn those many degrees distant from himself and from a holy life by degrees, and they rejected mercy sufficient for such steps. "...they that have help and mercy sufficient, *in suo genere*, to have drawn them nearer God, and refused to obey it," forfeit further helps of mercy and are justly forsaken by God.[3]

All nations who are without the gospel do have certain means for their salvation which they are obliged to use in hope, and which in neglecting add to their sin. The world compared to the catholic church is much like it was compared to the Jewish church before the incarnation, when, though the Jews had many advantages, God was also the God of the gentiles who had a law written in their hearts. Gentiles, whether heathen or Mohammedan, and Jews are not now saved by their religion, for that is either false or insufficient. Christianity is the only true religion.[4] Likewise, mere nature is an insufficient revelation, through which men are rarely if ever saved. How imperfect and insufficient are the attainments of the best of heathen philosophers![5] The truth in false religions is so small and so oppressed by errors that it gives no sound hope for salvation.[6]

But this is not to say that the heathen are remediless. The covenant of grace made to Adam is unrepealed. Those not under the full-gospel covenant are yet under the lesser edition.[7] Therefore, although none but God's people shall enter into the promised rest,

> the description of God's people in England, and in America, must not be the same; because as God's revelations are not the same, so neither is the actual faith which is required in both the same; and as the written and positive laws in the church were never given them, so obedience to those mere positives is not required of them. Whether, then, the threats against unbelievers be meant of unbelief privative and positive only, and not negative (such as is all non-believing that which was never revealed); or, whether their believing that God is, and that he is a rewarder of them that seek him, will serve the turn there; or, whether God hath no people? I acknowledge again is yet past my understanding.[8]

---

[1] II, 72, RCR : NR (1666).
[2] *Ibid.*, 74.
[3] *Idem.*
[4] II 247, UI (1655).
[5] II 545, NN (1663); III 116, SER (1649).
[6] II 954, RMeth (1653).
[7] II 979, GGV (1671).
[8] III 118, SER (1649).

God's giving to all men the duty of using certain means and providing them with certain mercies is a "promulgation of a law of grace, according to the first edition," which distinguishes men from unredeemed devils.[1] Thus, God has other ways of teaching than by the gospel.[2] No man can prove universal negative with regard to the possible salvation of the heathen.[3] Nor is the question clear as to their children, though they are not known to be saved.[4] But the "over-doing" divines who pretend to be certain that all the world are damned that are not Christian do add to God's word.[5] Though such over-zealous persons may

> ...curse all that hope that some are saved, who never heard of the name of Christ, and that his Spirit and grace go farther than the knowledge of his name, I will not curse such. All were not accursed that hoped well of Socrates, Antonine, Alexander Severus, Cicero, Epictetus, Plutarch, &c. There is no name, that is, no other Messiah, to be saved by but Christ. But, 1. God judgeth men by no other law but that which they were under; and the law of grace made to fallen mankind in Adam and Noah, was not repealed by the Jews' peculiarity. 2. God had more people than the Jews and proselytes of old. 3. The old Jews knew less of Christ than his apostles before his resurrection. 4. The apostles then believed not his dying for our sins, his resurrection, ascension, heavenly intercession, &c. 5. It is no christianity now that believeth not these. If I durst curse all the world who now believe no more than the old Jews and the apostles then did, yet durst I not curse all christians that hope better of them.[6]

Although all that is necessary for a holy, virtuous life may be found in *natura rerum*, yet very few attain it. The law of nature is of great difficulty to those without supernatural light to help them. Common people have not time to discover it, nor are they inclined to. Philosophers learn much, but widely disagree. They raise many questions but gain uncertain answers. What is sufficient for sound minds is not sufficient to darkened and diseased ones. Such diseases call for physicians, spectacles to see and crutches to walk.

> I must therefore conclude that the light and law of nature, which was suitable to uncorrupted reason and will, and to an undepraved mind, is too insufficient to the corrupted, vitiated, guilty world, and that there is a necessity of some recovering, medicinal revelation.[7]

Every man is in a state of corruption, thus in a state of death. Yet he retains somewhat of God's image: a reason and a will. These the Spirit must redirect. However, to these faculties we must address the gospel. The redemption of Christ secured a general and sufficient grace to all, and a special and effectual grace to those who believe. General grace, which also gives good gifts of educa-

---

[1] II 979, GGV (1671).
[2] II 145, RCR : Chr (1666).
[3] IV 627, TKL (1689).
[4] III 936, OP (1683); IV 855, SJ (1654).
[5] I 718, CD : CEccl (1673).
[6] IV 1045, SA (1689).
[7] II 77, RCR : Chr (1666).

tion, and civilization, is a preparatory help to conversion, though insufficient in itself. A moral qualitative difference distinguishes universal and special grace, though the former proceeds by degree to the latter. Those who resist preparatory grace must not expect to enter the kingdom. Men are judged by the law they are under: law, nature, or gospel. No man is saved apart from the redemption of Christ. Whether men are saved today who have no knowledge of Christ incarnate, we can not know. Nor can we prove a universal negative regarding their salvation. Nor may we condemn Christians who hope some may be saved.

### B. THE ROLE OF THE CHURCH

The conversion of man is, for Baxter, at the heart of the gospel message. That message is committed to appointed instruments, primarily to the church. A brief discussion of the nature of the church will be sufficient to indicate Baxter's general agreement with Sibbes. We next consider the means God uses in bringing his grace to men, and we conclude this section by presenting several methods suggested by Baxter for spreading the gospel.

#### 1. *The Nature of the Church*

The holy catholic church is the universality of Christians headed by Jesus Christ.[1] From this "holy kingdom" of which all sincere Christians are members, Christ has instituted

> ...a holy Christian society for ordinary holy communion and mutual help in God's public worship and holy living, consisting of pastors authorized and obliged to teach, and guide, and speak for the flock in God's public worship, and administer his sacraments according to Christ's word, and of a flock to hear them, learn, obey, and follow such their conduct to the foresaid ends... No man can deny that to be a christian church which hath this definition.[2]

The universal church and the local particular church are the two forms of church government of divine institution.[3] Particular churches are duty-bound to co-operate, but no one church has authority over the other.[4] Councils were early held in the history of the church, but they had only an advisory capacity; their degeneration to governmental authority came later.[5] The duty of church reformation rests with private persons, bishops and rulers. When need arises, they may call a synod of churches.[6] Yet, faithful ministers and the exercise of

---

[1] IV 96, CF (1682); Ms. Treatises, V, Item No. 165 (= 5/35), ff. 199–200.
[2] IV 722, OTN (1684).
[3] I 666, CD : CEccl (1673); A "Treatise on Government" is found in Ms. Treatises, I, Item No. 10, ff. 151–206.
[4] "... union and communion of Churches is not indifferent but necessary." III 475, TS–D (1659); IV 478, RP (1656).
[5] I 670, CD : CEccl (1673).
[6] *Ibid.*, 709.

discipline is enough to secure effective church reformation.[1] All presbyters, that is, pastors, have the right to lay on hands in confirmation of fellow ministers.[2] The pattern of the "Primitive Churches" ought to be followed.[3]

The door of the visible church is incomparably wider than the invisible actually is.[4] All who make a credible profession of faith are to be accounted members of the church.

> ...a Profession is credible *as such*, of itself, till he that questioneth it doth disprove it. Else the Rules of Human Converse will be overthrown: for who knoweth the Heart of another as well as he himself....[5]

Thus, the existential church has two kinds of people in it: those called by a common vocation, by an external acceptance of Christ, not common and unclean in the sense Jews and pagans are, but holy in the sense that the nation of the Jews was; and those called by a special vocation, by accepting of Christ and internal, sincere covenanting to be the people of God.[6] That these latter ones, the people of God, are but "a small part of lost mankind" is evident from Scripture and experience.[7] The presence of the former group in the worship of the church makes preaching an urgent matter. Are matters of forms and gestures, vestures and ceremonies our primary business? "O no, sirs! it is the converting and saving of souls that is our business." [8] Discipline, exercised only in consultation with two or three neighboring pastors [9] and in accordance with the command of Christ is necessary for the good of the church [10] and has for its object "...Heretics and notorious wicked men, who are impenitent after due admonition." [11]

Every worshiping congregation of Christians is in fact a church.[12] To be accounted as Christians are all who are baptized in infancy and who solemnly own their baptism at age, and those baptized as adults.[13] These join for worship on the Lord's Day, which day "keepeth up the christian religion in the world."[14] The ends of worship are "the honour of God; the edification of believers; the communicating of spiritual knowledge, holiness and delight to others; and the increase of God's actual kingdom in the world." [15] To attain these ends no form of worship which is an enemy to knowledge ought to be used.[16] Therefore, ignorant and childish worship (such as that used by papists) is a great hindrance to the conversion of sober heathen and Mohammedan nations.[17]

---

[1] IV 447, RP (1656).
[2] IV 332, CR (1658).
[3] Ms. Treat. IV, Item No. 81, ff. 171.
[4] II 171, RCR : Chr (1666); III 282, SER (1649).
[5] RB, I 114 (1664).
[6] III 10, SER (1649).
[7] *Ibid.*, 61.
[8] IV 449, RP (1656).
[9] *Ibid.*, 416–417.
[10] RB, I 92–93 (1664); cf. IV 390, RP (1656); 722, TOW (1679).
[11] II 171, RCR : Chr (1666).
[12] IV 153, CF (1682).
[13] IV 942, HGM (1682); cf. II 124, RCR : Chr (1666).
[14] III 909, DA (1671); cf. *Ibid.*, 880.
[15] I 554, CD : CEccl (1673).
[16] *Idem.*
[17] *Idem.*

## 2. The Means of Grace

For the communication of spiritual knowledge to others, God entrusts certain instruments to the church.[1] He gives grace in the use of means. No man can "expect to attain the end, that will not be persuaded to use the means."[2] Such a person ignores that God's common way to work is by means and thus imitates nature in his works of grace.[3] "God who appointeth severall means doth usually worke according to them."[4] As souls use bodies, so the Spirit uses means [5] which we neglect at our peril.[6]

> The very command of God, to use his appointed means for men's recovery, doth imply that it shall not be in vain; and doth not only show a possibility, but so great a hopefulness of the success to the obedient, as may encourage them cheerfully to undertake it, and carry it through.[7]

Some of the means are more general in nature: reading and hearing the Word of God, public worship, private prayer, confession of sin, holy conversation with experienced Christians, meditation on the life to come, and seeking counsel from a faithful guide.[8] But three are most essential for our illumination: the Word, the ministry, and the Spirit.[9] The three, all necessary, are the means Christ has resolved upon.[10]

The Word, given by divine inspiration, is the trustworthy and infallible guide for the church.[11] Though God is the full object of faith, Scripture is the *principium certitudinis*.[12] The cause of uncertainty of salvation usually rests in weakness of faith about the truth of Scripture.[13] Evidences for the authority and dependability of the Scriptures abound.[14] As such, the Word becomes the rule for worship,[15] the source for preaching,[16] and the guide for duty.[17] The Bible has two parts: history and doctrine. "Common evidence" establishes the history, and history establishes the doctrine.[18]

The proper perfections of Scripture intended by the Spirit of God do not exclude certain human imperfections in accident and mode. "As Christ cured the blind with clay and spittle... The excellency of the means must be estimated by its aptitude to its end."[19] The holy Scriptures are a perfect law to us for matters of divine faith and obedience, universal moral necessities, doctrines of the Christian religion, sacraments and way of salvation, institution of ministers

---

[1] I 16, CD : Eth (1673).
[2] *Ibid.*, 23.
[3] II 507, CU (1657).
[4] Ms. Letters, I, f. 38.
[5] IV 1046, RM (1676).
[6] I 71, CD : CEth (1673); II 498–499, TCon (1657).
[7] II 73, CD : CEth (1673).
[8] I 23–24, CD : CEth (1673); cf. also *Ibid.*, 55; IV 203, PM (1672); 320, CR (1658); II 411–412, 476–479, TCon (1657); II 979, GGV (1671).
[9] II 305, UI : ChW (1655); II 623, DP (1658).
[10] II 623, DP (1658).
[11] I 80, CD : CEth (1673); III 117, SER (1649); IV 573, TKL (1689).
[12] III 82, SER (1649).
[13] *Ibid.*, 88.
[14] I 167, CD : CEth (1673); II 124, RCR : Chr (1666); 254–255, UF : SpW (1655); 717–720, SB (1662); III 81, 91–92, 94, SER (1649).
[15] I 556, CD : CEccl (1673).
[16] *Ibid.*, 718.
[17] II 720, SB (1662).
[18] *Idem.*
[19] II 161, RCR : Chr (1666).

and churches, times of worship, and rules for holy living.[1] The Scriptures are not to be considered our perfect rule in the following respects: natural sciences and other fields of study, subordinate duties of societies, political principles, proprietorship, natural actions (what we eat or wear), and religious ordinances not specifically commanded.[2]

There are many Christians who have true faith but who are uncertain of some matters in Scripture.[3] Here one must first distinguish between what Scripture really teaches and what particular men say it teaches.[4] How one reads is of great significance.[5] Those who yet believe there are mistakes are at a disadvantage but are certainly saved by acceptance of what is essential.[6] If a man doubts much of Scripture, even

> ...all the Old Testament, and much of the New; yet if he believe so much as containeth all the covenant of grace and the aforesaid summaries [creeds, Lord's Prayer, and Ten Commandments],...he may and will be saved.[7]

For this reason an explicit belief in Scripture was never required in the church of those baptized, nor of all or any man that entered the ministry. If a man should doubt the canonicity of Job or Esther, he should not therefore be forbidden to preach Christ's gospel. Should Luther, or Althamer, or others that questioned the Epistle of James have been silenced? [8]

Thousands have been saved without having ever seen or heard the Scriptures.[9] Those, who now do not and cannot believe the Bible, must first know that its message is certain.[10] They must settle their belief in Christianity, "that is, of so much as baptism containeth."[11] There are many varying degrees of certainty in the Bible,[12] but there ought to be no uncertainty in "the christian religion, which is the vital part or kernel of the Scriptures."[13]

The heart of the Scriptures is what God, Father, Son, and Holy Spirit, offers in the gospel.[14] All of Jewish and Old Testament history must be seen as God's preparation for the history of the gospel of Christ.[15] He purposes through Christ's work [16] to exercise his grace in us and advance us to communion with himself.[17] Thus Christ came not to teach archeology or medicine [18] but to declare the love of God to sinners.[19] He is the *only* Saviour of the world.[20]

> Let this name or description of Christ be engraven as in capital letters upon your minds, THE ETERNAL WISDOM OF GOD INCARNATE TO REVEAL AND COMMUNICATE HIS WILL, HIS LOVE, HIS SPIRIT TO SINFUL... MAN.[21]

---

[1] I 706, CD : CEccl (1673).
[2] *Idem*; on pp. 724–725, Baxter enumerates 12 instances in which men undervalue the Scriptures and 20 instances of overevaluation.
[3] II 210, MR (1671).
[4] II 269, UI : SpW (1655).
[5] I 477–478, CD : CEc (1673).
[6] I 724, CD : CEccl (1673).
[7] IV 576, TKL (1689).
[8] *Idem.*
[9] II 279, UF : SpW (1655).
[10] III 72–74, SER (1649).
[11] III 603, LF (1669); cf. 601–604.
[12] IV 571–574, TKL (1689).
[13] III 602, LF (1669).
[14] I 21, CD : CEth (1673).
[15] IV 59, MC (1701).
[16] II 610, 616–617, DP (1658).
[17] I 65, CD : CEth (1673).
[18] II 148, RCR : Chr (1666).
[19] *Ibid.*, 97.
[20] *Ibid.*, 163.
[21] III 633, LF (1669).

Someone may say it is as unreasonable for God to become man as for a prince to become a fly to save flies. But this analogy is wrongly put. In becoming man God did not cease to be God. He assumed in Christ a human nature unto himself. The analogy should be that of a prince bringing so low a creature as a fly into a close relation to himself. Through such love God brings man into relation with himself.[1] Christ's righteousness is imputed to all true believers.[2] Upon them, the image of Christ and his holiest servants ought to be deeply imprinted.[3]

Ministers are appointed by God to preach [4] redemption through Jesus Christ as the message of the holy Scriptures.[5]

> Read the Scripture, or hear it read, and other holy writings that do apply it; constantly attend upon the public preaching of the word. As God will lighten the world by the sun, and not by himself alone, without it; so will he convert and save men by his ministers, who are the lights of the world.[6]

God speaks by them.[7] They are commissioned instruments and messengers of grace.[8] As such they are not to dominate the church nor to act as lords, nor to use external force, but to be spiritual fathers.[9] A note of seriousness and urgency becomes them as ambassadors of Christ.[10] Because of men's disaffection and hardness, the truths must be preached with the greatest plainness, convincing evidence, holy reverence, powerful and winning motives, life and fervency, constancy, seemly expressions, concord, and by the example of holy practice.[11] The words and works of God [12] are to be presented in such a way as to accomplish the salvation of others.[13] Ministers are to interpret God's law and to guide men, not seduce or lead them blindfolded into the kingdom.[14] Men need not to become learned but to practice holy piety.[15] God knew that common people would have neither heart nor time for this and therefore appointed pastors.[16] To them men should go for help.[17] So long as personal defects remain, a continuing ministry is as necessary as are physicians.[18]

---

[1] II 396, UI : AR (1655).
[2] III 683, LF (1669).
[3] *Ibid.*, 620.
[4] I 82, CD : CEth (1673); II 617, DP (1658); Baxter appeals to Matthew 28 : 19, 20 here.
[5] I 586–588, CD : CEccl (1673); II 502, CU (1657).
[6] II 538, CU (1657).
[7] II 869, MS–I (1661).
[8] II 112, RCR : Chr (1666); 502, 506, CU (1657); IV 1046, RM (1676).
[9] I 82, CD : CEth (1673); 756, CD : CP (1673); II 985, GGV (1671); IV 394, RP (1656).
[10] I 175, CD : CEth (1673).
[11] IV 151–152, CF (1682); cf. III 230–239, SER (1649).
[12] IV 378, RP (1656).
[13] *Ibid.*, 372.
[14] II 871, 883, MS–I (1661).
[15] IV 626, TKL (1689).
[16] II 317, UI : US (1655).
[17] II 433–437, 452, 416, TCon (1657); 966ff., RMeth (1653); III 290, SER (1549).
[18] II 887–888, RMeth (1653); 1058, CSCC (1669); Baxter met William Penn in a debate on the subject of the necessity of a paid ministry. Baxter pressed his affirmative view in subsequent letters. Cf. Ms. Letters, V, Item No. 59. In "Vs. Quakers inner light and Unchurching of the whole Christian world," Baxter says: "And I take for a heynous aggravation of their sin, that when they do all this against Love, unity, & prair, against Christs Ministers, and their work, against Gods faithfull people, even as Satan would have them do, they yet father it all on *The Spirit of God* – a thing that should make us all Quake to think on it." Ms. Treatises VI, Item No. 192, ff. 7–10.

But alas! How men refuse the faithful pastors,[1] how they quarrel with the Word of God[2] and applaud superficial sermons,[3] how they hate preachers who distinguish between the godly and the ungodly.[4] The time may come when exhortation will do more harm than good to a sinner; then is time for silence. Give no pearls to swine.[5] That there are unfaithful pastors[6] who preach formal, frozen, lifeless sermons,[7] who not only teach falsely and have no holy diligence but ridicule those who do,[8] only confirms the ungodly. A dead nurse will not give warm and vital milk.[9]

The first duty of the sacred ministry is to make the world Christian and gather men into the church by teaching and baptizing them.[10] "Alas! The misery of the unconverted is so great, that it calleth loudest to us for our compassion."[11] The ministry is not unnecessary to spiritual men. A believer's fall will be recovered.[12] Because of the "lamentable necessity of the unconverted," Baxter felt forced to neglect the godly.[13] Because of the inordinate size of many parishes, he advises his fellow-ministers: "O, therefore, brethren, whomsoever you neglect, neglect not the most miserable!"[14] What a lamentable impediment to the reformation of the church and the saving of souls when for a congregation of many thousand souls there are only one or two ministers. "Is this not a sad case in a nation that glorieth of the fulness of the gospel?"[15]

Baxter indicates fifteen duties of the minister; the first four have to do with missions: preaching to the unconverted, entreating repentance, receiving and baptizing believers, and gathering converts into churches.[16] It is well to note that "Preaching to the unconverted comes first." It is simply "the work of faithful ministers, to save men's souls."[17] True pastors and bishops thirst after the conversion and winning of men to Christ.[18] They know that to deal with an ignorant soul is much harder than to compose a sermon.[19] Necessity orders a minister's life and study. Life is short. We are dull. Eternal things are necessary. Souls are precious.[20] So many are for atheism, bestiality, and infidelity, that preaching becomes urgent.[21] The same applies to pagans, infidels, and Jews.[22] For all such, ministers are directors to life eternal.[23]

---

[1] IV 821, TD (1659) 857, SJ (1654).
[2] II 806, MS-I (1661).
[3] *Ibid.*, 866.
[4] *Ibid.*, 868.
[5] III 696, LF (1669).
[6] II 867, MS-I (1661).
[7] III 158, SER (1649).
[8] II 558–563, NN (1663).
[9] IV 974, HS (1678).
[10] IV 151, CF (1682); 639, TKL (1689).
[11] IV 381, RP (1656).
[12] II 306, UI : ChW (1655).
[13] Yet Baxter himself spent two days a week calling on his parishioners. He spent over an hour at each family and with his colleague visited fourteen each week in an attempt to visit most of the 800 families in his parish each year. III 910, DA (1671). He maintained that it was possible to gain more in a half hour private discourse than in ten years of preaching. IV 443, RP (1656).
[14] IV 381, RP (1656).
[15] *Ibid.*, 437.
[16] I 556, CD : CEccl (1673); cf. *Ibid.*,6 39; IV 381–391, RP (1656); II 97, RCR : Chr (1666).
[17] I 908, MP (1661).
[18] II 157, RCR : Chr (1666).
[19] IV 456, RP (1656).
[20] *Ibid.*, 392.
[21] RB III 151.
[22] III 87, SER (1649).
[23] I 556, CD : CEccl (1673).

The Great Commission of Christ (Mt. 28:19, 20) makes it undeniably evident that part of the minister's work is "to teach, convert, and baptize men, to bring them out of the world into the church."[1] This commission was not restricted to the apostles for the following reasons:[2]

> 1. Because [it is...] the first great business of the gospel and ministry in the world.
> 2. Because others as well as the apostles did it in that age, and ever since.
> 3. Because the promise is annexed... "I am with you always to the end of the world."
> 4. Because it was a small part of the world comparatively that heard the gospel in the apostles' days. And the far greatest part of the world is without it at this day....
> 5. Even where the gospel hath long continued, for the most part there are many still that are in infidelity. And so great a work is not left without an appointment suitable for its performance: and if an office was necessary for it in the first age, it is not credible that it is left to private men's charity ever since.
> 6. Especially considering that private men are to be supposed insufficient; (1) Because they are not educated purposefully for it, but usually for something else. (2) Because that they have other callings to take them up. (3) Because they have no special obligation. And that which is no man's peculiar work, is usually left undone by all.[3]

Not everyone is to go forth and preach in the same way that the twelve and the seventy were sent forth by Christ. Besides the three elementary qualifications: natural capacity, ready speech, and serious piety,[4] the ministerial office demands solid learning and hard study.[5] Ministers should be judicious, experienced, humble, holy, heavenly, faithful, lively, and peaceable.[6] Such men can be as confidently consulted concerning God, the Word, and the soul as one might consult a lawyer about titles and legal matters.[7]

---

[1] *Ibid.*, 639.

[2] W. F. Dankbaar points out that Calvin, in reaction to the doctrine of the apostolic succession in the Roman Catholic Church, did not apply the great commission of Mt. 28 : 19–20 to later church history. When Hadrian Saravia, who accepted the episcopal succession of the Anglican Church, defended (1590) the continuing applicability of the Great Commission, Beza wrote against him (1592). One Reformed Confession, the Helvetic of 1562, shared this judgment. Dankbaar concludes: "Overziende hetgeen wij tot nu toe vonden, komen wij tot de slotsom, dat Calvijn ontegenzeggelijk oog had voor de universaliteit van het christelijk geloof en de christelijke verkondiging, maar dat hij, gedwongen door zijn begrensde opvatting van het apostolaat, dit, om zo te zeggen tussen de mazen van zijn theologisch net door, óf op bepaalde predikers en vooral op christelijke overheden liet overgaan, óf er een uitweg voor zocht in de particuliere naastenliefde en het gebed der christenen." ("Het Apostolaat bij Calvijn," 177–192, in *Nederlands Theologisch Tijdschrift*, Vierde Jaargang, 1949–1950).

[3] I 639–640, CD : CEccl (1673).

[4] IV 253, PM (1672); IV 19, CC (1681).

[5] II 312–313, UI : CW (1655).

[6] II 1013, DW (1668).

[7] II 870, MS–I (1661).

The ministers are of two sorts: the unfixed ministers "who employ themselves in converting infidels, and in an itinerant service of the churches," and the stated, fixed ministers "having a special charge of each particular church."[1] The former is in the general ministry and, as such, is "a pastor in the universal church,"[2] preaching to "the unbelieving world (Jews, Mahometans, or pagans) as one that hath given up himself to that work, and is separated and set apart to it."[3] The latter preaches to the congregation as their ordinary teacher.[4] However, a man may be made at once "a minister in general, and the pastor of this or that church in particular: and in kingdoms wholly inchurched and christian, it is usually fittest so to do; lest many being ordained *sine titulo*, idleness and poverty of supernumeraries, should corrupt and dishonour the ministry...."[5]

This distinction between such extraordinary and ordinary ministers results from the character and scope of their work, not from a difference in the office itself.

> Yet it seemes to me that those Generall officers have no other kind or degree of Power (quod *naturam* actus) than the ffixed Ministers of p[ar]ticular Churches: but only their Power extendes its. as to its exercised act, to a larger (& lesse-punctuall, & more Generall) charge & so differs objectively. Much less have they any coercive, or Lordly Power over Minister or People. It is rather a greater worke & burden that they have, then a greater Power in kind.[6]

The main part of the work remains the same for both. Before his ascension Christ instituted "unfixed Ambulatory Ministers" as a "standing necessity" in the church.[7] This is clear from the Great Commission given in Matthew 28:19. The office and duties there enumerated are continuing; all ministers are to disciple, baptize, and teach. Only the special gifts, privileges, and honors do not continue. That some ministers disciple, baptize, and teach in fixed places is evident; some of the apostles also remained for a longer or shorter time in fixed places. The Commission itself evidences both the continuing nature of the ministerial office by the words "to the End of the world" and the world-wide scope of the office by the words "Teach all Nations &c."[8]

Where the same important work continues, the office continues. Though infallible preaching is no more, yet "Discipling Infidells, Baptizing them, & Teaching Disciples, is a worke that Continueth."[9]

> Breerwood sayeth, that of 30 partes of the world 19 are yet Idolators or Pagans: 6 Mahometans & but 5 Christians, taking the Greeks, Abassines, Jacobites & Papists & all: Doubtles then here is important worke for all

---

[1] I 556, CD : CEccl, 1673; cf. also IV 377, RP (1656).
[2] I 641, CD : CEccl (1673).
[3] IV 383, RP (1656).
[4] *Idem.*
[5] I 641, CD : CEccl (1673).
[6] MF Treatises, V, Item No. 165 (= 5/35) 24°, ff. 199–200.
[7] *Ibid.*; Baxter gives seven arguments in this passage to prove the continuance of an unfixed ministry.
[8] *Idem.*
[9] *Ibid.*, 2.

> those that have pity, opportunity & call to gather new churches as the Apostles did (& as Mr. Eliots doth in N. Engl:) & to Baptize them, & to ordaine Elders in them, & to have a care over them for their p[r]eservation.[1]

No man has the right to revoke an office instituted by Christ. Therefore the apostle, writing of that ministry which will continue till the body be perfected (Eph. 4:8), makes apostles and evangelists distinct, not in office, but in gifts, "...intimating that though the Eminencye of Guiftes cease, yet the offices & common worke of all those sortes shall continue to the Church."[2] Paul established men like Timothy, Titus, and others as unfixed ministers.

Unfixed ministers are necessary where:

> 1º Churches are to be newly gathered from among Infidells; 2º or Rude Materialls be be newly ordered & Ministers fixed in them by ordination; 3º or corrupted Infected, declining Churches to be restored.[3]

These general officers, although not bound to a fixed church, are not bound always to wander from place to place, but "to distribute their labors with prudence to the greatest advantage of the whole Church."[4] However,

> None of these Generall officers can appropriate a province to his owne care or oversight, excluding other unfixed or Generall officers; except by common consent together.[5]

The general officers are of "Christs planting in the church" and are necessary, in the above mentioned cases, to the furtherance of the church.[6] Ministers are appointed by God to bring blessing:

> 1. Christ maketh them the chief instruments for the propagating of his truth and kingdom in the world, for the gathering of churches, and preserving and defending contradicted truth....
> 2. And thus God useth them as his special instruments for the convincing, converting, edifying, comforting, and saving of souls....
> 3. And in this they are co-workers with Jesus Christ, the great Saviour of souls, and with the Holy Spirit, the Regenerator and Sanctifier....
> 4. In a word, churches, states, and christian kingdoms, are chiefly blessed and preserved by the labour of the faithful part of the ministry....[7]

As ministers are the usual means in the conversion of the heathen, so are parents in the conversion of their children through Christian education.[8] God's first great means of salvation comes in childhood.[9] The first work in reformation of the church and the commonwealth lies in the good education of children.[10]

---

[1] *Idem.*
[2] *Idem.*
[3] *Idem.*
[4] *Ibid.*, 3.
[5] *Idem.*
[6] *Idem.*
[7] IV 23, CC (1681).
[8] IV 940, HGM (1682).
[9] II 910, RMeth (1653).
[10] III 241, SER (1649); I 479–481, CD : CEc (1673).

If parents do not do this, preaching is the children's only hope for salvation.[1] Proper education of the youth is one-half the business of a man's life.[2] Godly parents seek to bring their children up in faith;[3] for this, they know that good and regular Christian education is necessary.[4] Families are sacred nurseries for church and kingdom.[5] Children have souls to save. They cannot begin learning too soon.[6]

> Family reformation is the easiest and the most likely way to a common reformation; at least to send many souls to heaven, and train up multitudes for God, if it reach not to national reformation.[7]

Children have original sin which must be pardoned or they are lost;[8] they are sinners and need a redeemer.[9] God is not so prone to wrath, rather than mercy, as to condemn them for their first father's covenant breaking and to allow them no help from their present parents' covenant keeping.[10] Children are through their parents included in the covenant[11] and as such are to be baptized.[12] Children of servants or those adopted or bought should be baptized where a pro-parent, or domestic educating relationship exists, even though their case is less certain than for children of believers.[13] Assurance of children's salvation[14] rests not upon a sort of child faith[15] but upon the faith of the parents.[16] This does not mean that children of believers, who are not baptized, are consequently not saved.[17] Christ considers all children of believers as his own and does not look upon children at so great a distance as the Anabaptists do.[18]

Yet we are not to presume regeneration[19] nor to count children as church members when they are of age.[20] Their own consent to the baptismal covenant must be given at age, or the meaning of baptism ceases. (Otherwise heathen, Turks, and Jews could be church members.)[21] In the same covenant as that of its parents, a believer's child is saved by a promise which legitimate hindrance of baptism does not thwart. Yet, though confirmed grace is never lost, the grace given to infants is as "losable" as was Adam's if not confirmed at age.[22] Every child must be converted, whether this occurs consciously or unconsciously, early or late in childhood or youth. When, is not the question, but rather, do you have the necessary points now?[23] Can the baptismal covenant be

---

[1] III 241, SER (1649).
[2] IV 3, CC (1681).
[3] III 663, LF (1669); 246, SER (1649).
[4] IV 1, CC (1681); II 954, RMeth (1653).
[5] IV 3, CC (1681).
[6] I 728, CD : CEccl (1673); II 1047, CSCC (1669).
[7] I 427, CD : CEc (1673).
[8] IV 292, CR (1658); I 427, CD : CEc (1673).
[9] III 791–792, DL : KG (1663).
[10] IV 291, CR (1658).
[11] III 501, CW (1657).
[12] II 499, TCon (1657); I 559–562, CD : CEccl (1673); III 737, LF (1669).
[13] I 652, 656, 657, CD : CEccl (1673); III 239 ff., SER (1649); IV 292, CR (1658).
[14] I 651, CD : CEccl (1673).
[15] IV 293, CR (1658).
[16] I 223, CD : CEth (1673).
[17] IV 154–155, CF (1682).
[18] II 427, TCon (1657).
[19] RB, I (1664); RB, II 328 (1665).
[20] IV 342, CR (1658).
[21] IV 293–295, CR (1658); I 161, CD : CEth (1673); II 842, MS-I (1661).
[22] III 937, OP (1683).
[23] II 437, TCon (1657); 842, MS-1 (1661).

renewed "understandingly, deliberately, freely, and seriously"?[1] If so, admission to the church, what Calvin and many Protestants call confirmation,[2] ought to be made in the open congregation.[3]

We have seen that the way to the spread of the gospel is basically through the Spirit's use of the minister as the bearer of the message of the Scriptures. Whether attached to a local church or itinerant to the unconverted, the minister's first and foremost concern is conversion. Even behind the concern that believing parents educate their children in the Christian faith lies the knowledge that all must be converted, not in a limited momentary experience usually, but in a life turned to God and dedicated to his purpose.

## 3. The Methods of Approach

The church in its outward manifestation must now be considered. The interest of the church is three-fold:

1. *Intensive*, in its holiness.  2. *Conjunctive*, in its unity, concord and, order.
3. *Extensive*, in its increase and the multiplication of believers.[4]

These are not isolated interests. He who promotes unity and seeks the souls of others most effectually promotes "his own consolation and salvation."[5] Contrariwise, holiness promotes unity and missions. So is the interaction between each in the triplex.[6]

We shall consider various aspects of the church's interest insofar as they are related to our subject. Baxter has much to say, for example, about the holiness of the Christian, which is the "intensive interest" of the church. This holiness involves (a) the witness of the believer to his fellow men and (b) the promotion of the public good in order to bring men to conversion. Likewise, the "conjunctive interest" of the church involves, (c) a concern for the disunity which hinders the progress of the gospel and (d) a concern for essential doctrine as the means for overcoming disunity. Both the "intensive" and "conjunctive" interests of the church involve the "extensive interest"; this latter we shall consider in detail in the next main section.

### a. Witnessing by the Church Member

The believer's plain and urgent duty through the church, weak and struggling as it is, is to witness to unredeemed humanity at home and abroad and to exercise compassion for men's bodies as well as their souls.[7] As light comes into the world by the sun, so good must come into the world by us.[8] We must be employed in joyful service of God. This is done on the one hand by happy and thankful worship. The primitive church celebrated the Eucharist every Lord's Day as a feast of thanksgiving. Such worship acquaints the world with

---

[1] II 665, SB (1662).
[2] I 690, CD : CEccl (1673).
[3] IV 312, 291, CR (1658).
[4] II 168, RCR : Chr (1666).
[5] *Idem.*
[6] *Ibid.*, 167–172.
[7] I 81, 254, CD : CEth (1673).
[8] *Ibid.*, 111.

the true nature of religion.¹ On the other hand, the Christian must be set on doing good. The sun does not hide itself; neither should we hide what God has entrusted to us.² Alas, how few Christians live as men that are made to do good. No thanks to us if heaven be not empty and the souls of our brethren perish not forever.³ Idleness which deprives us of the great delight of doing good,⁴ iniquities that hurt our families and neighbors,⁵ false slanders⁶ and instigation of public scandals⁷ that indicate want of love for neighbor and enemy,⁸ weak faith that hinders multitudes of the ignorant, and ungodly, unsettled minds that cause troubles and divisions in the church,⁹ short-sighted lamentation over our own little concerns while the world lies in darkness,¹⁰ a separation from the world that minds only the life to come,¹¹ "over-doing" on secular matters while ignoring education of self and children,¹² maintaining silence when heaven and hell are at stake¹³ – all these hinder the progress of the gospel and rob unbelievers of one means for salvation.¹⁴

There are two ways to see the Christian religion: in the gospel message itself, and in men professing by their lives.¹⁵ Many who are unconvinced by the former are often converted by the latter.

> Labour by your holy examples, by love, and concord, and meekness, and sobriety, and contempt of the world, and a heavenly life, to "shine as lights in the midst of a dark and crooked generation". Preach all of you, by the examples of your blameless, humble, holy lives. Oh how abundantly would this course promote the success of the public preaching of the gospel!¹⁶

The universal speech of a good life speaks in all languages of the world.

> You should all be preachers, and even preach as you go up and down in the world, as a candle lighteth which way ever it goeth. As we are sent to save sinners, as ambassadors of Christ, by public proclamation of his will; so are you sent to save them as his servants and our helpers, and must preach by your lives and familiar exhortations, as we must do by authoritative instruction. A good life is a good sermon; yea, those may be won by your sermons, that will not come to ours, or will not obey the doctrine which they hear.¹⁷

If we would rather have our neighbors reclaimed than destroyed, love and gentleness is the way.¹⁸ Well-governed families attract others.¹⁹ Since God

---

1. *Ibid.*, 147–149.
2. II 1044, CSCC (1669).
3. III 213, SER (1649).
4. III 719, LF (1669).
5. II 984, DW (1668).
6. I 195, CD : CEth (1673).
7. I 802, 859, CD : CP (1673).
8. II 853, MS-I (1661).
9. II 990, DW (1668).
10. III 937, OP (1683).
11. III 974, DT (1683).
12. IV 137–138, CF (1682).
13. IV 1047, RM (1676); III 758, LF (1669).
14. II 992, DW (1668).
15. II 79, RCR : Chr (1666).
16. I 589, CD : CEccl (1673); cf. II 308, UI : ChW (1655); I 807, CD : CP (1673).
17. II 992, DW (1668); cf. III 739, LF (1669).
18. I 785, 870, CD : CP (1673).
19. I 426, CD : CEc (1673).

chooses to communicate his goodness through human instruments,[1] we should be more studious of our duty to others.[2] We are members of the world and the church and are duty-bound to do good to many.[3] Rational souls are God's image in which we must see and love him.[4] There are to be no bounds to our endeavors to seek the good of multitudes [5] and to exercise a healing love to all mankind.[6]

> Be sure at least that your holy, loving, and blameless lives, be an example to those that are about you. If you cannot convert kingdoms, nor get other men to do their duty towards it, be sure that you do your part within your reach: and believe that your lives must be the best part of your labours, and that good works, and love, and good example must be the first part of your doctrine.[7]

But it is particularly to the verbal witness that we are called.[8] A new heart has a new tongue; a converted man talks of his everlasting condition and laments the inconsistency of his sinful life. He will warn others of the ways of sin. They need to know their need of Christ and his grace. This is of greater moment than all else in the world. Why cannot Christians keep their faith to themselves? Is it possible to be religious in secret? Can Christ and his Spirit dwell in man's heart and the tongue conceal them? Is it right to jest and talk foolishly and tell idle tales, and then to be silent on matters of greatest weight?

> What! have the love of God shed abroad in their hearts, and say nothing of it? have the pardon of sin in the blood of Christ, and say nothing of it? What! see many hundred souls in danger of damnation, and say nothing, but let them perish? It cannot be; it must not be; it is a most unreasonable thing to desire it.[9]

A silent, lay Christian is to be blamed as much as such a minister.[10] The great, plain duty of Christians is to tell their friends and neighbors the gospel in private conversation.[11] "Nature hath made the tongue the index of the mind."[12] Three of the duties of the tongue are to pray for conversion, to teach others, and to communicate the love of God.[13] That is to say, every Christian bears these duties and ought to exercise them.[14] He ought to do all he can for the conversion of others: [15] study for skill to discourse,[16] pray for the conversion of all the nations of the world to Christianity,[17] yearn over the ignorant and

---

[1] I 111, CD : CEth (1673).
[2] II 1041, CSCC (1669); I 562–564, CD : CEccl (1673).
[3] III 974, DT (1683).
[4] IV 149, CF (1682).
[5] IV 937, HGM (1682).
[6] IV 703, TOW (1679).
[7] III 739, LF (1669).
[8] III 228, SER (1649).
[9] II 432, TCon (1657).
[10] I 816, CD : CP (1673).
[11] II 939, RMeth (1653).
[12] II 830, MS–I (1661).
[13] I 342–343, CD : CEth (1673).
[14] IV 715, TOW (1679).
[15] IV 442, RP (1656); I 805, CD : CP (1673).
[16] I 150, CD : CEth (1673).
[17] I 489–490, CD : CEc (1673); II 1056, CSCC (1669); IV 709, TOW (1679).

careless multitude,[1] and be a friend to serious preaching.[2] There is a "common obligation on all men to do their best in their places to propagate the gospel and church, and to save men's souls."[3] Our goodness must be communicative if we will be like God.[4] We should go to ignorant people in our neighborhood and teach them the catechism as ambassadors of Christ.[5]

> ...this is certain, that whenever God converteth the soul, he maketh men very desirous of other men's conversion, and very compassionate to them that are yet in darkness and in bondage by their sins. Not only Paul and the preachers of the gospel say, "Necessity is laid upon me, and woe unto me if I preach not the gospel!", but every christian in his place doth find a necessity upon him to endeavour the good of others; and he findeth an earnest desire to it, and a delight in that which God hath made so necessary.[6]

In several lengthy passages Baxter sets out the believer's duties for the conversion of others. In *A Christian Directory*[7] fifteen general directions are given for furthering the salvation of others: inculcate by repetition, a hundred times if necessary, the simple and basic principles of sound doctrine; bring others to faithful pastors who teach such doctrine; establish concord among teachers and private Christians, "that they all may be one... that the world may believe that thou hast sent me";[8] preach every one of you by "blameless, humble, loving, heavenly lives... to all your neighbours whom you desire to save";[9] keep those you would save in a humble and learning attitude, place them in good families and marry them to fit helpers and steer them away from bad and into good company, for a drunkard is not cured in an alehouse nor a glutton at a full table; use the circumstances of afflictions and other warnings to engage in profitable and serious talk; encourage the reading of the Scriptures and other good books and the constant practice of prayer whether with a book or form, or without; show all hearty love and do all kindness that you can to men's bodies and to their souls for "Love is the most powerful preacher in the world"; avoid quarreling and bad feelings with those you would save, even though you lose in business by it; neither concur with men in sin nor run from them in lawful things, rather, like Paul, "become all things to all men, to save some."

> To place religion in things indifferent, and to cry out against lawful things as sinful, or to fly from others by needless singularities, is a great cause of the hardening and perdition of multitudes, turning their hearts against religion, and making them think that it is but unnecessary scruple, and that religious persons are but self-conceited, brain-sick people, that make

---

[1] III 158, SER (1649); IV 705, TOW (1679).
[2] IV 892, SR (1660).
[3] IV 152, CF (1682).
[4] II 940, RMeth (1653).
[5] *Ibid.*, 937.
[6] II 433, TCon (1657).
[7] I 813–814, CD : CP (1673).
[8] *Idem.*
[9] *Idem.*

to themselves a duty of their superstition, and condemn all that be not as humorous as they. Lay not such stumblingblocks before any whose souls you desire to save.[1]

In *The Saint's Everlasting Rest* a lengthy section is devoted to "an exhortation to those that have got assurance of this rest, or title to it, that they would do all that possibly they can to help others to it also."[2] The subjects discussed are: wherein this duty consists, why it is so neglected, some persuasions to its performance, and applications to particular groups.

The duty to help others to everlasting rest does not consist in an invasion of the minister's office by self-conceited intruders, nor in a zealous proselytizing to private opinions, nor in telling others' faults behind their backs while avoiding faithful and right admonition. Rather the duty consists first in getting one's heart affected by the misery of men's souls, being compassionate towards them, and yearning for their recovery to salvation. Then, second, the duty is to take every opportunity that you possibly can to confer privately about men's souls, and to instruct and help them to attain salvation.

But the manner in which this duty is done is of the greatest importance. Right performance increases success. Sincerity and rightness of intention require that the glory of God in the person's salvation be the only end of our work. The depth of need makes urgent a speedy application to this duty. Exhortation must proceed from compassion and love, for earnestness, not scorn, shows unselfishness of motive. Plainness and faithfulness demand a simple and open confrontation of eternal issues; no hiding of misery and danger or extenuation of sin will do. Labor seriously, zealously and effectually; heaven and hell are not to be jested about or to be passed off with a few careless thoughts. Yet, lest any run into extremes, this duty must be done with prudence and discretion; observe when sinners are fittest to hear instructions; suit the exhortation to the character of the person; be wise in using the most apt form of expression. Back all exhortation with the authority of God; turn to the very chapter and verse where he commands. Be frequent in exhortation and repeat your solicitations often. Bring the exhortation to an issue; do not stick with the issue, but keep working until the desired end is reached. Finally, be sure that not only one's word, but one's example exhorts.[3]

Besides the duty of private admonition, men must be brought to the profitable use of public ordinances. To this end every Christian should labor to procure faithful ministers where they are lacking, labor to provide suitable men (perhaps men of means can educate promising boys), draw the unconverted and weak to large and small group meetings of Christians to repeat the truths and pray and sing, and hold the ordinances and ministry in high esteem before all.[4]

The reasons for men's neglect of so great a duty are manifold: men's own gracelessness and guiltiness, secret infidelity, want of charity and compassion for men's souls, a base man-pleasing disposition, sinful bashfulness, impatience

---

[1] *Ibid.*, 814.
[2] III 213–248, SER (1649).
[3] *Ibid.*, 215–219.
[4] *Ibid.*, 219–221.

and laziness, self-seeking and self-minding (the "Am I my brother's keeper?" attitude), pride and haughtiness to lower-class people, and ignorance of duty.[1] Excuses for not witnessing abound.[2]

Motives for diligence in bringing men into everlasting rest rise from a consideration of the following truths:

1. Consider how nature and grace teach the communication of good, the neglect of which is, thus, a sin against both nature and grace.
2. Consider what value Christ placed upon souls and how he thought them worthy of his blood and sufferings.
3. Consider what fit objects of pity are men, unconverted and without hope of salvation.
4. Consider what was once your own case, in the way of perishing.
5. Consider that it is thy brother and thy neighbor that perish.
6. Consider what guilt of soul-murder, dishonor to God, and judgments upon the nation, your neglect brings upon you.
7. Consider what it will be to see your poor friends suffering eternally in flames of judgment.
8. Consider what a joy it will be to meet those you have helped to heaven.
9. Consider how many we have hardened in sin whom we ought to have drawn to life.
10. Consider how diligent the devil, inward lusts, sinful companions, and seducing teachers are to win men, and how we should be much more diligent to win them for Christ and life.
11. Consider how deeply the neglect of this duty wounds the conscience when it realizes what is left undone.
12. Consider what a seasonable time it now is to work while we yet live.
13. Consider this is a work of greatest charity which everyone, rich as well as poor, may perform.
14. Consider the happy consequences of such work when it is faithfully done:

one is God's instrument in saving souls; such souls will bless you now and forever; God will be much glorified by it; the church will gain from it; purity and the discipline of Christ will be furthered, and much personal advantage will accrue. That personal blessing includes an increase in glory through God's reward, much peace of conscience from faithful witness, a natural rejoicing which follows every good work according to its degree of goodness, an abundant honor, and a rich increase in grace.[3]

> ...those that have practised this duty most conscionably, do find, by experience, that they never go on more speedily and prosperously towards heaven than when they do most to help others thither with them. It is not here as with worldly treasure, the more you give away, the less you have; but here, the more you give, the more you have. The setting forth Christ in his fulness to others, will warm your own hearts and stir up your love.[4]

---

[1] *Ibid.*, 221–223.
[2] *Ibid.*, 223–225.
[3] *Ibid.*, 225–228.
[4] *Ibid.*, 227.

This duty which lies upon all Christians rests particularly on those with more responsibility and means. Those strong in faith and spiritually gifted are made so in order to help the weak. Those who have special familiarity with ungodly men may be, as Christ was, the means to bring sinners to God. Physicians who are much with dying men have a triple advantage: they are present at such a time, sick men are often more open and less stubborn than when they are well, and such men receive a physician's advice with great regard. Men of wealth and authority have the greatest opportunity of all men for doing good in the world. Tenants and neighbours need compassionate care and concern. Ministers and parents, likewise, must use their grave responsibilities effectually.[1]

b. Promoting the Public Good

The Christian, in his love to humanity, will seek the highest good for all men. Faith has much to do with the unconverted world.

> True morality, or the christian ethics, is the love of God and man, stirred up by the Spirit of Christ, through faith; and exercised in works of piety, justice, charity, and temperance, in order to the attainment of everlasting happiness, in the perfect vision and fruition of God.[2]

The "love of God and man... exercised in works" is the key to true Christianity. Faith itself is a sort of middle state between the unregenerate and the regenerate heart, being but the *"initium* of the latter," i.e., the coming to a real love of God.[3] The expression of love to God necessarily involves a love for holiness, self-love (which does not deny the rejection of our carnal selves), and love to others.[4] The latter three never use love of God as a means to attain themselves, but rather the action is inverse.[5] Only those who love God above all are saved.[6] There is thus not as wide a difference between faith and gospel obedience or works as some judge.[7] For good works contribute to God's glory and to our own and others' benefits. This God delights in.[8] Public service is God's greatest service; we should do our utmost for the church and the commonwealth.[9] Even bringing praises to God is a public service, for it acquaints the world with the true and joyful nature of religion.[10]

All the believer's life is characterized as "heart work and heaven work."[11] This "heaven work" includes being messengers of God's bounty. God's great mercy to mankind is that he will use us all to do good to one another, and that he gives us a sense of concern for every particular man's necessity. We best please God when we readily receive his gifts and most fully communicate them to others,[12] that is, to men of all sorts, "high and low, rich and poor, old and young, kindred, neighbours, strangers, friends, enemies, good and bad; none

---

[1] *Ibid.,* 229–248.
[2] III 686, LW (1669).
[3] I 160, CD : CEth (1673).
[4] *Ibid.,* 154.
[5] *Ibid.,* 158.
[6] III 352, SER (1649).
[7] *Ibid.,* 13; I 36, CD : CEth (1673).
[8] I 111, CD : CEth (1673).
[9] *Ibid.,* 115.
[10] *Ibid.,* 147–149.
[11] I 559, CD : CEccl (1673).
[12] IV 940, HGM (1682).

excepted that are within our power."[1] Such good works which are for the good of many include: do as much good as you are able to men's bodies in order to accomplish the greater good of souls; promote practical knowledge of great truths necessary to salvation; be more zealous in communication with neighbors; be such as you would have others be. Teach by example.[2]

In consonance herewith Baxter counsels ministers who are able to give somewhat for the relief of the poorer sort who come to them, also to help pay for the time and earnings they have lost from their work and thus encourage them to do their best in learning the catechism.[3] He also warmly commends the gracious actions of many for their gifts of charity after the disastrous London fire of 1665, especially Mr. Henry Ashurst for his solicitation from the rich abroad and direction of relief for the poor.[4] He extols, as well, Mr. Thomas Foley who "built a well-founded Hospital near *Stourbridge*, to teach poor children to read, and write, and then set them Apprentices, and endowed it with about five hundred pounds *per annum*...."[5] If only many more would follow their example, the outward reach of the gospel would be advanced. We shall illustrate Baxter's way of emphasizing this method of spreading the gospel from four of his writings.

The consequences of faith for the unconverted world are partially drawn out in a chapter from *The Life of Faith*: "How by faith to order our affections to Public Societies, and the Unconverted World."[6]

> Take heed that you lose not that common love which you owe to mankind, nor that desire of the increase of the kingdom of Christ, which must keep up in you a constant compassion to the unconverted world, viz. idolaters, infidels, and ungodly hypocrites.[7]

The "unchristian senselessness" of most zealous professors of religion is pitiful. They care only for their own sects and particular churches, rarely giving a thought to the rest of England and Wales or to the other reformed churches. Perhaps an occasional word of prayer for the poor Jews is uttered by some, but the miserable concerns of the vast heathen nations are neglected – and this when five parts in six of the world are heathen and Mohammedan, and of the sixth part the Protestants are about a sixth compared to the poor ignorant Abyssinians, Syrians, Armenians, the Greek churches, and the papists, to say nothing of in what a low state most Protestants are. Yet all these are taken care of by a few passing words in a prayer now and then! Is this man's love to God for the kingdom of Christ and for mankind? Are we to pray only for our party as if it were all the church or all the world? Is God so narrow as we? We must not only pray for the unconverted, but study what is within the reach of our power to do for their conversion. Common men can do little in comparison

---

[1] *Ibid.*, 936.
[2] *Ibid.*, 940 ff.
[3] IV 463, RP (1656).
[4] RB, III 17 (1670).
[5] RB, III 93 (1670).
[6] III 738–739, LF (1669).
[7] *Ibid.*, 738.

with Christian princes. Yet merchants and their chaplains might accomplish something if skill and zeal were united, as also would the writing and translation of fit books.

> "And greater matters might be done, by training up some scholars in the Persian, Indostan, Tartarian, and such other languages, who are for mind and body fitted for that work, and willing with due encouragement to give up themselves thereto. Were such a college erected, natives might be got to teach the languages: and no doubt but God would put it into the hearts of many young men, to devote themselves to so excellent a service; and of many rich men, to settle lands sufficient to maintain them; and many merchants would help them in their expedition." But whether those that God will so much honour, be yet born, I know not.[1]

When we see the wickedness of the world and the seeming impossibility of its cure, we should search the Scriptures for promises of its conversion and believe that God will fulfill them in his time. We must look as well to that better world, where all is light, love, and peace, rather than despair. If we fear God has deserted a great part of the world, our minds should find comfort in submission to his infinite wisdom and goodness. Do we dare think we are more gracious and merciful than God?

> And think withal, how little a spot of God's creation this earthly world is; and how incomprehensibly vast the superior regions are in comparison of it. And if all the upper parts of the world be possessed with none but holy spirits, and even this lower earth have also many millions of saints, prepared here for the things above, we have no more reason to judge God to be unmerciful, because this lower world is so bad, than we have to judge the king unmerciful, when we look into the common gaol; nor to judge of his government by the rogues in a gaol, but by his court, and all the subjects of his kingdom.[2]

Of the nine doctrines that Baxter sees in Matthew 5:16, his sermon on that text emphasizes only one: *What Light Must Shine in our Works*.[3] By way of introduction, he notes that God is his own glory and ours. Our candle does not try to show men there is no sun, but to persuade men to come into its light. When they see little lights, they will desire the greater who is the source of all light.

They are led in this way. First, they see the goodness of our works. This assumes that there are works which believers and unbelievers alike agree are good. If we could agree on no common principles, we could neither preach nor convince nor even converse with each other. However, there are many common things, approved by nature, which may be taken as granted principles. From these we lead to those principles yet denied. Second, the goodness of the deed

---

[1] *Ibid.*, 738–739.
[2] *Idem.*
[3] IV 905–920, WL.

shows the goodness of the doer. It is his subordinate honor under God to receive praise for such. Third, the goodness of Christians leads men to see the superiority of their religion. Through the doctrine and example of Christ and through the inward leading of the Spirit, Christians should be better than others. If only they were notoriously and usually so, the world would believe the gospel and the Christian religion to be the best. Finally, from the goodness of the works, that of the doer, and that of the Christian religion, men must conclude the goodness of the Spirit and the Saviour and the Father who make all the rest to be good. Thus men are led to know and glorify God by our works.[1]

A sermon to Christian merchants based on Galatians 6:10, entitled: "How to do Good to Many: or, The Public Good is the Christian's Life. Directions and Motives to It,"[2] concludes with an appeal to men of means. Could not more be done to promote the gospel in factories and foreign plantations? Mr. Eliot in New England and the Jesuits elsewhere have shown what can be done with diligence. Could not chaplains be sent to those factories in heathen lands, the kind of chaplains who "thirst for the conversion of sinners, and the enlargement of the church of Christ, and would labour skilfully and diligently therein?"[3] Could not short and fit Christian books be translated and distributed in the languages of the infidels? Could not Bibles, catechisms, and practical books be translated and sent to the poor ignorant Armenians, Greeks, Muscovites, and other such Christians? Could not more be done in other American plantations, as well as in New England, for those English who have no serious piety and for the Americans? Could not our planters be taught how to behave themselves more christianly to the natives to win them to Christ?

One of the ways this may be accomplished Baxter indicates in *A Christian Directory*:

> It is not only lawful, but one of the best works in the world, for fit persons to go on a design to convert the poor infidels and heathens where they go. Therefore the preachers of the gospel should not be backward to take any opportunity, as chaplains to ambassadors, or to factories, &c. to put themselves in such a way.[4]

c. Seeking Church Unity

The unity, concord, and peace of Christians in the Spirit is necessary: for the spiritual growth of each particular Christian; for the strengthening and accomplishment of the purpose of the church and all Christian societies, kingdoms, cities, schools, and family; for the good of the uncalled world; and for the glory and well-pleasing of Jesus Christ and of the Father.[5]

The Spirit in the church is God's appointed means to quicken and convert the infidel world. As this uniting Spirit of love works inwardly in ourselves, so

---

[1] *Ibid.*, 906–907; the nature of these works are described in detail, done as they must be in the context of holy families, well-ordered churches, and Christian kingdoms. IV 907–920.

[2] IV 935–950, HGM (1682).

[3] *Ibid.*, 949.

[4] I 841, CD : CP (1673).

[5] IV 704–715, TOW (1679); I 152, CD : CEth (1673).

it works outwardly "by attraction and communication, to draw in and assimilate others."[1] The church's unity of spirit fortifies and fits it for the conversion of the world; "A united army is likest...to be victorious."[2] Divisions have ruined Christian opportunity: the Eastern Christians were separated from the Greeks; divisions of the Greeks brought defeat by Turks; divisions of western nations furthered their conquest; divisions lost Palestine, Armenia, and the beginnings of the conversions of the Tartars. The guilt of the church is "unexcusable."[3]

> That which hath done so much to destroy churches and kingdoms...must needs unfit us all to recover the world, and convert unbelievers. ...were but christian preachers united, instead of their pernicious, church-destroying contentions, how great things might their united diligence have done.... What a happy case had the world been in![4]

The union of Christians tends to convert the world, while divisions hinder its conversion.

> They that reverence united Christians, despise them when they see them fall into divisions, and learn of themselves to condemn them all, by hearing them revile and condemn each other.[5]

Christ would not have made it so great a part of his prayer to his Father that Christians might be one, even as he and the Father were one, except to this end "that the world may know that the Father sent him" (John 17), if "this their union had not been a special means of convincing unbelievers."[6] Unity strongly invites the "reverence and consent of those without."

> By wilful dissensions we are scandals and snares to unbelievers; and if christians live not in unity, love, and peace, they rob the world of a great appointed means of their conversion....the love of christians to one another is made almost as needful as preaching to the winning of men's love to faith and holiness....so would the sweet consent of christians have won unbelievers to the love of christian faith and piety, when their divisions and wicked lives have had contrary lamentable effects.[7]

Undoubtedly if all Christians would truly establish concord and peace, it "would do more to win the heathen world, than all other means can do without it."[8] This would convince Mohammedans and an other infidels and "draw them home to Christ."[9] Not only should we be deterred from divisions, but we should "zealously study and labour with all our interest and might, for the healing of the lamentable divisions among Christians, if we have the hearts of Christians, and any sense of the interest of Christ."[10]

---

[1] IV 713, TOW (1679).
[2] Idem.
[3] Ms. Letters, II, f. 237.
[4] IV 713, 714, TOW (1679).
[5] Ibid., 714.
[6] Idem.
[7] Idem.
[8] I 602, CD : CEccl (1673).
[9] Idem.
[10] Ibid., 603, 601–607. Here Baxter gives a detailed presentation, similar to that in IV 713–715, TOW (1679); cf. also II 167–172, RCR: Chr (1666).

We must pray and "labour for the reformation and concord of all the christian churches; as the most probable means to win to Christ the world of heathens and unbelievers."[1]

Holy and charitable churches would win papists nearby; reformed papists and other Christians could win heathens and Mohammedans. They would be the salt of the earth, the lights of the world, and leaven for the whole lump.

The greatest guilt for the brokenness of the church rests at Rome's doorstep. Not satisfied with all Christian men being "mere Catholicks,"[2] papists have added their own devices to "patch up...conversion"[3] and condemn others for not accepting them.[4] But when papists make worship incomprehensible and therefore soulless, and when they worship bread as God himself, which is idolatry,[5] Protestants recoil. These and other vanities of their worship seal men in unbelief.[6] Romanists differ twenty times more among themselves than does any other "sect."[7]

We use tradition to establish history; they, to determine great matters in the resolution of faith. They take the judgments of the Roman clergy to be tradition; we take "the concurrent testimony of friends and foes, orthodox and heretics; and of all the churches throughout the world, both Greek and Latin, Ethiopian, Armenian, Protestants, &c." This testimony has "evidences of infallible moral certainty, in the very history."[8] Papists undervalue Scripture; Protestants, tradition.[9]

Papists have become cruel persecutors and in ignorant zeal have murdered thousands,[10] engineered the dastardly powder plot,[11] spread odious lies about the Reformers: Luther, Calvin, Zwingli,[12] perhaps even started the tragic London fire.[13] But still worse, they are the greatest dividers of the Christian world.[14] Rome, which is a third or fourth part of all Christians in the world, is guilty of the grand schism by cutting off all the others.[15] Its *extra ecclesiam nulla salus, ecclesia* meaning the Roman faction, has made of itself the greatest sectarian of all time.[16] One extreme is to silence Christians by the hundreds and thousands as England has done; another is to unchurch most of the world.[17]

Division tends to ruin the whole church, hinders the progress of the gospel, and injures the common interest of religion.[18] Further, it blocks the conversion of the infidel, heathen, and ungodly world;[19] it makes men seem like raging and malicious devils incarnate,[20] and it has thrown thousands into contempt

---

[1] III 739, LF (1669).
[2] RB, I 97 (1664).
[3] II 585, DP (1658).
[4] II 812, MS-I, (1661).
[5] I 599, CD : CEc (1673); IV 158, CF (1682).
[6] I 153, CD : CEth (1673).
[7] IV 745, TC (1659).
[8] I 589, CD : CEccl (1673).
[9] II 160, RCR : Chr (1666).
[10] I 39, 113, CD : CEth (1673); 607, CD : CEeccl (1673); 859, CD : CP (1673).
[11] II 347, UI : US (1655).
[12] I 186, CD : CEth (1673); III 451, TS-D (1659).
[13] RB, III 18 (1670).
[14] III 426, TS-D (1659).
[15] I 599, CD : CEccl (1673); IV 269, PM (1672).
[16] IV 738, TC (1659); II 345, UI : US (1655); RB, II 224 (1665).
[17] IV 1003, JC (1682).
[18] I 150, CD : CEth (1673).
[19] III 701, LF (1669); IV 730, TC (1659); 915, WL.
[20] III 965–966, OP (1683).

of all religion.¹ Church-tearing scandals are the great stumbling-block to conversion.² Has anything in the world done more to disable us for God's service than this? Unity might do wonders for the church of Christ.³

The sin of division, nearly catastrophic for the church's establishment in the world,⁴ necessitates plain warnings of the damnable character of this sin and utter abhorrence for it,⁵ and strenuous attempts to re-establish divinely-intended unity.⁶ For this Baxter expended rigorous personal efforts,⁷ vigorously supported the world-wide efforts of the ecumenist John Dury⁸ and as vigorously opposed the separatist views and actions of John Owen.⁹ He wrote twenty whole treatises and parts of many others directing serious Christians to ways of unity,¹⁰ and sought to remedy the tragedy of past schisms¹¹ by close analysis of their self-centered causes¹² and by careful delineation of true church unity in Christ and essential doctrine.¹³

d. Teaching Essential Doctrine

In the attempt to re-establish church unity, in the requirements for church membership, and in the instruction of new Christians, Baxter constantly accents essential doctrine. In the communication of the gospel, begin with the greater

---

[1] IV 407, RP (1656).
[2] IV 915, WL.
[3] IV 431, RP (1656); 712, TOW (1679).
[4] Of the countless passages concerning the abject *sin* of division, some examples are: I 804, CD : CP (1673); II 309, UI : ChW (1655); 669, SB (1662); 888, RM (1653); III 54, SER (1649); 356, TS-D (1659); 650, 704, LF (1669); IV 126, 133, CF (1682); 398, 406, 465, RP (1656); 528, CAM (1662); 686, CathU (1657); 695, TOW (1679); 742, TC (1659); RB, I 74–78 (1664).
[5] I 273, CD : CEth (1673); 759, 895, CD : CP (1673); RB, Appendix 72–73.
[6] Ms. Treatises VI, Item No. 201, ff. 203–204 (=6/7).
I 90, CD : CEth (1673); 739, 927, CD : CP (1673); II 1050–1056, CSCC (1669); III 54, SER (1649); 578, LF (1669); IV 395, RP (1656); 611, TKL (1689); 942, HGM (1682); 1026, FS (1683).
[7] I 190, CD : CEth (1673); 613, CD : CEccl (1673); II 547, NN (1663); 731, SB (1662); 982, DW (1668); 1030–1031, CSCC (1669); RB, II 437 (1665); III 123, SER (1649).
[8] IV 581, TKL (1689); 730, TC (1659); RB, I 117 (1664), II 295–297 (1665); Ms. Letters II (to "John Durie," 1658), ff. 74–75, 76, 77, 96–97.
[9] II 547, NN (1663); RB, I 111, 125–126 (1664); II 198–199 (1665); III 197–198 (1675ff.).
[10] I 590, 595, CD : CEccl (1673); II 723, SB (1662); 1057, CSCC (1669); III 3, SER (1649); IV 324–328, 337, CR (1658); 428–431, 463–468, RP (1656); 588, TKL (1689); 687, CU (1657); 695, TOW (1679); 946–947, HGM (1682); 1010, JC (1682); RB, I 97 (1664); II 181, 186 (1665); Appendix 73, 123, 127ff.; Ms. Treatises IV, Item No. 80, ff. 168–169 and Item No. 107, f. 377.
[11] Discussed in some detail in II 345, UI : US (1665); 983, DW (1668); III 745 ff., LF (1669); 965–966, OP (1683); IV 269, PM (1672).
[12] I 189, 213, CD : CEth (1673); 761, 877, CD : CP (1673); II 166–167, RCR : Chr (1666); 241, UI (1655); 344, UI : US (1655); 807, MS-I (1661); 990, DW (1668); 1022, CSCC (1669); III 356, 371, TS-D (1659); 699, LF (1669); IV 225, PM (1672); 553, 590, TKL (1689); 750, TC (1659); 942, HGM (1682); RB, I 74–78 (1664); Appendix 130.
[13] I 646, CD : CEccl (1673); II 269, 286, UI : SpW (1655); 499, TCon (1657); 673, 708, SB (1662); 1050, CSCC (1669); III 636, LF (1669); IV 95–97, CF (1682); 497, VR (1660); IV 733–740, 758, TC (1659); RB, I 118–119 (1664); Appendix, 69.

common truths.[1] Put the essential necessary truths first.[2] Demonstrate the "primitive fundamental verities" and their importance.[3] Teach all that is of "flat necessity to salvation" and as much of the rest as possible.[4] No one that "hath not the vitals of theology is capable of going beyond a fool in philosophy."[5] Teach the greatest, most certain, and necessary things: "Hence it is that a preacher must oft be upon the same things, because the matters of necessity are few."[6] Repetition of the essential truths of Christianity is as necessary as daily food.[7] Communicate that "square foundation which will bear up all the faith of the saints...."[8] Hold fast the substance of the Christian religion.[9] Knowledge of the true nature of Christianity is essential, and understanding is the passage-way to the heart.[10] Use Christ's method (Matthew 28:19-21): disciple, baptize, teach–in that order.[11] Seek the ancient fundamental truths:[12] "By the fundamentals we mean the essentials of the christian faith, or religion."[13] Keep the smaller controversial truths in the background; put the essential necessary truths first.[14] Distinguish between the universal laws of Christ and particular restricted ones such as immersion, women's hats, and the holy kiss.[15]

Too many men plunge themselves into inordinate expositions of the book of Revelation and other prophecies, or insist on smaller points of doctrine to the undervaluation of greater; this does great wrong to themselves and to the Church of God. "...God hath made the points that are of necessity to salvation, to be few and plain."[16]

So few of the multitudes of Christians have a clear idea of the real grounds of faith.[17] Take as examples the matters of the infallibility of the Scriptures and the making of confessions. Some insist belief in the infallible Scripture is one of the absolute essentials of Christianity.[18] But thousands are saved without believing such.[19] Some parts of the Scripture are not necessary to salvation; many have been saved who doubted the authenticity of portions of the Scriptures; others have been saved through preaching and catechisms without personal knowledge of the Scripture; and many were Christians before the Scriptures were written or known. Thus it is evident that a certain faith may rest

---

[1] I 592, CD : CEccl (1673).
[2] I 40, CD : CEth (1673); II 546, NN (1663).
[3] I 269. CD : CEth (1673).
[4] II 387, UI : AR (1655).
[5] IV 424, RP (1656).
[6] Ibid., 392.
[7] II 400, TCon (1657).
[8] II 965, RMeth (1653).
[9] I 50, CD : CEth (1673).
[10] II 378, UI : US (1655); 586, DP (1658).
[11] II 389, UI : AR (1655); H. Boer makes this point in his *That My House May Be Filled*, Chapter 5: "The Method"; "The basic method of all mission work and evangelism has been laid down by our Lord Himself in the great commission .... The order to be followed which is here plainly set forth is: 1. disciple, 2. baptize, 3. teach." (53).
[12] II 634, DP (1658).
[13] IV 731, TC (1659); Baxter enumerates five fundamentals in Ms. Treatises IV, ff. 168, Item No. 80.
[14] I 40, 177–178, CD : CEth (1673); II 242, UI (1655).
[15] I 557–558, CD : CEccl (1673); II 308, UI : ChW (1655).
[16] III 739, LF (1669).
[17] II 242, UI (1655).
[18] Baxter disagreed with John Owen on this point; cf. Ms. Treatises V, Item No. 10.
[19] II 279, UI : SpW (1655).

upon the principles of the Christian religion, though it may be uncertain of certain parts of the Scripture.[1] Explicit belief of all the Scripture itself was never required from primitive times to the present of every one that was baptized, nor of any man who entered the ministry.[2]

The making of new confessions and enlarging our creeds, making more fundamentals than God ever made, and the composing (and thus imposing) of our creeds and confessions in our own words and phrases rather than using those of the Scriptures, have plagued the church for a thousand years.[3] Dogmatical Christianity cheats many thousands into hell.[4] So many, who agree on essential points of doctrine, accuse brothers for differences of opinion.[5] It is the bane of unity when men make inferred opinions the seat of unity and will not unite in the essentials of Christianity, and endeavor to live in accord and love in the rest.[6] We may "lay the unity of the church upon nothing but what is essential to the church."[7] All true churches are agreed in the substance of their religion.[8] Nothing may be made necessary to the unity of the Church or the communion of Christians which God has not himself directed.[9] Therefore, we may take nothing as necessary to Christianity and salvation which is not in Scripture and held necessary by all Christians in every age and place. To do so is to unchurch the church.[10] "Mere Christianity" is a sufficient qualification for love and concord.[11]

> He is a christian fit for our communion, who is baptized in infancy, and owneth it solemnly at age; and so is he that was not baptized till he himself believed.[12]

There is always the danger and sin of two extremes: despairing of concord and a consequent laxation into liberty for all and unjust toleration on the one hand, and making too much necessary for church union and communion on the other.[13] Therefore it is necessary to distinguish between certainties and uncertainties, necessary things and unnecessary things, catholic verities and private opinions. The former include that which has been received by all Christians everywhere and always ("*quae ab omnibus, ubique et sember sunt retentea*" – Vincent Licensius).[14] The latter include a "variety of fallible, mutable church laws, and terms of concord" which "will be the engine of perpetual discord."[15] Baxter warns his Kidderminster flock in his farewell sermon:

> Maintain union and communion with all true christians on earth; and therefore, hold to catholic principles of mere christianity, without which you must needs crumble into sects.[16]

---

[1] I 713, CD : CEccl (1673); II 210 ff., MR (1671); IV 574, TKL (1689).
[2] IV 576, TKL (1689).
[3] III 83, SER (1649).
[4] III 624, LF (1669).
[5] IV 508, VR (1660).
[6] IV 748, TC (1659).
[7] *Ibid.*, 757.
[8] I 762, CD : CP (1673).
[9] I 607, CD : CEccl (1673).
[10] I 595, CD : CEccl (1673); IV 929.
[11] IV 942, HGM (1682).
[12] *Idem.*
[13] IV 724–728, TOW (1679).
[14] IV 395, RP (1656).
[15] IV 942, HGM (1682); cf. III 235, SER (1649).
[16] IV 1026, FS (1683).

The method of the ancient Christian church was to teach the people first the creed and sum of Christianity. The right order, thus, of grounding and settling one's faith is not first to require proof that all the Scripture is the word of God, but first to "prove the marrow of them which is the christian religion."[1] This conformed to the practice of the apostles who first preached the sum of the gospel, then baptized, and only then taught them all the things of Christ, i.e., the rest of the Scriptures.[2] The universal primitive church sets the standard as well for the spirit of reverence and charity with which all controversy is to be judged.[3] Heretics like Simon and Marcion were judged for denying the fundamentals of the faith.[4] Synods may have to judge in certain cases today,[5] for likely no universal general church council will ever be held due to age of the bishops, difference of languages, and great distances.[6]

All the ancient church accepted the Apostles Creed, the Decalogue, and the Lord's Prayer as containing all that is necessary to salvation as the sum of their religion.[7]

> ...the primitive, pure, simple christianity consisted in the daily serious use of the great materials of the *Creed, Lord's Prayer*, and *Ten Commandments*, contracted in the words of our baptismal covenant.[8]

The baptismal covenant, as explained in the three forms above, is the summary of all that is essential to Christianity.[9] This covenant is not simply being baptized into the Triune Name, but it involves a necessary consent to our relations and duties to our Creator, Redeemer, and Sanctifier,[10] which consent must be expressed in our lives.[11]

Both Scripture and tradition establish the baptismal covenant and the three forms: Apostle's Creed, Lord's Prayer, and Ten Commandments, as the essential principles and fundamentals of the Christian faith.[12] Baxter often marvelled that the authority of the apostles, the miracles, and the authority of the Scriptures were not included in the creed, but later understood these to be implicitly included under the confession of the Holy Ghost.[13] The heads of doctrine to be taught beyond the minimum for faith are legion,[14] but of primary signif-

---

[1] III 602–603, TKL (1689).
[2] *Idem.*
[3] I 559, CD : CEccl (1673); II 266–267, UI : SpW (1655); III 481, CW (1657).
[4] II 298, UI : ChW (1655).
[5] III 235, SER (1649).
[6] IV 111, CF (1682).
[7] RB, II 198 (1665).
[8] III 764, DL : KG (1663).
[9] I 480, CD : CEc (1673); II 279, UI : SpW (1655); 843, MS–I (1661); IV 65, CF (1682); 179, PM (1672); RB, Appendix, 127.
[10] II 659, DP (1658).
[11] II 843, MS–I (1661); In *The Poor Man's Family Book*, Baxter presents the simplest statement of the baptismal covenant twice: first, in the form of *The Holy Covenant* which a person must believe to be Christian, and, second, in the form of *The Shortest Catechism*, IV 199, 261–262, PM (1672).
[12] II 1003, DW (1668); IV 576, TKL (1689).
[13] IV 95, CF (1682).
[14] I 559–562, CD : CEccl (1673); II 84–87, RCR : Chr (1666); 571–572, NN (1663); 648, DP (1658); III 246, SER (1649); 622, LF (1669).

icance is to see that the three forms be observed: "then no error or difference will be damning to you."[1] The baptismal covenant, or covenant of grace,[2] is "nothing else but the universal promise in the gospel,"[3] that all who are truly repentant are saved.[4] The essence of holiness, thus, lies bound up in consent to the three articles of this gracious covenant:

> 1. That we give up ourselves to God, as our God and reconciled Father in Jesus Christ. 2. That we give up ourselves to Jesus Christ, as our Redeemer and Saviour, to recover us, reconcile us, and bring us unto God. 3. That we give up ourselves to the Holy Ghost as our Sanctifier, to guide and illuminate us, and perfect the image of God upon us, and prepare us for glory.[5]

The three forms are the means to the fulfillment of our baptismal vow: the creed as "the summary rule to tell us what our understandings must believe." The Lord's Prayer as "the summary rule to tell us what our wills must desire and our tongues must ask," and the Ten Commandments as "the summary rules of our practice." And after these, the Holy Scripture is taken as "the more large and perfect rule of all."[6] In consonance with these, Baxter requires only two things for church membership:

> And therefore if any man do but these two things: 1. By yea or nay, do signify to me, that he understandeth the truth, when I put the matter of nothing but the baptismal covenant into my questions; 2. And do manifest serious willingness accordingly, by avoiding evil, and using God's means; I dare not, I will not refuse that person from the communion of the church; though I would do as much as the most rigid censurer to bring such up to greater knowledge.[7]

If the covenant and the three forms be granted as the essence of Christianity, the name Christian applies to all who accept these.

> The reformed churches, the Lutherans, the Abassines, the Coptics, the Syrians, the Armenians, the Jacobites, the Georgians, the Maronites, the Greeks, the Moscovites, and the Romanists, do all receive baptism in all its visible essentials, and profess all the essentials of the christian religion, though not with the same integrity.[8]

We are saved as members of the holy catholic church. The name of a Christian is more honorable than that of any division or subdivision among Christians, "whether Greek, or papist, or Protestant, or prelatist, or Presbyterian, or Independent, or Anabaptist."[9] Perhaps some things are absolutely essential to

---

[1] I 595, CD : CEccl (1673).
[2] II 856, MS–I (1661).
[3] I 560, CD : CEccl (1673).
[4] II 144, RCR : Chr (1666).
[5] II 856, MS–I (1661).
[6] I 481, CD : CEc (1673); cf. RB, I 119 (1664).
[7] IV 561, TKL (1689).
[8] I 627, CD : CEccl (1673); cf. also Ms. Treatises IV, Item No. 8, ff. 168.
[9] II 571, NN (1663); cf. II 269, UI : SpW 1655).

all of us which are not so to Indians and Turks.[1] But for those under the last edition of the covenant of grace, the essentials are clear.[2] The tragedy is that Turks and pagans agree in wickedness better than Christians in the truth; the cause of all our trouble is making dark parts of doctrine to be our creed.[3] Demanding unnecessary things causes church divisions and sends men to Rome,[4] though papists and Protestants have basically much in common.[5] To be of a party is easy, to be a Christian is not. To love a sect or particular group is easy, to have catholic charity is not. The cause of Christ and the progress of the gospel are lamed by men who are zealous for private opinion but are enemies to the love of saints.[6]

Only a return to primitive and essential doctrine, as expressed in the three forms, can bring Christians to unity of purpose in the fulfillment of the church's calling to preach the gospel, by word and by deed, to all the world.

### C. THE REDEMPTION OF THE WORLD

The "extensive interest" of the church (as Baxter calls it) has a double dimension: the unbeliever and the non-Christian world. Both are objects of the believer's witness at home and the church's witness abroad.

*1. The Need in England and Abroad*

The church situation in England and in foreign countries leaves a great deal to be desired. In England where the gospel abounds more than in any other nation in the world, hosts of the common people live in sensuality and religious unconcern. Men forget that prayerless families make powerless lives. Religiously uninstructed children and servants are too often brought up by cursing householders, indifferent hypocrites, and worldly drunkards.[7] The abuse of money and time in outright sins of immorality and drunkenness, in needless dice and cards, in often foul stage-plays and cruel gaming, in useless play-books and feigned histories, in wilful laziness and slothfulness of spirit, while the soul remains under God's curse and while God's work is undone, is self-deluding blindness.[8]

Not that money and time spent in lawful recreation is wrong; there is a time for jesting, for comedies and tragedies, for hawking and a drink of wine, even perhaps for a game of cards and courting.[9] There are millions of things which are indifferent in themselves; each natural being is good in itself.[10]

---

[1] III 92, SER (1649).
[2] IV 111, CF (1682).
[3] III 57, SER (1649); I 630, CD : CEccl (1673).
[4] I 807, CD : CP (1673).
[5] I 595, CD : CEccl (1673).
[6] II 571, NN (1663).
[7] II 504, CU (1657).
[8] I 22, 56, 310–313, 318, CD : CEth (1673); 478–479, CD : CEc (1673); II 376, UI : US (1655); 778, SB (1662); 821, 833, MS–I (1661); 940, RMeth (1653); III 115, 286, SER (1649); 411–412, TS–D (1659); 902, DA (1671); IV 17, 23, CC (1681); 522, FP (1659).
[9] I 377, 388, CD : CEth (1673); 556, 566, CD : CEccl (1673); III 998, DT (1683); I 840, CD : CP (1673); III 197, SER (1649).
[10] I 566, CD : CEccl (1673).

> The world and all God's works are good; and to the pure they are pure; to the sanctified they are sanctified; that is, they are devoted to the service of God.... But yet I must tell you, the world, and all God's creatures in it, are too good to be sacrificed to the flesh and to the devil; and not good enough to be loved and preferred before God, and your innocency and salvation.[1]

The abuse of time and opportunity has been the downfall of most men. Rich men and masters, while over-working and under-paying for their own gain, plead that their workers need the Lord's Day for recreation.[2] Ignorance of God results.[3] Ignorant men plunge into useless waste of opportunity and licentious excess.[4] Such foolish delight distorts life. Men love not eternity, but flesh. Blind fools forget this body will soon be worm-eaten and rotten.[5]

Although the world is "that wilderness which is the way to the promised land of rest", we are not to secede from it.[6] To throw away talents is easier than to use them.

> It is one thing to creep into a monk's cell, or an anchorite's cave, or a hermit's wilderness, or Diogene's tub; and another thing truly to be crucified to the world; and in the midst of the creatures to live above them unto God....[7]

He who commanded us to "use the world as not abusing it" never meant to forbid us the use of it. Rather are we to exercise our lawful trades and labors.[8] Self-denial does not denounce marriage, secular trades, or public office.[9]

The soul's greatest advantage and the other's greatest good combine to guide in the choice of a Christian calling.[10] Those callings useful to public good are "magistrates,...pastors and teachers of the church, schoolmasters, lawyers, & husbandmen... and next to them are mariners, clothiers, booksellers, tailors, and such other that are employed about things most necessary to mankind." [11] Other occupations, though possibly lawful in themselves, such as, tobacco-sellers, lace-sellers, periwig-makers, etc., are of so little use that we should choose one where more good to others is done.[12]

But it is diligence in one's providential place that is crucial. To please oneself while multitudes go hungry and to be slothful in one's calling is as culpable as fornication and drunkenness.[13] "We are members of the world and church, and we must labour to do good to many." We must propagate the truth, honor God's cause, bring souls home, edify the church, and further the salvation of as many as we can.[14]

---

[1] III 707, LF (1669).
[2] III 904, DA (1671).
[3] II 504, CU (1657).
[4] Cf. III 355–475, TS–D (1659).
[5] I 305–318, 337, CD : CEth (1673); III 417, 445, TS–D (1659); cf. II 795, MS–I (1661).
[6] I 750, CD : CP (1673).
[7] III 496, CW (1657).
[8] *Idem*; II 670, 675, SB (1662).
[9] III 454–456, TS–D (1659); cf. II 551, NN (1663).
[10] III 561, CW (1657); 719, LF (1669).
[11] I 377, CD : CEth (1673).
[12] *Idem.*
[13] III 716 ff., LF (1669).
[14] III 974, DT (1683); cf. IV 188, PM (1672).

Especially magistrates have great opportunity for God's service and public good. They are God's officers for the public good. As such they are to be obeyed,[1] except when to do so demands disobedience of the Scriptures.[2] A learned ministry, unity and concord of the churches, subservience to the laws of God, restraint of sin, and promoting faith and holiness abroad, require magistrates' efforts.[3]

> ...what mortal enemies those men are to their souls, that would persuade them that they must not, as rulers, do good to the souls of men, and to the church as such; nor further the reformation, nor propagate the gospel, nor establish Christ's order in the churches of their country, any otherwise than by a common maintaining the peace and liberties of all.[4]

As Dr. Owen has rightly said, if rulers become "no more for Christ than for Mahomet," the "Lord Jesus will forsake them, as they have forsaken him...."[5] Should magistrates in tolerating heretics and Quakers rule as if there were no Christ or church or heaven or hell?[6] The pastor's office is to judge of Christian profession and life without use of force,[7] but it is the magistrate's duty to punish wrongs.[8] Care needs to be taken not to give magisterial power to the clergy.[9] In godly rule, magistrates perform highest service to God.[10] They will find the godliest Christian to be the most loyal subject and best help to the Commonwealth.[11]

Tragically enough, says Baxter, neither private persons were taking their calling to divine service seriously, nor were rulers exercising their responsibility to God as they should. Under Queen Mary was this notoriously so.[12] Fortunes rose and fell under succeeding rulers.[13] Great problems were created by the usurpation of Cromwell and the royally favored sectarians.[14] Relations between the state and religion had steadily deteriorated.[15] Moral conditions were as bad as the political.

But ecclesiastical problems, if anything, were worse. The Savoy Conference had gone into unjustifiable deliverances, led by the "overorthodox doctors" Cheynell and Owen.[16] The Westminster Assembly deliverances were useful, so long as subscription was not required.[17] But primitive episcopacy is not Presbyterianism.[18] Wide divergences ruin church unity in England. Elsewhere deadliest enemies live together: Turks and Christians in Hungary; Orthodox and heretics in Poland, Helvetia, and Holland. But Protestants cannot live with Protestants in England.[19] "Christ hath been pleading with England these four-

---

[1] RB, III 162 (1670).
[2] I 761, CD : CP (1673).
[3] I 741–743, CD : CP (1673).
[4] II 941, RMeth (1653).
[5] *Idem.*
[6] III 356–357, TS-D (1659).
[7] I 673, CD : CEccl (1673).
[8] IV 303, CR (1658).
[9] I 766, CD : CP (1673).
[10] II 552, NN (1663).
[11] I 766, CD : CP (1673); II 723, SB (1662); 1047, CSCC (1669).
[12] III 197, SER (1649).
[13] II 282, UI : SpW (1655).
[14] RB, I 71–72, 98–100 (1664).
[15] II 347, UI : US (1655).
[16] RB, I 104 (1664), II 199 (1665).
[17] RB, I 73–74, 122 (1664).
[18] RB, II 371 (1665).
[19] IV 526, CAM (1662).

score years and more, by the word of his gospel" to forsake her sin. Yet even bloody arguments have failed to persuade.[1] Four years of war should have convinced the people that God is dead serious with them.[2] But it has not. "O sinful! O miserable land!"[3]

Some have tried for reformation and holy living. All serious-minded men are labelled Puritans and Precisionists and viewed as Lot in Sodom. "O England! Hadst thou none to make the football of thy scorn, but the servants of the most high God?"[4] Impositions by the Protestant prelates became the engines of division in the church.[5] The prelates, though not they only, became the sect-makers.[6] The church splintered on this rock into three types of conformists and four of Noncomformists.[7] Yet the difference is not so great as to make separation from the church lawful even now.[8]

The great question centered upon whether the priest should refuse communion to those who for conscience sake refused to kneel for it.[9] Conformity to the manner of worship where one is would be wisest, whether standing, sitting, or kneeling.[10] One is not to follow his conscience in errors.[11] Certainly there is no wrong *per se* in using the Book of Common Prayer[12] or form prayers.[13] Though simplicity in worship is usually preferable since it is "the ordinary attendant of sincerity,"[14] much of church liturgy should be optional, e.g., printed images (as in the Genevan Bible),[15] ministerial laying on of hands,[16] fasting,[17] observance of saints' days,[18] use of words such as "sacrifice," "altar," and "priest,"[19] and use of the cross and surplice.[20] Reformation is not casting out a few ceremonies, changing some vestures and gestures and forms.

> O no, sirs! It is the converting and saving of souls that is our business. That is the chiefest part of the reformation that doth the most good and tendeth most to the salvation of the people. ...I am verily persuaded... you will do much more for a true reformation, and that peaceably without meddling with controverted points....[21]

But imposition left no choice; conform or be silenced.[22] Two thousand were silenced.[23] Thousands of ungodly who needed ministering were ignored.[24] Min-

---

[1] III 155, SER (1649).
[2] *Ibid.*, 57–58, 164.
[3] IV 528, CAM (1662).
[4] II 745–746, SB (1662); II 952, GGV (1671); III 368, TS–D (1659); 533, CW (1657); 899, DA (1671); IV 188–190, PM (1672); 399, RP (1656); 524–525, CAM (1662).
[5] RB, II 395 (1665); cf. 247–248.
[6] RB, III 43 (1670).
[7] RB, II 386 (1665).
[8] RB, II 438 (1665).
[9] RB, II 360 (1665).
[10] I 617, CD : CEccl (1673); 273, CD : CEth (1673).
[11] I 499, CD : CEc (1673).
[12] *Idem*; IV 486, VR (1660).
[13] I 486, 499, CD : CEc (1673); 555, 679, CD : CEccl (1673); II 539, CU (1657); 558–559, NN (1663); IV 237, PM (1672); 486, VR (1660). In IV 272–288 Baxter offers several form prayers for private, family, and church use.
[14] IV 494, VR (1660).
[15] I 698, CD : CEccl (1673).
[16] IV 306, CR (1658).
[17] I 690, SB (1662); IV 161, CF (1682).
[18] I 620–622, DP (1658).
[19] IV 160, CF (1682).
[20] IV 399, RP (1656).
[21] IV 449, VR (1660).
[22] RB, II 393 (1665).
[23] RB, Appendix, 121.
[24] IV 695, TOW (1679).

isters had no salary; common people were without pastors.[1] Persecution followed.[2] Morley (Bishop of Winchester, 1597–1684) claimed that strong measures were necessary to remove the "hindrances which Calvin had laid in the way."[3] But such a "prelacy is no part of the Christian Religion."[4] The Christian Kingdom, which England has been for many ages, is thereby threatened.

> ...the Church of *England*, as it is a Christian Kingdom, containing Confederate Churches under a Christian King and Laws, is that very Form that Christ offered to settle in *Judea*, and did settle by *Constantine*.[5]

The troubled church in England[6] was but a little wind compared to the storms brewing throughout Europe. Only one-sixth of the world can be called Christian,[7] and so few of those are orthodox reformed Christians.[8] There are but three Christian kingdoms in all the world.[9] Persecution of Christians by Christians has killed hundreds of thousands,[10] hindered the progress of the gospel and damned millions of souls.[11] Tyranny on the part of cruel princes and Roman Christians is the great sin which keeps the gospel from the heathen and infidel world by keeping away the means of knowledge.[12] We are all troubled by the confused state of the church abroad.[13] The poor churches in Ethiopia and Greece have no pastors.[14] Ignorance of the gospel prevails in vast regions.[15] Sins of the unreformed church in Rome and of the Eastern and Southern churches against the second commandment hinders acceptance of the gospel by the Mohammedan and heathen world, and confirms them in their infidelity.[16]

> Whereas, if the unreformed churches in the east, west, and south were reformed, and had a learned, pious, able ministry, that clearly preached and seriously applied the word of God, and worshipped God with under-

---

[1] III 121, SER (1649).
[2] *Ibid.*, 233.
[3] RB, II 218 (1665).
[4] RB, III 169 (1670).
[5] RB, Appendix, 77–78.
[6] Baxter believes that English divines are the soundest in the world [ III 191, SER (1649)] and exercised a moderating influence at the Synod of Dordrecht. I 651, CD : CEccl (1673); III 189–190, 194, 206, SER (1649); IV 581, TKL (1689); 1010, FS (1683); RB. I 113 (1664). Advice given by Puritan advisors at the Synod of Dordrecht is in the records of that gathering. (*Acta Ofte Handelinghen des Nationalen Synodi*. Inden Name onses Heeren Jesu Christi. Ghehouden door Authoriteyt der Hoogh: Mogh: Heeren Staten Generall des Vereenichden Nederlandts Tot Dordrecht, Anno 1618. ende 1619., Ghedruckt 1621.) Material is located in Book I: 14, 24–26, 32–34, 63; Book III: 3–18, 114–120, 183–195, 269–292.
[7] I 300, CD : CEth (1673); II 146, RCR : Chr (1666); IV 526, CAM (1662).
[8] I 144, CD : CEth (1673).
[9] I 752, CD : CP (1673). Baxter does not say which Kingdoms he means.
[10] I 779, 859, CD : CP (1673); 913–914, MP (1661); II 345, UI : US (1655); IV 594, TKL (1689); 938, HGM (1682).
[11] I 791, 847, CD : CP (1673).
[12] II 134–135, 157, RCR : Chr (1666).
[13] III 709, LF (1669).
[14] II 869, MS–I (1661).
[15] IV 20, CC (1681); 594, TKL (1689).
[16] I 153, CD : CEth (1673).

standing, gravity, reverence, and serious spirituality, and lived a holy, heavenly, mortified, self-denying conversation, this would be the way to propagate christianity, and win the infidel world to Christ.[1]

But there are few such teachers; "the Greek church, the Muscovites, the Abassines, Syrians, Armenians, papists, and most of the christians of the world" are in a sad case for want of them.[2] What help and grace is sorely needed for God's scattered flock in this wilderness.[3]

> The other...that are called christians, alas! consist most of people bred up in lamentable ignorance, mostly barbarous or debased by the oppression of tyrants, such as the Muscovites, most of the Greeks, the Abassines, Armenians, and many eastern sects and nations. What ignorance the vulgar papists are bred in in Italy, Spain, Germany, Poland, France, and other countries, and what an enmity to true reformation prevaileth in princes, priests, and people; and by what lying and cruelty they fight against truth, and what inquisitions, murders, and inhuman massacres have been in their powerful means, I need not use many words to tell. And are the protestant reformed churches free from fleshly, wordly, wicked men? From ignorant, malignant, cruel enemies to truth, and piety, and peace?...hell [has] found [a] cloak for malicious accusations, enmity, and discord.[4]
>
> Alas poor England (and more than England, even all the Christian world) into what confusion and misery hath selfishness plunged thee! Into how many pieces are thou broken....[5]

## 2. The Great Hindrances

The indifference, quarrelling, and ignorance in England and throughout the world make plain that the grand war in heaven is being fought out in human history. Satanic armies are near at hand. As the head of the war in heaven must be broken, so must the earthly heads of satanic power. These exist within Christian lands–monarchs and prelates, and without – Mohammedans and heathen.[6]

---

[1] *Idem.*

[2] I 797, CD : CP (1673).

At a later date, Baxter wrote: "But I must recant some former apprehensions: I have thought the Armenians, the Syrians, the Georgians, the Coptics, the Abassines, the Greeks, more miserable for want of polite literature, than now I judge them. Though I contemn it not as the Turks do, and the Muscovites; yet I perceive that had men but the knowledge of the holy Scriptures, yea, of the summaries of true religion, they might be good and happy men, without much more.

I will not cease praying for the further illumination and reformation of those churches: but I will repent of my hard thoughts of the providence of God, as if he had cast them almost off, and had few holy souls among them. For aught I know they may be better than most of Europe." IV 620, TKL (1689).

[3] II 1063, CSCC (1669).
[4] IV 526, CAM (1662).
[5] III 372, TS–D (1659).
[6] IV 552, CAM (1662).

a. Within the Christian Church

Monarchs not true to their calling hinder the progress of the gospel. The grand crime which keeps out the gospel from nations of infidels and pagans throughout the earth and eclipses its glory in popish principalities is the sin of tyranny.[1] Although almost all men are of the religion of their home country, whether Turks, "Bonzii," Chinese, "the people of Peru," Siamese, Americans, Brazilians, or "Lappians,"[2] having been trained in it from youth,[3] the common opinion of one's countrymen is no ground for one's personal faith.[4] The duty of Christian countries adjoining Mohammedan and heathen lands is to do their utmost to convert them by teaching, through a uniting spirit of love. "...the Spirit in the church... is God's appointed means to quicken and convert the infidel world."[5] Yet, when monarchs hinder this work, they are to be resisted.

Baxter presents seventeen arguments to prove an affirmative answer to the question: "Whether it be the duty of any who cannot work miracles to preach or publicly propagate true Religion when the Supreme Ruler or Lawes forbid it."[6] In doing so, Baxter especially opposes Spinoza (*Tract. Polit. Theolog.*) but also Hobbes (*de Cive* and *Leviathan*) and those called Seekers. All Christians, Baxter maintains, agree on the affirmative except some doubters of the faith who think Mohammedans and heathen do not need the gospel, since they will be saved without it. Those who agree on the affirmative do not mean to say, that a minister should leave greater obligations at home to seek opportunity elsewhere, that one sickly or aged is bound to go to foreign lands to preach, or that one should go where certain death awaits him (even Paul left Damascus in a basket!). Not that life is to be preferred above duty, but actions are subject to common sense and reason. No man is bound to be a fool. If I know that preaching a particular sermon will make it impossible to preach any more, it is a sin to so cast myself out of the vineyard.

> I ought not to preferre preaching once to an hundred before a probability of preaching some yeares to thousands. It is for future labour that men must lawfully preserve their lives.[7]

But when "I have reason to think that my martyrdome will do more good than my preaching longer, I must preach though I die for it...."[8]

Not only the natural law of love requires propagation of the true religion; the principles of Christianity clearly require it as well. Men cannot be saved in every religion; the gospel of Christ must therefore be preached. Christ himself, the apostles, and the martyrs in the early church preached against the will of the rulers. That which they did is a duty for us. In addition, Christ instituted a ministry unto the end of the world "to preach to & disciple & baptize all

---

[1] II 157, RCR : Chr (1666).
[2] III 384, TS–D (1659); IV 603, TKL (1689).
[3] I 427, CD : CEc (1673); IV 24, CC (1681).
[4] IV 163, CF (1682).
[5] IV 713, TOW (1679).
[6] Ms. Treatises V, Item No. 146 (5/15), ff. 74–75.
[7] *Idem.*
[8] *Idem.*

nations, without excepting those whose Lawes forbad it."[1] Matthew 28:19, 20 leaves no doubt about this.

> That is Lawfull and a duty by which Christ planted his churches and saved souls for the first 300 yeares. But by preaching the true religion against the Lawes & will of sovereigne rulers, Christ gathered his church and saved soules for 300 yeares: Therefore &c. // He that denyeth the Major is no Christian: And he that denyeth the Minor knoweth not the common history of the church.[2]

The propagation of Christ's kingdom is the best, most necessary and grateful work to be done in the world. "To leave the world justly to the Devil & damnation, if we can helpe it, is inhumane & unchristian."[3] About four-sixths of the world is heathen, one-sixth Mohammedan, and most of the last sixth are papists. In nearly all of these lands, the princes and laws keep out Christianity; most of the people would hear the gospel if men were permitted to preach.

> I take it to be the greatest duty encumbent on Christian Princes and people uppon earth to endeavour the conversion of all these lands. If they can procure the consent of their kings, – it's best: But if they cannot they should their best without it.[4]

Those who disagree condemn most of the propagation of Christianity throughout the past and in present times.

> Now the adversaries of this practice: 1º Condemne the work of the propagators of Christianity as is said in the three first ages, & many afterwards in Persia, India, Tartarie, Bulgaria, Germany, Swedan, Denmarke, &c. 2º They condemne our king who by a Corporation encourageth the preaching of the Gospell to the Indians in New England. 3º They condemne Mr. Eliots & his helpers that have long preacht to them: If you say, *They have no Kings, that are against it*; thats not true; A greater Ruler and a Lesser vary not the case; They have Sachems or petty Kings who mostly have bin the greatest enemies of the gospell: Obj.: *But they have no Lawes*: Ans: *writing* is not essentiall to a Law. They have *verbal Lawes*. 4º They condemne all that write bookes to convert Infidels & heathens & Mohametanes: as Mr. Eliots that translated the Bible: Mr. Boile & Dr. Pococke that translated into Arabike Grotius de Verit Rel. Christ. & sent it into Persia, &c. 5º They condemne the best worke that even the Jesuites did in the world: Though by the corrupt End of subjecting Kingdomes to the Pope, & by much corruption in managing their worke they disgrace & hinder it, yet I take it to be my duty *greatly to honour them*, for what they have done in Congo, Japan, China & other countryes, if Maffaeus & many others are to be believed: Yea I thinke them much more laudable that did those great things though in a culpable manner, than those Prot-

---

[1] *Ibid.*, Arg. III.
[2] *Ibid.*, Arg. IV.
[3] *Ibid.*, Arg. V.
[4] *Idem.*

estants that ever had opportunity, & have done nothing themselves, but find fault with them that did it. We have had preachers & chaplaines, at Aleppa Surat, & many other such places: But I never heard of any great matters attempted or done by any English Protestants, save excellent Mr. Eliots & his helpers in New England. // Its true that the Jesuites & Fryars have made their chiefe attempts on princes: But: 1º That is not because they thought it unlawfull to preach to the people against their wills: but because prudence directed them to it as the way of most generall successe if it could be attained: 2º And against the will of princes they converted many thousands in Japan, China, &c. And though a bloodye p[er]secution extirpated Christianity in Japan, yet multitudes by martyrdome are gone to heaven: (woe to those Dutchmen that caused it if that be true that is written of them). And it better beseemeth Christians to encourage martyrs & preachers, than p[er]secuting tyrants.[1]

No man has the authority to make laws prohibiting the public propagation of Christianity or the necessary parts of true religion. Laws thus made lose their authority; they are both unlawful and unnecessary. Prudence may make it unwise to disobey such laws, but no one can rightly enforce obedience to them. They are made at the devil's instigation, not by God. They flatly contradict God's will. He commands us to pray daily "*Thy name be hallowed. thy Kingdome come, Thy will be done on earth as it is [in] heaven,*" and we must likewise "pray most earnestly for the world's conversion." [2]

Not to endeavor that for which we pray is absurd. How absurd to condemn the apologists of the early church, the Reformers, and others who have written against ruler's laws to convert heathens and infidels! How absurd to condone public killings simply because the rulers so ordered: by the Turks of Greeks and other Christians for preaching openly against Mohammed, by the Japanese emperor of so many Christians, by the Spanish and Belgian inquisitions of those who preached against popery. How absurd to condemn all the Protestant churches that began against the wishes of rulers and all Christians who may not preach openly what they believe. How absurd to put the salvation of the people into the hands of kings, when God says: "How shall they believe without a preacher?" God must then beg of the king to be God and to be openly worshipped! Monarchs who make laws against the true religion are a serious hindrance to the propagation of the gospel.

Prelates of the Roman Church, and sometimes of other churches also, are great impediments to the conversion of the heathen and Mohammedan world. Dishonorable worship of God with images, oil, candles, holy water, kissing the pax, dropping beads, praying to Mary, fasting by feasting on fish instead of flesh, adoring bread as no bread, carrying relics, praying unknown words in Latin, offering before images, and the like, confirms the unbelieving world in its infidelity. Such forms of worship are a scandal to Turks and other infidels.[3]

---

[1] *Idem.*
[2] *Ibid.*, Arg. VII.
[3] IV 912, WL.

As "if our God were like a little child that must have pretty toys bought him in the fair and brought home to please him."[1] If such would be reformed, the word clearly believed and preached, and God worshipped with understanding, "this would be the way to propagate Christianity and win the infidel world to Christ."[2]

Though some Protestants take "Mohamet" as the Antichrist, most take the papacy.[3] Together they form the two grand impediments to the spread of the gospel.[4] One is certainly reminded of Rome in the description in II Thessalonians 2 of the wicked one, the son of perdition.[5] The universal church as political is headed by Jesus Christ. But the pope, pretending to hold sovereignty from and under Christ, commits treason by setting up a universal government without Christ's consent. As such he is the "usurping head of a rebellion against Christ, and in that sense by protestants called antichrist."[6] The devil's design is thus to corrupt the Church of Jesus Christ. Whether the pope be the antichrist or not...

> I am sure the devil shows himself as an antichrist in his exaltation and usurpation. The millions of souls that have been drowned in superstition, and led blindfold in commended ignorance, do show who hath been the pilot in that sea. The blood that hath been shed in Germany, France, Spain, Italy, England, and other nations, by fire and sword, for the suppression of a reformation, and extinguishing of the light, do show, that he, who was a murderer from the beginning, hath led on the inquisitors and bloodsuckers to the work. ...and so unchurching all the churches of Christ in the world, except their own, and these that make themselves their subjects, and by proclaiming themselves infallible, putting us out of all hopes of a cure of the least of their abuses, injuries, or errors, till the sword cure it, or God open their eyes.[7]

Leaders of the Roman church, the papists, have grosser principles than most of the common people.[8] Therefore, though the Roman church as papal be a false church having the policy of a usurper, the Christians in it may be true.[9] Some papists are sober and godly men [10] and better than impious, hypocritical Protestants. One ought not to speak "against any christian love to papists, or amicable correspondence with them as our neighbours: much less... passing any sentence on their souls, or countenancing those who run from them into any contrary extreme."[11]

---

[1] I 153, CD : CEth (1673).
[2] *Ibid.*, cf. also I 554, CD : CEccl (1673); II 272, UI : SpW (1655); IV 912, WL.
[3] I 871, CD : CP (1673).
[4] II 133–135, RCR : Chr (1666).
[5] RB, II 224 (1665). This was written in 1665. It is significant that most of Baxter's militantly anti-papal treatises were written in the first half of his writing career.
[6] I 599, CD : CEccl (1673).
[7] II 345, UI : US (1655).
[8] II 267, UI : SpW (1655).
[9] I 862, CD : CP (1673).
[10] RB, II 446 (1665); cf. II 286, UI : SpW (1655); 546, NN (1663); I 631–632, CD : CEccl (1673).
[11] IV 1031, LM (1665).

Others within the Christian part of the world also work against God's great redemption. Socinians are worse than heathen, for they even deny the immortality of the soul, which doctrine most heathen maintain.[1] The "odious heresies" of the Quakers mislead many.[2] Quakers pretend simplicity in plainness of garb, but are pretentious in their doctrine of continued inspiration.[3] Atheists who might have believed if they would are great stumbling blocks to religiously ignorant ones. Lord Bacon suggests four causes of atheism: the "many divisions in religion, the Scandal of Priests, a Custom of Profane Scoffing about Holy Matters, corrupting Prosperity."[4] Those who do such things are false Christians who may bear the name but at heart are heathen.[5]

b. Outside the Christian Church

The devil's first army in the world are the heathen and pagan nations.[6] These, who number two-thirds of the world, inhabit vast regions of Africa, "Tartary," Asia, and the newly discovered West Indies,[7] greatly outnumbering the other two religions in the world besides Christianity – Mohammedanism and Judaism.[8] Though there is some good in all religions,[9] the heathen are the "sort of men that are likest unto beasts, except some few at Siam, China, the Indian Bannians, the Japonians, the Ethnic Persians and a few more."[10] The generality of the heathen are "foolish idolaters, and ignorant, sensual, brutish men."[11] Indians in America are unmannered savages.[12]

Some among the heathen attain to better things. The good they achieve we recognize; some have a very great care of their souls; many industriously seek after knowledge of the works of God; some have bent their minds higher to know God and the invisible world; most believe in a life of retribution after death, and the wisest of them attain to what is set out in the *Reasons of the Christian Religion*–such as Seneca, Cicero, Plutarch, Plato, Plotinus, Porphyry, Julian the Apostate, Epictetus, et al.

> ...they thought that the universe was one animated world, and that the universal soul was the only absolute, sovereign God, whom they described much like as christians do; and that the sun, and stars, and earth, and each particular orb, was an individual animal, part of the universal world; and,

---

[1] IV 955, LW (1661); III 73, SER (1649); RB, I 79 (1664).
[2] II 996, GGV (1671).
[3] III 713, LF (1669); 979, DT (1683); II 1036, CSCC (1669); cf. IV 738, TC (1659).
[4] In Essay 16, p. 91; RB, I 102 (1664).
[5] II 416, TCon (1657).
[6] II 346, UI : US (1655).
[7] IV 594, TKL (1694).
[8] II 286, UI : SpW (1655); Baxter points his readers to Brerewood's *Enquires* and Attendius's *Encyclopedia* for more information on the widespread heathen nations of the world. II 340, UI : US (1665). Edward Brerewood (1565?–1613) was an antiquarian and mathematician. His *Enquires touching the Diversities of Languages and Religions through the chief part of the world*, was published in London in 1614, 1622, 1635, 1647, etc. (8 vols.).
[9] II 91, RCR : Chr (1666).
[10] *Ibid.*, 77, 247, UI (1655).
[11] II 77, RCR : Chr (1666).
[12] II 247, UI (1655).

besides the universal, had each one a subordinate, particular soul, which they worshipped as a subordinate, particular deity, as some christians do the angels: and their images they set up for such representations, by which they thought these gods delighted to be remembered, and instrumentally to exercise their virtues for the help of earthly mortals.[1]

Those few among the heathen who have the most knowledge commonly destroy what is good by the mixture of it with wrong. So the *literati* in China deny the immortality of the soul, or some, at least, say that only the souls of the good survive. The sect "Sciequia," or "Siacca," also in China, though clearly affirming the unity of the Godhead, the joys of heaven and the torments of hell, and some admission of the Trinity, deny all with their Pythagorean foolishness, affirming that souls after a time of bliss or torment enter again into bodies and so continue with frequent changes eternally. Their third sect, called "Lauru," is filled with "fopperies," sorceries, and impostures. All twelve of the "Japonian" sects teach the eternity of the world and perpetuation of souls through infinite transmigrations. The Siamese ("Siamenses") seem the best of all and nearest to the Christian faith, yet they worship the devil for fear as they do God for love. The "Indian Bramenes, or Bannians," incorporate Pythagorean errors and worship brutes because these have souls which once were human. The Persians dispersed in India confess God, heaven, and hell, but limit the world to a thousand-year existence, after which souls are released from hell and a new world begun.[2]

The great darkness and gross errors apparent are shown by the large number of sects and differences among them; Varro in his *de summo bono* listed two hundred and eighty-eight sects in his day. Asia, Africa, and America abound in sects, as do the more beastly sorts found in Brazil, the Cape of Good Hope (Soldania), and the islands of the cannibals.[3]

> I find not myself called or enabled to judge all these people, as to their final state, but only to say, that if any of them have a holy heart and life in the true love of God, they shall be saved; but, without this, no form of religion will save any man, be it ever so right. ...But I find it to be my duty to love them for all the good which is in them, and all that is true and good in their religion I will embrace; and because it is so defective, to look further, and try what I can learn from others.[4]

Though the heathen have only the book of nature as teacher, they have much to teach us.[5] "The wiser any heathen philosopher is, the nearer he is to the

---

[1] II 77, RCR : Chr (1666).

[2] *Ibid.*, 77–78; Cf. *Ibid.*, 109. Elsewhere, Baxter cites Ludovicus Vives (*De Veritate Fidei*, lib. i), a Roman Catholic, to the effect that "among the savages in America nothing is more common than to hear and see spirits ... both day and night." III 113, SER (1649).

[3] II 78, RCR : Chr (1666).

[4] *Idem*; cf. also I 649, CD : CEccl (1763): "... what God may do for others, unknown to us, we have nothing to do with."

[5] I 53, 55, 156, 167, CD : CEth (1673); II 148, RCR : Chr (1666); 558, 560, NN (1663); 593, DP (1658); 729, SB (1662); III 73, 211, 326, SER (1649).

doctrine and way of christians."[1] Heathen, like Aristotle, Plato, and Seneca, are only instruments having several parcels of God's truth which they have naturally or supernaturally received.[2] Yet, heathenism knows so little compared to Christianity that the advantage of the latter over the former is beyond comparison.[3]

The persistence of depravity in all men, and especially in heathen, is exemplified by the savages of Sardonia. They live naked, feed upon carcasses of beasts, and use the "guts" for ornaments. Some were enticed into ships and brought to England. When they had stayed long enough to know civility and order and were thought to be ready to communicate such to their countrymen, they were set on shore in their own country to draw others to the ships and to the things purposely chosen and directed for their enjoyment. But upon landing, they leapt for joy and cried "Soldania", threw away their clothes and came again in sight of the ships naked except for ornaments of "guts."[4] Such heathen darkness and confusion call loudly for help.

> The most eminent work of charity, is the promoting of the conversion of the heathen and infidel parts of the world: to this princes and men of power and wealth might contribute much if they were willing; especially in those countries in which they have commerce and send ambassadors: they might procure the choicest scholars, to go over with their ambassadors and learn the languages, and set themselves to this service according to opportunity; or they might erect a college for the training up of students purposely for that work, in which they might maintain some natives procured from the several infidel countries, (as two or three Persians, as many Indians of Indostan, as many Tartarians, Chinese, Siamites, &c.) which might possibly be obtained; and these should teach students their country languages. But till the christian world be so happy as to have such princes, something may be done by volunteers of lower place and power; as Mr. Wheelock did in translating the New Testament, and Mr. Pococke by the honourable Mr. Robert Boyle's procurement and charge, in translating "Grotius de Verit. Christ. Relig." into Arabic, and sending it to Indostan and Persia. And what excellent labour hath good Mr. John Elliot (with some few assistants) bestowed these twenty years and more in New England; where now he hath translated and printed the whole Scriptures in their American tongue, (with a Catechism and Call to the Unconverted) by the help of a press maintained from hence.[5]

Men should be provoked to do as much as the Jesuits have done. "If we be not better principled, disposed, and resolved to do or suffer in so good a cause, than the Jesuits are, we are much to blame."[6] When we work we are more likely to do good than they because they have the selfish motive of furthering

---

[1] II 270, UI : SpW (1655).
[2] II 1027, CSCC (1669).
[3] II 271, UI : SpW (1655).
[4] II 684, SB (1662).
[5] I 886–887, CD : CP (1673).
[6] III 491, CW (1657).

the interest of the pope and because they substitute a new set of superstitious practices for the heathenish ones. Much of this, the honest Jesuit, Joseph Acosta, relates to us.¹ Our conduct should be otherwise.

> Whereas if we went among them with the plain and pure gospel, not sophisticated by these superstitions, with a simple intention of their spiritual good, without any designs of advantage to ourselves, it is life we might do much more, and might expect a greater blessing from God; as Mr. Elliot and his helpers find of their blessed labours in New England, where, if the languages, and remote habitations (or rather no habitations, but dispersions) of the inhabitants did not deny them opportunity of speech, much more might be effected.²

If money and schools should be provided, doubtless the Spirit of God would animate some among us "to venture on the labour and apparent danger, for so great a work." ³

> An earnest desire° of the world's conversion, and of the bringing in the barbarous, ignorant, infidels, and impious, to the knowledge of Christ doth show a large degree of charity, and of the unity of the Spirit, which would fain bring in all men to the bond of the same unity, and participation of the same Spirit....
> °Such as now worketh in Mr. Eliot in New England, and **Mr. Thomas Gouge** in England, towards the Welsh; and in many ministers, who suffer the reproach and persecutions of men, because they will not consent to be as lights put under a bushel.⁴

There is nothing in the world that rests so heavily upon the heart than the thought that, of the miserable nations of the earth, so few should have the true profession of Christianity when compared to heathens, Mohammedans, and other infidels. We cannot be too affected by our own needs, and that of England, when the sad case of the heathen lands is considered.

> No part of my Prayers are so deeply serious, as that for the Conversion of the Infidel and Ungodly World, that God's Name may be sanctified, and his Kingdom come, and his Will be done on Earth as it is in Heaven: Nor was I ever before so sensible what a Plague the Division of Languages was which hindereth our speaking to them for their Conversion; nor what

---

¹ I 178, CD : CEth (1673); Baxter frequently cites Acosta, often in approving terms: I 23, 45, CD : CEth (1673); 554, 583, 585, 603, 608, CD : CEccl (1673). Joseph Acosta was born in 1540. He joined the Society of Jesus before he was fourteen in 1553. At the age of thirty-two he sailed to the new world as missionary to Lima and Peru. In 1586 he went to Mexico and returned to Spain in 1587 where his analysis of Indian natural and moral history was first published in Latin (1590). His work was entitled: *The Natural and Moral History of the Indians*. It spread rapidly to other countries, was translated and reprinted in several editions: Netherlands – 1598, 1627, 1727; France – 1597, 1600; Latin in Germany – 1602, 1603, 1624; German in Germany – 1601, 1623; and English – 1604.
² III 491, CW (1651).   ⁴ IV 704, TOW (1679).
³ *Idem*.

> a *great Sin tyranny* is, which keepeth out the Gospel from most of the Nations of the World. Could we but go among Tartarians, Turks, and Heathens, and speak their Language, I should be but little troubled for the silencing of Eighteen hundred Ministers at once in *England*, nor for all the rest that were cast out here, and in *Scotland* and *Ireland*: There being no Employment in the World so desirable in my Eyes, as to labour for the winning of such miserable Souls: which maketh me greatly honour Mr. *John Eliot*, the Apostle of the Indians in *New-England*, and whoever else have laboured in such work.[1]

Yet the heathen world remains out of our reach; we do not know how to send any likely means to them. Roman Jesuits and friars, dispatched and handsomely supplied by various kings (such as the king of Portugal), have worked hard in a praiseworthy manner among the heathen and have accomplished much in the Congo, Japan, and other countries. But their depravation of true Christian doctrine and the natural depravity of sensual heathen soon undid the good. In the Congo heathen quickly professed Christ, but when asked to leave their sin, they as quickly cast Christianity aside. In Japan and other places when the princes perceived the secular design of subjecting all kingdoms to the pope, new-made Christians were cruelly persecuted until Christianity there was utterly removed.

But, alas, Protestant princes and states contend about their own interests when they should join for the promoting of the gospel of salvation to the heathen for whom they have little regard. Merchants, too, who should make their factories serviceable to this end, strive only for their own gain. Neighboring nations of Christians are mostly of an ignorant sort, totally unfit for so great a work, such as Armenians, the transcaucasian peoples, Abyssinians, and most of the Jacobites and Nestorians, Greeks and Muscovites. Some are hindered by mastering conquerors as the Transylvanians and Hungarians. Only

> that old John Elliot and his helpers, have by long unwearied labour done much intensively, but not much extensively, in New England: and how to carry it farther they know not.[2]

"Is it like that Mr. John Eliot would ever have done half the good in England that he hath done in America?"[3] Translation of the Bible and other fit books, especially by Eliot, has reached many.[4] The *Call to the Unconverted* has been spread to many countries where ministers have not had leave to preach, and with good success.[5]

Masters in foreign plantations who have Negroes and other slaves must treat them as immortal souls, as capable of salvation as themselves. Nothing may be done to hinder their salvation, nor should be left undone to further it. Slaves and servants may be used only as subjects of God, and, if they believe the gospel, in no unseemly way as his beloved.

---

[1] RB, I 131 (1664).
[2] III 969, OP (1683).
[3] *Ibid.*, 954.
[4] II 171, RCR : Chr (1666).
[5] RB, III 190 (1675 ff.).

> Those therefore that keep their negroes and slaves from hearing God's word, and from becoming christians, because by the law they shall then be either made free, or they shall lose part of their service, do openly profess rebellion against God, and contempt of Christ the Redeemer of souls, and a contempt of the souls of men....[1]

What a contrast between such and New England men,

> And on the contrary, what an honour is it to those of New England, that they take not so much as the native soil from them, but by purchase! That they enslave none of them, nor use them cruelly, but show them mercy, and are at a great deal of care, and cost, and labour for their salvation! Oh how much difference between holy Mr. Elliot's life and yours! His, who hath laboured so many years to save them, and hath translated the holy Bible into their language, with other books; and those good men's in London who are a corporation for the furtherance of his work; and theirs that have contributed so largely towards it; and yours that sell men's souls for your commodity! [2]

But is it not possible to do more to convert our own black servants and slaves? Should not teachers be sent to "Barbadoes" and elsewhere for this work? How odious a crime it is for Christians to hinder the conversion of these infidels lest their service be lost! This is to sell souls for money, even as Judas did. If necessary, the government should permit the keeping of newly converted as free servants for a time, so that the means of knowledge should not be kept back. But then the governors should also force plantation owners by law to allow time in the week for the slaves' own work, so that they may congregate for instruction on the Lord's Days.

> Why should those men be called christians, or have any christian reputation or privileges themselves, who think both christianity and souls to be no more worth than to be thus basely sold for the gain of men's servilest labours? And what though the poor infidels desire not their own conversion, their need is the greater, and not the less.[3]

A certain degree of slavery is lawful but only by the necessitated consent of the innocent. Those captured in lawful war, or criminals, may be placed in forced servitude for so long as the situation warrants. It is well-done that princes make laws, however, that infidel slaves shall be free-men when they become christianized.

> To go as pirates and catch up poor negroes or people of another land, that never forfeited life or liberty, and to make them slaves and sell them, is one of the worst kinds of thievery in the world; and such persons are to be taken for the common enemies of mankind; and they that buy them

---

[1] I 461, CD : CEc (1673).
[2] *Ibid.*, 462.
[3] IV 949, HGM (1682).

and use them as beasts, for their mere commodity, and betray, or destroy, or neglect their souls, are fitter to be called incarnate devils than christians, though they be no christians whom they so abuse.[1]

If Christians own slaves who are unjustly slaves, they must free them and may in no circumstance resell the slave or return him to his former owner. Those who justly own slaves must "use them so as tendeth to win them to Christ, and the love of religion."[2] If they are infidels, baptize them only when they understand and believe the baptismal covenant; but be not so slow in baptizing as to let them linger in the state of those without the church.

Make it your chief end in buying and using slaves, to win them to Christ, and save their souls... and let their salvation be far more valued by you than their service.[3]

Heathen, thus, are largely inaccessible to the common Christian. Princes, merchants, and masters in foreign plantations as well as at home are to be encouraged to provide the means and, where possible, to perform the act. Then godly men like Eliot can learn the tongues and devote themselves to the work.[4]

Mohammedans are "the devil's second army."[5] They have gained as much of the world as Christianity, but their gains have been by the sword while ours have been by the Spirit and by the doctrine and holy lives of a few unarmed, inferior men.[6] Turks have built bridges of bodies over trenches.[7] Though God has used the Mohammedans as a dreadful scourge for the unfaithful church,[8] they with the Roman party have been the grand impediments to the progress of the gospel.[9] "How many kingdoms are left in the blindness of heathenism and Mahometanism, for hardening their hearts against the Lord!" [10]

Much good is to be found in the doctrines of the Mohammedan religion: a confession of one only God and a vehement opposition to all idolatry, a testimony of the veracity of Moses and Christ, a recognition of Christ as the word of God and a great prophet, and an acceptance of the holy Scriptures. Mohammedans have also fought for these beliefs and have gained by the sword what the preaching of the gospel had not attained in many idolatrous nations.[11]

But withal I find a man exalted as the chief of prophets, without any such proof as a wise man should be moved with; and an Alkoran written by him below the rates of common reason, being a rhapsody of nonsense and confusion; and many false and impious doctrines introduced; and a tyrannical means: all which discharge my reason from the entertainment of this religion.[12]

---

[1] I 462, CD : CEc (1673).
[2] I 463, CD : CEc (1673).
[3] *Idem*; cf. also I 136, CD : CEth (1673).
[4] I 491, CD : CEc (1673).
[5] II 346, UI : US (1655).
[6] II 147, RCR : Chr (1666); III 1043, DT : A (1683).
[7] III 293, SER (1649).
[8] III 1044, DT : A (1683).
[9] II 133–135, RCR : Chr (1666).
[10] I 173, CD : CEth (1673).
[11] II 78, RCR : Chr (1666).
[12] *Idem*.

That Mohammed was great is confirmed neither by miracle nor eminency of holiness and wisdom, nor by any other divine sign. Rather the irrationality and nauseous repetition of the Koran, showing less useful sense and reason than one page of some philosophers whom Mohammed opposes, proves the opposite. Likewise he can be no prophet of truth whose kingdom is of this world, erected by the sword, who barbarously suppresses all rational inquiry into his doctrine and disputes against it, and who teaches men to kill for their religion; such is not the kingdom of God but of the devil. Besides, the twisted doctrines of polygamy, a sensual heaven, a denial of the Trinity, and the murder of men to increase kingdoms are contrary to the light of nature and certain, common truth. Finally, the acceptance of Christ and Moses, as prophets, while at the same time contradicting them, and the bloodthirsty, raging against Christians proves Mohammed a false prophet.[1]

The great tragedy is that evil conduct of Christians is the great stumbling block for the conversion of Mohammedan nations.

> You boast of the holiness of christians, and we see not but they are worse than heathens and Mahometans; they are more drunken, and greater deceivers in their dealings; as lustful and unclean, as covetous and carnal, as proud and ambitious, as tyrannical and perfidious, as cruel and contentious; insomuch, as among the Turkish Mahometans, and the Indian Bannians, the wickedness of christians is the grand cause that they abhor christianity, and it keepeth out your religion from most nations of the earth; so that it is a proverb among them, when any is suspected of treachery, What, do you think I am a christian? And Acosta witnesseth the like of the West Indies.[2]

From the point of view of faith, it is usually less dangerous to go "among Turks and heathen (whose religion hath no tempting power to seduce men) than among Socinians or papists, whose errors and sins are cunningly and learnedly promoted and defended."[3] It might not be as safe, however, from a physical standpoint, especially among the Turks; still the duty remains.

> And though the Mahometans are more cruel than the heathens against any that openly speak against their superstition and deceit, yet God would persuade some, it is like, to think it worth the loss of their lives to make some prudent attempt in some of those vast Tartarian or Indian countries, where christianity hath had least access and audience. As difficult works as these are, the christian princes and people are exceedingly to blame, that they have done no more in attempting them, and have not turned their private quarrels into a common agreement for the good of the poor uncalled world.[4]

---

[1] *Ibid.*, 78, 79; cf. IV 526, CAM (1662); III 117, 202, SER (1649); II 303, UI : Chw (1655); 134, RCR : Chr (1666).
[2] II 158, RCR : Chr (1666).
[3] I 842, CD : CP (1673).
[4] III 491–492, CW (1657).

In a commentary on Arabic passages from the Koran, Baxter attempts to show that Mohammedans could find God in it. He says: Here, firstly, the marvelous providence of God shows itself in maintaining the truth of the gospel, even among unbelievers and enemies of the Christian name. He who in the midst of the superstitions of the heathen has not left himself without witness (Acts 14:17) has willed that the excellent testimonies of the Christian truth should stand out among the fables and lies of the Koran, by which a very great part of the miserable earth is enticed. Secondly, from this and very many other places in the Koran and words here and there, and from as it were the principles (basis, origin) of this sect, it is not difficult to prove that the followers of Mohammed must (even by order of the Koran) embrace the gospel & the doctrine of Christ.[1]

The third world religion besides heathenism and Mohammedanism, apart from Christianity, is Judaism. While heathens are to be pitied and deplored in their ignorance and Mohammedans have a few common truths, Jews are, as it were, but the porch of Christianity.[2] They were, in Old Testament times, not the whole of God's kingdom, though theirs was the benediction of being his peculiar, sacred people. As they had more means to know God and the Messiah to come, they were more answerable for faith and knowledge.[3] The positive part of their doctrine is confessed by both Christians and Mohammedans; the negative part, their denying of Christ, contradicts christianity.[4]

Cartwright [5] believed that the sin against the Holy Ghost was not to be found in papists, Turks, and Jews, but rather is to be found only among those who profess the gospel or at least formally approve it. Baxter does not agree.[6] Others maintain that the conversion of Jews seems hopeless and desperate because, although many believe the miracles of Jesus Christ, they ascribe the source of his power to the devil. Here, as with the papists, the leaders have grosser principles than do most of the common people. Yet while all nations flock in to Christ wherever the gospel has yet come, although the sword of the Turk has turned many away again, Jews come in only by twos and threes now and then. Perhaps some Jews have sinned against the Holy Ghost, and therefore "obstinate incurable infidelity" is most common with them. However, most Jews are not guilty of the unpardonable sin, for they attribute Christ's miraculous power, not to Satan, but to the right pronunciation of the ineffable name Jehovah. There is, therefore, no cause for discouragement in attempting their conversion.[7] The greatest reason for discouragement is that Jews, heathens,

---

[1] Ms. Treatises V, Item No. 38 (= 5/38). Hic miranda 1° Dei providentia elucet in asserenda Evangelii veritate, etiam inter infideles, & hostes Christiani nominis. Qui in mediis Gentilium superstitionibus sese ἀμάρτυρον houd reliquit (act 14.17) inter Alcorani fabulas & mendacia, quibus maxima erbis pars misere fascinatur, insignia Christianae veritatis testimonia extare voluit. 11° ex his, & allis quam plurimis Alcorani locis, & disertis verbis, & sectae illius quasi principiis, demonstratu houd difficile est, Muhamedis assedas debere (ipso Alcorano ixbente [Likely jubente]) Evangelium, & Christi doctrinam amplecti.

[2] II 164, RCR : Chr (1666).
[3] II 223, MR (1671).
[4] II 78, RCR : Chr (1666).
[5] *Supra*, p. 12.
[6] II 322, UI : US (1655).
[7] II 267–268, UI : SpW (1655).

and Mohammedans have not been converted because of the scandalizing lives of Christians and hypocrites. Thus, irreparable damage has been done to the progress of Christ's church in the world.

> These are the causes that christianity and godliness are so contemptible in the eyes of the world; that Jews, and heathens, and Mahometans, are still unconverted and deriders of the faith; because they see such scandalous tyranny and worship among the papists, and such scandalous lives among the greatest part of professed christians in the world: ...Christianity would then be in the eye of the world, as the sun in its brightness, and the glory of it would dazzle the eyes of beholders, and draw in millions to inquire after Christ, who are now driven from him by the sins of hypocrites and scandalous believers.[1]

### 3. *Motives for Involvement*

The basic motive for human redemptive action is to secure the glory of God and the felicity of man.[2] Though the glory of God may be called the final, ultimate motive, and the happiness of man the proximate end of the Christian religion,[3] so that the salvation of our souls may properly be called the end of our faith,[4] yet the two are inseparable. "...both God and our own felicity in the fruition of him, may be said to be our ultimate end, without any contradiction, yet so that it be eminently and chiefly God."[5]

> Many separate the glory of God and man's salvation, God and man, in assigning the ultimate end of man! As if a moral intention might not take in both! As if it were not *finis amantis*: and the end of a lover were not union in mutual love! As if love to God may not be for ever the final act, and God himself the final object: and as if, in this magnetic closure, though both may be called the end, yet there might not in the closing parties be an infinite disproportion, and only one be *finis ultimate ultimus*.[6]

God himself is the ultimate end and happiness of our souls;[7] he is our chief good. "To love him and to be loved by him, this is the Absolute perfection and end of man."[8] God is thus our End, "our Summum Bonum."[9] The final purpose of our personal lives and of all pastoral work, is God's glory joined to the glory of human nature in the incarnate Christ, in his church, and in individual Christians; the nearer ends include sanctification and holy obedience of God's people, unity and increase of the church, and right worship of God.[10] For Christians, however, "the glory of God is dearer than their own felicity, and the salvation of millions more precious than the mere hastening of their

---

[1] II 1062, CSCC (1669).
[2] I 87, CD : CEth (1673); III 812, DL : WG (1663); I 271, CD : CEth (1673).
[3] II 87, RCR : Chr (1666).
[4] II 885, RMeth (1653).
[5] III 804, DL : KG (1663).
[6] I 272, CD : CEth (1673).
[7] III 812, DL : WG (1663).
[8] II 35, RCR : NR (1666).
[9] *Idem.*
[10] IV 378, RP (1656); cf. I 773, CD : CP (1673).

own."[1] We are to set no bounds to our endeavors to seek the good of multitudes.[2] Doing good is the very thing for which we were created, redeemed, and sanctified.[3] But to love men or earthly things as ends in themselves is gross idolatry.[4] We may aim at no lower end than the pleasing of God, and move from no lower principle than the love of God planted within us. This love encompasses a common love to all men (a love for man as man) [5] and a special love to the saints.[6]

There is a natural law of love that binds us to seek the good of our fellow man. We must love all men as members of the same universal kingdom and as creatures of the same nature. This is true because there is "somewhat amiable in every man, for there is something of God in every man, and therefore something that is our duty to love." [7] No one who accepts even the light and law of nature can deny this duty, for the second of nature's moral laws is "*Thou shalt love thy neighbour as thyself* & *do him all the good thou canst without doing greater hurt by it....*" [8]

> The Naturall Law of Love requireth every man that hath capacity & opportunity, to do his best to make men good & happy, & save men's soules from everlasting misery & bring them to everlasting felicity. // But the propagating of the true Religion to men, is the true & only way to make men good & happy, and save men's soules &c. // Therefore, the Naturall Law of Love requireth every man that hath capacity & opportunity to do his best to propagate the true Religion to men. // [9]

It is not from fear of the wrath of God, first of all, but from love [10] that the Christian serves God as his Father, his felicity and end.[11] "The love of God constraineth him." [12] The Christian loves God for his goodness to himself, but most of all for his person and infinite perfections. "God is not finally for the creature, but the creature for God." [13] In redemption, God's justice, holiness, wisdom, and power are all seen, but it is his love and mercy which are the "most sweet and conspicuous end." [14] Other ends in Christ's blessed work are the glory of God in the praise and service of his redeemed ones, God's glory in the glorified manhood of the Redeemer, and reductively God's justice to those rejecting grace.[15] Christ shows God's perfections and mercy to the world; we should do no less. Our highest motive should be to be living images to show God to the world. To do so in a deformed and twisted manner is the grossest misrepresentation and sin.[16]

---

[1] IV 845, TD (1659).
[2] IV 937, HGM (1682).
[3] *Ibid.*, 948.
[4] III 250, SER (1649).
[5] I 271, CD : CEth (1673).
[6] III 490, CW (1657).
[7] II 33, RCR : NR (1666).
[8] Ms. Treatises V, Item no. 146 (5/15), ff. 74–75.
[9] *Idem.*
[10] II 1025, CSCC (1669).
[11] I 120, CD : CEth (1673).
[12] II 1025, CSCC (1669).
[13] *Idem.*
[14] II 611, DP (1658).
[15] *Ibid.*, 610–614.
[16] II 1002, CSCC (1669).

The ordering of ends in the Christian life around the one great end of human life and history leads from love for the greatest object to the lesser: God as the infinite simple good above all, the blessed person of our Mediator as glorified in his human nature, the heavenly church or society of angels and saints, the universal church on earth, particular churches and kingdoms, ourselves according as God has made such necessary to our duty and end, our Christian relations, all good Christians, every visible particular Christian, intimate and godly friends, neighbors, and civil relations, and all mankind—including enemies—as they are men. This order is to begin with God alone, proceed to God in the creature, and end in God alone.[1] Such an arrangement of ends indicates the proportionate degree of responsibility for the various duties of human life. The spheres of human duty, in order of dignity and importance, are: 1. private—our own souls, near relations, our whole family, neighbors, strangers, enemies; 2. public societies—the commonwealth (both governors and people) and the church; 3. universal—the whole world (whose good by prayer and all just means is to be sought); 4. Jesus Christ as our Mediator; and 5. "the highest ultimate termination of our returning duties, is the pure Deity alone."[2] By these ends, the significance of events in history, even the progress or decline of history itself, are to be judged.

All these lower ends are taken up in the highest, love for God which cannot but bring happiness to man. "And now, God and everlasting glory are his end; and Christ, and the Spirit, and word, and ordinances, holiness to God, and righteousness and mercy to men, these are his way."[3]

*4. Eternity and the Holy War*

The eternal issue of the soul, and thus of history, is entrance into the state of blessing or the state of judgment. These eternal states are, in the same kind but only in low degree, already present on earth.[4]

This is the time of apprenticeship when we should be learning a trade for the work to be done in heaven.[5] We must "grow as men that are growing up to glory."[6] The Christian makes it the business of his life to prepare for death.[7] He ought to use every object he sees as a lesson to remind him of heaven.[8] Luther and Calvin alike sought the heavenly work and avoided idleness even in their last sicknesses.[9] What is most desirable in this life is to do the will of God, do preparatory work for heaven, and give ourselves in service.[10] There will be executive powers and answering practice in heaven resultant from earthly work; our carefully prepared furniture for heaven will not go unused.[11]

The eye of faith sees through the glass of Scripture the world which is to

---

[1] III 691, LF (1669).
[2] *Ibid.*, 693.
[3] II 513, CU (1657).
[4] IV 526, CAM (1662); II 994, DW (1668).
[5] II 550, NN (1663).
[6] II 994, DW (1668).
[7] II 1059–1060, CSCC (1669).
[8] III 292, SER (1649).
[9] *Ibid.*, 303.
[10] III 974, DT (1683).
[11] *Ibid.*, 1023–1024.

come.[1] It sees the great assembly which before long will join in another world.[2] For heaven is the "very reason, the end, the life of all religion." [3] Then will be the personal perfection of our whole selves, the admission into the presence of God so far as our natures are capable and fit for it, the communion with the glorified church, fellowship with our beloved Saviour, beholding God in perfect love and joy, and being employed in his praise and service. In all this God's glory will shine forth and he shall be well pleased with us and his accomplished work of mercy and with the communication of his goodness to all creation. "And this is his ultimate end, and should be the highest point of ours." [4] The contemplation of such matters is a great duty.[5] "Can a poor deluded Mohametan rejoice in expectation of a feigned, sensual paradise; and shall I not rejoice in expectation of a certain glory?" [6]

Some men will be condemned. The purpose of punishment is first of all to restrain men from wrong; secondarily, justice.[7] If men will not respond to appeals of love and goodness, perhaps eternal issues will stop them short. The truth of future rewards and punishments is the great restrainer of sin in human societies, even among idolaters and pagans.[8]

Of course, men under judgment will always plead injustice to themselves. Even a child thinks his father unmerciful when he chastises, so also a murderer when his own life is at stake. But law with its penalties is the engine and instrument of government.[9] So there will be many millions of souls in heaven and in hell.[10] Those in hell will be there for deep guilt: idolatry of this world and traitorous conduct against the God of heaven, perfidious covenant-breaking with God, debasing human nature and its Owner, perverting the use of creatures, frustrating the purpose of creation and redemption, hatred of God, wilful self-murder, wasting of life and the gift of time, and high contempt of the kingdom of glory. Such sin is abominable madness and demands judgment.[11] In the face of such eternal issues: heaven and hell, glory and damnation, men choose the cup and the harlot. It is inconceivable.[12] Yet most of men shall be shut out of heaven.[13] And though the Christians

> ...are not the greater number, they shall be the everlasting demonstration of his wisdom, love, and holiness: and when you see all the worlds of more blessed inhabitants, you will see that the damned were the smaller number, and the blessed, in all probability, many millions to one. If the devil have the greater number in this world, God will have the greater number in the rest.[14]

Someone may object: Man has troubles all his life and most have hell at last. Is this the perfect goodness of God? We must begin with that which is clear

[1] I 250, CD : CEth (1673).
[2] II 469, TCon (1657).
[3] II 635, DP (1658).
[4] *Idem.*
[5] III 295 ff., SER (1649).
[6] *Ibid.*, 337.
[7] II 143, RCR : Chr (1666).
[8] II 275, UI : SpW (1655).
[9] *Ibid.*, 260.
[10] I 372, CD : CEth (1673).
[11] III 527–531, CW (1657).
[12] I 302, CD : CEth (1673).
[13] II 621, DP (1658).
[14] II 147, RCR : Chr (1666).

and fundamental truth, namely, that God is good, and not permit lesser matters to qualify the greater. For all we know there may be ten thousand good angels to one wicked man or devil; there may be thousands more "fixed stars" besides planets, perhaps inhabited with obedient creatures without sin and sorrow. God's goodness in the way of beneficence may be ten thousand times beyond the sorrows of which we complain.[1]

Baxter professes to have lived since the age of nineteen in expectation of his change to heaven. Consequently, he preached as "a dying man to dying men."[2] Men have a heaven to win or lose.[3] Of one who sought heaven, he could say, "She is gone home, and you and I are at the door."[4] He prayed: "...hasten, O my Saviour, the time of thy return.... O hasten that great resurrection-day."[5] In his *Dying Thoughts* he confessed, "But a better and glorious world is before me...."[6] And in his *Reliquiae*, he points to heaven as the great meeting place.

> ...I thought of Heaven...because I should there meet with Peter, Paul, Austin, Chysostom, Jerom, Wickliff, Luther, Zuinglius, Calam, Beza, Bullinger, Zanchy, Paraeus, Piscator, Hooper, Bradford, Latimer, Glover, Sanders, Philpot, Reignolds, Whitaker, Cartwright, Brightman, Bayne, Bradshaw, Bolton, Ball, Hildersham, Pemble, Twisse, Ames, Preston, Sibbs, Brook, Pim, Hambden.[7]

Eternity must be seen in the light of the holy war that is central to human history. All the world is of two armies; all men are servants of Christ or slaves of sin. Satan is the general of one as the prince of darkness and deceit; Christ is the general of the other as the prince of light and truth and holiness. Between these two armies there is no middle state, nor is there one man on earth that is not in one or the other of these armies. The commanders, Christ and Satan, are irreconcilable. On this all Christians agree, whether papists or Protestants, Calvinists or Lutherans, Arminian, Anabaptist or separatist. Even as Christ and Satan are of contrary natures, so are the converted and the unconverted, the godly and the ungodly,[8] those in a state of sin or in a state of grace.[9]

The converted are to battle against the flesh which is the end of all temptation, against the world which is the matter of temptation, and against the devil who is the first mover or efficient of temptation. It is presupposed that there is a devil, a fallen angel, who is the deadly enemy of Christ and us. Before the fall it seems our nature had no natural enmity against the tempter, not knowing his malice against mankind. But afterwards, God put a natural hatred against the diabolical nature in man. This natural hatred resists temptation until natural enmity is overcome by Satan's deceits. So this natural enmity is found in all the woman's natural seed, but moral enmity is put only into the spiritual seed by the Holy Ghost, except for what remnants are in the light of nature.[10]

---

[1] II 42, RCR : NR (1666).
[2] III 1030, DT (1683).
[3] IV 372, RP (1656).
[4] IV 978, HS (1678).
[5] III 345, SER (1649).
[6] III 973, DT (1683).
[7] RB, III 177 (1670), in reference to *The Saints Everlasting Rest*, 43. "Calam" is "Calvin" in SER.
[8] IV 662–663, CU (1657).
[9] II 831, MS-I (1661).
[10] I 91, CD : CEth (1673).

Satan is too strong an enemy for man alone. Therefore Christ has taken our part and become the captain of our salvation. He leads the cause of goodness against that of evil in the greatest conflict in the world, both within us and without us, by inward persuasions and outward means. Though the generals are both unseen, as is their power, their agents are visible. The soldiers fight against one another, but all for the general's sakes. "It is Christ that the wicked persecute in his servants, Acts ix.4; and it is the devil whom the godly hate and resist in the wicked." [1]

The principal means which Satan uses are: capitalizing on men's natural weaknesses and defects of character, getting fleshly interest on his team, using the common customs of the country to achieve crowd-sinning, deceiving educators to his side, and making the approved doctrines of the teachers to be on his side. "Mahometans, Jews, papists, and all heretics are the trophies and monuments of his victories by this way." [2] Satan seeks to gain worldly prosperity and good reputation for his side, enticing governments and powerful rulers to set up other religions. "...if the Turk be the emperor, the most of the vulgar are like quickly to be Turks: if a papist be their king, the most of them are likely to be papists. Look into the present state of the heathen, infidel, Mahometan, papal, and profane parts of the world, and into the history of all ages past, and you will see with grief and admiration, how much the devil hath got by this." [3] He wins our nearest companions and friends who have greatest opportunity to hurt us, and attempts to draw the appearance of virtue and piety to his cause.[4]

Christ uses means contrary to that of Satan; good elements of character, adaptation of temptations to ability, strength against evil, ministers as principal instruments, consecrated Christians,[5] instruction by parents and masters, power to princes and magistrates for good, exposing of evil, churches as receiving agencies for sinners, and providential direction of all things to the believer's good. "But the powerful inward operations of his spirit, give efficacy to them all." [6]

In *Of the Sin Against the Holy Ghost*, an exposition of Matthew 12:22-32,[7] Baxter portrays in detail the holy war between Satan's kingdom and that of Christ as it unfolds in history. In his work, Satan tries first to keep the gospel hidden from men, then if it is known to persuade men that it is foolishness, and if this is unsuccessful to convince men that not God but Beelzebub is the author of miracles. This he confirms by causing men to have apparitions or to bear evil spirits as witches. By God's grace such are far less numerous than in primitive and medieval times, but the trials and judgments in France, Lorraine, Germany, and Italy where hundreds were judged, establish their reality, as do those fewer found in England and America. Further, Satan in all ages strives to bring men into idolatry: nearly all except Israel in Old Testament times

---

[1] *Ibid.*, 91–92.
[2] *Ibid.*, 93.
[3] *Ibid.*, 94.
[4] *Ibid.*, 93–94.
[5] *Ibid.*, 96. "He maketh it the duty of every christian to do his part to carry on the work...."
[6] *Idem.*
[7] II 316–376, UI : US (1655).

were idolaters, as were the Athenians and Romans, and as are two-thirds of the world in paganism today.

> He that cannot see the inclination, interest, and design of the devil in all these effects of it, and in this planting, building, and maintaining of his own kingdom, is certainly very blind.[1]

Next, Satan endeavors to establish his kingdom by heresies. There were magicians against Moses in Egypt and false disciples against Christ's apostles. Their offspring were Simon Magus, Menander, Saturnius, Basilides, the Nicolaitans, Cerinthians, Ebionites, Marcionites, the corrupting teachers of Rome, and Mohammed. Renewed heresies today evidence the devil's malicious designs: Anabaptists, Schwenkfeldius, Paracelsus, John Arndt, Jacob Behmen. The overdoing prelates drove the undoing separatists into equal extremes. Lying spirits gave birth to Christ-denying Socinians who are far worse than almost all pagans and even the savage Americans. Thereafter came the sect called "ranters," the more fanatic sort who fall into trances and froth at the mouth, and the more sober ones who follow Jacob Behmen's teachings and those of the Rosicrucians. The truth is, the papists and the devil have conspired in most of the recent heresies to attempt to discredit the Scriptures and the ministry.[2]

Satan has been a murderer from the beginning and has by persecution evidenced his enmity to Christ. From Cain to Pharaoh, from Herod to Nero, from the Arians and the Turks to the papal bloodhounds, have the promised seed been subject to the rage of the enemy. From generation to generation hatred is propagated in the hearts and actions of cruel persecutors.

> It is not only one age, nor one emperor, that hath taken this course; but as at first, ten successively, with some breathing calms under the soberest rulers, of the heathen emperors; so afterwards when the heretics themselves got in power, they were as bloody and cruel as pagans. Also, it was not in one country, or under one prince's laws alone, but everywhere they found the same hellish malice and its effects.[3]

Not only heathen, heretics, and papists, have an inbred hatred and enmity to the kingdom and true subjects of Jesus Christ, but every wicked and ungodly man does also. Through them, the devil's purpose is to murder the souls of believers [4] by vilifying the work of grace in men's souls [5] and making men think they are saved, albeit in another religion, when they are not.[6]

Christ's part in the struggle is the story of the gospel, from the promised seed of the woman to the age of final glory.[7] The foundation of the kingdom of grace is in God's love and mercy.[8] He has been revealing that grace from the beginning until now by slow degrees.[9] The kingdom of God may be understood in three senses: all the world as it is subject to God, all those who bear

---

[1] *Ibid.*, 340.
[2] *Ibid.*, 341–350.
[3] *Ibid.*, 351; cf. I 778–779, CD : CP (1673).
[4] II 137–138, RCR : Chr (1666).
[5] III 563, CW (1657).
[6] III 201, SER (1649).
[7] II 616 ff., DP (1658); cf. II 80–84, RCR: Chr (1666).
[8] II 971, RMeth (1653).
[9] II 617, DP (1658).

*Courtesy of the British Museum, London*

RICHARD SIBBES

*Courtesy of the Dr. Williams's Library, London*

RICHARD BAXTER

the name Christian and are attached to a church, and all Christians that consent to his covenant. The true working of grace is in the last.[1] In the Christian, grace is growing; as such, it imitates nature. And as with the individual, so it is with the world of all mankind.[2] But why did Christ wait so long before coming as Saviour? Did he only care for a few Jews, or not care for the world's recovery until the latter age? The course of grace, as with nature, is from low degrees to the higher. The infancy of the church came before its maturity.[3] Now the heavenly city, the militant church, is planted on earth.[4] Do not now expect it to be holy: there is a Cain born of Adam, a Ham of Noah, and a Judas with Christ. Nor must we expect a bed of roses and worldly prosperity. Beyond a doubt, tribulation is God's common road to heaven.[5]

The suffering condition of the church on earth is not so bad as it might seem, for the infinite wisdom of God encourages the Christian in the greatest straits.[6] The grand design of the reconciliation and saving of lost mankind is moving forward.[7] There are millions more of saints in heaven than on earth.[8] We are not to sit idly by. "Do all that you can in this day of grace to promote Christ's present kingdom in the world." [9] Learn the many Scriptural promises of the increase of the church, its preservation and perfection.[10] Know that God's works are usually progressive to perfection.[11] Propagate grace and the kingdom of Christ in the world.[12] This is the time of the "Day-light of the gospel" when we must work.[13] As Christ has broken the head of Satan in heaven, so must now the earthly heads be broken.[14]

Although Christ caused a star of human learning to arise in Rome and Athens, it was but to usher a way for the Sun of righteousness and the gospel. Now that the gospel has come, God has given all the learning in the world worth mentioning unto the church. Not that the state of affairs in England is so wonderful! [15] The Christians there, as in all the world, are a people hated by the army of the ungodly; they are lambs among the wolves.[16] The times of godliness are indeed the best times in history, but how brief they are.[17] Most of the countries of the world have received the gospel, but their time of grace is past. They have rejected and sinned away the light.[18] How great is that darkness where the kingdom of the devil now reigns.[19]

Christ's kingdom bears no arms; it sets up no visible heads on earth.[20] The apostles began with a little success, a church here and there.[21] Some think

---

[1] II 228, MR (1671); IV 110, CF (1682); 269, PM (1672).
[2] II 224, MR (1671).
[3] II 144, RCR : Chr (1666).
[4] II 401–402, TCon (1657).
[5] II 964–965, RMeth (1653); III 210, SER (1649).
[6] III 783, DL : KG (1663); 970, OP (1683); IV 486, VR (1660).
[7] III 686, LF (1669).
[8] III 438, TS–D (1659).
[9] III 757, LF (1669).
[10] *Ibid.*, 664.
[11] IV 89, CF (1682).
[12] IV 63, MC (1701).
[13] IV 492, VR (1660).
[14] IV 552, CAM (1662).
[15] II 991, DW (1668).
[16] I 253, CD : CEth (1673); 911 ff., MP.
[17] II 727, SB (1662).
[18] III 107, 108, SER (1649).
[19] II 1056, CSCC (1669).
[20] II 1048, CSCC (1669).
[21] III 241, SER (1649).

that the kingdom established by Christ through Constantine was followed by the millenium.[1] Papal kingdoms are in abundance.[2] "But now, the kingdoms of the world are become the kingdoms of the Lord and his Christ." [3]

Although the kingdom of Christ is not of this world,[4] a very great part of it are believers at this day,

> ...if we consider besides Europe, all the Greek church, and all the believers that are dispersed in Egypt, Judea, and most of the Turks' dominions; and the vast empire of Prestor-John in Africa.[5]

There is little probability that the world will get better, rather, it may get worse.[6] God's providence, which is a kind of continued creation,[7] brings mercy to Christians and judgment to enemies of the gospel.[8] But whether such will bring a golden age or short reign of Christ on earth, as some believe,[9] or a thousand years of holy rest following six thousand of sin and sorrow, as others profess, is a matter of great uncertainty.[10]

But what is certain is that Christ's appearing and glorious kingdom will bring perfection to the church, and in the holy city of God perfect amiableness, concord, love, and joy will make all, though many, to be one.[11] Then "The great actions of the world [which] are but the conflictings" of the armies of Christ and Satan will have ended in final victory for God.[12] Seedtime is a time of small beginnings. Anyone who saw an egg or an acorn and knew not their harvest could hardly believe that a singing bird or spreading oak could come from such beginnings. Yet this difference is small compared to that between the kingdom of grace and the kingdom of glory.[13] As sin is the seed of shame, trouble, and everlasting torment, so grace is the seed of glory. The harvest comes at last.[14]

---

[1] RB Appendix, 70, 76, 78.
[2] II 1048, CSCC (1669).
[3] III 107, SER (1649); Prester John was a supposed Christian conqueror and potentate of the twelfth and thirteenth centuries who combined the characters of a priest and king and ruled over vast territories in Asia. In the late Middle Ages the legend changed and the royal presbyter was thought to have the seat of his kingdom in Ethiopia. Claims of his victories over Turks later inspired Protestant hopes for the further progress of Christianity. (cf. Vsevolod Slessarev, *Prester John, The Letter and the Legend*, Minneapolis, 1959).
[4] III 241, SER (1649).
[5] *Ibid.*, 1047.
[6] III 969, OP (1683).
[7] III 787, DL : KG (1663).
[8] III 109, SER (1649).
[9] III 944, OP (1683).
[10] III 608, LF (1669); MF Letters, I, f. 217, no date. In a letter to Increase Mather, Baxter refuses the millenial views propounded in Mather's book and indicates his own view: "I gladly read the full proofe that the conflagration must goe before the iudgment & resurrection & the great coming of Christ: But I see nothing yet to convince mee, that there will be another conflagration after it, & that the new heaven & earth shall be burnt or vanish at the end of a 1000 yeares, or that another resurrection shall follow it, or 1000 yeares end that Kingdome.... The Initial preparatory Kingdome before the Perfect and the Kingdome of fruition reward, shall continue when the Acquisition Kingdome is at an End."
[11] III 966, OP (1683).
[12] II 549, NN (1663).
[13] II 402, TCon (1657).
[14] II 596, DP (1658); 988, 994, DW (1668); 1063, CSCC (1669).

*A Psalm of Praise*       by Richard Baxter

3. [The world]
   All nations of the earth,
   Extol the world's great King:
   With melody and mirth
   His glorious praises sing;
   For he still reigns,
   And will bring low
   The proudest foe
   That him disdains.

4. [The church]
   Sing forth Jehovah's praise,
   Ye saints, that on him call!
   Him magnify always
   His holy churches all!
   In him rejoice,
   And there proclaim
   His holy name
   With sounding voice.

5. [My soul]
   My soul, bear thou thy part,
   Triumph in God above;
   With a well-tuned heart,
   Sing thou the songs of love.
   Thou art his own,
   Whose precious blood
   Shed for thy good
   His love made known.

15. With thy triumphant flock,
    Then I shall number'd be;
    Built on th' eternal Rock,
    His glory we shall see.
    The heav'ns so high
    With praise shall ring,
    And all shall sing
    In harmony.[1]

---

[1] IV 288–289, PM (1672).

*Conclusion*

Most historians have good words to say for Baxter. Epithets abound: "Passionate Pilgrim,"[1] "The holy Baxter,"[2] "the English Demosthenes,"[3] a "deep-rooted Puritan saint,"[4] "apostle of unity and a comprehensive Liturgy,"[5] a "priest of the church,"[6] "Idealtype des puritanische Pietismus,"[7] "der Friedensapostel,"[8] the "Origen of his century in literary output,"[9] and "the great apostle of evangelical fervency."[10] A. Grosart sees Baxter as dedicated to the common people, one whose preaching and writing of popular Christian literature was first of all for them. He became "the most successful preacher and winner of souls and nurturer of won souls, that England has ever had."[11] Likewise, Drysdale senses that Baxter's great desire was to "vitalize popular religion" and "to bring the quickening power of the gospel into direct contact with the masses."[12] F. Powicke, Baxter's biographer, writes: "He was Christ's ambassador—sent on a mission of life or death—called to speak a message which it must be his one and sole business to explain, commend, enforce."[13] Macaulay identifies him with "the mildest and most temperate section of the Puritan body."[14] He was a leader of learning and sanctity but, according to Cragg, "temperamentally quite unfitted for delicate negotiations."[15] Of Puritanism he is "sein Abschlusstypus," Chambon tells us, and "zugleich sein vollendetster Vermittlungstypus."[16]

The greatest disagreement among historians lies in the interpretation of Baxter's position and view, e.g., whether he was a presbyterian or not, a Biblical theologian or a scholastic, a Calvinist or an Arminian, a believer in free will or a determinist. We shall consider several of these questions shortly. Here, however, we may ask: Was Baxter presbyterian as various authors suggest?[17]

---

[1] Powicke, *A Life of the Reverend Richard Baxter*, II, 280.
[2] Baxter, *Practical Works*, Essay, xxi; Grosart, *Representative Non-Conformists*, 109.
[3] P. Doddridge, quoted by Nuttall, *Richard Baxter and Philip Doddridge*, 17.
[4] Ernest Parker, ed., *The Character of England*, 71.
[5] Horton Davies, *Worship and Theology in New England 1690–1850*, 284.
[6] Bruce Blaxland, *The Struggle with Puritanism*, 107.
[7] Lang, *Puritanismus und Pietismus*, 204.
[8] Joseph Chambon, *Der Puritanismus. Sein Weg von der Reformation bis zum Ende der Stuarts*, 284.
[9] Loane, *Makers of Religious Freedom in the Seventeenth Century*, 201. "... his works could not have been comprised in a uniform edition of less than sixty octavo volumes with a total of some thirty-five thousand closely printed pages." (*Ibid.*)
[10] Tulloch, *English Puritanism and Its Leaders*, 387.
[11] Grosart, *Representative Non-Conformists*, 142.
[12] A. H. Drysdale, *History of the Presbyterians in England*, 366f.
[13] Powicke, *op. cit.*, 281.
[14] Lord Macaulay, *History of England from the Accession of James II*, I, 484.
[15] Gerald R. Cragg, *The Church and the Age of Reason*, IV 51.
[16] Chambon, *op. cit.*, 281.
[17] Macaulay, *op. cit.*, III, 1394; Grosart, *DNB*, I 1349; Norman Sykes, *The English Religious Tradition*, 44; Henry Clark, *History of English Non-Conformity from Wycliff to the Close of the Nineteenth Century*, 325.

The question is basically one of terminology. Baxter himself refused to take the name. He explicitly asserts that the "primitive episcopacy," which he accepts as the Biblical position, is not "presbyterianism."[1] Moreover, the presbyter as lay elder does not exist for him; church government rests in the hands of ordained clergymen or pastors. He indicates that the term "presbyterian" is used loosely by his contemporaries in reference to a person seriously concerned with godly living and dissatisfied with the extent of reformation in the English church.[2] What Baxter objected to was that the taking of the name of a party tended to division in the church, as much as the making of a new creed or confession like that inspired by Owen and Cheynell at Savoy.[3] For this reason, as well as for the Biblical one, Baxter insisted on being called a "mere Non-conformist" when applying to the king for a license to preach in 1672. Though theologically Baxter's position approximated the group known in his day as "Presbyterians," this term does not correctly describe his position on liturgy and church government, and these were basic issues in the seventeenth-century English church reformation. For this reason, the terms preferred by himself, "mere non-Conformist" and "mere Catholick," more clearly reflect the position for which he stood.[4] For the fullest understanding of Baxter's view of the mission of the church in the world, we do well to keep his wishes on this matter in view as we discuss the mission principles, methods, motives, and goal operative in his thought.

The basic mission principles in God's work of redemption are the same for Baxter as for Sibbes. Some of the theological problems which they consider and the direction in which a solution is sought are different. The question we face, therefore, is whether these differences compromise or further the idea of missions present in Sibbes.

In the first principle, that the sovereign God is Lord of the mission, Sibbes let full weight fall upon sovereignty as seen in a comprehensive view of predestination in history and redemption. What does Baxter say? As we have noted, the radical nature of man's depravity makes redemption apart from divine grace an utter impossibility. Without Christ's redeeming death, no one can be saved; without the Spirit's regenerating work, no man can believe. Divine initiative indicates divine willingness; divine sacrifice secures the gracious covenant; and the divine gift of repentance accepts the divine invitation. Baxter explains man's inability to understand divine election and reprobation in two ways. First, time cannot be predicated of God. We can comprehend God's sovereign redemption only under the terms of past, present, and future, —bound as we are to categories of time. But all acts are one in God; there is no time in eternity; there is no *menta divina* or *preteritum vel futurum*; *predestinatio* is but *destinatio*. Our metaphysical notions ought to be laid aside. We speak of

---
[1] Baxter, *Reliquiae Baxterianae*, II, 371.
[2] Gerald R. Cragg, *Puritanism in the Period of the Great Persecution 1660–1688*, 252.
[3] Baxter, *Reliquiae Baxterianae* II, 199.
[4] "You could not (except a Catholick Christian) have trulier called me," Baxter wrote later, in his *Third Defence of the Cause of Peace* (1681), "than an Episcopal-Presbyterian-Independent." Nuttall and Chadwick, *From Uniformity to Unity 1662–1962*, 184.

God in borrowed phrase; we conceive him best as he is in the God-man, come down a little nearer to our understanding. Second, all our description of God is borrowed from his image on creatures. He cannot be contained by our logical categories. All our knowledge of him is anthropomorphic, for even a Person in the Godhead is not like the persons of men, which are so many substances divided from one another. To form God in our image is to make an idol of him in our minds. Because God is beyond both our time and our logical categories, we must bow before the mystery of his electing grace.

> Though God's eternal purpose gives us no right to the benefit whatever, (some lately say to the contrary) it being the proper work of God's law or covenant, to confer right or due; yet the event or futurition of it is made certain by God's unchangeable decree, his eternal willing it being the first and infallible cause, that, in time, it is accomplished or produced.[1]

With respect to the second principle, namely, the divinely appointed means accomplish the mission, the difference between Sibbes and Baxter is one of degree and not of kind. Both accentuate the primary significance of the proclamation of the gospel. Baxter, however, introduces two qualifications of significance. First, he introduces the general, unfixed minister who becomes the missionary beyond parish bounds in the homeland or in foreign lands, alongside of the regular, fixed ministers of the churches. This broader conception of the ministry made it possible for Baxter to advise Eliot to consider leaving his own parish in Roxbury for full-time mission work among the Indians.[2] Also, some of the methods he suggested for reaching heathen nations are made possible by this new and broader view of the ministerial office in English Puritanism. Second, Baxter makes explicit what perhaps is only implicit in Sibbes, that is, an emphasis on the essential message of the Scriptures. That message is positive, says Baxter, not negative. Ministers preach good news, not despair. So it is that both for Sibbes and Baxter the accent lies upon God's redemptive work and predestination to election, while the confessed truth of reprobation assumes a subsidiary role.[3] For this reason Baxter refused to subscribe to the

---

[1] Baxter, *Practical Works*, SER, III, 11; Essay, I, xlv: "Baxter is still more explicit in his Notes on the Ephesians: and as they were written for his own private use, and give his final judgment on controverted points, he ought to be judged by them. 'Election is from the foundation of the world. It is one decree or election of God, by which he chooseth Christ to be our Head, and us to be his members. It is one and the same election by which God hath chosen us to the praise and glory of his grace, and to be holy and blameless before him in love. That love is the sum of that holiness and blamelessness, to which we are predestinated. We are not only predestinated to life on condition of holiness; but we are predestinated to holiness itself; and, consequently, to faith and repentance; and not only on *condition* that we believe and repent. And so election is of individual persons, to faith, holiness, and salvation; and not only of believers, nor of persons to be saved *if* they believe. A conditional puts nothing into being or act. Were the Scriptures dark in the point of God's free electing of some to faith and repentance, more than others of equal guilt and pravity, experience might fully satisfy us of it . . .'."

[2] Ms. Letters, V, ff. 228 (1670).

[3] *Practical Works*, Essay, I xlv, quoting Baxter's "End to Controversies": "Election and reprobation go not *pari passu*, or are not equally ascribed to God. For election in God is the

anathematory portions of the Athanasian Creed. Anathemas and reprobation alike were God's business, not man's; faith and obedience are ours. "...all sin, and consequently punishment, is of ourselves; and all grace and deliverance is from God. Obey his Spirit, and you shall shortly understand his counsel." [1]

The willing response of man to the gospel as the object of the mission, the third principle, is dramatically set forth by Baxter's unceasing call for conversion. The emphasis of his appeal in his early ministry was upon repentance from sin, and later upon contemplation of God's graciousness, but throughout his life conversion of men was his earnest business. But granted that man must respond, the question arose for him, as it had for Sibbes, how can man respond, granting full weight as he did to predestination? In answer, Baxter developed ideas of common and special grace that have been judged Arminian [2] and a compromise between a Biblical and a rationalistic mentality.[3] For Baxter the relation between common and special grace may be seen as complementary to that between the natural and the moral powers of the will. Man's natural will is free in the sense that man is still image-bearer of God. He can think; he can be educated; he can choose for a good moral life. That these gifts remain in man is due to common grace. In this sense civilization itself may be called preparatory grace, as may sorrow for wrongs committed and fears for the future. But common grace and its consequent, civilization, are only aids. In themselves they are insufficient, because man's moral will is turned against God. Men no longer *want* to serve him; they are *dead* in sin. Only special grace saves a man, i.e., it brings a qualitative and moral change into man. Special grace does not reject common grace; the moral will does not reject the natural.

To become a new man, one must know what it is to be a man. God's redemptive love was for man as man and had a two-fold dimension: to all and to the elect. The love was universal in the sense that it procured common grace for all men and thus brought all men under the terms of the Covenant of Grace. No one is excluded. All who believe are forgiven. Christ's death was sufficient for all.

However, due to original sin and subsequent personal sin, man is caught in moral inability. For this, special grace is given to the elect, a grace which is not a feigned sufficient grace, leaving it to our wills to make it effectual, as

---

cause of the means of salvation by his grace, and of all that truly tendeth to procure it. But on the other side, God is no cause of any sin which is the means and merit of damnation; nor the cause of damnation, but on the supposition of man's sin."

Also from "Notes on the Ephesians": "The apostle tells us of no such decrees as causeth man's damnation. God causeth and giveth grace; and foreknoweth what he will give: but he doth not cause or give men sin, nor necessitate any to commit it; and therefore neither decreeth nor foreknoweth it as his own work, but as man's: so that election and non-election, or reprobation, are not of the same kind, degree, or order."

[1] *Ibid.*, IV, LB, 1045 (1680).
[2] Davies, *op. cit.*, 156: "In effect, Wesley's ethical sermons provided for the spiritual illiterates what another Arminian, Baxter, had given the spiritual élite in his *Christian Directory*." Tulloch, *op. cit.*, 381: "His reasoning ... is plainly Arminian."
[3] Chambon, *op. cit.*, 282: "... eine merkwürdige Brücke zwischen biblischen Christentum und rationaler Denkart...."

some think. Rather, what God purposes and foreknows he also effectuates.[1]

Baxter calls this position the "middle way" [2] and the "reconciling" way [3] on the question of redemption and universal grace.[4] On the one hand, he clearly maintains that he is no Arminian.[5] Likewise, he condemns "the error of the Pelagians and Arminians who say that nature is not quite dead."[6] On the other hand, he opposes those scholastic divines who maintain that there is no grace to mankind in general. Otherwise men would not be in a gray condition: neither saints nor devils. As man has a natural being which is good, so there is a metaphysical truth of being which he can know. He can know that it is good to preserve life rather than to kill. He can know that he is a man with reasoning and determining powers. As such, through common grace he can do natural good. So there are common duties such as almsgiving, fasting, and prayer that he may perform. These, however, do not gain special grace by any natural law or necessity, for salvation does not come to every one who performs such duties. Still, and this is significant, "a moral, specific difference is usually founded in a natural, gradual difference: if you confound these two specifications, you will lose yourselves in this point, and injuriously understand me."[7]

Between the natural and moral there is a difference of kind, not only of degree, but God *usually* builds the moral upon those who are faithful in the natural, those who are faithful with such powers as they have. According to Baxter, this is what Hebrews xi teaches: "He that comes to God (as the end and his happiness, or Creator and Preserver) must (first) believe that God is, and that he is (in the Redeemer) a rewarder of them that diligently seek him." [8] He that is diligent may be sure that God will be faithful to his promise. The condition in the Covenant of Grace may thus be understood to have a natural part and a supernatural part. The natural is written in the nature of every man; the supernatural condition cannot be "known to any man by the light of nature, but is supernaturally revealed to the world by the gospel."[9]

This view of grace has two direct consequences for Baxter's view of missions. First, theoretically one who fully uses common grace may be saved by the law

---

[1] Baxter deals with these matters extensively in MS Treatises V, ff. 220–265, Item No. 177 (= 5/47): "Disputation of Sufficient and Effectual Grace."
[2] III 3, SER (1649); II 1055, CSCC (1669); III 237, SER (1649).
[3] IV 1010, JC (1682).
[4] Following Baxter's death, "Baxterianism" came into being and was supposed to reflect his views "on the perseverance of believers, on the relation of grace to the moral law, and on the place of the moral law in the scheme of salvation." (Nuttall, *Richard Baxter and Philip Doddridge*, 3). According to Andrew Fuller, "*Baxterians* . . . hold with the gospel being a new remedial law, and represent sinners as contributing to their own conversion." (Fuller, *Works*, ed. by A. G. Fuller, ii, 552f., quoted by Nuttall, *op. cit.*, 31). With these views Fuller could not agree. Neither did Baxter.
[5] III 137, SER (1649): "I am no Arminian . . . ."
[6] Ms. Letters I, ff. 19, to Mr. Henry Oakland.
[7] III 199, SER (1649).
[8] *Ibid.*, 193.
[9] *Idem.*

he is under. However, practically, the awful distortions of the truth by pagans dim that hope to the point where one can make no positive judgment of the salvation of the heathen; but one may also make no universal negative, or at least one may not condemn those who refuse to do so. Second, one who uses common or universal grace faithfully may confidently expect that to the one who asks it will be given, and to those who knock the door will be opened. This is God's way of salvation. The "divine influx on the will in the working of grace" [1] no man can understand. But God's command to repent and believe, everyone can understand.

We have seen that Sibbes and Baxter alike hold to these three principles of the mission. In all three Baxter introduces new developments. In the first he illustrates the mystery of God's sovereign will in the decrees by emphasizing the beyond-time and beyond-logic position in which God is in relation to us and how we can conceive him best incarnate in Christ. In the second, he defines a second function for the one ministry of the Word, that of the unfixed minister. And in the third, Baxter closely defines common and special grace in such a way as to accent human responsibility to use such gifts as he has and to assure an answer to those who ask. But we "injuriously understand" Baxter if we take away the divine priority in the redemption of every man.

The first method by which the gospel is spread is the witness of every redeemed person; church members in their ordinary life are all preachers; regular ministers are witnesses to the gospel in their parishes; and general ministers (missionaries) go out to seek the unconverted wherever no churches are, at home or abroad. Second, promoting the public good, doing good to men's bodies and loving men as men will accomplish good for their souls. Responsible stewardship of our gifts and prayer are necessary, as is a full knowledge of the ignorant and unbelieving condition of the world. Colleges ought to be erected where natives could teach their language to the missionaries and those with philological abilities might learn foreign languages and teach natives so they might spread the gospel. Likewise, stimulating interest through foreign factories, embassies, and plantations, by sending properly motivated and qualified chaplains, and translating and distributing Bibles, catechisms, and practical books, would accomplish much. Third, since the brokenness of the church has hindered the gospel more than anything else, the guilt of the church is inexcusable. Unless concord and peace come to the church, we are unfit to recover the world and convert unbelievers. The love of Christians to one another is almost as needful as preaching to win the world to Christ. Fourth, the unity of the church and the conversion of unbelievers alike require putting the essential truths first. We must agree upon and teach what is necessary to salvation first; then we can go on to other things. The Great Commission gives the proper order: preach the gospel; baptize; teach all things.[2] For the essential matters the Apostles' Creed, the Decalogue, and the Lord's Prayer were enough for the primitive church; they are also enough for us.

---
[1] *Ibid.*, 3.
[2] Ms. Letters, Baxter to Eliot, III, ff. 133 (1668).

The Christian's basic motive for witnessing is the love of God. His glory is the ultimate end of all redemptive action. The happiness of man may be called a proximate end, since our happiness results from God's love to us and ours to him. God's glory is most clearly revealed to us in the incarnate Christ. In response to Christ's love and mercy, and not from fear of wrath and judgment, the Christian loves God.[1] The love of God constrains man to love by Christ's blessed example of mercy. Our highest motive should be as living images to show God to the world.

A resulting motive is a natural love for men as men, not as ends in themselves, but to the pleasing of God. We love men as creatures of the same nature because God's image is found in every man, and therefore there is something which we must love. Love seeks their happiness. This, only true religion can give, which, then, we must share according to our capacity. Thus we fulfill the end of our creation and redemption. Those who capture, trade, or abuse slaves break this natural law of love for mankind and are fitter to be called devils than Christians.

The motive of pity increasingly awakened Baxter to a sense of the need for foreign missions. The ignorance and tyranny in so-called Christian lands,[2] the miserable state of the heathen, and the plague of the division of languages, move him to confess: "...there is nothing in the World that lyeth so heavy upon my heart, as the thought of the miserable nations of the earth."[3] This deep concern, in addition to the love he had for heathen as men and for whatever good he found among them no matter how defective, made him think less in later life of the needs of his own family and country, and the Jews for whom he had been praying all along, and to think more of the heathen and Mohammedans. However, compassion for the misery of the unconverted had been, from the beginning to the end of Baxter's life, a compelling motive to most ardent preaching. The Sunday before he died, he exclaimed: "Lord, pity, pity, pity the ignorance of this poor city."[4]

Obedience to Christ's command receives more emphasis in Baxter than in Sibbes. Sibbes has referred to the commission of Christ incidentally; Baxter uses it as the foundation for the minister's duty to spread the gospel to unbelievers at home and abroad. He particularly defends the position that the authority conveyed by the commission did not end with the apostles but carries validity to the end of the world and necessitates preaching to the whole world.

---

[1] Roland Allen correctly indicates that Richard Baxter used the doctrine of a fiery hell to motivate men to care for the souls of others. What Allen does not point out is that for Baxter this doctrine should be used only secondarily and when all positive efforts to draw men with love have failed. (Allen, *The Spontaneous Expansion of the Church*, 51).

[2] Baxter makes this his plaint in his "Paraphrase of the New Testament" in Luke 10 : 2: "The Harvest truly is great but the labourers are few." This was one of the six texts for which he was judged and imprisoned. The charge was that Baxter's exposition was against the ejection of the two thousand ministers in 1662, which Baxter denied. He explained that he had the gross needs of the world in view. (MS Treatises I, No. 5, ff. 67–80.)

[3] Baxter, *Reliquiae Baxterianae* I, 131 (1664).

[4] *Ibid.*, Appendix, 16.

For Baxter, as well as for Sibbes, the communicative nature of the faith results in the spread of the gospel. Thankful worship and joyful service speak for all to hear. As light comes into the world by the sun, so good comes by the Christian. Christians must love their neighbors, shine as lights, preach by blameless lives, light the way like candles, speak of their faith, pray for conversion, and communicate goodness. A silent Christian is a contradiction in terms.

The immediate goal of the mission was primarily the conversion of unbelievers, to be followed by the establishment of churches which were to live in unity with one another. Although in his early ministry the establishment of *The Holy Commonwealth* (title of work written in 1659) [1] in England was proposed as a possible ideal, in his later years Baxter tended to emphasize more the eternal kingdom, indeed begun here in a spiritual way but fulfilled in eternity. The suffering state of the church on earth allowed no speculative prophecies concerning the nature or duration of Christ's reign on earth. Through the work of conversion and the unity of believers, God's kingdom would come. The fulfilment of history comes in eternity. Death is an ushering into life; love begun on earth is fulfilled in heaven; fellowship with believers on earth becomes communion with the saints of all history. The grand design of history is the reconciliation and saving of lost mankind. "...praise shall ring. And all shall sing In harmony." [2]

---

[1] Herbert W. Schneider treats this work of Baxter's as though it were the full formulation of Baxter's philosophy of history, rather than seeing it as his idea of the most practicable and desirable arrangement for a Christian government for his time. A literal reign of Christ on earth was increasingly (if not always) left out of Baxter's view of the progress of history. Even so, it was for Baxter one step in history and not to be identified with the whole nor to be seen as its goal. For him the Holy Commonwealth was only relatively holy in the sense of its direction towards God; in fact, not only its actual unholiness, but his philosophy of history as a whole kept him from the error of identifying a holy commonwealth with the city of God which concludes and transcends history. (*The Puritan Mind*, 14–17).

[2] IV 288, 289, PM (1672).

CHAPTER III

# JOHN ELIOT

THE ESTABLISHMENT OF THE MISSION

*Biographical Introduction*

When John Eliot came to New England in 1631 at the age of twenty-seven, Sibbes was preacher at Gray's Inn and Baxter was a lad of sixteen. Eliot had been born at Widford, Hertfordshire, in a well-to-do family. By 1623 he had received his B.A. at Jesus College, Cambridge. Here his special liking and aptitude for languages, particularly Hebrew and Greek, had been developed. In 1629 he had become assistant master at a school kept for one year by the distinguished Nonconformist Thomas Hooker [1] at Little Baddow. Through Hooker's influence Eliot was converted.

> To this place I was called, through the infinite riches of God's mercy in Christ Jesus to my poor soul: for here the Lord said unto my dead soul, *live*; and through the grace of Christ, I do live, and I shall live for ever! When I came to this blessed family I then saw, and never before, the power of godliness in its lively vigour and efficacy.[2]

Likely the closing of the school and the increasing pressure for conformity occasioned Eliot's transfer to the new land.[3] For one year he preached and taught in the Boston church during the absence of its pastor; then in 1632 he settled five miles away at Roxbury. Here he founded the church in whose service he remained until his death in 1690.

"Roxbury," wrote William Wood in 1634,

> ...is a faire and handsome countrey-towne; the inhabitants of it being all very rich.... Up westward from the Town it is something rocky, whence it hath the name Roxberry; the inhabitants have faire houses, store of cattle, impaled Corne-fields, and fruitfall Gardens.[4]

---

[1] Thomas Hooker (1586–1647) was one of the conspicuous leaders of Puritanism and was cited before the High Commission in 1630. Friends gave him money for bail and he fled to Holland. After serving the English churches at Amsterdam and Delft, he was briefly associated with William Ames. About 1635 he went as pastor to New England on the same ship with John Cotton.

[2] Quoted by Cotton Mather, *Magnalia Christi Americana*, I 336.

[3] "Sundry eminent divines removed to New England this year; and among others the famous Mr. Elliott, the apostle of the Indians, who not being allowed to teach school in his native country, retired to America, and spent a long and useful life in converting the natives, and with indefatigable pains translated the bible into the Indian language." Daniel Neal, *History of the Puritans*, ed. by Edward Parsons, I 446.

[4] William Wood, *New England Prospect*, 37.

"Woolves, Rattle-snakes, and Musketoes" were in that terrain as plentiful as Indians. The Indians began to doubt the power of their witchdoctors. Wood continues:

> ...since the *English* frequented those parts, they daily fall from his colours, relinquishing their former fopperies, and acknowledge our God to be supreame...they say he is a good God that sends them so many good things.[1]

Eliot had not been a year at Roxbury when he wrote to a friend in England that his people were in good relations with the Narragansett Indians,[2] who realized that the white man was additional protection against enemies and was in other ways a benefactor. "I trust," he wrote, "in God's time they shall larne Christ."[3]

At Roxbury his five sons and one daughter were born. Apparently all his sons planned to enter the ministry, but four died before their father, two before their studies were completed. Eliot had hoped that his oldest son, John, who with his father preached to the Indians, would be his successor in the Indian work. But in 1668 Eliot wrote sadly to Baxter:

> I...beg your prayers for me, who am sadly afflicted by the hand of the Lord in the death of my eldest son, a good workman in the vineyard of Christ, my assistant in the Indians work, a staffe to my age.[4]

John Eliot, Jr. was only thirty-five when he died, and his father carried on the work for twenty-two years more. When several of his sons had died, some friends asked him how he could bear the sorrow. To this he replied:

> My desire was that they should have served God on earth; but if God will chuse to have them rather serve him in heaven, I have nothing to object against it, but his will be done![5]

Great joy in his life was brought by the constant faithfulness and love of his wife Anne (Hanna). She had come to New England to marry him in 1633 and was his gracious companion for fifty-five years.

Cotton Mather's biography of Eliot gives a glimpse of how Eliot's contemporaries saw him. He was a man known for depth of piety and simplicity of life, refusing rich foods and strong drink. At visits with friends, meetings with ministers, and gatherings in the churches, one could expect an encouragement to prayer from him. To a family he knew well he would say, "Come, let us

---

[1] *Ibid.*, 83–84.
[2] The Narragansett and Mohegan dialects are closely related, both being variants of Algongquin, a family of languages of North American Indians, especially in the Northeast and New England regions, including the Chippewa, Cree, Delaware, Mohican, Mahican, Mohegan, Munsee, Narragansett, Naskapi, Potowatami, and Shawnee tribes.
[3] Letter to Sir Simonds D'Ewes, *Harvard Library Bulletin*, VIII 272. Quoted by William Kellaway, *The New England Company*, 82.
[4] Ms. Letters, I 55a (28 Sept., 1668).
[5] C. Mather, *op. cit.*, I 530.

not have a visit without a prayer; let us pray down the blessing of Heaven on your family before we go." [1] To a group of ministers, he would soon urge, "Brethren, the Lord Jesus takes much notice of what is done and said among his ministers when they are together; come, let us pray before we part!" [2] Eliot considered the Lord's Day a preparation for heaven and, therefore, for a heavenly walk on earth. Rigorous observance of religious duties inspires zeal for all our other duties. Faithfulness in God's service is living in heaven. "If thou art a believer, thou art no stranger to heaven while thou livest; and when thou diest, heaven will be no strange place to thee; no, thou hast been there a thousand times before." [3] Mather comments: "He was one who *lived in heaven while he was on earth.*" [4] For his charity to English and Indian alike the only bound was his own resources. When these were insufficient he pleaded with his congregation to give for others' necessity. He readily forgave his enemies, and once threw into the fire a bundle of papers that was occasioning dissension with the remark, "Brethren, wonder not at what I have done; I did it on my knees this morning before I came among you." [5] To feed his own soul, he attended the weekly lectures at Boston, Charlestown, Cambridge, and Dorchester.

The only guide he could consider worthy for life was the Holy Scriptures.

> It is to be confessed that the written word of God is to be regarded as the perfect and only rule for our lives; that in all articles of religion, if men "speak not according to this word, there is no light in them." [6]

In consonance with his character, Eliot's manner of preaching was simple and plain so that even children could understand. Besides being well-studied, his sermons centered on the person of Jesus Christ and reflected a passion dependent upon the Spirit of God. The approach he considered most acceptable in securing a *"well principled people"* was catechizing and the founding of schools. [7] He penned several catechisms accentuating the Christian life, and he was instrumental in founding a school for children at Roxbury.

Eliot's work went in two directions: to the English and to the Indians. Not only did he perform the pastoral duties at Roxbury nearly to the end of his life, though he had an assistant part of the time, but he served the interest of the New England church as a whole. He served on discipline committees, appealed for repeal of a law requiring that civil laws and penalties be read in the churches,[8] urged the establishment of schools in all New England communities, and supported the holding of synods for matters of mutual concern among the churches. The work in the Roxbury church hindered giving as much time to the Indian work as Eliot desired: "...Having little leasure...by reason of my continual attendance on my ministry in our own Church." [9]

---

[1] *Ibid.*, 532.
[2] *Idem.*
[3] *Ibid.*, 535.
[4] *Ibid.*, 534.
[5] *Ibid.*, 542.
[6] *Ibid.*, 544.
[7] *Ibid.*, 550, 551.
[8] *Massachusetts Historical Society Collections*, VIII 278–280. The law was adopted May 24, 1677, and repealed October 15, 1679.
[9] *Strength out of Weaknesse*, 17 (1652).

Yet he preached bi-weekly at Natick until he was past eighty, and for a shorter period to other Indian settlements. He travelled on foot and horseback, taxing his strength to the utmost, sometimes drenched for days at a time, all to bring the gospel to the natives. He brought cases to court to prevent defraud of Indian land, pleaded clemency for convicted Indian prisoners,[1] fought the selling of Indians into slavery, sought to secure lands and streams for Indian use, established schools for Indian children and adults, translated books, and attempted to train the Indians to adopt a settled way of life. No wonder that Jasper Danckaerts and Peter Sluyter, two representatives from the Labidist group in Friesland, went early in the morning to Roxbury before Eliot should be gone. (But Eliot had already left at 6:45 a.m.!) He was, according to these Dutchmen, an old man (this was 1680) but "the best of the ministers whom we have yet heard." [2]

Cotton Mather draws attention to the fact that the anagram for Eliot's name is "Toile." For his "faithfull and indefatigable labours in the propagacon of the gospell" [3] and for his deep sympathy with and concern for the salvation of his fellow-men he bears well the title "the Apostle of the American Indians." [4] He was more than eighty when he began instruction of a boy who was totally blind due to a childhood injury. As a result, the boy could repeat whole chapters from the Bible and passages in Latin from memory. In these last years, when others had taken much of the Indian work in hand, his concern turned to the black slaves on the English plantations.

> He had long lamented it, with a bleeding and a burning passion, that the English used their *negroes* but as their *horses* or their *oxen*, and that so little care was taken about their immortal souls; he looked upon it as a prodigy that any wearing the *name* of *Christians*, should so much have the *heart* of *devils* in them, as to prevent and hinder the instruction of the poor blackamores, and confine the souls of their miserable slaves to a destroying ignorance, meerly for fear of thereby losing the benefit of their vassalage.[5]

Eliot tried to secure permission from the masters to catechize those slaves serving within two or three miles of him. Before arrangements were accomplished, he was gone to that world to which he had shown many the way.

---

[1] Jeremiah Belknap wrote to Hazard Boston (1788): "I have this day been at Roxbury old church..." (looking over church records by Weld, Danforth, and Eliot). "Some things there are very curious, and some which I have heard you express, concerning the treatment which captive Indians met with from our otherwise good forefathers. Old father Eliot appears as an honest man, and expresses a parental affection for the unhappy Indians, and would have saved the life of one in particular, if he could; but the then Governour was inexorable. *Humanum est errare!*" *MHSC*, Fifth Series, III 56.

[2] "Journal of Jasper Danckaerts," quoted by P. Miller, *The Puritans*, II 407.

[3] G. P. Winship, *The New England Company of 1649 and John Eliot*, Records of the CPG, 146 (March 12, 1671).

[4] This name is used by Increase Mather in his much translated and published letter to Dr. John Leusden, professor of Hebrew in the University of Utrecht, dated July 12, 1687, and printed also in C. Mather, *op. cit.*, I 562–575; T. Thorowgood had used the title "The Indian Apostle" as early as 1660 in his *Jewes In America*.

[5] Mather, *op. cit.*, I 576.

The progress of the mission work with the Indians is given in what are frequently called the "Eliot Missionary Tracts." The tracts were written by a variety of authors, mostly from New England. Interested Puritans in Old England edited the first tracts and paid the costs for the rest. The "Corporation for the Propagation of the Gospel in New England," after its organization in 1649, took over the idea of publishing the tracts to secure support for the Indian work. The remainder of the missionary tracts were issued by them. Oliver Cromwell was an ardent supporter of the work. All the tracts except one were published before the Restoration in 1662. Most of the material for this chapter comes from these tracts.

### A. THE CONVERSION OF MAN

The theological views propounded in Sibbes' sermons and developed in Baxter's writings were also, for the most part, those of Eliot. His life in the New England mission, however, occasioned the application of Puritan theology in respects virtually unmentioned by the Old England men. Not only the nearly ideal opportunity for the establishment of a theocracy, but Eliot's character and the first-hand contact with savages as well, prompted such developments.

First, we will set forth briefly Eliot's theological position. Since he nowhere clearly outlines his views himself, we can best reconstruct them through the confessions of his Indian converts. We may assume that what they confessed is what they were taught, since they had no white teacher other than Eliot. In 1648 Eliot already broached the idea of Indian confessions, which we discuss later. Confessions were made by the Indians to their fellows in Sunday meetings, to the elders of the church at Roxbury, and to groups of official representatives ("messengers") from churches in the vicinity. Frequently, Indians were questioned by the elders following their confessions, and twice public examinations were scheduled (1654 and 1659). There are records in the missionary tracts of confessions made by seventeen Indians, some of whom made confession several times.

From the Examination at which the elders set forth questions and the Indians gave answer, the following is typical.[1]

[God]
Quest: What is God:
Answ: An Ever-living Spirit.
Quest: What are the Attributes of God?
Answ: God is Eternall, Infinite, Wise, Holy, Just.
Q.    In which of these are we like unto God?
A.    In Wisedome, Holinesse, and Righteousnesse: But in Infinitenesse and Eternity, God is onely like himselfe.

---

[1] *A Late and Further Manifestation of the Progress of the Gospel amongst the Indians in New England* ... London, 1655, 8–19. Parenthetical headings are mine. Questions do not all occur in the order here given since various Indians were being examined.

*Courtesy of the British Museum, London*

## COTTON MATHER

*No authentic photo of John Eliot is known.*

*Courtesy of the Walter De Gruyter Publishers, Berlin*

JONATHAN EDWARDS

Q. How many Gods are there?
A. There is one onely God.
[Creation]
Q. Was there alwayes an Heaven and Earth, how came they to be?
A. Jehovah made them, and Governeth them all.
Q. Were they ever?
A. No.
Q. How did God make the world?
A. Onely the Will of God.
[Providence]
Q. Now the world is made, can it keepe it selfe? By whose strength is it kept together?
A. God preserveth it, he made it, and keeps it all.
Q. How cometh it to passe that the Sun riseth and setteth, that there is winter and Summer, day and night?
A. All are the work of God.
[Man]
Q. In what condition was man made?
A. Very good, like unto God.
Q. What is the Image of God in man?
A. Holinesse, Wisedome, and Righteousnesse.
Q. Was there then any sin in the soule of man?
A. No.
[Covenant of Works]
Q. What Covenant did God make with Adam?
A. A Covenant of Works, Doe this and live, thou and thy Children, Sin, and dye, thou and thy Children.
Q. What was the sin of Adam?
A. He believed the Devil, and eat of the Tree in the midst of the Garden, of which God commanded him not to eat.
[Sin]
Q. When Adam sinned, what befell him?
A. He lost the Image of God.
Q. What is sin?
A. There is the root sin, an evill heart; and there is actuall sin, sin is a breaking of the Law of God.
Q. Wherein doe you breake the Law of God?
A. Every day in my heart, words, and works.
Q. What is the wages of sin?
A. All miseries in this life, and death, and damnation.
Q. Seeing but one man Adam sinned, how come all to dye?
A. Adam deserved for us all, that we should dye.
[Christ, Person of]
Q. Who is Jesus Christ?
A. Christ is God, born like man, God and man in one person.

Q. Why was Christ Man?
A. That he might dye for us.
Q. Why is Christ Jesus God?
A. That his death might be of great value.

[Christ, Work of]

Q. Why doe you say, Christ Jesus was a man that he might dye, doe onely men dye?
A. He dyed for our sins.
Q. What reason or justice is there, that Christ should dye for our sins?
A. God made all the world, and man sinned, therefore it was necessary Christ should dye to carry men up to Heaven. God hath given unto us his Son Jesus Christ, because of our sins.
Q. What else hath Christ done for us?
A. He hath kept all the Commandements of God for us, and also dyed for us.
Q. What hath Christ deserved, or merited for us?
A. Pardon of sin, and eternall life.
Q. The same Question was asked another, What hath Christ merited?
A. Pardon of all our sins, because he paid a ransome, the favour of God, and Eternall life.
Q. What doth Christ in heaven for us?
A. He appeareth for us before God, he prayeth for us, and giveth us the New Covenant.

[Covenant of Grace]

Q. What is the New Covenant?
A. The Covenant of Grace....
Q. Shall all men be saved by Jesus Christ?
A. All that believe in Christ shall goe to heaven, and be saved.
Q. What is repentance for sinne?
A. I am ashamed of my selfe, and broken is my heart, I hate, and am aware of all sin.
Q. What is faith in Jesus Christ?
A. I confesse I deserve to be damned for ever, and I am not able to deliver my selfe, but I betrust my soule with Jesus Christ.

This above is sufficient to indicate that the general structure of Eliot's theology closely reflects the thinking of Sibbes and Baxter, thus of Puritanism in its main lines. An added dimension appears in the confessions of faith by the Indian converts. In these the theological statement becomes living reality. Brief citations from the two Indians whose confessions are presented more often than any other in various of the missionary tracts, namely those of Nishohkou and Ponampam (iam) will illustrate. Moreover, Eliot wrote at the time that the Confessions were published: "...their Confessions, doth also demonstrate the Teachings of God's Spirit." [1] Because of Eliot's testimony, and because what

---

[1] *Tears of Repentance* ..., "To the Reader", 2 (1653).

they say is often reflected in the confessions of the other Indians, we may safely assume that they are good examples in both doctrine and life of the religious principles taught by Eliot.

Nishohkou gave two preparatory confessions about 1652. The first was read to the elders. In this one he says little about himself or his people. When he first heard the Word of God, he neither saw nor understood its meaning. He testifies that when he believed and prayed, he repeatedly fell back into temptation and doubt. Yet his doubt and sin were overcome by faith in God's promises.

> God who hath made the World, sent his own Son Jesus: and Jesus Christ hath died for us, and deserved for us, pardon and life, this is true; and he hath done for me all Gods Commandements, for I can do nothing, because I am very sinful. God in Heaven is very merciful, and therfore hath called me to pray unto God. God hath promised to pardon al their sins, who pray unto God, and beleeve in the Promise of Christ, and Christ can give me to beleeve in him.[1]

In his second Confession Nishohkou is more specific as to the nature of his previous sins, and the doubts he still experiences.

> I am dead in sin, Oh! that my sins might die, for they cannot give life, because they be dead: before I prayed to God, I did commit all filthynesse, I prayed to many gods, I was proud, full of lusts, adulteries, and all others sins, and therefore this is my first Confession, that God is mercifull, and I am a sinner, for God have given unto me instruction and causeth me to pray unto God, but I only pray words; when I prayed I somtimes wondered....[2]

However, he also feels guilt now for not performing positive duties. Though he came to Sabbath meeting, he confesses he did not truly hear the Word. Though usually he refrained from work on the Sabbath, he sometimes doubted if this were so important and thereby he feels a lack of reverence for the Word. Though he often prays, too often it is only with his mouth. These shortcomings serve to drive him to Christ.

> Again, sometimes I did think, true it is I can do nothing of my self, but Jesus Christ must have mercy on me, because Christ hath done for me all Gods Commandements and good Works, therfore my heart saith, Oh Jesus give me desires after thee....[3]

The reality of Satan and hell constitute a reminder of the urgency for repentance from sin.

> ...now I know what is hypocrisie, namely, when I know, what I should do, and yet do it not. Sometimes I think I am like unto Satan, because I do al these sins, and sin in all things I do; if I pray I sin, if I keep Sabbath

---

[1] *Tears of Repentance*, 33 (1653).
[2] *Idem.*
[3] *Ibid.*, 34.

> I sin, if I hear Gods Word I sin, therefore I am like the Devil. Now I know I deserve to go to Hell, because all these sins I have committed: then my heart is troubled, and I say, O God and Christ pardon all my sin....[1]

About seven years later, on February 15, 1659, the Indians made confessions before the elders of Roxbury, with some Christian men and women of the congregation also present. These confessions are longer with significantly more direct citations from the Bible, and they show greater depth of doctrine. That of Nishohkou, for example, is five and a half printed pages long, followed by a page of questions by the elders and his answers. It makes nineteen direct citations from or statements drawn from the Scriptures, and elaborates several doctrinal refinements not present in his first two confessions. One expanded doctrine is that of creation and the changes effected by the fall into sin.

> I confesse, that I have now learned out of *Gen.* 5.1. that God made man in the Image of God, and *Adam* lived 130 years, and begot a Son in his own Image, *ver.* 3. which then was not the Image of God, but by reason of the fall, was the Image of *Satan*; and that Image of *Satan* hee did communicate to us, so that wee are all born in sin, and so I lived.[2]

In this confession more biographical details come to light. He describes how the worst sins of his youth were those of lust and immorality. When the minister (Eliot) first came to preach, Nishohkou came to the meeting, but that was to look on women. It was two years before he began to understand what the minister preached. Even then it was hard to believe. Sometimes his heart said it was better to run wild as before. If he sinned now he would be punished or put in prison, but if he ran wild he could sin without danger. After such thoughts he would be ashamed, and repented. Yet he doubted. Then after another half year, a new part of the preacher's message became meaningful for him.

> That *Christ his death is of infinite value, but our death is little worth; God is satisfied with the death of Christ, and promiseth to pardon our sins for Christ his sake, if wee believe in Christ; wee deserve to die, but Christ standeth in our stead, and dyeth for us, and so saveth us from death.*[3]

During the next half year came many temptations, especially to drinking. On the Sabbath while at meeting the Indians were surprised by English soldiers who made the Indians bring all guns to them. This seemed to Nishohkou a flagrant violation of the command, Keep the Sabbath day holy. The Indians appeared before the magistrates, why we are not told, and the narration continues:

> ...I was thirsty, and I drank a great deal; and I was drunk, and was carried before the Magistrates, and then I was ashamed. Then I came to the Ministers house and I was greatly ashamed; and my heart said, Sure I have now cast off praying to God; but I repented and cryed to God, Oh God, pardon all my sins, and this my sin; for my sins are great.[4]

---

[1] *Ibid.*, 35.
[2] *A further Account* ..., 3 (1660).
[3] *Ibid.*, 5.
[4] *Ibid.*, 5–6. Cf. also pp. 40–41.

For two more years Nishohkou was one of the "praying Indians,"[1] but he wrestled with faith and doubt, with sin and assurance of pardon. More often now, despite inner turmoil and temptation at times, he felt God's Spirit was in his heart. Sometimes he read and taught on the Sabbath, though, as he confessed, in weakness. During this time the temptations of Satan seemed more real.

> And I saw Satan did thus follow mee with these temptations to misbelief and doubting. But now I see Satan tempteth mee, because hee desireth I should be ever tormented with him.[2]

Yet his many doubts, his fears of hell, his sense of his own weakness and sin, and his increasing knowledge of the Scripture teaching, made him desire the sacraments and full church-estate.

> Sometime my heart hated praying to God, and meeting on the Sabbath dayes, and therefore I see I deserve hell torments; and then I cryed, Oh Christ pardon all these my sins. Then afterward my heart desired strongly to pray unto God, but I saw I deserved misery and punishment, and I was weak. Then I desired my heart might be made strong by Church-covenant, Baptism, and the Lords Supper, which might be as a Fort to keep me from enemies, as a Fort keepeth us from our outward enemies.[3]
> Oh! I do therefore desire Church Ordinances, that I might be with Christ, and that I might have the Seals....[4]

The elders of the Roxbury Church were pleased by the confessions and therefore invited messengers to be present from ten neighboring churches on the Roxbury Lecture Day, June 5, 1659, for the public confession of the eight Indians preparatory to their being received into the Church. The counsel and judgment of these messengers was to be solicited.

At this occasion Nishohkou was the first Indian that Eliot asked to make his confession. This confession is half again as long as his previous one, and thirty-three times Scripture is cited or explained. The pattern of this confession is biographical, like the former one, but new material is presented.

Formed in his mother's womb in the image of Adam, Nishohkou, like his people, lived in the image of Satan due to the original sin rooted in his heart. He describes in detail the idolatry and lust that characterized the lives of his people.

> ...I confess that when I was a Child, my Parents and I were all wilde, we prayed to many Gods, and many other sins we did, and all the people

---

[1] The Indians who became Christians as a result of Eliot's work were already called "praying Indians" in his lifetime. Eliot explains the reason in *Strength out of Weaknesse*, 3 (1652): "Their frequent phrase of Praying to God, is not to be understood of that Ordinance and Duty of Prayer only, but of all Religion, and comprehendeth the same meaning, with them, as the word [Religion] doth with us...." (Cf. *Ibid.*, 20, 37.)
[2] *Ibid.*, 7.
[3] *Idem.*
[4] *Ibid.*, 8.

> did the same, both men and women, they lived in all lusts, they prayed to every creature; the Sun, Moon, Stars, Sea, Earth, Fishes, Fowl, Beasts, Trees, &c. all these things I saw when I was a youth, and all these things I liked and loved to do, and was delighted with these things; in all these things I lived, and with these things my memory was exercised, and in my youth I did what I listed, as *pauwauing*, or what else I would; when I was grown up, I loved lust, and delighted in it, I knew it not to be a sin, but an excellent delight: I loved all sin, but especially lust,...such things as women might like of; if I cut my hair, it was to please women; if I cut my hair in another fashion, and left a Lock on one side, it was with respect to lust; if I got fine cloaths, stockins, shoes, all was to serve lust; our meetings and drinkings were with respect to lust: so that this was the chief thing I did delight in; and these things were in my bones, and there grew; then the Minister came to *Channit* to teach us....[1]

We also learn in this confession that Nishohkou had earlier been chosen to be one of the Rulers at Natick, but he had refused since he did not yet believe the gospel. Thereafter his wife and child died. He himself became deathly sick. These events he viewed as possible warnings from God in the face of his own disobedience and refusal to believe the gospel. On this account, the keeping of the Sabbath took on new significance. Then the soldiers coming on that day and taking the weapons of his people threw him once more into doubt. After the episode of drunkenness followed by repentance and restoration, the command to Adam to cultivate, rule creation, and eat bread by the sweat of his face, made him see the need to work. When he was troubled about riches and poverty and land, he remembered that Dives was in hell and Lazarus in heaven. For troubles about salvation, the Scriptures gave ever new assurance of the way to heaven.

> Also I further heard, when my heart was troubled about Salvation, and doubted, I heard that there is no means of Salvation but Christ, not any thing in the world can carry us to heaven, only Christ, which I did believe, by *Gen.* 28. where *Jacob* dreamed a dream, and he saw a Ladder which stood on earth; and the top reached up to heaven, and that Ladder is Christ; who is Man, and so toucheth the earth; and God, and so is in heaven, and by believing in him we ascend to heaven as by a ladder. This helped me almost to believe, and I cried, Oh Christ be thou my Ladder to heaven![2]

Recurring attacks of doubt and temptation could only mean one thing: a greater need for the means by which God strengthens those weak in faith. The

---

[1] *Ibid.*, 37-38. The impulse of the part of the Christian Indian men to cut their hair seems to follow their general desire to imitate the English rather than from obedience to the Pauline text (Doth not even nature itself teach you, that, if a man have long hair, it is a dishonor to him? I Cor. 11 : 14, ASV). Eliot makes a point of saying that the English have not required this.

[2] *Ibid.*, 42.

last part of his confession evidences earnest desires for these means. One senses a note of urgency for the sacraments in the attainment of spiritual strength.

> And again it is said, that God loved his Son, and gave all things into his hand: I am weak, and though I pray, yet I am weak, therefore I desired to be in Christs hand, as in a Fort; in a Fort, we are safe from exercise, they cannot easily catch us; out of a Fort we are open to them: so I desire Church Estate, the Seals of Baptisme, and the Lords Supper, and all Church-Ordinances, as a Fort unto my Soul...so I desire to do all that is right, and I desire to be baptized. Again I confess, I fear I shall sin again, and defile my self, after I am washed and baptized, even as the dog returneth to his vomit; therefore I cry, O God help me for thy free mercies sake.[1] Therefore I desire to have the Ordinances of Christ, to be with Christ... And this I confess, that though I believe in Christ, yet I am still weak; and therefore I desire to be made strong by the Seals; but I fear I am unworthy,...and yet let me a dog come under thy Table to get a crum... let Free grace pardon me, and save me....therefore I desire to be...sealed with God's Seal.[2]

When the gospel first came to the people of Ponampam's tribe, he seriously considered for three nights whether he, too, should pray to God. He feared the reprisals of the unconverted sachems (Indian chiefs) and the ridicule of others. From the preacher he first learned the necessity of prayer.

> ...and the first word that I heard was, *That all from the rising of the sun to the going down thereof, shall pray unto God*; and I thought, Oh! let it be so. After I considered what the word may be, and understood by it, That God was mercyfull; afterwards when you always came to us, I only heard the word, I did not understand it, nor meditate on it, yet I found that al my doings were sins against God; then I prayed unto God.[3]

Afterwards, Ponampam learned of God's free mercy in Christ. Christ had himself

> taught through every town, and village, *Repent and beleeve*. If any one repent, and mourn, and beleeve, I will pardon him; then my heart thought I will pray to God as long as I live: but somtimes my heart was ashamed, and somtimes my heart was strong, and God seeth my heart: I now desire to repent, and beleeve in Christ, and that Christ will pardon me, and shew mercy to us all.[4]

In Ponampam's second confession before the elders he expanded on the above themes, adding one or two Scripture texts and certain doctrines he had learned from the catechism, including such teachings as creation, the incarnation, God's promise to Abraham and his seed, and the giving of the law to Moses. All of these doctrines were accepted questioningly at first, later, with more assurance.

---

[1] *Ibid.*, 43.
[2] *Ibid.*, 44.
[3] *Tears of Repentance*..., 20 (1653).
[4] *Ibid.*, 21.

> I heard that my heart must break and melt for sin, and beleeve in Christ, and that we should try our hearts if it be so; yet I could try but little, nor find but little, but still I sinned much. I heard that Word, That they which cast off God, God will cast off them; and I feared lest God should cast me away, because of my sins,... and my heart melted, and I thought I wil give my self to God, and to Christ, and do what he will for ever; and because of this promise of pardon to al that repent and beleeve, my heart desireth to pray to God as long as I live.[1]

The next recorded confession of Ponampam was given on the Fast day, before the great Assembly. Here the same themes and biographical details recur. Matters relating to prayer particularly troubled him. In his concern lest God cast him off before he believe, he expresses concern about perishing forever in hell. This drove him more fully to God.

> Then I heard that word, if ye repent and beleeve, God pardons all sins; then I thought, Oh that I had this, I desired to repent and beleeve, and I begged of God, Oh give me Repentance and Faith, freely do it for me; and I saw God was merciful to do it, but I did not attend the Lord, only sometimes; and I now confess I am ashamed of my sins, my heart is broken, and melteth in me; I am angry at my self; I desire pardon in Christ; I betrust my soul with Christ, that he may do it for me.[2]

Again in 1659 confessions were made satisfactorily before the Elders at Roxbury by eight Indians, including Ponampam. In this much longer confession than those of 1652 and 1654, more biographical details appear: the death of his father when he was only eight, the fear of being killed by the sachems if he would become a praying Indian before them, the lesson he taught at the request of fellow-Indians when no teacher came to the Sabbath meeting, the birth of his son, and the many passionate temptations to return to immorality and a life of sin. But most noteworthy is the confident testimony of a mature faith with which he concludes.

> ...but I saw Christ came to give eternal life, and therefore what Christ will do for me, so let it be. Therefore I believe only in Christ for eternal life; and what Christ will do with my soul, so let it be; and my soul desireth that I may receive the Seals to make strong my heart.[3]

When Ponampam gives his confession before the church at Roxbury and the elder representatives from the other churches, he makes nine references to Scripture, mostly quoting the verse, and concludes with a moving commitment to the purposes of God in Christ.

> Again I heard, Joh. 14. *I am the Way, the Truth, and the Life, no man cometh unto the Father but by me.* Then I fully saw that Christ only is our Redeemer, and Saviour, and I desire to believe in Christ; and my heart said, that

---

[1] *Ibid.*, 22.
[2] *Ibid.*, 24.
[3] *A further Account...*, 23 (1660).

nothing that I can do can save me, only Christ: therefore I beg for Christ, and a part in him. Then said my heart, I give my heart and my self to Christ, and my wife and children, let him do with us what he will. Then my mother and two children died, and my heart said, What Christ will do, so be it; I have given them to him, and I begged pardon and mercy, if God will please to pardon me a poor sinner, blessed be his name.[1]

The confessions of Nishohkou and Ponampam indicate the simple faith and life problems that concerned them and the Scripture-oriented teaching they had received. This seems to reflect Eliot's emphasis in his instruction and in most of his writing. He writes little about the various theological problems that concerned other Puritans. Questions such as the mystery of God's sovereignty and man's responsibility, the nature of the gospel offer, and the relation between common or general and special grace, are not discussed. Nor does Eliot himself clearly describe the Indian religion or the condition of unredeemed humanity.

In the Preface to his *Indian Grammar* he refers to the Indians as the "Ruines of Mankinde."[2] A contemporary of Eliot states: "Mr. Eliot had to do with another kind of people, that were every way naked and bare, Ezek. 16.7 in corporals, morals, intellectuals, and spirituals, who were...savage, and barbarous,...uncivil and untractable...."[3] The confessions of the Indians indicate reason for these judgments. "To be dead in sin," Eliot writes elsewhere, "is personal defilement by the loss of God's image...."[4] Likely it was difficult to conceive of Indians as image-bearers of God. Indeed, the confessions of the Indians show that Eliot taught them they were now image-bearers of Satan by virtue of sin. He refines the "image" idea in a letter to Baxter in June,1663. He suggests to Baxter that perhaps a distinction should be made between "immage" and "likeness." God's *image* in man, he writes, consists of knowledge, holiness, and righteousness. These moral qualities of the will have been lost and replaced by original sin. The *likeness* of God in man, on the other hand, lies in the spontaneity and freedom of the will. Man as such is the author of his own act, the determiner of his own choice. The spontaneity of the will has not been lost or changed. Now, however, the will freely acts to sin as before the fall it did to good. At conversion the will is again changed.[5]

> So likewise at Conversion, and in Sanctification, the Will suffereth the Powerful Work of the Spirit to change these Qualities, to kill the old Habits of Sin, and to create new Habits of Grace; that it may freely act according to Grace, as afore it freely acted in Sin.[6]

Spontaneity is the form and nature of the will. Without spontaneity we should cease to be men.[7]

---

[1] *Ibid.*, 57.
[2] *The Indian Grammar Begun*, Preface (1666).
[3] R. I. Thurston in a letter quoted by Tho. Thorowgood, *Jewes in America*, Prefatory material, 2 (1660).
[4] *Harmony of the Gospels*, 119 (1678).
[5] Richard Baxter, *Reliquiae Baxterianae*, I 293-295.
[6] *Ibid.*, 294.
[7] *Idem.*

Although Eliot is well satisfied with the explanation concerning free-will in fallen man which he has read in one of Baxter's treatises, Baxter, in a letter of answer in Nov., 1663, does not approve of Eliot's refinements on this point. He points out that the Schoolmen also make the distinction between "image" and "likeness," but it is only an argument *de nomine*, and as such it is a "groundless Conceit."[1]

Eliot conceives of the human soul as being comprised of several parts or powers: the understanding as the great light and commander of the whole man, the will as the sovereign uncompelled chooser, the conscience as the sovereign judge of all action, the memory as the storehouse of knowledge, and the imagination and affections as underservants of the soul[2] Through the understanding, Eliot makes his approach to the unredeemed Indian, expecting that, according as the understanding is enlightened by the Spirit, the will chooses. The Spirit's work is crucial. In the Indian examination the question is asked why some men believe God, and one Indian answers: "It is the work of the Spirit of God, teaching them to believe in Jesus Christ," and another answers: "Jesus Christ sendeth his Spirit into their hearts, and teacheth them."[3] Salvation thus is not simply the result of educating the understanding; it is the breaking of the sinner's heart to repentance by the Spirit and turning it to faith in Jesus Christ.[4] Educating the understanding is an avenue of the Spirit's approach; as such, Eliot emphasizes instruction and schools. This we shall consider in the next section.

We have seen that the general theological and anthropological position of Eliot coincides with the main lines of Puritan theology. Eliot's Indian converts were more than converts to the Christian faith; they were Anglicized Puritans. Though Eliot saw the Indians on the lowest rung of the ladder of civility, at the same time he saw them as educable and redeemable through the grace and Spirit of God.

### B. THE ROLE OF THE CHURCH

#### 1. The Nature of the Church

In order to place Eliot's work in proper perspective, his view on the nature of the church and its ordinances should first be considered. As we have noted, in main lines Eliot agrees with Baxter. However, in the matter of the church, its authority and power, certain differences are discussed in their correspondence.

For Eliot the local church is the heart of Christ's church on earth.

> A *church of Believers*, is a company of visible Saints combined together, with one heart, to hold Communion in all the instituted Gospel-worship, Or-

---

[1] *Ibid.*, 296. For Baxter's view, see above, p. 84; There does not seem to be any difference between Eliot's meaning and that secured by Baxter's distinction between natural and moral will.

[2] *Harmony of the Gospels,* 70 (1678).

[3] *A Late and Further Manifestation...,* 11 (1655).

[4] *Ibid.*, 18–19.

dinances and Discipline, which Christ hath fitted for, and given unto a particular Church. Such a Company are frequently called *A Church*.[1]

In 1668 Baxter had written to him: "...the *particular churches* could have no politie if the Universall Church had none."[2] The particular power is derived from the universal. So Christ is called King, not of a particular church, but of the universal one, even as a king is called, not the king of London, but of England. Eliot, however, wanted to begin with the single congregation. "...a p[ar]ticular visible Church is the supreme ecclessiastical politie instituted by Christ on earth."[3]

Eliot was jealous in his correspondence with Baxter lest the authority of the local church be underestimated; however, the longer they corresponded, the less difference there seemed to be between them. According to Baxter: "The anti-disciplinarians undervalue p[ar]ticular Church order. And some do so *much overvalue* such societies, as to give them the dignities of the *body of Christ*, & give to each corporation the priviledges of the *Kingdome*."[4] Baxter sought the middle way. Eliot's rejoinder is similar: "...some seeme to be too much for the Pr[es]bytery. The best issue of the matter is to joyne them both together, according to theire capacitys."[5]

The continued reformation of the churches, according to the rule of the primitive apostolic church, was for Eliot a *sine qua non*. The congregational way he judged the only scriptural one, lying as it does

> ...between *rigid* Presbyterianism and *levelling* Brownism; so that on the one side, the *liberties* of the people are not oppressed and overlaid; on the other side, the authority of the elders is not rendered insignificant, but a due balance is herein kept upon them both, and hence he closed with *our* "platform of church-discipline," as being the nearest of what he had yet seen to the directions of Heaven.[6]

Eliot feared an underestimation of the significance of the office of ruling elders and synods. Synods he judged necessary to suppress heresy, extinguish divisions, inquire into the holiness of the churches, and "send forth fit labourers into those parts of our Lord's harvest which are without the gospel of God."[7]

The duty of the organic part of the church (presbyters) is the calling of officers, the mission of officers to the service of Christ, the receiving of members, and the censuring of offenders.[8] One question discussed frequently by Baxter and Eliot in their correspondence was the channel through which the general officers (missionaries) received their authority. Though both believed the authority came from Christ, Eliot emphasized more than Baxter the particular local church as the channel through which such authority is given. Eliot, in one of his later letters (1669), points to the case of Matthew and of Paul and

---

[1] *Communion of Churches*, 1 (1666).
[2] Ms. Letters, III 133a (22 Sept., 1668).
[3] Ms. Letters, III 131a (June, 1669).
[4] Ms. Letters, III 133a (22 Sept., 1668).
[5] Ms. Letters, III 131a (June, 1669).
[6] Mather, *op. cit.*, I 552–553.
[7] *Ibid.*, 555.
[8] Ms. Letters, III 131a (June, 1669).

Barnabas to prove that even the Apostles, when they had opportunity to do so, sought the concurrence of their fellow-believers in appointments to office. We should do no less: "...much more we should doe so, in prudence & humility, though it is not of necessity." [1]

Even a council of churches, according to Eliot, has authority from Christ to appoint special officers when need requires. "These Ecclesiastical Councils," he writes, "are to do for all the Churches in an ordinary way, what the Apostles were to do in an extraordinary way." Besides the care of all the churches, "...they are to do for *all the World*, what lyeth in them, as the Apostles were to do, Matth. 28. *Go and teach all Nations*, &c." [2] The first three duties of councils have to do with the execution of the mission task of the church.

> ...first, if there be any Heathen people that yet know not Christ, it is a work well-becoming any of these *Orders of Councils*, and all of them in their harmony, to seek out, and *send forth fit labourers* to such a work and service of Christ, to carry the Gospel, and preach Jesus Christ unto them; to gather and *plant Churches* amongst them. And it is the duty of particular Churches, unto whose Society such Instruments, chosen by the Councils, do belong, by *Fasting and Prayer*, and *Imposition of hands*, to send them forth unto that Work; as the Church of Antioch did unto *Barnabas* and *Saul* when they were extraordinarily called, and sent fort unto such a Work as we are now speaking of, *Acts* 13.2,3. And this will be one holy way of improvement of *Church treasuries* raised by voluntary Contributions, to *spread* and *propagate the Gospel* to all the World.[3]

Second, councils are to also send missionaries to unbelievers in Christian nations. Third, it is likewise their duty to supply teachers where lack exists, and transfer "...where the gifts and labours of some special Instruments may be more fruitful to the glory of God, and the publick good of Religion, and all the Churches." [4] Ministers who are called to mission work should seek the consent and blessing of their own church where they are members. "The greater concurrence of the saints concerned, the stronger breath of prayer is raised in all the churches." [5]

Baxter replies (1670) that those men who are "called to goe preach & baptise Infidel nations" [6] are of two sorts: those who already serve a particular congregation, and those who do not. The first sort do well, of course, to seek the consent of the congregation they are serving, but such consent is not essential to their entrance into mission work, nor does it give the authority for the work. For the greater necessity and opportunity of mission work more fully shows God's will than the will of a particular congregation.

> Yet doubtlesse none of Gods people are to be despised; nor are they useles to us about our removes: It is meete that they fast & pray with us for Gods

---

[1] *Ibid.*
[2] *Communion of Churches*, 23 (1666).
[3] *Ibid.*, 23, 24.
[4] *Ibid.*, 24.
[5] Ms. Letters, III 131a (June, 1669).
[6] Ms. Letters, V 228a.

> direction & assistance; which they cannot do in faith, if they are before perswaded that our undertaking is sinfull.[1]

Baxter virtually suggests that Eliot consider leaving his particular congregation for full-time Indian mission work, only the great distance and thus uncertainty of the full implications of such a decision restrains him.

> And were I your neighbor, and did beleive that forsaking your Church, would enable you to do much more service, to the poore Indians, than your Church service cometh to, I should cast in my judgm[en]t that it were your duty so to do, and to be only the Apostle to the Indians.[2]

The second sort of "Unfixed Ministers", says Baxter, are those unattached to any particular church. The people of a local congregation do not *give* authority to their minister, they only choose the man who receives the authority from Christ as related to them. Such Christ-given authority does not entitle the congregation to dispense a general authority which itself is antecedent to a relation to a particular church. This last seems to be the only real point where Baxter and Eliot disagree concerning the authority of a missionary. In his previous letter Eliot had said:

> A fixed officer with the concurrence of the Fraternity, signifyeth more, as yet it seemeth to me, than one that hath only a general mission, unlesse it be one that is deeply ingaged and blessed in that general work.[3]

If Baxter agreed, as he likely did, that all missionaries must fulfill Eliot's last qualification above, the difference between the two men becomes primarily one of emphasis.

The same sort of situation appears in Baxter's and Eliot's view concerning the relation between churches. Already in 1657 Baxter asks that the New England pastors "...joyne in an earnest p[er]swasive to union, to the Presbyterian & Congregationall Brethren in England, & to p[ro]pound the termes in certaine Propositions?"[4]

Eliot replies later that year that though Baxter's desire for union is good, the New England church is too distant to function as mediator. The chief burden of the work is calming spirits and opposing the separatist way of forming

---

[1] *Idem.*

[2] *Idem.* Powicke says that perhaps Eliot wanted to do this, but that the Roxbury congregation demurred. "The early congregational view of ordination – that it was the seal of an indissoluble marriage between a man and a particular church – did sometimes induce this feeling of sole possession, and led to inconveniences which broke it down." Powicke, *op. cit.*, 151. The "lost letters" in the Baxter–Eliot correspondence, of which there were likely several, leave the matter uncertain. Certain passages in the tracts, however, lend weight to the thesis.

[3] Ms. Letters, III 131a (June, 1669).

[4] Ms. Letters, III 9a (20 January, 1656/7). Since England did not adopt the Gregorian calendar until 1752, the Puritans were still using the Julian calendar during most of the time span covered in this thesis. Accordingly, some of the dates used here are given under both calendars.

churches by calling the choicest persons out of various churches. He agrees with Baxter that godly Christians should remain in their own parochial churches and be salt to others. This he has insisted upon for his Indian converts rather than that they should leave the Indian villages and join the spiritually stronger English churches. "No, rather let them keepe Sabbath: worship together, & the strong help the weak." [1]

The "sad differences" and "distances of spirit" of the church in England prompted at least in part the writing of *The Christian Commonwealth* (before 1662) as Eliot testifies in the Preface to that work. As we have seen in Chapter II, Baxter favors a united church in which the various religious groups are taken up. This he writes to Eliot:

> And though my own Judgment & endeavours have still been to embody the Presbyterians, Independents, Anabaptists, & all that hold the essentialls of faith & church communion, yet...I will not totally leave out the best of the conformists.[2]

Because he will not leave out all conformists, though he judges himself to be of the same principle as Dod, Cartwright, Hildersham, and holds communion with "such a conformist as Sibs, Preston, Bolton," [3] the Nonconformists are hostile to him. In his lonely battle for unity, he feels a common bond with Eliot. Eliot had written in 1668 that he desires that

> ...we might come to such a complyance, as to walk together in unity, love, & peace & be one in o[u]r communion of Churches, which onenesse is [so] desireable in the eyes of Christ as that he hath prayed for it 4 times in a few lines of that mediatorial prayer John 17....[4]

And scarcely two weeks later he writes:

> The great want is, the uniting of Gods servants, w[hi]ch, were it attained, you would soone heare that p[ro]mised great voyce saying come up hither: for the resurrection of the saints is now past (Heb. xi.19).[5]

To this longing of Eliot for unity among the churches of Christ, Baxter expresses his "professed gladnes... for your zeale for unity in times when the common juvenile zeale doth worke all towards exasperations and divisions...." [6] And again:

> I gladly and thankfully rec[eiv]ed... your hearty breathings after Christian unity & pece. If we had here had the same spirit, we had bin healed long agoe.[7]

The *Communion of Churches*, written by Eliot in 1665, concretizes his desires for church unity. Four orders of Councils, each constituted by twenty-four representatives from the preceding order, would meet as follows: twelve churches,

---

[1] Ms. Letters, II 274a (7 October, 1657).
[2] Ms. Letters, I 59a (2 Sept., 1671).
[3] *Idem.*
[4] Ms. Letters, II 276a (10 January, 1667/8).
[5] Ms. Letters, II 229a (22 January, 1667/8).
[6] Ms. Letters, III 74a (27 March, 1668).
[7] Ms. Letters, III 133a (22 Sept., 1668).

each with two delegates, make one district council which meets monthly; provincial assemblies, similarly comprised out of district councils, meeting quarterly; so also national synods meeting annually; and the Ecumenical Council always in session in Jerusalem. Through this supreme council "...Christ will rule all the world–both of civil and ecclesiastical affairs–by the Word of His mouth delivered to His saints in the Hebrew language." [1]

Late in 1667 Baxter made animadversions on this little work of Eliot's, but with the general thought he agreed.[2] He feels that Eliot's proposals for unity are less broad than his own, yet they could be effective.

> Doubtlesse if your way of communicatory concordant Councills were set on foot, the concordant Churches, with the Glory & strength of their Unity, would in time weane out & shame the sects into nothing.[3]

In the same letter Baxter, in considering the tumultuous separatistic-minded parties about him in England, is concerned to put the brakes on extreme independentism, but remains equally wary of too much authority for Synods.

> To speake my heart to you, I greatly distinguish between *Independency* & *Separation*: & my owne judgment is for the Independency of particular Churches in point of Government; though for their Dependency in point (of) Concord & Councill. And yet in this, I goe not all so neere the Presbyterians as you doe: For I take Councills to be lesse of Divine right, & more variable by humane prudence, for statednesse, times, numbers, &c., than you seeme to doe.[4]

Again in 1671 Baxter emphasizes the proper authority of Synods.

> I heare your good motion for stated Synods is neglected. I am for avoiding all busy Lording and Law making Synods, where a major vote do thinke themselves authorized, to tyrannize over the minor, though the wiser part. But loving & free assemblies are very needfull for mutuall assistance & concord.[5]

Baxter also proposes in this letter that Eliot revise certain practical points of his *Communion of Churches*, as, for example, the number of delegates, and that he should offer the establishment of synods for council and concord, disclaiming church tyranny. To this proposal we have no answer, since Eliot's last remaining letter, dated eleven years later (1682), is brief and makes no reference to it.

From the foregoing it is clear that Eliot is concerned that the rights of the church members be protected, for they are no ordinary people but kings and priests. Yet church officers have fixed duties and authority as organic parts of the church. So also councils of churches and synods bear authority from Christ which is channelled through the wider bodies of church organization and fellowship. Each level of organization has its own missionary duties and is more

---

[1] Eliot, *Communion of Churches*, 17.
[2] Ms. Letters, VI 183a (1667).
[3] Ms. Letters, V 228a (5 Feb., 1669/70).
[4] *Idem.*
[5] Ms. Letters, I 59a (2 Sept., 1671).

than advisory in character. For Eliot as for Baxter lack of church unity hinders the progress of the Lord's work and preparation for his coming. Eliot mourned the disunity of the church, but his missionary work was, as he says, the "production of a Church, the building of a visible political Temple for Christ...." [1] Such he strove to build among the Indians.

## 2. *The Establishment of the Indian Church*

We turn now to an account of the establishment of the Indian church as given in the eleven missionary tracts which encompass the years 1630 to 1670. The significant dates during this period around which our discussion will center include: 1646–first preaching services, 1651–organization of civil government, 1652–first Indian confessions, 1654–examination of Indians for church membership, 1659–more Indian confessions and examination, and 1660–organization of the first Indian church.

The period from 1670 to 1675 marked a sharp increase of tension between the colonists and the Indians, followed by the war which devastated the Indian churches in 1675. The last fifteen years of Eliot's life were a period of partial rehabilitation of the Indian churches. But now we are ahead of the story.

### a. Small Beginnings and First Meetings

When the first of the missionary tracts (1643) was published, Eliot was busy learning the language from an Indian servant taken prisoner in one of the wars.[2] This tract, entitled *New Englands first fruits*, is a story of small and painful beginnings. Significantly, the title page includes as its texts: "Who hath despised the Day of small things?" Zach. 4.10, and "And though thy beginnings be small, thy latter end shall greatly encrease." Job. 8:6,7.

The anonymous author describes the Indians as those "who have ever sate in hellish darknesse, adoring the Devill himselfe for their GOD." [3] God has given

> some testimony of his gracious acceptance of our poore endeavours towards them, and of our groanes to himselfe for mercy upon those miserable Soules (the very Ruines of Mankind) there amongst us; our very bowels yerning within us to see them goe downe to Hell by swarmes without remedy.[4]

No one should wonder that only "firstfruits" are mentioned. The harvest will come in God's own time. Consider the difficulties:

> First their infinite distance from Christianity, having never been prepared thereunto by any Civility at all. Secondly, the difficulty of their Language to us and of ours to them; there being no Rules to learn either by. Thirdly, the diversity of their owne Language to it selfe: every part of that Countrey having its own Dialect, differing much from the other; all which make their comming into the Gospel the more slow.[5]

---

[1] Ms. Letters, III 131a (June, 1669).
[2] *Indian Grammar Begun*, 65 (1666).
[3] *New Englands first fruits*, 1 (1643).
[4] *Idem.*
[5] *Ibid.*, 1, 2.

But, in spite of such hindrance, God has done much for some. Ten adult Indians are presented as illustrative of the many who have seriously considered the gospel. One was startled into the way of obedience by the effective prayer meeting for rain by the Plymouth Church. He resolved "not to rest till he did know this great good God" who gives rain. To know this God he did "forsake the *Indians*, and cleave to the English." [1] Sagamore [2] John was friendly to the English from the beginning. He

> desired to learne and speake our Language, and loved to imitate us in our behaviour and apparrell and began to hearken after our God and his wayes, and would much commend English-men, and their God; saying (*Much good men, much good God*). [3]

A resolve to leave the Indians and join himself to the English was, for fear of the scoffing of his fellows, never carried out. This "sin" he confessed on his deathbed as he entrusted his only child to the care of Mr. Wilson [4] for its upbringing.

Many Indian boys and girls have long been in English homes. They are now civilized and industrious, English-speaking and reading, and well-grounded in the Christian faith. Some are convinced of their sinful estate, affected by thoughts of eternity sometimes to the point of tears, and concerned to live lives of prayer and obedience to God.

Much concern was evidenced for the English way of life. Faith and ethics went together. One loved the Word of God and labored to keep all the commandments, yet he said: "Me die, and walke in fire," that is "when I die I must to Hell." [5] Asked why, he said because he did not know Jesus Christ. But after he came to believe in Christ, he "went out amongst the *Indians*, and called upon them to put away all their wives save one, because it was a sinne against English-mans Saviour." [6] Other Indians, influenced by the English way, rebuked their fellows for cutting trees and killing pigeons upon the Lord's Day. Some rejected their Indian past, even their names, and abhorred dwelling with the Indians any longer. They forsook "their friends and Kindred" and "dwelt wholly with us." [7]

In initial stages, it thus appears that becoming Christian involved leaving all of Indian life and custom behind to identify oneself with the English way and the Englishman's God. The fact that these took obedience to God so

---

[1] *Ibid.*, 2.
[2] A great ruler, having sachems under his jurisdiction.
[3] *New Englands first fruits*, 3.
[4] Likely John Wilson, minister of Boston, d. 1667. Until Eliot began preaching to groups of Indians in 1646, converted Indians tended to identify themselves completely with the English. They were individually received as members of the English churches. This would indicate that no questions of racial hostility hindered the mission work. Later hostility was occasioned by other factors, e.g., the culture gap between the two groups. Eliot's *Communion of Churches* (1665) planned the geographic organization of all churches, regardless of race.
[5] *Ibid.*, 4.
[6] *Idem.*
[7] *Idem.*

seriously gave reason to believe that some might be saved. "All things weighed, we dare not but hope, that many of them, doe belong to the Kingdome of God." [1] As a matter of fact, one Blackmore maid from Dorchester experienced a saving work of grace in her heart. She desired church fellowship with the saints there. After private trial before the elders and later confession before the whole church, she was admitted a member "by the joynt consent of the Church with great joy to all their hearts." [2] She, too, came to live with the English but

> ...with teares exhorted some other of the *Indians* that live with us to embrace *Jesus Christ*, declaring how willing he would be to receive them, even as he had received her.[3]

Some English men who were well acquainted with his language were used as agents in the conversion of Wequash. Since he was probably associated with the Pequots and later moved to Connecticut, likely he came from the Massachusetts Bay Colony. But who these men were who already spoke the Indian language, the writer does not say.[4] It is significant to note the role of Wequash in the conversion of his fellows.

> Afterwards he went amongst the Indians, like that poore Woman of *Samaria*, proclaiming *Christ*, and telling them what a Treasure he had found, instructing them in the knowledge of the true *God*: and this he did with a grave and serious spirit, warning them with all faithfulnesse to flee from the wrath to come, by breaking off their sinnes and wickednesse.[5]

Some of the means God has used, the writer continues, to encourage the Indians to seek the gospel has been the fair bargaining and purchase of land, the extension of justice in all particular acts, and the humanity of the English in kind words and unoffensive deeds. Some other plantations have dealt scandalously and wickedly with the Indians. They have hardened those "poore wofull soules against the English, and all Religion for their sakes; and seale them up under perdition." [6] The Indians, however, are kept at a safe distance and not trusted too far, for they serve the Devil and are led by him. Except for one difficulty with the Pequots, God has kept away all hurt by Indians in the Massachusetts Bay Colony.

A report is given of work in several other English plantations, some several hundred leagues, others several hundred miles away, extending as far as Virginia and Barbados. The English on some of these plantations were "almost as darke and rude as the Indians themselves." [7] Letters were received from these places saying that there was no one, from one end of the land to the other, to break the bread of life unto the hungry. When these letters were read in the

---

[1] *Ibid.*, 5.
[2] *Idem.*
[3] *Idem.*
[4] *Ibid.*, 5–7; Page 7 is erroneously numbered 15.
[5] *Ibid.*, 7.
[6] *Ibid.*, 8.
[7] *Ibid.*, 9.

congregations, "we spared the bread from our own mouths to save their lives, and sent two of our Ministers for the present to *Virginia*...."[1] Some of the Indians in those places joined in worship with the English.

*New Englands first fruits* concludes with an exhortation. See the riches of God's free grace in Christ who is willing to impart mercy even to the worst of men. See how in the day of judgment the poor Indians will rise up against us and boldly condemn us if we do not share the gospel with them. Otherwise we who stand under great light shall see men from the East and from the West sit down in the kingdom of God, and we ourselves shall be cast out.

> Let the world know, that God led not so many thousands of his people into the Wildernesse, to see a reed shaken with the wind, but amongst many other speciall ends, this was none of the least, to spread the light of his blessed Gospel, to such as never heard the sound of it.[2]

This should "stop the mouths of the profane that calumniate the work of God in our hands...."[3] God is carrying his Gospel westward. Once it shone in the East. In these latter ages it bends West. Before God's sun sets it will brighten these parts of the world with his glorious lustre.

See how God takes the unlikely means of silencing ministers that they might speak in the uttermost parts of the earth. Despise not the day of small things. God will have his way. Only let others be stirred to pray and help that this great and glorious work may go forward.

> And desire the Lord to stirre up the bowels of some godly minded, to pitty those poore Heathen that are bleeding to death, to eternall death, and to reach forth an hand of soule-mercy, to save some of them from the fire of hell by affording some means to maintain some fit instruments on purpose to spend their time, and give themselves wholly to preach to these poore wretches.[4]

*New Englands first fruits* indicates that during the first decade of the plantation in Massachusetts, concern for the Indians was present. Individuals were converted, and at least one and perhaps more were admitted into the membership of the church. Many children were taken into English homes and carefully instructed in the Christian religion. Expeditions were made in answer to requests for spiritual help into other plantations. Here, too, was ministry to Indians as well as to the scattered English. These initial blessings were considered as an earnest of the greater harvest to come. For this gathering, help from England was sought already in 1643 to support full-time missionaries among the Indians. The early dream for such full-time preachers was long in becoming reality.

The title of the second tract (1647) gives increasing hopes for advance in the Indian work: *The Day-Breaking, If not the Sun-Rising of the Gospel with the Indians in New-England*. Four initial meetings between four ministers and

---

[1] *Ibid.*, 10.
[2] *Idem.*
[3] *Idem.*
[4] *Ibid.*, 12, erroneously printed 19.

a group of Indians are described by one of the ministers. At the first gathering on October 28, 1646, after an opening prayer in English, John Eliot, though here not named, preached an hour and a quarter. The sermon emphasized

> ...all the principall matter of religion, beginning first with a repetition of the Ten Commandements, and a briefe explication of them then shewing the curse and dreadfull wrath of God against all those who brake them,... and so applyed it unto the condition of the *Indians* present, with much sweet affection; and then preached Jesus Christ to them the onely meanes of recovery from sinne and wrath and eternall death, and what Christ was, and whither he was now gone, and how hee will one day come againe to judge the world in flaming fire; and of the blessed estate of all those that by faith beleeve in Christ, and know him feelingly....[1]

Eliot spoke, the writer continues, in the method which he saw most fit to edify the Indians, not meddling with too difficult matters, but familiarly opening the principal matters of salvation. Thus he stressed

> ...the creation and fall of man,...the greatnesse and infinite being of God, the maker of all things,...the joyes of heaven, and the terrours and horrours of wicked men in hell, perswading them to repentance for severall sins which they live in....[2]

Following the sermon, many present testified that they understood all the preacher had said. The Indians then propounded questions. The first, "How may wee come to know Jesus Christ?"[3] was answered by Eliot: if they could read the English Bible, the book of God, they would know; since they could not, much thought and meditation should be given to the preached message; prayers and sighing to God will not go unanswered for he hears Indians as well as English; and repentance with mourning for their sins and ignorance must open the way. One Indian wanted to know if Englishmen were ever as ignorant of God and Jesus Christ as the Indians. He was given to understand that even now there are two sorts of Englishmen, some ignore and disobey God; some, though once having done so, now repent from sin and seek him. The Indians can do the same. Other questions followed.[4]

Then came three questions from the ministers to the Indians: Did they not doubt there was a God since they could not see him? Was it not difficult to believe in one God who was yet present in Massachusetts, in Connecticut, in Old England, and in this wigwam all at the same time? Were they not troubled after committing sin, and what comfort did they have for the after-life when they must appear before God? The Indians confessed difficulty with these questions. Illustrations were used to clarify the minister's explanation. The impossibility of a fox or raccoon building a wigwam illustrated the impossibility of a world without God. The great house of the universe made by God was evidence enough without seeing him. The light of the sun was present in many

---

[1] *The Day-Breaking*..., 2 (1647).
[2] *Idem.*
[3] *Ibid.*, 3.
[4] *Ibid.*, 4–6.

places at once, so certainly could God be who made the sun. A "dolefull description...of the trembling and mourning condition of every soul that dies in sinne,"[1] given by the preacher, was clear enough to arouse concern for the life to come.

Thus ended three hours of consultation. The Indians were not weary, but the ministers "resolved to leave them with an appetite."[2] A time for a new meeting was arranged, apples for the children and tobacco for the men were given, and a promise was made to seek title for the hill on which the wigwams then stood.

Two weeks later, on November 11, the second gathering was held. The audience had grown, and seats had been prepared for the English guests. After prayer in English, the younger children were taught three questions and answers:

> 1. Quest. Who made you and all the world?
> Answ. God.
> 2. Quest. Who doe you looke should save you and redeeme you from sinne and hell?
> Answ. Jesus Christ.
> 3. Quest. How many commandements hath God given you to keepe?
> Answ. Ten.[3]

Each child present learned these answers. When this first catechism lesson was done, Eliot began his second sermon in the Indian language with the good news of the gospel.

> Wee are come to bring you good newes from the great God Almighty, maker of Heaven and Earth, and to tell you how evill and wicked men may come to bee good, so as while they live they may bee happy, and when they die they may goe to God and live in Heaven.[4]

Many of the themes of the first sermon recur in this one. Particularly stressed was how, in spite of God's anger against man's sin, he yet sent his Son to pacify divine justice by his sufferings in man's place. God's mercy, thus abundantly evident, will be withdrawn, however, and change to wrath should the Indians reject God's great salvation now offered to them. This one hour sermon was followed by questions set forth by the Indians themselves: Am I too old to become a child of God? Since English and Indian alike came from one father, why do English know more of God? How can we come to serve God? Why is sea water salty and land water fresh? If water is higher than earth, why does it not overflow? If a crime go unpunished on earth, is God still angry? With respect to the question about serving God, a three-fold answer was given: sinfulness must be lamented, forgiveness by the blood of Christ must be sought, and love for God must be evidenced by knowledge of and obedience to his will.[5]

---

[1] *Ibid.*, 6–7.
[2] *Ibid.*, 7.
[3] *Ibid.*, 8.
[4] *Idem.* This entire sentence is in italics in the original text.
[5] *Ibid.*, 10–13; Note here the recurrence of the three divisions of the Heidelberg Catechism.

Since "some houres" had now passed, the ministers posed the last two questions: What do you remember from the first sermon? Do you believe God is very angry for your least sin? To the first, the Indians, after consultation, offered much thanks for the wonderful things they had heard. To the second question

> They said yes, and hereupon wee set forth the terrour of God against sinners, and mercy of God to the penitent, and to such as sought to know Jesus Christ, and that as sinners should bee after death, *Chechainuppan*, i.e., tormented alive, (for wee know no other word in the tongue to expresse extreame torture by) so beleevers should after death *Wowein wicke Jehovah*, i.e., live in all blisse with Jehovah the blessed God: and so we concluded conference.[1]

The meeting ended with a prayer of fifteen minutes offered for the first time in the Indian language. Some of the Indians wept, and one could not stop. Many Indians could not sleep that night out of concern for what they had been taught. Two came on subsequent days to the preacher's house, much moved by the gospel. One of these reported that certain wicked Indians were beginning to oppose these beginnings.[2]

The writer pauses here in his narrative to comment on other matters. First he notes that they had thought to postpone further meetings until spring. Yet the evidences they had received of God's seal upon the work made them willing to go through frost and snow "lest the fire goe out of their hearts for want of a little more fewell...."[3]

He also observes that no one seems to know whence these Indians came. Those historians are likely right who consider them Tartars who passed from Asia to America by way of the straights of Anian and spread as far as the Atlantic shores. Close alliance to the wild beasts is likely evidence that these "dregs of mankinde" are inheritors of a divine curse. These natives are "the saddest spectacles of misery of meere men upon earth."[4]

> Yet notwithstanding the deepest degeneracies are no stop to the overflowing grace and blood of Christ, when the time of love shall come, no not to these poore outcasts, the utmost ends of the earth being appointed to bee in time, the Sonne of Gods possession.[5]

Many of our countrymen upbraid us, the writer continues, for not doing more for the hearts of the natives, "such men have surely more spleene than judgement, and know not the vast distance of Natives from common civility, almost humanity it selfe."[6] If we had forced Indians to baptism after teaching them a short answer or two to popish questions, as the Spaniards do in "Cusee,"[7] Peru, and Mexico, or if we allured them to it by giving coats and shirts as some

---

[1] *Ibid.*, 13.
[2] *Ibid.*, 13–14.
[3] *Ibid.*, 14.
[4] *Ibid.*, 14, 15.
[5] *Ibid.*, 15.
[6] *Idem.*
[7] Cuzco was the capital of the Incas. De Acosta, Joseph, *The Natural and Moral History of the Indies*, II 540, cf. I 155 and *passim*.

have done, we could have gained many hundreds or thousands under the name of a church. But we have not yet learned that art of coining Christians and stamping Christ's image on copper.

We should be humble that we have done too little for their conversion. Once we thought that there were reasons not to expect God's saving grace to operate upon the Indians:

> 1. Because till the Jewes come in, there is a seale set upon the hearts of those people, as they thinke from some Apocalypticall places.
> 2. That as in nature there is no progresses *ab extremo ad extremum nisi per media*, so in religion such as are so extreamly degenerate, must bee brought to some civility before religion can prosper, or the word take place.
> 3. Because wee want miraculous and extraordinary gifts without which no conversion can bee expected amongst these....[1]

Now it appears those who so thought were not altogether right. As once we thought New England soil too woody and rocky for grain but have discovered through tillage otherwise, so we thought Indians too rude and uncivil for conversion, but God has brought some to faith. Likely no great numbers will come till they are more civilized, but God works by degrees till more are brought in. Likely the English will not bring great numbers to God, since he ordinarily converts nations and peoples by some of their own countrymen who can best speak the language and best pity their own brethren. Both the preaching in their own tongue now being done and the repentance unto tears of some "argue a mighty and blessed presence of the spirit of Heaven in their hearts."[2]

Before reporting the third meeting, the writer makes several observations. (1) No Indians sleep during the sermon, as some English do, nor deride God's messenger. (2) Answering the philosophical questions of the Indians demands a learned gospel ministry with good knowledge of the arts. (3) There is no necessity for extraordinary gifts or miraculous signs for the conversion of the Indians, as the present working of the Spirit of God upon hearts of natives clearly evidences. Moreover, when one or two understand the gospel they usually talk about it to others as we do of news. (4) Englishmen, who are surfeited with fundamental doctrine while Indians weep when such is preached, will mourn too late their weariness of such truth. (5) The deepest estrangements of man from God are no hindrance to the Spirit of grace, for what people were ever so deeply degenerated since Adam's fall as this people? (6) If some are converted with so little light, what will happen in times of great light? Though some are very wicked, they are apt of understanding and melancholy of nature. These traits are likely to bring repentance and faith.

The writer could not himself be present for the third meeting on November 26, but he has a full report from those who went. More Indians had built their wigwams on the hill to enable ready attendance whenever the Word would be preached. Since opposition was increasing and threats of death made against

---

[1] *Ibid.*, 15, 16.      [2] *Ibid.*, 16.

those who attended preaching, Eliot spoke about temptations to sin by the devil. Various questions were again propounded by the Indians: Might they pray also to the devil to avert evil? What does "humiliation" mean? Why do the English call them "Indians?" What is a Spirit? Should they believe dreams? Could they have a place for a town and learn to spin? [1]

That night an English youth lodged with the Indians in Waaubon's [2] wigwam where the meetings had been held. He reported that Waaubon rehearsed the afternoon's preaching with all his company and prayed with them. Whenever he awoke during the night, he would again pray and speak to one or the other of the things he had heard. [3]

The Saturday night following, a wise Indian representative named Wampas brought four children, including his own son, ages nine, eight, five, and four, and two young men to the preacher's house. The Indian group desired to place these children in English homes so they would grow up to know God. The young men went to live at homes of elders in the Roxbury church, but so serious a matter as placing young children required more consideration. Wampas was satisfied with the promise that at the proper time the children would be accepted and educated or taught a trade. [4]

On December 4 Eliot preached to another group of Indians. Here he challenged a powwow (witch doctor) to answer two questions. Is God or Chepian (the devil) the author of all good? He answered, God. If God, then why do you pray to Chepian? This he refused to answer. Later Eliot spoke privately and kindly to the man, who then admitted that the question had struck terror into his heart. [5]

The writer uses this occasion to tell more of the evil called "powwowing." If an Indian dreams that Chepian appears to him as a serpent, he tells the other Indians about it. They dance and rejoice for two days for what has been learned about Chepian, and the Indian who dreamed becomes a powwow. His chief work is

> ...to cure the sick by certaine odde gestures and beatings of themselves, and then they pull out the sicknesse by applying their hands to the sick person and so blow it away: so that their Powwows are great witches having fellowship with the old Serpent, to whom they pray, and by whose meanes they heal sicke persons, and...will slew [*sic*–shew] many strange jinglings to the wonderment of the *Indians*. [6]

Should the powwow be ineffective, often he would be killed by the relatives of the dead patient, especially if he did not return the money paid to obtain the cure.

Meanwhile, the General Court decided to purchase land for the Indian town. In consultation with the English, the town was called Noonanetum, which means "rejoicing", because God and the English rejoice at the Indians' seeking

---

[1] *Ibid.*, 18, 19.
[2] Spelled Waubon in some later tracts.
[3] *Ibid.*, 19.
[4] *Ibid.*, 20, 21.
[5] *Ibid.*, 21.
[6] *Ibid.*, 21, 22.

to know God. The Indians, unaided by the English, had been busy making laws to govern themselves with stipulated penalties. Two of the ten laws have been forgotten, but the others included: idleness for a week, or at most a fortnight–five shillings; fornication–twenty shillings; beating one's wife–hands tied and severe punishment determined by the judge; women with loose hair or cut like a man's–five shillings; women with naked breasts–two shillings and six pence; men with long locks–five shillings; killing lice between one's teeth–five shillings. Concerning this last one, the writer adds: "This Law though ridiculous to English eares yet tends to preserve cleanlinesse among *Indians*."[1] The law which is perhaps most significant requires every young man, if not another man's servant and unmarried, to set up a wigwam and to plant for himself. He was not permitted to live shifting from one wigwam to the other.

This desire to settle and live ordered lives was an evidence of the sprinklings of the blood and spirit of Christ. So were the spontaneous prayers which the Indians began to offer:

> Take away Lord my stony heart.
> Wash Lord my soule.
> Lord lead mee when I die to heaven.[2]

Surely the Lord Jesus would never had made so fit a key for Indian locks had he not intended to open up the doors of some hearts.

> Hee that God hath raised up and enabled to preach unto them, is a man (you know) of a most sweet, humble, loving, gratious and enlarged spirit, whom God hath blest, and surely will still delight in, & do good by.[3]

Although the writer of this tract had never expected to be asking help from England to "further any good worke here," now he feels the burden to do so. To educate and train the Indian children already offered to the English, which meant providing schooling, clothing, and good food as well, is an expensive matter. Likely when other Indians learn of this way of civilizing and christianizing, many will want to avail themselves of the opportunity. Therefore, if any in England do something to encourage this work, gifts should be channelled through the college, so there will be no question of careless keeping and misuse. Yet, if no gifts are forthcoming, then "more weake meanes shall have the honour of it in the day of Christ."[4]

The fourth meeting held at Noonanetum in Wasupan's wigwam was on December 9. Again the children were first catechized; then Eliot preached concerning the passage in Ezekiel about the dry bones being opened, applying this to the Indian's condition. At this time the group offered all their children to be educated by the English, regretting that they could offer no payment in return. Since the English were making preparations for the children to be schooled near the Indian village, acceptance of the children was apparently postponed.

---

[1] *Ibid.*, 22.
[2] *Ibid.*, 23.
[3] *Idem.*
[4] *Ibid.*, 23, 24.

The usual interchange of questions followed. One Indian was asked: What is sin? He answered: A naughty heart. An old man complained that he was afraid whether he would go to hell or heaven, even though he was fully purposed to keep the sabbath. Hereupon "the justification of a sinner by faith in Christ was opened unto him as the remedy against all feares of hell." [1] Another complained that other Indians reviled them and called them rogues for cutting their hair in the English manner. The writer explains that no English man had mentioned the matter to the Indians, but they had themselves discerned what vanity and pride had been placed upon their hair. Likely the long hair was one of the most obvious differences between the Indian and the English men. This difference the Indians were eager to remove. Leading Indians present assured the fearful ones that they would stand by to help in persecution, and God would also help. Many Indians came only a few days to Noonanetum and went on again, but this group gave assurance of their full purpose to remain and keep the sabbath. Night was then drawing on. After encouraging the Indians in their purpose, the English went home.

b. Stabilization and Growth

The title of the third tract published in the series assures the reader that the "day-breaking" is past, and now one can speak of *The Clear Sun-shine of the Gospel Breaking Forth upon the Indians in New-England* (1648). The writer, Mr. Thomas Shepard (d. 1649), identifies John Eliot for the first time as the preacher whose work was praised in the previous publications. Also for the first time is included a letter penned by Eliot giving more light upon the nature of his work. This letter makes clear that Eliot's actual mission attempts had begun earlier than the story of the more recent successful meetings would suggest. Once again this tract appeals to Old Testament prophecy, suggesting by the use of Isaiah 2:2,3 on the title page that "God's Wonderfull Workings" evident in the coming in of the Indians in these "last dayes" is a fulfillment of prophecy.[2]

Two prefaces precede Shepard's account and Eliot's letter. Both are signed by twelve Puritan divines in England and repeat the judgments concerning the low, nearly sub-human level of Indian character. But the low estate from which the converts come serves to show the greatness of the mercy and glory of Christ. As God brought salvation to men through the cross of Christ and in the shipwreck of Paul, so good has come through the scattering of his ministers to the utmost ends of the earth. "Where the *Ministery* is the *Harbinger* and goes before, Christ and *Grace* will *certainly* follow after." [3] If in New England ministers must deal "with such *whom* they are to *make* men, before they can *make* them Christians," certainly they deserve all the strengthening and encouragement that Old England can offer.[4]

The appeal in the second Epistle is to the godly and well-affected in the kingdom of England. The divines cannot resist comparing New England with

---

[1] *Ibid.*, 25.
[2] *The Clear Sun-shine* . . ., "Epistle Dedicatory To the High Court of Parliament," 4 (1648).
[3] *Ibid.*
[4] *Ibid.*, 5, 6.

Old. The stirrings after grace and pleasure in the ordinances of the gospel by the natives serve as a warning. God may well seek other ground for his ordinances, seeing the old ground is bearing such poor fruit. The sad decline in England forms a sharp contrast to the rising sun in the western lands.

> The Ordinances *are as much* contemned *here, as* frequented *there; the* Ministry *as much* discouraged *here, as* embraced *there;* Religion *as much derided, the* ways *of godliness as much* scorned *here, as they can be* wished *and desired there;* generally *wee are* sick *of plenty, wee surfet of our abundance, the worst of surfets, and with our* loathed Manna *and* disdained *food,* God *is* preparing them a Table *in the wildernes; where our* satieties, *wil be their* sufficiencies; *our* complaints, *their* contents; *our* burthens, *their* comforts; *if he cannot have an* England *here, he can have an* England *there; & baptize & adopt them into those* priviledges, *which wee have* looked *upon as our burthens.*¹

Old England need not think that God will long continue the form where the power is gone, nor the light where the heat is gone. The lessons of the Jews and of the churches of Asia are too clearly written to make so great an error. Already in the new land the fields are white, the old land bears little fruit; there the feet of those that preach glad tidings are beautiful, here they are contemned; there they do much, and we do little; what a wonder that they should be men in their infancy and we children in our manhood. May those poor Indians be incentives to us.²

> ...*who knows but* God *gave* life *to* New England, *to* quicken Old, *and hath* warmed *them, that they might* heat *us,* raised *them from the dead that they might* recover *us from that consumption, and those sad* decayes *which are come upon us?* ³

This treatise is a sermon to every man to value the gospel, its ordinances, and its blessings. It is a sermon to all ministers not to despond at lack of gospel fruit for God has a fulness of time and his grace conquers the greatest degeneracy. It is a sermon to Christian merchants to propagate the gospel to dark corners of the earth. It is a sermon to serious Christians to rejoice to see "*the* bounds *of the Sanctuary extended,* Christ *advanced, the* Gospel *propagated, and* souls saved." ⁴ Let us give our prayers and assistance; children must be schooled and clothed, and parents trained and supplied with tools. Let those who have tasted God's mercy, be merciful.

Thomas Shepard continues the previously published narrative concerning the progress of the Indian work.⁵ An Indian sachem from Concord had attended one of the four meetings reported in the former tract. Upon returning to his own tribe he convinced most of his fellows that, contrary to the demanding practice of higher sachems, the English intended good and gave gifts. They desired to become more like the English and to cast off wild Indian customs. The three-fold effect of this decision was: an Indian was requested to write

---

¹ *Ibid.*, "Epistle to the Reader," 2, 3.
² *Ibid.*, 4.
³ *Ibid.*, 5.
⁴ *Ibid.*, 6.

⁵ The manner in which he calls attention to the previous tract and the similar style argue for his authorship of that document also, though there is no clear evidence.

down the laws they had agreed upon; Mr. Eliot was asked to come and preach to them; and property was requested within the bounds of Concord for a town near the English. Shepard views these as good signs, for the history of the Cuseo and Mexico Indians shows this to be a good means of civilizing men.

The twenty-nine "Conclusions and Orders," adopted by several sachems and other principal Indians at Concord in January, 1647, are quite comprehensive in comparison with those earlier made at Noonanetum. These also were drawn up without assistance from the English. Condemned, with appropriate penalties, were: too much strong liquor, powwowing, lying, stealing, polygamy, enmity, picking and eating lice (the fine is a penny per louse), greasing of themselves, fornication, adultery and murder (punishable by death), howling at funerals, and beating wives or others. The positive requirements were meant to establish ordered Christian conduct. Men are to be stirred up to seek God, and time is to be well used. Indians shall labor after humility, pay debts to the English, observe the Lord's Day, wear their hair properly, and set up prayer and devotions with their families. To accomplish this a town is to be established.

Due to, as Shepard says, "the neare relation between me and the fireside usually all winter time",[1] he did not again attend the bi-weekly Indian lecture at Noonanetum until March 3, 1647, when the fierceness of the winter was past. Others in attendance besides himself and Eliot included fellow-ministers Wilson and Allen, and President Dunster of Harvard College (founded–1636, charter secured–1650), "beside many other Christians." [2] Novel at this meeting were the two questions from Indian women asked via one of the men: Do I pray when my husband prays if my heart goes with what he says? And does a husband do well who prays with his wife but continues in his passions and anger with her? [3] An old man also asked counsel what to do with his son who refused to hear the Word of God and to give up drunkenness though commanded to do so. The son was providentially present, so Mr. Wilson spoke "so terribly, yet so graciously" to the son. The son, who understood English, exploded with anger, to which no answer was given, only the Word was left with him, "which we knew would one day take its effect one way or other upon him." [4]

The Order made by the General Court at Boston on May 26, 1647, brought a magistrate to the Indian lecture place quarterly to judge civil and criminal matters, not capital. The ministry of the Word, the Order points out, has brought some Indians to a sufficient state of civility to make this desirable. Indian sachems may bring offenders to these courts, and hold monthly courts themselves for the smaller cases. The sachems may themselves appoint officers to serve warrants and execute the judgments of the courts. All monies received in fines from Indians are to be used to build meeting houses, to educate poor children, or other public use, to be determined by the magistrates and Eliot or another elder who instructed the Indians in religion. The magistrates and Eliot,

---

[1] *The Clear Sun-shine . . .*, "Epistle to the Reader," 6.
[2] *Idem.*
[3] *The Clear Sun-shine . . .*, 7.
[4] *Ibid.*, 8.

or the elder, are to endeavor carefully to make the Indians understand the most useful English laws and the principles of reason, justice, and equity upon which they are grounded.[1]

During the summer, on the first day of the Synod's meeting at Cambridge, Eliot gave an Indian lecture to which a confluence of Indians came from the surrounding area. The purpose of holding the lecture in conjunction with the Synod's meeting was two-fold:

> ...partly that the reports of Gods worke begun among them, might be seen and beleeved of the chief who were then sent and met from all the Churches of Christ in the Countrey, who could hardly beleeve the reports they had received concerning these new stirs among the *Indians*, and partly hereby to raise up a greater spirit of prayer for the carrying on of the work begun upon the *Indians*, among all the Churches and servants of the Lord Jesus.[2]

The sermon was based upon Ephesians 2:1 to show the Indians their miserable condition without Christ, that they were dead in trespasses and sin, and to point them to the Lord Jesus who alone could quicken them. Following the sermon, public questions were asked: What countryman was Christ? How far is that away? Where is Christ now? How might they lay hold on Christ since he is now absent from them? The mourning of some Indians during the preaching, the asking of several spiritual questions, the aptness to believe the preached gospel and the answers given to their questions, and the ready answers of the poor naked children to questions in the Catechism

> did marvellously affect all the wise and godly Ministers, Magistrates, & people, and did raise their hearts up to great thankfulnesse to God; very many deeply and abundantly mourning for joy to see such a blessed day, and the Lord Jesus so much known and spoken of among such as never heard of him before.[3]

If any in England doubt the truth of what was formerly written or if any vilify what is now written, they speak too late, for what was done at Cambridge was done in open sun.

Near the end of 1647, Eliot, Wilson, and Shepard were asked to come to Yarmouth to settle a church controversy. This was quickly accomplished. Eliot, "as hee takes all advantages of time, so hee tooke this, of speaking with, and preaching to the poore *Indians* in these remote places about *Cape Cod*."[4] The Indians understood the language which Eliot spoke. For, Shepard writes, though other Englishmen may excel Eliot in speaking about common matters in the Indian language, he excels all in speaking about the sacred things of God. Both the variation in dialect which occurs every forty to sixty miles and the strangeness of sacred language about holy things of God made communication difficult, yet "they did understand him" assisted by variations of speech

---
[1] *Ibid.*, 15, 16.
[2] *Ibid.*, 11.
[3] *Ibid.*, 11, 12.
[4] *Ibid.*, 8.

and help of interpreters. Though there was strong opposition to Eliot's preaching by one fierce and furious sachem, yet another was willing to learn. This is significant, because what the sachem said and did, his men did also. One aged Indian informed them

> That these very things which Mr. Eliot had taught them as the Commandements of God, and concerning God, and the making of the world by one God, that they had heard from old men who were now dead, to say the same things, since whose death there hath been no remembrance or knowledge of them among the *Indians* untill now they heare of them againe.[2]

Shepard hereupon opines that such knowledge may have come to them by the French pastor cast upon these coasts many years before. Others of the Indians had the apprehension that their forefathers did know God but forgot him. One Indian testified that two years before he had dreamed of the English coming, and one dressed in black addressed them, and at last assured them that God's anger would turn to forgiveness for himself and his people. Since the Indian thought his dream fulfilled, the impression is that Eliot is dressed in black on this occasion.

Shepard did not attend the lecture at Noonanetum all summer, but when he returned in the fall of 1647, he was surprised at the large number of Indian men, women, and children clad in English apparel. Some clothing they had received from the English; some they have earned for themselves.

Shepard adds several episodes and a list of questions asked by Indians that have been reported to him during the past winter. One episode was related by Eliot himself and indicates his manner of working. An old Indian, about whom was also written in the previous tract, came naked to Eliot in the cold. Eliot told the man that, because he brought his wife and children regularly to the lecture, he would give him some clothes. At this the Indian was overcome with emotion and responded "God I see is mercifull." [2] At a lecture preceding the gift of clothes, this same Indian had testified publicly how good the Lord had been to send his Word to them who had been in gross ignorance so long.

Some of the questions the Indians had been asking indicate that acceptance of the Christian faith was not without its problems.

> How may one know wicked men, who are good and who are bad?
> If a man should be inclosed in Iron a foot thick and thrown into the fire, what would become of his soule, whether could the soule come forth thence or not?
> Why did not God give all men good hearts that they might bee good?
> How they should know when their faith is good, and their prayers good prayers?
> Why did not God kill the Devill that made all men so bad, God having all power? [3]

---

[1] *Ibid.*, 9.
[2] *Ibid.*, 12.
[3] *Ibid.*, 13, 14.

Many questions were more "Philosophicall," i.e., about the planets, elements, and the life hereafter. Some questions were called by the Indians "Papoose" questions, that is, childish questions. The seriousness with which the Indians went about their prayers and religious exercises indicates that more than curiosity prompted most of their inquiries.

Eliot's letter published in this tract was written at Shepard's request to describe the Indian work. It was dated September 24, 1647. He begins by stating the purpose of his work.

> That which I first aymed at was to declare & deliver unto them the Law of God, to civilize them which course the Lord took by *Moses*, to give the Law to that rude company because of transgression, Gal. 3:19, to convince, bridle, restrain, and civilize them, and also to humble them.[1]

But when he first tried, the Indians gave no heed, rather they despised what he said. Some time later a few wanted to adopt English fashions, but thought it would take forty years, or perhaps a hundred. Eliot hoped this desire was from the Lord and thus a preparative to the acceptance of the law and Word of God. His heart would not permit sitting still. He told the Indians there were only two differences between them and the English.

> First, we know, serve, and pray unto God, and they doe not: Secondly, we labour and work in building, planting, clothing ourselves, &c. and they doe not.[2]

If they would but do these two things, they would be one with the English. They said they did not know God nor how to pray and to serve him.

> I told them if they would learn to know God, I would teach them: unto which they being very willing, I then taught them (as I sundry times had indeavored afore) but never found them so forward, attentive and desirous to learn till this time, and then I told them I would come to their *Wigwams*, and teach them, their wives and children, which they seemed very glad of; and from that day forward I have not failed to doe that poore little which you know I doe.[3]

Eliot reports that he began at Noonanetum. Those at Dorchester refused at first, but later also desired to know God and pray to him. He emphasizes four effects which the preaching of the Word has had among them.[4] First, they have forsaken all their powwows, some of whom have also been converted. But other powwows have gone elsewhere and return only to mock and scoff at the praying Indians. Second, the Indians have learned to pray. They pray with their families morning and evening, as those who have visited their wigwams testify. They pray also at mealtime as they have seen the English do. They express their great joy that they know God and show great affection to those who teach them. Third, they are careful to instruct their children in the catechism. By

---

[1] *Ibid.*, 17.
[2] *Idem.*
[3] *Idem.*
[4] *Ibid.*, 18–20.

the oft repeating of it to the children, the men and women can also readily answer the questions. Fourth, they carefully try to sanctify the sabbath. They asked if it were best to come to the English meetings where they understood nothing, or to meet among themselves where they had none to teach them. Eliot had counselled that they meet together and let the wisest and best men lead in prayers and teach the rest such things as they had already been taught. When one had taught, a second and a third could do likewise. Then questions could be asked, and if no one could answer, Eliot would be asked at the next meeting. This became the pattern for the regular Indian sabbath meetings. No profaning of the sabbath by worldly talk and cutting trees was permitted. Some concluded that it must be wrong to split a piece of dry wood to put upon a dying fire on sabbath evening, but the matter was explained at Eliot's next lecture "for their better information." [1]

There are four parts besides prayer to the religious exercises which Eliot conducts semi-weekly with the Indians.

> First, I catechize the children and youth; wherein some are very ready & expert, they can readily say all the Commandements, so far as I have communicated them, and all other principles about the creation, the fall, the redemption by Christ, &c. wherein also the aged people are pretty expert, by the frequent repetition thereof to the children, and are able to teach it to their children at home, and do so.
> Secondly, I Preach unto them out of some texts of Scripture, wherein I study all plainnesse, and brevity, unto which many are very attentive.
> Thirdly, if there be any occasion, we in the next place go to admonition and censure; unto which they submit themselves reverently, and obediently, and some of them penitently confessing their sins with much plainnesse, and without shiftings, and excuses....
> Fourthly, the last exercise, you know, we have among them, is their asking us questions, and very many they have asked....[2]

Several examples of censure and admonition are given by Eliot. One of the most typical is that of Wampoowas.

> ...a man named *Wampoowas*, being in a passion upon some light occasion did beat his wife, which was a very great offence among them now (though in former times it was very usuall) and they had made a Law against it, and set a fine upon it; whereupon he was publikly brought forth before the Assembly, which was great that day, for our Governor and many other English were then present: the man wholly condemned himself without any excuse: and when he was asked what provocation his wife gave him? He did not in the least measure blame her but himself, and when the quality of the sinne was opened, that it was cruelty to his own body, and against Gods Commandement, and that passion was a sinne, and much aggravated by such effects, yet God was ready to pardon

---

[1] *Ibid.*, 21.   [2] *Ibid.*, 20–23.

it in Christ, &c. he turned his face to the wall and wept, though with modest indeavor to hide it; and such was the modest, penitent, and melting behavior of the man, that it much affected all to see it in a Barbarian, and all did forgive him, onely this remained, that they executed their Law notwithstanding his repentance, and required his fine, to which he willingly submitted, and paid it.[1]

The questions asked by Indians and reported by Eliot seem to be of the more problematical type: why did the English wait twenty-seven years to teach the Indians about God? Eliot's answer is both a confession and a reminder of guilt also on the Indian side.

To whom we answered, that we doe repent that wee did not long agoe, as now we doe, yet withall wee told them, that they were never willing to hear till now, and that seeing God hath bowed their hearts to be willing to hear, we are desirous to take all the paines we can now teach them.[2]

Other questions were: Since I am still so sinful and perhaps may fall back into bad sin, is it wrong to wish that I might now die? What happens to our little children when they die, since they have no sin? Since we are so sinful, is it possible that any of us shall be saved? What must we do when we are sick, now that we go no longer to the powwow?

To the question about children Eliot taught more about original sin and the damned state of all men, and about the Covenant of God made with all his people so that when he chooses a man or woman to be his servant, he chooses all their children to be his servants also. This cheered the Indians much. Concerning the difficulty of being saved, Eliot propounded Matt. 11:28–29 to them. The last question demanded action. The Indians were taught some rudiments of "Physick" and some anatomy. But Eliot suggests that a good work for England would be the maintenance of a school or college to train Englishmen and Indians for the skill that confounds the powwows. Then the people would also be "farre more easily inclined to leave those wayes, and pray unto God, whose gift Physick is, and whose blessing must make it effectuall." [3]

Those Indians who did not pray derided the praying Indians and asked what gain they had from believing in God and Christ. They pointed out that all Indians go naked, are poor, and have the same harvest of corn, while the unbelieving ones have more pleasure. To this Eliot replied that God gives both little things, showing them his little finger, and big ones, indicating his thumb, and added parenthetically – "for you know they use and delight in demonstrations." [4] The little mercies are food, clothes, liquor, houses, cattle, and pleasures. The great ones are wisdom, knowledge of God, Christ, eternal life, repentance, faith; such are for the soul. Besides, continues Eliot, you do have some clothes, and if you obeyed the commandment "Six days thou shalt work," God would give you clothes, houses, cattle, and riches as the English have.

---

[1] *Ibid.*, 21.
[2] *Ibid.*, 24.
[3] *Ibid.*, 26.
[4] *Idem.*

The Christian Indians learned not to gamble. But non-Christian creditors were pressing their claims for past gambling debts. Eliot often interviewed both debtor and creditor individually and got the creditor to agree to halve the debt.

Already the Indians were becoming industrious. Eliot was providing tools for those who would work. Women had products to sell each season of the year: in the winter handmade items, and the rest of the year mostly fruits and fresh meats. Properties were being fenced and two schools for Indian children were established. To solve problems like young men who were unfaithful laborers the Indians requested and received permission to have a court for government among themselves. The spontaneity of this request and its tendency "to civilize" pleased the English.[1]

In a postscript to this letter of September, 1647, Eliot says that the increased spiritual concern of these heathen for their relation to God and the mighty spirit of prayer for Indian conversion arising in all the churches convince him that the Lord's time to prepare for the coming of his grace and the establishment of his kingdom among the Indians has arrived.[2]

In the conclusion of this, the longest of the missionary tracts, Shepard takes up once again the narrative. The delay of the vessel gives him opportunity to add items that occur to him. He marvels that Indians who do not weep at the sorest torture do so much when the conquering power of Christ strikes them through the Word. Since the sun does not set as soon as it begins to rise, likely the Indians sunrise into the beams of the gospel will soon come to the full sun of God's grace. May it not be with us as Gildas, the British historian, observes concerning the early "Britaines", how that God permitted the Saxons to scourge and root them out because of their deep carelessness in the communication of the Christian religion to the Saxons. One of the greatest obstacles to the conversion of Indians is the "ill example" of the English, especially in the matter of loose sabbath observance.

After a seeming decline in the ardor of the Indians, Eliot preached about the danger of apostasy. This had the desired effect. Now the Indians were fencing in their town (Noonanetum) of several hundred acres for the sixpence a rod which Eliot paid to encourage them. Wigwams were as roomy as only sachems formerly had and had partitions to provide privacy between parents, children, and servants, "who formerly were never private in what nature is shamed of." [3]

More difficult questions are related: What should a man do when he had two wives and children only from the second? Should a man whose wife commits adultery and runs away receive her again when she repents? Why does God, who loves the repentant, still afflict them? What do English men think of Mr. Eliot because he associated with wicked Indians to teach them? This question was prompted by Eliot's sermon on Eph. 5.11: "Have no fellowship with unfruitfull workers of darkness." Wampoowas once commented that be-

---

[1] *Ibid.*, 28.
[2] *Ibid.*, 29.
[3] *Ibid.*, 32.

cause they prayed to God, other Indians hate them, and the English suspect that they are not sincere, but that God, who knows all things, knows their sincerity.[1]

In the fall of 1647 after the death of a little child, the Christian Indians broke for the first from superstitious heathen burial observances. They built a wooden box, and forty Indians accompanied the coffin to the grave. After the grave had been filled, they withdrew a short distance and spent a half hour in prayer under a tree in the woods with much sighs and tears. Indeed, many English are outstripped by Indians in piety.

Shepard, like Eliot, believes that the most hopeful time for the winning of the natives will come when pity arises in their hearts to move some of them to become missionaries to their own countrymen.[2] One difficulty is the variety of languages among the different tribes. Christ will surely, though perhaps slowly, conquer. However, such a conquering in blood as the Spaniards have done in the killing of nineteen million innocent natives in the southern parts of this continent, "as *Acosta* the Jesuite a bird of their own nest relates the story," [3] will be overthrown by some avenging hand. Perhaps then the oppressed remnants in those coasts will come into God's kingdom. Let us not be ashamed of the day of small beginnings, but, as the Jews of old, cry mightily to God.

The judgment that the Indian work is progressing is expressed in the title of the fourth tract. After the "first fruits," the "day-breaking," and the "clear sun-shine," comes *The Glorious Progress of the Gospel Amongst the Indians in New England (1649)*.

In the dedicatory epistle to the Parliament of England and the Council of State, Edward Winslow calls attention to the Ordinance approved March 17, 1647, by that body which was *"for the encouragement and advancement of Learning and Piety in New England."* [4] Nothing, however, has been done on this matter, despite the good intentions of Parliament. The letters contained in this tract are to indicate the continuing need. Perhaps it will serve as a stimulus to action. To the glorious work of enlarging the territory of Christ's kingdom, Winslow hoped the Parliament would commit itself.[5] He pointed out that the English had not been wholly negligent of their duty to bring the natives to a right understanding of God,

> ...but had in sundry parts of the Countrey long before brought divers to a pretty competency of right understanding in the mystery of salvation, who lived orderly, and dyed hopefully....[6]

The experience of the Indians with "the justice, prudence, valour, temperance, and righteousnesse of the English" [7] served to prepare them for the

---

[1] *Ibid.*, 33–35.
[2] *Ibid.*, 36.
[3] *Ibid.*, 38.
[4] *The Glorious Progress* . . ., "Epistle Dedicatory," 1–2 (1647).
[5] *Ibid.*, 6. Winslow discusses here the question of the possible identity of the Indians with the ten lost tribes of Israel, for which see below, section C. 2.
[6] *The Glorious Progress* . . ., 1.
[7] *Idem.*

present awakening. To describe that awakening, Winslow presents one letter from Thomas Mayhew, Jr., and two from Eliot.

Mayhew reports that the encouragements that advantaged his progress were God's glory and promises, the notable reason and capacity God has given to many Indians, their zealous desire for true happiness, the knowledge he himself possessed of their language, and several remarkable providences of healing after his prayers over sick Indians. He has heard from an old Indian who testifies of wise ancestors who once taught a knowledge of God now forgotten. This Indian with others (likely in the summer of 1647, since Mayhew's letter is dated Nov. 18, 1647) asked that Mayhew teach them the Word of God in their own tongue. This he does every fortnight.

One lengthy letter of Eliot's, written during 1648, has been lost. Winslow presents later letters of Eliot, the first written November 12, 1648, the second September 13, 1648, and the third December 2, 1648.[1] Eliot begins the first letter by thanking English friends for their efforts to provide for the New England mission to the Indians:

> ...which work I blesse the Lord goeth on not without successe, beyond the ability of the Instruments: It is the Lord, the Lord only who doth speak to the hearts of men, and he can speak to theirs, and doth, (blessed be his name) so effectually, that one of them I beleeve verily is gone to the Lord....[2]

There is, however, a great impediment to the further advance of the work. Many Indians want to be taught the knowledge of God, but they are scattered widely. One possibility is for Eliot to teach them where they live; the other is for them to live among or close to the English. For some reason, likely his work at the Roxbury church, Eliot says no more about the first alternative. The second is not presently possible because the Indians have neither tools nor skill nor heart to fence in their property; if it is not fenced, English cattle spoil their corn and their owners refuse to pay damages. The consequence is that few Indians come to live where Eliot teaches, but stay only a few days and then continue their wanderings. The way to do them good is this:

> A place must be found (both for this and sundry other reasons I can give) some what remote from the English, where they must have the word constantly taught, and government constantly exercised, meanes of good subsistance provided, incouragements for the industrious, meanes of instructing them in Letters, Trades, and Labours, as building, fishing, Flax and Hemp dressing, planting Orchards, &c. Such a project in a fit place, would draw many that are well minded together: but I feare it will be too chargeable, though I see that God delighteth in small beginnings, that his great name may be magnified.[3]

---

[1] *Ibid.*, 6–14. Though not chronological, this is the order in which the letters were printed.

[2] *Ibid.*, 6.

[3] *Ibid.*, 8.

Meanwhile, Eliot has been trying to get others to work. In response to the entreaties of the Indians of Martha's Vineyard,[1] Mr. Mayhew is teaching them in their own language, and not without success. Eliot believes all the ministers who live near the Indians should do the same.

> I have earnestly solicited many so to do, and I hope God will in his time bow their hearts thereunto.[2]
> ...it appeareth to me, that the Fields begin to look white unto the Harvest. Oh that the Lord would be pleased to raise up many labourers into this Harvest.[3]

Eliot himself went forty miles to Nashawog four times during the previous summer (1648) to teach a sizable group who are troubled that he does not come oftener and stay longer. Here the great sachem has embraced the gospel. At Pawtucket, at one of the falls of the Merrimac River, large groups of Indians come each spring for fishing. The occasion is like to a great fair in England. Eliot has met and taught the Indians here the past two years. This annual pilgrimage Eliot plans to continue, as well as to inaugurate a new one sixty miles away.[4] At the last gathering in Pawtucket Eliot preached on Malachi 1:11, which he translates to them:

> *From the rising of the Sun, to the going down of the same, thy name shall be great among the Indians, and in every place prayers shall be made to thy name, pure prayers, for thy name shall be great among the Indians.*[5]

After the sermon on the necessity and urgency for repentance and faith in Christ, one Indian asked whether it was so that "then all the world of Indians are gone to hell to be tormented for ever, untill now a few may goe to Heaven and be saved...?"[6] Eliot explains to the reader that he puts the principle of a two-fold estate after this life, heaven and hell, among the first truths taught to adults and children alike. This they readily accept, having a tradition concerning life after death with a good or bad character dependent upon conduct in this life. Hereupon a great sagamore and several of his sons who were sachems embraced Christianity. This is more than coincidence since Eliot endeavors "to engage the sachems of greatest note to accept the Gospel" because that

> ...doth greatly animate and encourage such as are well-affected, and is a damping to those that are scoffers and opposers; for many such there be, though they dare not appear so before me.[7]

The above-mentioned converted Indian leaders later proposed that Eliot live among them. For this purpose ground would be given, if only he would

---

[1] This book quotes Eliot as saying, "I entreated Mr. Mayhew to teach the Indians." This typesetting error Eliot himself corrects in *The Light appearing...*, 18 (1651).
[2] *The Glorious Progress...*, 8 (1649).
[3] *Ibid.*, 10.
[4] *Ibid.*, 11.
[5] *Ibid.*, 9.
[6] *Idem.*
[7] *Ibid.*, 10.

teach them. That this would have rendered more problems than that of language is clear. As it is, due to their barbarous life and poverty, there is no meat, drink, or lodging for those who go to preach among them. Rather, all necessities must be carried along, besides something to give to the Indians. This is just the reverse of Christ's situation. He and his disciples were poor and received care from the rich who accepted the gospel. But now, Christ comes with the rich to the poor, who receive from his ministers "externall benificence and advancement, as well as spirituall grace and blessings." [1] Therefore, Eliot never goes to the Indians empty-handed but carries something to distribute among them. Likewise, when they come to his home, no one leaves without some refreshment, and no gratuity is received that is not rewarded. One poor creature gave a penny-worth of wampam (an Indian bead) with a demonstration of hearty affection. This Eliot kindly accepted and responded with an invitation to his own home in order to show his love for the Indian.

Since the Indians have no means of treating illness, they are loathe to forsake powwowing. Eliot has himself used some cordials and medicines with success. This has served to convince many of the diabolical evil of the powwow.

The Indians near Roxbury receive the constant teaching with gladness and growth in faith and conduct. By degrees they are beginning to work. Eliot judges that the two and a half pages of questions he encloses show this growth. Their increased knowledge of the Bible is indicated by questions on Eve, Sodom, and Abimelech. Theological problems deal with the redemption by Christ, the nature of diabolical working, the possibility of seeing God, and the resurrection and heaven. Ethical struggles concern marriage with unbelievers, loving our enemies, anger at murderers, and lies of Englishmen. Questions of faith and Christian life include lack of love for prayer, the problem of pain, sabbath observance and sin after forgiveness.[2]

These questions show, Eliot believes, how Indian souls are searching for the things of God and Christ. He seems to be considering whether he should settle with them and give full time to the Indian work.

> ...I will say this solemnly, not suddenly, nor lightly, but before the Lord, as I apprehend in my conscience, were they but in a setled way of Civility and Government cohabiting together, and I called (according to God) to live among them, and could finde out at least twenty men and women in some measure fitted of the Lord for it, and soone would be capable thereof: And we doe admit in charity some into our Churches, of our owne, of whose spirituall estate I have more cause of feare, then of some of them: But that day of Grace is not yet come unto them. When God's time is come, he will make way for it, & enable us to accomplish it. In the meane time, I desire to wait, pray, and beleeve.[3]

Eliot concludes by asking the prayers of his friends that he may increase in the ability to converse in the language, since the lack of fluency slows the progress of the gospel.

---

[1] *Idem.*     [2] *Ibid.,* 12–14.     [3] *Ibid.,* 14.

The third letter [1] is dated only twenty days later than the first. His reason for writing is fear lest his other letters sent by different boats might be lost. He writes concerning the progress of the Indians because others are silent. He repeats the entreaty for prayers that the Lord send more laborers into the Indian harvest. He adds that the Indians have begun to "*enquire after baptisme and Church Ordinances, and the way of worshipping God as the Churches here do.*" [2] Eliot has responded by showing the Indians how incapable they are to be entrusted with such so long as they live unfixed, confused, and ungoverned lives, uncivilized and unsubdued to labor and order. Therefore they should choose a fit place for cohabitation where they may labor and settle down. Then they may have a church and all the ordinances of Christ. This proposal the Indians are seriously considering.

Two matters occasion gratitude. First, the act of Parliament to seek ways of assistance is surely a special smile of God upon the work. Eliot hopes their plan is already perfected. Second, an Indian who was taken prisoner in the Pequot Wars and who now lives with Mr. Richard Calicott of Dorchester has asked to join the church there. He was the first Indian to teach Eliot words and serve as his interpreter. Eliot must go that very day to the meeting of elders for the trial and examination of the young Indian in preparation for his admission into the church. If only the provisions Eliot has requested would be sent, the work can progress further. A list of necessary items has been enclosed, including well-tempered tools, medicines, surgical instruments, and clothing.

Five of the questions which Eliot appends are to indicate "the progresse they make in knowledge." [3]

The letter of September, 1649, [4] though brief, is significant. Directions are enclosed for the sending of new cloth and old clothes. The suggestion from his correspondent to have the Indians plant orchards and gardens, Eliot had already carried out. He personally reserved several hundred trees in the nurseries to be set out the next spring. They have no time to fence the orchards, however, since they are now fencing a large cornfield. Two hundred rod is already completed. The forty or fifty tools are nearly gone, and more are needed to continue the work. In the winter the Indians do well in sawing planks, only if Eliot could be among them oftener they would both attend it better and do it more orderly. They follow his advice in any reasonable thing.

Eliot agrees with his correspondent that Indians must not be expected to change all at once, as too many English assume. They must be bent slowly. Patience is necessary for the day of small beginnings. The best way is clear enough.

> I finde it absolutely necessary to carry on civility with Religion: and that maketh me have many thoughts that the way to doe it to the purpose, is to live among them in a place distant from the *English*, for many reasons;

---

[1] *Ibid.*, 17–21.
[2] *Ibid.*, 18.
[3] *Ibid.*, 19.
[4] *Ibid.*, 15–17.

and bring them to co-habitation, Government, Arts, and trades: but this is yet too costly an enterprize for *New-England*, that hath extended it self so far in laying the foundation of a common-weale in this wildernesse.[1]

The year preceding, a gentleman gave a gift of ten pounds for schooling of Indian children, five pounds of which went to a teacher at Cambridge and five to Dorchester. Unless more gifts come, both schools will have to close. The children will forget what they have learned, also the English language. Yet Eliot continues to catechize them every lecture day. Some Indians from Sudbury, Mestick, and Dedham are ingenuous and pray to God, coming to hear the word. Most Lynn Indians, on the contrary, do not, since their sachem refuses to believe and opposes the gospel.

An "Appendix," initialed J.D., minister of the gospel, concludes this tract. For the most part, it strikes themes developed earlier. As such, it emphasizes and enlarges on one or two of Eliot's ideas mentioned above.

He observes that the sincerity of the Indians is evidenced by their questions, rejection of powwows, melting under the word of grace, and the changing of their lives. In this day of God's power we should learn from his way of establishing his kingdom: he uses the bishops' persecution of the godly to promote the gospel; he works glorious accomplishments with small beginnings; he teaches old tired Christians by piety of poor heathen; he witnesses to you, "O ye *Apostate Christians in England!*" by the converted heathen in New England and their use of sabbaths for prayer.[2]

This should encourage all men to put their helping hand to the work.

1. *Arise ye heads of our Tribes in Old England*, and extend your help to further Christs labourers in *N.-England*. Rather steal from your sleep an houre, then suffer that good Ordinance to lye asleep so long; which if drawn into an Act, will exceedingly further this blessed work....
2. *Rouze up your selves my Brethren; ye Preachers of the Gospel*, this work concerns you. Contrive and plot, preach for, and presse the advancement hereof. Its cleare you may do much: Let not this be your condemnation, that you did nothing.
3. *Come forth ye Masters of money*, part with your Gold to promote the Gospel; Let the gift of God in temporal things make way, for the Indians receipt of spiritualls....[3]

Finally, pray earnestly that the Lord will further prosper the New England work, that he will bless Eliot, Mayhew, and all others in the work, and that he will incline more to take up the work. For the Lord says that the harvest is great, but the laborers few.

---

[1] *Ibid.*, 16.
[2] *Ibid.*, 27.
[3] *Idem.*

c. The Indian Town and Civil Government

*The Light appearing more and more*, the fifth tract, appeared in 1651 with Zephaniah 2:11 on the title page. The editor, Henry Whitfeld, who had been pastor at Gilford in New England and had returned to England, assures the Parliament in his dedicatory epistle of New England loyalty and decries those who suggest mismanagement of Indian funds and belittle the progress of the work. Further, he thanks the Parliament for their Act to further the work and asks that their hands be diligent in reclaiming the uttermost parts of the earth for Christ's possession. To that end the Act authorized the establishment of "the Corporation for the Propagation of the Gospel in New England", at whose request Whitfeld presents the Mayhew and Eliot letters in this tract.[1]

In his address to the reader, Whitfeld characterizes Mayhew, whose work on Martha's Vineyard he had visited, as about thirty years of age and a modest pastor who, though he had three children, received only about half the income of ordinary laborers in those parts, part of which he earned by manual labor. Mayhew's letter [2] testifies to his modesty and declares Hiacoomes to be the crucial figure to the work on Martha's Vineyard. This young Indian lad he had himself instructed each Lord's Day night, beginning in 1643. Hiacoomes received rejection and mockery from his own people, but by life and public testimony he remained a faithful witness of God's redeeming grace. The thirty-seven gods offered to him by one of the sagamores were no comparison to his God Jehovah. By 1645 a few began to listen to his teaching, and in 1646 some Indians asked Mayhew to preach to them in their language twice a month. During 1647 these Indians experienced the same ridicule as Hiacoomes, but by 1648 the conversion of a sagamore and a spontaneous meeting of Indians concerning religious matters indicated the tide was beginning to turn. Other Indians broke from the power of the powwows during 1649, and by 1650 thirty-nine men had committed themselves to the Christian faith, besides a larger number of women.

Mayhew sets forth three great obstacles to the advance of the gospel: the Indian way is more profitable in earthly things than the Christian, the sagamores are generally against the gospel, and the witchcraft of the powwows keeps the Indians in fear. The Christians have gotten over the first two hindrances and are progressively losing their fear of the powwows.

The method used by Mayhew to teach the Indians is similar to that of Eliot: "...and first I pray with them, teach them, chatechize their children, sing a Psalm, and all in their own language." [3] He also confers every Saturday with Hiacoomes, who preaches twice to the Indians every Lord's Day [4] about his subject matter of preaching on the next day, "...where I furnish him with...spiritual food...." [5] Mayhew's account ends, as Eliot's frequently do, with a request for prayer that he be strengthened for preaching to the praise

---

[1] *The Light appearing...*, 1651, 4.
[2] *Ibid.*, 3–13.
[3] *Ibid.*, 13.
[4] *Ibid.*, 1.
[5] *Ibid.*, 13.

and excellency of God's name and not his own. For the Indians in this small beginning are "Gods husbandry, and Gods building." [1] To aid Mayhew in his study and work, Eliot pleads for books and salary for him from the corporation.[2] Eliot hopes that the Indians at Martha's Vineyard will also soon be "ripe for this work of Civility and Cohabitation, if once they see a successful pattern of it" and "desire Church-fellowship, and the Ordinances of Gods worship." [3]

Six letters, addressees unknown, written between July 8, 1649, and Dec. 21, 1650, comprise Eliot's contribution to this tract. For the most part during this year and a half period, Eliot is continuing his regular ministry to the Indians, speculating concerning their possible Jewish origin [4] and patiently waiting for the requested tools and help from England.

Eliot judged that in England the black cloud of blood and confusion, heresies and errors, and, worst of all, toleration of gross impiety by the sword of authority under the pretence of conscience will undoubtedly delay Christ's coming. But come he will. The glorious work of bringing in his kingdom the Lord has of his free grace put in the hands of the renowned Parliament and Army. Eliot prays: Lord, make this their first design. Make them fit instruments further to promote the setting up of that kingdom among the poor Indians also.

The Lord knows, the need is great enough. The Indian work "Sticks in the birth for want of means." [5] How the Indians

> ...long to come into a way of civility by co-habitation, and by forming government among themselves, that so they being in such order might have a Church and the Ordinances of Christ among them.[6]

How necessary it is to bring them into ecclesiastical and civil polity. The "work of the day is to civilize them" but this will be an expensive matter.[7] What impedes the work is the lack of a supply of all kinds of tools and materials.[8] Letters enough have explained the need. Annual revenue for salary of teachers is essential to teach the youth to read Scripture. Ten pounds a year would maintain one Indian youth at school. Money to hire Indians to help translate the Bible cannot come either from the poor savages or from Eliot's eight-member family budget. "...want of money is the only thing in view that doth retard a more full prosecution of this work unto which the Lord doth ripen them apace." [9]

Eliot relates continued progress in 1649. Hired Indians have broken a path for horses to an inaccessible area sixty miles distant. At Pawtucket on his annual visit to the fishing site, the sachems again with many arguments "did exceeding earnestly, importunately invite me to come and live there and teach them." [10]

---

[1] *Idem.*
[2] *Ibid.*, 24, 25, 29.
[3] *Ibid.*, 42.
[4] See below, section C.2.
[5] *Ibid.*, 16.
[6] *Idem.*
[7] *Ibid.*, 23.
[8] In a letter to Hugh Peters, dated October 12, 1649, Eliot urges the providing of these by a collection from shops of such items as can be spared. *Of the Conversion of Five Thousand...*, 38.
[9] *The Light appearing...*, 17.
[10] *Ibid.*, 19.

The fact that these arguments incline Eliot to establish the Indian town in this area suggests that Eliot may have contemplated living in the town himself. Scarcity of good land and poor climate, however, argue for a site further south, unless "more townes than one" be begun, or "the Lord would raise up more and more fit labourers into this harvest." [1]

Inter-tribal wars hindered the work. Eliot's church took a dim view of its pastor going sixty miles west in the summer of 1649 but must have been put somewhat at ease when a local sachem with twenty armed warriors and other Indians went as bodyguard. Eliot took some English as well "so that hereby their good affection is manifested to me, and to the work I have in hand." [2]

About this time the Christian Indians became aware of the "communion of the saints." They discovered, to their own surprise, that when praying Indians who were total strangers came, a deep sense of love united them. But when their own non-praying relatives came from a great distance, the natural love present was not so deep as that for the strangers. Eliot asked the Indians why godly people in England, three thousand miles away, hearing of the Indians' conversion rejoiced and gave gifts for the work. He told them of past gifts and expected town-building materials to come. When they professed not to know, the truths about the unity of the spirit were explained.

After consultation with John Cotton, Eliot proposes that the civil and church government be wholly based on the Scripture pattern, taking up "*Moses* policie so farre as it is morall and conscionable...." [3] Only the Lord will be their law-giver, judge, and king. The governments of other nations are adulterate with anti-Christian and human wisdom. Even England stumbles before the present opportunity for a full change to the rule of Scripture. The great design of Christ in these latter days is to bring all nations to a common foundation, the Word of God. When the whole world is brought to such a frame, then Christ reigns, and government is in the hands of God's saints. Accordingly, "my work is to endeavor the setting up Christ Kingdome among the Indians." [4]

In the remainder of the letters in this tract, Eliot repeatedly affirms the Indians' continued longing for "cohabitation" and for church ordinances. [5] Continued delay discourages the praying ones and emboldens the adversaries so that powwowing is returning in some places where once it had stopped. [6] As frequently he emphasizes the need for tools and money to build the Indian town. [7] Should the supplies be forthcoming, a carpenter or two young men servants could also be sent from England, provided they be godly and well-conditioned. Otherwise they will do more harm than good. [8] The earnest spirit of prayer in both Old and New England is a great encouragement for the work. [9] Providential blessings among praying Indians and ravages like smallpox among despisers of God were strengthening the work.

---

[1] *Ibid.*, 20.
[2] *Ibid.*, 21.
[3] *Ibid.*, 29, 24.
[4] *Ibid.*, 24, 28.
[5] *Ibid.*, 27, 31, 35.
[6] *Ibid.*, 32.
[7] *Ibid.*, 25, 28, 32, 35.
[8] *Ibid.*, 25.
[9] *Ibid.*, 29, 30.

For three and a half years Eliot had preached and instructed, preparing the Indians for the next step forward. That step, however, cannot be taken until it is certain whether any help is coming from England or not. The size of the town depends upon the extent of supplies. Moreover, Eliot cannot show the church that God has called him for this work until the means are there to begin, with "probable hopes of supply" for the future. "...until that be done, the Church hath no rule to give me up to that work; nor I a rule to require it." [1]

Two of Eliot's Indians had gone to Providence and Warwick where Samuel Gorton lived. Why is it, they asked, that English people teach so differently from the same Bible? They had publicly opposed several of Gorton's teachings, such as: There is no heaven or hell except in the hearts of good and bad men; baptism of infants is a very foolish thing; and ministers and magistrates are needless things. Eliot approved the answers they had given. He thanked God for the Indians' ability to discern between truth and error and for their courage to stand for the truth against error. [2]

When in the summer of 1650 the ships came with no supplies, Eliot was disheartened at first. Then he saw in the disappointment the lesson that he had depended too much upon man and not enough upon God whose work it is. After consultation with his own elders and those at Boston, he held a day of fasting and prayer in Roxbury. It was decided to proceed with the work. That very night a ship came from England with letters of encouragement and some gifts from private friends.

So work began. The place chosen was the fruit of prayer. Grass was cut for hay, a large provision house was built from Indian hewn lumber, an eighty-foot bridge nine foot high was erected to span the river which divided the living and farming areas, and ground was prepared for spring planting. For construction of the provision house and such labour Eliot paid wages to encourage them to learn the working way of living, but the bridge was considered by all to be a labour of love.

Now not only the powwows and profane spirits oppose the gospel, but the sachems see that religion breaks their tyranny and decreases the amount of tribute they receive in corn, deer, skins, and labor. Even the Christian sachems opposed the building of a town for fear of losing power and income. However, in spite of opposition, the ways of the Lord will overcome by this great change in Indian life: bridling lust by laws of chastity, mortifying idleness by labor, and training of children in the way of God. And when such who do this live in fixed cohabitation, who can forbid their establishing a church, electing officers, and being baptized? [3]

In spite of opposition and hindrance the work will go forward. If there cannot be an arsenal of guns, powder, shot, and swords, one of slings and bows will have to do. The work of civilizing goes slowly with such few tools as can be purchased. If only there were means to support a man to direct the labor of the Indians! But the Lord will bless the day of small beginnings. A teacher has

---

[1] *Ibid.*, 32.
[2] *Ibid.*, 33–35.
[3] *Ibid.*, 36 ff.

already been hired to instruct Indian children daily. This is one of our "chiefest" cares. Daily school exercises to teach all men to read and write and all the women at least to read is the goal. For this some of the Scriptures must be translated into their own language. When a few Indians can spell, read, and write, the work will be most speedily advanced.[1]

Editor Henry Whitfeld closes this tract with the familiar moralizing by which the spirituality of the Indians is used to awaken indifferent and ungrateful English souls to spiritual renewal.

> Brethren, the Lord hath no need of us, but if it please him, can carry his Gospel to the other side of the world, and make it there to shine forth in its glory, brightnesse, power and purity, and leave us in Indian darknesse. [2]

*Strength out of Weaknesse* (1652), the sixth of the missionary tracts, is published to still rumors that only five or seven Indians are converted and the rest are Christian "but for the loaves" (i.e., sixteenth-century "rice Christians").[3] The seven letters of eminent gentlemen in New England, including the Governor of Massachusetts John Endicott, ought to be evidence enough to establish the true progress of the work.

The dedicatory epistles to the Parliament and the address to the reader are significant in that they evidence real commitment to the Indian mission in New England by the eighteen Puritans of Old England who signed one or both of these introductory documents. In the first, thankfulness is expressed for opening the door for assistance. The address to the reader is a straight-forward request for prayer and funds. Offered as motives for sacrificial giving are: hereby the kingdom of Christ is enlarged; the glorious gospel of Christ is propagated; the souls of men are rescued from the snare of the devil; the fullness of the Gentiles draws near to accomplishment; the successful labors of the brethren who were driven from English shores; and the possibility that these converted Indians are the first fruits of many nations to be brought unto Christ. Concerning the fullness of the Gentiles, Scriptural prophecy makes clear that the first conversion of the Gentiles will be brought in before the conversion of the Jews (Romans 11:25), while the second conversion will be after that of the Jews (Acts 15:16,17). We may rejoice that the time of fulfilling the first promise is here.[4]

The two letters from Eliot, one written April 28, 1651, and the other six months later, comprise nearly one-third of this tract. The first letter tells of Indian progress in spiritual awareness, which now includes a spirit of love and charity, previously unknown among that people. A sick old man had been abandoned by his family. The Christian Indians took him into their homes

---

[1] *Ibid.*, 42, 43.
[2] *Ibid.*, 46.
[3] *Strength out of Weaknesse ...*, (1652), Postscript, "The Corporation to the Reader," signed by William Steele, Pres., 40.
[4] *Ibid.*, "To the Christian Reader," 3. This means that the fact that the Jews have not yet been converted does not for the Puritans preclude missions to the Gentile, as some have suggested.

free of charge for several weeks, and for some weeks more paid for his care from public funds until these were depleted. Collections were then taken to relieve his need.

> I could with a word speaking in our Churches have this poore man relieved, but I doe not, because I thinke the Lord hath done it, for the tryall of their grace, and exercise of their love, and to traine them up in works of Charitie, and in the way of Christ to make Collections for the poore.[1]

During the winter just passed, the Christians learned that the Lord teaches his own by way of cross-bearing. Many had been sick and some died. No longer did they expect to escape trial; they saw it as chastisement. The best Indian carpenter died, so that the house being built for Eliot's use when he came to Natick, as the new village was called, remained unfinished.

Bright spots are also present. The ability of the Indian assisting in translating the Scriptures is rapidly increasing. Other Indians are improving in learning, so that Eliot judges they can become teachers in the Indian schools rather than Englishmen, as he had earlier judged necessary. Thus native teachers will be able to write as much of the Bible as Eliot is able to translate. Building the town is also proceeding: marking out lots and streets, planting orchards, building a public bridge with a wire for catching fish, and beginning the fort, schoolhouse, and meeting house. The great hindrance is still the lack of tools. "...when we cannot goe wee must be content to creepe." [2]

The summer of 1651, as the second letter reports, was the great forward push in cohabitation. First there was the school which Eliot judged so crucial to the future of the Indian work. Natick's school, now open, has two Indian teachers who daily pray, teach the brief catechism which Eliot has written, and instruct in reading and writing the Bible. Eliot's chief cares are two: translating as much of the Bible as possible, and training men and youths as evangelists to go to other parts of the country. He judges Indian preachers to be more effective than himself.

> There be severall providences of God appearing to worke, which make mee thinke that the most effectuall and generall way of spreading the Gospell will be by themselves, when so instructed as I have above-mentioned; as for my preaching, though such whose hearts God hath bowed to attend, can picke up some knowledge by my broken expressions, yet I see that it is not so taking, and effectuall to strangers, as their owne expressions be, who naturally speake unto them in their owne tongue.[3]

To train the Indians in teaching others, Eliot appoints two on the Lord's Days when he is there to teach and to pray as they have heard him do. The Indian schoolmaster now catechizes the children while Eliot catechizes the men, examining and trying their knowledge with care so as not to discourage the weak. Groups of two or more have been sent on expeditions to various

---
[1] *Strength out of Weaknesse...*, 2, 3.
[2] *Ibid.*, 5.
[3] *Ibid.*, 7.

places with a measure of success. The men remain a few days, answering questions and telling of the Lord's work at Natick. Thus this work will be

> ...a patterne and Copie before them, to imitate in all the Countrey, both in civilizing them in their order, government, Law, and in their Church proceedings and administrations; and hence great care lyeth upon mee to set them right at first, to lay a sure foundation for such a building, as I foresee will be built upon it, and in this matter I greatly need pray....[1]

Eliot's program is first to bring the Indians to civil government and then to form them into visible church-estate, by which he means an organized Indian church, with its own officers and the administration of sacraments. The first of these goals was achieved at Natick on August 6, 1651, after the building of the community fort was done. A great meeting was held at which Eliot once again expounded Exodus 18, following which one ruler of a hundred families, two of fifty, and ten of ten, were chosen. During the following month Eliot explained and taught the meaning of a Church Covenant, which the Indians could then accept as an act of knowledge and faith. On September 7, the long awaited and generous supplies from the Corporation were received, though somewhat damaged by a shipwreck in the harbor. The damage showed something of divine disfavor for sin. This, together with the beginning of their cohabitation, their choice of civil rulers, and their intention to enter into covenant to be God's people and to be ruled by his Word, occasioned the holding of the first day of fasting and prayer by the Indians on September 24. Six Indians preached, exercised as Eliot calls it, in two groups of three, each group followed by Eliot who preached on the right of fasting as a necessary outward act motivated by a believing heart (Ezra 9:3,9) and on Israel's entering into covenant with the Lord. (Deut. 29:1-16.) After this Eliot recited the Covenant, to which first the rulers and then all the people joyfully consented. "...by dark night wee finished our worke." [2]

Eliot notes that this "Act" of forming themselves into this "Government of God" is the first public record among the Indians. The initial words, up to "wee doe give our selves..." were suggested by John Cotton and incorporated into the Act which follows in its entirety.

> Wee are the sonnes of Adam, wee and our forefathers have a long time been lost in our sinnes, but now the mercy of the Lord beginneth to finde us out againe; therefore the grace of Christ helping us, wee doe give our selves and our Children unto God to be his people, Hee shall rule us in all our affaires, not onely in our Religion, and affaires of the Church (these wee desire as soone as wee can, if God will) but also in all our workes and affaires in this world, God shall rule over us. Isa. 33.22. The Lord is our Judge, the Lord is our Law-giver, the Lord is our King. Hee will save us; the Wisedome which God hath taught us in his Booke, that shall guide us and direct us in the way. Oh Jehovah, teach us wisedome

---

[1] *Ibid.*, 8, 9.      [2] *Ibid.*, 12, 13.

to finde out thy wisedome in thy Scriptures, let the grace of Christ helpe us, because Christ is the wisedome of God, send thy Spirit into our hearts, and let it teach us, Lord take us to be thy people, and let us take thee to be our God.[1]

On October 8, Governor Endicott of Massachusetts Colony and other dignitaries visited the new settlement. One of the Indians "exercised" before them all. The Governor was sufficiently impressed to ask Eliot for a written copy of his summary in English. The sermon was based on the parables of the treasure in a field and the pearl of great price. The summary for the first parable follows.

> ...for instruction he first propounded what is this treasure which is hid in a feild? he answered it is Repentance for sinne, faith in Christ, and pardon of sinne and all grace, as also praying to God, the worship of God, and his appointments, which are the meanes of Grace, on which he dilated, shewing what excellent pearles these are, exhorting all to account so of them, and on this point he did much insist: secondly, he asked what is the Feild where these pearles are to be found? he answered the Church of Christ, which they did desire to constitute in this place, and to that end come thither to dwell: Thirdly, he asked what it is to sell all that a man hath to buy this Feild? He answered, to part with all their sinnes, and to part with all their old Customes, and to part with their friends and lands, or any thing which hindereth them from coming to that place, where they may gather a Church, and enjoy all these pearles; and here he insisted much to stirre them up, that nothing should hinder them from Gathering together into this place where they might enjoy such a mercy.[2]

The other letters included in this tract confirmed the progress of the Indian work. Pastor John Wilson of Boston adds eyewitness description of the October 8 meeting. William "Leverick" enlarges on the Indian work at Sandwich to which he had been encouraged by Eliot. Anthoney Bessey of Sandwich testifies that some Indians come ten miles on Saturday and stay until Monday for the Lord's Day worship. Mayhew reports that one hundred ninety-nine Indians at Martha's Vineyard now profess the faith. They worship in two places twice each Lord's Day under the preaching of Hiacoomes and Mumanequem, who are tutored by himself on Saturday. He plans to establish a school for Indian children and young men and is endeavoring their cohabitation with all possible speed. Governor John "Endecott" sees the proceedings of the October 8 meeting as reason for thanksgiving and the fact that "there are some Schollers amongst us who addict themselves to the study of the *Indian* tongue" as reason for hope.[3] William French evidences the conversion of the Indians by recording an interview with an Indian of two years' profession. Thomas Allen, who recently returned from a pastorate in New England, attests to the converting work of four ministers there. William Steele, president of the Corporation, summarizes by calling the people of England on the basis of these testimonials to the support of earnest prayer and generous gifts.

---

[1] *Ibid.*, 12, 10.    [2] *Ibid.*, 14.    [3] *Ibid.*, 35.

d. Preparation for Church Estate

*Tears of Repentance* (1653) gains its title from the Indian confessions published for the consideration of the Christian world. To Eliot's dedication of his narrative to Lord Cromwell, William Steele concurs on behalf of the Corporation. Eliot indicates to Cromwell the Lord's double design in these times:

> First, To overthrow Antichrist by the Wars of the Lamb; and Secondly, To raise up His own Kingdom in the room of all Earthly Powers which He doth cast down, and to bring all the World subject to be ruled in all things by the Word of His mouth.[1]

As the Lord has used Cromwell to begin the first part of the work, so may the Lord use him to begin the accomplishment of the second by putting the government into the hands of the saints and under the Word of Christ. The rising of Christ's kingdom in "these Western Parts of the World" confirms that the Lord's time is come to advance and spread that kingdom which shall "in his season" fill the earth.[2]

Thomas Mayhew, Jr., describes in his letter to the Corporation certain Indian beliefs and practices and the progress of his work. The Indians worshipped gods innumerable: men-gods, women-gods, children-gods, fellowships and companies of gods, gods of many creatures, gods of corn and every color of it. But the Devil with his angels living among them and in them, they accounted the terror of the living and the god of the dead. Under his cruel power and into his deformed likeness all men are translated at death. Their word for "dead man" is the same as the word for "devil." The Devil hurt their bodies and distracted their minds. To appease him, they offered sacrifices through their powwows with vehemency of spirit and bodily violence. They were enslaved to a multitude of heathen traditions of their gods. Only an obscure notion of a god greater than all, called Mannit, remained. But his nature and how to worship him they did not know. Such a religion was dominated by fear: fear of powwows as agents of the Devil on earth and fear of the complete subjugation to the Devil in death.

Mayhew takes real joy in describing the feeling of release from fear that commitment to the Christian faith brought, sometimes at once, sometimes more gradually, but always surely. By the strength of God's power all the spirits of the powwows ("imps") "flee away like Muskeetoes."[3] The testimony of a converted powwow serves as an example:

> That ever since that very time God hath in mercy delivered him from them, he is not troubled with any pain (as formerly) in his Bed, nor dreadful visions of the night, but through the blessing of God, he doth lie down in ease, sleeps quietly, wakes in Peace, and walks in safety, for which he is very glad and praises God.[4]

---

[1] *Tears of Repentance*..., "To His Excellency, the Lord General Cromwel," 1 (1653).
[2] *Ibid.*, 2.
[3] *Ibid.*, "Mayhew's Letter," 6.
[4] *Idem.*

In the spring of 1652 the Indians of Martha's Vineyard spontaneously asked for an ordered way of life under a covenant and rulers comprised of Mayhew, his father, and certain of themselves. The group of two hundred eighty-three Indians, not counting the younger children and including eight converted powwows [1] held two appointed days of fasting and prayer during the summer at which they entered into covenant to serve God. The platform of the covenant, basically similar to that adopted by the Indians of Natick, comprises: a confession of ignorance and sin; a profession of faith in the triune God Jehovah; a commitment to the service of Jehovah God in Christ Jesus as Teacher, Lawgiver in the Word, King, Judge, and Ruler; and a doxology to God.

At the time of this letter, October 22, 1652, Mayhew's praying Indians are about to begin a town for cohabitation and civil government. Thirty children are now attending the school which began on January 11, 1652. The children are apt learners. The older Indians desire to learn and seek to be subject to Jehovah. They choose the most godly as their rulers. God has clearly shown his providential care over the praying Indians as compared to the unrepentant ones. The quality of Indian commitment to the gospel is shown by acts of love to their enemies, unheard of in their history, by their propagating the knowledge of God to others, and by the fact that they are neither compelled by force nor allured by gifts, having "received nothing for about seven years time." [2]

Eliot's narration concerning the first public profession of the Indians is brief. For four years, he says, the better and wiser sort have inquired about church-estate, baptism, and the rest of God's ordinances which the English use. Their requests have been periodically delayed until they had begun to live a settled community life. Until that time they were not to be entrusted with the treasures of Christ. If any should, for example, be placed under censure, he could easily run away unless he had a fixed habitation and a means of livelihood to lose. But now that the Indians have come under civil law and bent themselves to labor, as evidenced by their fences, buildings, and especially the fifty-foot long and twenty-five-foot broad meeting house, Eliot's argument for delay is gone. During the summer of 1652 Indians gave personal confessions of their former sins, of their knowledge of God, and of their experience of his grace before the regular Indian assemblies. These Eliot recorded.[3] All elders round about Roxbury were invited to hear these read. Since the elders were well satisfied, the Indians first held a day of fasting and prayer among themselves. Then another such day was appointed which was publicly announced with the names of the Indians who were to make confession on that day. The purpose of this day was

> ...to try whether the Lord would vouchsafe such grace unto them, as to give them acceptance among the Saints, into the fellowship of Church-Estate, and enjoyment of those Ordinances which the Lord hath betrusted his Churches withal.[4]

---

[1] *Ibid.*, 3.
[2] *Idem.*
[3] The content of these and subsequent confessions we have already discussed, 1–14.
[4] *Ibid.*, Eliot's "A Brief Relation...," 2.

October 13, 1652, was the great day of the first public assembly held to try Indians for church-estate. The day began with prayers and sermons by Eliot and two Indians, so that it was nearly eleven a.m. before the examination began. Eliot proposed that first a doctrinal examination with questions and answers on the fundamental points of religion be held, and thereafter the Indians could declare what they believed. After a brief discussion the elders decided to have the confessions of the Lord's work in their hearts first, because in so doing something would be discerned of their knowledge in doctrines of religion. Thereafter appropriate questions could be proposed. For lack of time the former professions recorded by Eliot during the summer were not read, though they are included in this tract.

John Wilson had proposed unsuccessfully that the former professions be read because it was evident the Indians were afraid to speak before so large an assembly and could not be expected to do their best. His fears were justified when the confession of Waban, the second to speak, was not as satisfactory as desired. Both Wilson and Eliot indicated that he was one of the most stable and respected of the Indians, having been chosen a ruler of fifty, and that he did much to win others to the faith—only public speaking was not his strong point. This satisfied most of the assembly.

By the time five had finished, much time being required for translation and recording, it was nearly sunset. The magistrates, elders, and other Christian people present decided to stop for that day due to lack of time and to the fact that only one interpreter, Eliot, was present. Mayhew and Leveridge had been asked to come but were not there. Eliot says: "...I was alone (as I have wont to be in this work)...."[1] Eliot explained to the Indians that it was God's ordinance there should be two or three witnesses present instead of only one, and that the work was so solemn a fitter season must be appointed to finish. So the day ended with prayers to God.

Eliot carefully, almost too carefully, explains that the postponement of church-estate is for the best.

> The Lord he knoweth, that with much fear, and care I went about this work, even unto the sensible wasting, and weakning of my natural strength, knowing that the investing these young Babes in Christ, with the highest, and all the external priviledges of the Church, the Spouse of Jesus Christ on Earth, would have drawn upon me much more labor and care, lest they should in any wise scandalize the same; unto which I have now more time assigned me by the Lord to prepare them....[2]

Besides, the Lord by the counsel of his servants and by the providential lack of interpreters, which Eliot had tried in every way to provide, spoke clearly that the day had not yet arrived. Much had been gained, however, for many hundreds of saints have been comforted and confirmed in their hopes for this work of Christ in New England.

---

[1] *Ibid.*, 25.   [2] *Ibid.*, 26.

Richard Mather's letter in this tract first makes clear that he believes Scriptural prophecy is being fulfilled by the conversion of the heathen, for *"the Heathen shall be his Inheritance, and the uttermost parts of the Earth his Possession."* [1] God's marvelous free grace to a people so wretched and unworthy, though thirty years of English history in New England is past, is plainly evident through the now published Indian Confessions. But how, Mather asks, do we know that these are truly related since we have the testimony of only one man to assure us? True, he answers, we have only one man's word for it, but

> ...a man whose pious and painful labors amongst this People, have rendered him approved and highly honored in the eyes of his Brethren about him, for indefatigable diligence, and earnest love to the Lord Jesus, and their poor souls; a man whose integrity and faithfulness is so well known in these Parts, as giveth sufficient satisfaction to beleev that he would not wittingly utter a falshood in any matter whatever, and much less so many falshoods, & that in such a publick manner, in the view of God & the World....[2]

One may ask, Mather continues, why were the Indians not combined and united into church-estate? First, he answers, that as the material temple in Solomon's day took many years in building, so one must expect that building a spiritual one "out of such rubbish as amongst Indians" could not be accomplished quickly.[3] Second, they "are not furnished with any to be an able Pastor and Elder over them, by whom they might be directed and guided in all the Affairs of the Church, and Administrations of the House of God." [4] This is a far more serious matter than admitting Indians into the membership of already established churches. However, language difference and distance makes this impossible.

To these two considerations may be added the two mentioned by Eliot, namely, shortness of time and lack of interpreters, which two were certainly the principal, if not the only reasons, insisted upon and publicly given for deferring the establishment of the Indian church.

Some people dare to deny the working of God's grace among the Indians. Such evil reports persist. That the Indian work is simply a scheme to get money is the accusation of some. The deferring of church organization ought to help disprove such conjectures. If the magistrates and elders wanted wordly advantage, they surely would have advised organization. Only spiritual motivation can explain the deferral.

Some divines in New England are concerned that the Indians do not apply themselves to duty and labor as they ought. There is some reason for their concern. Yet the buildings and cultivated ground show how much they have changed for the good. God's spirit is abundantly present among them.

*A Late and Further Manifestation of the Progress of the Gospel* (1655) tells of the working for church-estate through 1654. The foreword is signed by four Puri-

---

[1] *Ibid.*, "To the Christian Reader," 1.
[2] *Ibid.*, 6.
[3] *Idem.*
[4] *Ibid.*, 7.

tans [1] and encourages the continuance prayer of and liberal contributions for successfully "carrying on the hoped for Conversion of the Indians." [2]

Eliot's "Narration of the Indians Proceedings in respect of church-Estate" first reviews briefly the history to 1652. He adds that besides the Indian towns at Natick and at Ponkipog, another is being built, and three more towns are being planned. Eliot's first intention to gather all praying Indians into one town he now judges to have been impossible, for there were only fifty lots available at Natick. Now the Indians in various places find a better course of life through God's mercy and the bounty of good people in England.

Eliot had not proceded further toward church organization with the Indians during 1653 for two reasons. First, he had sent the *Confessions* to England to be printed so that he might hear the reaction of godly people there and so that copies could be spread in New England "unto the better and fuller satisfaction of many." [3] The printed books came to New England, however, with the last ships of the year, so there was insufficient time for reaction. Second,

> ...there fell a great damping and discouragement upon us, by a jealousie too deeply apprehended, though utterly groundlesse, viz. That even these praying *Indians* were in a conspiracy with others, and with the *Dutch*, to doe mischief to the *English*. ...it was no season for me to stir or move in this matter, when the waters were so troubled.[4]

Had Eliot known how that distrust would disrupt Indian work in the future, his discouragement would have been far greater.

Some time after the books had arrived, late in 1653, a great church meeting was held in Boston. Present were representatives from all the colonies and the commissioners, who also served as a liaison between the Corporation in London and the New England Mission to the Indians. To this august body, Eliot made a proposition:

> *That they having now seen their confessions, if upon further triall of them in point of knowledge, they be found to have a competent measure of understanding in the fundamentall points of Religion; and also, if there be due testimony of their conversation, that they walke in a Christian manner according to their light, so that Religion is to be seen in their lives; whether then it be according to God, and acceptable to his people, that they be called up unto Church-estate?*

Unto which I had I blesse the Lord, a generall approbation.[5]

Accordingly, in 1654 Eliot proposed to his elders a day of examination of the Indians in points of knowledge. Later another day for the constitution of the church could be held, at which time one Indian would make a doctrinal confession before the Lord and the people, to which the rest of the Indians

---

[1] Signatures are: H. Whitfeild, Simeon Ashe, Edm. Calamy, John Arthur.

[2] Joseph Caryl writes in his epistle "To The Reader" that if the one thing we desire most is to dwell in the house of the Lord forever, the next is that we earnestly desire that those hitherto strangers might also dwell there.

[3] *A Late and Further Manifestation of the Progress of the Gospel* ..., "To the Reader," 4.

[4] *Idem.*

[5] *Idem.*

could attest their consent. The elders could also attest at the public meeting to the competency of their knowledge. To these arrangements the elders agreed, since there was too much to be done in one day. Only there was still question whether there was fit matter for church officers!

June 13, 1654, the Indians were to be examined by the elders in Roxbury. "Brother Mayhu" promised to be present with an interpreter for this *Natootomuhtéae kesuk* (a day of asking questions). The Indians and the churches held a day of public fast to prepare.

About ten days before the important meeting, three of the weaker praying Indians got several quarts of "Strong-water," which, Eliot complains, too many for the sake of a little money sell to them to the grief of the better sort of Indians and the more godly English. Not only did they get drunk, but they got the eleven-year-old son of Toteswamp, an Indian ruler, drunk as well. One of the three was assisting in Eliot's translation of the Bible. Eliot found his hopes collapsing.

> I did judge it to be the greatest frowne of God that ever I met withall in the work, I could read nothing in it but displeasure, I began to doubt about our intended work: I knew not what to doe, the blacknesse of the sins, and the Persons reflected on, made my heart faile me.[1]

Eliot's ruling elder at Roxbury graciously encouraged him. That sin, he said, was but a transient act which would vanish, while the judgments of the Indian rulers were an ordinance of God and would remain. Eliot, he said, ought to be thankful how responsibly the Indians themselves had dealt with the matter. The three men had been judged guilty in four respects: the sin of drunkenness, wilfully making a child drunk, slandering the rulers, and fighting. After twenty lashes and much time in public stocks, the men heard admonitions to repentance and amendment of life from many of the Indian rulers before some two hundred of their community. The boy was in the stocks a little while and then whipped before his classmates at the school. These judgments would, the elder assured Eliot, "doe more good every way, then their sin could doe hurt." [2]

The assembly of examination was held on the appointed day. All in due order would have opportunity to ask what questions they had. If there was doubt of Eliot's translation, the other language experts could be consulted. On one question Mayhew doubted Eliot's translation of "Hohpoóonk" as "humility," but the interpreters authenticated Eliot's word.

Following the examination, Eliot was concerned that no questions had been asked on such matters as the grace of Christ wrought in us by the Holy Spirit, the ordinances of Christ (sacraments, offices, etc.), the resurrection, the estate of man after death, and the last judgment. But the elders had heard enough to be assured that the Indians knew their catechism. Words of acceptance and encouragement were spoken both to Eliot and to the Indians.

---

[1] *Ibid.*, 7.   [2] *Ibid.*, 9.

Now the question is, Eliot writes, when shall the Indians enjoy the ordinances of Jesus Christ in church-estate? To this question he gives no answer. Because of the solemnity of establishing this pattern church, because others do not know the sincerity of the Indians as well as Eliot and some others, because God's works among men usually go slowly, because the season is getting late and days are short, because there are so many other church meetings, because of the difficulty of getting interpreters together again, the time for organization has not yet arrived.

But above all the other reasons is the lack of laborers to take care of the Christian Indians. Some of the Indians need training and instruction to rule and direct the others in the fear of the Lord. They live in various towns and remote from each other, so that many leaders are needed. For this instruction Eliot hopes that the commissioners will give some aid to support this work.

The last, and supposedly greatest, reason actually has little to do with the organization of a church at Natick, for there leaders and rulers have been functioning in civil and "unorganized" church-estate since 1651. Rather, it serves as a bridge to a request for further help and some general concluding remarks. He believes that God's gracious supply for the Indians and his own family will continue and that church-estate will come in God's season. In God's sure promise "*Commit thy way unto the Lord, trust also in him, and he shall bring it to passe,*" [1] he finds strength and support.

> ...against all suspitious jealousies, hard speeches, and unkindnesses, of men touching the sincerity and reallity of this work, and about my carriage of matters, and supply herein.... And herein likewise I find supply of grace, to wait patiently for the Lords time, when year after year, and time after time, I meet with disappointments.... Thus I live, and thus I labour, here I have supply, and here is my hope, I beg the help of prayers, that I may still so live and labour in the Lord's work, and that I may so live and dye.[2]

One senses in these words that more than the incapability of Indians slowed their organization into a church.

Since four years separate the eighth and ninth tracts, it is disappointing to learn little of the work, though the title of the ninth (1659) does speak "of the Progresse of the Gospel amongst the Indians." [3] Besides a letter from the commissioners [4] for the united colonies concerning Pierson's *Catechisme* for the Indians and certain bills to be paid (Sept. 22, 1658), and a letter from John Endicott urging the sending of paper and letters and a journeyman for printing the translation of the entire Bible (Dec. 28, 1658), there are some letters from Reynolds and Eliot.

The first letter is the seven-page introduction by Ed. Reynolds addressed to

---

[1] *Ibid.*, 23.
[2] *Idem.*
[3] *A further Accompt of the Progresse of the Gospel...*, (1659).
[4] John Endicott, President; Simon Bradstreete, Thomas Trence, Josiah Winslow, John Winthorpe, John Talcot, Francis Newman, William Leete.

the Christian reader (April 1, 1659) in which, after the usual vigorous application of prophecy (twenty Scriptural references here) to the American Indian, two great works are described which further the progress of the gospel: the improvement of natural reason unto the knowledge of the true God, and the translation of the Scriptures into the Indian language by Eliot. Natural reason can profitably be used to "...*demonstrate unto* Pagans *the falsenesse of the way they are in, and so to prepare a way for entertainment of the Truth.*" [1]

The doctrine of the gospel, continues Reynolds, is supernaturally made known only by the revelation of the Holy Spirit, and as such cannot be investigated by the human mind. However, when the revelation comes, certain impressions in the natural conscience make men attend and prepare them for the preaching of the gospel. Some contact points are: the human desire for happiness rather than misery, the universal impression of a supreme god, an innate sense of immortality, a habit of moral principles and sense of guilt, a natural desire for good and recognition of a divine giver, and the awareness of the need for revelation and religion to find the true way of service to God.

Since these are present in some degree in the natural conscience, we may convince the heathen by "his own naturall and implanted light": [2] there is a righteous God who has implanted in all men a law of nature which man has violated. This guilt is punishable by death, a death from which the sinner wants to be delivered but, by his own strength and false way of worship, cannot be. In his extremity the sinner listens to the godly and is persuaded to see in the gospel evidence of its reliability: its inherent character of purity and the miracles. This "he hath no more reason to distrust than the truth of any other history." [3] He is persuaded to believe the gospel and reap those joys and comforts which make him know whom he has believed.

The other great work, Eliot's Bible translation, is a necessary and excellent work for which the reverend translator deserves great thanks and encouragement. For so large a work the cost will be much, yet for something that *"tends so immediately to the Salvation of souls and glory of...God"* [4] there should be many helping hands and cheerful assistance.

Eliot's first letter (December 28, 1658) is dated the same as Endicott's. This is due to Eliot's last-minute visit to him before the ship's leaving in order that his request and that of the president of the commissioners might lend weight to their joint appeal for help in printing the Indian Bible. The elders at Roxbury had requested the commissioners' approval without their pastor's knowledge. The commissioners asked the inevitable question: how far does the dialect Eliot uses extend? Eliot answers that he has read selections from his translation as far away as Connecticut, one hundred miles away, before many hundreds of English witnesses. The Indians present testified before all that they understood perfectly. His translations of Matthew and Genesis he had sent to all who knew the language best, but none could find any fault with it.

---

[1] *A further Accompt...*, "To the Christian Reader," 3 (1659).
[2] *Ibid.*, 5.
[3] *Ibid.*, 6.
[4] *Ibid.*, 7.

Eliot's second letter in the tract (though written earlier, December 10, 1658) bears tragic news: "The Lord hath given us this amazing blow to take away my brother *Mayhew*." [1] He and a native Indian preacher were lost at sea. Mayhew's aged father does what he can to continue the work. Eliot has encouraged him to do so by letters and successfully asked the commissioners to give him support. For the rest, Eliot sends notes of exhortations given at a day of fasting at Natick on November 15, 1658, and tells of the beginning of his second son's work with the Indians. Of the fast, he simply notes without further explanation: "The causes of this fast were partly in preparation for gathering a Church, and because of much rain, and sicknesse and other tryalls." [2]

All the Indian exhortations, as one might expect, are based upon passages from Genesis and Matthew which, along with a few Psalms in meter, were earlier printed in their language. It is plain to see, concludes Eliot in a postscript, how much the Indians use what Bible they have.

> I blesse the Lord, that the whole book of God is translated into their own language, it wanteth but revising, transcribing, and printing. Oh that the Lord would so move, that by some means or other it may be printed. [3]

e. Church Establishment

The tenth missionary tract, *A further Account of the progress of the Gospel Amongst the Indians in New England* (1660), comprises a six-page preface by Joseph Caryl similar in content to those in the earlier tracts, and a historical account by Eliot of the decision of the Roxbury elders to admit eight Indians into their church fellowship. In order to accomplish this the Indians (some of them) appeared for the third time in public trial of God's people to see whether they "be indeed Christians, as fit matter for a Gospel Church." [4]

Significantly, Eliot says he was stirred and quickened by letters from England "to move mee, before I moved." [5] When, in the spring of 1659, Eliot proposed action, the inclination of the magistrates, elders, and other saints, was that some of the principal Indians should be seasoned in the communion of the English churches before they should be organized into churches themselves. When it was objected that the other Indians would miss their most able leaders for sabbath worship, the solution was proposed that usually the Indians should keep sabbaths among their own people, only to be present with the English for the sacraments and discipline. All agreed Roxbury church should receive the praying Indians. At a regular Roxbury lecture the proposal was presented to the congregation and accepted. The elders called eight Indians to a "private preparatory Confession" on April 15, 1659, which was publicly announced, and many men and woman were in attendance. John Eliot, Jr., attested to the accuracy of his father's translations.

---

[1] *A further Accompt...*, 6.
[2] *Ibid.*, 8.
[3] *Ibid.*, 20.
[3] *A further Account...*, 1 (1660).
[4] *Idem.*

These confessions were well accepted by the church. Letters were sent to all the neighboring churches informing them of progress and asking whether they had either any just offence or word of encouragement concerning the eight Indians proposed for church membership. The greatest difficulty was the paucity of interpreters to attest Eliot's interpretation.

On the public day of confessions, July 5, 1659, was a church council consisting of "messengers" from the ten nearest churches. After prayer Eliot first pointed out the full supply of interpreters on hand. Mr. Pierson had come to sabbath the day before at Roxbury, spent half a day with Eliot hearing the Indians confess, and taking down these confessions in writing. Should the assembly so desire, therefore, not only the confessions before the elders written by Eliot, but also those taken by Pierson, could be read to augment and verify the confessions now to be made. In addition, five other interpreters, plus the Indian scholars from the school, could also assist.

Eliot declared that the Roxbury church was submitting itself to the guidance of the council and was asking their direction. The public confessions were made. Five interpreters individually testified after each confession that Eliot's written account read to the meeting accurately presented the substance of the confessions. After the first four lengthy confessions the remaining Indians were asked to be brief. When two of those were dones, the elders proposed that Pierson read the confessions of the last two Indians which he had taken the day before. This procedure the assembly approved.

When the confessions were completed, many catechetical questions were asked about grace, ordinances, sacraments, baptism, Lord's Supper, repentance and faith, and Christian life.

After the public meeting the messengers of the churches met together and unanimously declared the confessions satisfactory and the Indians fit matter for church-estate.

The last of the Eliot missionary tracts, published in 1671, contained only one letter from Eliot. He describes the state of Indian work, also that under Thomas Mayhew, Sr., and Richard Bourne who had replaced W. Leveredge at Sandwich. There a church was organized on August 17, 1670, Bourne was ordained pastor of the Indian Church, arrangements were made for an Indian ruling elder and a deacon, and the Indians with their children were baptized. The organization followed the usual pattern: a day of fasting and prayer, confession of the truth and grace of Jesus Christ, and entering into covenant to live under him according to the order of the gospel. Six magistrates and messengers from nearby churches were present.

Eliot reports a visit to Martha's Vineyard where many adults and children were baptized, the Lord's Supper was celebrated in the Indian Church with many Englishmen also participating, two teaching elders were ordained to serve as pastors, ruling elders and deacons were chosen, and encouragement was given for the organization of two new churches there as well as one for Nantucket. In Nantucket ninety were praying to God.

Though the Vineyard Indians pressed Mayhew, Sr., to be their pastor, he judged that his service to them in land and other affairs would be of greater advantage if his present relationship be maintained.

Advice was given that schools be established. Every child capable of learning should pay equally, regardless whether he attend or not. For parents to neglect the schooling if their children is a transgression censurable both by civil and ecclesiastical officers, the offence being against both. Eliot significantly adds: "So we walk at Natick." [1] Apparently, Natick serves as the pattern, as Eliot had intended it should.

Concerning the ordination of Indian pastors, Eliot adds an explanatory paragraph. It is "hopeless" [2] to expect English ministers to go to Indian churches. First, the work is full of hardship and hard labor. Second, the Indians cannot afford their support. Third, Englishmen cannot communicate the gospel nearly so well as the Indian evangelists, nor do they know the customs and manners. Such English as desire to teach Indians, and there are many good opportunities, must begin with the Indians who already pray to God. As one grows in ability to speak the language, one can communicate the gospel to them. But the first work is to train Indian pastors in the liberal arts and sciences as well as theology and in the ability to explain both the works and Word of God.

There are various ministers who live close enough to Indians to work with them. Eliot says he is going to stop "importuning" [3] ministers in general, and will concentrate on those having the greatest opportunity. The ministerial charge to all is "to preach to the World in the Name of Jesus, and from amongst them to gather Subjects to his holy Kingdom." [4] The Bible and the catechism drawn out of it are the general instruments for teaching and the foundation of community among the Indian churches and Christians. To further that work, Natick will send out in the fall of 1670 Indians to remoter places to teach the gospel. Only money is short. Eliot trusts the Lord will find a way for English Christians to encourage the work.

Eliot uses the remainder of the tract to describe the present situation in Natick, the chief Indian town, with between forty and fifty communicants, and that in the other Indian towns: Ponkipog, Hassunnimesut, Ogquonikongquamesut, Nashope, Wamesut, Panatuket, Magunkukquok, and Quanatusset.

Eliot's attitude at this time to certain troubling moral problems among the Indians is illustrated in a remarkable passage concerning an elder in Ogquonikingquamesut.

> One that was a Teacher in this place, is the man that is now under Censure in the Church; his sin was that adventitious sin which we have brought unto them, Drunkenness, which was never known to them before they knew us *English*. But I account it our duty, and it is much in my desire, as well to teach them Wisdom to Rule such heady Creatures, as skill to get them, to be able to bridle their own appetites, when they have means

---

[1] *A Brief Narrative...*, 5 (1670).
[2] *Idem.*
[3] *Idem.*
[4] *Idem.*

and opportunity of high-spirited enticements. The Wisdom and Power of Grace is not so much seen in the beggarly want of these things, as in the bridling of our selves in the use of them. It is true Dominion, to be able to use them, and not to abuse our selves by them.[1]

## 3. *Hindrances and Helps*

Before considering Eliot's conception of the purpose of history and defining what mission principles were operative, a summary is necessary of the main helps and hindrances in the establishment of the Indian church. The account of the Indian Mission recorded in the missionary tracts gives a sufficient picture of the method of approach and the basic mission principles from which to make certain observations. First, the hindrances to the progress of missions to the Indians should be considered. Second, those factors which most constantly and effectively furthered the work will be enumerated.

The hindrances to the Indian work may be appropriately classified as those intrinsic to the given Indian situation and those involved in the relationship between the English and the Indian. In the former class may be considered the low state of civilization and morality of the Indian, his nomadic way of life, and the language with its many dialects.

All of the Puritans were agreed that the barbarous standard of Indian life was such as to make civilization an absolutely essential partner to evangelization in the Christianization of the natives. The much-used description of the Indians as the "ruines of mankind," which Eliot ascribes to Thomas Hooker [2] was to be taken literally. It was Satan's image, not God's, that the Indians confessed they bore. Both the boarding of Indian children with Puritan families and the school approach were attempts to overcome what seemed an insurmountable problem and what proved often to be so.

The Indian nomadic way of life made the necessary regular instruction an impossibility. The Indians, Eliot and others often complain, come for a few days, then move on. Word of the Christian faith spread and aroused curiosity. But the gospel, as the Puritans understood it, was a way of life, not simply a few doctrines to be accepted. Too often the Indians accepted the doctrines as "gospel truth." Who were they to deny that the English, who were so obviously superior in nearly everything, were not also superior in the knowledge of God? But the way of life they did not easily accept. What was necessary was, Eliot judged, the creation of a patterned way of life which would both be Christian in its structure and provide opportunity for unbroken training in Christian doctrine and life.

Finally, there was the difficulty of an unknown and unwritten language, which varied in dialect from tribe to tribe within the same general area. Henry Newman pinpoints the gravity of the problem in a letter of gentle warning to John Wesley in Georgia.

---

[1] *Ibid.*, 8.   [2] *The Indian Grammar Begun,* Preface (1666).

> I wish you find the the Indians as tractable to religious instruction as you expected, but the method of conveying that instruction is so laborious that it seems insuperable without a miracle (considering the brevity of Human Life), for you must either learn their language or they yours before you can instill the first rudiments of Christianity into their minds. To do the former, there is neither Dictionary nor Grammar to lead you and you must endorse the mortification of living Savage, as they do, at least a year, to make any proficiency in it, but where these difficulties have been surmounted, as in New England, it served only for a small district not so big as Yorkshire; beside the barrenness of their language, would puzzle a learned man that is master of it to express divine truths in the clearness they are made to appear in a language that has been for several ages polishing; for which reason the people of New England seem now convinced after 100 years experience that the shortest way to instruct the Indians is to teach them English and good manners in order to instruct them in the Christian Religion.[1]

Newman continues by suggesting that the adults are hardly capable of instruction, but perhaps the young can be instructed gradually so that language and common civility may be diffused until, as in Ireland, the old language falls into oblivion. But even then, progress is difficult. In New England, where the Indian college was built, the Indians could not be coaxed to accept a gratis education and to quit their old liberty, except one Indian only, Caleb Cheeshateaumuck, who became a bachelor of arts, but he killed himself with drink, "though all possible care was taken to restrain him from it." There also, the Bible was printed, but it was of no value beyond a very limited area.

> And as for the Impression of the Bible the language of it was so much altered in 70 or 80 miles distance that a Chinese Bible would have been as edifying to the Natives, as Mr. Eliot's Impression.[2]

Newman is repeating the criticism which was so often made against the translation during Eliot's own lifetime. However, Eliot and Mayhew, as the account above indicates, repeatedly insisted that the translation was sufficiently familiar to most dialects over a wide area.

One example of this is found in the Baxter–Eliot correspondence. In a postscript to his letter of September 22, 1668, Baxter asks: "I pray tell me how farre that Indian language reacheth into which you have translated the Bible and how numerous their languages there are...."[3] To this question Eliot replies on June 20, 1669,[4] that the Narragansett language into which the Bible is translated can be understood as far north as Canada, two hundred miles to the south, nearly one hundred miles to the east to Cape Cod, and sixty or seventy miles to the northwest, which is as far that direction as Eliot has gone.

---

[1] June 12, 1736, S.P.C.K. Archives, Miscellaneous (draft) Letters – CN 2.2, p. 37.
[2] *Idem*.
[3] Baxter's Letters, vol. iii, 133a.
[4] Baxter's Letters, vol. iii, 131a.

He lists three reasons for the "wonderful extent of this language."[1] The Narragansett and their kin, the Pequots, have been great conquerors and rulers over a vast area, so that their language is basically known; the Narragansett Bay is the chief place where the shellfish are found from which the Indians make their jewelry, even royal ornaments as far away as Mexico are fashioned from these; and the geographic location for fishing, water transportation, and cultivation of soil, is such as to attract other Indians. The fact that Eliot first used a Pequot captive from Long Island for language study establishes the similarity of that language to that of the Massachusetts Indians, the Narragansett.

Roger Williams at an earlier date shared this perhaps too optimistic view of the one language reaching from the New York Dutch plantation to that of the French in Canada:

> There is a mixture of this *Language North* and *South*, from the place of my abode about six hundred miles...their *Dialects* doe exceedingly differ; yet not so, but (within that compasse) a man may, by this *helpe*, converse with *thousands* of *Natives* all over the *Countrey*: and by such converse it may please the *Father* of *Mercies* to spread *civilitie*, (and in his own most holy season) Christianitie; for *one Candle* will light *ten thousand*, and it may please *God* to blesse a *little Leaven* to season the *mightie Lump* of those *Peoples* and *Territories*.[2]

In a letter written in 1722, Experience Mayhew emphasizes the basic unity of language between Long Island and Massachusetts. The difference between the dialects

> ...was formerly somewhat greater than now it is, before our Indians had the use of the Bible and other books translated by Mr. Eliot; but *since that, the most of the little differences that were betwixt them have been happily lost*, and our Indians speak, but especially write, much as those of Natick do.[3]

Trumbull says that Eliot's Bible and tracts served

> ...as text-books in a well-defined dialect of that great Algonkin language which, at the beginning of the seventeenth century, was spoken over an extent of territory half as large as Europe....[4]

Jonathan Edwards, Jr., to mention a later and somewhat enlightening observation, indicates that in the New England areas, two radically different languages are used: Mohawk, which is the language of the Six Nations, and Mohegan, which is that of Stockbridge (where his father was missionary), of Farmington, and of New London. Eliot's translation of the Bible is in a dialect of the Mohegan. This language, the younger Edwards continues,

---

[1] *Idem.*
[2] *A Key into the Language of America*, "To the Reader," pp. 2–3.
[3] Quoted in J. H. Trumbull, *Origin and Early Progress of Indian Missions in New England*, 28 (1874).
[4] *Ibid.*, 3.

...appears to be much more extensive than any other language in North-America.... That the languages of the several tribes in New-England, of the Delawares, and of Mr. Elliot's Bible are radically the same with the Mohegan, I assert from my own knowledge.[1]

We may fairly conclude that the Narragansett language, referred to by Eliot, was basically understood over much of Massachusetts, Connecticut, Rhode Island, and Long Island, and reached out further to other areas through various of the nomadic tribes. However, throughout parts of these areas were likely whole tribal families speaking a radically different language, the likelihood increasing with distance, which made it impossible for them to understand Eliot's reduction of the Mohegan language to its written form.

Another sort of problem arose to hinder the progress of the Indian mission, namely, the growing English-Indian hostility, based on, and furthered by, several factors: the unchristian character of many English, the lack of full-time missionaries, quarrels over lands, treatment of captives from war on both sides, barbarous Indian reprisals, sale of liquor to Indians, diseases brought by the English which virtually eliminated whole families and depleted tribes, and consequent to all of these, a basic distrust of the Indian on the part of the English which many, no matter how Christian, could never repress.

That distrust came clearly to light in the war of 1675 between hostile Indians and the English. It had been long in building. During the 1650's, when fear of the Indians had arisen, the praying Indians had been dispossessed of their firearms, once even during a sabbath meeting. The Englishmen's desecration of the Lord's Day, as the Indians interpreted the act, had had an unsettling effect on the Natick community. In the 1660's Eliot had given arms and ammunition to Christian Indians from New England Company funds for self-protection and hunting. The Company had balked. Understandably enough, no funds were permitted for such use. Increasingly, to the colonists an Indian was an Indian, whether he prayed or not; therefore, he was not to be trusted. By 1674 there were fourteen towns of praying Indians; two years later, after King Philip's War, there were only four. Many of these Christian Indians were disarmed and deported to barren Deer Island in Boston harbor, there to undergo severe hardship during the winter of 1675–1676 with little food, shelter, or fuel. Many died. From this devastating blow the Indian work never fully recovered.[2]

Still another hindrance to the Christianization was the required Anglicizing of the Indian. This, and for good reason, seemed necessary because of the full identification of Indian religion with their way of life. To accept the Christian faith obviously involved a rejection of Indian religion, but such an act implicitly involved as well the rejection of the old Indian way of life, the known and familiar, the trusted and loved. It meant the acceptance of the will of strangers, some demonstrably bad, with the Indian remaining spiritually, economically, and militarily subject to the newly arrived superior race.

---

[1] *Observations*, see Occum, 5.
[2] For much of this I am indebted to Kellaway, *The New England Company*, 116–119.

Among the helps to the work should be counted the fluctuating, but encouraging, financial assistance of the New England Company for the Propagation of the Gospel from 1649 on, the learning of the Indian language by Eliot and some fellow-workers, and the numerous publications in the Indian language. Colonists furthered the work by the acceptance of Indian children into their homes for the express purpose of bringing them up in the Christian faith. Schools were established which the Indian children could attend for little or no cost. Regular lectures and sermons were given by several English pastors. From the beginning the Indians witnessed to each other. As the work progressed, Indian evangelists preached regularly to worshiping groups, served as interpreters, and went to evangelize areas inaccessible to the English.

Eliot's work as a translator deserves special mention here. There were thirty-six books published in the Indian language between 1653 and 1721. Of these, Eliot was responsible for twenty and a half, Cotton Mather for seven, and other Puritans for the remainder. About ten of Eliot's publications, one of Mather's, and half of one other were second editions or, in Eliot's case, portions of Scripture included in the publication of the full Bible in 1663. No work is known to have been published in the Indian language of New England between 1722 and 1775.[1] Up to the time of Eliot's death the only Indian work not published by Eliot was a brief catechism by Abraham Pierson.[2]

C. THE REDEMPTION OF THE WORLD

*1. The Divine Mission in History*

Eliot saw the world's history as a great spiritual war between the forces of Jesus Christ and those of evil. "The Spiritual War is a principal part of our Religion...."[3] To Christ's forces belonged godly people, also godly commonwealths; to the evil forces belonged Satan and his antichristian parties, including the Roman Church. Eliot intended that *The Christian Commonwealth* should be a structure for the rising kingdom of Jesus Christ on a national level.[4] This proposal, though written before the restoration of the king in 1662, was published afterwards. It was dedicated "To the Chosen, and Holy, and Faithful, who manage the War of the Lord, against Antichrist, in great *Britain*...."[5] The dark and confused clouds which have descended upon England may for a long time obscure the great and glorious coming of Christ, but some day men will see that those clouds were needful.

The prayers of the saints and the prophecies of Scripture are for the downfall of Antichrist and the establishment of Christ's kingdom. By his government and law in the Holy Scriptures, Jesus "will reign over all the Nations of the earth in his due time...."[6]

---

[1] J. H. Trumbull, *op. cit.*, 33–50.
[2] *Some Helps for the Indians* (1658).
[3] Eliot, *Harmony of the Gospels*, 63. Cf. also 62.
[4] *The Christian Commonwealth or, the Civil Policy of the Rising Kingdom of Jesus Christ*, London, 64 pages.
[5] *Ibid.*, Preface, 1.
[6] *Ibid.*, 3.

...the Lord Jesus will bring down all people, to be ruled by the Institutions, Laws, and Directions of the Word of God; not only in Church-Government and Administrations, but also in the Government and Administration of all affairs in the Commonwealth. And then Christ reigneth, when all things among men, are done by the direction of the Word of his mouth: his Kingdom is then come amongst us, when his will is done on earth, as it is done in heaven....[1]

The prophecy of Daniel 2:34ff. has been mostly fulfilled in the downfall of most of the monarchies there referred to. Only the last and the strongest, the Roman monarchy, remains, "...so mixed and interwoven in many States, by the combining of that dirty Roman Religion, with civil Powers...."[2] When the Christ stone shall, by his faithful instruments, beat down the Roman Religion, supporting civil states will also be destroyed. Then all men will submit "to be ruled by the Word, in civil, as well as Church-affairs."[3]

Victory in Scotland is the beginning of the destruction of the Roman image. A beginning has also been made in England. People make much of the rightful heir of the crown, "but Christ is the only right Heir of the Crown of *England*."[4] England has the honor of being first in the setting up of the blessed kingdom of Jesus Christ. In England, Roman religion and the government of Antichrist have been beaten down, while the civil state which stuck fast unto it, also fell. God now calls England to adopt the "forme of Civil Government instituted by God himself in the holy Scriptures...."[5] God is about to destroy the "*Roman-Image*"; the part of wisdom is to search out the divine platform. We should derogate from the sufficiency and perfection of the Scripture if we should deny the existence of such a platform.

> The Scripture is able throughly to furnish the man of God (whether Magistrate in the Commonwealth, or Elder in the Church, or any other) unto every good work.[6]

Eliot explains in an "Apology" that though he is not a statesman, but only one who spends his time in the study of the holy book of God, yet his experience with the Indians has brought him to this Scripture form for government.

> I think it needful to insert this word of Apology for my self; That it pleased the Lord of his free mercy to me (in myself being no way fitted for such a work) to put me on, to instruct our poor, blind, and dark Indians, in the good knowledge of the Lord: who when (through grace) they tasted of the knowledge of God, of themselves, of Christ and redemption by him; they desired to leave their wild and scattered manner of life, and come under Civil Government and Order; which did put me upon search, after the mind of the Lord in that respect. And this VOW I did solemnly make unto the Lord concerning them; that they being a people without any

---

[1] *Idem.*
[2] *Ibid.*, 4.
[3] *Ibid.*, 5.
[4] *Ibid.*, 6.
[5] *Ibid.*, 8.
[6] *Idem.*

forme of Government, and now to chuse; I would endeavour with all my might, to bring them under the Government of the Lord only: Namely, that I would instruct them to imbrace such Government, both Civil and Ecclesiastical, as the Lord hath commanded in the holy Scriptures; and to deduce all their Laws from the holy Scriptures, that so they may be the Lords people; ruled by him alone in all things. Which accordingly they have begun to do through grace, covenanting with the Lord, in a day of fasting and prayer, to be the Lords people; and to receive that forme of Government, which they had learned to be a Divine institution in the holy Scriptures.[1]

Such a form, Eliot pleads, the "holy...Saints" who have fought the "Lords Battels against Antichrist" in England should surely need no persuasion to adopt. Insofar as his platform is purely deduced from the holy Scriptures, "your onely *Magna Charta*," it is a divine institution.[2] The time has come when Christ will shake all the earth, throwing down human governments and setting up his own Scripture-government in their stead.

The platform sets out in eight chapters the following prescriptions: the necessity of entering into "Scripture Covenant" with the Lord (1); the setting up of orders of men in tens, fifties, hundreds, thousands, and so on higher (2); the setting up of courts of judgment on various levels (3); the right of appeal up to the Supreme Council made up of both magistrates and of teaching and ruling elders, with the magistrates in the majority (4,5); the duty of all rulers to apply both tables of the divine law, which includes maintaining the purity of religion, promoting the propagation of religion, and calling of ecclesiastical councils (6, 7); and, the Scriptures to be the perfect frame of laws from which human laws are drawn (8).[3]

Though Eliot does not often refer to the Roman Catholic Church, his identification of it with Antichrist is clear. In a letter to Baxter, written a few years after *The Christian Commonwealth* appeared, he states the matter clearly.

The Jesuits' missions by their Provincials into the East and Westr'n worlds and into all Protestant nations, is a notable means of upholding Anti-Christ. The man of sin siteth in the Temple of God, the p[ri]est and ordinance of God; and it p[ro]ves a vigorous way of p[ro]moting their superstition and darknesse. But when the Churches and Councils of Churches are awakened to their duty, and shall vigorously undertake that service of Christ, it will shine downe all their Jesuitical abuses into the bottomlesse pit from which they ascended. The man of sin shall be destroyed by the brightnesse of Christ his coming.[4]

---

[1] *Ibid.*, 9.
[2] *Ibid.*, 15, 17; This view of Eliot is directly contrary to that of Roger Williams, who writes: "... the state of the Land of Israel ... is proved *figurative* and *ceremoniall*, and no patterne ... for any Kingdom or civill state in the world to follow." *Bloudy Tenant*, Preface, 2.
[3] *The Christian Commonwealth*, 1–35.
[4] Baxter's Letters, vol. iii, 131a. This identification was common Puritan doctrine in the mid-seventeenth century. So Roger Williams, for example, also believed that the time

It is Satan who uses Antichrist to lead men astray. As he tried to hire Jesus Christ to Devil-worship by a false pretense, so many in our day "are hired against their light, from the Truth, and Protestant Religion, unto Popery by a fat Bishoprick, a Cardinals cap, a tripple crown." [1] Satan's inner kingdom reaches into the hearts and imaginations of men.[2] He has a strange power over their phantasies. Yet the Lord overcomes his greatest efforts. Eliot writes to Baxter in 1671:

> I never found such violent opposition by Satan; and yet the L[or]d doth outwork him in all, & the Kingd[o]me of Christ doth spread and rise the more by his so violent opposition.[3]

God is working out his great design in the world. He made the whole world of mankind to glorify his justice.

> And he purposed and chose out a certain number, a scattering out of mankind in all Ages to be vessels of mercy, in whom he would glorifie his free grace and mercy, and all this, by and through Jesus Christ, Eph. 1.4,5,6....Hence Gods Elect were in Christ before they were in Adam.[4]

After creation, man sinned and can escape condemnation only through Christ's fulfillment of the covenant of redemption. By Christ's active and passive obedience, God's elect are made to be vessels of mercy.

God's great will moves through history. Eliot teaches the Indians:

> *Ques. 18. Why do I say, The Power is thine?*
> Answ. Because He is the Allmighty God, what he pleaseth he doth in the whole world.[5]

He interposes with a divine hand in history,[6] and by degrees draws men to himself.[7] "God's works among men, doe usually goe on slowly." [8] His wonderful acts of providence are much to be treasured by his people. But wrathful acts of persecutors are not divine punishments, though they accomplish his ends.[9] Christ Jesus is knocking at our door in the perplexing troubles of life.[10] World history is full of examples of how the church and saints have been delivered from persecution by the death of persecutors.[11] Ordinarily bodily infirmities are medicinal to the souls of God's people,[12] and temptations are God's school, "...Gods usual preparatorys of his Children for great services...." [13]

---

would soon come that the Church of Rome would be "a poore desolate naked whore, torn and consumed." *Bloudy Tenant*, 246. And John Cotton wrote: "Antichrist shall be abolished and Rome ruinated." *The Churches Resurrection*, London, 1642, 14.

[1] Eliot, *Harmony of the Gospels*, 60.
[2] Ibid., 63.
[3] Baxter's Letters, vol. iii, 264a, June 27, 1671.
[4] *Harmony of the Gospels*, 2.
[5] *The Indian Primer*, 17.
[6] *A Brief Narrative...*, 9.
[7] *Harmony of the Gospels*, 32.
[8] *A Late and Further Manifestation...*, 21.
[9] *The Christian Commonwealth*, Preface, 16.
[10] Ibid., 13.
[11] *Harmony of the Gospels*, 51.
[12] Ibid., 46, 56.
[13] Ibid., 64.

God has made two great changes in ecclesiastical polity since the beginning of the world. Both were marked by earthquakes, the Mosaic polity and the Gospel polity. By the former the ancient paternal government was begun; by the latter "...Christ hath opened Heaven for all that will come unto him, Gentiles as well as Jews...."[1] We are in the "...last and best Age of the Church in this militant world...."[2] However,

> ...it is God's designe and purpose, that the state of his Church and Saints in this world should be poor, the most part of them, and therefore he hath prepared poverty for them by taking the curse out of it.[3]

Poverty must not be considered a sin, but an affliction and punishment of sin.[4] Even the prophets and apostles, saints and martyrs of the Church "...who did eminent good works for the World, yet they did basely abuse them, and ill reward them...."[5] So God's dearest children may be rejected and banished from the church, longing for the presence of God in instituted worship.[6]

> What better and more seasonable Subject canst thou...exercise thy soul about in these black, and suffering dayes, then in the sufferings of our Lords Jesus Christ.[7]

The church will not continue in such a low condition. In the latter days of this age, Jesus Christ will "more plentifully pour out prosperity, grace,...in the more glorious times of the Church in this world as may be gathered out of the Prophesies of *Isaiah* from the sixty Chapter and so forward: and from many other Scriptures."[8] It is significant that Eliot here speaks in a different tone than he did nearly twenty years earlier in *The Christian Commonwealth, the Rising Kingdom of Jesus Christ*. Then, plans for the type of government for Christ's Kingdom had priority. Now in 1678 Eliot is using the suffering of Jesus Christ to comfort a suffering church. Now, promises of Scripture that the "low condition" will not continue are the order of the day.[9]

In 1675, Eliot wrote to John Winthrop, Jr., that men must take God's visitations more seriously lest "...God chastise us 7 times more by his next visitation, as he threatens to do to such as profit not by former rods."[10] The visitations undoubtedly referred to the increasing hostility between the English and the Indians, and the beginning of King Philip's War. Eliot's conviction that "New-England is a preface to New-Jesusalem" must have been shaken.[11]

---

[1] *Ibid.*, 126.
[2] *Ibid.*, 59.
[3] *Ibid.*, 38.
[4] *Ibid.*, 36.
[5] *Ibid.*, 56–57.
[6] *Ibid.*, 17.
[7] *Ibid.*, Title Page.
[8] *Ibid.*, 42.
[9] Eliot's change on this matter is reminiscent of Baxter's change after the writing of his *The Holy Commonwealth* (1659). He had not finished writing when news of the reversal of political fortunes in Parliament and the army reached him. That, with official displeasure for his book against popery (*A Key for Catholicks*), made him realize how impossible it was for Christians to find acceptance in the world. Thereafter Baxter concerned himself even less with political matters.
[10] *Mass. Hist. Soc. Coll.*, Fifth Series, Vol. I, 424–426 (July 24, 1675).
[11] *Ibid.*, Sixth Series, Vol. II, 202, quoted in a letter by S. Sewell to Experience Mayhew, dated March 19, 1726.

The kingdom of God, according to Eliot, is fourfold: "Our holy In-being in Christ; also our Church Communion; and also our being under his Government in this World, and also in Heaven forever." [1] Though many of his contemporaries stressed the thousand-year reign of Christ in a literal way and predicted the time of its beginning,[2] Eliot spoke in general terms and made no predictions except that he judged the time of the glorious kingdom on earth was near. He taught the Indian children thus:

> *Ques. 8. For what do I pray, Let come thy Kingdom?*
> Answ.: That Christ may cause me to return to God.
> Secondly, That he would by my Confession of him gather me into the Church.
> Thirdly. That Christ would hasten to come to the last Judgment.[3]

It is clear that Eliot's concept of the kingdom meant that all of God's people were under the government of God in this world, and that their condition would improve with the institution of Scriptural government in various nations. Beyond this, he looked forward to the return of Christ and the establishment of the perfect kingdom in heaven following the general resurrection and the last judgment. The consideration of the eternal state ought to move men to pray for forgiveness.

> *Ques. 13. Why do I pray, Forgive us our sins?*
> Answ. Because if it be not so we shall for ever be damned for our many sins.[4]

Those who refuse to seek forgiveness reject free grace.

> But Wo be to those unto whom this grace is freely offered, but they rather chuse the pleasures of sin for a season, and by their own choice plunge themselves into these flames of wrath, out of which Jesus Christ offereth to deliver them, but they refuse to accept his offer.[5]

The greatest sin is that against the light of the gospel. Eternal judgment is the harvest of man's own sin alone. "In Hell every soul feels the punishment due to his own sin only, he suffereth only for his own sins." [6]

God's purpose in history is not the condemnation of souls. By the word of the gospel he "doth indeed shake the hearts of men, but it is to repentance, and to embrace the offer of grace and mercy in Jesus Christ." [7] The story of Gethsemane makes clear how God carries out his purpose.

---

[1] *The Indian Primer*, 14–15.
[2] Thomas Parker, *The Visions and Prophecies of Daniel Expounded*, 1646, predicted that either 1649 or 1860 would be the beginning of Christ's millenial reign, ushered in by the conversion of the Jews, 153–155, or, as John Cotton thought, by the destruction of "Anti-Christ and Rome." *op. cit.*, 12 (1642).
[3] *Indian Primer*, 15.
[4] *Ibid.*, 16.
[5] *Harmony of the Gospels*, 70.
[6] *Ibid.*, cf. 119; *The Indian Primer*, 16.
[7] *Harmony of the Gospels*, 92.

We may also see in this story the sovereign wisdom of God in over-ruling and ordering the counsels of men to make for his own glory, and for the accomplishment of his own holy counsel, unknown and unconsidered by them that act them, that which they act for their own bad ends, God permitteth them, and over-ruleth them for his own holy ends.[1]

Christ as the second Adam stood in the stead of all; he suffered the punishment of sin due unto all.[2] He has set a pattern for us in the exercise of suffering graces.[3] He is the ingenuous Servant who fished for souls, as did Paul, "...for all the doings and Sufferings of Iesus Christ were to gain and save souls."[4] So he professed his intention to draw all men unto himself.

> ...the sovereign grace of Jesus Christ, is poured forth from the Cross, and draweth hearts to believe, and this power of grace is exercised by the sweet savour of the Cross of Christ, unto this day, yea, and will be so to the worlds end.[5]

So Jesus has set heaven's gates open for rich and poor, masters and servants, for parents and children. Especially those of low estate may take comfort from the suffering of their Lord.

> And at the great day we shall see many bond slaves, Servants, and underlings; men and women, *sit down with Abraham, Isaac, and Jacob in the heavenly Kingdome, but their Masters, Rulers, and such as made them slaves, cast out into outer darkness.*[6]

Death for believers is thus an entrance into glory and a waiting for the great day of resurrection.[7] They will forever be "Monuments of mercy" rather than "Vessels of Wrath."[8] Now, however, the godly are to look forward to the next two great acts and dispensations of Christ which all men shall see. First, Christ is sitting on the right hand of power, that is,

> ...you shall see the mighty power of Gospel grace of Christ Jesus, in the conversion both of Jews and Gentiles, and so going on until the last and final conversion of the Jews, which we hope for at this day.[9]

Second the "next and last act of Jesus Christ in this world" is that *"you shall see him coming in the Clouds of Heaven* viz. *in power and great glory, to judge the World."* [10]

2. *The Indians and the Ten Lost Tribes of Israel*

Eliot was greatly concerned about the expected conversion of the Jews. This was evident from the missionary tracts where he expressed his opinion that the Indians belong to the ten lost tribes of Israel. Eliot was not alone in this view. Edward Winslow describes the problem in a dedicatory epistle to

---

[1] *Ibid.*, 75.
[2] *Ibid.*, 126.
[3] *Ibid.*, 117.
[4] *Ibid.*, 43.
[5] *Ibid.*, 130.
[6] *Ibid.*, 46.
[7] *Ibid.*, 131.
[8] *Ibid.*, 47; cp. 118–119.
[9] *Ibid.*, 79–80.
[10] *Idem.*

the Parliament of England. Two questions, Winslow says, have troubled ancient and modern writers, namely, what became of the ten tribes of Israel? And what people first planted America?[1] Rabbi-ben-Israel, in a letter to a London minister, proposed that there were "infallible tokens" that the ten lost tribes first peopled America.[2] This "Dr. of the Jewes"[3] living in Amsterdam had support in New England for his views. Regulations from the ceremonial laws of Moses concerning the purification of women were observed by the Indians but by no other known people. Belief in the Deity, soul of man, immortality of the soul, and eternity of happiness or misery after death added weight to this conjecture. Moreover, the prevailing idea among the Indians that their ancestors once possessed knowledge of God and the way to worship Him, of the general deluge, and of one man who alone had seen God, fit in with such a view as to their origin. And now, just when many divines had foretold from Scripture prophecy of the nearing conversion of the Jews, God was opening the hearts of the Indians to accept the gospel. Such an unlikely coincidence must be more than speculation. Yet, should this happy identification not be true, what is of greatest significance of all is "the work of communicating and encreasing the light of the Gospel...to *Jewes* & Gentiles."[4]

To this tract an "Appendix", initialled "J.D., minister of the gospel," is attached. This minister describes why he believes the Indians are possibly to be identified with the ten lost tribes of the Jews. He notes that some of the wisest Jews then living expect that about the year 1650 "*Either we Christians shall be Mosaick, or else that themselves Jewes shall be Christians.*"[5] In addition "*Jewes of the Netherlands...informe that after much inquiry they found some of the ten Tribes to be in America.*"[6] Because Indian beliefs suggest a Jewish origin, the author hopes that the work of Christ among them may be a preparation for his own coming. Though this view concerning Jewish origins be not sure, all can rejoice that these poor souls, captives of Satan for many ages, have received the gospel. The early Christians, when scattered abroad, went everywhere preaching the Word.

> And I wish from my soul, that all these *Ministers of the Dispersion* (as I may call them) *in New-England*; would stirre up themselves to this work of the Lord....[7]

Meanwhile, in 1649 and 1650 Eliot joined the discussion. He would like to hear more of the opinions of Rabbi-ben-Israel concerning the grounds for his beliefs about the Jewish origins of Indians. How did he come to this view? When did they come to America? How were they transported? How many came? To what parts first? Should it be possible to establish such origin, "it is a ground of faith to expect mercy for them,"[8] since God is faithful to ancient covenants and promises.

---

[1] *The Glorious Progress*..., "Epistle Dedicatory," 1–2 (1649).
[2] Ibid., 4.
[3] Idem.
[4] Ibid., 5, 6.
[5] *The Glorious Progress*..., 22.
[6] Ibid., 23.
[7] Ibid., 25.
[8] *The Light appearing*..., 14 (1651).

Eliot believes that as surely as the English are children of Japhet, Indians are of Shem. Shem is likely Melchizedek, to whom Abraham paid tithes. Eber, Shem's son, is portrayed by Scripture as having settled farthest east and, as Broughton [1] testifies, some of his descendants went into America. The sureness of God's Covenant with his people, the many promises in Scripture of the gospel's spread to the going down of the sun, which seems to include America, and the multitude of nations to be included in Christ's kingdom, argue not only for the conversion of the Eastern nations but for that of the Indians as well, especially if their Jewish origin be established. Such Scriptural grounds "do minister comfort & encouragement" to Eliot's heart.[2] On Scripture alone, the precious and perfect Word of God, does he desire to build. Captain Cromwell's [2] testimony that many of the Southern Indians in America are circumcised gives additional credibility to this interpretation of Scriptural promise.[3]

Ten years later, Eliot's views had developed further. The evangelism of the Indians he saw as part of the fulfillment of God's promise that the Jews would be converted in the next great act of Christ in history. The idea expressed by some that missions in New England were hindered because the church must wait for the conversion of the Jews, could hardly have been true for Eliot, since he tended to identify the Indians with the lost tribes. This view would sooner be a stimulus than a hindrance.[4]

In a twenty-two page letter printed in Thorowgood's *Jewes in America* (1660), Eliot traces his conjectures in detail. Conjectures they remained:

> ...I thought, I saw some ground to conceive, that some of the Ten Tribes might be scattered even thus far, into these parts of *America*, where we are according to the word of God, *Deut. 28.64*.[5]

In that passage Moses tells Israel what the fearful consequences of her disobedience will be:

> And Jehovah will scatter thee among all peoples, from the one end of the earth even unto the other end of the earth; and there thou shalt serve other gods, which thou hast not known, thou nor thy fathers, even wood and stone.[6]

Here Eliot found an accurate picture of the true state of the Indians as a life dominated by uncertainty and fear.

> ...Jehovah will give there a trembling heart...and thy life shall hang in doubt before thee; and thou shalt fear night and day, and shalt have no assurance of thy life. In the morning thou shalt say, Would it were even! and at even thou shalt say, Would it were morning! for the fear of thy heart which thou shalt fear, and for the sight of thine eyes which thou shalt see.[7]

---

[1] *Ibid,*, 15.
[2] *Idem.*
[3] *Ibid.*, 24 (1651).
[4] See Trumbull, 7.
[5] Thorowgood, *Jewes in America*, 1.
[6] American Standard Version.
[7] *Ibid.*, vs. 65–67.

The following verse found literal fulfillment, in Eliot's view, when Indians taken captive in King Philip's War were shipped to Egypt to be sold and no buyers were found.

> And Jehovah will bring thee into Egypt again with ships, by the way whereof I said unto thee, Thou shalt see it no more again; and there shall ye sell yourselves unto your enemies for bondmen and for bondwomen, and no man shall buy you.[1]

The western world was peopled, Eliot believed, by the descendants of Japhet and Ham, two of Noah's sons. Further, Scripture indicates that Shem's descendants settled easterly, first in Persia, also called Elam after Shem's first son. Eber, the grandson of Arphaxed, Shem's third son, was born about the same time as Nimrod and opposed his rebellion. The fathers of the church called the holy language of the church Ebrew by Eber's name. Eber's grandchildren, the narrative continues, migrated eastward and possessed all countries east of Elam or Persia. The word of God says that the distribution of lands made to the children in the holy line of Seth were the settled demarcations.

> Hence therefore we may, not only with faith, but also with demonstration, say, that fruitful *India* are *Hebrewes*, that famous civil (though Idolatrous) nation of *China* are *Hebrewes*, so *Japonia*, and these naked *Americans* are *Hebrewes*, in respect of those that planted first these parts of the world....[2]

The paternal polity of church and state of the Hebrews remained in effect until God displaced it by the Mosaic. The family of Abraham, which God sent westward, he chose to bear the holy line, thus rejecting the rest of Shem's line. And, when Christ came to institute the gospel-polity of congregational churches, even Abraham's branch was outside the church, which then entered the western world among families of Japhet and Ham. Apart from the visit of Thomas to one part of India, of which history tells us, all the eastern world has been without the gospel. Is it possible that God is entering the eastern kingdom by its most eastern portal, as Israel used to do in the Old Testament temple? Shall there not be a glorious Church in all the eastern world?

> And God grant that the old bottles of the Westerne world be not so uncapable of the new wine of Christ his expected Kingdom, that the Easterne bottles be not the only entertainers thereof for a season.[3]

But since the confusion of languages did not fall upon Seth's line, how is it that the Hebrew language is lost and the families yet fell under that confusion of tongues? The holy language was likely intended for the use of the church. Thus, as families degenerated from the church and the holy ways of God, they fell into confusion of that language also. It would be worth searching after, Eliot observes, whether all the eastern world is not more similar in language

---

[1] *Ibid.*, vs. 68.
[2] *Jewes in America*, 17.
[3] *Ibid.*, 18.

to the Hebrew, at least grammatically, than all the western world. He judges "...that the gramatical frame of our *Indian* language cometh *neerer to the Hebrew*, than the *Latine*, or *Greek* do...." [1]

The dispersion of the ten tribes to the eastern countries was among the posterity of Eber whose language and spirit were not wholly strange, whereas Judah was dispersed westward, throughout the western world among peoples and tongues utterly strange to them, and where they received greater affliction. Since the ten tribes were captives first, and sinned against less light of the gospel than Judah, is it not likely they will be first in the return of the Jews to God? [2]

One of the works of God in the last days is to find lost Israel and bring it into his kingdom. This moves the hearts of God's people to search after Israel. [3] He that can resurrect dead bodies can also find lost Israel. Now is the time, as is confirmed by the interpretation of holy prophecies concerning them, by the spirit of intercessory prayer on their behalf, and by the earnest search and inquiry after them. [4]

Christ has set his servants upon the search. That should be done. Whether the light will soon dawn upon Israel, we do not know. [5] Eliot has reasons which to him seem weighty which make him silent on this matter. In a private letter to Thorowgood (Oct. 16, 1656) he concludes by saying:

> I am called of God to labour among them, [the Indians] but not so far, as I yet see to be engaging in that point: your labours and letters have drawn me forth further that way, than otherwise I should have gone, but I desire you to spare me in this, and give me leave to hear and observe in silence, what the Lord will teach others to say in this matter. [6]

---

[1] *Ibid.*, 19. Roger Williams did not agree with Eliot. He concedes that some Indian words are similar to Hebrew, and some Indian customs are like those of the Hebrews, such as anointing their heads, paying dowries for wives, and separating the women at their monthly sickness for four or five days. But, for his own reasons, he prefers the theory of the Greek origin of the Indians. (*A Key into the Language of America*, 6.) Jonathan Edwards, Jr., about a hundred years later, wrote: "Besides what has been observed concerning prefixes and suffixes, there is a remarkable analogy, between some words in the Mohegan language and the correspondent words in the Hebrew." How far the usages "go towards proving, that the North American Indians are of Hebrew, or at least Asiatic extraction, is submitted to the judgment of the learned." (*Observations*, see Occum, 14.)

[2] *Jewes in America*, 20.
[3] *Idem.*
[4] *Ibid.*, 1, 2.
[5] *Ibid.*, 20.
[6] *Ibid.*, 34. Baxter wrote to I. Mather, Ms. Letters I, f. 217 – no date:
"As to the Doctrine of the Jewes conversion, I have told you somewhat of the reasons of my dissent: I am past doubt that the ten tribes were sent back with the rest, that (though mixt with corruption) the Romans found them there, and that allmost all the Infidell Jewes were killed by Tiberius, Trajan, and Adrian, and the scattered Jewes are but the progeny of the nation left, and had the liberty of their country, (too small and barren to continue them), and that the fullness of the Gentiles coming in by Christ's assuming visibly the Imperiall sword, Judea was the noblest of all Nationall Churches, proportionate to its greatness, Though the Christian Jewes soon lost their names by marrying and joyning with the Gentile Christians."

Eliot will give himself to his call. The service of his Lord required the redemption of man and the salvation of souls.[1]

> We must not sit still, and look for miracles: *Up, and be doing, and the Lord will be with thee*. *Prayer* and *Pains*, through faith in Christ Jesus, will do anything. *Nil tam deficile quod non* – I do *believe* and *hope*, that the Gospel shall be spread to all the Ends of the Earth, and dark Corners of the World, by such a way, and by such *Instruments* as the Churches shall send forth for that end and purpose. Lord hasten those good dayes, and pour out that good Spirit upon thy people. *Amen.*[2]

*Conclusion*

The monumental work of John Eliot towers above the low level of mission consciousness in seventeenth-century Protestantism. Not that there were no other missionaries dedicated to the propagation of the gospel. This was, after all, within a century of King Gustav Wasa (Swedish mission to Lapland) and Leibniz (plea for missions in *Novissima Sinica*, 1697), of August Hermann Francke (father of German Pietism) and the Dutch colonial missions (Justus Heurnius: *De legatione evangelica ad Indos capessenda admointio*, 1618). But to Eliot belongs the title of the "evangelical missionary" of the seventeenth century [3] due to the length and character of his work. It cannot be doubted that Eliot was quite typical of basic Puritan thought in his general religious, political, and social views.[4] In ecclesiastical spheres he represented, like most of his Puritan contemporaries, the New England blend of Presbyterian-Congregationalism.[5] But in missionary thinking and doing, as we have seen, Eliot was indeed the "notable exception," [6] the "great luminary" of the century.[7]

---

[1] *Idem.*

[2] *Indian Grammer Begun*, 65.

[3] Gustav Warneck says: "Dieser edle Mann hat den Ruhm, der erste evangelische Missionar zu sein, der aus den lautersten Motiven und unter den grössten Opfern und Beschwerden sein Leben der Bekehrung von Heiden widmete und sich auch wirklich apostolischer Mittel in diesem Bekehrungswerke bediente." *Geschichte der Protestantischen Missionen*, 48–49.

[4] Herbert Schneider, *The Puritan Mind*, 25–26.

[5] A. H. Drysdale defines Eliot's position in *History of the Presbyterians in England*, 337, as "essentially Presbyterian," in reference to Eliot's *Communion of Churches* (1666). There Eliot states: "Christ, who hath *all power*, Mat. 28.20, hath derived all Ecclesiastical Power first unto the Apostles, that they by Institution might distribute the same unto several Officers in the Church. Hence, As all Church officers, especially Elders, and more especially *Teaching Elders*, are ordinary Successors of the Apostles, in their several branches of Church-power: So *Councils of Churches* are their eminent ordinary Successors, in point of Counsel..." (4). Hugh Martin calls him the "Presbyterian 'Apostle of the Indians' in New England...," *Puritanism and Richard Baxter*, 164. Mather, however, says: "It was his as well as his master, the great Ramus's principle, 'that in the reformation of churches, to be now endeavoured, things ought to be reduced unto the order wherein we find them at their primitive, original, apostolical institution.' And in pursuance of this principle, he justly espoused that way of church-government which we call the *congregational* . . . .," *Magnalia Christi Americana*, I, 552.

[6] Geoffrey Nuttall, *Visible Saints*, 161.

[7] Edmund D. Soper, *Philosophy of the Christian World Mission*, 121–122.

The three missionary principles which we discussed in the chapters on Sibbes and Baxter are found in Eliot's writings as part of his theological framework. First, the sovereign good pleasure of God, Eliot says, is seen in the over-ruling of human sin by God's holy counsel. The sovereign grace of the cross sets the doors of heaven wide open and draws men who have lost the divine image of true knowledge, righteousness and holiness. Original sin leaves men with the image of Satan. The almighty God chooses out of history a certain number whom he elects to receive his free grace and mercy. Man has sinned and escapes judgment only through Christ. The Lord speaks by his Spirit to human hearts, and in his time they are brought to himself. The deepest estrangements of men from God are no hindrance to the sufficient grace of Christ, to the Spirit of his grace. Eliot holds, thus, to divine sovereignty in redemption as expressed in election and to man's helplessness apart from saving grace. The theological position of Sibbes and Baxter is clearly fundamental also for Eliot, but he, unlike Baxter, does not discuss the difficulty of man's comprehending God's way. For him, it is enough to say "God's way is best." [1]

In the second place, Puritanism had always emphasized that preaching is God's appointed means to accomplish redemption. In this light we must see Eliot's frequent appeal for more laborers in a white harvest field, and his encouragement of fellow-ministers to evangelize Indians in their vicinity. Eliot was as concerned as his fellows to make Scripture and the preaching of its message central. He was, according to Mather, a "Bible theologian." [2] Elders, and especially teaching elders, are the ordinary successors of the apostles. Upon them falls the apostolic mantle of responsibility to "Go and teach all nations." This responsibility they are to carry out by means of the ecclesiastical councils of churches whose prime duties are to send out fit laborers to bring the gospel to heathen peoples and to those in spiritual darkness in Christian lands, and to supply teachers and ministers where special needs exist. [3]

Thus, Eliot agreed with Baxter that ministers might be ordained for full-time mission work in the church, though for the proper prayer for and support of the work he judged it better to seek the approbation of a particular church. Baxter agreed that normally this would be wisest, only he insisted that *in principle* such attachment to a local church was not necessary. Like Baxter, Eliot believed that "God gave us two books," [4] the book of Scripture and that of creation. In the book of creation "...every creature was a word or a sentence...." [5] Eliot could point to evidence of God's presence in nature and in the beliefs of the Indians themselves. However, true knowledge of God and right religion came through the preaching of gospel grace. For Eliot, as for Sibbes and Baxter, no question was raised concerning the connection between sovereign, elective grace and the appointment of means. The presence of the latter was itself a guarantee of God's gracious disposition to the deepest degeneracy of man.

---

[1] *Strength out of Weaknesse...*, 33 (1652).
[2] *Magnalia Christi Americana* I, 546.
[3] Eliot, *Communion of Churches*, 23, 24 (1666).
[4] *Strength out of Weaknesse...*, 26 (1652).
[5] *Idem.*

Third, Eliot believed that every man to whom he preached could respond to the gospel. Without qualification he preached to the Indians that all who "by faith beleeve in Christ, and know him feelingly" are children of God. The way to come was by repentance, by seeking forgiveness in Christ as Saviour, and by love for God evidenced in knowing and obeying his will. As philological expert and practical missionary of the first order, Eliot's whole life is a living testimony of his faith in the redeemability of men. He had preached, and the Indians had learned, as the confessions of Nishohkou and Ponampam make clear, that redemption comes from overpowering grace and not human goodness. Man possesses a likeness to God in the spontaneity of his will. This sort of will-freedom is not able in itself to make a spiritually dead Indian or Englishman alive to God. But it can choose to use the means at hand. God's law, "civility," and prayer serve as preparatives. These Eliot unhesitatingly challenges the Indians to use, knowing that, as the Puritans in England had professed, "where the *Ministery* is the *Harbinger* and goes before, Christ and *Grace* will *certainly* follow after." [1]

The preaching of the law of God was intended to convince, restrain, civilize, and humble the Indians. When some Indians took the message seriously and began to imitate the English, Eliot hoped this was a preparatory step for the confession: "...broken is my heart...I am not able to deliver my selfe, but I betrust my soule with Jesus Christ." [2] To secure a believing response like this, Eliot preached and worked exhaustively, as had Sibbes and Baxter.

Because of his involvement in the work, the methods used by Eliot are more specific than those found in Sibbes and Baxter. However, their general methodology undergirds his approach as well. Eliot firmly believed that the nature of faith was communicative; hence, he was deeply concerned for spiritual character, or lack of it, in Englishmen's lives, and he highly approved of the Indian-to-Indian witness. With respect to the former, we have noted that unholy, rude, and dishonest Englishmen's lives, (as Eliot wrote to Baxter in 1657), were the greatest hindrance to the work. The witness of Indian Christians reminded Eliot of the praiseworthy example in the early church, and he increasingly stressed the importance of sending teams of Indians rather than whites to witness to their own and other tribes.

Baxter's advice to do good to men's bodies and to love them as men in order to benefit their souls was expanded by Eliot into a full program of civilizing the Indians. Not only did he give to the poor and defend the Indians from abuse; he set in motion a whole process of community living and self support. This foundation upon which he built, Eliot called the work of "civility," from which a settled church and its ordinances might result. Eliot, like Baxter, also believed that separation from the church was wrong and pointed to the fact that disunity in the church hinders the advance of the kingdom and the coming of Christ. His concern was evidenced in the elaborate and visionary scheme

---

[1] *The Clear Sun-shine of the Gospel* . . ., Epistle Dedicatory, 4 (1648).
[2] *A Late and Further Manifestation* . . ., 18, 10 (1655).

for church unity worked out in the *Communion of Churches* (1666). Congregational and Presbyterian unity was its local implication, but unity of church organization, including Indian and English alike, throughout the world was its ultimate goal.

In preaching to the Indians Eliot placed the simple truths of the gospel in the foreground: repentance for sin, faith in Christ, and loving service of God. We hear Indians confessing, not foreordination and election, but that all good is from God's grace, all evil from man's sin. Christ's death is of infinite value; God promises to forgive if we believe; Christ stands in our stead and saves.

The main emphases of Eliot's methodology should be noted. First, the heart of his approach is the establishment of the church among the Indians. His deep concern for the conversion of the individual Indian involved the setting up of Christ's kingdom among them. This was accomplished by stages: preaching to groups and dealing with individuals who responded and sought further counsel, encouraging the communion of believers by community living, the organization of the community dwellers into political units, and finally, nearly ten years later, the establishment of local churches where the sacraments were administered. That this process took nearly a decade and a half is not the fault of Eliot. Within two years he was speaking of the importance of the sacraments for the Indians. From that point on he repeatedly urged the hearing of confessions and holding of examinations, while from year to year, though favorable reactions inevitably followed these events, reasons were found by delegates of the Roxbury church and the neighboring churches to postpone approval. The Indian confessions pointedly show that the Indian converts earnestly desired church-fellowship and the seals of grace. "Godly hearts long for the enjoyment of God's presence in his instituted worship. They can find no rest in their souls, so long as they are at a distance from the visible presence of God." [1] What might be called a cultural motive, namely, the establishment of community living and political organization, was a preparatory step for the full establishment of the church with its ordinances.

Second, Eliot emphasized the teaching method both in winning converts and in their growth in grace. He taught them the history and doctrine of the Scripture. He established schools to train Indians to read the Bible and devotional materials. He translated books into the Indian language. He trained natives as teachers and evangelists. He wrote and taught catechisms to children and adults. The composition of the *Indian Grammar Begun* had in view "the help of others who have an heart to study and learn the same for the sake of these Ruines of Mankind...." [2] In this light must also be considered his translation of the *Logick Primer* "to initiate the Indians in the knowledge of the Rule of Reason" [3] so that they could not only read the Scriptures but understand them. Two examples of how Eliot used his writings to teach the Christian message may be given.

---

[1] *Harmony of the Gospels*, 17 (1678).   [2] *The Indian Grammar Begun*, Preface, (1666).
[3] Perry Miller, *The New England Mind: The Seventeenth Century*, 114. Miller points out that "Reason" does not at all mean for the Puritans what later thinkers understood by it. For

Eliot's *Indian Grammar Begun* was written, as the sub-title indicates, "for the furtherance of the Gospel among them," and, as the preface points out, to help those who desire to learn the language for the sake of Christ. One who used this book learned theology in the process. For example, in discussing what Eliot called the "Suffix form advocate, or *in stead form*, when one acteth in the room or stead of another," he adds:

> This form is of great use in *Theologie* to express what Christ has done for us; as
> Nunnuppoowonuk, *He died for me.*
> Kenuppoowonuk, *He died for thee.*
> Kenuppoowonukgun, *He died for us.*
> Kenuppoowonukoo, *He died for you.*[1]

So also, when Eliot deals with the five modes of verbal action, he says of the second:

> The *Imperative*, or *Hortative*, or *Praying* and *Blessing Modes* is when the action is *Commanded*, or *Exhorted to be done*, or *Prayed* for. When a Superiour speaks in this *Mode*, he *prays* and *intreats*. When a Minister speaks in this *Mode*, he *exhorts* and *blesseth*.[2]

One can detect a tinge of humor, when after giving a list of words to be learned, he comments; "And these will be enough to busie the heads of *Learners* for a while." [3]

*The Indian Primer* was a first reading book for Indian children. The beginning of a Biblical vocabulary can be seen in the first list of noun words for the child to learn: Christ, Lord, keep, God, us, wage, may, keep, nag, week.[4] The first piece to read was the Lord's Prayer and a brief catechism of twenty questions and answers on the phrases in it.[5] This was followed by the Apostles Creed and a catechism based, for the most part, upon it, entitled: "The Christian Belief in twenty and four Questions and Answers concerning Christian Doctrine." [6] Some questions beyond the articles of the Creed dealt with the Ten Commandments, the Christian life, prayer, the officers of the church, the sacraments, and a rule of discipline.[7]

For Eliot the Christian faith was, in part at least, beyond reason, but not contrary to it. Therefore, Eliot accented teaching the way of God to the Indian,

---

the Puritans, "Reason ... is not an instrument but a doctrine; logic is the instrument by which doctrine is made evident." Like Ramus, they tended "to regard truth as a body of received, inviolable, and objective dicta" (*Ibid.*, 150–153). The "Achilles heel" was that this body of truth was considered to be subject to rational analysis and systematic catagorization, and, therefore, mysteries in religion, such as the Trinity and the double nature of Christ, became indefensible. The development of Deism with its emphasis on the reasonableness of Christianity and elimination of mystery was a logical consequent drawn in later times.

[1] *Indian Grammar Begun*, 18 (1666).
[2] *Ibid.*, 19.
[3] *Ibid.*, 18.
[4] *The Indian Primer*, 8 (1669).
[5] *Ibid.*, 8–17.
[6] *Ibid.*, 18.
[7] *Ibid.*, 18–29.

which teaching itself required a settled and ordered way of life. "Civilizing" assists the believing response to the regular preaching and teaching of the gospel and makes possible the establishment of the church.

The third emphasis in Eliot is what we have referred to above as the Indian-to-Indian witness. Contrary to the opinion of many Englishmen, Eliot believed that Indians should be approached in their own language. English was taught as a subject at the schools for Indian children, but the basic language at Natick was Indian, and the teachers were natives. Indians, far better than the English, could address the gospel to their own people. When God is ready to do a great work in any people, he uses members of that people to do the work. Early in his work, Eliot wanted to pastor the first Indian church that should be organized. If there were fifteen or twenty Christian Indians who so desired, and a call from a particular church for this task were received, he was ready to serve. However, Eliot was fifty-six when the first Indian church was organized. By that time he believed that Indian pastors could best serve. In their approach to the Indians, as in his own, attempts were made to convert the sachems, though these were usually unsuccessful.[1]

Many forces worked together to bring Eliot to his missionary labors. Cotton Mather mentions several motives that encouraged his work. Among the more external factors was the call to missions expressed in the royal charter, namely,

> To win and incite the natives of that country to the knowledge and obedience of the only true God and Saviour of mankind, and the Christian faith, is our royal intention, and the adventurer's free profession is the principal end of this plantation.[2]

All good men in the plantation encouraged him, especially the ministers who did pulpit and pastoral work at Roxbury to relieve him for the Indian work. The remarkable zeal of the Roman Catholic missionaries made Eliot feel that New England ought to more than equal their efforts. Likewise, the organization of the Society for the Propagation of the Gospel in New England, its generous support and assurances of England's concern and prayer for the work, proved a great stimulus. All this evidence of the Lord's favor, worked a spirit of thankfulness in Eliot which made him yet more desirous to gain the heathen and the utmost parts of the earth for God's possession.[3]

Eliot does not describe in detail the motives that prompt his mission concern. He rarely writes autobiographically. The motive most often attributed to him by contemporaries is that of love and compassion. He had, writes Richard Mather, "earnest love to the Lord Jesus, and their poor souls." [4] Grandson Cotton Mather attributed to him "a pitty for the dark souls of those natives, whom the 'god of this world had blinded', through all the bypast ages." [5]

---

[1] The following interesting notation appears in the Records of the New England Company: "And it was further Ordered That a Sword & Belt & Coate be sent to the Indian called King Robert of the like value of those which were formerly sent to King Unces." *Records of the C.P.G.*, March 22, 1677, 183.
[2] Mather, *Magnalia Christi Americana* I, 557.
[3] *Ibid.*, 557, 558.
[4] *Tears of Repentance...*, 6 (1653).
[5] Mather, *Magnalia Christi Americana* I, 557.

Eliot's concern was to rescue, Cotton Mather says, as many of them as he could from the devil, "that old usurping *landlord* of America." [1] It was the Holy Spirit that moved him to the work of evangelizing the Indians. The Spirit "laid before his mind that which was on the *seal* of the Massachusetts colony: *a poor Indian having a label going from his mouth, with a* COME OVER AND HELP US." [2] Eliot firmly believed there was no salvation without the knowledge of Christ, therefore he sought to bring the gospel to the "perishing" ones.[3]

A second primary motive, and, at the same time, his goal, was eschatological; that is, he viewed the work of missions as a part of the progressive establishment of God's eternal kingdom. God's kingdom comes in four stages: union with Christ, church communion, Scriptural government, and the eternal kingdom. Eliot believed the accomplishment of the first three would usher in the last. He could not understand why there were so few laborers to assist in bringing men into union with Christ. Nor could he approve of the church divisions which ruined church communion and thus hindered Christ's coming in his kingdom. His view that the Indians were likely of Jewish extraction was part of a larger perspective, though not essential to his view of history. Both the conversion of the Jews and the calling of the Gentiles were steps forward in God's redemptive program. Whether the Indians were Jews, as Eliot thought most likely, or Gentiles, their conversion was necessary for the further establishment of Christ's kingdom. Eliot stated: "My work is to endeavor the setting up Christ Kingdome among the Indians." [4] By Christ's kingdom, Eliot had in mind Scriptural government by which the Indians made the Word to be their constitution. The establishment of Indian towns and churches continued to his death. Though he saw in the periodic regression of the work reason to doubt the durability of human arrangements (including his own) for the coming kingdom of Jesus Christ, he nevertheless believed to the end that the Indian work was a significant step forward in its attainment.

---

[1] *Ibid.*, 556. Mather reflects the common notion that when the gospel began to spread rapidly during the first centuries of the Christian era, Satan retreated to the unknown parts of the world to set up his kingdom where he thought the gospel would not reach the heathen. This idea gave impetus to the judgment that the return of Christ was near since the gospel was being preached for the first time in the "ends of the earth," and the last stronghold of the devil was being overcome.
[2] *Ibid.*, 556–557.
[3] *Idem.* To claim that Eliot is "der erste evangelische Missionar" is to put the matter too strongly. *Supra*, 235, n. 3.
[4] *The Light appearing more and more...*, 24, 28 (1651).

CHAPTER IV

# COTTON MATHER AND JONATHAN EDWARDS

THE PROGRESS OF THE MISSION

A. COTTON MATHER AND THE *Magnalia Christi Americana*

*Biographical Introduction*

Cotton Mather stemmed from a family of ministers. His name combined those of his two grandfathers who emigrated in the prime of their lives to New England. John Cotton (1585–1652) was converted at twenty by the preaching of Richard Sibbes and, after twenty years of ministry at Boston, Lincolnshire, escaped persecution by coming to Boston, Massachusetts. Richard Mather (1596–1669) preached fifteen years before he was suspended for Nonconformity. He then drew up reasons for removal to New England, came in 1635—the same year as John Cotton—and fathered a new church in Dorchester. Both Cotton and Mather were leaders of the troubled young colony. Increase Mather (1639–1723), Richard's youngest son, studied and preached in England for four years, returned to the home of his father (who had meanwhile married the widow of John Cotton), and married the widow's daughter Maria. Of this marriage Cotton Mather (1663–1728) was born.

Plymouth Colony was then just over forty years old, and Massachusetts was nearly thirty-five. Cotton Mather grew in a spiritual climate that asked constant introspection and evidence of repentance for one's evil nature and acts. Cotton was a precocious lad. At twelve he could read, write, and speak Latin, had read most of the Greek New Testament, and had progressed in Hebrew. No wonder that at that early age he was admitted to Harvard College. Here one hundred ten of the ministers officiating in the congregational churches in 1696 had attended (only eleven were not graduates of Harvard). At fourteen he began his lifelong practice of setting aside days of prayer with fasting; at sixteen he joined the Second Church at Boston and that same year presented himself for the bachelor's degree at Harvard, the youngest who had ever applied—only two have done so since at a younger age. At his commencement President Urian Oakes said:[1]

> ...if this youth bring back into being the piety, the learning, the elegant accomplishment, the sound sense, the prudence, and the gravity of his very reverend grandfathers, John Cotton and Richard Mather, he may

---

[1] J. L. Sibley, *Harvard Graduates*, III 6,7, quoted in Barrett Wendell, *Cotton Mather: The Puritan Priest*, 29.

be said to have done his highest duty. Nor is my hope small that in this youth Cotton and Mather shall, in fact as well as in name, join together and once more appear in life.

There are many indications that Oakes' hopes became those of Cotton Mather. After receiving his Master of Arts in 1681, he began preaching and serving as assistant to his father at Second Church; in 1683 he was called to be one of the two regular ministers there, and, after a period of uncertainty, he was ordained in 1685. This church he served for life, many years together with his father, excepting the four years he was its sole pastor while his father was securing the new charter in London (1688–1692). He also served alone for five years after his father's death.

The relation of Cotton Mather's active ministry to missions may be judged from different perspectives; we shall deal particularly with his own ideas for missions reflected in his diaries (begun in 1681) and with the fulfillment of these ideals as illustrated by his published books. We shall briefly organize our further biographical description around them.

First, then, his *Diary* gives evidence to certain relevant aspects of his character. Basic was the sense of divine calling and mission for his life. As early as 1681 he wrote:

> *I beleeve that I am a chosen Vessel, and that the Lord will pour mercy unto mee, till I have arrived unto a Fulness of eternal Glory! Lord, help me to serve thee, love thee, glorify thy Name. Fill mee with thy Spirit. It will be so!* [1]

This sense of mission was confirmed by a sense of "Particular Faith" that some event (usually good) was about to happen after a period of intense prayers, often uttered prone upon the floor of his study and with many tears. These "Rayes from the invisible world" are described thus:

> All this while, my Heart had the Coldness of a Stone upon it, and the Straitness that is to be expected from the bare Exercise of Reason. But now all on the Sudden, I felt an inexpressible Force to fall on my Mind; an *Afflatus* that cannot be described in words; *none knowes it, but he that has it;* if an *Angel* from Heaven had spoken it articulately to me, the Communication would not have been more powerful and perceptible. It was told mee that the Lord Jesus Christ, lov'd my Father, and lov'd me, and that Hee took Delight in us, as in two of His faithful Servants; and that Hee had not permitted us to be deceived in our *Particular Faith*.... [2]

But to what was Mather called, and what was his mission? After an "*Afflatus*" in 1702, he testifies:

---

[1] Mather, *Diary*, I 6 (1681). Unless otherwise indicated, all further references in this section of the chapter will be from the *Diary*.
[2] I 355 (1700). For similar examples see 344, 374, 376, 394, 411, 421–422, 431–433, 438, 473, 594, etc. The "Particular Faith" in this instance was not fulfilled. This was readily accepted by Mather. The fact that this happens on more occasions indicates that these "inspirations" tended to be dramatic assurances of answer to specific prayer and were not considered to be infallible or revelatory in character.

> *My Father*, will make me *a chosen Vessel*, to do good in the World. *My Father* will yett use me to glorify His Christ, and my Opportunities, my precious Opportunities to do so, shall be after a most astonishing Manner continued and multiplied.[1]

The fact that he mentions the publication of one of his books in this connection is not accidental. In the last diary extant (1724), Mather takes stock of his life by asking the question: *"What has a gracious Lord given me to do...?"* [2] In fourteen answers he points to sailors, Negroes, the female sex, the college, the country, and others whom he has assisted to the best of his ability, including writing books and giving alms for the welfare of those in need. Then, in the twelfth answer he writes:

> *What has a gracious Lord given me to do, in the Writing of many Books*, for the Advancing of Piety, and the Promoting of His Kingdome, *Glory to GOD in the Highest and Good will among men?* There are, I suppose, more than three Hundred and thirty of them.[3]

That Mather considered the writing of books one of his prime duties for advancing the kingdom of Christ cannot be doubted. Frequent remarks in the *Diary* evidence that special providences made publication possible. But Mather, true Puritan that he was, considered preaching to his church, which he called the largest in New England,[4] his first task. Many of his more than five hundred publications are sermons. His *Diary* frequently records the text preached for each Sunday and for his mid-week lectures. Themes appealing for conversion, found in his first years of preaching to 1685, recur frequently through the years: Invitation to Christ (ten sermons on Mt. 11:28), Be ye Reconciled, Almost Persuaded, Effectual Calling, and the *"Works*, by which the Holy Spirit *praepared* men for the Lord Jesus" – Election, Vocation, Marks, Preparation, Conviction, Contrition.[5] In 1702 he preached on the winning of souls, Gentiles sharing in salvation, and the wrong of despising souls – especially those of black servants.[6] And in 1724 the subjects included personal preparation for the Lord's coming, the offers of the gospel, a call to life in Christ, the free offer of the living water and how that offer is to be received.[7]

Besides his sense of personal calling to further the kingdom of Christ and the significance that he attached to preaching, the "G.D." (Good Devised) references, "Ejeculations" and other good intentions indicate concern for missions. Upon seeing a Negro he said: *"Lord, wash* that poor Soul *white* in the *Blood* of thy Son."[8] That his concern for Negroes went further than words is evidenced by his helping to establish a Negro fellowship group for spiritual edification [9] and his later resolves to strengthen the Religious Society for Negroes: "G.D. I would send for the *Negro's* of the Flock, which form a religious Society;

---

[1] I 438 (1702).
[2] II 706 (1724).
[3] II 707 (1724).
[4] I 360 (1700).
[5] I 115–120 (1685/6).
[6] I 459–464 (1702/3).
[7] II 787–790 (1724/5).
[8] I 83 (1681).
[9] I 176 (1698).

and entertain them at my House, with suitable Admonitions of Piety." [1] He baptized Negroes and accepted them in his church. "I baptised four Negro's; and the Lord helped mee, to make this Action, a special Occasion of my glorifying Him: especially, with what I then spoke unto the rest of that Nation." [2] In 1702 Mather notes the reception of two aged Negroes into the church. In 1711 two Negroes were baptized: "I would make it an occasion to glorify the great Saviour of all men, in several Instances; especially in such Admonitions to that black Part of the Flock, as may be needful for them." [3] He sought to convert his own Negro servants. Especially one 'Onesimus' was of great trouble. After stealing, he was kept and taught to read, write, and recite the catechism; he was given leisure hours and was later given conditional liberty after payment of five pounds.[4] Mather successively got at least two other servants, one of whom sought baptism in 1716.[5] He established an evening charity school for the education and evangelization of Negroes, [6] which he periodically revived [7] and supported alone: "I have at my own single Expense for many years, maintained a *Charity-Schole* for the Instruction of *Negro's* in Reading and Religion." [8] He gave books and catechisms written for Negro instruction and conversion,[9] and quoted with emphatic approval Baxter's denunciation of trading in men's souls.[10] He also wrote letters to eminent persons to promote the Christianization of the Negroes,[11] and he appealed to the general public to reconsider the ill-treatment of slaves.

> ...there can be nothing more seasonable and reasonable than for us, to Consider whether our Conduct with relation to our African Slaves, be not one thing for which our God may have a Controversy with us.
> Are they always treated according to the Rules of Humanity?
> And much more, Christianity which is improved and Ennobled Humanity.
> Are they treated as those, that are of one Blood with us, and those that have Immortal Souls in them, and are not meer Beasts of Burden?
> Are they instructed, and made to know
> Such things, which if they knew, would restrain them from Exorbitancies and Enormities which are Complained [against] them, and render them notable Blessings in the Families they belong unto.

---

[1] II 364 (1716); 532 (1718).
[2] I 278 (1697).
[3] II 43 (1711).
[4] I 139 (1711); 222, 271 (1713); 383 (1716).
[5] II 477 (1717); 547, 562 (1718) [Obadiah]; 576 (1718); 603 (1721); 672–673 (1721/2) [another]; 683 (1721/2); 698 (1723/4); 710 (1724).
[6] II 379 (1716).
[7] II 478 (1717).
[8] II 663 (1721).
[9] I 598 (1706). He resolved in 1707 to give every family with Negroes a copy of his *The Negro Christianized: An Essay, to excite and assist that Good Work; the Information of the Negroes in Christianity*, and to send copies to the West Indies. I 564–565 (1706).
[10] Mather, *Theopolis Americana*, 21–23, cited by Thomas J. Holmes, *Cotton Mather: A Bibliography*, III 1069. Passage quoted by Mather is from Baxter, *Christian Directory*, II, Chap. 14.
[11] "I not only write Letters, unto the most eminent Persons, in all the Islands, to promote the Design of Christianizing the *Negroes*; but I also apply myself unto Sir *William Ashurst*, and by him unto the Parliament, to procure an *Act of Parliament* for that Intention." I 570–571 (1706).

> The Common Cavil, that they are the worse servants, for being taught the Knowledge of CHRIST, is a Cursed Falsehood; Experience confutes it; It is a Blasphemy; and it is fitter for the Mouth of a Devil, than of a Christian, to utter it.
>
> But then, there is a Voice of Heaven, to the Slaves, on what this poor Creature is Left unto....
>
> To become the Servants of CHRIST.[1]

Mather's concern for the evangelization of the Indian was much greater than for that of the Negro, if one judges by the number of references in the *Diary*.[2] His personal approach to the Indians was mainly through writing books and catechisms for them, through letters and appeals to fellow-colonists to further the Indian work,[3] by his diligent service as one of the commissioners for the Corporation for the Propagation of the Gospel for thirty years,[4] and by his personal mediation on behalf of the Indians and his personal approaches to them. Mather made the conversion and spiritual growth of the Indians a matter of personal and public prayer,[5] opposed English oppression,[6] proposed

---

[1] II 687–688 (1723).

[2] Ford lists sixteen references to the Negroes, one hundred fourteen to the Indians and the Corporation for the Propagation of the Gospel, and twenty to the Jews. Cf. *Diary*, II, Index, 843, 849.

[3] I 342 (1700) – against those who debauch Indians by selling them strong drink; I 571 (1706) – "I write Letters to the General Assembly at *Connecticut*, to awaken their Zeal, to Christianize their *Indians*; and our Commissioners for the Indian-Affayrs do join with me, in signing them." Cf. also II 531 (1718), 803 (1725), II 233 (1713) – "Besides my drawing up Instructions for Agents to go from the Indian-Commissioners to *Martha's Vineyard*, I must prevent some indirect Proceedings in *Connecticot*, whereby our Attempts to Christianize the Indians there, may meet with Obstruction; and Letters must be written for that Purpose. There are several other Intentions of Piety, to be sett forward among the Indians." II 512 (1717) – "After I had ineffectually sollicited the Governor of N.Y. who was too much encumbred with High-church, to do the Good he wished for; The Ministers on *Long-Island* have promised me, to do their best for Christianizing the Pagan Indians there, whose Children are now generally in *English* Families." He attempted to provide a missionary for the Eastern Indians: II 537 (1718), 615 (1721); II 581 (1719) – "Some letters unto the Scotch Ministers arrived in our East Countrey, may have a Tendency to hearten them in that Work of GOD, which they have to do, in those new Plantations; and more particularly for the christianizing of the Indians there." II 554 (1718) – He sought the conversion of a French missionary priest by corresponding in Latin with him.

[4] This aspect of Mather's Indian work is well summarized by Kellaway, *op. cit.*, 203, 206–211, 222, 228, 234–235, 242–243. Kellaway points out that Cotton Mather was the second minister to serve as a commissioner for the Indian work. The first, his father, showed little interest. The appointment of Cotton Mather, with that of Samuel Sewell, "inaugurated a more vigorous period in the Commissioners' affairs. If neither man possessed the passionate purpose with which John Eliot had goaded the Commissioners, they were nevertheless strong advocates of his cause." (*Ibid.*, 203) Rarely more than six commissioners were present to carry on the work and usually less. Mather, however, "devoted much time and thought to his duties...." (*Ibid.*, 208–209) For more specific material on Mather's intentions to enlist the support of the commissioners, see *Diary*, II 78, 130–131, 132–133 (1711); 344, 345–346, 466 (1716); 576 (1718); 604, 682 (1721); 732 (1724).

[5] II 443 (1717).       [6] II 48 (1711).

a conference of Indian ministers to discuss problems and methods,[1] sought missionaries to carry on the work,[2] devised ways of furthering the Indian cause,[3] and supported the evening school for Indians and Negroes.[4] To the end of his ministry he proposed ways of stimulating the work. In a letter dated 1725 he stated his concern for the "dying Religion among those miserable objects,"[5] points to the need of revived efforts, and asks the appointment of a functionary to review and redirect the work.

> The work of Gospellizing the Aboriginal Natives of this Countrey is one of *New Englands* peculiar Glories. That it Labours under grievous Difficulties and Discouragements, is not at all to be wondred at, considering what lies at the Bottom of all. But the Greater they are, the stronger must be the Application of the Instruments to surmount them. The conduct of the Commissioners has many eyes upon it; yea, Greater Eyes, than those of the Governour and company on the other side of the water.
>
> To Retrieve what is wanting, and produce numberless Good Effects, I could make an Humble Proposal to your Honour and the Board; That the Commissioners find out a Man of Discretion, and Probity, and Activity, and constitute him, *A Visitor of all the Indian Villages.*
>
> This *Visitor* may with an Exact Scrutiny, find out, what may be found among the Indians that wants to be Redirected and Reformed or better provided for. And He may by Enquiry of the most prudent and best affected among the *English*, Learn, what would be most Advisable to be done for the *Indians*.
>
> And He may Return from his Visitation, furnished with Proposals, which the Commissioners may without needless Retardations under the Notion of writing and Waiting for further Informations, (which may confound the best proposals, and has often, it may be, done so,) Immediately find ways and means to putt in Execution.
>
> The Visitor may carry Instructions from the Commissioners, and a copy of all the Articles, which his Enquiries are to proceed upon. The Visitation also may be renewed and repeated, as often as the commissioners may judge Convenient. And if their Servant be well-paid, the Money may be well-spent.[6]

A word should be added about Mather's concern for the conversion of Jews throughout his ministry. He made this one goal of his ministry:

> This Day, from the Dust, where I lay prostrate, before the Lord, I lifted up my Cries.... For the Conversion of the *Jewish Nation*, and for my own having the Happiness, at some Time or other, to baptise a *Jew*, that should by my Ministry, bee brought home unto the Lord.[7]

---

[1] II 143 (1711).
[2] II 248 (1713); 396, 445, 493 (1717).
[3] II 248 (1713); 550–551 (1718); 370, 396 (1716); 445, 493 (1717).
[4] II 442 (1716), 500 (1718). Likely the same school mentioned for Negroes above.
[5] To Lieutenant Governor Dummer of Massachusetts, II 807 (1724/5).
[6] II 808 (1724/5).
[7] I 200 (1696).

In 1699 he had "for diverse Years, employ'd much Prayer for, and some Discourse with, an infidel *Jew* in this town; thro' a Desire to glorify my Lord Jesus Christ in the Conversion of that Infidel...."[1] He resolved to renew his prayers and to write a letter to the Jew, enclosing two books, one of which was *Faith of the Fathers*. Five months later, letters from Carolina told him of a Jew who had been converted to the Christian faith by that same book.[2] He continued to pray regularly for the conversion of his Jewish friend in Boston.[3] He heartily approved the work of charity being done for Jewish children in Berlin and their conversion, and he sent the account of it to the grammar schools to be read to the children.[4] Upon hearing of the arrival of a Jew in the vicinity, Mather decided to have a conversation with him.[5] In a 1717 lecture he likewise encouraged his people to be concerned for the conversion of the Jews.[6] At a communion service he reflects that not only the "Jewes" but "*my Lusts,*" "killed the Lord Jesus Christ...."[7] As far as we know, Mather never saw the fulfillment of his hope to baptize a converted Jew.

Second, we can measure in part Mather's concern for the mission by those of his published works which relate to our subject,[8] particularly since Mather views his publications to be one of the chief fulfillments of his calling. His first mention of an Indian publication was the *Indian Primer* in January, 1700, shortly after his appointment as a commissioner for the Indian work. Of this book he writes:

> ...An INDIAN PRIMER, was ordered for to bee composed and published. The Gentlemen that were to *translate* it, requested of *mee* to *compose* it. I did so; and with as much Artifice and Contrivance as I could, I interwove into it, such Things, as I thought it of most Consequence, for young persons to have their Minds tinged withal, and such Things also, as were more peculiarly agreeable to the Conditions and the Temptations of the Indians.[9]

Four months later the *Diary* mentions the writing of *An Epistle unto the Christian Indians* (*Wussukwhonk en Christianeue asuh Peantamwae Indianog*).[10] The full title is: *An Epistle unto the Christian Indians, Giving them a Short Account, of What the English Desire them to Know and to Do, in order to their Happiness*. The twenty-eight pages (printed in the Indian language on the left and the English on the right) comprised

---

[1] I 300 (1699).
[2] *Ibid.*, 315.
[3] II 41 (1710/11); 62 (1711); 219, 233 (1713); 500 (1717/18).
[4] II 378 (1716); 492, 494 (1717); 503, 524 (1718).
[5] II 469 (1717).
[6] Sewall, *Diary*, III 123; cf. Mather, *Diary*, II 439 (1716/17).
[7] I 64 (1683).
[8] This survey is based upon Holmes, *op. cit.*, 3 vols.; Kellaway, *op. cit.*, 147–164; Trumbull, *op. cit.*, 33–50; and Mather, *Diary*, 2 vols.
[9] I 328 (1699/1700). This book, as all others printed by the New England Company except one, was in the Narragansett dialect of the Mohegan language.
[10] I 347 (1700).

the Sum of the *glorious Things* Reveled unto them in the Gospel; and the *Godly Things* which the Lord Jesus Christ expected from them; and the *Snares* and *Sins* whereof they were most in Danger: and the most pungent Considerations to awaken them unto a Sense of their Duty and Interest. [1]

The work, which was reprinted in 1706, ends as follows:

My dear *Indians,* If you do forsake the wayes of the Lord Jesus Christ, I *earnestly testify* unto you, That you shall *utterly perish.* God will kill you, with one Thunderstroke of His wrath after another. And in Hell, you shall cry out, *I am Tormented! I am Tormented!* for more years, than you now see Leaves upon the Trees.

But, if you do follow the wayes of the Lord Jesus Christ, you will be Rich above those people that have Money, and all Riches. At your Death, God will take your Souls to be among the Angels. The Lord Jesus Christ shall Raise you from the Dead unto everlasting Life, at the Day of Judgment. You shall be Blessed with the Lord Jesus Christ, infinitely more years, than you see stars in the Sky, or stones on the Earth, or Drops of water in the Rivers.

Now, *Consider what I say, and the Lord give you understanding.*[2]

*Hatchets to Hew Down the Tree of Sin, Which Brings Forth Fruit of Death* (English and Indian, 1705) gives twenty laws for conduct with prescriptions of harsh punishment, even death in a few instances, for violation.[3] Two years later, the Indian translation of an English sermon which had been published in 1703 was addressed to the Indians. Printed with Indian on one side and English on the other, these forty pages emphasize Mather's concern for Indian conduct: *The Day Which the Lord hath made, A Discourse Concerning the Institution and Observation of the Lords-Day.* A translation of the first thirty-eight verses of the gospel of John was appended.

The most interesting of Mather's Indian publications was the Corporation's only attempt to print in the Iroquois language.[4] This was a little catechism of sixteen pages with fifteen questions and answers, written in Indian, Latin, English, and Dutch. It was entitled:

---

[1] *Idem.*
[2] Holmes, *op. cit.,* I 321.
[3] Mather, *Diary,* I 511–512 (1704–5).
[4] Holmes shows Mather's relation to Godefridus Dellius and establishes the likelihood that the Iroquois translation was secured from Dellius, based upon a Jesuit catechism. (Holmes, *op. cit.,* I 49–52). On the other hand, Holmes' judgment that Mather's last question ("How many commandments has Jesus Christ given us?") has "inadvertently betrayed him into ... Modalistic Monarchianism" is hardly justifiable. Undoubtedly, Mather simply took over the work of Dellius verbatim, since Mather knew no Indian language. Dellius (1624–1664) arrived at Albany, New York, in August, 1683, as minister to the Dutch and missionary to the Iroquois. (A. Eekhof, *De Hervormde Kerk in Noord-Amerika,* I 164, 's-Gravenhage, 1913).

> Another Tongue brought in, to Confess the Great SAVIOUR of the World
> OR
> Some COMMUNICATIONS of Christianity,
>
> Put into a Tongue used among the
> Iroquois INDIANS
> in America
>
> And, Put into the Hands of the ENGLISH and the DUTCH Traders: To accommodate the Great Intention of Communicating the CHRISTIAN RELIGION, unto the SALVAGES, among whom they may find any thing of this Language to be Intelligible. (1707) [1]

The book in its address to the English and Dutch traders is concerned that the Roman Catholic missionaries are pressing westward into the country of the Iroquois Indians. Mather is anxious to further the spread of "*Pure Christianity...* advantaged with the *Protestant Reformation*." [2] Therefore the traders are asked:

> You are now earnestly Solicited, *That* you, who are Traders for *Bever-Skins*, would be as Instrumental as you can to Convey the *Garments* of *Righteousness* and *Salvation*, among the Naked Salvages.[3]

This idea to use traders as missionaries to the Indians was an attempt to apply to Indians what Protestant and Roman Catholic traders had long been doing in other lands.

Mather's last two works to be translated into Indian (none of the translations were by himself) were intended to strengthen the faith of Christian Indians. *Family Religion Excited and Assisted* (1714) was intended to stimulate family devotions and was followed by examples of prayers, the Ten Commandments, and the Lord's Prayer. *A Monitor for Communicants, An Essay To Excite and Assist Religious Approaches to the Table of the Lord* had been addressed by several New England pastors to the English people in 1714, but five hundred copies were printed in Indian two years later.

Several others of Mather's works promoted the Indian cause among the colonists and abroad. *Triumphs of the Reformed Religion in America*, the biography of John Eliot (editions: 1691, 1694, 1755, 1820) is Mather's most widely known work on missions in New England. No doubt that work helped more than any other to keep alive Eliot's vision and example. The *Short History of New-England* (1694) spoke of the great problem of Indian-English relationships and reminded the too-complacent New Englanders of the unhappy controversies that ruined the new plantation of Protestant colonies in Brazil "which the great

---

[1] Holmes, *op. cit.*, I 48.
[2] *Another Tongue Brought In* ... (1707), quoted in Holmes, *op. cit.*, I 49.
[3] Quoted in Kellaway, *op. cit.*, 149.

Calvin had sought to establish under the influence of the French Admiral Coligne." [1] The application was obvious: the same awful possibility might recur in New England. *A Monitory, and Hortatory Letter, to those English, who debauch the Indians, By Selling Strong Drink unto them* (Written at the Desire of some Christians, to whom the Mischiefs arising from that *Vile Trade* are matters of much *Apprehension* and *Lamentation*, 1700) carries Latin quotations from Johannes Hoornbeek (*De Conversione Indorum et Gentilium*) and Joseph Acosta (L 3.C.22) in support.[2] Others of Mather's writings, either wholly or in part, concern themselves with reports on the progress of the Indian work, accounts of special events, and proposals for furthering the work.[3] There are also expressions of disgust for the wicked and traitorous Indians. Several of Mather's writings (from 1699 to 1718) concern themselves with the Jews, as well as with the Negroes (from 1693 to 1716). There is one work in Spanish to bring the gospel to the Indies,[4] and another in French: one for refugees in New England and another for Protestants in France. (Mather claimed to be able to write seven languages.)

In the *Nets of Salvation, A Brief Essay, Upon the Glorious Designs & Methods of Winning the Minds of Men unto Serious Religion*, (Matthew 4:19 – I will make you fishers of men), 1704, Mather challenges his fellow-countrymen to fruitfulness by winning others to the Christian faith. If Christians will not learn of God, Christ, and good men how to win others, they should learn from the devil. He does all he can to win them.

> The *Mahometans* out-do us; The *Quakers* out-do us; The *Socinians* out-do us; The *Papists* make us Ashamed. With what a *Zeal* do their Missionaries *compass Sea & Land*.... What Hazardous Travels, what Marvellous Fatigues, do their *zealots* undergo, that they may *Win* the Souls of men, only to change the Old Chains of Death for New ones? They will bear the Loathsome and Irksome Wigwams of the Indians in an howling Wilderness, if they may but *Win* over the Salvages to their Superstitions.... No

---

[1] *A Short History of New England* (1694), 65–67; quoted in Holmes, *op. cit.*, III 978. For the attempted mission to Brazil (Calvin, Coligny), see C. Baez-Camargo, "The Earliest Protestant Missionary Venture in Latin America", *Church History*, XXI, 1952, 135–145.

[2] Cf. I 342, Holmes, *op. cit.*, II 704. For Acosta, *supra*, 132. Johannes Hoornbeek (1617–1666), one of the Second Reformation men, had published *Pro convincendis et convertendis Judaeis* in 1637. The work Mather cites was published in 1669.

[3] See Holmes, *op. cit.*, and *Diary*, I 347, 509, 570, etc.

[4] On October 2, 1696, Mather records:
>  Moreover I find in myself, a strong Inclination to learn the *Spanish* Language, and in that Language transmitt Catechisms, and Confessions, and other vehicles of the Protestant-Religion, into the *Spanish* Indies. Who can tell whether the *Time* for our Lord's taking Possession of those Countreyes, even the *sett Time* for it, bee not *come?* This Matter I now solemnly pray'd over; beseeching the Lord, that He would accept of my Service in it; and I have, of late often done so! (*Diary*, I 206).

Just over two years later (January 2, 1699) Mather writes that he has sent his "Little Body of the *Protestant Religion*, in certain Articles, back'd with irresistible Sentences of Scripture" to the printer under the title: *La Religion Pura, En Doza palabras Fieles, dignas de ser recebidas de Todos*. (*Ibid.*, I 284–285.)

less than Six Hundred Clergymen, in that one Order of the Jesuits, did within a few Years, Embarque themselves at several times, for *China*, that they might *Win* over that mighty Nation unto their Bastard-Christianity. No less than Five Hundred of them lost their *Lives*, in the Difficulties of that Enterprise; and yet the Survivors go on with it, Expressing a sort of Trouble, that it fell not unto their share to make a *Sacrifice* of their *Lives*, in Enterprising the Propagation of *Religion*.[1]

We have seen that Mather's publications to the Indians are basically of two sorts: the doctrinal (e.g., catechisms), which is for conversion and for deepening the knowledge of the gospel, and the ethical, which encourages an upright Christian life. His writings to the Negroes also bear that double character, while those to the Jews are more polemic than winsome. His efforts reached a variety of language groups. But Mather did not forget to scold the rum-traders and dishonest English and to urge the compassion of his fellows for the unconverted. The fact that writings with a mission emphasis are fairly evenly scattered over his entire career coincides with his continuance as one of the most active commissioners for Indian affairs until his death. After Eliot's death, no person in New England, with the possible exception of Sewall,[2] could match Mather's record of effort for the New England mission.

It is important to keep this fact in mind when we turn to the *Magnalia Christi Americana*, which was completed when Mather was thirty-five and published four years later. The *Magnalia* is the Puritan monument to the seventeenth century. It makes the case for the New England Israel. The planting of the church in a new land takes precedence over the evangelizing of the natives. We turn to the *Magnalia* for a classic expression of that aspect of the mission which Voetius a quarter-century before had called *plantatio ecclesiae*.[3]

*1. The Planting of the Church in America*

a. The Background

The *Magnalia Christi Americana* is a special kind of history. It does not follow the course of the development of New England in an orderly, progressive manner. Nor does it pretend only to record man's struggles to conquer a primitive land with its people. Rather, it is structured as a piece of redemptive history, as God's mission, claiming human lives as its instrument. So the *Magnalia*[4] commences:

---

[1] *Nets of Salvation* . . ., 35–36 (1704), quoted in Holmes, *op. cit.*, II 727–729.
[2] Judge Samuel Sewall (1652–1730), who held political positions of importance in Massachusetts, served as Commissioner for Indian Affairs from 1699 to 1730: he was secretary 1700–1724 and treasurer 1701–1724. His literary fame stems from his *Diary*.
[3] Gisbertus Voetius, *Politicae Ecclesiasticae*, III, Lib. II, Tract. II, (1676, [Amsterdam] Amstelodami). Cap. I, "De Prima Plantatione & Collectione Ecclesiae . . .," 293–322. Cap. II is "De Missionibus Ecclesiasticus," 323–348, and Cap. III, "De Missionibus & Missionariis Papatus," 349–355. An analysis of Voetius' teaching on missions may be found in H. A. van Andel, *De Zendingsleer van Gisbertus Voetius*, Kampen, 1912.
[4] Hereafter, *Magnalia* as shortened form for the title.

I WRITE the WONDERS of the CHRISTIAN RELIGION, flying from the depravations of Europe, to the American Strand; and, assisted by the Holy Author of that Religion, I do... report the wonderful displays of His infinite Power, Wisdom, Goodness, and Faithfulness, wherewith His Divine Providence hath irradiated an Indian Wilderness.[1]

This "Indian Wilderness" becomes the stage wherein God's power is displayed and the growth of His Church recorded – not simply in the establishment of churches, but as well in the spiritual progression of His Church. The book's crusading spirit and pure-church ideal record what men desired to be accomplished, but what yet lies beyond the grasp and experience of us all; the land where God's will is supreme and man willingly and humbly serves his fellow and his Lord. No greater mission could one claim than this: to bring all men whether savage or Puritan, Catholic or Quaker into the service of God. The mission of establishing God's kingdom in the new world was the determinative factor in life.

The *Magnalia* records this mission in seven books. The beginning of the drama is described in the first book and some lives of the principal actors in the second and third. An account of educational progress, of church policy and acts, of special confirmatory providences, and of the afflictions endured comprise the books four to seven. Each of these books reflects the spiritual purpose upon which, in the author's vision, the colonies were founded.

That purpose, in briefest compass, was the extension and deepening of God's church and kingdom in New England. The idea of missions reflected in the *Magnalia*, and thus also in the seventeenth-century Puritan mind, was to a large degree identified directly with the establishment of the organized church in new places and indirectly with the maintenance of its purity. The basic concept, thus, is not the conversion of the heathen, though this takes its place in the larger whole.

We see this exemplified in Cotton Mather's grandfather, Richard, who had come to Boston in 1635 during the great decade of Nonconformist immigration. Before coming he had in his careful way compiled the reasons for leaving England for America. These were, said Cotton, "the very reasons that moved the first fathers of New England unto that unparalleled undertaking of transporting their families with themselves, over the Atlantic Ocean." The reaons were:

1. A removal from a *corrupt* church to a *purer*.
2. A removal from a place where the truth and professors of it are *persecuted*, unto a place of more *quiet* and *safety*.
3. A removal from a place where all the *ordinances* of God cannot be enjoyed, unto a place where they *may*.
4. A removal from a church where the discipline of the Lord Jesus Christ is wanting, unto a church where it may be practiced.

---

[22] Mather, *Magnalia*, I 25 (1702). All citations are from the edition of 1855.

>
> 5. A removal from a place, where the ministers of God are unjustly inhibited from the execution of their functions, to a place where they may more freely execute the same.
> 6. A removal from a place, where there are fearful signs of *desolation*, to a place where one may have well grounded hope of God's protection.[1]

Richard Mather came to these conclusions on the basis of the old Puritan principles that "all *religious worship* not *commanded* by God is *forbidden*; and that all *symbolical ceremonies* enjoined on men in religious worship, are made parts of it." [2] Not every New Englander, however, was as moderate in his language. Grandson Cotton reflected the spirit of many when he refers to those who conformed with the rites of the Church of England as the "Satanical Party." [3] So Hooker in his farewell sermon draws the fearful conclusion:

> And, thou, England, which hast been lifted up to heaven with means, shall be abased and brought down to hell; for if the mighty works which have been done in thee, had been done in India or Turkey, they would have repented ere this.[4]

It was common practice to call down Scriptural judgments upon England's head for her sins.[5]

The required conformity to English liturgy against conscience was the bane of every true Puritan. John Cotton, maternal grandfather to Cotton Mather, gave this account of his refusal to conform:

> The grounds were two: *first*, The *significacy* and *efficacy* put upon them [the ceremonies], in the preface to the book of Common Prayer.... The second was the limitation of church power... [by] Christ, Mat. xxviii 20. Which made it appear to me utterly unlawful for any church-power to enjoyn the observation of *indifferent ceremonies*, which Christ had *not commanded*....[6]

Samuel Mather, uncle of Cotton, argued the impossibility of agreement between conformity and Nonconformity on the ground that the former

> excluded the Scripture from being the rule of Church-administrations, and made unscriptural Rites, with promiscuous admissions to the Lord's table, and the denial of church-power unto the proper pastors of the churches, to be the terms of communion....[7]

Those who conformed to the various Acts of Uniformity, especially that of 1662, were bitterly condemned. Those imposing conformity were judged in uncompromising fashion. "...they were Atheists, with the inventions of ceremonies habited like Christians, for the service of the devil, to corrupt and destroy true Christianity." [8] One of the most pointed cries of opposition came from the mouth of uncle Samuel Mather.

---

[1] *Magnalia*, I 449. Unless otherwise indicated, all further citations are from the *Magnalia*.
[2] II 506.
[3] I 260.
[4] I 341.
[5] I 345, 361.
[6] I 260.
[7] II 52; cf. also 383.
[8] I 618.

> When you have stopt our mouths from preaching, yet we shall pray; and not only we, but all the souls that have bin converted, or comforted and edified by our ministry, they will all cry to the Lord against you for want of bread, because you deprive them of those that should break the bread of life unto them.[1]

It was that "Act of Uniformity" which appeared in Cotton Mather's year of birth that "silenced" his uncle and was "the general *death* upon the ministry of the non-conformists, at the black Bartholomew Day, August 24, 1662...," affecting some two thousand clergymen in all.[2] The somber view of this event taken by the Puritans is well reflected in the silenced William Hook's treatise title: *The Slaughter of the Witnesses*.[3]

It was little wonder that the century of oppression, though now and then stemming also from the Puritan side, occasioned the emigration from England of ninety-four ministers (of which twenty-seven later returned).[4] What was the greater wonder was the attitude these ministers and their New-England-educated sons could take towards the Church of England. Persecution was increasing. Ceremonies were absolutely required. Hope of the removal of the "Antichristian *ceremonies*" and the "*stinted liturgies*"[5] grew dim. Yet separation from the Church of England was unthinkable. Even John Robinson counseled the first settlers of the New England Colonies before they left the shores of Holland:

> I must also advise you to abandon, avoid and shake off the name of Brownist: it is a mere nick-name, and a brand for the making of Religion, and the professors of religion, odious unto the Christian World... For there will be no difference between the *unconformable* ministers of England and you, when you come to the practice of evangelical ordinances out of the kingdom. And I would wish you by all means to close with the godly people of England; study *union* with them in all things, wherein you can have it without sin, rather than in the least measure to affect a division or separation from them.[6]

At the beginning of the Massachusetts Colony, the ministers were charged with "*departing from the orders of the Church of England;* adding, 'That they were Separatists, and would be shortly Anabaptists'...."[7] The ministers answered pointedly:

> That they were neither Separatists nor Anabaptists; that they did not separate from the Church of England, nor from the ordinances of God there, but only from the corruptions and disorders of that Church....[8]

The irreconcilable contradiction between the severe judgments upon the Church of England and the steadfast refusal to separate from her fellowship

---

[1] II 50.
[2] II 51.
[3] I 586–587.
[4] I 588.
[5] II 51–52.
[6] I 64; cf. also II 311.
[7] I 73.
[8] *Idem.*

seems strange to us. Separation in England was legally impossible. Yet the thousands of miles that made it possible in New England, also made it unnecessary. The religious convictions of the colonists would not permit it. Besides, they were too heavily dependent upon religious and political England to want divorce. Cotton Mather says concerning the farewell request by the Massachusetts settlers to the Church of England for their prayers and for the removal of suspicions concerning the motivation for the new plantation:

> In this address of theirs, notwithstanding the trouble they had undergone for desiring to see the Church of England *reformed* of several things, which they thought its *deformities*, yet they now called the Church of England their *dear mother;* acknowledging that such *hope* and *part* as they had obtained in the *common salvation* they had *sucked from her breasts*....[1]

In explanation Mather continues:

> ...if it now puzzle the reader to reconcile these passages with the *principles* declared, the *practices* followed, and the *persecutions* undergone, by these American Reformers, let him know, that there was more than one *distinction*, whereof these excellent persons were not ignorant. First, they were able to distinguish between the Church of England, as it *contained* the whole *body of the faithful*, scattered throughout the kingdoms... and the Church of England, as it was *confined* unto a certain constitution by *canons*.... Again, they were able to distinguish between the Church of England, as it kept the true *doctrine* of the Protestant religion... and the Church of England, as limiting that name unto a certain *faction*, who, together with a *discipline* very much *unscriptural*, vigorously prosecuted the *tripartite plot* of Arminianism and conciliation with Rome, in the church, and unbounded *prerogative* in the state... then, say I, the planters of New-England were *truer* sons to the Church of England, than that part of the church which, then by their misemploying their heavy *church-keys*, banished them unto this plantation.[2]

Let this be sufficient to indicate how strictly the New Englanders insisted upon "the unwarrantableness of separation from churches for certain defective circumstances."[3] Brownism they despised.[4] There is reason for their repeated insistence upon this point. The whole case for the perspective in which they viewed themselves and presented their claims to the world depended in large measure upon it. They were part of the continuing church of God; more, they were the continuing church, the true church, the hope of the other churches. To this claim we shall presently turn.

Cotton Mather and the New Englanders evidenced sensitivity to the direct speaking and acting of God in nature and history. The great mission of God, they believed, was being accomplished in New England. Life was as uncertain

---

[1] I 74.
[2] I 75–76.
[3] I 348, in reference to Thomas Hooker's *A Survey of Church Discipline;* II 496.
[4] I 453; II 311.

and tragic for Cotton Mather as for most of his fellows. His life was long, compared to many. He had three wives, two of whom preceded him in death, and fifteen children of whom only six grew to maturity and but two lived as long as Cotton himself. Whether he thought these events were to be counted as evidence of God's favor or judgment is difficult to say. To him, all that happened reflected God's attitude toward man's faith or sin. New England was a "spot of *earth*, which the God of heaven *spied out*...." [1] "God...rocqued three nations, with shaking dispensations, that he might procure some rest unto his people in this wilderness!" [2] All those who seek "to undermine the churches of the Lord Jesus Christ, shall be...overtaken by his judgments." [3] Against such: "the terrors of the Almighty shall beset...you...the heavens shall frown upon you,...and the dangers of death shall threaten you." [4] The furtherance of the colonies welfare is "the furtherance of *his work*," and "prosperity depends...on the light of God's countenance." [5] Many remarkable if not miraculous answers to prayer for sick, sinful, and troubled people are recorded as evidence of divine favor upon piety. [6] A distressed church prayed for the life of their beloved pastor "but Heaven determined otherwise." [7] That the New Englanders continued to exist in the face of overwhelming opposition, also of the Indians, is ascribed to "a *strange operation* of God upon the *minds* of men, to curb, and check, and blind the *evil-minded*." [8] The "Heavenly Father put a *rod* into the hands of base Indians, and bid *them* to scourge his *children!*" [9]

These suggest a certain sense of God's nearness and concern with human lives. More, they point to his direct control of nature, to his purposeful acts in history. New England was a part of that history. God's mercies and judgments must be seen as approbation or disapproval of her existence and progress. The suggestion that Mather's "constant efforts to derive religious meaning from every experience, however small, savour today of artificiality" [10] may bear some truth, yet it fails to note his conviction with regard to the fundament of God's close purpose in and guidance of New England history. God and New England are inseparable, at least insofar as the latter is concerned. All of Mather's five hundred published books,[11] his societies for assorted good causes, his distribution of literature at home and abroad,[12] his defense of New England's cause against those abroad who belittled her existence and qualities,[13]...these were offered for God's cause in New England. There Mather rests his case.

---

[1] I 45.
[2] I 284; cf. 240, 249.
[3] I 283.
[4] *Idem*.
[5] I 161.
[6] I 314–317; II 37–38.
[7] II 138.
[8] II 657.
[9] II 672.
[10] *Dictionary of American Biography*, Vol. 12, p. 388.
[11] Samuel Drake numbers three hundred eighty-three ("A Memoir of Cotton Mather," *Magnalia*, I xxxi), while the *Dictionary of American Biography* (Vol. 12, 388) suggests over four hundred fifty. Perry Miller maintains there are over five hundred printed titles (*The American Puritans*, 60).
[12] *Dictionary of American Biography*, Vol. 12, 388.
[13] *Magnalia*, I 414–429; II 317–581.

b. The Divine Mission

The great mission of God is the planting of his divinely regulated church in the uttermost parts of the earth. This church becomes the instrument for the conversion of men, but the church always remains primary. This can best be seen by examining the idea of the church and its function in God's purpose in order to make plain the primary reason for the establishment of the church in America.

The test for the authenticity of the church was to be found in primitive Christianity as reflected in the Bible and the apostolic church. William Bradford, the first governor of Plymouth Colony, decided to "keep close unto the *written word* of God as the *rule* of...worship," since he beheld how "fearfully the evangelical and apostolic *church-form*, whereinto the churches of the primitive times were cast by the good spirit of God, had been *deformed* by the apostacy of the succeeding times." [1] The epitaph to John Wilson paints the picture clearly:

> The ancient apostolic Age of Gold,
> Obscured so sadly in the mists of Time,
> Our WILSON, cast in apostolic mould,
> Seems to restore in all its pristine prime. [2]

The venerable Davenport sought to "embark in a design of reformation where in he might drive things...as near to the precept and pattern of *Scripture*, as they could be driven." [3] Testing of applicants for church membership ought to follow the example of the apostles. [4]

In church government the "Congregational way...is the very same way that was established and practiced in the 'primitive times', according to the institution of Jesus Christ." [5] Some of the Nonconformists opposed the practice of preaching at funerals, maintaining "that in the Primitive churches they were not practiced until the apostacy began." [6] By way of highest eulogy it was written that Thomas Shepard "had in him that spirit of the primitive Christions." [7] The title page of the Fifth Book, which concerns church polity and acts, carries the following inscription:

> We ought not to assert in matters of Church Government every thing which mere human reason would dictate, but only such observances as were instituted by Christ himself, and practised in the church from its very foundation. [8]

In the Fifth Book frequent appeal for various questions of church polity is made to "the primitive times of the New Testament." [9] Even when divine judgment comes because of degeneration in the church, an analogy is drawn

---

[1] I 110.
[2] I 321.
[3] I 325; cf. also II 98, 108.
[4] I 328.
[5] II 79–80.
[6] II 125.
[7] II 119.
[8] II 177.
[9] II 238, 239, 245, 246, 249, 251, 265–267, 318.

to the "dismal calamities [which] befel the primitive Christians" for like apostasy.[1] And when it became time to argue against physical reprisal for spiritual error, the answer was to be found in the practice of the primitive church.[2]

Since they judged the church had so far departed from its pristine purity, as we noted in Section II-A above, the Puritan and Nonconformist cry was for a new or a continued reformation. It is true that New England was considered a "retreat for persecuted non-conformists."[3] Yet at heart it was more. In his General Introduction, Cotton Mather presents the fundamental basis for the New England churches.

> The sum of the matter is, that from the very beginning of the REFORMATION in the English Nation, there hath always been a generation of Godly Men, desirous to pursue the Reformation of Religion, according to the Word of God and the Example of the best Reformed Churches.... And there hath been another generation of men, who have still employed the *power* which they have generally still had in their hands, not only to stop the progress of the desired Reformation, but also, with innumerable vexations, to persecute those that most heartily wished well unto it... many of the Reformers... cried out earnestly for purer Administrations in the house of God, and more *conformity* to the *Law of Christ* and *primitive Christianity*: while others would not hear of going any further than the first Essay of Reformation. 'Tis very certain, that the first Reformers never intended that what they did should be the absolute boundary of Reformation, so that it should be a sin to proceed any further.... It is the History of these PROTESTANTS that is here attempted: Protestants that highly honoured and affected the Church of ENGLAND, and humbly petition to be a *part* of it: but by the mistake of a few powerful brethren, driven to seek a place for the exercise of the Protestant Religion... in the desarts of America.... I perswade myself, that *so far as they have attained*, they have given great examples of the methods and measures wherein an Evangelical Reformation is to be prosecuted, and of the qualifications requisite in the instruments that are to prosecute it, and of the difficulties which may be most likely to obstruct it, and the most likely Directions and Remedies for those obstructions.... I do not say, that the Churches of New-England are the most *regular* that can be; yet I do say, and am sure, that they are very like unto those that were in the first ages of Christianity.... In short, the *first* Age was the *golden* Age: to return unto *that*, will make a man a Protestant, and, I may add, a Puritan....[4]

This Reformation is to be considered "nothing in *doctrine*, little in *discipline*, different from that of Geneva."[5] Edward Winslow, an early governor of Plymouth Colony, gives us to understand that "they are entirely of the same faith with the reformed Churches in Europe, only in their Church-government

---

[1] II 316.
[2] II 536.
[3] I 619.
[4] I 26–27.
[5] I 40.

there are endeavourers after *a reformation more thorough*... yet without any un charitable *separation* from them." [1] Thus it could justly be affirmed that "the *beginnings*,...the *foundations* of those colonies...afforded a singular prospect of churches erected in an American corner of the world, on purpose to express and pursue the Protestant Reformation." [2] Stronger yet: "our Lord Jesus Christ... carried into an American wilderness a people persecuted for their desire to see and seek a reformation of the church, according to the Scripture...." [3] It was the "Romanizing faction in the Church of England" that made this necessary, not "the *true* Protestant Reforming church of England" whom

> ...the first planters of New-England, at their first coming over...call...their *dear mother*, desiring their friends to "recommend them unto the mercies of God, in their constant prayers, as a Church now springing out of their own bowels:" nor did they think, that it was their *mother* who turned them out of doors, but some of their angry *brethren*, abusing the name of their mother, who so harshly treated them. [4]

One may justly conclude that the call for a return to primitive Christianity was meant to be a reformation within and not outside the Church of England, and that the New England enterprise was viewed as the instrument by which this reformation would be achieved.

Freedom of religion is popularly cited as the chief motive for the settlement of New England. That it was a motive cannot be denied. So Mather affirms:

> The *design* of these *refugees*, thus carried into the wilderness, was, that they...might maintain the *power* of *godliness* and practice the *evangelical worship* of our Lord Jesus Christ...without any *human* innovations and impositions. [5]

The New England father John Norton put it:

> 'Our liberty to walk in the faith of the gospel, with all good conscience, according to the order of the gospel,' was the cause of our transporting our selves...into the vast wilderness. [6]

It was conjectured that America had been added to English dominions to make the "evangelical worship of our Lord Jesus Christ" possible. [7] From the very beginning, a whole theory of missions was associated with the settlement of New England. Reformation according to primitive Scriptural purity was the goal. This was impossible to achieve in England. Therefore, in America the continuing reformation would leap forward. A church-state would be erected, and the Israel of New England would be a reality. Thus the colonies are repeat-

---

[1] I 62; cf. also II 117–118, 276.
[2] I 86.
[3] I 248.
[4] I 249–250.
[5] I 240.
[6] I 296; cf. I 388.
[7] I 289.

edly called the "NEW ENGLISH ISRAEL" [1] and the American Jerusalem.[2] Many analogies are made to the Old Testament Israel, as though it and the Israel of New England are complementary to each other.[3]

Attention is called to themselves as the special people of God who have escaped into the wilderness of New England.[4] They are summoned to "serve the King of Israel" in the "ecclesiastical kingdom of our true David." [5] These Old Testament concepts make clear their claim to be the continuation of the true people of God. A poem written in dedication to one of their greater divines, Urian Oakes, upon his return to American shores from England, reflects this spirit:

> Welcome, great prophet, to New-England shore,
> The fam'd Utopia of more famous More,
> Unfabled, for New-England is by thee,
> Now Twisse's guess too must accomplisht be:
> That for the New Jerusalem there may
> A *seat* be found in wide America.[6]

It was little wonder that, when Cotton Mather elaborates his point near the end of the *Magnalia*, he can say: "But New England is by a more eminent profession that 'Immanuel's land'." [7]

c. The American Theocracy

Essential to the program was the organization of the "New-English Israel" into a kind of theocracy. Mather describes it by way of comparison with that of the Old Testament Israel:

> When the great God of heaven had carried his "peculiar people" into a wilderness, the *theocracy*, wherein he became (as he was for *that reason* stiled) "the Lord of Hosts," unto them and the four squadrons of their army, was most eminently displayed in *his* enacting of their *laws*, *his* directing of their *wars*, and *his* electing and inspiring of their *judges*. In some resemblance hereunto, when four colonies of Christians had marched like so many *hosts* under the conduct of the good spirit of our Lord Jesus Christ into an American wilderness, there were several instances wherein that army of confessors was under a theocracy; for their *laws* were still enacted, and their *wars* were still directed by the voice of God, as far as they understood it, speaking from the *oracle* of the *Scriptures*: and though their judges were still elected by themselves, and not inspired with such extraordinary influences as carried them of old, yet these also being singularly furnished and offered by the special providence of God unto the government of his New-English people, were so eminently acted, by *his graces*, and *his precepts*, in the discharge of their government, that the blessed people were still sensibly *governed by the Lord of all*.[8]

---

[1] I 44, 284; II 117, 334, 674.
[2] I 121.
[3] I 90–104, 107, 342.
[4] I 372, 403, 414, 464.
[5] I 414, 404.
[6] II 115.
[7] II 661.
[8] I 143.

Because of this special relationship, God could be understood as saying over the sinning people: "How shall I give thee up, O *New England*? how shall I give thee up, O *Massachusets*?"[1] Governors could be called *"vicegerent[s]* of GOD."[2] Regarding some magistrates it was reported:

> ...these are...worthy to be found in our Church-History...when it is considered, not only that they were the members of Congregational churches, and by the members of the churches chosen to be the rulers of the Commonwealth; and that their exemplary behaviour...was generally such as to "adorn the doctrine of God our Saviour"...but also that their love to, and zeal for, and care of these churches, was not the least part of their character.[2]

It is significant that this last, i.e., "zeal for," and "care of," includes the right of the magistrate to exhort and admonish the churches regarding the performance of their spiritual duties. An official document, for example, sent in 1668 from the governor and council of Massachusetts "To the Elders and Ministers of every Town" includes concern for the following: catechizing, preaching, teaching the children English reading, rebuking evil, instructing all in their parochial bounds in the gospel, etc.[4] They base their right to do this, interestingly enough, upon the practice of the Old Testament magistrates. This illustrates the practice of the civil rulers subsequent to the adoption of the "Cambridge Platform" of 1649. In that Document itself the following statements are noteworthy: "Magistrates have power to call a synod...but yet the constituting of a synod is a church-act."[5]

> Church-government stands in no opposition to civil government of commonwealths...whereas the contrary is most true, that they may both stand together and flourish, the one being helpful unto the other, in their distinct and due administrations.[6]
>
> It is the duty of the magistrate to take care of matters of religion, and to improve his civil authority for the observing of the duties commanded in the first, as well as for observing of the duties commanded in the second table.[7]
>
> Idolatry, blasphemy, heresie, (Deut. xiii; I Kings xx.28. 42) venting corrupt and pernicious opinions, that destroy the foundation, (Dan. iii.29) open contempt of the word preached, (Zech. xiii.3) prophanation of the Lord's Day, (Neh. xiii.31) disturbing the peaceable administration and exercise of the worship and holy things of God, (I Tim. ii.2) and the like, (Rom. xiii.4) are to be restrained and punished by civil authority.[8]

The power of the magistrates in matters religious was quite inclusive, sufficiently so for Cotton Mather to say:

---

[1] II 674.
[2] II 680.
[3] I 142.
[4] I 142–143.
[5] II 234.
[6] II 235.
[7] II 236, 328.
[8] II 236.

"Wherefore, magistrates, and that in Scriptures referring to the days of the New-Testament, are said to be the church's nursing fathers, (Is. xlix.23,) for that it concerns them to take care that the churches be fed with the bread and water of life." [1]

Magistrates must likewise look upon themselves "as concerned to effect a reformation (Neh. xiii.10.)" [2] when this is necessary in the church. Thus, it was the General Court of Massachusetts which called the Reforming Synod of New England in 1679.[3]

In this new theocracy, the form of church government judged best suited to fulfill the needs of the "New Israel" was the congregational way. We noted in the preceding section that especially in this respect the settlers viewed themselves as having advanced beyond the continental Reformation. They had come to their new form with difficulty, but with conviction. Nathaniel Rogers, one of their more highly respected ministers, recognized that: "Frequently a Reformation is embarrassed by the difficulty of making churches conform to a sound system of government." [4] Because of this the New England fathers judged it crucial to begin their revived primitive Christianity in the right way. So Thomas Shepard asserts: "Tis true, where there is no church-relation, but a people are ready to begin a new constituting of churches, reformation is to be sought in the first constitution: this is our case." [5] One of the principles operative was that given by A. Spalatensis in his work on the *Christian Commonwealth*, quoted by Mather on the title page of Book V in the *Magnalia*.[6]

Yet a primary concern was how "the Christian religion must be preserved, with a true and pure church state... and conveyed and secured unto posterity." [7] Here the "kingdom of Christ" and the "commonwealth," which are closely correlative to one another,[8] were to work in close harmony. An interesting conflict between the claims of the two is symbolized by the dispute occasioned when some one (reportedly as a consequence of the ministry of Roger Williams) cut the red cross out of the king's colors in 1633.[9]

We have seen that the New England Israel was instituted not only because of persecution for Nonconformity to the Church of England, but in order to advance the Reformation begun on the continent, by a closer return to primitive Christianity and a unique relationship wherein church and state exercised reciprocal responsibilities. The kingdom of Christ and the commonwealth were jointly concerned to preserve the cause of true religion, to fulfill the divine mission to which they were appointed by heaven. They were together what we should term today the responsible agents of the mission.

Now we may proceed to ask more specifically: What are the means by which the primary mission of planting the kingdom of Christ in America is to be accomplished? Moving from the broadest to the narrowest, we may suggest

---

[1] II 328.
[2] *Idem.*
[3] II 318.
[4] I 422.
[5] I 387.
[6] *Supra*, 258.
[7] II 105.
[8] I 387–388.
[9] II 499–503.

three stages: (1) the propagation of the gospel, (2) the planting of churches, and (3) the maintaining of the purity of the churches. We shall illustrate each briefly, as it comes to expression in the *Magnalia*.

First, America was planted "on a design of enjoying and advancing the true *reformed religion*, in a *practical* way,"[1] indeed, "the one main end...of all these undertakings was to plant the gospel in these dark regions of America."[2] In the early colonial days John Davenport published a pamphlet entitled "*A Discourse About Civil Government, in a New Plantation, whose design is Religion.*"[3] For the settlement of the Massachusetts Bay Colony in 1629 it was determined "to send none...but godly and honest men, professing that religion which they declared was the *end* of this plantation" and those who would further the "design of establishing and propagating *reformed Christianity* in the new plantation."[4] Thus John Higginson could declare upon embarking: "...we go to practise the positive part of church reformation, and propagate the gospel in America."[5] So thousands transported "themselves and their families into the deserts of America, to prosecute and propagate the glorious designs of the gospel, and spread the *light* of it in those 'goings down of the sun.'"[6]

Second, the kingdom is advanced by planting churches.

> "The *original design* of New-England was to settle *congregations*, wherein the Lord Jesus Christ should be known and served according to his gospel; and instruct *families* that should be the nurseries of those congregations."[7]

In a dedication of "The Life of Mr. Thomas Hooker" to the churches in the colony of Connecticut, Mather writes: "'Tis a great work that you have done, for our Lord Jesus Christ, in forming a colony of evangelical churches for him, where Satan alone had reigned without controul in all former ages."[8] What is testified concerning one, a Mr. Peter Bulkey, could well have been written of many:

> Nevertheless, the concern which his *renewed soul* had for the *pure worship* of our Lord Jesus Christ, and for the planting of *evangelical churches* to exercise that worship, caused him to leave and sell *all*, in hopes of gaining the 'pearl of great price' among those that first peopled New-England upon those glorious ends.[9]

Thus "the main business of this new plantation...was, 'to settle and enjoy the ordinances of the gospel.'"[10] This was accomplished by making "one of their *first works*...to gather a church into the *covenant* and *order* of the gospel."[11]

The propagation of the gospel assumed the character of church extension within America once the colonies were well established and had begun to grow. The Cambridge Platform of 1649 stipulates in Chapter XV, Paragraph

---

[1] I 15.
[2] I 45.
[3] I 330.
[4] I 360–361.
[5] I 362; cf. 363.
[6] I 376.
[7] II 660.
[8] I 332.
[9] I 400.
[10] I 308.
[11] I 79.

4, the propriety of this manner of organization of new churches.[1] So also the divines of New England are represented as being "solicitous that the *propagation* of our churches might hold pace with that of (their) offspring." [2]

Third, maintaining the purity of the churches was considered necessary to the continuance and growth of the kingdom of Christ in America. Hopes of fulfilling the goal of a more perfect church in a new land were fading, as we shall note in the following section. It is evident that every means was used to hold the line. Attempts were made to hold high the standard of church membership, though in the latter part of the seventeenth century the efforts slackened and standards were lowered. In early days some wanted to require acceptance of the separatist principle with regard to the Church of England. This both the pastor in Leiden, Mr. Robinson, and Elder Brewster refused, "shewing them that we required no such thing at their hands; but only to hold faith in Christ Jesus, holiness in the fear of God, and submission to every ordinance and appointment of God." [3]

In addition to belief in the message of repentance and faith [4] and regeneration and union with Christ,[5] both of which were accentuated in preaching, a careful examination in matters of life and conduct was required for admission to the Lord's Supper.[6] The reasons given for this are significant.[7]

1. "Clear Scripture proof" requires it.
2. Otherwise "the holy Lord Jesus Christ" will be displeased.
3. The church must judge who "are fit" to be there.
4. Christ's practice makes such "a divine institution".
5. "To use all lawful means to keep church communion pure" is the duty of every church.
6. In the "primitive and purest times of the church" this was done.

Interestingly, Mather appeals to the fact that in England some Presbyterians and other reformed churches agree in *"substance"* with the New England practice. He especially refers with approval in this connection to Dr. Hoornbeeck, "that learned and worthy professor of divinity in the university of Leyden." [8] After the formulation of the Westminister Confession in England, a New England synod at Cambridge in 1648 declared "consent thereunto for the substance thereof," except for that section on *"church-government* and *discipline"* [9] for which reference was made to their own document, the "Platform of Church Discipline" adopted in 1649.[10] Acceptance of these two statements was required for church membership.

Because of the concern to maintain a deep experiential profession of faith as indispensable for membership, the ministers made a real conversion and

---

[1] II 233.
[2] II 278.
[3] I 63; cf. also 485.
[4] I 416; II 225–226.
[5] I 411.
[6] II 68–69, 102–103, 243–247.
[7] II 70–75.
[8] II 75, in reference to Johannes Hoornbeek (1617–1666): *Epistola ad Johannes Duraeum Scoto-Britannum, qua respondetur Examini Johannis Beverley de Inde penditissimo,* 1660, 299.
[9] II 179–180.
[10] II 207–236.

reconciliation to God points of sermonic emphasis.[1] Often special note is taken of many who were converted and brought home to God.[2] The winning of and building up of souls were alike the pastor's task [3] since all within or without the parochial bounds rightly deserved his call to repentance [4] whether Christian or not.[5] It was regarded, however, "a *tyranny* to enjoin upon every man, 'a relation about the precise time and way of their conversion unto God.'"[6] When many covenantal and baptized youth did not assume adult membership in the churches,[7] special concern was evidenced for the conversion of "the rising generation."[8] When they or adult church members showed declension of spiritual vitality and fell into sin, they were admonished and placed under church discipline.[9] By these means an attempt was made to hold the purity of the churches, and thereby to progress the kingdom cause.

d. The Great Apostasy

The slowness and frequent regress in the attainment of their heaven-appointed goal made the religious leaders' disillusionment the more painful as the century wore on. They vigorously decried what was judged to be the moral and spiritual falling away of the second and third generation. Many of the early leaders seemed to have had a "prophetic apprehension of the declensions which would attend the Reforming churches...when they came to enjoy a place of liberty."[10] They feared moral decay and apostasy from the faith.[11] New England, they thought, would surely lose "her holiness, her righteousness, her peace, and her liberty."[12] Earlier in the century, England's apostasy was held up for all to see:[13] later, other Protestant lands were included.[14] By comparison there were "a *larger* number of the *strictest* saints in this country, than in any other on the face of the earth."[15]

Now the fact of declension became too apparent in the Israel of America. It was variously described: "...the *power of Godliness* is now grievously decayed among us,"[16] "I saw a fearful *degeneracy*,"[17] a minister's dying plea was to "look after...the dying power of godliness" in the churches,[18] the "old spirit" was dying out with the "old saints,"[19] and the like.[20]

To counteract this "evil spirit of apostasy,"[21] the great Reforming Synod of New England was summoned in 1679 at Boston. It judged that the basic problem was "God's...controversie with his New-England people."[22] This was verified by a series of disasters which had come upon them. In their view of special and confirmatory providence, this could only mean one thing: God

---

[1] I 471; II 276.
[2] I 379, 418, 430, 452, 590; II 140.
[3] I 424, 588.
[4] I 142–143.
[5] I 72.
[6] II 68, 246.
[7] II 398.
[8] II 156, 167, 657.
[9] I 72; II 229–230, 309, 338.
[10] I 342.
[11] I 147; II 655–657.
[12] I 601.
[13] I 361, 389, 410, 510.
[14] II 317, 385.
[15] II 317–318.
[16] I 103.
[17] I 249.
[18] II 138.
[19] II 334.
[20] I 156, 388–389.
[21] II 319.
[22] II 320.

was terribly displeased with them. Why? The Synod enumerates the reasons: decay of godliness, pride, neglect of the church and its institutions, profanation of God's name, Sabbath-breaking, poor family relationships, inordinate passions, intemperance, lack of truth, inordinate affection unto the world, opposition to reformation, lack of public spirit, and sins against the gospel.[1]

Because of these, God's judgment came. The lamentations increased each year. Mather's writing of the *Magnalia* hoped to assist in keeping alive the "dying religion."[2] He cried with the rest: "Alas, how little of an 'evangelical church state' (is) there to be seen among all our *eastern settlements*!"[3] They "hop'd the war [with the Indians], would now come to an immediate end; but the great God who *creates that evil*, had further intentions to chastise a *sinful people* by those who are *not a people*."[4] Thus this war could be termed: "God's war with us."[5] Jeremiads without number flooded the worldly wilderness.[6] Repent, or "Ichabod" will be written over you.[7] The objects of our sins have been the engines of our plagues.[8] The unspiritual churches will be broken apart.[9]

A classic expression of the mind of the times is given in "God's Controversie with New England," a poem by Michael Wigglesworth published in 1662. In seemingly unending stanzas he pours out his plaint. In the verses that follow God's intentions are clear:

> For think not O backsliders, in your heart,
> That I shall still your evil manners bear;
> Your sins Me press as sheaves Do load a cart.
> And therefore I will plague you for this gear.
> Except you seriously, and soon, repent,
> I'll not delay your pain and heavy punishment.[10]

> What shall I do with such a stiff-necked race?
> How shall I ease me of such Foes as they?
> What shall befall despisers of my Grace?
> I'le surely beare their candle-stick away,
> And Lamps put out. Their glorious noon-day light
> I'le quickly turn into a dark Egyptian Night.[11]

---

[1] II 321–326; cf. also I 313, 413; II 148; Smith, Handy, and Loetscher in *American Christianity; Interpretation and Documents* (1607–1820) suggest six reasons for the lamentations: (1) decline of the growth rate of church members after 1650, (2) the disappointing turn of events in England after Cromwell, (3) the disruption of religious uniformity, (4) social and economic improvement, (5) disasters such as fire, drought, Indian wars, and the witch plague, and (6) the lack of interest in higher education. pp. 199–201.
[2] I 251.
[3] II 659.
[4] II 589.
[5] II 671–672.
[6] II 387–391, 557, 668.
[7] II 661.
[8] II 323, 664.
[9] II 660.
[10] Quoted from *The American Puritans*, ed. by Perry Miller, 299.
[11] Quoted from *American Christianity: Interpretation and Documents* (1607–1820), Vol. 1, Smith, Handy, and Loetscher, 198.

Most of the New England theologians would by the time of Mather's prime have subscribed to the colorless but true judgment of Walker: "In general, it may be said, however, that, though New England remained a religious land, the zeal of its founders had burned low by the opening of the eighteenth century...." [1] The following passage indicates the general concern of all the colonies in this matter, indicated by leaders both of church and state:

> The Massachusetts Colony was not alone in such essays of reformation: but the colonies of Plymouth and Connecticut shewed themselves in like manner concerned; that they might avert the *tokens* of divine displeasure, "whereat they who dwelt in these uttermost parts were afraid." The rulers both in *church* and *state*, had their serious deliberations with one another, and they together "enquired of the Lord," as the oracle of his written word, what might be the grounds of the divine-controversie.[2]

We have seen, therefore, that the basic sense of mission was the establishment of the pure church of God in America whose duty in closest harmony with the spiritually oriented state was to preserve the cause of true religion, not only for New England, but for the world. A variety of means were used (and abused) to achieve this end, yet when the curtain fell on seventeenth-century ecclesiastical history the achievement of the high goal seemed further away than ever before. Two convictions helped to keep the dim hopes burning: faith in the coming age of the Spirit and a wide agreement upon the essentials of the eternal gospel. But before we continue this development of the major thesis, we ought first to consider a secondary sense in which the New England mind conceived of mission.

## 2. *The Evangelization of the Indians*

In our discussion thus far it has become evident that missions in the sense of preaching the gospel to the unconverted natives of America did not play the primary role. Other factors motivated the great migration. In this light it must come almost with surprise that the remarkable seal of the Massachusetts Bay Colony pictured "*a poor Indian having a label going from his mouth with a* COME OVER AND HELP US." [3] John Eliot, the great Indian missionary, Mather informs us, was

> awakened by those expressions in the royal charter, in the assurance and protection whereof this wilderness was first peopled; namely, "To win and incite the natives of that country to the knowledge and obedience of the only true God and Saviour of mankind, and the Christian faith, in our royal intention, and the adventurer's free profession is the principal end of the plantation." [4]

---

[1] Walker, W., *A History of the Christian Church*, 568.   [2] II 333-334.
[3] I 556. That the image on this seal represented an Indian has not been questioned. For a comparison with the image on the seal of the Society for the Propagation of the Gospel, see J. van den Berg, *op. cit.*, 46-48.   [4] I 557.

It is significant that direct reference to this "principal end of the plantation" is made rarely in the two volumes, and that in connection with Eliot, while that of establishing the American Israel is repeatedly brought to the fore. To understand this fact we should describe more fully the Indian situation into which the colonists entered; we should consider the conflicts which arose, and finally we should summarize the concrete achievements of the Indian mission.

There was an inherent contradiction in motives for the establishment of the church in America. Theoretically, there need be no conflict between establishing an improved church and winning natives for Christ. Practically, the opposite proved to be true. On the one hand, there was a general concern for those both within and without the parochial bounds of the church,[1] a recognition of the duty to promote the salvation of souls [2] and the general welfare of the Indians,[3] and examples of humanitarian concern.[4] Concerning the founding of the Plymouth Colony, Mather observes that " 'twas much wished by the holy Robinson, that some of the poor heathen had been converted before any of them had been slaughtered." [5] Occasional references are made to Indian origins,[6] practices,[7] and characteristic sins.[8] Some close association with neighboring natives existed.[9]

On the other hand, after suggesting that perhaps Satan kept America hidden to hinder the conversion of its inhabitants,[10] God is reported to have "brought a vine out of *England*," and to have "cast out the heathen" [11] in order to "make room for a *better growth*," for the "*chosen generation*." [12] A considerable accumulation of uncomplimentary names are illuminating: pernicious creatures,[13] diabolical Indians,[14] hypocritical wretches,[15] inaccessible enemy,[16] Scythian wolves,[17] and like to devils.[18] Besides their character weaknesses of lying, laziness, and insubordination,[19] their base religion was a "sort of *devil worship*." [20] In a dedicatory epitaph to Sir William Phips, a governor of Massachusetts Bay (died 1695), it is asserted that:

> The wolfish Pagans, at his dreaded name,
> Tam'd, shrunk before him, and his dogs became! [21]

But, far worse, they filled a sort of diabolical role against God's chosen ones: "Lord...the *salvage hounds*...worry thy dear *flocks*." [22] Because of the savages' wickedness, winning a battle meant to the New Englanders "a *blast* from

---

[1] I 71, 142–143.
[2] I 142–143, 413; II 486.
[3] I 71, 373; II 338.
[4] I 308.
[5] I 59.
[6] II 594.
[7] II 607.
[8] II 663.
[9] I 81, 329.
[10] I 41–42, 556.
[11] I 81.
[12] I 51.
[13] Idem.
[14] I 213.
[15] I 215.
[16] Idem.
[17] II 665.
[18] II 78.
[19] II 663.
[20] II 552.
[21] I 230.
[22] II 613.

heaven upon their Indian Amalekites." [1] It was judged to be "*the most unexceptionable piece of justice to extinguish them.*" [2] Likely, at least the conclusion is correctly made in the claim that: "The evident hand of Heaven appearing on the side of a people, whose *hope* and *help* was alone in the Almighty 'Lord of Hosts', extinguished whole *nations* of salvages." [3]

The attitudes and judgments existing between the Indians and settlers were both developed by and issued into the various conflicts already suggested. To the savage mind, a threat, whatever the cause, was removed by war and the greatest imaginable barbarities. These Mather vividly describes.[4] The real question was: Why could not the Indians and settlers peacefully co-exist? Was it because of inability or lack of proper spirit and approach? This problem reaches beyond the scope of our investigation. Yet it is helpful to note several of the crucial issues at stake.

First, Mather claimed that the patent for the land was "fairly purchased." [5] Roger Williams' "pretence of *wrong*...done unto the Indians" [6] was based upon his conviction that the king of England had no right to sell the Indians' land. A certain Tom Moule "exposed unto the publick a volume of *nonsensical blasphemies and heresies*" in which he defends the Indians' rights against New England. Mather laconically concludes that "The fittest way to answer him, would be to send him to *Boston Woods!*" [7] Mather admits that the real reason for the conflict between the English and the Indians was a difficult point.[8] One author lists five reasons: (1) failure of the English to pay the corn agreed upon, (2) invasion of Indian fishing areas, (3) difficulty of pasturage place for cattle, (4) granting and patenting of lands to the English, and (5) common abuses in trading: drunkenness, cheating, and the like. He judges the fourth to be the "*main* provocation." [9] Mather is concerned to demonstrate that the New Englanders have dealt fairly with the Indians when he says:

> ...the good people of New-England have carried it with so much tenderness toward the tawny creatures among whom we live, that they would not own so much as one foot of land in the country, without a fair *purchase* and *consent* from the natives that laid claim to it.[10]

He recognizes that some may be surprised when the late secretary Randolph affirms that "This barbarous people were never civilly treated by the late government, who made it their business to encroach upon their lands, and by degrees to drive them out of all." [11] Mather answers:

> It was one of our laws, "That for the further encouragement of the hopeful work among them, for the civilizing and Christianizing of them, any Indian

---

[1] I 344. One need only imagine what visions were conjured up by the word Amalekites to the Old Testament minded divines. The name Ammonites carries the same connotations (II 553).
[2] I 215.
[3] II 582.
[4] II 596–597 ff.
[5] I 79.
[6] II 497.
[7] II 644–645.
[8] II 583.
[9] II 584.
[10] I 573.
[11] I 574.

that should be brought unto civility, and come to live orderly in any English plantation, should have such allotments among the English, as the English had themselves." [1]

In common with most of the New Englanders, Mather here assumes the right of the English to determine private ownership of the land. He assumes as well their right to require men to be like the English before occupying it.

Second, there was the problem of divine punishment. Book VII presents the troubles and disasters which came upon New England with the sub-title: "A Book of the Wars of the Lord." [2] This was the vertical dimension which was basic to the whole theocratic mission. When Tom Moule says, "God hath well rewarded the inhabitants of New-England for their unrighteous dealings towards the native Indians," perhaps Mather had reason to be indignant. [3] But in contemplative moments the New English divines did say that the Indian persecutors were a judgment upon their sins, [4] and a "rod of God's anger" against them. [5] In this perspective the reason for the continuing conflict between the Indians and the English was the continuing sinfulness of the Israel of New England.

Third, Roman Catholic Missions to the north in Canada were flourishing. Walker states:

> No brighter page of missionary sacrifice is to be found than that written by the Jesuits in Canada, beginning in 1611. Though aided by other orders, the strongly Roman provinces of Quebec is their monument to this day. [6]

This sounds commendable in a history book, but it made the New England Church tremble. In some "General Considerations for the Plantation of New England" the first was:

> It will be a service unto the Church, of great consequence, to carry the Gospel into those parts of the world, and raise a *bulwark* against the kingdom of anti-christ, which the Jesuites labour to rear up in *all* parts of the world. [7]

That carrying the gospel to other parts of the world meant a "bulwark" of the New England Israel and not of Indian churches is made clear by the third and sixth considerations which point out the unworthiness of the natives to remain and the importance of the "Lord's *garden*" here to be tilled and improved by the English. [8] But the significant point is that the Roman mission enterprise is identified with that of Antichrist. The Jesuits "seduced Indians" to their faith, [9] and made bizarre claims of French ancestry for the Lord. The Indian Wars were thought to be stimulated by the popish and Frenchified Indians. [10]

---

[1] *Idem.*
[2] II 487.
[3] II 645.
[4] II 660.
[5] II 663–665.
[6] Walker, W., *A History of the Christian Church*, 565.
[7] I 69.
[8] I 70.
[9] I 197–216.
[10] II 610–612.

Fourth, all but one of the reasons mentioned under number one above indicate a few of the deeply rooted social and economic difficulties. One more should be added. It is clear that some of the Indians were captured and used as slaves both at sea [1] and at home.[2] Of Hope-Hood it is said: "...that hellish fellow (was) once a servant of a Christian master in Boston." [3] Apart from the holding of captives as hostages, little more light is shed on this subject in the *Magnalia*.

Untold efforts were made to secure an amicable relationship. Under terms of the peace treaty agreed upon in 1693 by the Eastern Indians with Sir William Phips, an enforced solution to some of the above problems was attempted. The Indians pledged to be loyal to the crown of England, to abandon and forsake the French interest, to release all claim to title of lands and of former settlements,–and these for "all time and times for ever." [4] Five years later, Mather could only in exasperation hold the treaty up to heaven and cry out, "Ah, Lord God of truth, wilt thou not be revenged upon the false wretches that have broken this league!" [5] He urged all to prayer "for a total dissipation of those *Amalekites*." "Then will our God, 'thunder with a great thunder' of his consuming wrath upon our Indian Philistines!" [6] Their doom is read from Psalm 21:8, 9, 10 –

> Thine hand, O Lord, shall find out all thine enemies;
> thy right hand shall find out those that hate thee;
> the Lord shall swallow them up in his wrath,
> and the fire shall devour them;
> their fruit shalt thou destroy from the earth,
> and their seed from among the children of men.

To secure this judgment, repentance and reformation are indispensable. On this note the great *Magnalia* ends.

Considering the situation just described, the amount of mission work accomplished is nothing less than amazing. How much more could have been done under more favorable circumstances is pleasant to imagine. What was done was mostly through the dedicated selflessness of some persons like Roger Williams, the Mayhews, and John Eliot. Others played a smaller but significant role. The second son of Mather's grandfather, John Cotton, preached to five native groups and "was a minister of the gospel, at Plymouth; and one by whom not only the English, but also the Indians of America, had the 'glad tidings of salvation' in their own language carried unto them." [7]

In the "Ecclesiastical Map of New-England," among the 132 churches and 124 pastors in the eleven counties of the three colonies, Mather lists for Martha's Vineyard: "Mr. Ralph Thatcher, Mr. Denham, besides *Indian* churches and pastors," and for Nantucket: "Indian pastors." [8] Elsewhere in the *Magnalia* occasional reference is made to Indian pastors.[9]

---

[1] I 171.
[2] II 438, 589.
[3] *Idem*.
[4] II 625–626.
[5] II 678–679.
[6] *Idem*.
[7] I 285. The same is said of Mr. Peter Thatcher of Milton. I 494.
[8] I 86–88.
[9] I 216–217; II 559.

In one section of the *Magnalia*, "a further account concerning the present State of Christianity among the Indians in other parts of New-England," [1] additional information is given concerning the work following the death of Eliot. At Easthem, 505 adult Indians heard the gospel regularly in four assemblies, "having a great desire to be baptiz'd"; at Stonington one or two Pequots died praying and some captive servants were baptized; at Sandwich, 214 attended worship regularly; in Plymouth Colony John Cotton ministered to about 500; and elsewhere, Thomas Tupper preached to 180 Indians, while Grindal Rawson, Mr. Bondet, Daniel Gookin, and Mr. Dellius attempted to reach the natives in their areas. Three others seem to have carried the brunt of the load in bringing the gospel to the natives. Roger Williams won a reluctant compliment from Mather:

> He used many commendable endeavours to Christianize the Indians in his neighbourhood, of whose language, tempers and manners he printed a little relation with observations, wherein he *spiritualizes* the *curiosities* with two and thirty chapters, whereof he entertains his readers. [2]

Martha's Vineyard and Nantucket Island, just off the New England shore, were perhaps the most successful missionary ventures. Here at the high point some three thousand adults were claimed as Christian. [3] Young Thomas Mayhew had become pastor in 1644 at the first named island to a small group of settlers. He was ordained by God, reports Mather, as an evangelist "for the conversion of these Gentiles." He had a "holy zeal and resolution to assay what success he might find in that work; he takes opportunity to insinuate the love and good will he bore to that people; and soon finds occasion to let them know their 'deplorable condition' under Satan." [4] When he was not permitted by the Indians to lecture in public assemblies, he began to go privately from house to house. The Indians worshipped many gods and professed "*familiarity* with the infernal spirits." [5] By 1657 many hundreds of men and women were believers. Thomas Mayhew, Sr., together with John Cotton organized a native congregation on August 22, 1670. Grandson John Mayhew later took over much responsibility for the work until he died in 1682. After this the work was cared for primarily by the native Indian clergy. [6] Particularly noteworthy was the native attitude to missions:

> ...as in the apostolick times, the church sent forth from among themselves, for the conversion of the nations, so these Indians on Martha's Vineyard did: not only to the island of Nantucket, being about 1500 adult persons, but likewise to the mainland. [7]

The final form of civil government on the islands inclined to the New England type, though the prince's assent had to be obtained for decision of councils. The fullest loyalty was pledged and observed in peace and war to the laws

---

[1] II 437–440.
[2] II 499.
[3] II 430.
[4] II 427.
[5] II 425.
[6] II 428–431.
[7] II 432.

and crown of England.[1] One can fairly conclude that these Indians were colonialized and Christianized. Both processes proceeded simultaneously, although the motivation for beginning the work decidedly favored the latter.

The section in the *Magnalia* on John Eliot is appropriately called: "The Triumphs of the Reformed Religion in America."[2] The twenty nations of Indians on territory occupied by the Three United Colonies aroused Eliot's life-time concern. Mather states:

> This was the miserable people which our Eliot propounded unto himself to teach and save! And he had a double work incumbent upon him; he was to make men of them, ere he could hope to see them saints; they must be *civilized* ere they could be *Christianized;* he could not, as Gregory once of our nation, see anything *angelical* to bespeak his labours for their eternal welfare: all among them was *diabolical*. To think on raising a number of those hedious creatures unto the elevations of our holy religion, must argue more than common or little sentiments in the undertaker; but the faith of an Eliot could encounter it![3]

Eliot immediately set himself to the task of learning the language, writing a grammar, and translating the Bible and other books of piety. This type of work was the essential first step, because the Indians were

> ...so stupid and senseless, that they would never do so much as enquire after the religion of the strangers now come into their country, much less would they so far imitate us as to leave off their beastly way of living, that they might be partakers of any spiritual advantage by us: unless we could first address them in a language of their own.[4]

Eliot was not satisfied to labor alone. He cried for fellow-laborers to assist in the great work. Several soon joined him. In addition to those already mentioned, Mr. Fitch and Mr. Pierson worked in Connecticut with but little success, due to the opposition of the local chiefs. A letter from Increase Mather written in 1687 to Dr. Johannes Leusden of the University of Utrecht summarizes:

> In short, there are six churches of baptized Indians in New-England, and eighteen assemblies of catechumens, professing the name of Christ: of the Indians there are four-and-twenty who are preachers of the word of God.[5]

---

[1] II 433–436.
[2] I 526.
[3] I 560.
[4] I 561.
[5] I 570–571. Leusden (1624–1699) was the well-known Dutch orientalist with a deep interest in missions. He reported receipt of this letter to the synodical meeting of the Hervormde Kerk at Utrecht in 1690. The chief matters in the letter are set forth, and the account concludes:
> De Christelijke Synode verheugt zich over deze progressen en de uitbreiding van de Kerken en het Rijk van Jezus Christus in die Amerikaansche Gewesten, en bedankt den heer professor Leusden voor zijn gedane communicatie dienaangaande. (*Archief voor de Geschiedenis der Oude Hollandsche Zending*, II, Utrecht, 1884 117.)

See further J. C. Budde, "Johannes Leusden," in Nederlands *Archief voor Kerkgeschiedenis*, Nieuwe Serie, XXXIV 1944–1945, 163–186.

Eliot despised the Roman Catholic missionaries for their adoption of heathen usages in the worship of God; nothing but "a *pure, plain Scripture worship*" would do.[1] The industry of the papists in missionizing certainly ought to spur Protestant Christians into action. Though perhaps not in money and numbers, yet "that little handful of reformed churches in this country... has in divers regards outdone the furthest efforts of Popery."[2]

> ...the proselyted Indians of New England have been instructed at a more noble rate; we have helped them to the "sincere milk of the word;" we have given them the *whole Bible* in their own language: we have laid before them such a *creed* as the primitive believers had.... And God has blessed our education of these poor creatures in such a measure, that they can pray and preach to better edification... than multitudes of the Romish-clergyman.[3]

## 3. The Coming of the Kingdom

We have considered the situation which gave birth to the double thrust of the New England Mission: the primary and foundational mission in the establishment of a purer form of the church of God on American shores, and the secondary and ancillary mission in the preaching of the gospel to the natives. Before we specify more closely the principles, methods and motives which were operative, we shall examine two theological aspects of the mission: the first, inherent in the mission itself, revolves around the relation between the mission and the better age, imminently expected; and the second, a consequent of the mission, involves a felt need for ecclesiastical cooperation at the least, and for church union at the deepest level.

New England at its inception embodied the closest possible interworking between church and state. The theocratical machinery frequently needed oiling, and, as often, its breakdown was alternately feared and lamented. Yet through all these temporary disappointments, the hope for a better day burned sometimes dimly, sometimes more brightly.

When the emigrants left the shore of their mother country, many, if not most, nursed the same hopes as did Mr. John Sherman.

> ...upon mature deliberation,...with several famous divines who came over in the year 1634, hoping that by going over the *water*, they should in this be like men going under the *earth*, lodged "where the wicked would cease from troubling and the weary be at rest."[4]

But through the century there had been little rest for the weary, and wickedness was painfully discovered not to be the exclusive property of Europe. The picture faded of that "*old world* in Europe, where a flood of iniquity and calamity carried all before it," and that "*new world* in America; where...an hedge of *piety* and *sanctity* continued...."[5] During the first decade (1636) it was possible for the venerable John Cotton to write:

[1] I 571.
[2] I 572.
[3] I 572–573.
[4] I 512.
[5] I 355.

> That the order of the churches and the commonwealth was now so settled in New-England, by common consent, that it brought into his mind the new heaven and the new earth, wherein dwells righteousness.[1]

Likewise it seemed a reasonable if not required goal for Mr. Davenport to do all possible "to render the renowned church of New-Haven like the New-Jerusalem." [2] But as the years wore on, the shroud of lamentation obscured the identity of the "American Jerusalem." [3] The identity was not lost. The vision of "A Reformation of the Church is coming on" began slowly to comprehend the meaning of not yet "perfect before God... whereto they are quickly to be awakened." [4] The "not yet" expresses the hope still present at century's end.

The lamentations concerning the fulfilment of the prophesied falling away [5] had increased. So fierce were the evils that "the last conflict with antichrist" was judged to have arrived.[6] The call came to be less thoughtful of the earthly in order to escape the torments of hell,[7] and served as a stimulus to conversion.[8] Yet these were but a necessary prelude, a cleansing in preparation for that great and notable day of the Lord. He would soon come [9] in order to establish a millennial kingdom.[10] Samuel Mather was making prophetical calculations about the millennial kingdom before 1650,[11] but it was near century's end before Increase and Cotton Mather made much of it. By 1697 Increase, while warning against apostasy, could say: "The day is near when the Lord Jesus Christ will make his churches more pure and reformed than in the former ages." [12] Cotton explains that, though the primitive church universally believed in the millennial kingdom, the rise of the kingdom of Antichrist obscured the doctrine so that it fell into reproach.

> So the *mystery* of our Lord's "appearing in his kingdom," lay buried in Popish darkness, till the light thereof had a fresh *dawn*, since the antichrist entred into the last *half time* of the *period* allotted for him; and now, within the last few sevens of years, as things grow nearer to accomplishment, learned and pious men, in great numbers every where, come to receive, explain, and maintain the *old faith* about it.[13]

A number of years before, "...in both Englands the true notion of the Chiliad was hardly apprehended by many divines of note." [14]

But the mood of New England had changed a great deal. What was thought to be the beginning of the heavenly New Jerusalem in 1629 was through the always-correcting influence of history now seen as a prelude. But the fact of its coming was not altered, nor that of its imminence; rather, the manner of its coming was changed. In the youth of the colonies, the establishment of the theocratic commonwealth was the decisive event. A century of years made

---

[1] I 325.
[2] I 328.
[3] I 121.
[4] I 26–27.
[5] I 251.
[6] I 332.
[7] I 607.
[8] *Idem.*
[9] I 137, 509–510.
[10] I 331; II 57.
[11] II 57.
[12] II 79.
[13] I 331.
[14] *Idem.*

them doubt the efficacy of human establishments and a too easy identification of human and divine interests. Now the accomplishment of the mission would be achieved by the Lord's personal return. So the election sermon of 1696 evidences.

> The tidings which I bring unto you are, that there is a REVOLUTION and a REFORMATION at the very door, which will be vastly more wonderful than any of the deliverances yet seen by the church of God from the beginning of the world. I do not say that the *next year* will bring on this *happy period;* but this I do say, the bigger part of this assembly may, in the course of nature, live to see it. These things will come on with horrible commotions, and concussions, and confusions: The mighty angels of the Lord Jesus Christ will make their descent, and set the world a *trembling* at the approaches of their almighty Lord.[1]

One must not conclude that the establishment of New England had been a mistake. On the contrary, this was seen to be a means in God's hand by which the goal of the mission was to be achieved. His all-inclusive providence had determined events so that

> ...the gospel, in the power and purity of it, might come into these dark corners of the earth, and that here might be seen a specimen of the new heavens and a new earth wherein dwells righteousness, which shall ere long be seen all the world over, and which according to his promise we look for.[2]

What scandalized the gospel and the church as its bearer perhaps as much as the indifference of the second and third generations was the disruption of the new model of church reformation. In the light of the belief that New England represented the New Jerusalem on the earth, this is to be expected. To bring a division in the New England church was to divide what was essentially *not able to be divided*. It was to attempt the thwarting of God's purpose for the new world.

The whole idea of separation, even from the English church with its catalogued corruptions, was reprehensible; still worse, it was sin.[3] New England cried: "...we are not seditious as to the interests of Caesar, nor schismatical as to the matters of religion." [4] "We dare not be guilty of...schism." [5] As the century continued, the bewailing of public and private sins included those of factionalism and divisions.[6] Schismatical churches merited civil rebuke and punishment.[7] Those places and churches born or living in factionalism and strife soon reaped the divine judgment of destruction.[8]

The leaders of New England are repeatedly credited with a deep desire for unity.[9] Communicants from French, Dutch, and Scottish churches are wel-

[1] II 653.
[2] I 248. Written by Increase Mather in 1695.
[3] II 496; I 35, 72.
[4] I 296.
[5] I 250.
[6] I 388–389, 436.
[7] II 236.
[8] II 396.
[9] I 35, 379, 601; II 100–101.

comed in their churches.[1] Presbyterians, Independents, and Congregationalists are urged to adopt a charitable attitude to one another as brothers in the Lord.[2] When John Dury, who had been working for the union of the reformed churches in Europe from 1635, requested the concurrence of the New England ministers for his design, they heartily approved.[3] Davenport wrote, with the agreement of the rest of the ministers:

> You have done right well, reverend *brother*, in that you have, after a brotherly manner, unto the promoting of this affair, in the *communion of saints* invited us, who belong to the same mystical body with your selves, under one head, our Lord Jesus Christ....
>
> For we reckon that as well to *judge* what things are *errors*, as to *bear* with such errors in weaker brethren, are *both* of them agreeable to what we have been taught by the apostles. The *toleration* of our erroneous brethren should not be without *rebuking*, but it should be without *rejecting* of those brethren.[4]

There were efforts to unite the various parties of the church in New England. Samuel Mather endeavored to secure a union between the Presbyterians, Independents, and Baptists.[5] Differences between them he judged circumstantial.[6] Increase Mather had been instrumental in the union of the Congregational and Presbyterian believers in England.

The English "Heads of Agreement Assented to by the United Ministers formerly call'd 'Presbyterian' and 'Congregational'" were urged upon the New England churches to formalize what in effect already existed.[7] Niceties of "controversial divinity" do not justify separation from fellowship.[8] Wide theological differences existed among the fathers of the primitive church but did not occasion division.[9] These differences exist also among the New England fathers and thus may not occasion division of the church.[10]

There was a limit to which the New England divines would go. Heretics were denounced in fiery terms: "Let (their errors) go to the devil of hell, from which they come." [11] The black list of heretics was not small: Antinomians and Familists,[12] Brownists and Separatists,[13] old style Quakers,[14] Pelagians and Arminians,[15] and the Roman Papists "whose religion is antichristian." [16] All these were marching another road to another Jerusalem than the true one. With such there could be no fellowship. It was not that Cotton Mather and

---

[1] I 62.
[2] II 490–491.
[3] I 299–301.
[4] I 326–327.
[5] On May 21, 1718, Mather preached the sermon at the ordination of a Baptist minister in Boston (Elisha Callender, 1692–1738). This was an unusual occurrance, and Mather expected criticism for his participation. (*Diary*, II 530, 535, 537).
[6] II 53; note Cotton Mather's willingness to receive Anabaptists, II 531.
[7] II 272–276.
[8] I 300–301.
[9] I 331.
[10] I 410.
[11] I 310.
[12] I 266, 418.
[13] I 339.
[14] I 492–493; II 499, 527–528.
[15] II 78–79.
[16] I 316; cf. also I 414, 440 and II 610–612.

many others now approved (as they had only a few years before) of the horrible persecutions and hangings of heretics which persisted nearly to the end of the century.[1] Rather they appealed to the practice of the primitive church which penalized heretics during the first three hundred years "by *sound preaching*, by *discipline*, by *catechising*, and by *disputation*." [2]

But how can one decide which believers are to be judged fellow-believers and which not? The key is what Mather alternately calls: "the *substantials* of the Christian religion,"[3] "essential doctrines" [4] and "fundamentals of doctrine." [5] The letter to John Dury mentioned above puts it:

> In whatever assemblies amongst the whole company of those that profess the gospel, the fundamentals of doctrine, and essentials of order, are maintained, though in many niceties of controversial divinity they are at less agreement with us, we do hereby make it manifest, that we do acknowledge them all and every one for brethren, and that we shall be ready to give unto them the right hand of fellowship in the Lord, if in other things they be peaceable, and walk orderly.[6]

It is beyond our immediate purpose to inquire further into what Cotton Mather and his contemporaries included in essential doctrine. The conflict with conformity made clear that church liturgy and government was not included. Constant skirmishes as well as head-on theological battles with the heretics made clear that the central New Testament doctrines of Christ and the gospel, of grace and reconciliation, were required. Subscription to the simple gospel without the many theological and liturgical accretions after the fourth century was the heart of true worship and faith. The return to primitive Christian doctrine and life was the mission which New England judged itself appointed to fulfil. That many of the New England Church still sensed this calling presaged hope for the future.

*Conclusion*

On the basis of the New England Church story given above, we ought now to gather the various threads. This can best be done by noting successively the mission principles which were operative, the various mission methods which were employed, and the motives that compelled men and churches to the mission deed.

---

[1] I 298.
[2] II 536.
[3] I 250.
[4] I 259.
[5] I 300.
[6] I 300–301. Ernst Benz maintains that: "This doctrine of the *evangelium aeternum* and of the approaching epoch of the Holy Spirit gives us the deepest insight into the real religious fundamentals of Puritanism." Benz, "Pietist and Puritan Sources of Early Protestant World Missions" in *Church History*, Vol. XX (a.) 48.

a. Mission Principles

First, missions is a divine enterprise. The establishment of the mission in America was divinely planned and executed. God was considered the direct ruler and captain of the New England Pilgrims. He spoke and judged as specifically and painfully to them as he had to Israel of old. The success or failure of the whole enterprise depended upon a recognition of and subjection to his external will and divine plan for humanity.

Second, the church is both the primary bearer and the goal of the mission. The church's chief calling in the world and reason for existence is to reflect God's will in all aspects of human life. As such, the profession of the true doctrine of God and the perfect obedience to his holy will serve to promote the Lordship of Christ and the extension of his kingdom. Thus, correct doctrine and holy living become the test points for the church's faithfulness to the divine mission.

This makes the church at the same time bearer and goal of the mission. It becomes goal in that God's great purpose in history is to establish his perfect church. Insofar as this goal is achieved, the divine mission is attained. The Puritans thought their church form and personal piety quite unique and further along than any other in truly reflecting what God would have his church to be.

Third, the state bears a divine calling to function as the auxiliary agent in the mission. The colonial Christians envisioned a perfect harmony between church and state in which each actively participated in the achievement of the divine mission. Both were equally responsible for purity of life and doctrine and for mutual admonition should one fall short of its task. Yet more, they were united in basic purpose: the attainment of a church-state commonwealth in which God's will is final and supreme. To the magistrates were thus given concrete responsibilities in the furtherance of the Christian religion.

Fourth, the Bible as lived by the primitive church is the norm for the mission. The knowledge of God's will in the Bible was still more clarified by the concreteness of the primitive church experience. Ecclesiastical history from the fourth century on is the story of useless additions in church practice and inner decay in church doctrine. Nothing less than a full return to the plain and simple Christian life and forms of the primitive church will do. Appeal to the lived-out reality of the Bible in that golden age was the final appeal to unquestioned truth and practice.

Fifth, divine blessing and retribution existentially judge the mission. The knowledge of the truth or falsity of church decisions, political programs, and personal lives came through God's subsequent acts in history. The progress and fruition of a national cause or personal state meant divine approval. War, sickness and death, harvest failure, and the like, clearly revealed God's wrath consequent to national or personal sin. The quality of the mission cause was proved at every step by the immediacy of divine blessing or judgment.

b. Mission Methods

The planting of Christian churches was the primary task. Propagation of the gospel meant the bringing of the church to places where it had never been before. Most of the Puritan effort concentrated upon the gathering of immigrant believers on American shores into churches. It included, however, the gathering of assemblies of believers among the Indians with gradual church organization.

A herculean effort was made to maintain the purity of the church. The church existed not only as agent but also as goal of the mission. Its qualification for this calling and task was vital. The constant cry for further reformation and the lamentation of spiritual compromise must be seen as attempts to purify the instrument for the mission. The maintenance of high requirements for church membership and for admittance to the Lord's Supper, the encouragement of the heresy trials, and the issue of the Reforming Synods meant life or death for the church. The most concentrated effort was spent upon this *sine qua non* for the fulfillment of the divine mission.

First, the official preaching of the gospel had central place in the approach. By way of reaction to the "silencing" activity of the Church of England, teaching by preaching became the heart of New England worship. One and two hour sermons were to the older generation a delight. Ministers were duty bound to minister the Word to all those within their parish. For those who individually felt the calling, preaching was extended to the pagan Indians in the near vicinity of the churches. The cry for conversion reached both those in the shadow of the church and those in the wilds of nature. Only through the preached gospel of Jesus Christ was salvation to be found.

Second, education through catechizing and the establishment of schools rapidly became common in New England, sometimes even for Indians. The teaching ministry of the church found channels in the catechizing of children within the church, and of adults as well among the Indians. Knowledge of doctrine was highly valued. For one to profess belief in Christ without knowing the essential doctrines of salvation was foolishness.[1] Well-grounded converts and proselytes over against the mass superficiality of Jesuit teaching was New England's boast. An early emphasis upon schools especially by John Eliot is noteworthy. Consistent with this was the emphasis upon the close relationship between civilizing and Christianizing in the making of Christians.

Third, for the first time mission societies were established. The "Society for the Propagation of the Gospel in New England" was erected in 1649 in England and provided vital assistance to the work of John Eliot. This was the first such organization in England. The first in America was to come a century later. Exemplary is Mather's prophetic call to the three kingdoms to

> ...procure well-composed *societies*, by whose united counsels, the noble design of evangelizing the world may be more effectually carried on...and vast *contributions* (may be gathered) from all well-disposed people, to assist and advance this progress of Christianity.[2]

---

[1] I 365.   [2] I 582.

Fourth, personal witnessing in the New England churches functioned in terms of admonitions to piety, calls for repentance, and urges to make and to be faithful to one's contract with God. Not usual but "most savoury," is a treatise written by John Higginson entitled: "*Our dying Saviour's Legacy of Peace to his Disciples in a troublesome world; with a Discourse on the Duty of Christians, to be Witnesses unto Christ; unto which is added, Some Help to Self-Examination.*" [1] Mather's *Nets of Salvation* also struck this note.

Fifth, in the primary mission of establishing God's church on American shores, much emphasis was placed upon the goal of church unity. Church polity might not hinder the rapprochement of the Christian churches. However, common acceptance of primitive church doctrine constituted the minimal fundament. On this basis Congregational, Baptist, Presbyterian, and charitably inclined Independents could stand together. The openness in accepting believers from other national churches at communion and in accepting gifts for Eliot's work from English Christians testifies to a deep-felt unity. However, no concrete steps were jointly taken in advancing the gospel among the heathen.

Sixth, literature distribution was used in the seventeenth century, both to promote the zeal of the colonists for witnessing and to reach the unconverted natives. From the end of the century to 1728, Mather wrote voluminously to further the mission.

c. Mission Motives

First and foremost of the motives operative in the establishment of the New England Church was the glory of God. Constant cries of unworthiness by the divines were not meant to testify to the shakiness of the cause; rather, they meant to confirm their own human unworthiness before the majesty and supremacy of their Lord. Salvation was of God. New England was his gift. One's self and one's land could only be offered to him in worshipful obedience. The accomplishments of New England were his triumphs and her failures the disgrace of his name by a sinful people. Selflessness and sacrificial obedience were only a small part of what one owed to God. So Cotton Mather appropriately ends the introduction of his great *Magnalia*: "What am I? Nothing. – Sovereign Grace alone Lives in my life, and does what I have done." [2]

The desire to secure the glory of God issued into theocratic forms. There burned in the New England hearts a deep hope for restoration. They turned to the primitive New Testament standards in matters of worship and life. But they drank deeply at the Old Testament fountains, also. The close harmony and near identity of political and religious life seemed closest to reality for them. The state as well as the church must express the glory of God and obedience to him. One uses the sword of force, the other the sword of persuasion, but both are one in purpose. Only thus can we understand the uniqueness of the religious state as it was born in America and as it traveled its troubled road.

---

[1] I 365.      [2] I 38.

Of increasing importance toward the century's end was a second motive, the eschatological. A sense of urgency was created by the expectation of an imminent appearance of the Lord Jesus for the institution of his millenial kingdom. Though belief in this event and in its imminence was not universal, the Mathers could claim considerable support for it. Perry Miller says: "The two Mathers were...possessed by the true apocalyptic spirit, they marched into the Age of Reason loudly crying that the end of the world was at hand.... From 1693 on, the Mathers hourly expected the day." [1] And again, "The Magnalia...is a summation and synthesis of the New England apocalypse." [2] Though this is somewhat overdramatized, it is indeed true that the eschatological vision impelled Eliot, the Mathers, and some other Puritans to vital concern for the conversion of their countrymen and the Indians.

Third, the motive of love and compassion was of great importance in the mission to the Indians. John Eliot truly reflected a fitting Christian response to the challenge presented by the seal of the Massachusetts colony. His near half century of unremitting and self-giving labors speak, as Richard Baxter wrote, twice as loudly as Mather's voluminous writings.[3] But what was true for him could equally be said for the many others who received no official call from the churches, but who felt deeply the call of compassion for unbelieving souls.

Fourth, this motive was accompanied by that of duty and obedience. It was not that the end of converting the heathen enunciated in the charters pressed so heavily upon them. Likely those words were all too soon forgotten in the hard business of keeping oneself alive. There was, however, an awareness of the significance of the great commission of Christ and its relevance for the seventeenth century.[4] Sensitivity to the duty inherent in a bearer of the Christian name for those who cannot be saved apart from Christ finds occasional expression. The great disasters and wars with the Indians were seen as evidence

---

[1] Miller, *The New England Mind*, 185, 188.  [2] *Ibid.*, 189.
[3] *Magnalia*, I 583. On his deathbed, Baxter, after reading Cotton Mather's *Life of John Eliot*, wrote to Increase Mather:
"Dear Brother: I *thought* I had been near dying at twelve o'clock in bed; but your book revived me: I lay reading it until between one and two. I know much of Mr. Eliot's opinions, by many letters which I had from him. There was no man on earth whom I honoured above him. It is his *evangelical work* that is the *apostolical succession* that I plead for. I am now dying, I hope, as he did. It pleased me to read from him my case, ["my understanding faileth, my memory faileth, my tongue faileth, (and my hand and pen fail) but my charity faileth not."] That word much comforted me. I am as zealous a lover of the New-England churches as any man, according to Mr. Noyes', Mr. Norton's, Mr. Mitchel's, and the Synod's model.
"I loved your *father*, upon the letters I received from him. I love *you* better for your learning, labours, and peaceable moderation. I love *your son* better than either of you, for the excellent temper that appeareth in his writings. O that godliness and wisdom thus *increase* in all families! He hath honoured himself half as much as Mr. Eliot: I say, but *half as much*; for *deeds* excel *words*. God preserve you and New-England! Pray for
"Your fainting, languishing Friend,
August 3, 1691.                                                  Ri. Baxter."
[4] II 429.

that the New Englanders had not used divinely-given duty "to make a vertuous people" of the Indians.[1] A sub-motive of fear for more such punishment is evidenced here.

The fifth motive of significance was the cultural one. The settlers generally, and the missionaries as well, took a dim view of Indian life and culture. They lived a near-animal existence. To Christianize such as these was an utterly impossible thought. First they must be brought to a more reasonable and civilized form of existence before the possibility of converting existed. Apparently more is made of this by Eliot than by the Mayhews. One thing is certain. Cotton Mather, who normally reflects something of the spirit of his times, makes it clear where he stands.

> Wherefore, may the people of New-England...be encouraged still to prosecute, first, the *civilizing*, and then the *Christianizing* of the barbarians in their neighbourhood; and may the New-Englanders...make a *mission* of the gospel unto the mighty nations of the Western Indians.[2]

Ancillary in the mission to the Indians was the motive of competition with the Roman Catholics. The success of the French Jesuits in the Canadian territory bordering on the north hurt more than New England's pride. A secondary political motive involved itself in the French use of the Indians to advance their own cause against the English. Mather vigorously defends the depth of his people's proselyting against the extensiveness of the Roman activity. Yet one Canadian Indian who had formerly been English said: "...had the English been as careful to instruct [me] in [their] religion...as the *French* were to instruct [me] in theirs, [I] might have been of [English] religion."[3] How that must have hurt!

d. A Pattern for the World

New England, believes Mather, sets a pattern for the world. The hard and demanding life of the frontier quickly broke any tendency to a romantic motive. Neither did the Puritan activistic and crusading spirit favor an ascetic one. Yet Mather saw in the purest church form of America a consequence for missions. The American experiment was an example to the world not only in church organization and real Christianity but as well in mission zeal. Mather will have this example serve as stimulus for the world. His prophetic call to mission zeal and activity by New England is paralleled by one to old England and Europe. He claims America's example has already stimulated the Dutch to an East Indies Mission. He cries for England to do likewise in Wales and Ireland; for the great trading companies to do so in Asia, Africa and America; for all to assume responsibility for the Greeks, Armenians, and Muscovites in the eastern countries in the battle against the Turks. Far from accepting the criticism from across the sea that the Americans have "hindred the conversion of the poor pagans," he pleads:

---

[1] I 581.   [2] I 580–581.   [3] II 357.

But let that which has been the *vindication* of New England, be also the *emulation* of the world; let not poor little New-England be the only Protestant country that shall do any notable thing "for the propagation of the faith", unto those "dark corners of the earth which are full of cruel habitations"...it is possible that the great God who "despises not the prayer of the poor", may, by the influences of his Holy Spirit upon the hearts of some whose eyes are upon these lines, give a blessed answer thereunto.[1]

The idea of missions in the *Magnalia Christi Americana* is plain. The further-reformed church patterned after the example of the primitive believers and rooted deeply in Old Testament theocratic ideals was being established in the ends of the earth. This was God's great mission for the seventeenth century. Nowhere else in the world were so many thousands of European Christians brought into close contact with pagan tribes. Slowly the Christian conscience awakened first in a few, gradually in many. The gospel was preached and churches were gathered. Yet the deep consciousness of divine appointment for New England was never forgotten. Hope for a better fulfillment of her destiny and calling was hung upon the maintenance of a minimum of essential doctrine and the expected age of the Spirit which would make all things right. The final accomplishment of the mission rests yet in the future, but its coming is sure, – as sure as God himself.

### B. JONATHAN EDWARDS AND THE *History of Redemption*

*Biographical Introduction*

In 1740 Northampton was a frontier town of two hundred families. Boston could boast thirteen thousand inhabitants. Yet Northampton carries the fame for the beginning of the Great Awakening in New England. To find the reason for this, we must look to a parsonage farmhouse where Timothy Edwards and Esther Stoddard bore their eight daughters and only son Jonathan (gift of Jehovah). Timothy was full cousin to Cotton Mather, and Esther was the daughter of "the pope" of Connecticut Valley, Solomon Stoddard, minister at Northampton for nearly sixty years. Jonathan was born in the frontier town of New Windsor in 1703, only three months after John Wesley was born in another parsonage across the ocean. The two spiritual leaders never met, but their quite different lives bore common fruit, influencing the religion of many thousands in Old and New England.

Jonathan was educated with other students at home. He entered Yale at twelve when his thousand-word essay on "flying spiders," famous for its close scientific observations, had already been written. At college, stimulated in part by Locke and Newton, he wrote his reflections on the mind and on natural

---

[1] I 580.

science, and he began his "Notes on the Scriptures" and "Miscellanies." He graduated from Yale in 1720, only three months short of a century after the Mayflower had docked at Plymouth.

After two years of graduate study in New Haven, he left Yale in 1722, the year Timothy Cutler, its president, and Samuel Johnson shocked the constituency by declaring for episcopacy. Edwards served a Scotch Presbyterian Church in New York for a year and thereafter was a tutor at Yale for two years. Grandfather Stoddard had chosen young Edwards to inherit the Northampton throne. This he occupied, following a period of illness, until his dismissal after a painful controversy in 1750. At Stockbridge he served as missionary to the Indians for eight years until he moved to assume the presidency of Princeton a few weeks before his death.

Edwards' significance for missions stems from his influence in the Great Awakening, the inspiration later missionaries received through his writings, and the eight years of work in the Indian mission. We shall briefly consider each of these.

In 1731 Edwards was invited to give the Thursday morning public lecture at Boston. In Stoddardian fashion he accentuated the radical nature of divine sovereignty and the absolutely dependent character of conversion. The lecture was entitled: "God Glorified in the work of Redemption, by the Greatness of Man's Dependence upon Him in the Whole of It." The die was cast: Edwards would countenance no diminution of basic Puritan doctrine though, as we shall see, he cast it into significantly new molds.

The scattered flames of revival touched New Jersey under Frelinghuysen and Gilbert Tennant in the 1720's before igniting in Northampton in 1734. The letdown following the conversion of several hundred souls bothered Edwards in the succeeding years. He pointed his congregation back to those brighter days when "the town seemed to be full of the presence of God." [1] His *Faithful Narrative of the Surprising Work of God in the Conversion of many Hundred Souls in Northampton and the Neighboring Towns and Villages* was published in 1737. Two years later, as part of his attempt to re-arouse his congregation, he preached the thirty sermons which constitute the *History of Redemption*.[2]

These sermons undergirded the great new wave of revival that enveloped Northampton (and New England) in 1740. They were not "threatening, imprecatory" sermons, but, like most of his preaching, they were Biblical and ethical in character.[3] His simple, unrelenting logic persuaded men of their need. With quiet voice and only an occasional gesture, he was able to communicate the depth of man's dependence upon God and the greatness of God's

---

[1] Jonathan Edwards, *The Works of President Edwards*, III 15, *Faithful Narrative* . . ., 1737.
[2] Perry Miller, *Jonathan Edwards*, 130. "Of the six hundred full-length manuscript sermons extant, about 25 per cent are tentatively classified as evangelistic and only a few of these are of the threatening, imprecatory sort. A much larger percentage is typed as theological or as dealing with the Christian experience and with personal and social ethics. Of the seventy or so sermons already published, only about eight are denunciatory."
[3] Douglas J. Elwood, *The Philosophical Theology of Jonathan Edwards*, 163.

concern for man.[1] *A Devine and Supernatural Light, Immediately Imparted to the Soul by the Spirit of God, Shown to be Both a Scriptural, and Rational Doctrine* (published in 1734) and other sermons prior to the 1734 revival were also on "positive themes: the joy of the saints, the beauty of holiness, the rest the true believer enjoys in Christ, the practical Christian virtues, especially benevolence and honesty."[2] A subsequent series of sermons on "Justification by Faith"[3] prepared his congregation for the first revival as the *History of Redemption* series did for the second. Edwards' most famous imprecatory sermon, *Sinners in the Hands of an Angry God*, vividly pictured God's judgment upon human sin. It was preached in its final form at out-of-the-way Enfield and ended upon the note of judgment, an infrequent occurrence for him.[4] Since it came at the high point of religious enthusiasm in 1741 (actually just before this wave of excitement began to decline), we may view it more as typical of contemporary sermonization than as Edwards' main method to secure revival. However, this sermon is typical of his theological pattern in demonstrating that man's moral judgments and his seeking of God through repentance cannot earn God's favor. Man's seeking lies in the universal realm of common grace and natural ability. Nothing but saving grace born of God's transcendent will can rescue a sinner from judgment. What made God's anger for sin and unbelief so vivid for Edwards was his own mystical sense of the beauty and holiness of God. In his own spiritual experience lies the key to his preaching.

During his early ministry he felt a growing concern for the advancement of Christ's kingdom and the conversion of men. In 1723 he often walked with a friend on the banks of the Hudson River, and he records: "...our conversation used to turn much on the advancement of Christ's kingdom in the world, and the glorious things God would accomplish for his church in the latter days."[5] After his illness in 1725 he began "to long for the conversion of some I was concerned with; I could gladly honour them, and with delight be a servant to them, and lie at their feet, if they were but truly holy."[6] At Northampton the broader reaches of the kingdom attracted him:

> My heart has been much on the advancement of Christ's kingdom in the world. The histories of the past advancement of Christ's kingdom have

---

[1] H. Richard Niebuhr judges that Edwards' sermons on judgment indicate his
...intense awareness of the precariousness of life's poise, of the utter insecurity of men and of mankind which are at every moment as ready to plunge into the abyss of disintegration, barbarism, crime and the war of all against all, as to advance toward harmony and integration. He recognized what Kierkegaard meant when he described life as treading water with ten thousand fathoms beneath us. Elwood, *op. cit.*, 4.

[2] Ola E. Winslow, *Jonathan Edwards, 1703-1758*, 151.

[3] Concerning these sermons Ola Winslow, his biographer says: "Read on the printed page, these sermons seem too heavily doctrinal and too argumentative to make revival history." *op. cit.*, 152-153.

[4] Isaac Watts wrote in his copy of the printed sermon: "A most Terrible sermon, which should have had a word of Gospell at the end of it, tho I think tis all true." Winslow, *op. cit.*, 180.

[5] "Extracts from his Private Writings," *Works*, I 35.      [6] *Ibid.*, 36.

been sweet to me. When I have read histories of past ages, the pleasantest thing in all my reading has been, to read of the kingdom of Christ being promoted.... And my mind has been much entertained and delighted with the scripture promises and prophecies, which relate to the future glorious advancement of Christ's kingdom upon earth.[1]

During this period the mystic sense of the presence of God continued:

> Once, as I rode out into the woods for my health, in 1737, having alighted from my horse in a retired place, as my manner commonly has been, to walk for divine contemplation and prayer, I had a view, that for me was extraordinary, of the glory of the Son of God, as Mediator between God and man, and his wonderful, great, full, pure and sweet grace and love, and meek and gentle condescension. This grace that appeared so calm and sweet, appeared also great above the heavens. The person of Christ appeared ineffably excellent with an excellency great enough to swallow up all thought and conception—which continued, as near as I can judge, about an hour; which kept me, the greater part of the time, in a flood of tears, and weeping aloud. I felt an ardency of soul to be, what I know not otherwise how to express, emptied and annihilated; to lie in the dust, and to be full of Christ alone; to love him with a holy and pure love; to trust in him; to live upon him; to serve and follow him; and to be perfectly sanctified and made pure, with a divine and heavenly purity. I have, several other times, had views very much of the same nature, and which have had the same effects.[2]

The "sweet communications" of the Holy Spirit brought the sense of God "as an infinite fountain of divine glory and sweetness; being full, and sufficient to fill and satisfy the soul...."[3] But that very presence brought as well a "vastly greater sense of my own wickedness, and the badness of my heart, than ever I had before my conversion."[4] His sin seemed to him the "very worst of all mankind" since the beginning of the world; if God should judge him he would "have by far the lowest place in hell." When others came to discuss the concerns of their souls and expressed their own sense of wickedness, theirs seemed weak and feeble compared to his own, which were "like an infinite deluge, or mountains over my head.... When I look into my heart, and take a view of my wickedness, it looks like an abyss infinitely deeper than hell."[5] Now it appears to him

> ...that were it not for free grace, exalted and raised up to the infinite height of all the fulness and glory of the great Jehovah, and the arm of his power and grace, stretched forth in all the majesty of his power, and in all the glory of his sovereignty, I should appear sunk down in my sins below hell itself; far beyond the sight of every thing, but the eye of sov-

---

[1] *Ibid.*, 38.
[2] *Ibid.*, 38, 39.
[3] *Ibid.*, 39.
[4] *Idem.*
[5] *Ibid.*, 39–40.

ereign grace, that can pierce even down to such a depth. And yet it seems to me, that my conviction of sin is exceeding small, and faint; it is enough to amaze me, that I have no more sense of my sin. I know certainly, that I have very little sense of my sinfulness. When I have had turns of weeping and crying for my sins, I thought I knew at the time, that my repentance was nothing to my sin.[1]

We must keep Edwards' testimony of his own spiritual life in view to understand his preaching. He portrayed the abysmal depths of human sin against the highest reaches of divine beauty and holiness. In this sense he himself is the microcosm of humanity. His sin was that of every man. His sense of grace could be that of those men who sought it earnestly. The spider suspended over the fiery pit was Jonathan Edwards. His wickedness deserved yet deeper judgment. But the miracle of pure grace brought him to an ecstatic sense of union with the holiness and beauty of God. By this vivid personal experience of sin and grace Edwards communicated to his hearers a sense of the awfulness of sin and judgment and a fervant desire for forgiving grace. That many did find forgiveness, or were seeking it, is attested by those who came for counsel to his study each Monday.[2]

Edwards' writings have wielded a still greater influence than his preaching. Not only did his *Narrative of Surprising Conversions* spark the second wave of the Great Awakening, but his *Distinguishing Marks of a Work of the Spirit of God* (1746), while discrediting excesses, pointed out the eschatological significance of the revivals. America was considered the scene of the latter-day glory and renewal of mankind. Prophecy was being fulfilled. The revivals were but the beginning of the still greater glory of God. The *Narrative* was followed the next year by *Some Thoughts Concerning the Present Revival of Religion in New England*, a series of sermons which would become the basis of the *Treatise Concerning Religious Affections* (1746). The *Treatise* attempted to define the nature of religion in order to come to terms with the extremists who identified religion with violent emotion, on the one hand, or with right conduct on the other. Edwards distinguishes between the understanding and the will as the activities of the mind. To the will belong the affections and the power to choose. Doctrinal knowledge is necessary but insufficient. Even devils know doctrine. A sense of the beauty and holiness of God gives man a new discernment of Scriptural truth, brings him into vital union with Christ, and molds his affections into exquisite harmony with the divine. Edwards makes this experience of religion concrete in his *An Account of the Life of the Late Reverend Mr. David Brainerd* (1749).

Two years before, he had supported a number of Scottish divines, with whom he corresponded extensively, in their institution of regular prayer meetings for the coming kingdom of Christ. He published *An Humble Attempt to Promote Explicit Agreement and Visible Union of God's People in Extraordinary Prayer for the Revival of Religion and Advancement of Christ's Kingdom on Earth*. It refers to the

---

[1] *Ibid.*, 40.
[2] On one Sunday a hundred new members were received *en masse*, including his oldest daughter, Sarah, age seven. Winslow, *op. cit.*, 155.

widespread conviction, which he also shared, of a thousand-year reign of peace and obedience to God, which would serve to prepare the way for the second coming of Christ. But the chief importance of the work was that, as Beaver has shown, "it became on both sides of the Atlantic the most potent means of missionary education and support." [1] Based upon Zechariah 8:20–22, the appeal is for fervent and constant prayer that Christ will "advance his spiritual *kingdom* in the world, as he has promised." [2] New Testament promises make clear that "a time will come when the gospel shall universally prevail, and the kingdom of Christ be extended over the whole habitable earth...." [3] Since nothing comparing to universality has yet occurred, we must expect the fulfillment when "religion and true christianity shall in every respect be *uppermost* in the world...." [4] Again he discounts the "errors and extremes" and undue glorification of "instruments" in the "late wonderful season" of revival. Many have fallen into "infidelity, heresy, and vice" but our hope is that "a happy change is nigh." [5] Edwards calls to mind evidences of the Spirit's work first in Germany, then in New England, England, Wales, and Scotland, followed by "remarkable" happenings in the United Netherlands, a reformation of Indians in Jersey and Pennsylvania, and an awakening in the southern colonies. "The late remarkable *religious awakenings*, in many parts of the christian world, may justly encourage us in prayer for the promised glorious and universal outpouring of the Spirit of God." [6] Such united prayer will realize the pious union which Scripture makes "the peculiar beauty of the church of Christ." [7]

When the separation came from the Northampton church, Edwards became missionary at Stockbridge on the farthest edge of civilized America. Two hundred fifty Housatonic and twelve English families were his parishioners. John Sergeant, earlier a pupil of Edwards, had been the post's only missionary since its founding in 1734. In order to strengthen the Indian settlement, the commissioners for Indian affairs had encouraged Mohawks to settle alongside the Housatonics. The Mohawks were feared by every other tribe in the area and, because Catholic missionaries had been active, they inclined to favor the French rather than the English.

Edwards carried responsibility for the boarding school for Indian boys; he made regular reports to the commissioners for Indian affairs and the London Society for the Propagation of the Gospel (from whom much of his salary came) and sought their approval for his actions. Other facets of his work involved discriminating between English commercial and religious interests, administering funds, and unraveling duplications of work by rival missionaries.

The sermons Edwards preached through an interpreter were "mostly New Testament sermons, explaining very simply the joys of heaven to which drunken Indians do not go, the anger of God against sinners,... and the practical virtues

---

[1] R. Pierce Beaver, *Ecumenical Beginnings in Protestant World Mission*, 19.
[2] *Works*, II 437, *An Humble Attempt to Promote Explicit Agreement and Visible Union of God's People, in Extraordinary Prayer*..., 1748.
[3] *Ibid.*, 451.
[4] *Ibid.*, 457.
[5] *Ibid.*, 478.
[6] *Ibid.*, 480.
[7] *Ibid.*, 482.

of Christian living...."[1] But in 1754 war broke out, and many Christian Indians enlisted. Murders of whites in the vicinity by hostile Indians brought a state of alarm. The parsonage became a fort where numbers of settlers sought refuge. The frail Edwards was severely ill during that autumn and winter.

The Stockbridge parsonage provided hospitality to students and missionaries. As Brainerd had found a second home earlier at Northampton, so now Gideon Hawley (missionary to the Iroquois since 1751) enjoyed pleasant days in company with others who stayed at Stockbridge. Traveling missionaries glimpsed the deep attachments in the Edwards family and their pleasant submission to what they firmly believed to be God's will. Edwards was one of the theological instructors most sought after by Presbyterian students [2] and missionaries preparing for the work.[3] Here in the wilderness came the long sought opportunity to write. From Stockbridge Edwards still speaks.

The lines from Edwards to the subsequent great mission efforts are not difficult to trace. His brief contact with George Whitefield was prophetic of what his writings and example would mean to later generations. During the crest of the Awakening, Whitefield had stayed at the Edwards home during four days of revival meetings in Northampton. Whitefield wrote in his *Journal*: "Our Lord seem'd to keep the good Wine till the last. I have not seen four such gracious Meetings together since my Arrival." [4] Under date of October 19, 1740, he wrote warm words of the Edwards family: "Felt wonderful Satisfaction in being at the House of Mr. *Edwards*. He is a Son himself, and hath also a Daughter of *Abraham* for his wife. A sweeter Couple I have not yet seen." [5] He viewed Edwards as "a solid, excellent Christian, but at present weak in Body. I think, I may say I have not seen his Fellow in all New England." [6]

Undoubtedly the facts that Edwards had been a spiritual father to the self-sacrificing Brainerd, and that at the Edwards home his life had slowly ebbed away, served to identify the Brainerd spirit with that of Edwards himself. Jerusha Edwards had cared for the twenty-nine year old missionary through the last months. Four months later she died, age seventeen, unaware that Brainerd's contagious disease had been tuberculosis. Everyone knew that the work Edwards put into the publication of Brainerd's *Diary* and *Journal* was more than the writing of another book; it was a labor of love. Gideon Hawley carried the book in his saddle bag so that "when it seemed he could not endure loneliness and hardship another day, he read a chapter and was spurred to emulation." [7]

---

[1] Winslow, *op. cit.*, 261. Though he could communicate practical matters in the Housatonic language, his repeated efforts to learn the tongue well enough to preach were unsuccessful.

[2] L. J. Trinterud, *The Forming of An American Tradition*, 128.

[3] Kellaway, *op. cit.*, 266.

[4] *Continuation of the Journal*, quoted by Winslow, *op. cit.*, 176.

[5] *Ibid.*, 176–177.

[6] *Ibid.*, 175; These remarks of Whitefield support E. A. Payne's statement: "Whitefield's zeal had been quickened by his contacts in America with Jonathan Edwards." "Toleration and Establishment: A Historical Outline," essay in *From Unity To Uniformity*, G. F. Nuttall and O. Chadwick, eds., 268.

[7] Winslow, *op. cit.*, 252.

Contacts were close between Edwards and the Scottish evangelicals who were the driving power behind the Society in Scotland for the Propagation of Christian Knowledge. Peter Kawerau [1] rightly calls attention to Edwards' own proposal for a Concert of Prayer published at the end of his *Some Thoughts concerning the Present Revival of Religion In New England and the way in which It Ought to be Acknowledged and Promoted* (1742). He proposes that each one consider the needs of his own soul, that ministers should enter actively into the work of advancing the kingdom of Christ, that rich men should contribute temporal goods, that God's people should abound in united fasting and prayer, and that Christians should attend to the moral duties involved in true love for their neighbor.[2] He outlines the proposal for a specific day for united fasting and prayer as follows:

> I have often thought it would be very desirable, and very likely to be followed with a great blessing, if there could be some contrivance for an agreement of all God's people in *America*, who are well-affected to this work, to keep a day of fasting and prayer; wherein we should all unite on the same day, in humbling ourselves before God... that he would continue and still carry on this work, and more abundantly and extensively pour out his Spirit, and particularly upon ministers; and that he would bow the heavens and come down, and erect his glorious kingdom through the earth. – Some perhaps may think that its being all on the same day, is a circumstance of no great consequence; but I cannot be of that mind. Such a circumstance makes the unison and agreement of God's people in his worship the more visible, and puts the greater honour upon God, and would have a great tendency to assist and enliven the devotions of Christians.... Christ delights greatly in the union of his people, as appears by his prayer in the 17th of John: and especially is the appearance of their union in worship lovely and attractive unto him.[3]

Edwards suggests that a group of ministers from all the provinces prepare proposals for such a united day of prayer, then secure the consent of their congregation and forward the signed proposals to a printer. The printed sheets would then "be sent abroad again with the names, that God's people might know who are united with them in the affair." [4] The lack, however, in Edward's proposal is a regular, *recurring* day of prayer. This is taken up in the Concert of Prayer of 1744 by the Scottish ministers and is approved by Edwards in his *Humble Attempt* of 1748.

Besides those awakened to mission interest through the revivals,[5] many were stimulated by Edwards' writings. Wesley was quickened as he read the *Nar-*

---

[1] Kawerau, *Amerika und die Orientalischen Kirchen*, 68, 69.
[2] *Works*, VI 194–206, *Some Thoughts Concerning the Present Revival of Religion in New England...* (1742). Unless otherwise indicated, all further citations will be from *The Works of President Edwards*, 1817.
[3] VI 198.    [4] VI 199.
[5] D. Brainerd, S. Occum (a converted Indian), E. Wheelock, J. Sargeant. Van den Berg, *op. cit.*, 92.

*rative of Surprising Conversions* one day as he walked from London to Oxford.[1] Later he prepared an abridgment of Edwards' *Religious Affections* for publication. William Carey, Samuel Marsden, Henry Martyn, and Philip Doddridge were influenced by Brainerd's *Diary*.[2] Doddridge's book *Rise and Progress of Religion in the Soul* in turn influenced Wilberforce's conversion. Andrew Fuller, a friend of Carey, altered his hyper-Calvinist views as a result of reading Edward's *Discourses on Justification*. Inspired by the plea for united prayer, Fuller and small Baptist groups began prayer meetings in 1784. Carey's famous *Enquiry* and the organization of the Baptist Missionary Society (1792) followed.[3] The London Missionary Society likewise began a monthly Concert of Prayer for missions.[4] As late as 1795, Edwards' early call to united prayer was answered by a group of ministers in Connecticut. This example was followed in various parts of the land, though with no uniform method or specified time. These activities form the prelude to what Latourette has rightly called the great century of mission expansion. Jonathan Edwards was, during the eighteenth century, one of the chief links between the Great Awakening in America and the missionary awakening in Britain. "...without any doubt, the British missionary awakening owes a great deal to the stimuli given by this great Reformed theologian." [5]

Perhaps Edwards' best claim to originality in theology is found in the thesis of the *History of Redemption*. It is clear that this, a theology structured in historical form,[6] was a radical break with the dogmatical structure of traditional Puritan theology. "The real thesis," says Miller, "of the *History of Redemption* is the unity of history." [7] Kawerau stresses the heart of its message: "Die Erlösung durch Christus ist ein allmählicher Prozess, der sich in der Geschichte vollzieht und in der Bekehrung der ganzen Welt seinen Abschluss findet." [8] The divinely directed movement of seventeenth-century church history is seen through Northampton's porthole and expanded to cosmos-embracing dimensions. There God's great redemptive mission clearly and mysteriously moves ahead.

The sermons of 1739 were put into treatise form by John Erskine and first published in 1774 in Edinburgh. Erskine added:

> Though the acute philosopher and deep divine appears in them, yet they are in the general better calculated for the instruction and improvement

---

[1] *Wesley's Journal*, quoted by V. Ferm, *Cooperative Evangelism*, 51.
[2] G. Warneck, *Geschichte der Protestantischen Mission*, 72.
[3] *Ibid.*, 90, 91.
[4] Beaver, *loc. cit.*
[5] Van den Berg, *op. cit.*, 123; cf. also 92–93.
[6] Nelson R. Burr, *op. cit.*, p. 983; J. Ridderbos observes: Al was Edwards' plan om eene theologie in historischen vorm te geven, niet het gelukkigste, dat hij heeft opgevat, toch is het geene geringe verdienste, dat hij hierdoor reeds op het bestaan eener historia revelationis heeft gewezen," in *De Theologie van Jonathan Edwards*, p. 295.
[7] Perry Miller, *op. cit.*, p. 313; cf. also C. C. Goen, who says there are "no discontinuities in history" for Edwards. "A New Departure in Eschatology," *Church History*, Vol. 28, p. 25.
[8] Peter Kawerau. *Amerika und Die Orientalischen Kirchen*, p. 18.

of ordinary Christians, than those of President Edwards' writings, where the abstruse nature of the subject, or the subtle objections of opposers of the truth, led him to more abstract and metaphysical reasonings.[1]

Subsequent publications rapidly followed: Boston, 1782; New York, 1788, 1839, 1840; Worcester, 1808, etc.

It was Edwards' hope and intention shortly before his death to complete "(which I long ago began, not with any view to publication) a great work, which I call a *History of the Work of Redemption*, a body of divinity in an entirely new method, being thrown into the form of a history." [2] These words, written to the trustees of Princeton, were never fulfilled. He arrived at Princeton on February 16, 1758. One week later he was innoculated for smallpox. On March 22 he died.

### 1. The Message of the "History of Redemption"

#### a. God's Great Purpose for the World

The introductory sermon (Isaiah 51:8) grounds the work of redemption upon God's saving acts for the church and his "carrying on" to victory.[3] The saving acts began before the Fall in the Trinitarian "covenant of redemption." [4] When their purpose is achieved, the world ends.[5] All is summed up in the word "redemption," used in a narrower and in a larger sense. In the narrower sense redemption was "begun and finished with Christ's humiliation." In the larger sense it includes "all God's works that were properly preparatory to the purchase, and accomplishing the success of it." [6] Upon this larger sense Edwards builds. "Carrying on," as Edwards likes to call it, binds the parts into the whole. "From generation to generation" in the sermon text means from the beginning to the end. "Redemptively carrying on" points to the purposeful relatedness of history. This is the key to the introductory paragraph:

> The design of this chapter is to comfort the church under her sufferings, and the persecutions of her enemies; and the argument of consolation insisted on, is the constancy and perpetuity of God's mercy and faithfulness towards her, which shall be manifest in continuing to work salvation for her, protecting her against all assaults of her enemies, and carrying her safely through all the changes of the world, and finally, crowning her with victory and deliverance.[7]

As redemption may be understood narrowly or broadly, so with its effect. On the one hand God's work converts, justifies, and glorifies particular souls. But this effect upon individual subjects is taken up into the universal subject and end. Here, like a temple in building, the "many successive works and dispensations of God" are united into one grand goal.[8] The last is the greater, as the whole is greater than the part.

---

[1] V 9, *A History of the Work of Redemption . . .*, 1739.
[2] Quoted from P. Miller, *op. cit.*, 307.
[3] V 11–18, *A History of Redemption* (1739).
[4] V 15.
[5] V 276.
[6] V 14.
[7] V 11.
[8] V 17.

What is the design of this one great work? There are five aspects in it:

It is to put all God's enemies under his feet, and that his goodness may finally appear triumphant over all evil.

God's design was perfectly to restore all the ruins of the fall, so far as concerns the elect part of the world, by his Son....

Another great design of God in the work of redemption, was to gather together in one all things in Christ, in heaven and in earth, i.e., all elect creatures....

God designed by this work to perfect and complete the *glory* of all the elect by Christ.

In all this God designed to accomplish the glory of the blessed Trinity in an eminent degree.[1]

Of these designs, God's great purpose is the salvation of all within the purview of the covenant. That means "the whole course of nature" is subservient to it.[2] It means "every thing in the state of mankind" is taken up into "this great design."[3] The events of providence are all "an orderly series of events, all wisely directed in excellent harmony and consistence, tending all to one end."[4] To this "glorious scheme of providence"[5] even the history of the creation forms only an introduction.[6] "The *glorious issue*" of God's work "shows how much greater the work of redemption is, than the work of creation."[7] Creation is building the house, redemption is using it. Using is more than making. Great events and small "suit the great design of redemption."[8] Redemption so defined is the purpose of all history.

b. God's Purpose Progressively Realized in Three Stages

In the first period of general history, from the fall to the incarnation, the keynote is preparation for Christ's coming. Great revolutions took place. Souls were saved, earnests of the greater harvest. The church, however, was yet a minor.[9] God had laid the foundation immediately after the Fall. The Messianic promise (Gen. 3:15) broke gospel light into dark souls. That light gradually increases.[10] "Christ and his redemption are...the great subject of the history of the Old Testament from the beginning all along."[11]

Not that the growth was steady. Great apostasies, terrifying revolutions and leprous hands thwarted God's building. So at least it seemed. Yet what seemed to be decline turned out to be a gathering of strength. Sometimes swiftly, sometimes painfully slowly, inevitably the new surge came. God was still carrying on.

---

[1] V 18.
[2] V 65.
[3] V 132.
[4] V 275.
[5] V 131.
[6] V 130, 15.
[7] V 272.
[8] V 40.
[9] V 21, 22.
[10] V 51.
[11] V 130.

...so wonderfully were things ordered...that whatever happened was ordered for good to this general design, and made a means of promoting it.... The very decline itself, was one thing that God employed as a further preparation for Christ's coming.[1]

Each decline was followed by a new wave which rose to unprecedented heights. Surges of God's grace were followed by a curse of sin and despair. But the greater crest would come; God's design demanded and his saving acts accomplished it.

The greater preparatory crests came to Adam in Eden, to Noah, Abraham, Moses, and David. The deeper troughs behind the waves came with the Curse, the Flood, the scattering at Babel, the bondage of Egypt, the Wilderness, and the Captivity. But even the greater crests and deeper troughs were made up of the lesser events of empires, seasons, and beggars. Always God was delivering his church in preparation for Christ's kingdom. To quarrel with God's method is nonsense. He could have converted the world instead of drowning it. But He did not. The tide is coming in. Babel and Pharoah must go. In their place will come a new season of building for the eternal kingdom.[2]

Remarkable communications of the Holy Spirit push forward the redemptive purpose. The constant influence of the Spirit attends all of God's ordinances.[3] Yet special new outpourings bring revival. It did in the times of Enoch, Joshua, and Josiah.[4] It is "God's manner, in every remarkable new establishment of the state of his visible church, to afford a remarkable outpouring of his Spirit." [5] The first was during Enoch's life. Men had been saved before, but now there was brought in "a harvest of souls to Christ." [6] This work of the Spirit was but a foundation stone for future outpourings "for the lasting benefit of his church, thenceforward continued in those establishments." [7] Marks of these occasions are always prayer and humility, destruction of God's enemies and the saving of His people.[8]

A grave decline prepared the way for Christ. The glory of Solomon and the temple had marked a glorious crest. But it was long between the full moons of the hand-made temple and the heaven-made one. The dead legal dispensation, the narrowing political horizon, and flickering spiritual hopes darkened Israel's future.[9] The enemy forces multiplied. Heathen philosophers, Caesars, and goddesses were plentiful. Here God took two ways contrary to human reason:

> He brought his own visible people very low, and made them weak; but the Heathen, his enemies, he exalted to the greatest height, for the more glorious triumph of the cross of Christ.[10]

The keynote to the second great period, from the incarnation to the resurrection, is "procuring and purchasing redemption." [11] Thousands of years had

---
[1] V 89.
[2] V 34, 37, 39.
[3] V 30.
[4] V 30, 92, 114.
[5] V 114.
[6] V 30.
[7] V 114.
[8] V 30, 31, 39.
[9] V 90, 91.
[10] V 123.
[11] V 21.

passed. God's saving acts had gone steadily forward, yet the accounts were all debit. Christ's full act of humiliation from the cradle of the womb to that of the grave paid the whole account. The giving of his life was at once the deepest and the highest of suffering and satisfaction for the human sin.[1] "Then was finished that great work, the purchase of our redemption, for which such great preparation had been made from the beginning of the world." [2]

In the last period of world history, from the resurrection to the end of the world, the keynote is accomplishment. This period is that of *"the latter days," "the end of the world," "a new heaven and a new earth," "the kingdom of God."* [3] The design of Christ's humiliation was identical to the design of God's saving work.[4] In principle it was accomplished by Christ's redemptive deeds. Now God is actualizing redemption in the world. Four great crests usher in the perfect age. Each in Scripture is called Christ's coming in his kingdom.[5] With each coming God advances the glorious redemption of his church step by step: to the glorious state of the gospel; to liberty from persecution; to a state of prevalence with truth, liberty, peace and joy; and to consummate glory in heaven. The bitter enemies of the church in each period are terribly destroyed: the Jews at the destruction of Jerusalem, the heathen and heretics to the time of Constantine, the Antichrist in the destruction of papacy and the Mohammedan empire, and all the ungodly in the Gog and Magog battle.[6] What is attained in each is not provisional. In each the world is ending; the eternal kingdom has begun.

> So far as the *kingdom of Christ is set up* in the world, *so far* is the world brought to its end, and the eternal state of things set up – *so far* are all the great changes and revolutions in the world brought to their everlasting issue, and all things come to their ultimate period....[7]
> 
> ...there is in each of these comings of Christ an ending of the old, and a beginning of new heavens and a new earth; or an end of a temporal state of things, and a beginning of an eternal state.[8]

Each new period is thus loaded with eternal meaning. New impulses of the Spirit bring higher crests.[9] Revival and conversion of souls follow in their wake.[10] History presses on to consummation.

The Reformation brought Antichrist half-way to ruin. The pope's authority and dominion were greatly diminished. Satan recast his forces. He would fight to the death. The Council of Trent, secret Roman plots, open wars, and inquisitional persecutions were his agents of fury. When Bohemia and Hungary were overcome, Daniel 7:20, 21 and Revelation 13:7 were fulfilled. Prophecy was ripe. Holland and France, England and Scotland, Spain and Italy were

---

[1] V 133, 142, 143, 150.
[2] V 158.
[3] V 169–171.
[4] V 168.
[5] V 172.
[6] V 171–174.
[7] V 171.
[8] V 173.
[9] V 180, 186, 187, 224, 227.
[10] V 185, 187, 238–240.

drenched with Protestant blood. Now Satan has invaded the sacred precincts of the true Church. Anabaptists, enthusiasts and Quakers, Socinians, Arminians, and, of late, ancient Arianism and Deism—all are agents of the devil, no less.[1]

But the tide is changing. Successes attend the Protestant way. First, there is a great reformation of doctrine under Peter the Great in Muscovy. Second, the gospel is preached to the heathen in America, Muscovy, and the East Indies. Third, a great revival of the practice and power of religion has come through "August Herman Frank" in Germany, and through an outpouring of the Spirit in New England, in Northampton especially.[2]

Only Scriptural prophecy can describe the fall of Antichrist. A very dark time of little faith and infidelity precedes. Such a time has now come. The falling of Antichrist and the rising of the kingdom occurs "swiftly yet *gradually*."[3] God's Spirit will qualify instruments to preach; some converted will win others; one nation will reach out to another. So the Daniel stone "gradually grows."[4] Opposition will be fierce. Heretics, Antichrist, Mohammedans, will be totally overcome. The conversion of Jews and heathen ends their evil.

The prosperous age of the church follows.

> ...this is most properly the time of the kingdom of *heaven upon earth*. Though the kingdom of heaven was in a degree set up soon after Christ's resurrection, and in a further degree in the time of Constantine; and though the Christian church in all ages of it is called *the kingdom of heaven;* yet this is the principal time of *the kingdom of heaven* upon earth, the time principally intended by the prophecies of Daniel whence the Jews took the name of the kingdom of heaven. Now is the principal fulfillment of all the prophecies of the Old Testament which speak of the glorious times of the gospel in the latter days. Though there has been a glorious fulfillment of those prophecies already, in the times of the apostles, and of Constantine; yet the expressions are too high to suit any other time entirely, but that which is to succeed the fall of Antichrist. This is most properly the glorious day of the gospel. Other times are only forerunners and preparatory to this: those were the seed-time, but this is the harvest.[5]

It will be a time of great light and knowledge. Then many of the "Negroes and Indians will be divines" and "excellent books will be published in Africa, in Ethiopia, in Tartary, and other now the most barbarous countries."[6] Other glorious characteristics of the true church prevail: holiness, universal religion

---

[1] V 214–221.

[2] V 221–224. Elsewhere Edwards says: "It is not unlikely that this work of God's Spirit, ... is the dawning, or at least, a prelude of that glorious work of God, so often foretold in scripture, which, in the progress and issue of it, shall renew the world of mankind.... And there are many things that make it probable that this work will begin in *America* ... if these things be so, it gives us more abundant reason to hope that what is now seen in *America*, and especially in *New England*, may prove the dawn of that glorious day...." VI 54, 59, *Some Thoughts Concerning the Present Revival of Religion in New England*..., 1742.

[3] V 238, *A History of Redemption*, 1739.

[4] V 239.   [5] V 250–251.   [6] V 251.

and peace, excellent order in the church, rejoicing, temporal prosperity.[1] Great apostasy cuts the beauty and glory short. Christ comes in judgment. Never shall another soul be converted. Of the many millions brought into the kingdom through all of time, not one shall be lost. Complete is the mystical body of Christ. The decisive words in the work of redemption are uttered: "Come, ye blessed...." "Depart, ye cursed". Heaven has been attained or lost.[2]

## 2. *The Nations and Their Religions*

The condition of the heathen by reason of the Fall is one of total spiritual darkness.[3] Their custom, therefore, of sacrificing to the gods to atone for their sins was derived from the Jews. "The light of nature did not teach them any such thing." [4] Since they practiced this idea of atonement, a way was made for their receiving this great doctrine of the gospel.[5] The scattering of Babel was done in such a way around Canaan as most suited to the design of the future propagation of the gospel. Canaan was strategically located as the center by which Rome and the other countries could be reached.

Edwards believes that all true ideas of God, creation, sacrifice, judgment, and immortality have entered heathenism through outside influences and have been handed down by tradition. Thus Socrates, though greater than Plato, knew less of true religion because he had never been out of Greece, while Plato had contact with Eastern traditions. If the finding out of truth had been a matter of time, the Tartars, Americans, and Africans would have known theology.

> The doctrine of St. Paul, concerning the blindness into which the Gentiles fell, is so confirmed by the state of religion in Africa, America, and even China, where, to this day no advances towards the true religion have been made, that we can no longer be at a loss to judge of the insufficiency of unassisted reason, to dissipate the prejudices of the Heathen world, and open their eyes to religious truths.[6]

This blindness was not due to man's lack of natural capacity or of opportunity to know, but it is due to an evil principle that "hinders the exercises of his *faculties* about the things of religion: exercises for which God has made him well capable, and for which he gives him abundant opportunity." [7]

The counter-strategy of Satan was to lead some nations to the inaccessible regions of America and the northern cold regions.[8]

> Here the many nations of Indians worshipped him as God from age to age, while the gospel was confined to the opposite side of the globe. It is

---

[1] V 252–255.
[2] V 255–270.
[3] V 24.
[4] V 27; cf. also 161.
[5] V 27.
[6] VIII 193, *Miscellaneous Observations*. See especially Chap. VII, "The Insufficiency of Reason as a Substitute for Revelation" (196–214).
[7] II 392–393, *Man's Natural Blindness in the Things of Religion.*
[8] V 40, *A History of Redemption* (1739).

probably supposed, from some remaining accounts, that the occasion of first peopling America was this: that the devil, being alarmed and surprised by the wonderful success of the gospel the first three hundred years after Christ, and by the downfal of the Heathen empire in the time of Constantine – and seeing the gospel spread so fast, and fearing that his Heathenish kingdom would be wholly overthrown through the world – led away a people from the other continent into America, that they might be quite out of the reach of the gospel, that here he might quietly possess them, and reign over them as their god.... However small the propagation of the gospel among the Heathen here in America has been hitherto; yet I think we may well look upon the discovery of so great a part of the world, and bringing the gospel into it, as one thing by which divine providence is preparing the way for the future glorious times of the church.[1]

Heathen philosophies were used by God to reveal the bankruptcy of human wisdom. All the nations, except Israel, were given up to idolatry.[2] Their guilt, by reason of lack of divine revelation, is less than that of those under the preaching of the gospel.[3] Yet, the heathen who opposed God's purpose in history encountered fearful ends "dying miserably, one after another, under exquisite torments of body, and horrors of conscience, with a most visible hand of God upon them." [4] That the gods they worship are no gods, both the gospel and redeemed reason clearly demonstrate.[5] When the western kingdom of Antichrist (the papacy) and the eastern kingdom of Mohammed are destroyed, the glorious times of the church will have arrived.[6] The great pouring out of the Spirit at the end of the age will turn "many from heresy, from Popery, and from other false religions," [7] and Satan's heathen kingdom will be overthrown.[8]

The total incapacity of human reason underscores the absolute necessity of the divine revelation. Mankind is "utterly insufficient to deliver themselves from that gross darkness and misery." "...all the wisdom of the heathen philosophers" could bring no deliverance.[9] Before the coming of Christ, God permitted natural man to do his best towards self-salvation.

> God was pleased to suffer men to do the utmost that they could with human wisdom, and to try the utmost extent of their own understandings in order to find out the way to happiness, before the true light came to enlighten the world. God suffered these great philosophers to try what they could do for six hundred years together; and then it proved by the events of so long a time, that all they could do was in vain; the world not becoming wiser, better, or happier under their instructions, but growing

[1] V 221–222.
[2] V 56, 122.
[3] V 160.
[4] V 198.
[5] V 200–201.
[6] V 207.
[7] V 240.
[8] V 246–247.
[9] V 56–57.

more and more foolish, wicked, and miserable. He suffered this, that it might be seen how far reason and philosophy could go in their highest ascent, that the necessity of a divine teacher might more convincingly appear.[1]

All this served to secure "the more glorious triumph of the cross of Christ."[2] The limitations of human reason confounds the revelation-denying deists as well as the Messiah-denying Jews.[3] The gospel of the crucified Saviour made futile all the learning, philosophy and wit of the Romans, Celsus and Porphyry included.[4] The philosophers tried in vain, but knew not God.[5] "The light of nature, their own reason, and all the wisdom of learned men, signified nothing till the scriptures came." Only these have been successful in bringing men to God.[6] Redeemed reason, as opposed to natural, sees God's design and glory in his works.[7]

### 3. Mission Principles in the "History of Redemption"

#### a. God is the Founder and Lord of the Mission

Redemption is God's great mission in the history of nature, man, and the world. God's righteousness is the cause or root, while his salvation work is the effect or fruit.[8] Salvation is the sum of all God's works. Time itself is the dispensation in which the whole of redemption is worked in the preparation, the purchase, and the accomplishment of the Trinitarian purpose.[9] When man fell, darkness reigned, total darkness. God sent the first gospel light through words to a serpent.[10] He instituted sacrifice and poured out his spirit.[11] He steadily increased gospel light[12] and brought in a harvest of souls.[13] Though his grace seems alternately to prevail and to languish, yet it is growing.[14] God frustrates evil designs and purposes.[15] He fences in his church[16] and renews his covenant in the face of human unfaithfulness.[17] The written word of Scripture is his directory for the way to heaven.[18] Nature fulfills his will.[19] All is gathered into the fulfillment of his purpose in Jesus Christ.[20]

The sovereign pleasure of God is a keystone to Edwards' theology. God is in no way dependent upon His creatures.[21] Mystery clouds His being.[22]

---

[1] V 122.
[2] V 123.
[3] V 125.
[4] V 193.
[5] V 200.
[6] Idem.
[7] V 276.
[8] V 12.
[9] V 14.
[10] V 24.
[11] V 27, 92, 96, 114.
[12] V 32, 33.
[13] V 30.
[14] V 32.
[15] V 34, 37, 39, 65.
[16] V 43.
[17] V 44, 50.
[18] V 57, 58.
[19] V 66, 102.
[20] V 89.
[21] "God stands in no need of creatures and is not profited by them." In *The Philosophy of Jonathan Edwards. From His Private Notebooks*, ed. by H. G. Townsend, 138.
[22] *Ibid.*, 233; P. Miller, *Jonathan Edwards*, 303-304.

Words describing Him are used analogously, but cannot themselves bear the full weight of revelation.[1] The majesty and sufficiency of God is the clue to the theology and philosophy of Edwards.[2] His trembling God-consciousness rejected the humanism in Arminianism and the mechanism in Deism.[3] What one commentator calls Edwards' "emphatic theocentricity"[4] should not be viewed abstractly, but existentially.[5] God is acting, and none can stay His hand. Edwards stands squarely in the tradition of classic Calvinism.

Two matters should be noted here. First, A. A. van Schelven leaves the impression[6] that Edwards' classification as Calvinist is more formal than essential. The fuller quotation in J. Ridderbos[7] correctly suggests that Edwards' views are based upon a deeper source than Calvin. The context from which Edwards is quoted[8] clearly indicates the correctness of the latter interpretation. V. L. Parrington dryly comments: "He was called to be a transcendental emancipator, but he remained a Calvinist."[9] Second, some commentators believe Edwards' views compromised the basic doctrine of God's sovereignty. Note, for example: "Thus the same Edwards who first gives himself so entirely to teaching the absolute sovereignty of God, contributes equally to the bridging of the gulf between God and man. And in the long run his last contribution exerts the stronger influence.... And by so doing he marks the beginning of the end of Puritan theology."[10] H. E. Runner judges Edwards to have compromised Calvinism through a fatal synthesis of it with the idealism of the Cambridge Platonists.[11] The crucial question is whether Edwards is building a new bridge between God and man (i.e. basically using the Platonic one) or whether he is pointing to the bridge in Christ which God has built and which needs to be held in spite of the apparent contradiction inherent in it, the contradiction between absolute sovereignty which creates the gulf and divine love which spans it.

b. Man is the Responsible Object of the Mission

Reproof and encouragement are the two dimensions of the gospel application. First, there is reproof for unbelief. Unbelievers have never "opened the door of their heart to him, but have kept him shut out."[12] They have been deaf to all his calls.[13] They "slight the glorious person, for whose coming God made such great preparation in such a series of wonderful providences from the beginning of the world."[14] This brings greater guilt than the sins of the

---

[1] Ibid., 211–212.
[2] B. B. Warfield, "Jonathan Edwards" in Encyclopedia of Religion and Ethics, Vol. V, 223; V. L. Parrington, The Colonial Mind 1620–1800, 152.
[3] V. L. Parrington, op. cit., 155.
[4] G. Hammar, Christian Realism in Contemporary Theology, 89.
[5] H. Richard Niebuhr, The Kingdom of God in America, 173.
[6] Het Calvinisme gedurende zijn bloeitijd II, Schotland–Engeland–Noord-Amerika, 396.
[7] Ibid., 44.
[8] Freedom of the will, Preface, iii-vi.
[9] Ibid., 163.
[10] W. A. Visser 't Hooft, The Background of the Social Gospel in America, 93.
[11] "The Relation of the Bible to Learning" in Christian Perspectives – 1960, 151–155.
[12] V 159, A History of Redemption (1739).
[13] Idem.
[14] V 160.

worst of heathens.¹ Second, there is reproof for self-righteousness. Since God's work of providence is greater than that of creation, to attempt one's own redemption is greater than to create a world.² Such self-saving effort attempts to make Christ's redemptive acts and God's providences "wild...and transcendent folly." ³ Third, there is reproof for neglect of salvation. Christ's hard labor and suffering certainly merit our labor in seeking salvation.

> God may, through wonderful patience, bear with hardened careless sinners for awhile; but he will not long bear with such despisers of his dear son, and his great salvation, the glory of which he has had so much at heart, before he will utterly consume without remedy or mercy.⁴

The other aspect of the gospel application is encouragement to seeking ones.⁵ Pardon is full and free. Justification in Christ is complete. One need only to come, accept God's salvation and be saved.⁶

---

[1] *Idem.*
[2] V 162.
[3] *Idem.*
[4] V 166.
[5] On the basis of his study of the Edwards sermons in manuscript, Gerstner writes: "Directions for seeking salvation are found in almost every sermon Edwards ever preached. No theme was so much on his heart and lips as this. This was the point of contact between sinners and the gospel, and he was constantly urging it on them." (*Steps To Salvation*, 78.) Some examples from his unpublished sermons follow (all cited from Gerstner on page indicated): "... sinners under concern and distress of mind about the condition of their souls ought to take encouragement from the infinite mercy of God in Christ." – Acts 16 : 29 (21). The call of the gospel is "to sinners universally" – Rev. 3 : 20 (22). "The reason why they don't use the means is not because they could not if they were disposed but because they are not disposed." – Eccles. 4 : 5 (69). "... persons ought to do what they can for their salvation." – Eccl. 9 : 10 (89). "When persons do what they can God usually does that for them that is not in their own power." – Eccles. 4 : 5 (97). "God is pleased commonly to bestow his saving grace on those that diligently .. seek it." – Rom. 3 : 11 (98).
[6] V 166, *A History of Redemption* (1739). The first wave of revival at Northampton in 1734 followed a series of sermons on "Justification by Faith Alone," followed by what Edwards called more practical sermons, e.g. "Pressing into the Kingdom of God," "Ruth's Resolution," and "The Justice of God in the Damnation of Sinners." When they were published in expanded form (*Five Discourses on Important Subjects Nearly Concerning the Great Affair of the Soul's Eternal Salvation*, 1738), Edwards appended a fifth sermon entitled "The Excellency of Christ" with the comment: "... something of the excellency of the Saviour was proper to succeed those things that were to shew the necessity of *salvation*." (VI 211, *Some Thoughts Concerning the Present Revival of Religion in New England*, 1742).

In these sermons Edwards stacks promise upon promise to those who earnestly seek God. "So that it is in mercy to us, as well as for the glory of his own name, that God has appointed such earnest seeking, to be the way in which he will bestow the kingdom of heaven." (from "Pressing into the Kingdom of God" – Lk. 16 : 16, VI 324). But it is the last sermon, "The Excellency of Christ", that page after page gathers the invitations of Scripture to encourage the broken sinner in his "choosing Christ." (VI 427). One passage will illustrate. (Rev. 3 : 20).

> Christ condescends not only to call you to him, but he comes to you; he comes to your door, and there knocks. He might send an officer and seize you as a rebel and vile malefactor; but instead of that, he comes and knocks at your door, .... but he stands there waiting, while you are backward and unwilling. And not only so, but he makes promises what he will do for you, if you will admit him, what privileges he will admit you to; he will "sup with you, and you with him." (VI 423, 424).

Therefore you may be sure Christ will not be backward in saving those who come to him, and trust in him: for he has no desire to frustrate himself in his own work. Neither will God the Father refuse you; for he has no desire to frustrate himself in all that he did for so many hundreds and thousands of years, to prepare the way for salvation of sinners by Christ. Come, therefore, hearken to the sweet and earnest calls of Christ to your soul. Do as he invites and as he commands you, Matt. xi.28–30.[1]

Divine sovereignty and human responsibility are thrown into bold relief. The stark absoluteness of the first could be a fatal compromise with Platonic idealism and rationalism. The urgent necessity for the second could be an equally fatal compromise with Arminian individualism.

Commentators vary widely in their critique of Edwards here. W. A. Visser 't Hooft maintains that through Edwards, Puritanism became Pietism on the one hand [2] and a rationalization of the idea of God on the other.[3] H. E. Runner sees New England Puritanism as different from Genevan Calvinism and, especially through Edwards, the introduction of rational theology.[4] J. Ridderbos finds Edwards' preaching methods Methodistic... "dat den mensch gaarne losmaakt uit zijn kosmisch verband" [5] ...and his theology basically anthropocentric.[6] E. Wolf relates the contradictory elements: "Das theologische Interesse nimmt die (idealistische) Philosophie bewust in Dienst und richtet sich vor allem auf die Lösung des Problems von Determinismus und Freiheit im Rahmen eines kräftigen Harmoniedenkens." [7] Edwards himself elsewhere says: " 'Tis very true that God requires nothing of us as condition of eternal life but what is in our own power, and yet 'tis very true at the same time that it's an utter impossible thing that ever man should do what is necessary in order to salvation, nor do the least towards it, without the almighty operation of the Holy Spirit of God – yea, except everything be entirely wrought by the Spirit of God." Yet this does not "at all excuse persons for not doing such duties as loving God, accepting of Christ...." [8] Edwards held these two aspects in a healthy Biblical tension similar to the genuine Christian paradox of Paul in Phil. 2:12–13.[9] The emphasis upon the free offer of grace to all men and the necessity of conversion both added living depth to the Puritan notion of the full sovereignty of God and opened the wider doors of the Great Awakening in New England.[10]

c. Biblical Revelation is the Norm and Fundament of the Mission

The giving of the written Word was for the advancement of redemption.[11] It serves as "the main instrument employed by Christ" in order to carry on

---

[1] V 167, *A History of Redemption* (1739).
[2] *Op. cit.*, 138ff
[3] *Op. cit.*, 171–172.
[4] *Op. cit.*, 152–153.
[5] *Op. cit.*, 300.
[6] *Op. cit.*, 314.
[7] "Jonathan Edwards," *Die Religion in Geschichte und Gegenwart II*, 309–310.
[8] Townsend, *Philosophy of Jonathan Edwards*, 155, 161.
[9] Hammar, *op. cit.*, 88.
[10] Van den Berg, *op. cit.*, 87.
[11] V 58, *A History of Redemption*, 1739.

his work and to regulate faith, worship, and practice.[1] During the first period of world history additions were gradually made to advance the great building of God's work.[2] Scriptures give account of the whole chain of redemptive events from the beginning to the end in two ways: by history and by prophecy. Hereby is exhibited the "wise and holy designs of the supreme governor in all." The men who wrote were no ordinary penmen but immediately inspired as prophets of the most high God.[3] The same Spirit which prompted them must guide the reader who will learn at Scripture's fountain.[4] Its message serves as "an infallible and perpetual rule of faith and manners to the church." The record of miracles recorded in these writings are "a standing proof of the truth of Christianity to all ages." [5] After the apostles the canon of Scripture is "completed and settled, and a curse denounced against him that adds any thing to it, or diminishes any thing from it." [6] Upon these divine revelations "the church of God has always been built." [7] The future of the church, as the fall of Antichrist, can only be discerned by the prophecies of Scripture.[8] Without the divine light of the Bible, all mankind would be left "in miserable darkness and confusion." [9]

Both the divine initiative in revelation, which had been accentuated by the Puritans all along, and the inner and immediate leading of the Holy Spirit for the believers' understanding of the written Word, which the Separatists were inclined to stress, are held in tension by Edwards.[10] The Bible message is vital for every man. Elsewhere Edwards points out that one does not judge history by history, but by the written word of Scripture.[11] To natural reason Edwards allows no credit in the divine-human reconciliation.[12] And this is evident, that the Scriptures were designed of God to be the proper means to bring the world to the knowledge of himself, rather than human reason, or any thing else." [13] For redeemed reason to remain idle is contrary to God's purpose,

---

[1] *Ibid.*, 58-59.
[2] V 76.
[3] V 126.
[4] V 131.
[5] V 180.
[6] V 183.
[7] V 228, 232.
[8] V 236.
[9] V 277.
[10] H. Richard Niebuhr calls this "the Reformation's paradoxical doctrine of the Word of God" (*op. cit.*, 109).
[11] VI 20-21, from *Some Thoughts Concerning the Present Revival of Religion*, 1742.
[12] J. Ridderbos judges that Edwards leaves Reformed ground on this doctrine: "Zijn pogingen om aan de specifiek Gereformeerde leerstukken een filosofische onderbouw te geven, hebben door overschatting van de rede gefaald." "Jonathan Edwards," *Christelijke Encyclopaedie*, Tweede druk, II, 544. Edwards held "that grace and the exercise of grace is given entirely by the Spirit of God by His free and most arbitrary motions . . . ." (Townsend *op. cit.*, 109) However, the Spirit ordinarily uses "preparatory" convictions of sin to bring men to salvation. "In the more unthinking people, such as husbandmen and the common sort of people who are less used to much reasoning, God commonly works this conviction by begetting in their minds a dreadful idea and notion of the punishment. In the more-knowing and thinking men, the Holy Spirit makes more use of rational deductions to convince them that 'tis worth their while to seek earnestly for salvation. For God makes use of those things, viz., good nature, a good understanding, a rational brain, moral prudence, etc., as far as they hold." (*Ibid*, 110; cf. also 110-113, where Edwards discusses the law of nature, the Spirit's operation, nature, grace, common grace, and common illumination.)
[13] V 201, *A History of Redemption* (1739).

but it operates only on the presupposition of divinely given meaning and light.¹ This light is "immediately imparted to the soul by God, of a different nature from any that is obtained by natural means." ² Revelation through the Scripture and illumination by the Holy Spirit, rather than by reason, is the norm and fundament of the mission.

d. The Spirit working through the Church is the Agent of the Mission

The forward surges of the divine mission inevitably followed new outpourings of the Holy Spirit. The present progress of redemption, as in the past, depends in full upon such divine activity. At the "appointed time" will come the "glorious out-pouring of the Spirit of God" when He "by his own immediate influence" will advance the kingdom of his Son.³ This pouring out will be directed to "the wonderful revival and propagation of religion," ⁴ "reviving those holy doctrines of religion," "turning many from their vice and profaneness," and "bringing vast multitudes savingly home to Christ." ⁵

The pouring out at Pentecost was unique. It marked the beginning of the Christian Church formed from Israel. The Jerusalem church became the "mother of all other churches in the world." ⁶ Then began "that first great dispensation which is called *Christ's coming in his kingdom*." ⁷ "For Christ, having ascended, and received the Holy Spirit, poured it forth abundantly for the conversion of thousands and millions of souls." ⁸ But though the dispensation altered, the church of God in its essentials abides through all time. The pouring out of the Spirit marks each advance in God's redemptive plan.

After the resurrection God established certain specific "means of success" for the propagation of the gospel. These included: ⁹

> 1. The abolishing of the *Jewish dispensation*.
> ...their ceremonial law...would have kept the Gentiles from complying with the true religion. This wall therefore was broken down to make way for the more extensive success of the gospel....
> 2. The next thing in order of time seems to be the appointment of the *Christian Sabbath*.
> ...that joyful day, is appointed to be the day of the church's holy rejoicing to the end of the world, and the day of their stated public worship. And this is a very great and principal means of the success which the gospel has had in the world.
> 3. The next thing was Christ's appointment of the *gospel ministry*....
> (1) The appointment of the *office* of the gospel ministry. – For this com-

---

[1] H. Richard Niebuhr says: The Puritans "differed from the humanist rationalists of their day not in rejecting reason but in refusing the presuppositions of humanism and in making the presuppositions of the Christian revelation their own." (*op. cit.*, 107–108).
[2] VIII 5, from "A Divine and Supernatural Light ...," (1734).
[3] V 227, *A History of Redemption* (1739).
[4] V 239.
[5] V 240.
[6] V 186.
[7] V 187.
[8] V 185.
[9] V 179–180.

mission which Christ gives to his apostles, in the most essential parts of it, belongs to all ministers....[1]

(2) Something peculiar in this commission, viz. to go forth *from one nation to another*, preaching the gospel in all the world.

(3) Here is an appointment of Christian *baptism*...established as an ordinance to be upheld in the Christian church to the end of the world. – The ordinance of the Lord's supper had been established before, just before Christ's crucifixion.

Other means of success were: full revelation of more obscure Old Testament doctrines, appointment of deacons, the work of the apostle Paul, institution of ecclesiastical councils, and the written word of God.[2] Edwards has no patience with those who undervalue the divinely appointed means.[3] The church remains "under the means of grace" to the end of history.[4]

This work will be accomplished by *means*, by the preaching of the gospel, and the use of the ordinary means of grace, and so shall be *gradually* brought to pass. Some shall be converted, and be the means of others conversion. God's spirit shall be poured out first to raise up instruments, and then those instruments shall be used with success.[5]

God's whole work of redemption includes the conversion of particular persons but this is taken up into the larger purpose of the union of all elect in Christ.[6] Through the covenant of grace this is accomplished.[7] The "great condition of the covenant of grace" is faith.[8] Through this everlasting covenant Christ "offers to poor sinners... the same sure mercies" in every age.[9] The success of Christ's purpose "consists in the bestowment of grace on the elect."[10] The gathering of the elect is not as individuals, but as part of "the mystical body of Christ, which has been growing since it first began in the days of Adam" until it becomes complete "having every one of its members."[11] "What is *real* in the union between Christ and His people, is the foundation of what

---

[1] Elsewhere Edwards says: "It is God's revealed will that whenever that glorious revival of religion and reformation of the world, so often spoken of in his Word, is accomplished, it should be principally by the labors of his ministers." (In *Thoughts on the Revival of Religion*, II, J. C. Wolf, *op. cit.*, 49).

[2] V 180–183, *A History of Redemption* (1739).

[3] In *Thoughts on the Revival of Religion*, Wolf, *op. cit.*, 63–64. In the unpublished sermons, Gerstner found that Edwards repeatedly emphasized to his congregation the necessity of the use of the means of grace. Cf. *Steps to Salvation*, 20, 48f., 72, 89ff., 106ff.

[4] V 259–260, *A History of Redemption* (1739).

[5] V 238.

[6] V 16, 19.

[7] V 12. Gerstner found frequent sermon references to the covenant of grace. These he presents in his concluding chapter (xix: "The Covenantal Frame of Reference") and observes: "We have considered Edwards' doctrine of the covenant that we may understand the frame of reference in which the various steps to salvation are to be comprehended. These steps are but the realizations of this covenant" (188).

[8] V 44.

[9] V 80.

[10] V 259.

[11] V 258. "The covenant of grace was revealed and established all along."

is *legal*."¹ The church on earth is thus inseparable from that in heaven and the embodiment of God's redemptive purpose in and beyond time. The preaching, the ordinances, the written word of God, and through these the Holy Spirit, work the covenant of grace through the church.

e. The Establishment of God's Eternal Kingdom is the Goal of the Mission

The "age of the Spirit" as Increase and Cotton Mather had understood it at the turn of the century was taken up into Edwards' periodization of world history corresponding to the cycles of the book of Revelation.² It was stage three in the series of the four comings of Christ in his kingdom. Each of these kingdom comings in the New Testament period was a real and permanent step forward.³ The kingdom of heaven is "that evangelical state of things in the church, and in the world, wherein consists the success of Christ's redemption in this period."⁴ Insofar as the kingdom is set up, insofar is the eternal state of things set up, so far also are the first heavens and the first earth come to an end and the new, everlasting heavens and earth established in their place.⁵ This great work of God is wrought gradually. Certain signs and events might suggest a sudden fall of Satan's kingdom, yet "all will not be accomplished at once, as by some great miracle, like the resurrection of the dead."⁶ Towards the end of this period of Antichrist, conversion will break forth in an unprecedented way.

> God, by pouring out his Holy Spirit, will furnish men to be glorious instruments of carrying on this work; will fill them with knowledge and wisdom, and fervent zeal for the promoting the kingdom of Christ, and the salvation of souls, and propagating the gospel in the world. The gospel shall begin to be preached with abundantly greater clearness and power than had heretofore been. This great work of God shall be brought to pass by the preaching of the gospel....⁷

What in modern mission theology is called the "already" and the "not yet" is in Edwards the clue to his eschatological vision.⁸ The "gradually growing" signifies the already, and the final judgment of history, the not yet. "The *glorious issue* of this whole affair [is] in the perfect and eternal destruction of the wicked, and in the consummate glory of the righteous."⁹ This decisive

---

¹ Quoted by T. A. Schafer in "Jonathan Edwards' Conception of the Church," *Church History*, 24 (1954).
² V 172–175, 207, *A History of Redemption* (1739).
³ V 171.
⁴ *Idem.*
⁵ *Idem.*
⁶ V 238.
⁷ V 239–240.
⁸ This distinction made in the Dutch report to the International Missionary Council at Willingen (1953) at heart reflects Edwards' concern to consider present kingdom gains as real and abiding and kingdom expectations as future. Cf. W. Andersen, *Toward a Theology of Missions*, 57.
⁹ V 272, *A History of Redemption* (1739).

judgment of history has its beginnings in God's judgments in time. But like the act of redeeming grace, it finds its ultimate fulfillment when time is full. It will not do to philosophize the concreteness of the historical end of human history into the niceties of rational thought.[1] With stark realism and utter simplicity Edwards expects at God's appointment the final trumpet call.

The unity of God's design and way of working in history can everywhere be seen. Most particularly in the conversion and subsequent blessings and trials of a single person or community is the character of the Whole clearly described. What happened to Abigail and Phoebe, made famous by the *Narrative*, and to Sarah, Edwards' wife, happens to the world. The history of their redemption adequately reflects that of the church of God. Revival at Northampton was an earnest of that one which will sweep in the glorious age.[2]

A particular soul is converted. Gospel light so begun increases. Sometimes it burns brightly, sometimes dimly. Corruption threatens, but grace revives. Through it all grace is growing, growing to perfection. One day, in glory, the kingdom of Christ in the soul will be complete.[3] Precisely so is it in Northampton, ...in America, ...in the world, ...in all of history. Grace is growing, the kingdom is building, the waves of the Spirit are rising higher, the end is becoming reality.

---

[1] Perry Miller suggests that on the surface level Edwards' version of history is rude, primitive and pedantic. However, Edwards had, Miller continues, a deeper meaning. Judgment is an eternal event, incommensurate with time and matter-of-factness. He "preached a final judgment that does not arrive in time, but is every moment renewed. It does not, in scientific fact, belong to history at all, but must be told for the sake of the artistic coherence of the historical conception ... it is pronounced anew every moment, and is declared as much at this moment as it shall be in any hypothetical future" (*op. cit.*, 330). This seems not so much like Edwards' philosophy of history as Miller's.

[2] P. Miller comments: "... the *History of Redemption* ... is the history of Northampton writ large." (*op. cit.*, 315).

[3] V 32, *A History of Redemption* (1739).

# CONCLUSION

The attitude of the Puritans towards missions was a positive one. We have seen how Sibbes' theological position stressed the need for conversion and for spreading the gospel. The implications were drawn out by Baxter, especially for the evangelization of heathen lands. Eliot's commitment to Reformed theology and lifetime dedication to the Indians united to form a powerful incentive to Protestant missions. The practical Mather and the theologically-minded Edwards combined the chief Calvinistic doctrines, as understood by Sibbes, with active participation in the New England mission to American and Indian unbelief. The themes we have found to be determinative for the Puritans are significant elements in the recent emphasis on what J. Blauw has called the consideration of missions as a commission from God, a commission for which "the question of a Biblical and theological foundation for mission becomes important." [1]

### A. THE CONVERSION OF MAN

The soteriological consideration that men must be brought to personal conversion dominates the Puritan message. The practical use of doctrine was at the heart of Puritan preaching, no doubt influenced by Petrus Ramus (1515–1572).[2] The idea behind William Perkins' "golden chain of salvation" was akin to that of the Heidelberg Catechism. What does this doctrine "benefit" you? [3] The direct application of spiritual truth to man's situation was the Puritan purpose in preaching.

What was the human need to which they preached? Their anthropology was essentially a realistic one, accenting man's total depravity. Ever since Adam, all the Puritans proclaimed, man has been a slave to sin. Not only ignorance of the divine will, but obstinate perversion from the divine way, make up the human character.[4] Adam's sin left man's nature dead. This, however, did not

---

[1] J. Blauw, *The Missionary Nature of the Church*, 9.
[2] G. P. Hartvelt has indicated the implications of Peter Ramus' idea of "logic," also incidentally for the Puritans, in his perceptive article concerning the analytical and synthetical approaches to dogmatics. Hartvelt cites for his Puritan sources Perry Miller's explicit treatment of this matter in Miller's *The New England Mind*, the 17th Century. Cf. especially 116–153. ("Over de methode der dogmatiek in de eeuw der Reformatie" in *Gereformeerd Theologisch Tijdschrift*, LXII [1962], 97–149.)
[3] This phrase recurs frequently in the Heidelberg Catechism, e.g., Question 28: "What benefit do we derive from the knowledge of God's creation and providence?" (Thomas F. Torrance, *The School of Faith*, p. 73. Cf. also questions 1, 2, 36, 43, 45, 49, 51, 52, 57, 58, 59. *Ibid.*, 67–79.)
[4] The *perversion* of what good remains in man as God's image-bearer and as constant receiver of God's gifts is central here. J. H. Bavinck calls this activity of the unbeliever "verdringen en vervangen," (*Religieus Besef en Christelijk Geloof*, 171–180) as based upon his interpreta-

destroy man's rational and volitional faculties. In these God's image in a broad sense remains imprinted. To man's rational faculty God addresses himself[1] in the books of nature and of Scripture.[2] Although nature may point to some general truths and fulfill certain preparatory functions,[3] Scripture provides the knowledge of God's way of salvation in Jesus Christ. Such knowledge informs man's intellect, but only the direct working of the Holy Spirit can change man's corrupted will. Thus, only God's electing grace in Christ can account for a changed heart in man.[4]

---

tion of Romans 1. W. Freytag describes man as having an evil will that opposes God and a religious life that "imprisons him against Christ.... His ears are stopped to the message of Christ." (*The Gospel and the Religions*, 42–43.)

[1] The fact of man's "addressability" is what has come to be called the "contact point" for the gospel. Bavinck points out that the only true "aanknopingspunt" lies in general revelation, which becomes real in "de symbiose van mens en wereld." Missionary preaching is secure only when it bears the certainty that God has been concerned with man for a long time, but man has not understood. (*op. cit.*, 163–165.) So H. Kraemer says:

> General revelation can henceforth only mean that God shines revealingly through the works of His creation (nature), through the thirst and quest for truth and beauty, through conscience and the thirst and quest for goodness, which throbs in man even in his condition of forlorn sinfulness, because God is continuously occupying Himself and wrestling with man, in all ages and with all peoples. (*The Christian Message in a Non-Christian World*, 125.)

Kraemer also places a great deal of emphasis upon the character of the missionary: "This one point of contact" upon which all others depend "is the disposition and attitude of the missionary." (*op. cit.*, 140.) Van Ruler overemphasizes Kraemer's latter statement without giving full weight to the former, with which he agrees: "God zelf is het aanknopingspunt voor alle apostolische arbeid; God zelf, gelijk Hij van overlang bij de natuurlijke mens is, met hem bezig is en met hem worstelt." (*Theologie van het Apostolaat*, 30.)

[2] F. W. A. Korff insists that mankind in the whole of his existence is continually being addressed by God. "Het is een onbijbelsche, onchristelijke gedachte, dat de zondige wereld geheel buiten betrekking tot God zou staan. De mensch heeft in zijn zonde God verlaten, maar daarom heeft God den mensch nog niet geheel verlaten" (*Het Christelijke Geloof en de Niet-Christelijke Godsdiensten*, 79 f.); and later: "Dat beteekent dus, dat de mensch in zijn religie niet slechts met zijn goden te maken heeft ... maar de theologie weet iets anders, zij weet, dat de mensch in zijn geheele existentie en dus ook in zijn religie, te maken heeft met God." (*Ibid.*, 80.)

[3] Kraemer seems to disagree here: "The function of natural theology will henceforth be, not to construe preparatory stages and draw unbroken, continuous lines of religious development ending and reaching their summit in Christ, but in the light of the Christian revelation to lay bare the dialectical condition not only of the non-Christian religions but of *all* the human attempts towards apprehension of the totality of existence." (*op. cit.*, 125.) However, the Puritans, though they spoke of preparatory steps, pointed always to the qualitative difference between the unbeliever and believer.

[4] Max Warren succinctly describes the change: " 'The structure of evil' here referred to is that solidarity of mankind in its sheer need, born of its unwillingness to be in unity with the will of God, which Paul laconically calls sin. The argument of Romans 5.12–21 is based on the two structures – the structure of sin which is matched by the structure of grace. Man in the solidarity of his sin is rescued and set in a solidarity of grace. As we might say, paraphrasing Paul in the setting of our contemporary problem, the collective 'Adam' is by grace refashioned into the collective 'Christ'. According to the New Testament this collective 'Christ' is Christ in His Church." (*The Christian Mission*, 80.)

The message of the Scriptures is Jesus Christ. By his work redemption has come for God's people. Not that the operation of grace is restricted to them. The Puritans emphasized that by his death Christ has procured grace for all men. What the Puritans called common or universal grace brought blessings for every man.[1] As a result of this grace man can perform formal actions of approach to the Christian faith. The fact that, to use Baxter's figure, drunkards could have avoided the saloon and indifferent people could have gone to church illustrates man's natural (Eliot says "spontaneous") will. But the common grace that makes fulfillment of general duties possible does not heal a man's will. Universal grace is sufficient for salvation in the sense that God will give the special grace to find salvation, provided man faithfully does what he can in order to seek it. Universal grace is insufficient in the sense that man cannot be saved without receiving special grace. Baxter, who particularly develops the implications between universal and special grace, makes clear that although all grace alike flows from Christ's redemptive work, yet a qualitative difference comes when man is reconciled to God. Baxter held, with regard to the heathen who never knew Christ incarnate, that the possibility of their salvation could not be summarily dismissed. However, from what he knew of the heathen, he judged the possibility of their salvation to be slight. His objection was to the categorical universal negative that some insisted upon.

The work of the Holy Spirit was particularly emphasized in Puritan thought.[2] The Spirit constituted the core of the mystery of salvation. He brought God's presence into human hearts. He changed corrupt wills. He persuaded sinners to seek salvation. He made Scriptural truths take root in stony hearts. But more still, he formed the connecting link between divine sovereignty and human accountability.[3] Upon these two poles every Puritan insisted. If grace is really grace, free and unmerited, God dispenses it as he wills. The truth that this

---

[1] For a recent discussion on common grace, see G. C. Berkouwer, *De Algemene Openbaring* (also published in English under the title: *General Revelation*.) For our problem, see especially Chapter VII, "Openbaring en Kennis," pp. 107–145. Cf. also J. H. Bavinck, *op. cit.*, 177ff. Both of these theologians, like Korff and Kraemer, disagree with Barth in his rejection of common grace.

[2] G. F. Nuttall has clearly shown the centrality of the work of the Holy Spirit in Puritan theology in his *The Holy Spirit in Puritan Faith and Experience*. The doctrine of the Holy Spirit, Nuttall affirms, "received a more thorough and detailed consideration from the Puritans of seventeenth-century England than it has received at any other time in Christian history." (*op. cit.*, viii.)

[3] "This same dialectical structure is the core of the whole problem of the point of contact: divine grace and human responsiveness are its components; yet the fact of human responsiveness does not impair the exclusive causality of grace in the whole process." God, after all, makes the seed grow. (H. Kraemer, *op. cit.*, 134.) The use of the word "causality" has occasioned much confusion in the matter of God's relation to man. When it is understood in a mechanistic way, as Berkouwer has indicated, the danger is great – if not inevitable – that one falls into either determinism or synergism. (*op. cit.*, 221.) Though Kraemer uses "causality" (see above), he does not use it in a scholastic way. Rather, he is concerned about "the divine initiative" to restore the "fundamentally defective" relation between man and God. The essence of this divine initiative is "the forgiveness of sins as God's sovereign act of grace through Christ." (*op. cit.*, preface to the second edition.)

special grace goes to some and not to others, no man can understand.[1] We only know according to both the Scriptures and experience, that this is so.[2] No logical principle is operative here.[3] Predestination is the Biblical way of describing God's free and sovereign good will in dispensing saving grace.[4] History is the theatre in which divine providence is fulfilling the divine purpose.[5]

Election and reprobation are not to be considered equally ultimate.[6] Election has primary reference to grace. All grace is redemptive in character. Election has to do with God's redeeming activity in Christ.[7] Men are elect in

---

[1] "The doctrine of the universal Sovereignty of the divine will is paralysing so long as it is doctrine only; but when it is matter of personal experience, it becomes impulse and energy and inspiration." (W. Temple, *Nature, Man and God*, 381.)

[2] "Yet we cannot escape the doctrine of Election in some form; it is not so much an inference as the only possible reading of the facts when Theism is accepted." (Temple, *op. cit.*, 403.)

[3] "No man can make a general or individual judgment on this question when it falls outside the correlation of faith." (P. Tillich, *Systematic Theology* I, 269-270.)

[4] Van Ruler sees predestination as an expression of the living God, active in his world. "Hij zelf is bezig! Hij zelf is een instantie! Alle eschatologisch-historische denken zal met onvruchtbaarheid en onzuiverheid geslagen blijven, zolang men weigert, deze praedestinatiaanse dimensie, deze dimensie van God zélf, die handelt, er in op te nemen." (*op cit.*, 19.)

[5] This is nowhere (to my knowledge) better expressed than in Herbert Butterfield's *Christianity and History*, Chap. 5, "Providence and the Historical Process." He concludes:

> All these things considered I do not see why Christians should be shy of trusting in Providence, therefore, floating on it so to speak, leaning on it and making alliance with it, regarding it as a living and active agency both in ourselves and in its movement over the length and breadth of history. It is a special Providence for the religious mind and in the history of Christianity – a special Providence for those who consciously seek to be in alliance with it – but we cannot make terms with it or demand that it give us either victory in war or exemption from cataclysm, and even for Christians Richard Baxter provided an object-lesson when he wrote concerning the Great Plague:
> 'At first so few of the religiouser sort were taken away that (according to the mode of too many such) they began to be puffed up and boast of the great differences which God did make. But quickly after that they all fell alike.'
> From which we must conclude that Providence at least is not a thing to be presumed upon; and indeed the Christian knows that it gives him no guarantee against martyrdom for the faith. What it does guarantee so exultantly in the New Testament is a mission in the world and the kind of triumph that may come out of apparent defeat – the kind of good that can be wrested out of evil. (112.)

[6] On this matter, Berkouwer (*De Verkiezing Gods*, 214, 222) disagrees with C. van Til (*The Defense of the Faith*), who affirms that rejection of the "equal ultimacy" necessarily involves Arminianism. Berkouwer shows that Calvin, though he, with help of the "cause" concept, affirms that nothing occurs outside the counsel of God, yet he directly proceeds to emphasize man's sin as the real "cause" of judgment. Man is so surely the cause of his own reprobation, according to Calvin, that he asks why man should even look in heaven for a cause. (Berkouwer, *op. cit.*, 222.) Cf. James Daane, "The State of Theology in the Church", *The Reformed Journal*, VII September (1957), 3-17.

[7] True missions depend upon election. "Wie de verkiezing en het daarin geschonken *heil* misverstaat, kán geen ware zending meer drijven, omdat de souvereine vrijheid der genade is weggenomen." (Berkouwer, *op. cit.*, 388.) The doctrine of election, he continues, is the powerful divine stimulant to preaching: "Deze belijdenis der verkiezing is geen bedreiging van die prediking, maar haar geweldige Goddelijke stimulans." (*Ibid.*, 290.)

Christ, only by his grace. Election in grace, therefore, becomes a change from being dead in sin to being alive in Christ. Reprobation is a concept of a different order. God does not have to will that man shall be condemned. By sin man is condemned already. God does not will a nothing. It would be ridiculous to maintain that God must will not to will what will not come to pass. The possibilities for such negating decisions are infinite. Before the mystery of why God does not effect the salvation of all, man must be silent. God's ways are incomprehensible. We do know, these Puritans affirm, that judgment is just and that every man is punished for his own sin – inherited and personal. Man wills his own judgment; he chooses momentary pleasures above eternal joy, sinner-hood above saint-hood. To use Baxter's summary again: all evil is of man, all good is of God.[1]

The soteriological motive stems from the above anthropological considerations. The utter lostness of man apart from God and the utter impossibility of salvation apart from grace were problems calling for resolution. In this respect all men, whether the lawyers at Grey's Inn or the Indians in America, were alike. Sibbes and Baxter were as deeply filled with compassion for their hearers and as vitally concerned for their souls, as Eliot, Mather, and Edwards were. There was no distinction here between Jews and Indians, between unbelievers in the church and those outside. The sense of urgency for conversion was frequently heightened by an appeal to the last judgment, especially by Baxter, Eliot, and Edwards. However, this fear motive remained secondary; Baxter stated this explicitly, Eliot turned Indians to constructive action, and Edwards' judgment sermons constituted but a small part of his preaching. Rather, love for the sinner and concern for his present and eternal state provided the basic motivation in the attempt to secure his conversion. The love of Christ constrains me,[2] says Baxter, to seek the conversion of my neighbor. When I thus love my neighbor, my own love for God grows.

Here is one key to the Puritan sense of missions. Sibbes affirmed that the nature of light and love is to be communicative. Divine love has come through

---

[1] Others must judge to what extent nuances of interpretation are present in Calvin's teaching (original Calvinism). Like Calvin, the Puritans develop the concept of common grace and attribute it solely to the working of the Holy Spirit. Likewise, they do not coordinate election and reprobation as if God were ultimately the author and cause of both. However, the pointing to preparatory steps to or the seeking of salvation seems to me to receive more emphasis in Puritanism than it did for Calvin. Brunner says on this point of doctrine: "The *sola gratia* and Predestination mean the same thing, namely, that the true Good lies only in the power of God and not in that of man; that no other human goodness and good conduct exists save that which is based on the free gift of God." (*The Divine Imperative*, 58.) It is difficult to reconcile this judgment with his subsequent comment: "... how deep, at all points, is the gulf between the Reformed Faith and Puritanism." (*Ibid.*, 502.)

[2] In this Biblical phrase, J. van den Berg finds the key to the missionary awakening of the eighteenth century. (*op. cit.*, 213.) George Mosse puts the question well, whether, rather than seeking to relate the political theory of the Puritans with the growth of the democratic idea, it would not be better to consider the stress they laid upon the public good over private interest in restructuring society. As we have seen, this emphasis on the public good played a significant role in Baxter's writings. (*Archiv für Reformationsgeschichte*, LV, Germany [1964].)

Christ into human hearts.[1] Every Christian must, therefore, show Christ. It is not a matter of choice.[2] Mather stresses this in his *Nets of Salvation*, and he himself sought out the Boston Jews. The primary methodology for the spread of the gospel is primarily based upon this conception of the nature of faith. In an age when Protestant eyes were generally dimmed to white harvest fields in other lands, here was a truly Biblical and evangelical call for every Christian to witness in his place. Teaching and preaching the message of redemption issued from a true recognition of the depth of man's need.[3] To those who were the chief agents in this we shall turn in a moment. But here we should recall that condemnation of the sinner was due to perverted knowledge or ignorance of the message of salvation and a perverted will. Man could do two things: he could learn about the way of salvation, and he could will to take certain steps which, though not in themselves saving, at least placed him in the context in which God usually brought salvation. The minister and the ordinary Christian alike could, out of concern for a man's need, teach him the gospel and encourage him to use the divinely appointed means. Baxter preached, wrote,

---

[1] Kraemer concludes his *Christian Message:*
> The undying fire, however, without which all our endeavours are nothing and all our missionary enthusiasm is powerless, is only kindled by the faith and prayer which are born from the vision of the triumphant Divine Love that burns in the heart of the Universe and which became incarnated in Jesus Christ, our Lord. (445)

[2] Harry Boer compares the command to witness with the commands "to be reproductive, to subdue the earth, and to rule over the animals that inhabit it." These commands are more than simply commands. They are the "*organic law* which enters into the very fibre of man's being, which penetrates and permeates his entire constitution." Awareness of this law is not necessary in order to obey it.
> Men observe this law because their nature, their whole being, drives them to obey it. Not to live in accordance with this law is to deny the human nature with which man was created. Men can rebel against its requirements, they can limit its effectiveness, but essentially they cannot escape it, they cannot not-obey it. Even those who are aware of the primordial promulgation of this law and who willingly observe it, do so not so much consciously as instinctively, spontaneously. It is only when men try to evade or escape the law of their natural being that this law becomes a command for them. (*Pentecost and Missions*, 121.)

Command is external, Boer continues; this law is part of being. So is it with the command to witness.
> The Great Commission as the divine mandate to the Church to be a witnessing Church, is not only a law similar to that which was promulgated at the beginning of human history, but *it is its spiritual counterpart in the new creation*. It is a statement of the task of the renewed humanity as the other is a statement of the task of old humanity. The urge to witness is inborn in the Church, it is given with her nature, with her very being. She cannot not-witness. She has this being because of the Spirit who indwells her. Pentecost made the Church a witnessing Church because at Pentecost the witnessing Spirit identified Himself with the Church and made the Great Commission the law of her life. (*Ibid.*, 122.)

[3] Only a true recognition of the depth of human need and the little the world has to offer in meeting that need places preaching in the right perspective. Men are addressed, not out of election, but as personally elected out of darkness into light. "Deze blijvende herinnering is de enige bescherming tegen alle lijdelijkheid en tegen alle verschraling van haar [nl. de gemeente] missionaire roeping in de wereld." (Berkouwer, *op. cit.*, 308.)

and taught in homes. He insisted that fathers ought to teach their families, masters their servants, and every man his neighbor. English and American Puritans alike made wide use of the catechetical approach and asked a substantial knowledge of Christian doctrine as a condition for church membership.[1] Eliot's plea for schools in every New England town and his establishment of Indian schools stem from a conviction that God requires education to the truth. Mather's personal literature crusade and Edwards' demand for sound Christians and his doctrinal sermons further indicate the intellectual approach.

But human depravity rested as well in a corrupt will. Men must be convinced to choose the right way. God holds each man accountable for his own sin. Your sin, the Puritans boldly announced, damns you. This does not please God, nor the preacher, nor your Christian friends. All desire your conversion. At this point we find various emphases in the appeal for conversion. Sibbes was usually gentle, though he judged that sometimes harsh and threatening words were needed. Baxter pleaded God's desire for man's conversion but used nearly every conceivable motive to stimulate response. Eliot commonly began with the two states of heaven and hell, speaking in a didactic and catechetical manner. Mather's *Magnalia* shows that the New England Puritans frequently saw misfortune as God's judgment. These "special" providences frequently became sermonic meat for pronouncement of woes and encouragement to repentance. Sermon titles indicate an increasing concern for the Christian life. Missions by the beginning of the eighteenth century were being directed more and more to the non-churchgoer and to the heathen. Edwards, however, addressed himself to guilty men in the church, under the judgment of God. Again, as in seventeenth-century Puritanism, the urgency and necessity of personal conversion was thrust into the foreground. No unconverted man enters heaven or escapes hell. In Mather's prime, men had gotten into the habit of judging most people Christian by their conduct. Now Christians sure of their faith were few indeed! Thousands of uncommitted, indifferent, and uncertain people became converted. Once again motives for conversion ranged the full gamut from the beauty and marvel of God's redeeming love to fear of coming into judgment. The emphasis was, still, that men are condemned because they so choose, and saved while seeking; for those who seek, they were assured, would find.

To a great extent the goal of the mission was simply the conversion of souls. No matter was greater, since this was God's concern in sending his Son. Jesus

---

[1] This is similar to the practice of the second-century church. A. Harnack writes: "No less important than baptism itself was the preparation for it . . . . The pagan who desired to become a Christian was not baptized there and then. When his heart had been stirred by the broad outlines of the preaching of the *one* God and the Lord Jesus Christ as saviour and redeemer, he was then shown the will and law of God, and what was meant by renouncing idolatry. No summary doctrines were laid down, but the 'two ways' were put before him in a most comprehensive and thoroughgoing fashion; every sin was tracked to its lurking-place within. He had to renounce all sins and assent to the law of God, nor was he baptized until the church was convinced that he knew the moral code and desired to follow it." (*The Mission and Expansion of Christianity in the First Three Centuries*, 391.)

was the greatest soul-winner that ever lived, and Paul followed his example. God will be satisfied with no less from us, and our neighbors need nothing more.

The Puritans addressed themselves to man's temporal need as well. The concern for education, gifts for the poor, charity schools, and other forms of philanthropy, are evidence enough. Baxter's *Christian Directory* has intense passages crying for social justice. Eliot's encouragement of the Indians to care for their own poor and Mather's efforts and generosity for the schooling of Negro and Indian children and the collections of his church for the poor indicate a deep humanitarianism that implemented their soteriological concern. Though Puritans generally did not totally reject slavery, for example, yet men like Baxter and Eliot were forerunners in asking for limitations upon the conditions under which men could be put into slavery, e.g., prisoners of war and criminals, and frequently in calling for limitations to length of servitude.[1] Eliot, Mather, and Edwards fought for civil justice for the Indians. The establishment of the Corporation for the Propagation of the Gospel was due both to a pity for the poor natives and to a genuine desire to bring God's love.

The humanitarian motive, however, was not permitted to eclipse the soteriological one. The burning conviction was that the souls of men were of far greater importance than their bodies. The greatest danger was that an experiential concern for one's own soul tended to dim the wonder of the gospel message, the height and the depth of God's love in Christ to man. Thus, there are moments when particularly Baxter and Edwards hammer home the despicableness of man's sin and the awfulness of his eternal state. This emphasis sometimes tended to eclipse the good news of God's love for man which must be the fountain from which flows the message of forgiveness and reconciliation to the sinner. Edwards' "Sinners in the Hands of an Angry God" is deficient on this score. However, this sermon indicates the negative aspect of a total message that rarely was absent, God's free grace in forgiving repentant and seeking sinners. Compassionate love demanded the awakening of men to a sense of need for reconciliation with God.

### B. THE ROLE OF THE CHURCH

For the Puritan the church had a double nature. First, she was the mystical body of Christ, the communion of all true believers. Membership in the church, in this sense, did not depend upon attendance at the preaching and the sacraments or living a holy life, though all of these were considered important. Rather, membership in the body of believers depended upon faith as fulfillment of the covenant of sovereign grace,[2] knowing God feelingly, as Eliot had put it.

---

[1] Lauber, *Indian Slavery In Colonial Times*, 305.
[2] G. van der Leeuw (Theologia II, *Inleiding tot de Phaenomenologie van den Godsdienst*, 94) emphasizes this aspect of the church as the "fellowship." "Daarom is de kerk eigenlijk geen 'phaenomeen', doch slechts te benaderen voor het geloof. De kerk kan men niet beschrijven, men moet haar binnentreden." He seems, however, to leave room for the church as institute as well. The church "is zoowel gemeenschap als verbond. Men wordt in haar geboren, maar ook gedoopt; men is er in, maar men treedt ook toe." (*Idem.*)

But not all who had knowledge of God had it experientially. These, with those of the first group, were members of the institutional church. There is then, in the second place, the organized form of the church which bears the divine sanction and call. To her are entrusted the ordinances of furthering and consolidating the advance of Christ's kingdom. The church thus has a two-fold character: as gathering of the members of the body, and as means to further the gospel.[1]

In order to fulfill the call of spreading the gospel, the Puritans we have considered stressed the need for the unity of the church. Sibbes' ecclesiology left no room for men to break from the church on non-essential matters. Eliot, Mather, and Edwards are cited by Yoder as having made significant contributions to the beginnings of the ecumenical awakening.[2] Eliot fully agreed with Baxter in his distress concerning the brokenness of the church. Baxter judged that there was no greater hindrance to missions than disunity.[3]

Yoder points out that "the more conservative and less irenic colony of Massachusetts produced in the 17th and 18th centuries at least three prophets of Christian unity – John Eliot, Cotton Mather, and Jonathan Edwards." [4] Eliot, particularly in his *Communion of Churches*, urged cooperation of all churches for the furtherance of missions in foreign lands, in professing nations where spiritual darkness exists, and in the establishment of churches in new settlements. He proposes an "Oecumenical Council" but does not outline its duties, leaving that for those "whose happy portion it shall be, to see those *glorious times*, when such Councils shall be called." [5] Mather, according to Yoder, was "New England's second contribution to the gallery of ecumenical pathfinders." [6] Mather strove for Presbyterian-Congregational unity, included the Baptists in his plans as Baxter had done, corresponded with Francke and others, sought the union of all Protestant groups, and contributed fourteen fundamentals as a basis for unity. Baxter had proposed the three formularies as ideal: the Apostles' Creed, the Lord's Prayer, and the Ten Commandments. Edwards

---

[1] L. Newbigin defines the church as "fundamentally missionary" in nature. ". . . a salvation whose very essence is that it is corporate and cosmic, the restoration of the broken harmony between all men and between man and God and man and nature, must be communicated in a different way. It must be communicated in and by the actual development of a community which embodies – if only in foretaste – the restored harmony of which it speaks. A gospel of reconciliation can only be communicated by a reconciled fellowship." (*The Household of God*, 141.)

[2] R. Rouse and Stephen Neill, *A History of the Ecumenical Movement*.

[3] Newbigin concludes his book, *The Household of God*, by pointing to the "close relation between the Church's mission and the Church's unity. The connection may be exhibited in a twofold way; firstly, in that unity is in order that the world may believe, and secondly, in that the act of witness sets the Church in the situation in which disunity is seen for what it is." (149). Melvill Horne wrote in 1794: "Let liberal Churchmen and conscientious Dissenters, pious Calvinists and pious Arminians, embrace with fraternal arms. Let the press groan no longer with our controversies and let the remembrance of the petty interests we have contended for be buried in everlasting oblivion." (*Letters on Missions*, 2.)

[4] *Op. cit.*, 227.

[5] *Communion of Churches* (1665), 34.

[6] *Op. cit.*, 127.

believed the spiritual union of believers "should be manifested, and become visible." [1] His *Concert for Prayer* was dedicated to this goal and accomplished much. The comment of Melvill Horne a century after Baxter is interesting: "Let liberal Churchmen and conscientious Dissenters, pious Calvinists and pious Arminians, embrace with fraternal arms. Let the press groan no longer with our controversies, and let the remembrance of the petty interests we have contended for be buried in everlasting oblivion." [2]

These five Puritans made a clear distinction between essential and non-essential doctrine, although only Baxter and Mather got down to listing which were essential. One of the chief purposes, we should add, in their making the distinction between essential and non-essential doctrine was to bring about unity among like-minded Christians and churches.[3]

There are two quite different relations which the church bears to the mission. In the first place, she has been appointed to channel the truth, to preach the gospel. And secondly, she must grow by self-establishment. So we speak of the church's double mission character, as bearer of the message [4] and as goal of the mission.[5]

First, then, the church is bearer in the sense that she has the divine appointment to spread the gospel.[6] Here various factors come into focus: the Great Commission, the centrality of preaching, the minister as missionary, and the urgency of prayer. The Great Commission does not occupy a large place in Puritan thought.[7] In itself this is not strange, since the command to evangelize had played but a small part in mission motivation in the primitive and medi-

---

[1] *Ibid.*, 228.
[2] *Letters on Missions*, 21, 22.
[3] Melvill Horne also summarizes the "grand forcible truths" of the gospel (*op. cit.*, 49). Another factor, however, was the Puritans' attempt to deal with rapidly changing systems of thought. The openness with which they accepted new discoveries while trying to preserve what they judged essential to the faith may seem incongruous to us, but likely no more so than we will appear to future generations. H. Butterfield has a profitable word on this subject. "There are times when we can never meet the future with sufficient elasticity of mind, especially if we are locked in the contemporary systems of thought. We can do worse than remember a principle which both gives us a firm Rock and leaves us the maximum elasticity for our minds: the principle: Hold to Christ, and for the rest be totally uncommitted." (*Christianity and History*, 146.)
[4] As in A. A. van Ruler: "Het wezen van het apostolaat der kerk ligt daarin: niet, dat de kerk uitgaat, getuigt en staat in de wereld, maar daarin: dat zij gebruikt wordt! Zij is instrument!" (*Theologie van het Apostolaat*, 20.)
[5] L. Newbigin views the church also in this way, both as a means and an end. Here he disagrees with J. C. Hoekendijk's exclusive emphasis on the church as only means. (Newbigin, *op. cit.*, 147.) For Calvin's view of the two aspects of the church, see T. F. Torrance, *Kingdom and Church*, 115.
[6] The church is set by God in the world. "Daar 'bevindt' zij zich niet, existentialistisch, maar daar is zij gestéld, praedestinatiaans." (Van Ruler, *Theologie van het Apostolaat*, 21.)
[7] Melvill Horne makes a strong appeal to the Great Commission. Its validity must not be limited to the Apostles. "Shall we say, these injunctions were laid upon the Apostles only? Impossible! The genius of Chr'ty, and the spirit of the precept, forbid such an interpretation." (*Letters on Missions*, 14.)

eval church.[1] Nor did Luther and Calvin see its significance. The Puritans did point to the continuing validity of its call to mission duty. Sibbes cited it, Baxter expounded it, and Eliot fulfilled it. Especially Baxter concerned himself with the old lands of Asia and Europe and the new ones of the Indies and America. The "into all the world" assumed great significance for him. He saw the duty of fulfilling the Great Commission by Christians who went abroad, diplomats and traders alike. He called for chaplains to accompany the adventurous abroad, for teachers to establish colleges for Englishmen or natives in preparation for the work. Such as these deserve the support of every Christian and of the church. However, in these proposals Baxter calls upon the church as organism rather than as organization to further the work. He points to the binding character of the Great Commission for every age. Every church and every minister bears the assignment to evangelize.

The mission duty of the institutional church is carried by ministers.[2] God has appointed them primary agents in redemption.[3] Ordinary ministers are ambassadors of God to their parishes. Their duties are not only to the church members; rather, *if necessary*, these should be neglected and the unbelievers sought out. Believers, after all, will recover from a fall into sin. Missionaries to serve beyond the reach of the local church should be appointed, with the approbation of a local church when possible, to reach dispersed Christians, teach ignorant Christians, supply ministerial deficiencies – also in other lands, and evangelize the heathen. Baxter's call for "unfixed ministers" constituted a needed antidote to the lifetime marriage of ministers and churches in seventeenth-century New England. Eliot's attachment to the Roxbury church seems to have hindered giving his full attention to the Indian work. He insisted, however, that the first duties of broader Christian church councils were missions abroad (a sort of cooperation still visionary today!). By the end of the seventeenth century, the vocational missionary was an accepted fact in the Puritan church; Mather was contriving to secure more men for the work, and later Edwards entered the missionary ranks.

The awareness of the duty to evangelize, rising out of the missionary command of Christ and illumined by broken lives of men,[4] struck deep root in

---

[1] J. van den Berg, *op. cit.*, 177.
[2] Concerning G. Warneck's view that missions should be carried out by an *ecclesiola in ecclesia*, J. H. Bavinck indicates that this position is not substantiated in the Scriptures. Rather, "the church, the body of Christ ... forms the organ through which and in which the glorified Christ will reveal his great work of salvation to the world." (*Science of Missions*, 58-59.)
[3] Van Ruler points to man as partner with God through the Covenant: "In de notie van het verbond wordt de mens verstaan als partner, die omsloten is door en opgenomen is in de gemeenschap, welke de levende God in zijn historische handelen om zich heen sticht." (*Theologie van het Apostolaat*, 28.)
[4] Max Warren concisely relates "Christ in His Church" and the church as institution. "... the Church in history cannot help taking on an institutional aspect, being in a genuine and proper sense an institution. Otherwise it could not render unto Caesar the things that are Caesar's, and God would not be the God of politics but only and exclusively the God *in* the Church. But the Incarnation bids us believe that God came down into the

Puritan soil as it had in the Dutch Second Reformation [1] and was beginning to do in Scotch Presbyterianism. These Calvinistic tributaries were preparing to join with those of German Pietism and later with English Methodism to make the mighty stream of what Latourette has called the great century of advance. Jonathan Edwards sparked the prayers that roused the church. His conviction that not human methods but only sovereign grace could reach the sinner, made urgent prayer necessary for the progress of the gospel. In this light we see his *Concert of Prayer*, which proved to be one of the greatest factors in awakening the Protestant churches to their mission calling.

In the second place, the Puritans saw the establishment of the church of Christ as the goal of the mission.[2] The further reformation of the church was viewed as a step forward in God's great program for the world. To this program

---

life of man in order to redeem that life. And the life of man is life lived out in an inescapable network of relationships. Only in the network of relationships is man known as man at all. Only as involved in the collective of humanity can man know full salvation. And it is only into the Church that he can be saved, for the Church is the means by which the human collective can be transmuted into the divine Community. It is in its institutional aspect that the Church in its corporate capacity plays its part in the Christian Mission." (*The Christian Mission*, 81.)

[1] The Second Reformation movement (H. Witsius, W. a Brakel, W. Teellinck, J. Heurnius, J. van Lodensteyn) during the seventeenth century in the Netherlands, is a re-emphasis upon "pneumatology in both its aspects: the work of the Spirit in man's soul as well as on the broad face of life, the renewal of man's inner life and the renewal of the 'face of the earth.' The Second Reformation shows at least in its first stages a remarkable blending of the soteriological and the theocratic elements in Calvinism; its weakness was an under-accentuation of the objective value of the *justificatio impii*, which would bring the movement in a later stage into the narrow waters of a sterile mysticism. The men of the Second Reformation in Holland have formed a bridge between the British Puritans and the German Pietists." (J. van den Berg, *op. cit.*, 18.) In some respects the Second Reformation is similar to Puritanism. "The Second Reformation vacillated between a world-affirming Calvinism and a world-denying Mysticism, and the same traits are to be found in British and American Puritanism." (*Ibid.*, 179.)

[2] The church is "the community of the Holy Spirit, who is the earnest of our inheritance. The Church can only witness to that inheritance because her life is a *real* fortaste of it, a real participation in the life of God Himself." (Newbigin, *op. cit.*, 147.) In this light we must also see Calvin's relation to the mission. Torrance tells us that Calvin teaches that all "members of the Church are engaged in the work of gathering the Church together on every side.... It is that impulse under what Calvin called the incredible force for the Gospel that accounts for the amazing extension of the gospel to all parts of Europe from Geneva.... It is the business of the Church to be continuously restoring its true face, and in making that face public both in a godly life and in a form and order of the Church on earth through which by Word and Sacrament God may be known familiarly and face to face." (*op. cit.*, 163-164). In this light, as well as in the teaching of the Puritans on missions, Weber's view that Calvin and Calvinism have not contributed their part to the "expansion of the Church" cannot stand. He says: "Calvinism as such is not responsible for those feats of missionary zeal, since they rest on an interdenominational basis. Calvin himself denied the duty of sending missions to the heathen since a further expansion of the Church is *unius Dei opus*." (Max Weber, *The Protestant Ethic and the Spirit of Capitalism*, 225-226.) The Puritans clearly teach that the mission is *unius Dei opus*, but because the church is God's mystical body, by the nature of the case the divine mission is also that of the church.

we shall turn in the next section. The *plantatio ecclesiae* in new places and among the heathen had priority in the propagation of the gospel.[1] Men must be converted, it is true. But to be converted they must come under the divinely appointed means of grace. How naive to think that a heathen could simply accept a gospel of a redeeming Christ sent by a God of whom he had never heard. When Baxter heard of the barbarity of American Indians he could only thank God for the revelation of the Scriptures. Eliot taught and taught and taught. After two years he thought some Indians ready for the sacraments. He wanted to establish the Indian church, and later he did.

But the seventeenth-century Puritans saw the planting of the church in America as a great step forward. This was God's work. Their calling was to claim the land and possess it for God. Their sense of the oneness of life and the Lordship of Christ made them sure that this was a sacred calling. The great tragedy was that they too often failed to see this primarily as a calling to serve others, to see that their election was to service in a broader sense than they generally understood. To mention the hardships of frontier life and the hostile character of many Indian tribes does not remove the blind spot that many Puritans had concerning the challenge for Indian mission work. The fact that few missions of other groups to the Indians were of continuing significance confirms the difficulty of the task. Cromwell's establishment of the Corporation and the support it received from leading Puritans in England was a stimulant to the New England mind. However, the sacrificial work of men like Eliot and the Mayhews accomplished more than anything else on both sides of the Atlantic in showing the need and arousing interest in the mission. The church awakened slowly, but its sense of calling, like the Daniel-stone, grew.

The two greatest hindrances to the establishment of the Indian church were the deep distrust that intermittently broke into the open and finally erupted into the disastrous war in 1675, and the ill-fated attempt to Anglicize the Indians. The causes of the distrust were rooted in non-church matters: social, economic, and political. The failure to deal realistically with these matters and the inability of the English to read the mind and heart of the Indian severely crippled the work almost before it began. Lack of sensitivity to Indian ways, in the second place, was aggravated by the attempt to transmit a foreign, and in many ways, opposite culture.[2] The too-close association between colony and mission made paternalism inevitable. Elders and ministers who were not missionaries judged whether Indians were spiritually qualified for baptism and church membership, and whether they were suitable as officers in the projected

---

[1] For a full discussion of the concept "plantatio ecclesiae" as it is used in Gijsbert Voetius, see H. P. van Andel, *De Zendingsleer van Gisbertus Voetius*.

[2] Roland Allen judges that this tendency has wrongly found a large place in our missionary work. "We are accustomed by long usage to an elaborate system of church organization, and a peculiar code of morality. We cannot imagine any Christianity worthy of the name existing without the elaborate machinery which we have invented. We naturally expect our converts to adopt from us not only essentials but accidentals. We desire to impart not only the Gospel, but the Law and the Customs." (*Missionary Methods: St. Paul's or Ours?*, 6.)

Indian church. That men not personally involved in the work should hold to standards too high for Indian attainment is understandable, even though inexcusable.

The positive side to the emphasis on the planting of the church as organization was the securing of a continuing ministry. The destructive factors in the mission in the case of the Indian church were chiefly external to the work: disease, war, and distrust. The founding of the Indian church and the training of native leadership held promise for the future of the work. These steps were an anticipation of the idea of an indigenous church, an anticipation that waited two centuries for realization.[1]

### C. THE REDEMPTION OF THE WORLD

What is the relation of the kingdom to the church? Is it to be established on earth or in heaven? How is the spiritual character of the kingdom to be related to the temporal? What is the missionary to achieve – the redemption of souls, the establishment of churches in order to cultivate Christians, or the transmission of a Christian cultural pattern?[2]

To answer these questions, we must first ask, what did the Puritan mean by "kingdom"? He meant far more than church. The church was, as we have seen, of a double character: essentially, it was an inner circle of Christians, but it was also a convocation of men and women needing conversion. The kingdom of God also had a four-fold reference. The conversion of souls, namely, Christ reigning in man's heart, was the first step. Believers gathered in church-fellowship, Christ reigning in the church, was the next. Then followed Christ's reign in the state, when the national government proclaimed God's will supreme. Finally, when there were sufficient Christian (political) kingdoms, the universal

---

[1] John L. Nevius describes the difference between the "Old System" used in the nineteenth century in China and the "New System" by the "principles of independence and self-reliance" applied in the native situation "from the beginning" of the work. The "indigenous" method does not pay all costs for the natives nor teach that many should be appointed to official functions. Rather, believers are expected to work in their original environment and to be self-supporting, self-governing, and self-propagating. (*Planting and Development of Missionary Churches*, 8. Cf. also 27, 28.) David M. Paton puts it: "Let us first make a vigorous native ministry in order to obtain numerous Christians." (*Christian Missions and the Judgment of God*, 58.)

[2] G. F. Vicedom relates the purpose of God's redemptive work as follows: "Ich meine, man kann das Handeln Gottes mit den Menschen sachgemäss genauso unter dem Gedanken der Herrschaft Gottes erfassen wie unter dem der Missio Dei. Beide Begriffe beschreiben wohl nicht denselben Vorgang, haben aber vieles gemeinsam. Sehen wir die Missio Dei in dem Gottsein Gottes begründet, so hat auch die Herrschaft Gottes dort ihren letzten Ursprung. Das Ziel der Missio Dei ist, die Menschen in die Basileia tou Theou, in die Gottesherrschaft einzugliedern und ihnen deren Gaben zu vermitteln.... So könnte also das Reich Gottes als das Ziel der Mission Dei beschrieben werden. Eine weitere Beziehung ist in dem Gegenüber gegeben, das sowohl die Missio Dei als auch die Basileia haben, nämlich der Menschenwelt. Von diesem her wird das Handeln Gottes in seiner Liebe veranlasst und auf dieses ist es ausgerichtet." (*Missio Dei*, 18.)

reign of Christ would be established. The first two we have discussed above.

That the third stage of the kingdom had arrived was evident to the Puritan from the Reformation and the subsequent establishment of Protestant political kingdoms. By this measuring stick, England, for example, was a Christian kingdom. Baxter considered many of the Eastern churches as places where Christ might soon come in his kingdom in this sense. This stage asked that all of national life, social, political, ecclesiastical, be placed under the Lordship of Christ. Baxter's *Holy Commonwealth*, as well as Eliot's, was intended to be a national guide for Protestant politics in this in-between time of history.[1] This basically theocratic structure [2] was an attempt to unify human life in its totality under the Lordship of Christ.[3] Christ's kingship was not to be restricted to comfortable churches and emergency bridge-building in times of personal and national disaster. What God had said once for all in Christ through the Scriptures was relevant to politics, to economics, to statutory law. Governors no more than farmers and periwig-makers could ignore the divine purpose in their calling. The sort of work one did, the bargain one made with the Indian beadmaker, the prayers one said with the children and servants, had an eternal referent. The storms in the village, like the tempests of one's soul, were alike in the hand of God. Mather and Edwards were forerunners in the acceptance of astronomical and other scientific discoveries, but whether through natural law or through spiritual crises, God still was the sovereign Lord of all.

That this theocratic structure of society carried grave dangers became evident. Spiritual leaders tended to call the signals for political moves. Voting members of the "Christian kingdom" were restricted to church members. Tolerance reached to the Quaker fence on the one side and at first only to the Anglican fence on the other. Roger Williams and Mrs. Hutchinson were welcome only if they conformed to the Puritan rule! The failure to take serious

---

[1] "It is clear then that Calvin thinks of the Kingdom of God in terms of two great eschatological movements, the *initium* and the *complementum* . . . ." (T. F. Torrance, *Kingdom and Church*, 113. Cf. also 113–122.) O. Cullman has particularly pointed, in his *Christ and Time*, to the significance of our stage of history as the time between the center time of Christ's redeeming acts and the end time. (Cf. especially Chap. II.4: "The Present Stage of Redemptive History and its Relation to the Christ-Event at the Midpoint," 144–174.) Christ is "the one who 'became flesh' at the centre of time," as well as the one whose "second coming" is the fulfillment of "Heilsgeschichte." (*The Christology of the New Testament*, 315–328.) Cullman's view of the unity and progress of history is strikingly like that of Edwards: "This view of Christology from the standpoint of *Heilsgeschichte*, which leads us from creation through the reconciliation in the cross and the invisible present lordship of Christ to the still unaccomplished consummation in the new creation, is defined by two essential aspects which we have repeatedly encountered in our investigation of the various solutions to the problem of Christ: the principle of *representation* according to which this whole history occurs; and the idea of *God's self-communication*, which connects the various phases of the history . . . ." (*Ibid.*, 324.) Cf. also, W. Anderson, *op. cit.*, 55.

[2] J. van den Berg judges that the "theocratic tendency was transplanted to Britain, where it became rooted in the circle of Puritanism, and, from there, to New England." (*op. cit.*, 169.)

[3] The living God, says Van Ruler, does more than use his Church; he wrestles with every human heart and he participates "in het grote spel en de grote strijd der volkeren om een politieke, sociale, economische en culturele vormgeving van het leven." (*op. cit.*, 20.)

account of the inevitability of power pressures and prejudice destroyed the theocratic state from within. It was the story, often repeated, of the identification of interests, earthly and heavenly. The medieval *corpus christianum*, the monolithic society, was slow in breaking down. [1]Even nineteenth-century missionaries still were often transmitters of western culture.

The Puritan spirit did not die with the break-down of the Puritan state. The Puritan vision for the religious claim upon all of life remains.[2] Divine sovereignty asks more than individual souls. Every structure of life must be subject to God's will.[3] Here was the heart of the Puritan mission in England and America. The divine mission asks the redemption of the soul, the perfection of society, and the accomplishment of history.

In this perspective we can understand the methods used by the Puritans. Christianization of society was not primarily the desire of strong-willed clergymen for power; it was meant as a surrender to the universal Lordship of Christ. Baxter's voluminous writings, which pressed the Christian ethic to every nook and cranny of private and public life; Eliot's Indian villages which, though effecting segregation of Christian Indians from their fellows, required total commitment to the Christian cause; and Mather's five hundred books were, after all, but expressions of that same vision: "...all authority is given me in heaven and upon earth." The realization of Christ's rule among the nations, the Puritan strived to attain.

The final stage in the achievement of Christ's kingdom finds its fulfillment in the future but is anchored firmly in the present. The emphasis Sibbes placed upon the "grace is growing" concept was central to Puritan theology. The

---

[1] According to Kraemer (*op. cit.*, 58, 59), the "dissolution of this *Corpus Christianum* and the chastening lessons which the Christians of the modern age have learnt thereby have made this a deflated ideal." Thus, "the well-considered purpose of modern missions [is] to plant a Church that lives in and with the community, but which is always distinct from it by its inward autonomy which again is founded on obedience to God...." Cf. also Benz, *Kirchengeschichte in Ökumenischer Sicht*, 4ff., and A. A. Koskinen, *Missionary Influence as a Political Factor in the Pacific Islands*, Chap. II. D. Paton remarks that there is no such thing as a pure gospel, since it is always incarnating itself in a cultural form of expression. (*op. cit.*, Chap. I, Sec. B.) J. van den Berg discusses the problem in "Corpus Christianum en Zending", *De Heerbaan* XIII (1960), 159–178.

[2] J. Blauw indicates this dimension of the mission as grounded in the Great Commission: "Whereas 'all nations' indicates the extensive area of authority of the exalted Lord, 'all that I have commanded you' contains a reference to the intensive range of authority: *all life and the whole man is claimed by Christ*." (*The Missionary Nature of the Church*, 86, 87.)

[3] J. C. Hoekendijk points out the implication of the universal Lordship of Christ in this sense. "*Uitgangspunt en basis* zijn duidelijk: De intensieve universaliteit van het heil, de radicale toepassing van Christus' koningschap over het gehele leven, vereisen, dat men zich op de mens richt in zijn totale omgeving. Het comprehensieve karakter van onze methode moet een reflex zijn van 'the comprehensive will of God, that life as a whole should be redeemed', 'a reflection of the concern of Christ for the needs of the whole man'." *Kerk en Volk in de Duitse Zendingswetenschap*, 277. He is quoting here his article "Comprehensive Approach" in *Zending in Indonesie*, (1947) 90–98. Van Ruler states that the Christianizing of man's social life is no accidental by-product, but it is an essential part of God's purpose. (*op. cit.*, 47.)

kingdom is like a mustard seed. It begins small but becomes a tree that covers the earth. So the kingdom, planted early in history, is gathering momentum.[1] No grace or divine gift is wasted. All are included in the divine purpose. Eternal values and spiritual qualities attained on earth are taken up into the eternal kingdom.[2] Edwards gave classic expression to what the Puritans had believed all along when he pointed to the total incapacity of man to find God. But divine initiative, acting through revelation and the immediate operation of the Spirit, is redeeming souls, establishing churches, sparking revivals of religion, and gathering the mystical body of Christ. Insofar as the evangelical state of things is already accomplished, so far is the kingdom of God already set up. This accomplishment of the eternal state is gradually accomplished. When time is full, Christ will come in judgment and the eternal kingdom will be realized.

The temporal and eternal dimensions of the final kingdom need to be held in constant tension. The temporal dimension meaningfully relates the events of history to God's purpose, while the eternal one, the eschatological, casts a note of urgency to the fulfillment of the mission. Both aspects could, and often were, side-tracked. When the temporal is too exclusively emphasized, men tend to forget the coming judgment and the high goal of missions.[3] Then the this-worldly part of life is withered into philanthropy, institutionalism, and social improvement programs. Not that these are unimportant. The good and necessary emphasis found in the comprehensive approach [4] to the unbeliever must

---

[1] A. A. van Ruler begins his discussion of the apostolate with a consideration of eschatology: "Dit is reeds aanstonds een merkwaardig gevolg voor de theologische systematiek, dat de apostolische visie op het wezen en de functie van de kerk er krachtig toe bijdraagt, de locus over het einde zózeer naar voren te halen, dat hij met noodzakelijkheid het uitgangspunt van het denken wordt." Eschatology "legt dit accent uiteraard in eerste aanleg vanwege haar vragen naar de plaats van de zending in het plan van God met de wereld." (*op. cit.*, 14.)
The end waits, according to Paton, until the gospel is spread. The "Christian witness is dynamically related to the consummation of God's purpose in history." (*op. cit.*, 30.)

[2] The "eschaton" means that God's kingdom is on the way. It is not simply future "zodat wij er naar toe zouden gaan, maar dat het veeleer op ons toekomt en reeds elk moment in het heden stempelt." (Van Ruler, *op. cit.*, 18.)

[3] J. van den Berg (*Constrained by Jesus' Love*, 180ff.) presents a pertinent statement on the relationship between Church and Kingdom in church history.

[4] "Here, I think," Blauw observes, "lies the most pregnant justification for what is ordinarily called the 'comprehensive approach'. But at the same time the character and the boundaries of this comprehensive approach are shown in the personal form ('all that *I* have commanded you'): the approach must be carried by and must lead to a more distinct discipleship of the exalted Lord. Though personally I shrink a bit from burdening Scriptural data such as these too heavily with our present-day phrasing of questions (the danger of eisegesis is very great!), I still think that we may find here a directive for the present relationships between older and younger Churches. Can one, in the complicatedness of today's relationships, 'teach them to observe all that I have commanded you' in every respect without the experience of the whole Church in the whole world? Even if no 'abridged gospel' were passed on by the 'older' Churches to the 'younger' ones, nevertheless, the evangelical *perspective* is often abridged as a consequence of a conception of 'what is commanded' which is all too spiritualized. Here a deficiency from the past can be made up without the 'older' Churches lapsing into a nineteenth-century method of pedagogy in missions." (*op. cit.*, 163, 164.) Cf. also J. van den Berg, *Constrained by Jesus' Love*, 172.

receive a significant role. But when the radical nature of conversion, the depths of men's alienation from God, and the inadequacy of human patches for healing the brokenness of man's life are forgotten, the heart of missions suffers. The burning zeal and compassion of an Eliot and a Baxter cannot be missed.

On the other hand, when the eternal dimension is accented to the exclusion of the temporal, two equally bad effects follow: man lives in an other-wordly realm which is as far from the true kingdom of God as is its opposite extreme, and the accomplishment of missions is crippled because the temporal dimension, through which God is bringing his kingdom to pass, is negated. In the first case we have not taken seriously enough the command to love our brother.[1] We too often forget that "he that loveth not his brother whom he has seen cannot love God whom he has not seen" (I John 4:20). Sometimes the Puritans, like so many of their time, also lived for a future day without catching the eternal significance of this one. The tens of calculations concerning the coming end of the world, speculations about its nature, and the superficial reading of current history, were not permanent gains for the kingdom. This failure, found not in Sibbes and Baxter but rather frequently in certain groups of English Puritans, was also present in the New England church. Warnings of impending judgment and cries for repentance began to sound less urgent and more hollow through the sobering and correcting passage of time. Eliot got down to the work, and Mather, though he warned enough, balanced this with a zealous concern for men's bodies as well as their souls. Edwards struck hard with eternal hammers, but the temporal anvils, he believed, were made for that. Time is not destroyed by eternity, but it is made for it. Revival excesses, indeed, made Edwards pause in his study long enough to warn the superficially-minded of his congregation that conversion was more than emotion. One may be emotionally "saved", but real salvation strikes deep into a man's heart and alters the farthest reaches of his life.

The second danger involved in other-worldliness is the negation of one's temporal responsibility. The divine pattern for brotherly concern is set by Christ. He identified himself with suffering humanity; he became the "suffering Servant." His path was not that of earthly glory and political kingdoms, but the way of the cross. The church militant tends often to forget that it is not the church triumphant that rules and reigns. Perfection is the *sine qua non* for such glorious responsibility. Again here, the Puritans were deeply tempted to over-emphasize earthly structures, though, it must be granted, they identified these with the spiritual ideal of subjection to Christ's Lordship. And it was not long before experience and providence taught those Puritans whose views we have studied to see the identification of the suffering church with the suffering Servant. Here is where the theology of missions must begin and where it shall

---

[1] "The implication of a true eschatological perspective will be missionary obedience, and the eschatology which does not issue in such obedience is a false eschatology." (Newbigin, *op. cit.*, 135.)

end. Those who bear Christ's name must bear his character.[1] He is the divine Redeemer.[2] His followers must be redeemers too, the means through Christ's Spirit to save and to heal. *Custodimus etiam cum non custodimus.*

---

[1] "The Christian individual in his understanding of holiness will, then, from the outset of his approach to his fellows see them as already involved in a network of relationships which are part of their very selves. Only in so far as he can so identify himself with those to whom he goes and become part of their relationships so that he shares in their burdens, can he introduce a new pattern of relationships – create wholeness. This involves a quality of fellowship very difficult indeed to achieve and extremely costly. Any approach as from a superior with something to give to an inferior whose only need is to receive, will be foredoomed to failure. It is at this level that the problem of race-relations is most acute." (M. Warren, *op. cit.*, 123.)

[2] Wilhelm Andersen emphasizes that men are not going to evangelize the world. "Since God Himself is responsible for the missionary enterprise, since He Himself guarantees its continuity, He will also guide it to the destiny that He has appointed for it." (*Towards a Theology of Mission*, 47.)

# ABBREVIATIONS

### RICHARD SIBBES

AA  Angels' Acclamations: or The Nativity of Christ, celebrated by the heavenly Host. (Luke II.13, 14) 1638.

AC  The Art of Contentment. In one Sermon. (Philip. IV.11, 12, 13) 1629. This sermon was No. 1 of the first edition of the "Saint's Cordials."

ACN  Antidotum Contra Naufragium Fidei et Bonae Conscientiae. Concio Latina Habita Ad Academicos Cantabrig. in Ecclesia S. Mariae 9 die Octobris, 1627.

AM  The Art of Mourning. Sermon III of the four sermons entitled "Josiah's Reformation." (2 Chron. XXXIV.27) 1629.

BD  The Beast's Dominion over Earthly Kings. A Sermon preached upon the 5th of November, in remembrance of Our Deliverance from the Papists Powder-Treason. (Rev. XVII.17) 1639. This is one of the three gunpowder-plot anniversary sermons contained in "Evangelical Sacrifices." 1640.

BG  A Breathing After God, or A Christians Desire of Gods Presence. (Ps. XXVII.4) 1639.

BL  The Bride's Longing for her Bridegroom's Second Coming. A Sermon preached at the funerall of the right Worshipfull, Sir Thomas Crew, Knight, Sergeant at Law to his Maiestie. (Rev. XXII.20) 1638.

BO  Bowels Opened, or A Discovery of the Neere and deere Love, Union, and *Communion betwixt Christ and the Church*, and consequently betwixt Him and every beleeving soul. Delivered in divers Sermons on the Fourth Fifth and Sixt Chapters of the Canticles. 1639.

BR  The Bruised Reed and Smoking Flax. Some Sermons contracted out of the 12. of Matth. 20. At the desire, and for the good of weaker Christians. 1630.

CB  Christ is Best; or, St. Paul's Strait, a Sermon Preached at the Funerall of *Mr. Sherland*, late Recorder of Northampton. (Phil. I.23, 24) 1634. It was included in "Saint's Cordials" in 1637 under the title: Christ is Best; or, A Sweet Passage to Glory.

CCC  The Church's Complaint and Confidence. In three Sermons. (Isaiah LXIV.6–8). This sermon forms a portion of the "Beams of Divine Light." 1639.

C2C1  A Learned Commentary or Exposition upon The first Chapter of the Second Epistle of S. Paul to the Corinthians. 1655.

C2C4  A Learned Commentary or Exposition, upon The fourth Chapter of the Second Epistle of Saint Paul to the Corinthians. 1656.

CE  Christ's Exaltation Purchased By Humiliation. Wherein you may see *Mercy* and *Misery* meete together. *Very Usefull* I. For Instructing the Ignorant. II. For Comforting the Weake. III. For Confirming the Strong. (Rom. XIV.9) 1639.

ChE  The Church's Echo. In one Sermon. (Rev. XXII.17). This forms one of the sermons included in the "Beams of Divine Light."

CP  A Christian's Portion; or, The Christian's Charter. Wherein is unfolded the unsearchable *Riches* he hath by his interest in *Christ*. Whom injoying hee possesseth all things else. (I Cor. III.21–23) 1638.

CV  The Church's Visitation. (I Pet. IV.17, 18, 19). This is the name of the first sermon appearing in a volume bearing this same name, forming an expository treatise of five sermons on I Pet. IV.17–19. The sub-title follows: Discovering The many difficulties and tryalls of Gods Saints on earth: Shewing wherein the fountaine of their happinesse consists: Arming Christians how to doe, and suffer for Christ; And directing them how to commit themselves, and all their wayes to God in holinesse here, and happinesse hereafter. 1634.

| | |
|---|---|
| CW | The Christian Work. (Phil. II.12). The first part of a volume entitled "An Exposition of the Third Chapter of the Epistle of St. Paul to the Philippians." 1639. |
| CWa | The Christian's Watch. (Luke XII.37) 1639. Appended after "An Exposition of the Third Chapter of the Epistle of St. Paul to the Philippians" in the work entitled "The Christian Work." |
| DAB | Dictionary of American Biography. |
| DB | The Danger of Backsliding. (2 Tim. IV.10) Originally appeared in the 1629 edition of "Saint's Cordials" under the title: Experience Triumphing; or the Saint's Safety, from 2 Timothy iv.17, 18. In One Sermon. Wherein is shewed, how the Comfort of Former Experiences of Gods Goodness and Mercy, doe and ought support and stay the soule for the expectation and assurance of Deliuerances and helpe for time to come, &c. |
| DC | A Description of Christ. His neerenesse to God, His calling, His qualification, His execution of his calling. In three Sermons. (Matt. XII.18) 1639. |
| DGC | The Demand of a Good Conscience. In one Sermon, upon I Pet. 3.21. 1640. This forms one of the sermons which compose "Evangelical Sacrifices." |
| DM | The Dead Man, or The State of Every Man by Nature. In one Sermon. (Eph. II.1) 1639. |
| DMHC | Divine Meditations and Holy Contemplations. 1658. "These 'Meditations' seem to have been taken from Sibbes's Commonplace book, or from his lips as they occurred in his Sermons, as many of them will be found scattered up and down his writings." (A. Grosart). |
| DNB | Dictionary of National Biography. |
| DR | Discouragement's Recovery. Wherein the sovle by Refexion of the Strength of Vnderstanding, quarrelling with it selfe, is at length reduced and charged to doe that, which must and should be the true vpshot of all Distempers. (Ps. XLIII.5) 1629. |
| DS | The Difficulty of Salvation. (I Peter. IV.18) This is Sermon III of "The Church's Visitation," 1634. |
| EG | The Excellency of the Gospel Above the Law. Wherein the Liberty of the Sonnes of God is Shewed. With the Image of their Graces here, and Glory hereafter. Which affords much Comfort and great incouragement, to all such as Begin Timely, and Continue Constantly in the wayes of God. (II Cor. III.17, 18) 1639. |
| EP3 | An Exposition of the Third Chapter of the Epistle of St. Paul to the Philippians. 1639. Appeared in a volume by that name, of which "The Christian Work" formed the first part. |
| FC | The Faithful Covenanter. In two Sermons upon Gen. 17.7. 1639. These two sermons form a portion of the miscellaneous sermons of "Evangelical Sacrifices." 1640. |
| FL | The Fruitful Labour for Eternal Food. (John VI.27). Appeared originally in "Beames of Divine Light, Breaking forth from severall places of holy Scripture, as they were learnedly opened, In XXI. Sermons." 1639. |
| FO | The Fountain Opened: or, The Mystery of Godliness Revealed. (I Tim. III.16). This sermon is one of the four treatises which compose "Light from Heaven." 1638. |
| FS | A Fountain Sealed: or The *duty* of the sealed to the Spirit, and the *worke* of the Spirit in Sealing. *Wherein* Many things are handled about the Holy Spirit, and grieving of it: As also Of assurance and sealing what it is, the priviledges and degrees of it, with the signes to discerne, and meanes to preserve it. (Eph. IV.30) 1637. |
| FSe | First Sermon. From "Two Sermons, Vpon the first words of Christs last Sermon, Iohn 14.1. Being also the *last* Sermons of Richard Sibbs D.D. Preached to the honourable society of Grayes Inne, Iune 21. and 28. 1635. Who the next Lords day following, dyed, and rested from all his labours." This is from the title page of the fourth edition, 1638. |
| FT | Faith Triumphant. In five Sermons, on Heb. 11.13. 1639. First appeared in "Evangelical Sacrifices", 1640. |

GG     A Glimpse of Glory. In One Sermon. (2 Peter I.3) Wherein is shewed, The excellency and necessity of a particular calling. What our calling to glory is. Divers particulars to ravish the soule in admiration of it. &c. Originally published in "Saint's Cordials," 1629.

GH     A Glance of Heaven; or, A Precious Taste of a Glorious Feast. Wherein thou mayst taste and see those things which God hath prepared for them that love him. (I Cor. II.9) 1638.

GI     God's Inquisition, In two Sermons. (Jer. VIII.6, 7) This sermon forms part of the "Beams of Divine Light." 1639.

GR     The General Resurrection. In One Sermon. Declaring, The manner, time, and certainty of our Resurrection. In what estate our Bodies shall rise againe. Wherein the glory and excellency of the Saints shall consist after the Resurrection, shewed in sundry particulars. Together with the deplorable estate of the wicked in that day, &c. (John XI.23, 24) 1629. Printed in the first edition of "Saint's Cordials."

HC     A Heavenly Conference Between Christ and Mary After His Resurrection Wherein, The intimate familiarity, and near relation between Christ and a Beleever is discovered. (John XX.16) 1656.

HL     The Hidden Life. In two Funerall Sermons upon Col. 3, 4. 1639. Printed in "Evangelical Sacrifices." 1640.

JR     Judgment's Reason. In Two Sermons. Wherein that great Qvestion is Decided, and the Afflicted Satisfied; Why God sends so many crosses and troubles in this life; both upon his best Seruants; and those who are not yet brought into the way of life. (I Cor. XI.30, 31) 1629. These two sermons appeared originally in "The Saint's Cordials."

KDE     King David's Epitaph: or An Epitome of the life and death of King David. In three Sermons. (Acts XIII.36) This sermon appeared originally in the "Beams of Divine Light." 1639.

LC     Lydia's Conversion. This is the former of two short treatises published in a volume entitled "The Riches of Mercie." (Acts XVI.14, 15) 1638.

LF     The Life of Faith. In three Sermons. Wherein is shewed, What this Life of Faith is: Why Faith has so much attributed unto it: And how to live this glorious Life in all the severall passages of our Pilgrimage. (Gal. II.20) In the edition of "Saint's Cordials" published in 1629.

MC     Mary's Choice. Wherein is laid down some directions how to choose the better part. Comforts for them that have chosen it. Signes whereby we may know we have chosen the better part. (Luke X.38–40) 1637.

MF     The Marriage Feast Between Christ and His Church. A series of nine sermons on Isaiah 25.6–9 under the title "The Glorious Feast of the Gospel. Or, Christ's gracious Invitation and royall Entertainment of Believers." 1650.

ML     The Matchless Love and Inbeing. In two Sermons. Wherein is shewed,
That we may be Assured of Gods loue vnto vs:
Helpes for Weake Christians how to attaine vnto this loue:
Helps how to know that we haue it in vs:
That Christ is in all beleeuers:
How to know that Christ is in vs:
How in a seeming absence he is discouered to be in the Soule:
How to keep Christ there, and how to recouer him being lost, &c.
(John XVII.26) 1629.

OPG     Of The Providence of God. (Phil. II.24) This sermon is part of a volume entitled "An Exposition of the Third Chapter of St. Paul to the Philippians: Also Two Sermons of Christian Watchfulnesse. The first upon Luke 12.37. The second upon Revel. 16.15. An Exposition of part of the second Chapter of the Epistle to the Philipp. A Sermon upon Mal 4.2.3." 1639.

| | |
|---|---|
| PF | The Privileges of the Faithful. (Romans VIII.28) This is the second half of a little volume entitled "Yea and Amen: or Pretious Promises, and Priviledges. Spiritually unfolded in their nature and use. Driving at the assurance & establishing of weak believers." 1638. |
| PP | The Pattern of Purity: Wherein is shewed, What Purity of heart is. The necessitie and excellency thereof. The meanes how to purifie our selves. (I John III.3) No. 13 of the original edition of the "Saint's Cordials." 1629. |
| RB | The Returning Backslider: or, A Commentarie upon the whole XIV. Chapter of the Prophecy of the Prophet Hosea. Wherein is shewed the large extent of Gods free Mercy, even unto the most miserable forlorne and wretched sinners that may be, upon their Humiliation and Repentance. In 16 sermons. 1639. |
| RBo | The Redemption of Bodies. In one Funerall Sermon upon Phil. 3.21. 1639. Printed in "Evangelical Sacrifices," 1640. |
| RD | A Rescue from Death. (Ps. CVII.17, &c.) The second of two short treatises published in a small volume entitled "The Riches of Mercie," 1638. |
| RMJ | The Ruin of Mystical Jericho. A Sermon preached upon the 5th of November, in remembrance of Our Deliverance from the Papists Powder-Treason. (Heb. XI.30) 1639. Included in "Evangelical Sacrifices." |
| RP | The Rich Poverty; or, The Poor Man's Riches. (Zeph. III.12). The last of the four treatises included in "Light From Heaven." 1638. |
| RPe | The Rich Pearl. In a Sermon upon the Parable of a Merchant man seeking good pearles. Matth. 13.45. Shewing what that Pearle is, how we may know we have it, how to improve it, &c. 1637. This sermon forms the second of the four Sermons appended to "The Saint's Comforts." |
| S | The Spouse, Her Earnest desire after Christ her Husband. Or, A Sermon preached on Cant. 1. Vers. 5. (The verse is evidently a misprint, since the sermon is based on Vers. 2. See Sibbes, *Complete Works*, II, 200.) 1638. |
| SA | Salvation Applied. In one Sermon. Wherein is shewed, The more speciall and peculiar worke of Faith, in apprehending Christ as our *owne*; the grounds thereof are shewed, with meanes to attaine it, and most of all the knotty objections against particular assurance of Gods love answered. (Gal. II.20) This forms the third of the three Sermons which compose "The Life of Faith." 1637. |
| SAnt | Sin's Antidote. In One Sermon. Wherein is shewed, What sinne is. The misery of it. How it bindes over to condemnation. How and in what sense it is said to be remitted. How Iustice and Mercy joyne in this act of remission of sinnes. That all the benefits of the new Covenant are given with remission of sins. That it is possible to attaine unto the knowledge that our sins are remitted. Lastly, how this knowledge is attained by the spirits threefold conviction. (Mat. XXVI.28) 1629. In the original edition of "Saint's Cordials." |
| SC | The Soul's Conflict With Itself, And Victory Over Itself By Faith. A Treatise of the Inward Disquietments of Distressed Spirits, with Comfortable Remedies to Establish Them. (Ps. XLII.II). 1635. |
| SF | The Spiritual Favourite at the Throne of Grace. (Neh. I.11) 1640. |
| SG | The Success of the Gospel. Shewing the diverse entertainements it hath in the World. In a Sermon Preached upon the 7. of Luke and 31. verse. 1637. |
| SH–P | The Saint's Hiding-Place in the Evil Day. (I Peter IV.19) This is the name of Sermons IV and V in the series entitled "The Church's Visitation." 1634. |
| SJ | The Spiritual Jubilee. (Rom. VIII.2) 1638. Published originally in "Beams of Divine Light." |
| SM | Spiritual Mourning: In Two Sermons. Wherein is laid open, *Who are spirituall mourners, and what it is to mourne spiritually. That all godly mourning is attended with comfort. How spirituall mourning is known and discerned from other mourning. Together with the meanes to attaine it, and the tryall thereof, in sundry instances*, &c. (Mat. V.4) 1629. Originally published in the first edition of "Saints Cordials," 1629. |

| | |
|---|---|
| SMA | The Spiritual Man's Aim. Guiding a *Christian* in his *Affections* and *Actions*, through the sundry passages of this Life. So that *God's glory* and his Salvation may be the maine end of all. (I Cor. VII.29–31.) 1637. |
| SP | The Saint's Privilege, or a Christians constant Advocate; Containing a short but most sweet direction for every true Christian to walke comfortably through this valley of teares. (John XVI.8–10) 1638. |
| SPC | Saint Paul's Challenge. In one Sermon. (Rom. VIII.31) 1638. First published in "Beams of Divine Light." 1639. |
| SR | The Saint's Refreshing. (2 Chron. XXXIV.28) This is Sermon IV in a series of four sermons entitled "Josiah's Reformation... Wherein is Shewed the Tvrnings and Windings of the Soule in this great worke of Reformation: and how the stout heart may so be brought low, as to be made humble, melting, and compassionately mournfull: even to the comfort of a sweet Assurance." 1637. |
| SRi | The Sun of Righteousness; A Sermon upon Malachi. (Malachi IV.2, 3) Appended to "An Exposition of the Third Chapter of the Epistle of St. Paul to the Philippians," 1639. |
| SS | The Saint's Safety in Evil Times. Two Sermons. (Ps. VII.14 and II Tim. 4.17, 18) 1633. Delivered at St. Maries in Cambridge the fift of November upon occasion of the Powder-Plot. |
| SuS | The Successful Seeker. In two Sermons, on Psalme 27.8. 1639. Appeared originally in "Evangelical Sacrifices." 1640. |
| TH | The Tender Heart. (2 Chron. XXIV.26) Sermon I in the series entitled "Josiah's Reformation." 1637. |
| TR | The Touchstone of Regeneration. In One Sermon. Wherein the Vndovbted and true Signes of Regeneration are discovered, and the Soule pointed to such a frame and temper of disposition, which having attained, it may be comforted. (Isaiah XI.6–9) 1629. |
| UB | The Unprosperous Builder. A Sermon preached upon the 5th of *November*, in remembrance of Our Deliverance from the Papists Powder-Treason. (Joshua VI.26) 1639. Printed in "Evangelical Sacrifices," 1640. |
| UM | The Ungodly's Misery. (I Peter IV.17) This is the second of five separate but related discourses on I Peter IV.17–19, published as "The Church's Visitation." 1634. |
| VV | Violence Victorious: In two Sermons. (Mat. XI.12) Appeared originally in the "Beams of Divine Light." 1639. |
| WS | The Witness of Salvation: or, God's Spirit Witnessing with ovr Spirits, that wee are the Children of God. In One Sermon. Wherein is shewed, What the spirit of Bondage is. Why God suffers his Children to be terrified therewith. The paralleling of the Witnesses in Heaven and Earth. What the witness of our spirit is. How to discerne of it. The order of the Witnesses. What the witnesse of Gods Spirit is: and, How to discerne the truth thereof. (Rom. VIII.15, 16) 1629. |
| YA | Yea and Amen; Or, Precious Promises Laid Open out of 2 Cor. I.19–23. From the volume entitled "Yea and Amen; Or, Precious Promises and Privileges." 1638. |

RICHARD BAXTER

| | |
|---|---|
| ASC | A Sermon of the Absolute Sovereignty of Christ; and the Necessity of Man's Subjection, Dependence, and Chiefest Love to Him. Psalm ii.10–12. (1654). |
| CAM | Cain and Abel Malignity, that is, Enmity to Serious Godliness; that is, to a Holy and Heavenly State of Heart and life.... (1689). |
| CathU | Catholic Unity: or the only Way to bring us all to be of one Religion. Ephesians iv.3. (1659). |

| | |
|---|---|
| CC | Compassionate Counsel to all Young Men: especially, I. London Apprentices; II. Students of Divinity, Physic, and Law; III. The Sons of Magistrates and Rich Men. (1681). |
| CD | A Christian Directory: or, a Sum of Practical Theology, an[d] Cases of Conscience. (1673). |
| CD:CEth | Part I. Christian Ethics, (or Private Duties). |
| CD:CEc | Part II. Christian Economics, (or Family Duties). |
| CD:CEccl | Part III. Christian Ecclesiastics, (or Church Duties). |
| CD:CP | Part IV. Christian Politics, (or Duties to our Rulers and Neighbours). |
| CF | The Catechising of Families. A Teacher of Householders how to Teach their Household: useful also to Schoolmasters, and Tutors of Youth. (1682). |
| CR | Confirmation and Restauration, the Necessary Means of Reformation and Reconciliation, for the Healing of the Corruptions and Divisions of the Churches. (1658). |
| CSCC | The Character of a Sound, Confirmed Christian; as also of a Weak Christian, and of a Seeming Christian. (1669). |
| CU | A Call to the Unconverted to Turn and Live, and accept of Mercy while Mercy may be had, as ever they would find Mercy in the Day of their Extremity: From the Living God. Ezekiel xxxiii.11. (1657). |
| CW | The Crucifying of the World by the Cross of Christ. Galatians vi.14. (1657). |
| DA | The Divine Appointment of the Lord's Day, Proved; as a Separated Day for Holy Worship, especially in the Church Assemblies: and Consequently the Cessation of the Seventh-Day Sabbath. (1671). |
| DA:AC | An Appendix for further Confirmation of God's own Separation of the Lord's Day, .... (1671). |
| DL | The Divine Life: in Three Treatises. (1663). |
| DL:KG | Part I. Of the Knowledge of God. John xvii.3. |
| DL:WG | Part II. The Description, Reasons, and Reward of the Believer's Walking with God. Genesis v.24. |
| DL:CG | Part III. The Christian's Converse with God: or, the Insufficiency and Uncertainty of Human Friendship; and the Improvment of Solitude in Converse with God. John xvi.32. |
| DP | Directions and Persuasions to a Sound Conversion. For Prevention of that Deceit and Damnation of Souls, and those Scandals, Heresies, and Desperate Apostasies that are Consequents of a Counterfeit or Superficial Change. (1658). |
| DT | Mr. Baxter's Dying Thoughts upon Philippians i.23. Written for his own Use in the latter times of his Corporal Pains and Weakness. (1683). |
| DT:A | An Appendix. A Breviate of the Helps of Faith, Hope, and Love. A Breviate of the Proof of Supernatural Revelation, and the Truth of Christianity. I Timothy iii.16. (1683). |
| DW | Directions for Weak, Distempered Christians, to grow up to a Confirmed State of Grace. Col. ii.6, 7. (1668). |
| FP | The Fool's Prosperity the Occasion of his Destruction. Prov. i.32, 33. (1660). |
| FS | The Farewell Sermon of Richard Baxter; Prepared to have been preached to his Hearers at Kidderminster at his Departure, but Forbidden. John xvi.22. (1683). |
| GGV | God's Goodness Vindicated; for the Help of such (especially in Melancholy) as are tempted to deny it, and think Him cruel, because of the Present and Future Misery of Mankind; with respect to the Doctrine of Reprobation and Damnation. (1671). |
| HGM | How to Do Good To Many: or, the Public Good is the Christian's Life. Galatians vi.20. (1682). |
| HS | A Sermon Preached at the Funeral of that Holy, Painful, and Fruitful Minister of Christ, Mr. Henry Stubbs .... Acts xx.24. (1678). |
| JC | A Sermon Preached at the Funeral of that Faithful Minister of Christ, Mr. John Corbet. II Cor. xii.1–9. (1682). |

| | |
|---|---|
| LB | Mr. Baxter's Letter to Mr. Bromley, 1680, Containing his Judgment about Free-Will, in as Few Words as Possible, for the Satisfaction of Some Persons, who Misunderstood Some of his Books. |
| LF | The Life of Faith. In Three Parts. Hebrews xi.1. (1669). |
| LM | Mr. Baxter's Letter in answer to the case of Marrying with a Papist. (1665). |
| LW | The Last Work of a Believer; His Passing Prayer, Recommending his Departing Spirit to Christ, to be Received by Him. Acts vii.59. (1661). |
| MC | The Mother's Catechism; or, a Familiar Way of Catechising of Children in the Knowledge of God, Themselves, and the Holy Scriptures. (1701). |
| MP | A Moral Prognostication, first, What shall befall the Churches on Earth, till their Concord, by the Restitution of their Primitive Purity, Simplicity, and Charity: secondly, How that Restitution is Likely to be Made, (if ever) and what shall befall them thenceforth unto the End, in that Golden Age of Love. (1661). |
| MR | More Reasons for the Christian Religion, and No Reason against it .... (1671). |
| MS-I | The Mischiefs of Self-Ignorance, and the Benefits of Self-Acquaintance .... 2 Cor. xiii.5. (1661). |
| NN | Now or Never. The Holy, Serious, Diligent Believer justified, encouraged, excited, and directed. And the Opposers and Neglecters convinced by the Light of Scripture and Reason. Ecclesiastes lx.10. (1663). |
| OP | Obedient Patience: Its Nature in General; and its Exercise in Twenty Particular Cases. (1683). |
| PM | The Poor Man's Family Book .... With a Form of Exhortation to the Sick; Two Catechisms; A Profession of Christianity; Forms of Prayer for Various Uses, and some Psalms and Hymns for the Lord's Day. (1672). |
| RB | Reliquae Baxterianae. The Autobiography of Richard Baxter. |
| RB I | Part I. pp. 1–138: Written for the most part in (1664). |
| RB II | Part II. pp. 139–448: Written in (1665). |
| RB III | Part III. pp. 1–177: Written for the most part in (1670). pp. 177–200: Of the Additions of the years 1675, 1676, 1677, 1678, &c. |
| RB Appendix. | pp. 1–132: (followed by funeral sermon by M. Sylvester). |
| RCR | The Reasons of the Christian Religion (1666). |
| RCR:NR | Part I. Of Natural Religion, or Godliness. |
| RCR:Chr | Part II. Of Christianity, and Supernatural Revelation. |
| RL | The Reformed Liturgy. The Ordinary Public Worship on the Lord's Day. (1661). |
| RM | Reasons For Ministers using the Greatest Plainness and Seriousness Possible, in all their Applications to their People. (1676). |
| RMeth | The Right Method for a Settled Peace of Conscience and Spiritual Comfort. In Thirty-two Directions. Matt. xi.28–30. (1653). |
| RP | Gildas Salvianus. The Reformed Pastor; showing the Nature of the Pastoral Work: Especially in Private Instruction and Catechising: with an Open Confession of our too Open Sins. Acts xx.28. (1656). |
| RT | Of Redemption of Time. (1667). |
| SA | Mr. Baxter's Sense of the Articles of the Church of England: In answer to the Scruples Proposed to him by Some that were Called upon to Subscribe Them. (1689). |
| SB | A Saint or a Brute. The certain Necessity and Excellency of Holiness ... to be Communicated by the Charitable, that Desire the Conversion and Salvation of Souls, while the Patience of God, and the Day of Grace and Hope Continue. (1662). |
| SER | The Saints' Everlasting Rest: or, A Treatise of the Blessed State of the Saints in their Enjoyment of God in Glory. (1649). |
| SJ | A Sermon of Judgment. 2 Corinthians v.10, 11. (1654). |
| SM | Short Mediations on Romans v.1–5. Of the Shedding Abroad God's Love on the Heart by the Holy Ghost. |
| SR | A Sermon of Repentance. Ezekiel xxxvi.31 .(1660). |

| | |
|---|---|
| TC | The True Catholic, and Catholic Church Described; and the Vanity of the Papists, and all other Schismatics, that Confine the Catholic Church to their Sect, Discovered and Shamed. (1659). |
| TChr | True Christianity; or, Christ's absolute Dominion, and Man's Necessary Self-resignation and Subjection. 1 Corinthians vi.19, 20. Psalm ii.10–12. (1654). |
| TCon | A Treatise of Conversion, Preached and now Published for the Use of those that are Strangers to a True Conversion, especially grossly Ignorant and Ungodly. Matthew xviii.3. (1657). |
| TD | A Treatise of Death, the last Enemy to be Destroyed. Showing wherein its Enmity Consisteth, and how it is Destroyed. I Corinthians xv.26. (1659). |
| TKL | A Treatise of Knowledge and Love Compared. In Two Parts: I. Of Falsely Pretended Knowledge. II. Of True Saving Knowledge. I Corinthians viii.2, 3. (1689). |
| TOW | The True and only Way of Concord of all the Christian Churches. Ephesians iv.3. (1679). |
| TS–D | A Treatise of Self-Denial. Luke ix.23, 24. (1659). |
| UI | The Unreasonableness of Infidelity, manifested in Four Discourses. (1655). |
| UI:SpW | Part I. The Spirit's Witness to the Truth of Christianity. Gal. iii.1, 2. John xx.29. |
| UI:ChW | Part II. Christ's Witness Within Us, the Believer's Special Advantage against Temptations to Infidelity. John xv.26, 27. |
| UI:US | Part III. For the Prevention of the Unpardonable Sin against the Holy Ghost: A Demonstration that the Spirit and Works of Christ were the Finger of God. Matthew xii.22–32. |
| UI:AR | Part IV. The Arrogancy of Reason against Divine Revelations, Repressed; or, Proud Ignorance the Cause of Infidelity, and of Men's Quarreling with the Word of God. John iii.9. |
| VR | The Vain Religion of the Formal Hypocrite, and the Mischief of an Unbridled Tongue, as against Religion, Rulers, or Dissenters. James i.26. (1660). |
| WL | What Light Must Shine in our Works. Matthew v.16. |

In most cases Baxter dated his own works in the preface or dedicatory epistle. Where he did not do so, we have used the chronological list published by A. B. Grosart.

# BIBLIOGRAPHY

PRIMARY SOURCES

(Works written during the time covered by this study
are included under primary sources.)

ACOSTA, FATHER JOSEPH DE. *The Natural and Moral History of the Indies, Reprint from the English translation of 1604*, I, II, London, 1880.

*Acta Ofte Handlinghen des Nationalen Synod, Gehouden door Authoritijt der Hoogh: Mogh: Heeren Staten Generall des Vereenichden Nederlands Tot Dordrecht, Anno 1618 and 1619*, Ghedruckt 1621.

*Archief voor de Geschiedenis der Oude Hollandsche Zending I, Aanteekeningen uit de Acta der Provinciale Synoden van Noord Holland*, Utrecht, 1884 (including sections of meeting of 1690).

BAXTER, RICHARD. *A Paraphrase on the New Testament, with Notes, Doctrinal and Practical*, London, 1811.

—. *The Practical Works of Richard Baxter*, I–IV, London, 1888.

—. *Reliquiae Baxterianae, or Mr. Richard Baxter's Narrative of the Most Memorable Passages of His Life and Times. Faithfully published from his own Original Manuscript by Matthew Sylvester*, London, 1696. Much of the *Reliquiae* is republished in *The Autobiography of Richard Baxter* by J. M. Lloyd Thomas.

—. Mss. Letters, I–VI, and Treatises, I–VII, are located in the Dr. Williams's Library in London. These handwritten papers have been microfilmed. The letters in the Baxter-Eliot correspondence have been transcribed by F. J. Powicke in "Some Unpublished Correspondence of the Rev. Richard Baxter and the Rev. John Eliot, 'The Apostle to the American Indians', 1656–1682" in *Bulletin of the John Rylands Library Manchester*, 15, Manchester, 1931. On some minor points our transcription differs.

COTTON, JOHN. *The Churches Resurrection*, London, 1642.

EDWARDS, JONATHAN. *The Works of President Edwards*, I–VIII, London, 1817.

—. *The Philosophy of Jonathan Edwards from His Private Notebooks*, edited by Harvey G. Townsend, Oregon, 1955.

ELIOT, JOHN. "Missionary Tracts":
  1. *New Englands first fruits; in respect, first of the conversion . . . of Indians. Second, of the progresse of learning in the Colledge at Cambridge in Massachusetts Bay*, London, 1643.
  2. *The Day Breaking, If not the Sun-Rising of the Gospel with the Indians in New England*, London, 1647.
  3. *The Clear Sun-shine of the Gospel Breaking Forth upon the Indians in New-England. Or, an Historical Narrative of Gods Wonderful Workings upon Sundry of the Indians, both Governors & Common people . . . etc.*, London, 1648.
  4. *The Glorious Progress of the Gospel amongst the Indians in New England, etc.*, London, 1649.
  5. *The Light appearing more and more towards the perfect Day. Or, a farther discovery of the present state of the Indians in New-England concerning the progresse of the Gospel amongst them*, London, 1651.
  6. *Strength out of Weaknesse; or a glorious manifestation of the further progresse of the Gospel among the Indians in New-England*, London, 1652. Although this tract is referred to in the preface as the fifth tract, it is sixth in our listing, since we have included *New Englands first fruits*.
  7. *Tears of Repentance: or, A further Narrative of the Progress of the Gospel amongst the Indians in New-England. . . . Related by Mr. Eliot and Mr. Mayhew. . . . Published by the Corporation for propagating the Gospel there, etc.*, London, 1653.

8. *A Late & Further Manifestation of the Progress of the Gospel amongst the Indians in New England – – Being a narrative of the examinations of the Indians about their knowledge in religion by the Elders of the Churches*, London, 1655.
9. *A further Accompt of the Progresse of the Gospel amongst the Indians in New-England*, London, 1659.
10. *A further Account of the progresse of the Gospel Amongst the Indians in New England, etc.*, London, 1660.
11. *A Brief Narrative of the Progress of the Gospel amongst the Indians . . . in 1670*, London, 1671.
—. *The Christian Commonwealth; or the civil policy of the rising kingdom of Jesus Christ*, London.
—. *Communion of Churches; or the divers management of gospel-churches by the ordinance of councils; as also the way of bringing all Christian parishes to be particular reforming congregational churches, etc.*, Cambridge (Mass.), 1665.
—. *Of the Conversion of Five Thousand and Nine Hundred East Indians, In the Isle Formose, neere China, To the Profession of the true God, in Jesus Christ; By meanes of M. Ro: Junius a Minister lately in Delft in Holland. Related by . . . M. C. Sibellius . . . with a postscript of the Gospels good Successe also amongst the West-Indians, in New England*, London, 1650.
—. *Harmony of the Gospels*, Boston, 1678.
—. *The Indian Grammar Begun*, Cambridge, 1666.
—. *The Indian Primer*, Cambridge, 1669.
—. *The Logick Primer*. Some Logical Notions to initiate the INDIANS in the knowledge of the Rule of Reason; and to know how to make use thereof . . . . Composed by J.E. for the use of the Praying Indians, Cambridge, 1672.
Letters. Published in the *Massachusetts Historical Society Collections*, Boston, 1791.
 President DUNSTER to Professor RAVIS (RAVIUS) of Berlin, [1648?].
 JOHN HIGGINSON to INCREASE MATHER, Sept. 30, 1678.
 JEREMIAH BELKNAP to HAZARD BOSTON, 1788.
 JOHN ELIOT to JOHN WINTROP, Jr., July 24, 1675.
 SAMUEL SEWELL to EDWARD TAYLOR, Oct. 28, 1696.
 SAMUEL SEWELL to WILLIAM ASHURST, May 3, 1700.
 SAMUEL SEWELL to EXPERIENCE MAYHEW, March 19, 1725/6.
 JOHN WINTHROP to JOHN ELIOT, etc., Aug. 22, 1704.
MATHER, COTTON. *Magnalia Christi Americana; or, The Ecclesiastical History of New-England, From its first planting, in the year 1620, unto the year of our Lord 1698*, I, II, Hartford, 1853.
—. *Diary of Cotton Mather*. Edited by Worthington C. Ford, I, II, New York.
Minutes, 1655/6–1685/6. *The New England Company of 1649 and John Eliot*, edited by G. P. Winship, Boston, 1920.
PARKER, THOMAS. *The Visions and Prophecies of Daniel Expounded*, London, 1646.
PERKINS, WILLIAM. *The Works of that Famous and Worthie Minister of Christ . . .*, I-III Cambridge, 1608-1609.
SIBBES, RICHARD. *The Complete Works of Richard Sibbes, D.D.*, edited by Alexander B. Grosart, I-VIII, Edinburgh, 1862.
Society for the Propagation of Christian Knowledge, Archives. Miscellaneous (draft) Letters – CN2.2, June 12, 1736. Letter from HENRY NEWMAN to JOHN WESLEY.
THOROWGOOD, THO. *Jewes in America, or, Probabilities that those Indians are Judaiical, made more probable by some Additions to the former Conjectures. An Accurate Discourse is premised of Mr. John Elliot, (who first preached the Gospel to the Natives in their own Language) touching their Origination, and his Vindication of the Planters*, London, 1660.
VOETIUS, GISBERTUS. *Politicae Ecclesiasticae*, Tom. III, Amstelodami, 1676.
WILLIAMS, ROGER. *The Bloudy Tenent of Persecution for Cause of Conscience Discussed: and Mr. Cotton's Letter Examined and Answered*, London, 1848.
—. *A Key into the Language of America or, an help to the language of the natives in . . . New England. Together with briefe observations of the customes, manners, and worships, etc., of the aforesaid natives, in peace and warre, etc.*, London, 1643.
WOOD, WILLIAM. *New England Prospect*, London, 1634.

## SECONDARY SOURCES

ALLEN, ROLAND. *Missionary Methods: St. Paul's or Ours?*, Grand Rapids, 1962.
—. *The Spontaneous Expansion of the Church*, Grand Rapids, 1962.
ANDEL, H. A. VAN. *De Zendingsleer van Gisbertus Voetius*, Kampen, 1912.
ANDERSEN, WILHELM. *Toward a Theology of Missions*, London, 1955.
BAVINCK, J. H. *An Introduction to the Science of Missions*, Philadelphia, 1961.
—. *Religieus Besef en Christelijk Geloof*, Kampen, 1949.
BEAVER, R. PIERCE. "The Concert for Prayer for Missions," *Ecumenical Review*, X (1957-1958), 420-427.
—. *Ecumenical Beginnings in Protestant World Mission. A History of Comity*, New York, 1962.
—. "Eschatology in American Missions," *Basileia*, Walter Freytag zum 60. Geburtsdag, Stuttgart, 1959.
BENZ, ERNST. *Kirchengeschichte in Ökumenischer Sicht*, "Oekumenische Studien" III, Leiden, 1961.
—. "Pietist and Puritan Sources of Early Protestant World Missions," *Church History* XX (1951), 32-55.
BERG, JOHANNES VAN DEN. *Constrained By Jesus' Love*, An Inquiry into the Motives of the Missionary Awakening in Great Britain in the Period Between 1698 and 1815, Kampen, 1956.
—. "Corpus Christianum en Zending," in *De Heerbaan*, XIII (1960), 159-178.
BERKOUWER, G. C. *De Verkiezing Gods*, Kampen, 1955.
BLAUW, JOHANNES. *The Missionary Nature of the Church*, London, 1962.
BLAXLAND, BRUCE. *The Struggle with Puritanism*, London, 1910.
BOER, H. *Pentecost and the Missionary Witness of the Church*, Franeker, 1955.
—. *That My House May Be Filled*, Grand Rapids, 1957.
BRUNNER, EMIL. *The Divine Imperative*, Philadelphia, 1947.
BURR, NELSON R. *Religion in American Life*, II, Princeton, 1961.
BUTTERFIELD, HERBERT. *Christianity and History*, London, 1949.
CHAMBON, JOSEPH. *Der Puritanismus, Sein Weg von der Reformation bis zum Ende der Stuarts*, Zürich, 1944.
CLARK, HENRY W. *History of English Nonconformity from Wyclif to close of 19th Century*, I, II, London, 1911-1913.
CRAGG, GERALD R. *The Church and the Age of Reason*, 1648-1789, Middlesex, 1960.
—. *Puritanism in the Period of the Great Persecution*, 1660-1688, Cambridge, 1957.
CULLMANN, OSCAR. *Christ and Time*, London, 1962.
—. *The Christology of the New Testament*, Philadelphia, 1959.
DAANE, JAMES. "The State of Theology in the Church," *The Reformed Journal*, VII (September, 1957), 3-17.
DANKBAAR, W. F. "Het Apostolaat bij Calvijn," *Nederlands Theologisch Tijdschrift*, IV (1949-1950), 176-192.
DAVIES, HORTON. *Worship and Theology in New England*, 1690-1850, Princeton, 1961.
DRYSDALE, A. H. *History of the Presbyterians in England: Their Rise, Decline and Revival*, London, 1889.
EDWARDS, JONATHAN, Jr. "Observations on the language of the Muhhekaneew Indians," Published with *A Sermon at the Execution of Moses Paul*... by Sampson Occom, New Haven, 1788.
ELWOOD, DOUGLAS J. *The Philosophical Theology of Jonathan Edwards*, New York, 1960.
FERM, ROBERT O. *Cooperative Evangelism*, Grand Rapids, 1958.
FREYTAG, W. *The Gospel and the Religions*, London, 1957.
GEORGE, CHARLES and KATHERINE. *The Protestant Mind of the English Reformation 1570-1640*, Princeton, 1961.
GERSTNER, JOHN H. *Steps to Salvation, The Evangelistic Message of Jonathan Edwards*, Philadelphia, 1960.
GOEN, C. C. "A New Departure in Eschatology," *Church History*, XXVIII, (1959), 25-40.

GROSART, ALEXANDER B. *Representative Nonconformists*, London, 1879.
HALLER, WILLIAM. *The Rise of Puritanism*, New York, 1957.
HAMMAR, GEORGE. *Christian Realism in Contemporary American Theology*, Uppsala, 1940.
HARNACK, ADOLF. *The Mission and Expansion of Christianity in the First Three Centuries*, New York, 1962.
HARTVELT, G. P. "Over de methode der dogmatiek in de eeuw der Reformatie," *Gereformeerd Theologisch Tijdschrift*, LXII (1962), 97–149.
HOEKENDIJK, J. C. *Kerk en Volk in de Duitse Zendingswetenschap*, Amsterdam (s.n.).
—. "The Church in Missionary Thinking," *International Review of Missions*, XLI (1952), 324–336.
HOLMES, THOMAS J. *Cotton Mather: A Bibliography*, I–III, Cambridge, Mass., 1940.
HORNE, MELVILL. *Letters on Missions*, Bristol, 1794.
HOWSE, ERNEST MARSHALL. *Saints in Politics*, London, 1963.
JORDAN, W. K. *The Development of Religious Toleration in England*, London, 1936.
KAWERAU, PETER. *Amerika und die Orientalischen Kirchen*, Berlin, 1958.
KELLAWAY, WM. *The New England Company, 1649–1776*, London, 1961.
KORFF, F. W. A. *Het Christelijk Geloof en de niet-Christelijke Godsdiensten*, Amsterdam, 1946.
KOSKINEN, A. A. *Missionary Influence as a Political Factor in the Pacific Islands*, Helsinki, 1953.
KRAEMER, H. *The Christian Message in a Non-Christian World*, London, 1961.
LANG, AUGUST. *Puritanismus und Pietismus*, Neukirchen, 1941.
LAUBER, A. "Indian Slavery in Colonial Times," *Studies in History, Economics, and Public Law*, LIV, 3 (1891, etc.) 352 ff.
LEEUW, G. VAN DER. *Inleiding tot de Phaenomenologie van den Godsdienst, Theologia II*, Haarlem, 1948.
LOANE, MARCUS L. *Makers of Religious Freedom in the Seventeenth Century*, London, 1960.
MACAULAY, THOMAS B. *History of England* from the accession of James II, I–IV, London, 1913–1914.
MARTIN, HUGH. *Puritanism and Richard Baxter*, London, 1954.
MILLER, PERRY, ed. *The American Puritans. Their Prose and Poetry*, New York, 1956.
—. *Errand Into The Wilderness*, Cambridge, 1957.
—. *Jonathan Edwards*, Cleveland, 1959.
—. *The New England Mind*, I, II, Boston, 1961.
—. and THOMAS H. JOHNSON, eds. *The Puritans*, I, II, New York, 1963.
MORGAN, EDMUND S. *The Puritan Dilemma*, Boston, 1958.
MORGAN, IRVONWY. *The Non-Conformity of Richard Baxter*, London, 1946.
MORISON, SAMUEL ELIOT. *The Intellectual Life of Colonial New England*, New York, 1956.
MOSSE, GEORGE. "Puritanism Reconsidered," *Archiv für Reformationsgeschichte*, LV, Germany (1964), 37–48.
NAUTA, D. "Die Verbreitung des Katechismus, Übersetzung in andere Sprachen, moderne Bearbeitungen," *Handbuch Zum Heidelberger Katechismus*, ed. L. Coenen, Neukirchen, 1963.
NEAL, DANIEL. *History of the Puritans*, I, II, London, 1811.
NEILL, STEPHEN. *Christian Faith and Other Faiths*, London, 1961.
NEVIUS, JOHN L. *The Planting and Development of Missionary Churches*, Grand Rapids, 1958.
NEWBIGIN, LESSLIE. *The Household of God*, London, 1957.
NIEBUHR, H. RICHARD. *The Kingdom of God in America*, New York, 1937.
NUTTALL, GEOFFREY F., ed. *Richard Baxter and Philip Doddridge*, London, 1951.
—. *The Holy Spirit in Puritan Faith and Experience*, London, 1947.
—. *Visible Saints*, Oxford, 1957.
—, and OWEN CHADWICK, eds. *From Uniformity to Unity, 1662–1962*, London, 1962.
PARKER, ERNEST, ed. *The Character of England*, Oxford, 1947.
PARRINGTON, VERNON LOUIS. *The Colonial Mind, 1620–1800*, I, New York, 1927.
PATON, DAVID M. *Christian Missions and the Judgment of God*, London, 1953.
POWICKE, FREDERICK J. *A Life of the Rev. Richard Baxter, 1615–1691*, I, II, London, 1924.
RIDDERBOS, J. *De Theologie van Jonathan Edwards*, 's-Gravenhage, 1907.

Rouse, Ruth, and Stephen Charles Neill, ed. *A History of the Ecumenical Movement*, London, 1954.
Ruler, A. A. van. *Theologie van het Apostolaat*, Nijkerk (s.n.).
Runner, H. Evan. "The Relation of the Bible to Learning" in *Christian Perspectives*, Pella, 1960.
Schaefer, T. A. "Jonathan Edwards' Conception of the Church," *Church History*, XXIV (1955), 51–66.
Schelven, A. A. van. *Het Calvinisme Gedurende Zijn Bloeitijd, Schotland, Engeland, Noord-Amerika*, Amsterdam, 1951.
Schmidt, Martin. *Der junge Wesley als Heidenmissionar und Missionstheologe*, Gütersloh, 1955.
Schneider, Herbert Wallace. *The Puritan Mind*, Ann Arbor, 1961.
Slessarev, Vsevolod. *Prester John, the Letter and the Legend*, Minneapolis, 1959.
Smith, H., R. Handy and L. Loetscher. *American Christianity, Interpretation and Documents, 1607–1820*, New York, 1960.
Soper, Edmund Davison. *The Philosophy of the Christian World Mission*, New York, 1943.
Sykes, Norman. *The English Religious Tradition*, London, 1953.
Temple, William. *Nature, Man, and God*, London, 1951.
Tillich, Paul. *Systematic Theology*, I, Chicago, 1951.
Torrance, Thomas F. *Kingdom and Church*, Edinburgh and London, 1956.
—. *The School of Faith*, London, 1959.
Trevelyan, G. M. *England under the Stuarts*, A Pelican Book, Middlesex, 1960.
Trinterud, L. J. *The Forming of an American Tradition*, Philadelphia, 1949.
Trumbull, J. H. *Origin and Early Progress of Indian Missions in New England with a List of Books in the Indian Language*, Worcester, 1874.
Tulloch, John. *English Puritanism and Its Leaders*, Edinburgh and London, 1861.
Vicedom, Georg F. *Missio Dei*, München, 1958.
Visser 't Hooft, W. A. *The Background of the Social Gospel*, Haarlem, 1928.
Walker, Williston. *History of the Christian Church*, New York, 1918.
Warneck, Gustav. *Abriss einer Geschichte der Protestantischen Missionen, von der Reformation bis auf die Gegenwart*, Zehnte Auflage, Berlin, 1913.
Warren, Max. *The Christian Mission*, London, 1951.
Weber, Max. *The Protestant Ethic and the Spirit of Capitalism*, New York, 1958.
Wendell, Barrett. *Cotton Mather: The Puritan Priest*, New York, 1963.
Winslow, Ola E. *Jonathan Edwards*, New York, 1941.
Wolf, J. C. *Jonathan Edwards on Evangelism*, Grand Rapids, 1958.
Ziff, Larzer. *The Career of John Cotton*, Princeton, 1962.

# INDEX OF PERSONS

(References to R. Sibbes, R. Baxter, J. Eliot, C. Mather, and J. Edwards are not given for the section where each is discussed or for the conclusion of the book.)

Abigail, 309
Acosta, J. de, 132, 182, 195, 251
Allen, R., 154, 188, 322
Allen, T., 208
Althamer, A., 95
Ames, W., 12, 17, 142, 156
Andel, H. P. van, 252, 322
Andersen, W., 308, 324, 328
Aristotle, 131
Arminius, J., 12
Arndt, J., 144
Arthur, J., 213
Ashe, S., 213
Ashurst, W., 245
Attendius, 129
Augustine, 45, 142

Bacon, F., 16, 129
Baez-Camargo, C., 251
Ball, T., 142
Barth, K., 312
Basilides, 144
Bavinck, J. H., 310, 311, 312, 320
Baxter, Margaret, 67
Baxter, R., 13, 14, 32, 160, 162, 169, 170, 171, 172, 173, 174, 175, 176, 221, 226, 227, 228, 234, 235, 236, 237, 245, 247, 283
Bayne, P., 52, 63, 142
Beaver, R. P., 290, 293
Behmen, J., 144
Belknap, J., 159
Benz, E., 279, 325
Berg, J. van den, 64, 69, 268, 292, 293, 304, 314, 320, 321, 324, 325, 326
Berkouwer, G. C., 312, 313, 315
Bessey, A., 208
Beverly, J., 265
Beza, M. T., 12, 142
Blauw, J., 310, 325, 326
Blaxland, B., 148
Boer, H., 115, 315
Bolton, R., 142, 174
Bondet, M., 273
Boston, H., 159
Bourne, R., 218

Boyle, R., 69, 126, 131
Bradford, W., 142
Bradford, Wm., 258
Bradshaw, W., 142
Bradstreet, S., 215
Brainerd, D., 289, 291, 292, 293
Brakel, W. à, 321
Brerewood, E., 99, 129
Brewster, W., 265
Brightman, T., 142
Bromley, M., 83
Brooke, R., 142
Brunner, E., 314
Budde, J. C., 274
Bulkely, P., 264
Bullinger, J. H., 142
Butterfield, H., 313, 319
Burr, N. R., 293

Calicott, R., 199
Callamy, E., 213
Callender, E., 278
Calvin, J., 13, 15, 23, 61, 63, 98, 113, 123, 140, 142, 224, 251, 275, 276, 313, 314, 319, 320, 321
Carey, W., 293
Cartwright, T., 12, 137, 142, 174
Caryl, J., 213, 217
Casas, B. de las, 15
Catlin, Z., 15
Celsus, 300
Chadwick, O., 68, 149, 291
Chambon, J., 148, 151
Charles I, 66
Charles II, 66
Charles IX, 57
Chauncey, C., 16
Cheeshateaumuck, C., 221
Cheynell, F., 121, 149
Chrysostum, 142
Cicero, 129
Clark, H. W., 17, 148
Coligny, G., 251
Constantine, 298, 300
Cotton, J., 16, 156, 203, 207, 227, 229, 242, 254, 272, 273

342

Cragg, G., 148, 149
Cromwell, C., 232
Cromwell, O., 66, 160, 209, 322
Cromwell, R., 66
Cullmann, O., 324
Cutler, T., 286

Daane, J., 313
Danckaerts, J., 159
Danforth, S., 159
Dankbaar, W. F., 98
Davenport, J., 258, 264, 276, 278
Davies, H., 148, 151
Delius, G., 249, 273
Denham, M., 272
D'Ewes, S., 157
Diogenes, 120
Dod, J., 174
Doddridge, P., 70, 148, 293
Drake, S., 257
Drysdale, A. H., 148, 235
Dummer, W., 247
Dunster, H., 188
Dury, J., 114, 265, 278, 279

Edward VI, 35, 56
Edwards, J., 13, 14, 208
Edwards, J. Jr., 222, 223, 224
Edwards, Jerusha, 291
Edwards, Sarah, 289, 309
Edwards, T., 285
Eekhof, A., 249
Eliot, Anne, 157
Eliot, J., 13, 14, 69, 84, 100, 111, 126, 127,
  131, 132, 133, 134, 135, 153, 250, 252,
  268, 272, 273, 274, 275, 281, 282, 283,
  284
Eliot, J. Jr., 157, 217
Elizabeth I, 17, 56
Elwood, D. J., 16, 60, 61, 286, 287
Endicott, J., 205, 215, 216
Epictetus, 129
Erskine, J., 293
Everard, J., 61

Fawkes, G., 57
Ferm, R. O., 293
Fitch, J., 274
Ford, W. C., 246
Francke, A. H., 235, 298, 318
Frelinghuysen, T. J., 286
French, W., 208
Freytag, W., 311
Fuller, A., 152, 293
Fuller, T., 16

George, Catherine, 60
George, C., 60
Gerstner, J., 303, 307
Gildas, 194
Glover, R. H., 142
Goen, C. C., 293
Goodwin, T., 33
Gookin, D., 273
Gorton, S., 204
Gouge, T., 132
Gouge, W., 16
Grosart, A., 15, 16, 17, 35, 60, 66, 67, 148
Grotius, H., 126, 131

Haller, W., 60, 61
Hambden, J., 142
Hammar, G., 302, 304
Handy, R., 267
Harnack, A., 316
Hartvelt, G. P., 310
Hawley, G., 291
Herbert, G., 16, 66
Herbert, H., 66
Heurnius, J., 15, 235, 321
Hiacoomes, 201, 208
Higginson, J., 264, 282
Hildersham, A., 142, 174
Hobbes, T., 125
Hoekendijk, J. C., 319, 325
Holmes, T. J., 245, 248, 249, 250, 251, 252
Hook, W., 255
Hooker, T., 156, 220, 256, 264
Hooper, J., 142
Hoornbeek, J., 251, 265
Hope-Hood, 272
Horne, M., 318, 319
Howse, E. M., 70
Hitchinson, Anne, 324

James I, 17, 35, 57
James II, 66, 67
Jeffreys, J., 67
Jerome, 142
Johnson, S., 286
Jordan, W. K., 60
Julian the Apostate, 129

Kawerau, P., 292, 293
Kellaway, W., 69, 157, 223, 246, 248, 250, 291
Kierkegaard, S., 287
King Philip, 228, 233
King Robert, 240
King Unces, 240
Knox, J., 15

Korff, F. W. A., 311, 312
Koskinen, A. A., 325
Kraemer, H., 311, 312, 315, 325

Lang, A., 60, 70, 148
Latourette, K. S., 293, 321
Lattimer, H., 142
Lauber, A., 317
Laud, W., 17
Leete, W., 215
Leeuw, G. van der, 317
Leibniz, G. W. von, 235
Leusden, J., 159, 274
Leveridge, W., 208, 211, 218
Licensius, V., 116
Linde, S., van der, 60
Loane, M., 66, 68, 70, 148
Locke, J., 285
Lodensteyn, J. van, 321
Loetscher, L., 267
Luther, M., 56, 95, 113, 140, 142, 320

Macaulay, T. B., 148
Maffaeus, 126
Manton, T., 16
Marcion, 117
Marsden, S., 293
Martin, H., 66, 70, 235
Martyn, H., 293
Martyr, P., 12
Mary, Queen, 35, 121
Mather, C., 13, 14, 16, 156, 157, 158, 159, 171, 224, 235, 236, 240, 241, 285, 308
Mather, I., 146, 159, 234, 242, 274, 276, 277, 278, 283, 308
Mather, R., 212, 240, 242, 253, 254
Mather, Maria, 242
Mather, S., 254, 276, 278
Mayhew, E., 222, 228
Mayhew, J., 273
Mayhew, T., 218, 221, 273
Mayhew, T., Jr., 196, 197, 200, 201, 202, 209, 210, 214, 217, 273
Mede, J., 16
Menander, 144
Menasseh ben Israel, 231
Miller, P., 16, 17, 62, 159, 238, 257, 267, 283, 286, 293, 294, 301, 309, 310
Milton, J., 16
Mitchel, J., 283
Mohammed, 121, 128, 136, 137, 144, 300
More, T., 261
Morgan, E., 16
Morgan, I., 60
Morison, S. E., 12

Morley, G., 123
Mosse, G., 314
Moule, T., 270, 271
Mullinger, J. B., 12
Mumanequem, 208

Nauta, D., 32
Neal, D., 156
Neill, S., 318
Nevius, J. L., 323
Newbigin, L., 318, 319, 321, 327
Newman, F., 215
Newman, H., 220, 221
Newton, I., 285
Niebuhr, H. R., 287, 302, 305, 306
Nishohkou, 162, 163, 164, 165, 166, 169 237
Norton, J., 260, 283
Noyes, J., 283
Nuttall, G., 68, 70, 149, 152, 235, 312, 391

Oakes, U., 242, 243, 261
Oakland, H., 152
Obadiah, 245
Occom, S., 292
Onesimus, 245
Owen, J., 16, 114, 121, 149

Paracelsus, 144
Paraeus, 142
Parker, E., 148
Parker, T., 229
Parrington, V. L., 302
Parsons, E., 156
Paton, D. M., 323, 325, 326
Payne, E. A., 291
Pemble, W., 142
Penn, W., 96
Penny, F., 69
Perkins, W., 12, 17, 76, 310
Peter the Great, 298
Peters, H., 202
Philpot, J., 142
Phips, W., 269, 272
Phoebe, 309
Pierson, A., 215, 218, 224, 274
Piscator, J., 142
Plato, 61, 131, 146, 299
Plotinus, 146
Plutarch, 26, 129
Pococke, A., 126, 131
Ponampam, 162, 167, 168, 169, 237
Porphyry, 146, 301
Powicke, F. J., 66, 70, 148, 173
Prester John, 146

Preston, J., 12, 16, 17, 142, 174
Pym, J., 142

Ramus, P., 12, 239, 310
Rawson, G., 273
Reynolds, Dr., 142
Reynolds, E., 215, 216
Ricci, Matteo, 15
Ridderbos, J., 293, 302, 304, 305
Robinson, J., 15, 255, 265, 269
Rogers, N., 263
Rous, F., 61
Rouse, Ruth, 318
Ruler, A. A. van, 311, 313, 319, 320, 324, 325, 326
Runner, H. E., 302, 304

Sagamore John, 177
Sanders, 142
Sargeant, J., 290, 292
Sarovia, H., 98
Saturnius, 144
Schaefer, T. A., 308
Schelven, A. A. van, 302
Schmidt, M., 60, 61, 64, 65
Schneider, H. W., 155, 235
Schwenkfeldius, K., 144
Scudder, H., 54
Seneca, 26, 129, 131
Sewell, S., 228, 246, 248, 252
Shepard, T., 186, 187, 188, 189, 190, 191, 195, 258, 263
Sherman, J., 275
Sibbes, R., 13, 14, 76, 92, 142, 149, 150, 151, 153, 154, 155, 160, 162, 174, 236, 237, 242
Sibley, J. L., 242
Simon, 117
Slessarev, V., 148
Sluyter, P., 159
Smith, H., 267
Socrates, 61, 299
Soper, E. D., 235
Spalatensis, A., 263
Spinoza, B., 125
Spurgeon, C., 70
Steele, W., 205, 208, 209
Stoddard, Esther, 285
Stoddard, S., 285, 286
Sykes, N., 148
Sylvester, M., 66, 67

Talcot, J., 215
Taylor, J., 16
Teellinck, W., 321

Temple, W., 313
Tennant, G., 286
Thatcher, P., 272
Thatcher, R., 272
Thorowgood, T., 169, 232, 234
Thurston, R. I., 169
Tillich, P., 313
Torrance, T. F., 310, 319, 324
Toteswamp, 214
Townsend, H. G., 301, 304, 305
Trence, T., 215
Trevelyan, G. M., 57
Trinterud, L. J., 291
Trumbull, J. H., 222, 224, 232, 248
Tulloch, J., 66, 148
Tupper, T., 273
Twisse, W., 142, 261
Tyerman, L., 70

Van Til, C., 313
Varro, 130
Vicedom, G. F., 323
Vives, L., 130
Voetius, G., 252, 322
Visser 't Hooft, W. A., 302, 304

Waaubon, 184, 211
Walker, W., 268, 271
Walton, L., 16
Wampas, 184
Wampoowas, 192, 194
Warfield, B. B., 302
Warneck, G., 293, 320
Warren, M., 311, 320, 328
Wasa, G., 234
Wasupon, 185
Watts, I., 70, 287
Weber, M., 321
Weld, T., 159
Wendell, B., 242
Wequash, 178
Wesley, C., 70
Wesley, J., 12, 65, 70, 220, 285, 292, 293
Wesley, Susannah, 12
Wheelock, E., 292
Wheelock, Mr., 131
Whitaker, W., 142
Whitefield, G., 70, 291
Whitfield, H., 201, 205, 213
Wigglesworth, M., 267
Wilberforce, W., 70
William III, 66
Williams, Roger, 222, 226, 234, 263, 270, 272, 273, 324
Wilson, D., 70

Wilson, J., 177
Winship, G. P., 159
Winslow, E., 195, 196, 230, 259, 289, 291
Winslow, J., 215
Winslow, Ola E., 60, 63, 287
Winthorp, J., 215
Winthrop, J., Jr., 228
Witsius, H., 321
Wolf, E., 304

Wolf, J. C., 307
Wood, W., 156
Wren, M., 16
Wycliff, J., 142

Yoder, D. H., 318

Zanchy, G., 142
Ziff, L., 16, 60, 63
Zwingli, U., 113, 142

www.ingramcontent.com/pod-product-compliance
Lightning Source LLC
Chambersburg PA
CBHW080421230426
43662CB00015B/2177